PAPARAZZi!

PHOTOGRAPHERS, STARS, ARTISTS

PAPARAZZI!

PHOTOGRAPHERS, STARS, ARTISTS

Edited by Clément Chéroux

Flammarion Centre Pompidou-Metz

CONTENTS

THE TEXTS ACCOMPANYING THE WORKS WERE WRITTEN BY CAMILLE LENGLOIS, ANAÏS FEYEUX, AND CLÉMENT CHÉROUX

Many of the essays indicate monetary values in euros, and on occasion in U.S. dollars or in pounds sterling. At the time of going to press, the conversion rate was €1 = $1.37 / £0.81.

Foreword

Alain Seban
President of the Centre Pompidou-Metz

For the past thirty years, art history has continually changed and redefined its areas of study, exploring new geographies and unprecedented mediums, combining anthropological and aesthetic readings, the history of forms and ideas, scholarly and popular culture. The Centre Pompidou-Metz, like the Centre Pompidou in Paris, offers a space for thought and the presentation of these new approaches and intersections between art and societal issues.

The exhibition *Paparazzi! Photographers, Stars, Artists* is an example of this approach. Through more than six hundred works, it explores the profession of the "picture hunter" in all its facets, revealing its specific techniques and methods. Although the first photographers of celebrities were popularized in the illustrated press at the turn of the twentieth century, this practice took off in the 1950s in Italy, where the cinema industry was flourishing at that time. The character embodied by Walter Santesso in *La Dolce Vita* by Federico Fellini, in 1960, thus gave his name to a new kind of photographer, forever on the lookout for an opportunity to reveal the private lives of stars to the public, by any means necessary. The phenomenon progressively increased in scale and reached a peak in the 1980s, before undergoing profound changes as the profession adapted to the development of digital techniques.

The saga of "paparazzism" traced here illuminates the complex and passionate relationships established between the photographer and his prey, forever oscillating between attraction and repulsion in a theater of infinitely repeated attitudes and poses. It is through this gestural vocabulary, composed of raised hands, shielded faces, closed fists, or pointing fingers, that a popular and subversive genre was built, shattering the traditional codes of portraiture. Since the 1960s and 1970s, it has incessantly spread its influence beyond the photographic field. By associating historical paparazzi figures with works by artists who have questioned this modern myth, this exhibition and its catalog aim to define the characteristics of a paparazzi aesthetic. The porosity of these worlds is evident, notably through the reappropriation of tabloid images, and the use of paparazzi techniques and vocabulary, thereby contributing to the normalization of this practice.

The representation of intimacy and the ideal of transparency, which lie at the heart of the paparazzi aesthetic, are also signs of societal developments over the last decades. At a time when digital technology allows us to infiltrate everything, this exhibition and catalog implicitly question the fate of images in a society of the spectacle that has reached its height.

I would like to thank Clément Chéroux, the chief curator of the exhibition, as well as the team of associate curators with whom he worked, and all of the artists, lenders, and those who have contributed to the making of *Paparazzi! Photographers, Stars, Artists*. Through the historical and aesthetic nature of its approach and the relations established between the paparazzi and artists during its research, this exhibition and accompanying catalog give us the opportunity to discover a hitherto unexplored area of the history of photography.

Foreword

Laurent Le Bon
Director of the Centre Pompidou-Metz

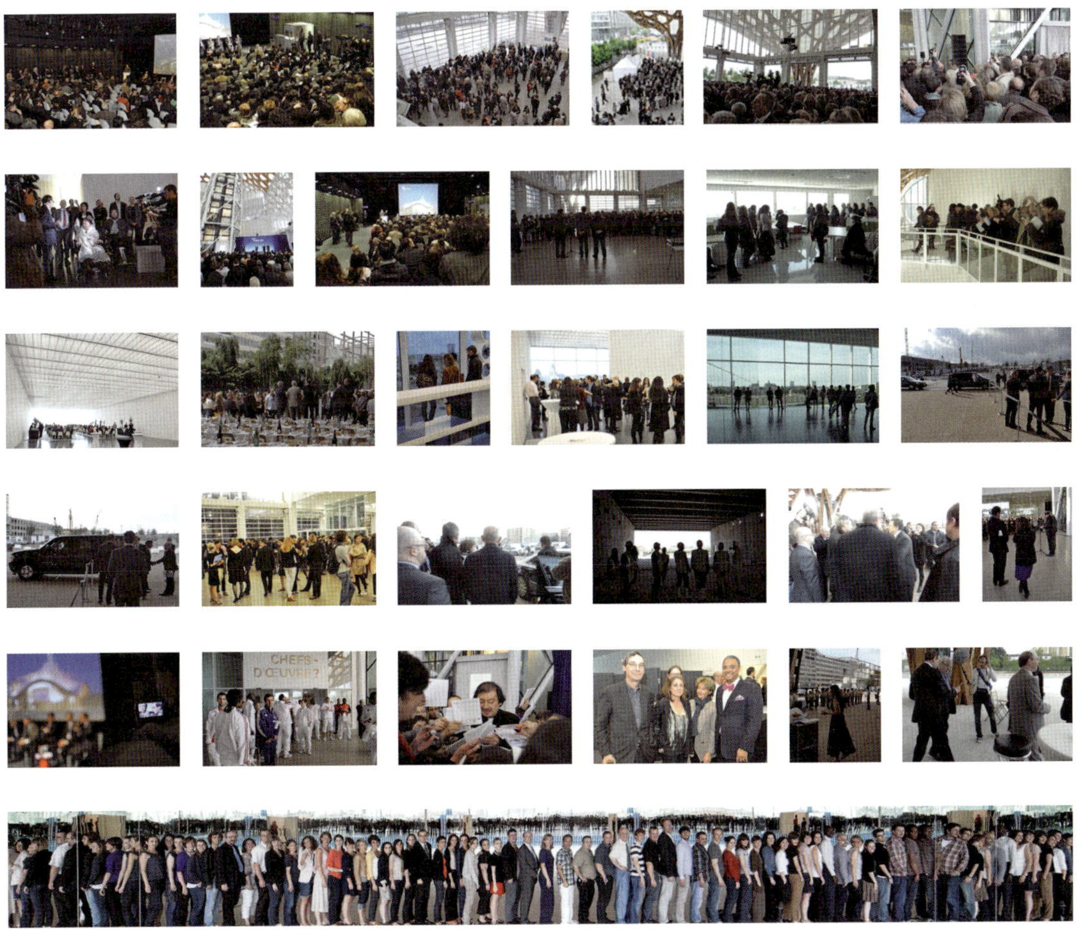

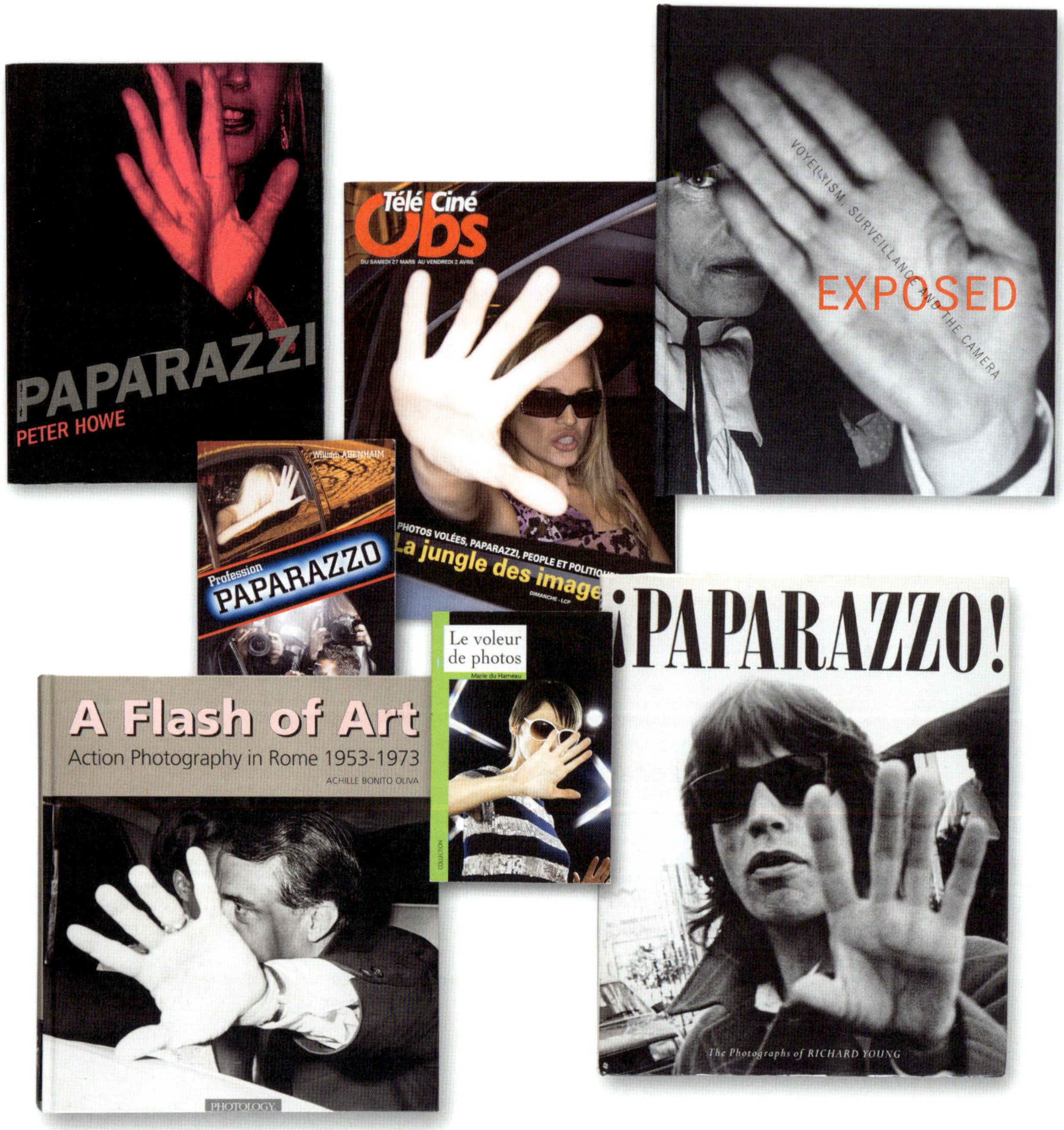

Peter Howe, *Paparazzi: And Our Obsession with Celebrity* (New York: Artisan, 2005); "Photos volées, paparazzi, people et politique," *Télé Ciné Obs*, no. 2368, March–April 2010; **Sandra S. Phillips**, ed., *Exposed: Voyeurism, Surveillance, and the Camera Since 1870* (London: Tate Publishing, 2010); **William Abenhaim**, *Profession paparazzo* (Paris: Nouveau Monde Editions, 2009); **Achille Bonito Oliva and Davide Faccioli**, *A Flash of Art: Action Photography in Rome, 1953–1973* (Milan: Photology, 2004); **Marie Du Hameau**, *Le Voleur de photos* (Paris: Groupe Mondadori, 2010); **Richard Young**, *Paparazzo! The Photographs of Richard Young* (London: Virgin, 1989).

Thirteen and a Half Theories on the Concept of Paparazzi Photography

Clément Chéroux

1. Stars, Flashes, and Overexposure

To what—or perhaps to whom—does the term "paparazzi" refer? Today the word is so bandied about that it ends up covering quite different types of photographs. All authors of pictures that are taken furtively, or of photographic indiscretions, tend to be labeled paparazzi. The mere amateur who happens to capture the distant silhouette of a celebrity in the street is now considered a paparazzo. "We are all paparazzi," as a French newspaper recently headlined.[1] In the hyper-mediatized society in which we live, the term "paparazzi" is almost synonymous with "photographer." Here, it is evidently understood in a more precise sense. This practice of photography first implies that the image has been neither given nor negotiated, but rather snatched. The paparazzo can be an amateur or a professional, but in most cases he takes his photographs without the consent of his subjects. The latter—and this is a second compulsory condition—receive a public recognition that goes beyond their simple socioprofessional circles. They can be internationally recognized celebrities or occasional stars. It is this double determination—the photograph is snatched and the subject is a celebrity—that has guided the choice of works for the exhibition *Paparazzi!* Therefore (with a few exceptions, particularly in this introductory section), images of stars taken during posing sessions, or snatched shots of anonymous people have been excluded. The project is organized around this confrontation between the paparazzi and celebrities, which can occasionally be extremely violent. The photographer, as the word's etymology indicates, writes with light. The star shines brightly. In both cases, it is all about light. To satisfy the public's curiosity, the paparazzi want to cast full light on the celebrities, even when they are nowhere near a spotlight. The latter react in order to preserve a portion of shadow over their personal lives. The exhibition and this work focus on this conflict of interest which is, in short, the eternal battle between light and darkness.

1. "Nous sommes tous des paparazzis," *Le Parisien*, May 19, 2012.

ANONYMOUS
Plaque in honor of Coriolano Paparazzo, placed on the Albergo Centrale of Catanzaro, c. 2000

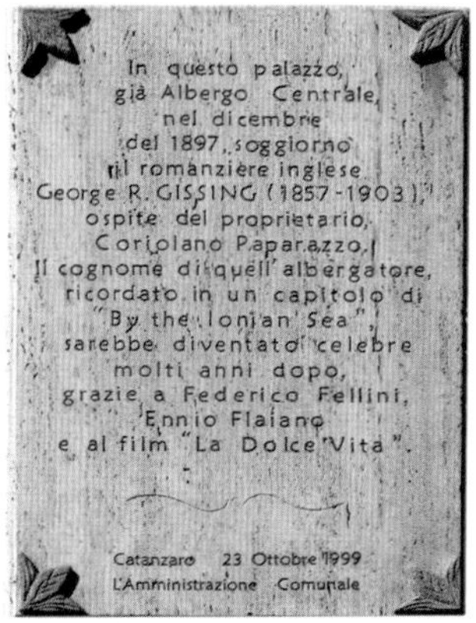

2. Homer and Photography

Argos, Athens, Chios, Colophon, Cumae, Pylos, and Smyrna: according to the *Palatine Anthology*, no fewer than seven Greek cities wrangle over the claim to being Homer's birthplace—the blind poet, who in fact was probably not even born in Greece, and perhaps was never even born at all. The same applies to the birth of the paparazzi phenomenon. The majority of specialists situate it in Rome in the 1960s.[2] In a recent article in the journal *Études photographiques*, the American historian Vanessa R. Schwartz readily pushed it back to the previous decade in the context of the Cannes Film Festival.[3] Others see it occurring with the great rise of Hollywood in the 1920s. In short, everyone has his own point of view. In the canonical texts, the genre's inventor is, more often than not, Italian: Tazio Secchiaroli, Marcello Geppetti, or even Felice Quinto. For certain photography historians, there is no need to wait for neo-realistic Italy for the appearance of the first paparazzo. As early as the 1930s, Weegee in New York or Erich Salomon in Berlin were already practicing the profession of "picture snatcher." Even earlier, toward 1910, Jacques Henri Lartigue photographed courtesans in their Sunday best on the avenues of the Bois de Boulogne.[4] In 1889, Giuseppe Primoli surprised the painter Edgar Degas leaving a public convenience in the streets of Paris, and at the same period Carl Størmer immortalized the playwright Henrik Ibsen's walk along the main street of Oslo with the help of a camera hidden under his shirtfront.[5] We have chosen not to take part in this exercise as it seemed of little relevance, but there is no doubt that, with a little perseverance, it would be possible to find a few earlier examples of pictures of public figures taken against their will, and thus push back even further in time the invention of "paparazzism."

3. Where the Term Paparazzi Comes From

The same imprecision surrounds the origins of the word "paparazzi." Federico Fellini is said to have invented the word while working on *La Dolce Vita*, to designate a particularly intrusive photographer played in the film by Walter Santesso. However, Fellini himself frequently gave contradictory versions of this invention. When he named his character, he supposedly recalled a childhood friend from the local school in Rimini called "paparazzo."[6] He also tells of having found this name in a libretto.[7] According to other sources, he made up the name himself by contracting *papatacci*, the name of the ferocious little mosquitoes particularly present in the plains of Po where he came from, and *razzi*, the flash of the cameras.[8] But in an interview with the weekly newspaper *Oggi*, just after the film was released, Giulietta Masina, the director's wife, stated that it was she who suggested the name by associating *papatacci*, not with *razzi* but with *ragazzi*, which in Italian means young men.[9] Ennio Flaiano, the scriptwriter, has also given his side of the story: the word was found by chance in the English author George Gissing's book *By the Ionian Sea*, published in 1901, but translated into Italian in 1957, and in which the name of the hotel owner in a small town in Calabria, southern Italy, was Coriolano Paparazzo.[10] In the collective imagination, this version of the

2. See Karen Pinkus, *The Montesi Scandal: The Death of Wilma Montesi and the Birth of Paparazzi in Fellini's Rome* (Chicago: University of Chicago Press, 2003); Carol Squiers, "Class Struggle: The Invention of Paparazzi, Photography and the Death of Diana, Princess of Wales," in *Over Exposed, Essays on Contemporary Photography* (New York: The New Press, 1999), 269–303.

3. Vanessa R. Schwartz, "Grand angle sur la plage," *Études photographiques* 26 (November 2010): 132–50.

4. See Jacques Henri Lartigue, *Mémoires sans mémoires* (Paris: Robert Laffont, 1975), 80.

5. See Lamberto Vitali, *Un fotografo fin de siècle, il conte Primoli* (Turin: Einaudi, 1968), 79; Jonas Ekeberg and Harald Ostgaard Lund (eds.) *80 Millioner Bilder. Norsk kulturhistorisk fotografi 1855–2005* (Oslo: Forlaget Press, 2008), 144.

6. See Federico Fellini, *Photo* (French edition), March 1973, quoted by Michel Guerrin, *Profession photoreporter. Vingt ans d'images d'actualité* (Paris: Centre Georges-Pompidou/Gallimard, 1988), 213.

7. See Federico Fellini and Charlotte Chandler, *Moi Fellini, Treize ans de confidences* (Paris: Robert Laffont, 1994), 143.

8. This origin of the word is given by Enrico Giuffredi, a photographer in Rome during the 1950s. It is described by Bruno Mouron and Pascal Rostain in *Paparazzi, chasseurs de stars* (Paris: Michel Lafon, 1988), 7.

9. "Paparazzi," http://fr.wikipedia.org/wiki/Paparazzi#cite_note-1, accessed December 8, 2013.

10. See Pierre Coustillas, "Gissing in Italy," "Revisiting the Shores of the Ionian Sea," *Supplement to the Gissing Journal* 35, no. 4 (October 1999): 1–5 and 6–43.

word's origin now prevails, so much so that in 1999 a plaque was placed on the façade of the Albergo Centrale of Catanzaro paying homage to Coriolano Paparazzo for having inspired—both unintentionally and indirectly—Fellini in the invention of a character that was to embody, almost in itself alone, the failings of the society of the spectacle. The paparazzi are indeed the Homers of photography, with the difference that they are anything but blind and are rarely poets.

4. The Myth of Origins

"We tend to think," wrote Michel Foucault, "that [the birth] is the moment of their greatest perfection, when they emerged dazzling from the hands of a creator or in the shadowless light of a first morning."[11] Behind this desire to find the inventor of the word "paparazzi," to discover who was the first, or to try and identify the country in which this practice initially appeared, there is the belief that the origin is a place of absolute truth, that the essence of beings or things can be found folded within it, as if preserved in a state of virginal purity, at the dawn of all alteration. It would suffice, therefore, to return to the original phenomenon in order to retrieve its shining authenticity and thereby better understand it. This is far from being the case, however. New history, structuralism, Foucault's thinking, amongst others', has shown us just how much this frantic quest for origins—what the historian Marc Bloch called "the embryonic obsession"[12]—is a decoy. Firstly, because the search for origins is endless. It is a point in indefinitely receding time. It is always possible to find a predecessor to a precursor, and then a precedent to the predecessor of the precursor, and so on and so forth. But also because the origin is often deceptive. In French terminology, the word signifies both the beginning and the cause, yet these two meanings frequently contaminate each other, as Bloch explains: "For everyday vocabulary, the origins are a beginning that explains. Worse still, that suffices to explain. Here is the ambiguity; here is the danger."[13] Learning about the beginnings of a historical phenomenon can help to understand it, but it is not enough to explain it. "Discovering the seed does not disclose the cause of germination," adds Bloch.[14]

5. The Visual Form of Gossip

No one, then, invented the paparazzi. They are the spontaneous product of a very human curiosity and doubtless as old as humanity itself. It is the irrepressible desire to know about others' lives—and in particular the lives of those who are in the public eye—that gave birth to gossip and what is more commonly known as tittle-tattle, scuttlebutt, or dish. It was this same craving for familiarity that gave birth to the gazette *Le Mercure galant* as early as 1672. In its first issue, the editor already promised to "those curious for news, to provincials and foreigners who have no acquaintance with the people of high birth or great merit of which they have so often heard talk, [that they] will learn in this and the following issues how they are recommendable, and what makes them estimable."[15] It is again this desire to know everything about the great and good of this world that, in the following centuries, allowed for the exponential development of the gutter press, of sensation and scandal, up until today's tabloid press. The paparazzi phenomenon fits wholly within this change in the press, which has progressively replaced text with image. The appearance of picture snatchers is the direct result of an increasing demand for celebrity

11. Michel Foucault, "Nietzsche, Genealogy, History," in *The Foucault Reader*, ed. Paul Rabinow (New York: Pantheon Books, 1984), 79.

12. Marc Bloch, "L'idole des origines," *Apologie pour l'histoire ou Métier d'historien* (1949; Paris: Armand Colin, 1993), 54.

13. Ibid.

14. Marc Bloch, *Histoire et historiens* (Paris: Armand Colin, 1995), 105.

15. Théodore Girard, "Le libraire au lecteur," *Le Mercure galant* 1 (1672; repr., Paris/Geneva: Slatkine, 1982), 8–9.

LUC MAZEL, RAOUL CAUVIN
Les Paparazzi. Reporters de choc,
vol. V, Paris: Dupuis, 1999, p. 47
(Spot the difference ... "I'm telling you, there is no difference between you war correspondent-photographers and us paparazzi ...")

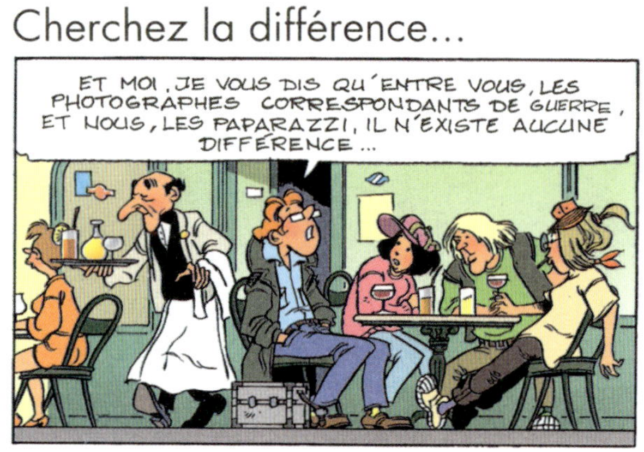

photographs. It is a question of economics—of supply and demand. From the moment stars were no longer able to satisfy the incessant requests for new, unpublished images, they had to be robbed of them. Paparazzi respond to an uncontrollable voyeurism, which, in short, is only a visual form of gossip. It is, however, important to remember that until the end of the nineteenth century, photography was not instantaneous, and, furthermore, that it had to be manually transformed into an engraving before being published. For paparazzi to exist, it was therefore necessary for a certain number of technical factors to come together, and this happened at the turn of the twentieth century. The first photographs of the genre appeared in the wake of the first periodicals illustrated by photographs—in France, *L'Excelsior* or *Femina*, for example.[16] The phenomenon increased during the 1910s and the 1920s with the rise of the photographic press. The 1950s and 1960s, with the development of the consumer society and the star system, represent a form of crystallization of this iconography. Fellini may not have invented the paparazzi but, by giving them a name that passed into posterity, he took them to the baptismal font of the capital of Christianity, Rome, which is probably more than just a matter of chance.

6. Telephoto Lens or Flash

Two distinct types of paparazzi exist. Those who photograph from a distance—generally hidden and armed with a telephoto lens—and those who work up close, within contact of the stars, and who more often use a flash. The former are discreet and secret; they resemble hunters on the lookout. They use all possible and imaginable strategies to avoid being spotted: masks, camouflage, automatic cameras. They tell the most unbelievable stories about their hideouts and their pursuits. The second kind is more aggressive and brazen. As Francis Apesteguy recalls in an interview published in the present catalog, these paparazzi behave deliberately like bullfighters who plant their banderillas until death ensues.[17] These are the ones most hated by the stars. Each of these two styles fits into a well-established tradition of street photography. The "hunters" (who are, in fact, poachers more often than not, as they have no license) descend from what Anglo-Saxon historiography calls candid photography. This approach to taking photographs appeared at the end of the nineteenth century with the advent of small-format cameras—and notably those called "detectives"—and was based on the premise that the subject could be represented more naturally if it was unaware that it was being observed. The "matadors'" style corresponds more to the kind of photograph that Henri Cartier-Bresson began taking in the 1930s and of which William Klein became the best-known representative after the war: a dynamic and provocative shot that aims to trigger a reaction from its subjects; a sort of shouting photograph. The former group fundamentally believes in a photographic truth. They are certain that their invisibility is a pledge of authenticity. The latter type knows that their presence inevitably

16. See *Femina*, January 1, 1902, cover; *L'Excelsior*, April 8, 1919, cover.

17. See the interview by Francis Apesteguy in the present catalog, p. 34.

Logo of the Mamarazzi photography website www.mamarazzi.com.au/

modifies the particulars of the observation experience. These two methods—situated at diametrically opposed ends of the spectrum of paparazzi practice—correspond, in short, to the significant difference in method between positivist ethnology and a more modern anthropological approach.

7. The Reverse Side of the War Reporter?

A "paparazzi" category does not exist in the important international prizes for photojournalism, such as World Press Photo or the Pulitzer, and with good reason: these prizes are intended to reward a concept of the profession that war reporters symbolize much more than the paparazzi. Moreover, in the collective imagination these two great figures of press photography are frequently seen as polar opposites. War reporters enjoy a real aura of respectability in the eyes of the public. They are willing to confront fear and danger, even if it means risking their lives, to defend the truth. They appear as veritable modern knights.[18] Conversely, the paparazzi are viewed as cowardly and lacking in probity. They will stoop to anything to earn money off celebrities' backs. In their pirate morality, no holds are barred. On the one side, we see heroism and abnegation; on the other, a lack of scruples and mercenary motives. In the public's mind, the paparazzi represent the opposite, the double negative, of the war correspondent. They embody the accursed side of photo reportage. They have passed over to the "dark side of the force." In reality, things are obviously much more complex than this. Many photographers practice the two activities by turns. Jacques Langevin—who was on duty at the Sygma agency on the evening of Princess Diana's death and photographed the moments running up to her fatal accident—is an esteemed reporter who has covered most of the important news events of the past decades: the fall of the Berlin wall, the demonstrations in Tiananmen Square, the American intervention in Saudi Arabia, the Gulf and the Iraq wars, the Rwanda genocide, to name but a few. In 1973, right in the midst of the Vietnam war, Nick Ut received the Pulitzer Prize for his famous photograph of Kim Phuc, a little girl screaming with pain, running from her village that had been bombed with napalm. In 2007, in Los Angeles, he photographed Paris Hilton crying in front of her car after receiving a sentence of twenty-three days' incarceration for a traffic offence. Between these two images of woe lies the entire evolution of the reporting profession. The photographer did not receive a prize for this second image, but he certainly earned a lot more money than he did with the first.

8. A "Gendered" Practice

The Internet is a particularly propitious field for the appearance of neologisms. *Urban Dictionary*, a website based in San Francisco, lists and comments on them. A few years ago the site created an entry for the term "mamarazzi," which was beginning an endemic spread across the Net. According to the definition posted by an anonymous Internet user, the word describes possessive mothers who constantly follow their children around with cameras or camcorders, documenting every single moment of their lives, both great and small. Communities of mamarazzi have started forming on the Net in order to share pictures, exchange advice, and organize

18. See Clément Chéroux, "Mythologie du photographe de guerre," in Thérèse Blondet-Bisch, Robert Frank, Laurent Gervereau, and André Gunthert (eds.), *Voir, ne pas voir, la guerre. Histoire des représentations photographiques de la guerre* (Paris: BDIC, Somogy, 2001), 306–11.

Publicis Graffiti Agency
Sunshade, advertising campaign for the Argentinean magazine *Paparazzi*, 2007
(Photograph: anonymous)

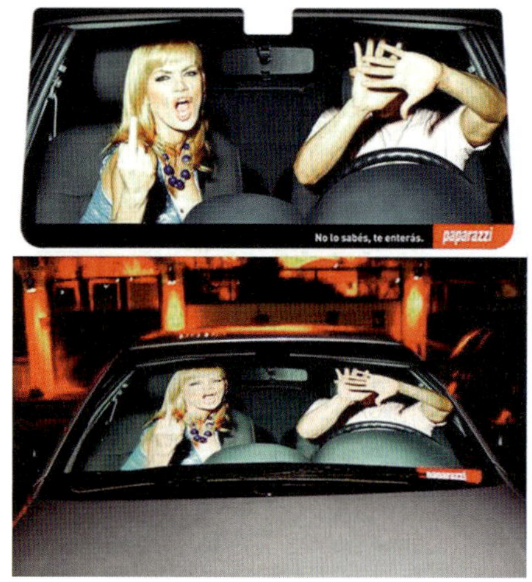

workshops or competitions. The appearance of this neologism as a play on words, where the supposedly paternal root of the word is replaced by a resolutely maternal prefix, provokes the awareness that the paparazzo is a fundamentally masculine figure. The picture snatchers have indeed always been men since the beginning of the profession. It is only very recently that a few female paparazzi have appeared in Hollywood, but they remain extremely rare. If historically and statistically the majority of paparazzi are men, their victims are, on the other hand, more generally women and, it must be noted, women who overtly assert their femininity. As Michel Guerrin recalls in his article for this catalog, a statistic established by the magazine *Voici* for its tenth anniversary demonstrated that out of the ten personalities most hunted down by photographers and published on magazine covers, eight were women.[19] The paparazzo is a man and his favorite subject is woman. It is, then, as we say today, a "gendered" practice.

8 ½. Theft and Rape of Images

There are indeed some men—Sean Penn, Hugh Grant, Patrick Poivre d'Arvor, to mention just a few—who have suffered at the hands of the paparazzi. But this cannot be compared with the physical and moral harassment that personalities such as Liz Taylor, Jackie Kennedy-Onassis, Brigitte Bardot, Caroline and Stephanie of Monaco, or, closer to our generation, Diana Spencer, Paris Hilton, and Britney Spears had to endure incessantly. This violence toward women is particularly noticeable in the vocabulary used in this context. The paparazzi, as has already been noted, describe themselves as hunters who track down their prey in packs, spy on their victims, arm their camera, take aim and fire until the kill. This predatory terminology is often substituted by a language of penetration with strong sexual undertones. It is about introducing themselves into the stars' intimacy. This is the reason why, among the top ten paparazzi shots that have hit the headlines over the past few decades, images in which the female body is openly exposed and thus sexualized are heavily featured. For example, there are the photos of Jackie Onassis naked on her island of Skorpios; those of Stephanie of Monaco wearing a monokini on a beach in Mauritius; or, more recently, those of Kate Middleton tanning her naked breasts at a villa in southern France. The image that Britney Spears has offered several times to photographers over the last few years, of herself getting out of a car with spread legs and no underwear, thereby constitute a pinnacle for the genre. The pictures achieve a penetration fantasy of which the photographic lens—particularly prominent in the case of paparazzi photography—is the symbolic instrument. It is not surprising that in return celebrities often declare that they feel they've been "raped." Something in the order of macho violence is being played out within the photographic field.

19. See Michel Guerrin, "The Market for Paparazzi Pictures" in the present catalog, p. 51.

Presse-Publicité, no. 5,
April 11, 1937, p. 11
(Photograph: anonymous)

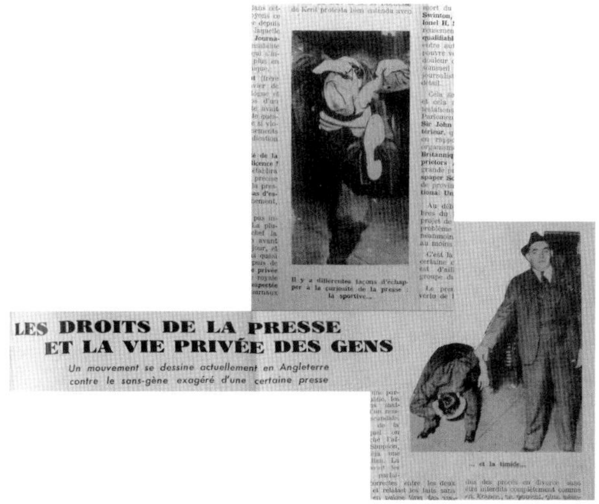
LES DROITS DE LA PRESSE
ET LA VIE PRIVÉE DES GENS

Un mouvement se dessine actuellement en Angleterre contre le sans-gène exagéré d'une certaine presse

Il y a différentes façons d'échapper à la curiosité de la presse : la sportive...

... et la timide...

9. Situationists Without Knowing It

Certain paparazzi are veritable bandits and are proud to be so. They readly use the most devious methods, creating setups and trapping stars. The Ducruet affair is a pertinent example of this. In 1996, Daniel Ducruet, Stephanie of Monaco's husband, was forced to divorce his wife after his sexual antics with a Belgian stripper around a swimming pool at a villa in the south of France were photographed and filmed by a paparazzo, who, according to the decree of Nice's criminal court, had organized the whole ambush.[20] In Paris during the 1980s, certain paparazzi were in the habit of provoking celebrities at the entrance of restaurants or nightclubs—because they knew that there was more money in an angry face, a middle finger, or an obscene gesture than in a normal shot, but also, no doubt, in the hope of seeing the dispute turn into a fight, just for the pleasure of having it out with a celebrity. One of them gladly tells how he held his camera by the lens, the case jutting out, and used it like brass knuckles to strike his victim with an uppercut.[21] The conflict between stars and paparazzi is somewhat similar to the class struggle, transferred to the media field. Many paparazzi do not hide their deep aversion to the system of show business: its inequalities, its easy money, its wealthy, and above all its stars for a day—personalities with no real talent who are suddenly thrown into the spotlight. No doubt this explains their boundless rampage against reality television stars. The paparazzi may not have read Guy Debord, but most of them abhor the society of the spectacle. They are situationists without knowing it. Photography is their revenge.

10. The Car: A Celebrity Trap

In the collective imagination, the paparazzo is most often represented in movement. He is inseparable from his means of locomotion. The paparazzi of the 1960s in Rome are unimaginable without their Vespas or Lambrettas. Today, they are more readily associated with helicopters and drones. But if there is a vehicle that has really counted in the history of this photographic practice, then it is the car. Several paparazzi have talked of the relationship they formed with their car during the long hours of waiting. "The car of the paparazzo in hiding," explain Pascal Rostain and Bruno Mouron, "is a soldier's trench from World War I, a survival tank, a tin can, and, depending on the season, an oven or a freezer."[22] For the paparazzo, his car is like a second home. The car is also a place in which he particularly likes to photograph stars, because once in the passenger seat, the celebrity cannot get away. The photographer can turn around him or her as much as he likes, photographing the star from any angle. The resulting pictures are often quite surprising, and the effects of transparency, of iridescence or reflection in the car windows play an important role. A few major pictures were taken in these circumstances. The star taken (in both senses of the word) in his or her car has even become a classic of the genre. A few years ago,

20. See Michel Henry, "Ducruet, la strip-teaseuse, le paparazzo et madame la juge," *Libération*, March 17, 2000.

21. A conversation by the author with one of the paparazzi presented in the exhibition.

22. Mouron and Rostain, *Paparazzi*, 147.

Noticias, no. 1001,
March 3, 1996, cover
(Photograph: José Luis Cabezas)

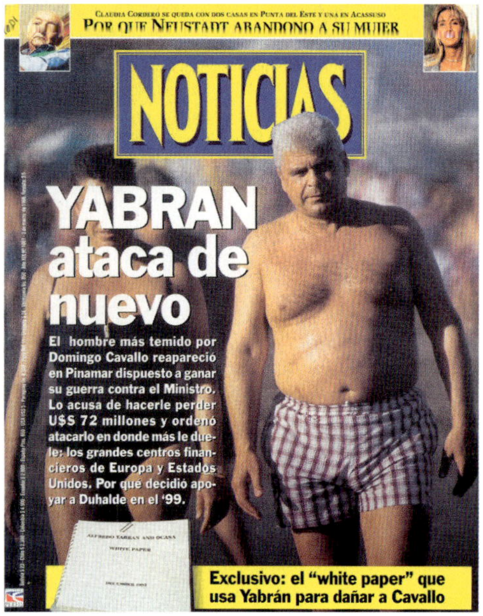

the Argentinean magazine *Paparazzi* based a promotion campaign on this situation. For its fiftieth anniversary it distributed sunshades—those pieces of foldable cardboard placed on windscreens in summer—depicting in trompe l'oeil celebrities caught by surprise in their cars. For the star, the situation is obviously less amusing. They find themselves caught in the car like a fish in an aquarium. For them, the car is a trap. The death of the Princess of Wales, imprisoned in her Mercedes under the Alma tunnel after a car chase with the paparazzi, is a particularly tragic confirmation of this.

11. Welcome to Media Hell

"A movement is currently taking shape in England against the exaggerated brazenness of a certain kind of press."[23] The remark seems acutely contemporary. It dates in fact from 1937. At the time, these words formed the opening of an article on "the rights of the press and people's private lives" in a journal for journalism professionals. The article was illustrated by two photographs showing different ways of escaping the prying lenses of those not yet known as paparazzi. In the first, a man attempts to hide his face behind his hands, his hat, and his foot. In the second, another man contorts his body in order to conceal his head between his legs. Indeed, a whole typology of attitudes exists for celebrities to protect themselves from nosy looks. But the most effective, the quickest, and the most prevalent still involves placing a hand between one's face and the camera lens. Since the beginning of the twentieth century, this gesture has been repeated so often that it has become a kind of visual signature for paparazzi photography. Most publications on this topic feature such an image on their cover and the present book is no exception. In his *Swingeing London 67* at the end of the 1960s, Richard Hamilton represented Mick Jagger and Robert Fraser hiding their faces with their hands after their arrest for drug possession. The art historian Hal Foster has noted how much this gesture recalls that of the famous fresco by Masaccio showing Adam and Eve banished from paradise having committed the original sin.[24] Today, this gesture of hiding one's face with one's hand is no longer a sign of the fall of man—it is instead a sign of the ascension to fame. For the person making it, it now marks not so much the expulsion from the Garden of Eden but rather the entry into media hell.

12. The About-Face of Violence

The practice of "hollaback" has developed a great deal over the past few years. If a woman is challenged or pestered in the street, she uses her smartphone to photograph her aggressor, and then posts the image on the Internet with an account of what took place.[25] This form of visual denunciation of everyday sexism is a complete reversal of the paparazzi principle. Moreover, several photographers have found themselves in a similar situation, with the tables turned on them in such a way. William Abenhaim tells of his surprise when he saw Kylie Minogue, whom he was tailing, suddenly turn toward him and compulsively photograph him.[26] However, the response is

23. Anonymous, "Les droits de la presse et la vie privée des gens," *Presse-Publicité*, no. 5 (April 11, 1937): 11.

24. See Hal Foster, *The First Pop Age: Painting and Subjectivity in the Art of Hamilton, Lichtenstein, Warhol, Richter, and Ruscha* (Princeton: Princeton University Press, 2011), 2–5.

25. See http://www.ihollaback.org/ accessed on December 8, 2013.

26. William Abenhaim, *Profession Paparazzo* (Paris: Nouveau Monde Editions, 2009), 101–2.

generally less sophisticated than this form of photographic hollaback. The star makes do with hurling abuse at the paparazzo, insulting him, throwing at him whatever can be found at hand. Sometimes the dispute turns into a fight. In 2010, the American actor Sean Penn was sentenced by a Los Angeles court to three years of probation and three hundred hours of community service for having violently punched a paparazzo.[27] The violence has gone much further in other cases. In February 2013, the Italian paparazzo Daniele Lo Presti—known for his photographs of celebrities and in particular those of Brad Pitt in the company of his alleged mistress—was found dead, a bullet in his head, under the Testaccio bridge in Rome. It is still not known to this day if he was killed for his photographs or in the context of a Mafia settling of scores. The situation is, however, perfectly clear in the case of José Luis Cabezas. In 1996, this Argentinean photographer managed to photograph on a beach one of the local Mafia chiefs whose portrait was as yet unknown. A few weeks later, the image appeared on the front page of the magazine *Noticias*. A short while after this, the photographer was kidnapped and then executed.[28] His picture had signed his death sentence. Much more than a hollaback, this is instead an ancestral expression of an eye for an eye. Visual violence is answered by physical, paroxysmal violence, which can lead to death.

13. The Paparazzi Aesthetic

Most paparazzi are not artists, but their pictures nevertheless often possess an astonishing aesthetic quality. As a consequence, there exists perhaps not a paparazzi *art* but a paparazzi *aesthetic*. This is the product of a group of technical determinants (the telephoto lens, the flash, the grain due to excessive enlargement), characteristic places (the car, the private pool, concert hall exits, or nightclubs), and gestural habits (the hand in front of the face, the surprised look or averted gaze). It is, for the most part, an aesthetic that is involuntary. From the 1960s, when Fellini baptized the phenomenon, artists began to be interested in this aesthetic. "The most exciting work I've seen lately," explains Andy Warhol, "are these paparazzi photos from the forties of movie stars and things that someone is printing on really good paper. They look so beautiful … like the greatest pictures in the world."[29] "I love the paparazzi," admits Helmut Newton. "I have always had a weakness for them. I have a certain admiration for their daring, their courage, and the strength of their work. I find it virile.… You know, I have never managed to do as well with Princess Caroline as the photos of certain paparazzi. As for the shots taken of Jackie Onassis naked, they are among the most disturbing images of this century."[30] The paparazzi aesthetic interests artists because it offers new visual forms, but also because it questions contemporary society's relationship with the media, with the spectacle, and with fame. Since pop art, and perhaps even more so with postmodernism, many artists have appropriated photographs taken by paparazzi. Others have played out again, in their own work, the characteristic codes of this iconography, or have temporarily transformed themselves into a paparazzo for a photographic series. Today, paparazzism has become a genre, a full-fledged stylistic category, and perhaps even one of the "-isms" of contemporary art.

27. See "300 heures de travaux d'intérêt général pour Sean Penn," *Le Monde* (May 15, 2010): 24.

28. See Marie-Monique Robin, "Mafia en Argentine," *Les 100 Photos du siècle* (Paris: Editions du Chêne/Hachette Livre, 1999), 97–98.

29. Andy Warhol, *I'll Be Your Mirror: The Selected Andy Warhol Interviews 1962–1987*, ed. Kenneth Goldsmith (New York: Da Capo Press, 2004), 316.

30. Helmut Newton, interview with Alain Morel, *Le Parisien*, May 26, 1995, quoted by Gilles Lhote, *Voleurs d'images. Les dessous des scoops* (Paris: Michel Lafon, 1995), 9.

RED CARPET

The hiss and crackle of camera flashes, screams, jostling, the surge of the crowd—when a star makes a public appearance everything happens quickly, but with extreme violence. If they are not held in behind barriers, as during traditional photo-calls, the paparazzi surround the celebrity, calling at them in an attempt to catch their gaze and shoot them with a thousand lights. The star is subjected to the slightest sway of the crowd, as if caught in a net. They can neither resist nor escape. It is a veritable photographic dismemberment led by a pack of jubilant hunters. Through works by Malachi Farrell, Frank Perrin, and a series of photographs taken by the paparazzi themselves, this opening section reveals the violence of the media pressure exerted against celebrities.

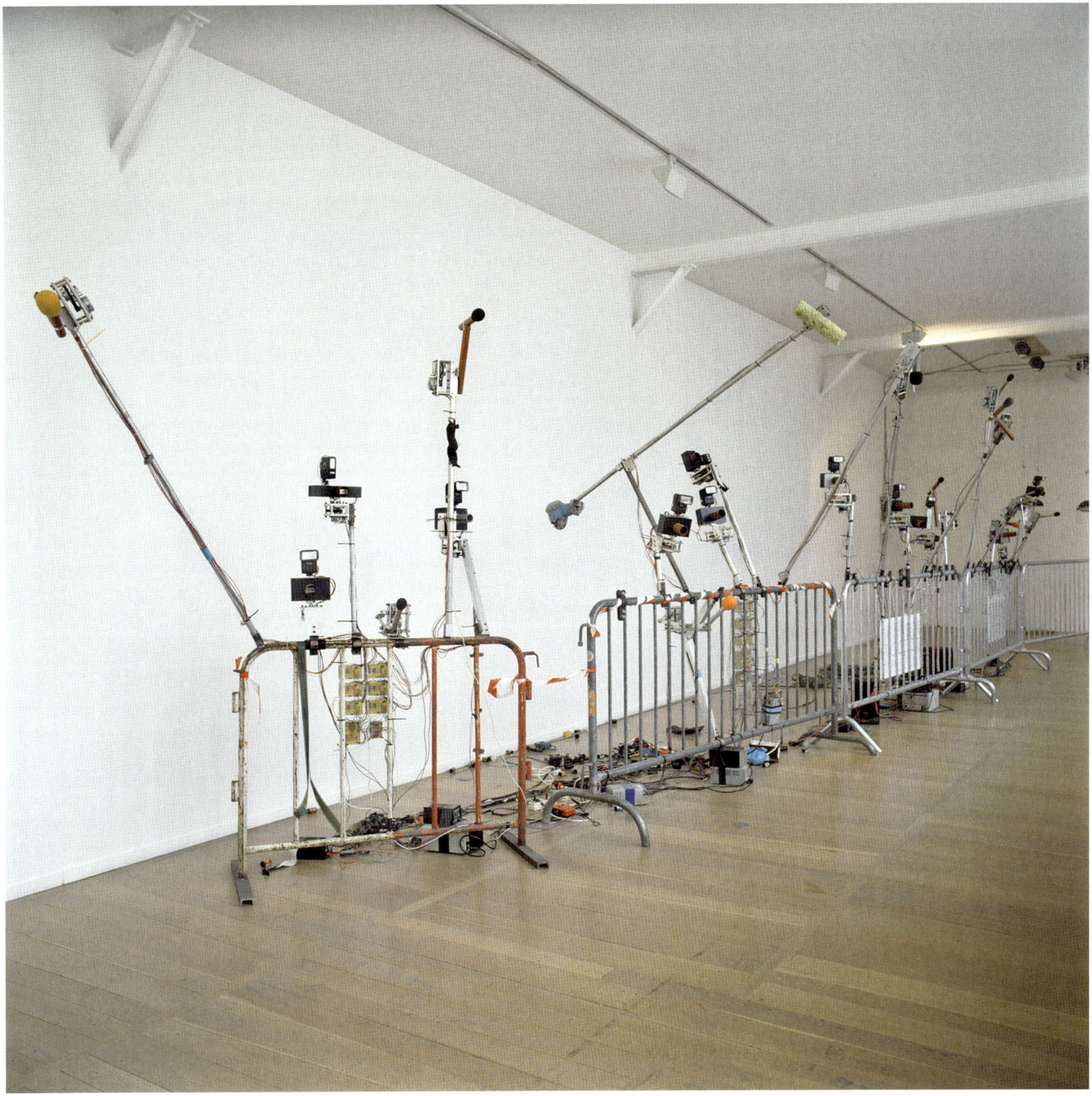

MALACHI FARRELL
Interview (Paparazzi)
2000

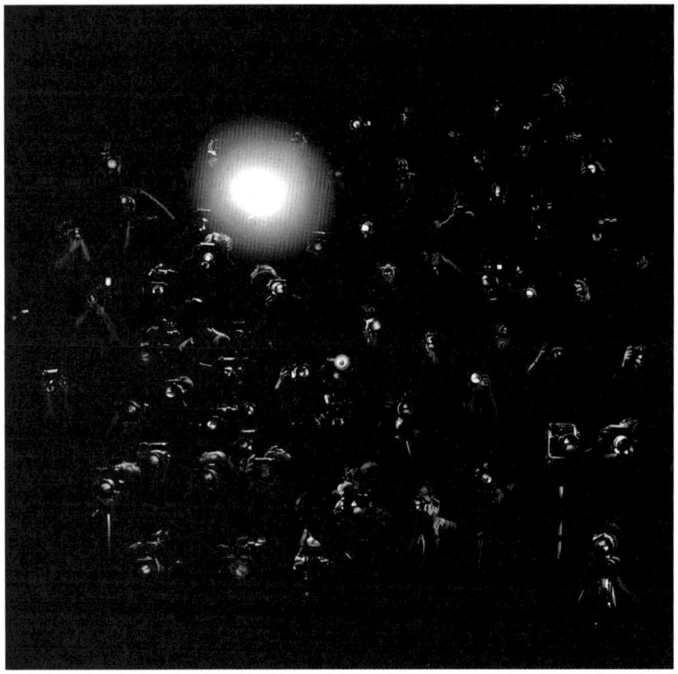

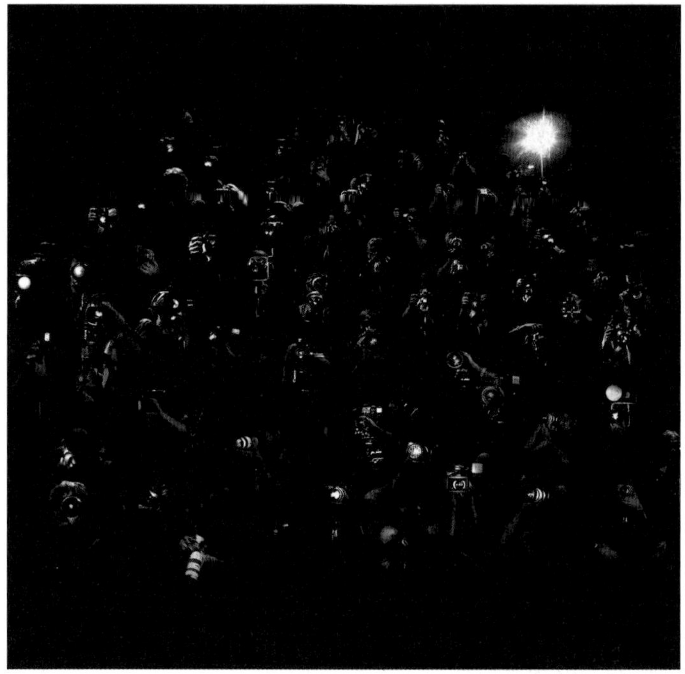

PAGE 21
MALACHI FARRELL, born in Ireland in 1970, created an installation entitled *Interview (Paparazzi)* in 2000. Atop the metal street barricades where paparazzi are stationed during photo calls, he mounted a phalanx of fictive photo devices equipped with bulbs and sensors that triggered flashes as viewers passed. Visitors were assaulted by blinding bursts of light as they advanced down a red carpet, becoming "stars" themselves. This "electromagnetic choreography," which combines sophisticated cutting-edge technology with more jerry-built touches, transposes the brutality of the contemporary media system into a museum setting. Providing an emotionally powerful experience, the installation demonstrates various practices that are all too prevalent in celebrity society, while retaining a certain playful—even humorous—quality.

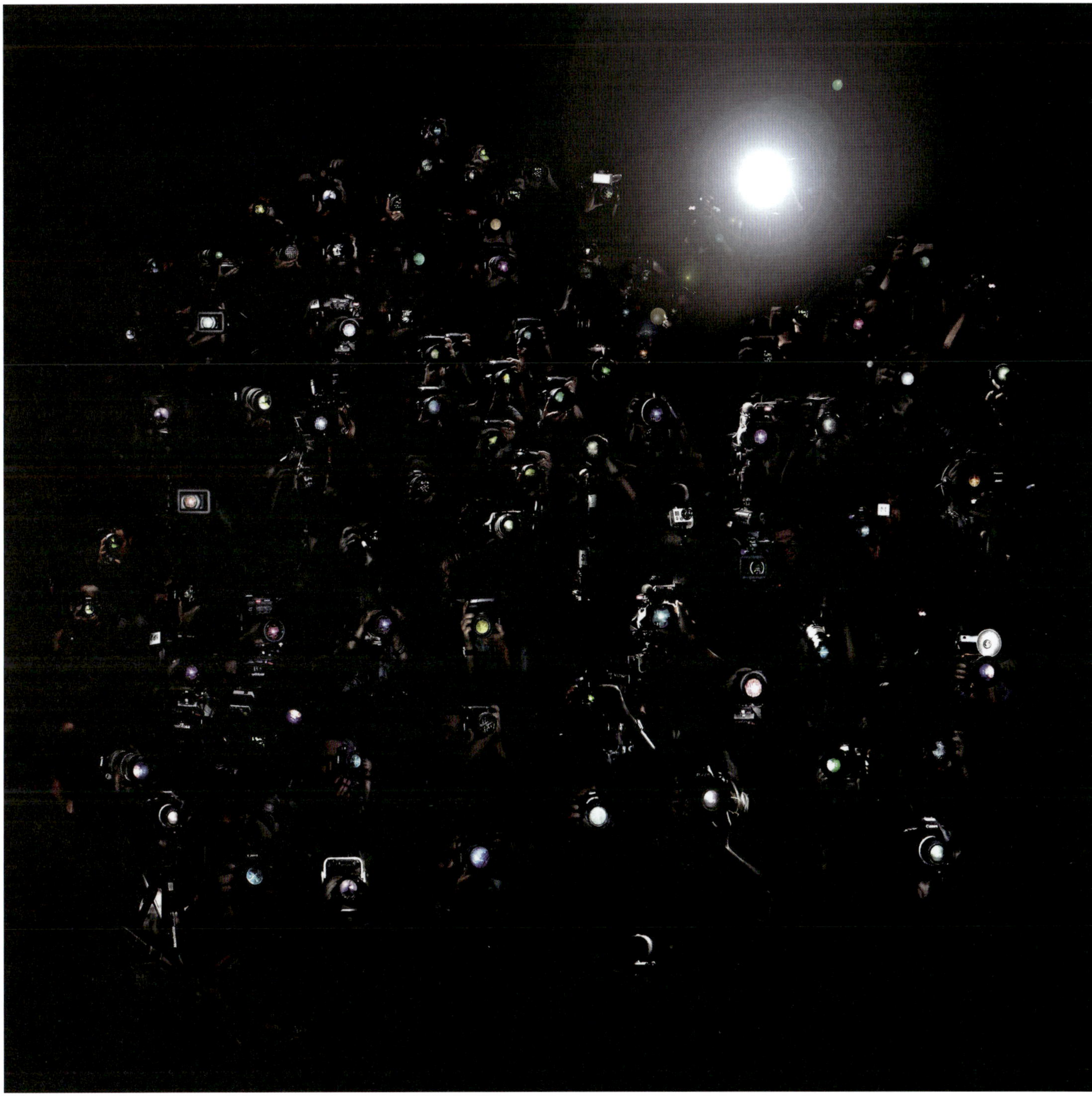

FRANK PERRIN
The Big Shot #01, #03, #04
(Postcapitalism Section 14)
2013

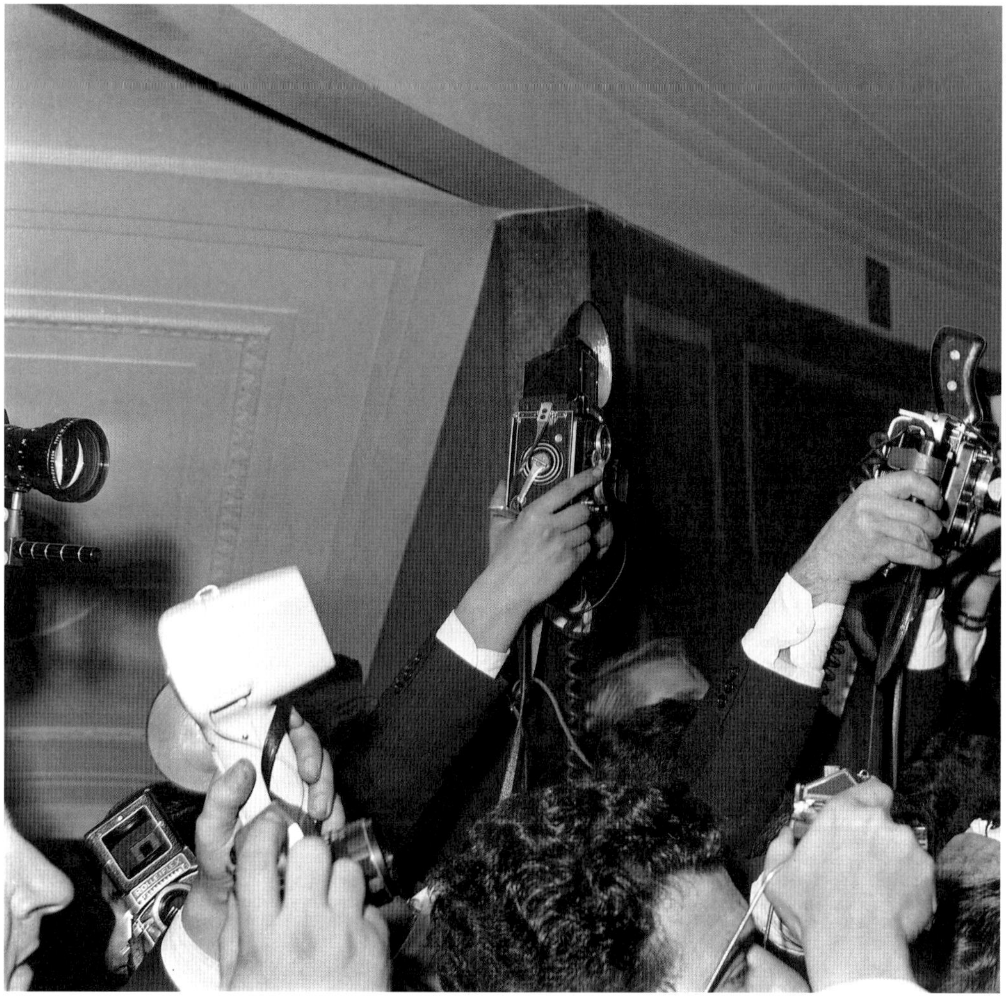

UMBERTO CICCONI
Paparazzi Photographing Sophia Loren at the Premiere of the Film Marriage Italian Style *by Vittorio De Sica at the Teatro dell'Opera, Rome*
December 18, 1964

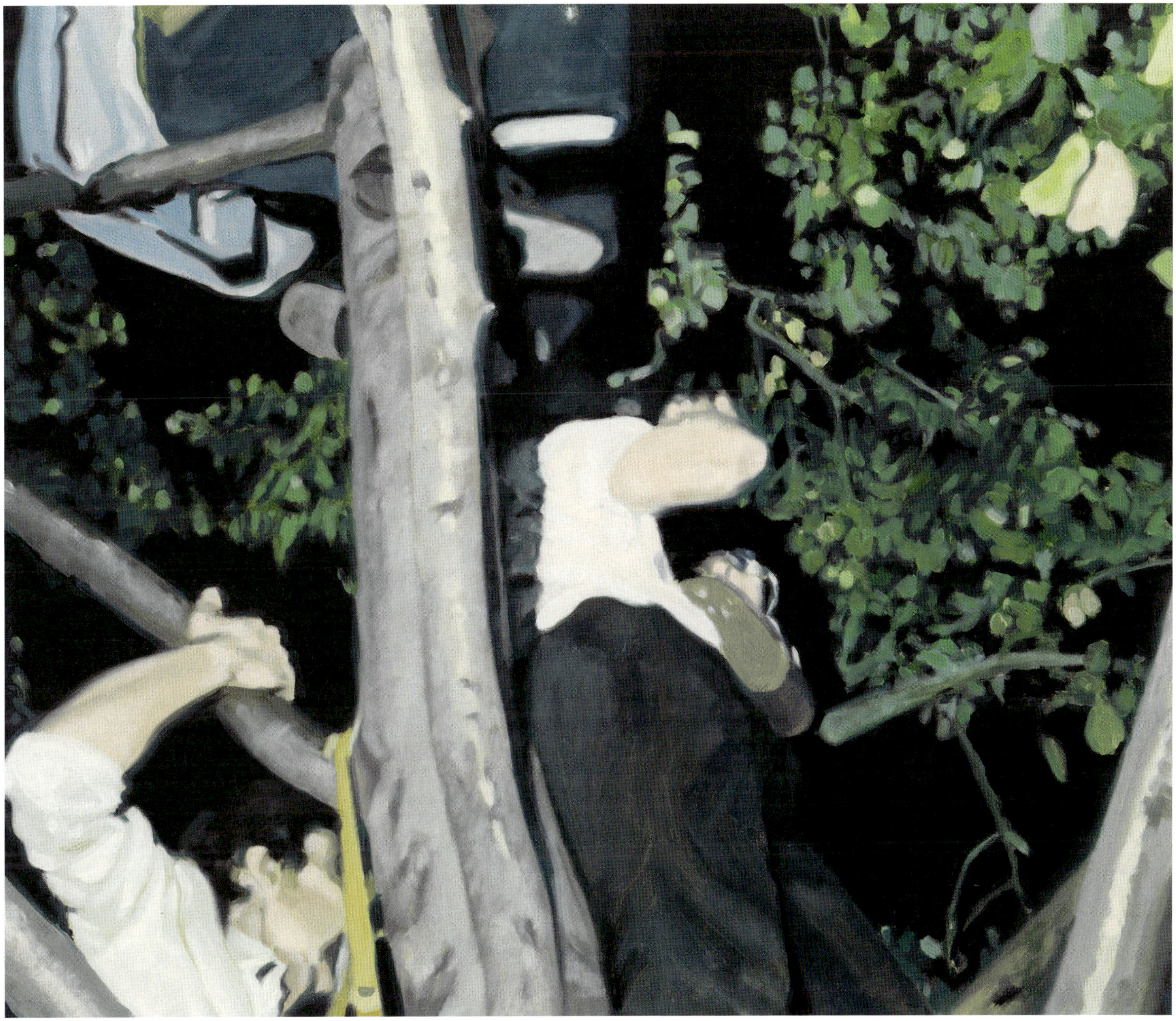

PASCAL DANZ
1972 (Paparazzi)
2007

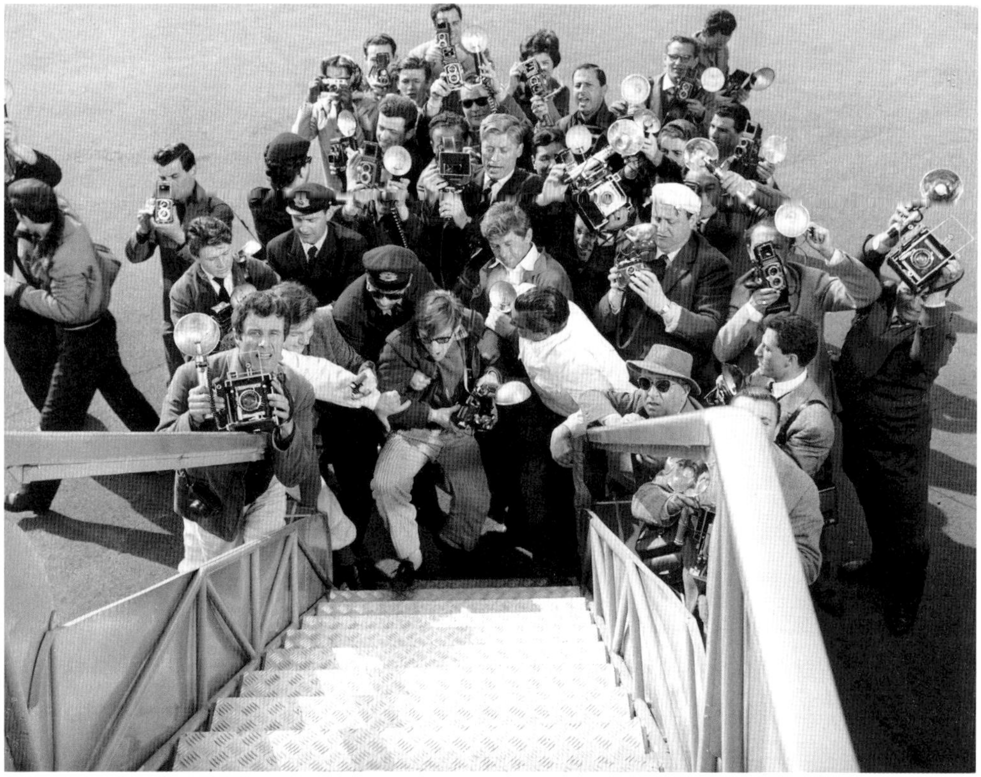

ANONYMOUS
(Pierluigi Agency)
Photographers Waiting for Anita Ekberg at an Airplane Boarding Ramp
1959

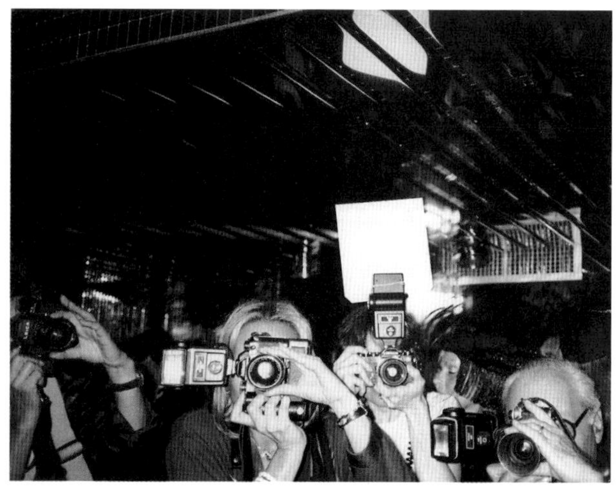

ANDY WARHOL
Paparazzi
1986

THE WOLF PACK. When Federico Fellini directed *La Dolce Vita* in 1960, he stigmatized a practice that had recently become widespread: the stalking of stars by photographers. Actors and actresses, perhaps more than any other celebrities, were subject to predatory pursuit by the media. Photographers "hunted" them in gangs, gathering in throngs that sometimes reminded observers of wolf packs. They targeted the star, encircling her, advancing closer and closer to seize her image with a violence that symbolically evoked a fatal attack. The crowd of lenses and the ever-tightening concentric circles of photographers around their prey contributed to a sense of oppression. "Celebrity culture," to use the terminology of sociologist Chris Rojek, is a modern idolatrous cult in which the star is relentlessly pursued until she finds herself cornered—to persevere with the metaphor of predator and prey.

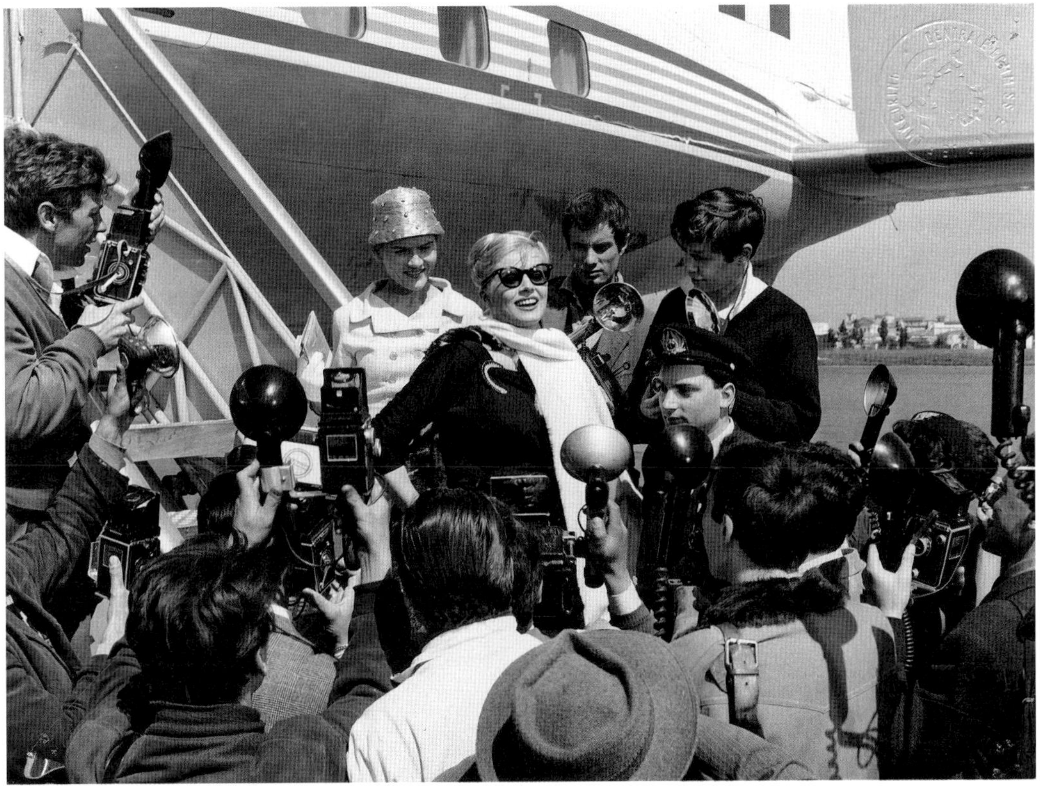

ANONYMOUS
(Pierluigi Agency)
Anita Ekberg Getting Off an Airplane
1959

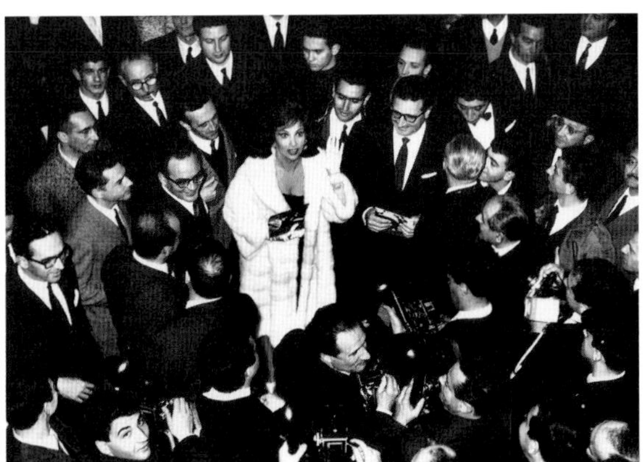

MASSIMO ASCANI
Gina Lollobrigida at the Maschere d'Argento (Silver Ribbon) Ceremony, Rome
March 29, 1962

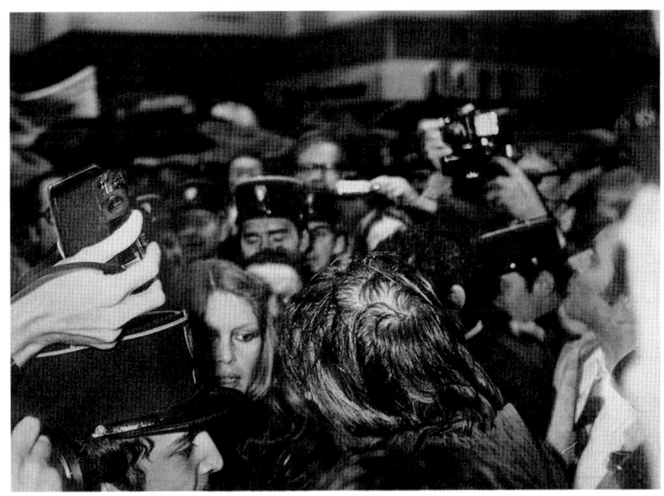

JEAN-JACQUES CECCARINI
Brigitte Bardot during a Demonstration against the Massacre of Baby Seals in front of the Norwegian Embassy, Paris
April 1976

PHOTOGRA

PHERS

A PROFESSION

The paparazzi are ingenious, often setting up complex and risky operations. Each of them possesses his own tricks and anecdotes that together construct a great chronicle of the profession. Through interviews with a few of the top paparazzi of our time and descriptions of their most common accessories (from the spy camera to the telephoto lens, as well as some of their disguises), this section explores the everyday details of the trade. Series of photographs by Olivier Mirguet, Jessica Dimmock, and Christophe Beauregard; an extract from *Reporters* by Raymond Depardon; and a video by Romain Dussaulx and Benjamin Lalande made in Los Angeles show the hideouts, the waiting, and, finally, the confrontation, allowing us to understand what being a paparazzo means.

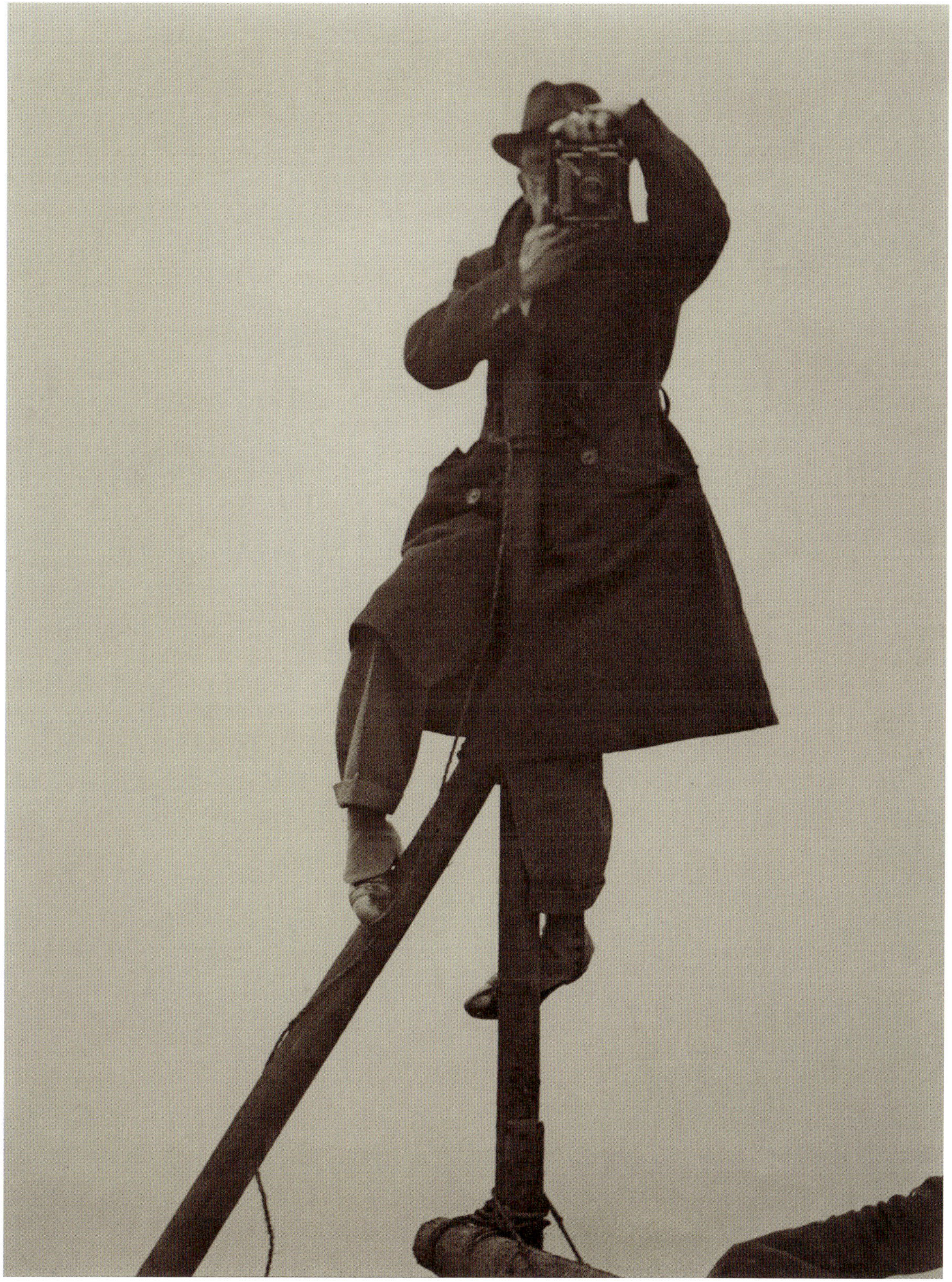

ANONYMOUS
(Fox Photos)
Reporter Hanging off Scaffolding, London
c. 1930

Hazards of the Trade: Interviews with Paparazzi

Clément Chéroux, Camille Lenglois, Véra Léon, Max Bonhomme

How did you become a paparazzo?

DANIEL ANGELI: I began at the age of sixteen. I wasn't a good student, and so I had to choose a job. My father worked in catering, but I didn't want to do that. I had never thought of taking photographs in my life. I first started work at *Jours de France*—but I was too young to be an intern—and then at Dalmas, a press agency that had a photographic laboratory called Photodal. And so I began work as a laboratory assistant for about a year.

BRUNO MOURON: A book was published by Robert Laffont [in 1970], *The Reporters* by Christian Brincourt and Michel Leblanc. I read all these accounts by photographers, journalists, and people from the radio: they were fabulous stories that revealed all the tricks for making a good photo ... or a news story. And I decided I wanted to do that job. So I studied in the photo department of the IDHEC film school. I didn't like it that much because we studied things like the decomposition of light or optical mathematics. I dropped out but I got lucky. Thanks to a friend of my parents I was able to get a foothold in the newspaper *L'Aurore*, and from there, little by little, I made my way up in the profession until I got a job with *Paris Match*.

FRANCIS APESTEGUY: One day, in front of the Castel restaurant, I came across three or four guys with cameras on the ground. I didn't understand what they were doing there, and so I asked them. They told me they photographed stars. I was just getting started as a photographer and had been an assistant, but I found this boring. So I joined them with my camera at night, and I observed and imitated their practice, and things followed on from there.

SÉBASTIEN VALIELA: I have always had a passion for photography. I got my first camera at about the age of eight. After the Baccalaureate exams, I went to a photography school and looked for a job in the field. "Paparazzi" was the area I liked the most.

RON GALELLA: I started out as a ceramic artist.... I got out of doing military service because I didn't want to take part in the Korean War. Instead, I enrolled in the US Air Force. And this was the beginning of my career as a photographer. I studied at the Art Center College of Design in order to become a photojournalist, then I went back to the Bronx where I was born, to my father's house. I didn't have enough money to rent a studio so I built a laboratory in the basement.... I was twelve miles from the center of Manhattan, where the action and celebrities could be found. I photographed stars at evening parties, at film premieres. That's how I began. It was easy to photograph on the spot, and it was great because it provided some realism. I like photographing people as they are, with their various links. I don't like the "one, two, three, smile!" poses, fixed in front of the camera lens.

What is your best paparazzi memory?

DANIEL ANGELI: It would probably be—even if they have been talked about too much—my photos of Agnelli, for example, or certain hideouts in the sun used to take snaps of Romy Schneider or Brigitte Bardot. It was at the start of my career. I was totally at ease because I was at a distance from my subjects. The choice of working with a telephoto lens is due in part to my shyness. Even at the Cannes Festival, I preferred using 400 mm on close-ups rather than working in close proximity to my subjects.

RON GALELLA: *Windblown Jackie* is my most sensational photo. I was photographing a fashion model in Central Park, near to Jackie [Kennedy]'s house, and I thought to myself that I might see her go for a run in the park, but it didn't happen. And then, as I left Central Park, across from her house, I saw Jackie leaving her home by the backdoor. She was walking toward the northern end of Madison Avenue and I jumped into a cab to catch up with her. Jackie was walking when the cab hooted. Jackie turned around and I photographed her. She hadn't recognized me, hidden behind my camera in the back of the cab. But as soon as I got out, she said, "Oh, it's you again!" Then she added, "Are you satisfied?" and I replied, "Yes, thank you. Good-bye." *Windblown Jackie* is my best photo—the most incredible, my favorite, the most sold, and the most published. It is my Mona Lisa.

FRANCIS APESTEGUY: The best memories are also the worst. When I get hit or when I punch back. If not, I have good memories of shots I've taken from a distance, without being seen, leaving the "prey" to their own devices.

PASCAL ROSTAIN: I don't know if we can talk about paparazzi memories or just memories, simply because they are about encounters. They are not necessarily the most famous photos that have been published the most or, let's be honest, earned the most money, . . . but rather memories of encounters. For me, there have been several, in particular that incredible meeting with Orson Welles, who we began "paparazzing" in 1982 when he came [to France] as President of the César Awards ceremony, and with whom I later became friends. I could also mention a recent photo taken at Castel Gandolfo where we hid from the ex-pope Benedict XVI, in gardens which, for thirty-five years, had had the reputation of being totally impregnable.

SÉBASTIEN VALIELA: The best memory, in my view, is the day the photographs of Mitterrand and Mazarine [Pingeot, Mitterrand's illegitimate daughter] were published, when we realized, with my friend Pierre Suu, what we had done and the consequences. We were watching the program *Les Guignols* [a satirical puppet show] which presented Mazarine's birth announcement, and it made us laugh.

What is your worst paparazzi memory?

RON GALELLA: The worst moment was in Cuernavaca, in Mexico, when I was following Elizabeth Taylor and Richard Burton on the shooting of *Hammersmith is Out*. I got caught on the set. Richard Burton recognized me and he sent three bodyguards to hit me. My nose and a few teeth were broken. They took my films and went to my hotel where they confiscated fifteen others, that is to say two weeks of work and over five hundred photos. They unrolled the films on the set, destroying my work. I pressed charges against Richard Burton and Elizabeth Taylor. But I lost the case because the hotel owner didn't want to testify that he had authorized me to photograph them. That was the worst—they even sent me to prison. A thrashing and no sleep; it was a nightmare. I stayed in prison for one hour before they let me go. I made the front page of the newspaper down there: "Life Photographer Sues Elizabeth Taylor and Richard Burton." Richard Burton wanted me to sign a press release saying that he wasn't implicated and offered me 1,500 dollars in exchange. I said no, but I lost the case.

SÉBASTIEN VALIELA: I haven't got any bad memories.

FRANCIS APESTEGUY: They are the same as the good ones, when I get beaten up, but that's the price to pay! Sometimes there can be a bad response.

DANIEL ANGELI: I have to think. My worst memory is in London. . . . I was taking a series of photos that would have been very important at the time, but there was no film in my camera!

BRUNO MOURON: The worst memories are inevitably when you bungle a shot!

What is the most annoying thing in the life of a paparazzo?

SÉBASTIEN VALIELA: Waiting!

DANIEL ANGELI: It's the waiting, when nothing happens. I like things that move very fast.

FRANCIS APESTEGUY: One might think it is the waiting, but in fact we have a totally different relationship to time. The first hour is tough, then the second hour is less so, and by the tenth hour it isn't difficult anymore. It is not the waiting that is the most annoying, but maybe the need to go to the bathroom.

PASCAL ROSTAIN: The most annoying thing in the paparazzi profession is when the information you have been given is incorrect.

BRUNO MOURON: Missing a story, otherwise we get used to the rest! Hiding out can be long, but at the same time it's not boring because we don't know what we are going to do when we get up every morning.

What is the most enjoyable thing in the life of a paparazzo?

BRUNO MOURON: The most enjoyable thing is obviously when you know that your photographs are going to be published, and, above all, the attraction of the scoop.

DANIEL ANGELI: Succeeding. Bringing back the pictures. Being in the swing of current events.

SÉBASTIEN VALIELA: The moment we take the photo, or just after, when we know we have obtained something we have been waiting a long time for.

Which star did you most enjoy photographing?

FRANCIS APESTEGUY: There are so many of them! I loved Catherine Deneuve, because she was such a rebel! We found ourselves in crazy car chases; it was like in Charlot's films, we ran all the red lights, it didn't make any sense. It was extraordinary, we didn't even realize—neither she nor I—that we were risking our lives for nothing, in vain. This is the memory that comes back to me now, but there are many more.

RON GALELLA: The person I most enjoyed photographing was Jackie, because she didn't pose; she was herself and I appreciated that. I was very good at catching people in an instant and Jackie was my favorite subject. I knew where she lived; I was in my car waiting for her, following her. It was a whole adventure and I loved that.

SÉBASTIEN VALIELA: I have really photographed a lot of people, especially during the time I was in the United States; we could snap three or four subjects a day. In France, it is always more or less about the same people, but I enjoy photographing anybody.

PASCAL ROSTAIN: It is somewhat paradoxical to imagine that we could enjoy photographing a star. Firstly, I find the word "star" very demeaning and vulgar—I prefer to use the term "celebrity." I really liked following and photographing Mitterrand, but maybe more for ideological reasons, because his personality was fascinating. It is not necessarily the important people who count. The royal family of Monaco has been photographed a lot; we lived with them, were their distant cousins, their hidden family. The celebrities that I really enjoy photographing are still politicians, as they always have something to hide and, as Pierre Lazareff used to say, our primary role is based on three rules: the first, verify; the second, verify; the third, verify.

BRUNO MOURON: Some paparazzi are in the profession because they are fans. We are not fans of the stars, but of our profession. We are more journalists than fans. We are not friends with the stars.

Are you more flash or telephoto lens?

PASCAL ROSTAIN: We began in the 1970s at a time when we were part of the celebrity environment. It was totally different; we weren't hidden but out on the pavements. There was, if not a sense of cooperation, then at least a certain elegance—the elegance of the people we were photographing, and, as a result, in our attitude toward them. Over time, the first English tabloids—which became increasingly aggressive—appeared, as well as telephoto technology that allowed us to photograph from a distance. I like both ways. The most important thing is that the pictures we take tell a story.... The technique is of little importance—it is the result that counts.

BRUNO MOURON: We have adapted. Before telephotography, it was nice because there was a certain proximity between people, like the paparazzi of *La Dolce Vita*. Obviously, with the telephoto lens our work is different. But it was more enjoyable when we worked in 35 mm.

FRANCIS APESTEGUY: I began as a "matador," in close contact, very provocative, planting my banderillas at every flash. I was snatching something, taking something that I wouldn't give back, even if I was beaten up. Later, I understood that it was smarter to let the prey go and to follow it around with the telephoto lens, as I would get something anyway. As Cartier-Bresson used to say, you mustn't want anything because otherwise you won't get anything. This is the approach I later adopted, with a bit more intelligence—and a few punches.

RON GALELLA: It really depends on your subject, on the circumstances. If I was in a building photographing Jackie, I would use a wide-angle lens, a 300-mm lens. If it was John Lennon or David Bowie, a long focal length. It depends on the situation, but most of the time I prefer the short focal length, a wide-angle.

Because people know me—for better or for worse—and celebrities react to me, they say "No photos!" Either they pose for me, or they throw me out. But most of the time, I prefer taking them by surprise five feet away, really fast. Then they see me and react, and I take another one and manage to capture their look of surprise: that's what I like taking.

DANIEL ANGELI: Everything depends on whether the picture needs to be good or not. I prefer working with a telephoto lens because I am shy, and I find the pictures are better.

SÉBASTIEN VALIELA: I use the telephoto lens—we can't use a flash anyway in France. With our laws, if we want the pictures to come out before any injunction, people mustn't see us. Photographers who use a flash are mostly based in the United States; in France, Italy, and Spain we work much more with the telephoto lens.

Do you consider yourself a collector of stars?

FRANCIS APESTEGUY: Not at all.

BRUNO MOURON: Not at all. I am not a fan of the stars. I enjoy my job. When you work for [*Paris*] *Match*, you don't only take paparazzi photographs, which means I get to do different things and it is more balanced.

PASCAL ROSTAIN: Not at all. I don't collect stars. I don't collect pictures. I only collect memories.

DANIEL ANGELI: I have met a lot of celebrities and had human relationships with many of these people—John Lennon, Johnny Hallyday, Onassis—but it wasn't calculated. For me, it was a normal relationship. I realize today that these pictures are important because the people are important, but at the time I was just doing my job as I would have done any other.

RON GALELLA: I am not really a collector. I don't collect autographs and other celebrity objects. My interest is limited to photographing stars. My art—photography—is the art of today and it is beautiful. For me, painting and sculpture have had their time. Photography is modern art.

Do you feel as if you reestablish a kind of truth about the stars?

DANIEL ANGELI: That is a very good question and one that has always bothered me about the profession. The pictures we take are destined to be published in newspapers according to how *they* want them to be interpreted. The text can give a certain interpretation of a photograph but it is not always the truth. I have seen some of my pictures published with false captions, telling a story that doesn't exist, for commercial reasons. It is a complicated question.

BRUNO MOURON: A photo has nothing to do with text. Depending on how the caption is formulated, it can make a photo say whatever one wants, but I think that a photo is truth, as long as it has not been doctored or reprinted. In its pure state, a photo bears real testimony.... The paparazzi are much closer to reality. The last photographer to have [really] photographed a star is [Bert] Stern who, when he photographed Marilyn, spent forty-eight hours alone with her. You can see the emotion, you can see everything in his photos. When you want to photograph a star or any celebrity today, there is a producer or a press agent there—there are fifteen different people behind them. You can't do anything; nothing happens and the photos show this. In addition, the photos are totally retouched. For me, it's about PR, and that's another profession.

SÉBASTIEN VALIELA: Yes, we reestablish the truth, and we are the only ones to tell it. The contents of the "official" magazines resemble advertorials more than reporting. Newspapers take care not to upset personalities, asking them the right questions, photographing them in a good light, with the right makeup. We don't bother with all that, we capture the brutal truth.... If we say something that goes against what they want us to believe, we just say it, that's all.

RON GALELLA: Yes, I capture the stars as they are, in action. Like Philippe Halsman, who photographed several covers of *Life* magazine. He managed to keep such a low profile that the stars forgot he was there and didn't look at the camera or the photographer, thereby retaining their natural expression. The key is ensuring that when stars do something, they are themselves.

PASCAL ROSTAIN: It's a game. There is no truth, there are no lies. It's a game of cat and mouse, of cops and robbers. Certain stars overuse it, abuse it, play with it. In the end, the day a real star no longer has any paparazzi in front of their house, they're not anything anymore.

FRANCIS APESTEGUY: It would be too long to answer in depth. We only capture a kind of monumental stupidity, a frivolity, a cheap drug authorized in the kiosks. All of this is just about frivolity.

Is there a paparazzi code of ethics?

RON GALELLA: I have limits. I wouldn't go into a star's home without being invited, but I have knocked at their doors. I went to Doris Day's house once. I took some photos until she asked me, "Are you a professional?" I said yes. Bang! She slammed the door in my face! When I knocked on Nathalie Wood's door, she said, "Come in. I'll be ready in five minutes!" And she let me take some good photos of her in a miniskirt.

PASCAL ROSTAIN: The limits are not fixed by our profession, nor by the people we photograph, nor by the magazines we work for. They are fixed by a baseline of decency. There are obviously things that we are not going to photograph, but it's not that common an occurrence in encounters between paparazzi and stars—it's much more common in cases concerning miscellaneous news items or conflicts, when it's often easy to trample all over decency every day. Increasingly, the stars open the doors of their apartments, their bathrooms, and—why not?—their clinics.... Indecency is not always on the side of the paparazzi or the public, it is also on the side of those we photograph.

FRANCIS APESTEGUY: Each person has their own limits. I have colleagues who photographed Romy Schneider's son at the morgue, by disguising themselves as doctors. I couldn't have done that, because I already had a child at the time and so other references, which wasn't their case. I might have done the same thing as them before I had a child—it is a question of mental references.

DANIEL ANGELI: There are barriers in this profession: for example, children or deaths, such as the death of Romy Schneider's son, which deeply marked me because certain photos were published that I would not have taken.

SÉBASTIEN VALIELA: There is obviously no written code of ethics. Everyone does as they choose. Apart from not touching on illness or people's physical weaknesses, the rest doesn't seem important, given that we concentrate mostly on happy events (love stories, pregnancies etc.) 99 percent of the time.

According to you, who creates the paparazzi? The magazines or the readers?

DANIEL ANGELI: I would say that initially it is the reader.... If the reader buys, he must be interested.

SÉBASTIEN VALIELA: In my opinion, the readers are the first; they are hungry for scoops and gossip. The magazines just give them what they want. We can see this clearly today on the Internet.

RON GALELLA: The creation of the paparazzi industry is the result of a combination of the public's desire to know—curiosity, in other words—and the photographer's. This is what motivated me, to see what the rich and famous were like, and it is the same for the public. Everyone wants to know how they live, what they are like, etc.

BRUNO MOURON: It is a vicious circle. People say that without the readers there would be no magazines, and if there were no magazines, there would be no readers. This shouldn't be taken as an excuse. It is completely untrue.

FRANCIS APESTEGUY: In Diana's case, there was talk of "Paparazzi assassins." It was a perfect spotlight. But the paparazzi who were there in that tunnel were commissioned, which implies a commissioner—they are the ones who create the paparazzi. [Who are the commissioners?] The press tycoons: [Rupert] Murdoch, Bernard Arnault, [Arnaud] Lagardère, people who have nothing to do with the press, who are salesmen and wheeler-dealers. There's an argument worthy of Mélenchon [French left-wing politician]!

PASCAL ROSTAIN: I think that neither the magazines nor the readers create the paparazzi. It is simply the celebrities and the people who refuse to be photographed. It is very complicated, because at some point they need the promotion,... they need the press, and allow this media intrusion into their private life. But the day they decide to close the door—and this is understandable—the public and the magazines want to know more.

What do you feel about the society of the spectacle in which we live?

SÉBASTIEN VALIELA: It is not all about glitter and celebrities, but people need this to relax. [Reading magazines like *OK!*, *National Enquirer*, or *Hello!*] provides a small break for people to escape a little.

FRANCIS APESTEGUY: If I was still a paparazzo today, I would necessarily be a part of it. We serve a frivolous system which does not better people's minds. We render them stupid. It is a free drug, as I said for the Diana affair. If there weren't any dealers, there would be no drug addicts.

RON GALELLA: I think there is an excess of media and that they overexpose everything—it's not good. They have become vulgar. They go and see the stars to demolish them, whereas I like to build them up, I like to see what is beautiful. That's why I photograph beautiful, natural expressions. But today the media focuses on their cellulite, on their legs; they want to make them ugly, show their obesity and everything else. I find it horrible.

DANIEL ANGELI: For me, it represents the end of my profession. I stopped twenty years ago to devote myself to something else—rock 'n' roll, cinema—when everything interesting about the job was coming to an end. I would not choose this job today. At the time, what interested me was the discovery. There were very few newspapers, it was difficult. You had to really want to do photography.

PASCAL ROSTAIN: The Internet has changed things enormously. It is a death sentence for the printed press. You really have to be more and more interested in all things digital. The problem with the Internet is that there is a huge amount of stupid things on there. We are back to the fundamentals of the profession, there are fewer and fewer journalists in the field. When we did a stakeout on General Rondot, when *Le Monde* published the Clearstream affair, people often said to us, "You are the best!" No, we weren't the best, we were the only ones in the field. Thirty years ago, there would have been fifty journalists.... The only rule, as Tom Wolfe—who was a journalist before becoming a writer—said, is to go out into the field.... We have to incite the younger generations to get out into the street. Learning on the streets is what's best.

Is there a political dimension to your job?

FRANCIS APESTEGUY: All our thoughts are political in some way.... I didn't do this job as a class struggle, it was about provocation. I have always been a provocateur. That said, you could always link this provocation to a class struggle—when I mentioned Mélenchon, it was for a reason!

PASCAL ROSTAIN: There is no political dimension, only the dimension of truth. If politics lie, if politicians are bullshitting, it is the journalist's role to show it.

RON GALELLA: There is nothing political in my photos of celebrities. I photograph in an objective manner. I do not lean to one side or the other. I give an account of what I see. What I do is photojournalism.

DANIEL ANGELI: I have touched upon politics. For me, political characters such as Sarkozy are a bit like showbiz stars.

SÉBASTIEN VALIELA: There is a political dimension only when I photograph politicians, because celebrity politics has started to come into our profession. But we always remain within the private sphere, we don't really deal with the politics.

Why are there no women paparazzi?

BRUNO MOURON: It is strange, because women are often more patient than men.

FRANCIS APESTEGUY: You should ask them!

SÉBASTIEN VALIELA: I met some in the United States, but it's true that it's quite rare and in France there aren't any. Why? I don't know. Maybe because it's not a profession that interests them.

DANIEL ANGELI: There are a few, but they don't last because it really is a difficult job. I don't think it is a job for women.

RON GALELLA: My wife Betty was a *paparazza*. We were in Johannesburg photographing Ted and Rose Kennedy during a parade; she fell, knocked over by another photographer, and fractured her knee. She stopped after that. The reason why there are no women is because it's tough, really tough.

What do you say to people who accuse you of violating other people's privacy?

FRANCIS APESTEGUY: They're right! I don't answer them, but I have realized that the people who make these accusations often know the contents of celebrity magazines much better than we do!

RON GALELLA: It's a point of view. Maybe sometimes I intrude upon their privacy and go too far. If celebrities want privacy, they should stay at home. They should expect paparazzi in public.

SÉBASTIEN VALIELA: The people who say that are probably the ones we photograph—it's understandable if they get angry! What we do is not very serious, we rarely reveal anything extremely important. There are limits though—defined by the law, not only by us. Generally, we announce, maybe two weeks before them, before a red carpet event or a film premiere, that so-and-so is with so-and-so, that's all. The term "violating their privacy" seems a bit strong; it is more that we get in their way on a commercial, publicity, or career level.

PASCAL ROSTAIN: Certainly, we can steal a picture, but we don't steal their souls! If they even have one.... "Robbers," "violators," that's fine, it's really aggressive, but aren't they stealing the truth? We haven't "stolen" pictures,... they are just *real* images. It's people's real lives, and that's why it works, because that interests the public.

DANIEL ANGELI: I have rarely been attacked.... What I think is bad about this profession is that we bother people just because they are well known and it sells. For my part, I have always tried to be in tune with current events, to have a cause, a reason for taking my photo. For example, my photo of Agnelli jumping naked into the sea was taken because of the Revelli-Beaumont affair at the time. What is the boss of Fiat doing at the moment a ransom is being asked for the life of the man who represented Fiat? Afterward, the photo can be interpreted in a different way, but I took it in this spirit.

What do you think about the fact that certain people consider you as predators yet take great delight in your pictures at the same time?

FRANCIS APESTEGUY: [Laughs] I still don't understand it!

RON GALELLA: There is a lot of hypocrisy in this fear of celebrity photography, a lot of contradiction. Stars maybe don't like it, but at the end of the day they want to see themselves in the magazines and on TV. We are considered parasites and intruders. For me, it's not true, and it doesn't affect me!

SÉBASTIEN VALIELA: I don't feel I am perceived as a predator at all! When I take photos in the street, people come and talk to me, sometimes they ask me questions—it is never aggressive. When I am at a dinner party and people find out what I do they ask me a lot of questions and people are fairly favorable. I don't really have a feeling of aggression. I think that traffic wardens in the street are more badly perceived than me.

PASCAL ROSTAIN: I am very comfortable with this contradiction. Firstly, it is a very Gallic attitude, very French. We like to burn our icons, we like consuming this kind of information, but we also like saying that it's despicable. It's a global market, and what's interesting is to see how we are considered abroad. In certain countries such as Spain, Italy, or the United States, it is totally accepted—we are considered as journalists doing a job that is not at all deplorable. It is true that this happened in France, after August 31, 1997, after Princess Diana's accident, when we were condemned and lambasted by our journalist colleagues, who, when we get a scoop that makes the cover of a magazine, love talking about it or showing it on screen. So we're comfortable with it because we're not naïve. We have no remorse or regrets. I have perhaps had more regrets when photographing miscellaneous news stories or conflicts.

BRUNO MOURON: People need truth, and know very well that it sometimes appears straight up in these photos. You also have to resituate everything in time and look at the photos that were taken twenty, thirty, or forty years ago. Today people look at them differently and appreciate them; they are even hung on museum walls!

Have you noticed any developments in the profession?

BRUNO MOURON: There are many more photographers and the way of working is different today. It was much more relaxed for us; we worked with 35 mm, there was a certain proximity with people, a dialogue, we talked to them. Sometimes we took photos and then we went for a drink with them. Something happened.... Now, there are two kinds of journalists: those who remain behind their desk and work on the Net, and thousands of paparazzi in the street, working in packs. They are more aggressive because there is no contact.

DANIEL ANGELI: When I started out, I had very few media within my reach. There was *Paris Match*, *France Dimanche*, *Ici Paris*, and *Noir et Blanc*, which has since disappeared, and then the dailies, *Paris Presse, L'Intransigeant* with Edgar Schneider's pages, that interested us and kept us going. For a few years, it was really difficult to survive in this profession, and then suddenly there was the German press explosion, the birth of *Voici* in France, prices rose and that formed a kind of photographer similar to a picture hunter, which didn't exist when I started out.

FRANCIS APESTEGUY: It has gone dramatically downhill. Today, the methods are still the same, but the paparazzi trail Patrick Poivre d'Arvor—it's bullshit. In my time it was Sophia Loren, Catherine Deneuve, Brigitte Bardot. There was something there, it was glorious. When Stallone arrived in Paris, we followed him around; there were four or five of us, and we spent the day with him at Montmartre and he posed for us. I could give other examples.

PASCAL ROSTAIN: We started at a time when there were fifty paparazzi on the planet. We all knew each other, there were ten of us in France, twelve in England, there were two on the American East Coast, there was Phil Ramey on the West Coast. There were only a lot of them in Italy.... It was really the *dolce vita* at a more elegant time, where what counted was the demonstration of truth. There was a Robin Hood quality about it. We would have exclusivity for several months, today that lasts for ten minutes. News goes faster and faster—much too fast.

RON GALELLA: When I started, there were very few paparazzi in New York, only four or five. It was very easy to get exclusives, there was a lot of freedom. But this has changed today. Toward 1975, the celebrity magazines appeared—*US Weekly, Stars*—and it became difficult to get good photos: too many obstacles, too many bodyguards, too many PR agents, too many people in the way. And too many problems, too many restrictions. Thank God, I stopped photographing. For me, my best work is already in my archives, so I compile books.

SÉBASTIEN VALIELA: I arrived at the beginning of *Voici*; things had already changed in comparison to before. The profession has become more democratic, there are more and more media outlets. This means we can reach a range of different people; instead of confining ourselves to royalty or a few actors, we now attach ourselves to TV personalities or singers. The second change has been the Internet, which is in the process of upsetting everything. We are now in a transitional period between print and the Internet, which does not yet have the capacity or the money to pay the lawsuits etc., but which at the same time lowers the print runs of newspapers. Things will balance out, but it is not sorted yet.

What changes have been brought about by digital technology?

BRUNO MOURON: Digital technology has brought a lot on a technical level. You can take photos at night or in the dark. And then there are cell phones. People photograph every major event with their telephones.... To begin with we thought these images would be competition, but the pictures aren't sourced. If you take a photo of a celebrity waiting at the airport, just with your telephone, I don't know who will want to buy the photo.

DANIEL ANGELI: I don't think pictures have any value today: anyone can take them, cameras have developed so much that you don't need to learn any technique, and that kills the value of a picture. It's a new generation.

FRANCIS APESTEGUY: It's like the coal mines sixty years ago; it's what closed down the agencies. It has the same effect as the arrival of gasoline for the coalmines.... One day, I took the same photo, at the same time, with a 35-mm camera and with a high-quality digital camera. I scanned my slide—and so that also became digital—took the magnifying glass, and made two prints. Well, you could recognize immediately which one was the silver print and which one was digital. How? The volume. That's what the silver print had and the digital print didn't. What's perverse is that our eyes get used to this flatness.

How does it feel to see your pictures exhibited in a museum today?

RON GALELLA: It is very flattering. I would never have expected it.

SÉBASTIEN VALIELA: It's gratifying, but it's surprising, because we often hear people say—apart from Helmut Newton who liked our work—that we take unfocused, blurry, and unattractive pictures.

FRANCIS APESTEGUY: I think it is well deserved,... not only for me, but for the pictures themselves. Cartier-Bresson and Willy Ronis took the same pictures as Angeli, me, or any other. They were taken on the spot; it was life. When people ask me in the street, "Why did you photograph us?" I reply, "I am photographing life, that's all. I am not offending you, I am photographing life."

PASCAL ROSTAIN: It amuses us enormously to find ourselves hanging on museum walls.... But more seriously, I think that it is also the reflection of an era and part of the history of photography. Taken one by one, these photographs are not that interesting, but when you bring them together, they give meaning not only to the profession of the photographer, of the paparazzo, but also that of the journalist.

DANIEL ANGELI: I realize that we cannot show everything. Initially, these photos were taken for publication, and among them, from time to time, there is one that stands out from the rest, but the choice is always difficult.

BRUNO MOURON: The art world hadn't previously got into this field of photography yet. As I was choosing certain photos, I realized that it was a very good idea. It has given me a fresh look and I find that—as with fine wine—as they get older, certain photos are actually pretty good.

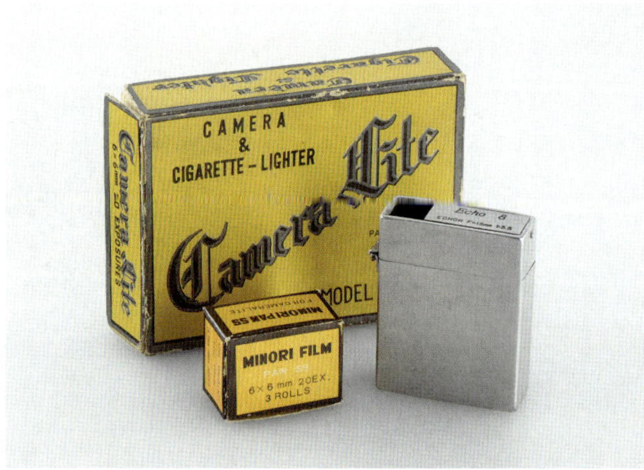

SUZUKI OPTICAL CO.
Cigarette Lighter Camera
Echo-8
c. 1955

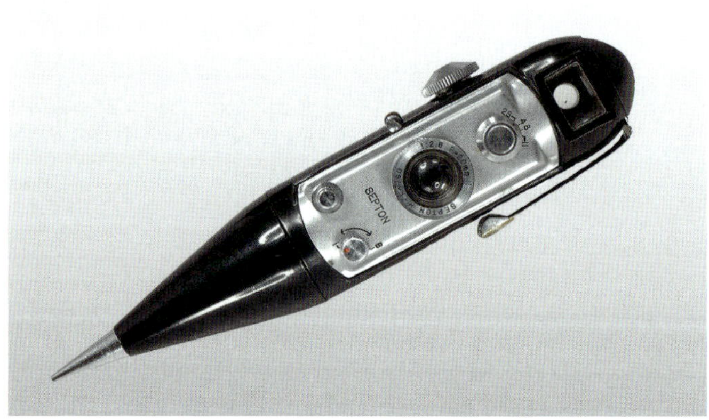

HARUKAWA TRADING CO.
Septon Pen Camera
c. 1953

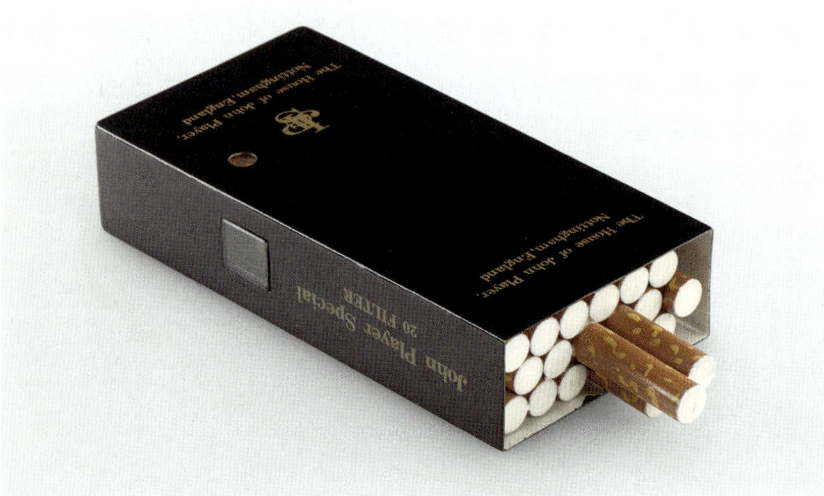

KIEV
John Player Special
Spy Camera
1970

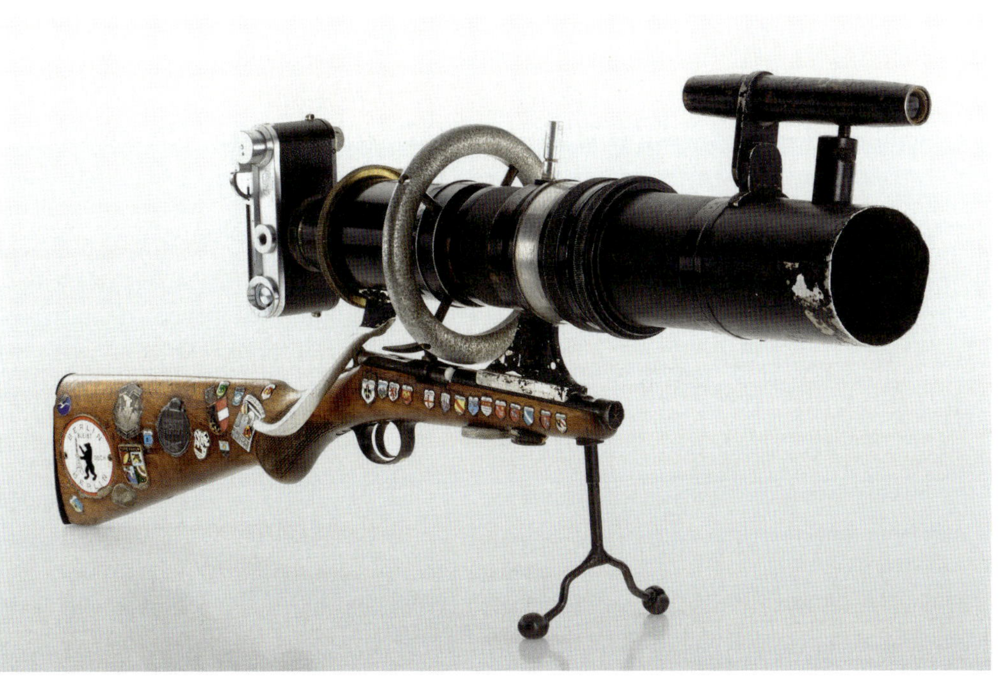

LEICA (camera)
ASTRO (lens)
Telephoto rifle
1940

SPYING DEVICES AND TELEPHOTO LENSES. The paparazzo and the spy have much in common. They share the same working methods—investigation, tracking, concealment—and use similar equipment, including telephoto lenses and miniature devices. The telephoto lens became the iconic accessory of image thieves in the early decades of the twentieth century. Miniaturized devices became popular during the cold war years. Numerous prosaic objects—watches, pens, ties—were transformed into tiny cameras. Photographers could deploy them to take pictures at trials or secretly capture celebrities in extremis. In 1996, François Mitterrand was photographed on his deathbed by a device concealed in a pack of cigarettes. This fascination with voyeuristic spying, spurred in large part by motion pictures, launched marketing campaigns for a number of devices whose putative powers exceeded the actual requirements of espionage. Nevertheless, there was an appetite for these often mediocre-quality toys with their inferior lenses, small-format film, and approximate framing. Such limitations make it easy to understand why these devices were rarely used by genuine paparazzi.

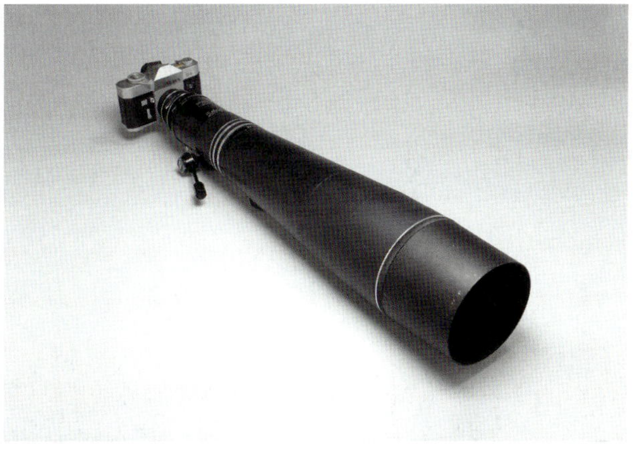

ALPA (camera)
KILFITT (telephoto lens)
Reflex Camera, Alpa 10D, and Kilfitt Telephoto Lens, Zoomar Sport-Fern-Kilar
c. 1968

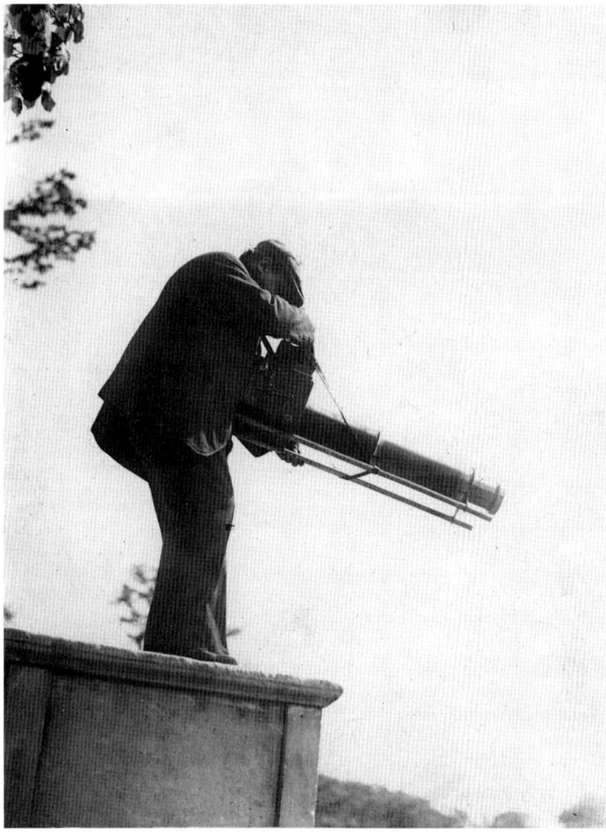

MAURICE-LOUIS BRANGER
King George V in Paris
1914

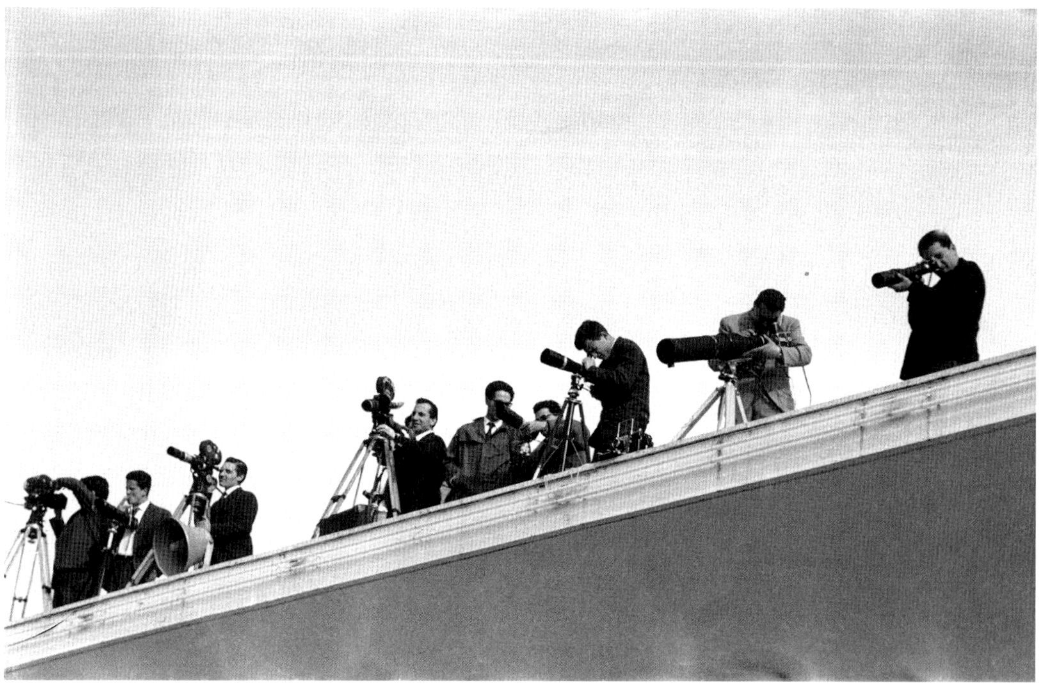

ANONYMOUS
(Reporters Associati)
Photographers Waiting for the Arrival of Soraya Esfandiary-Bakhtiari at Ciampino Airport
1959

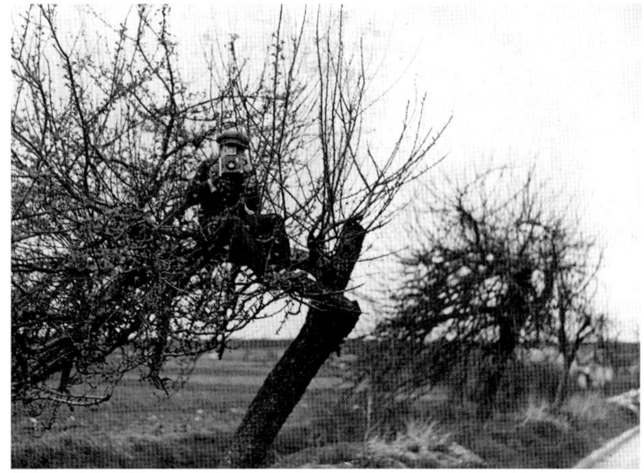

ANONYMOUS
Photograph Taken on the Film Set of Le Gamin de Paris *by Gaston Roudès*
1932

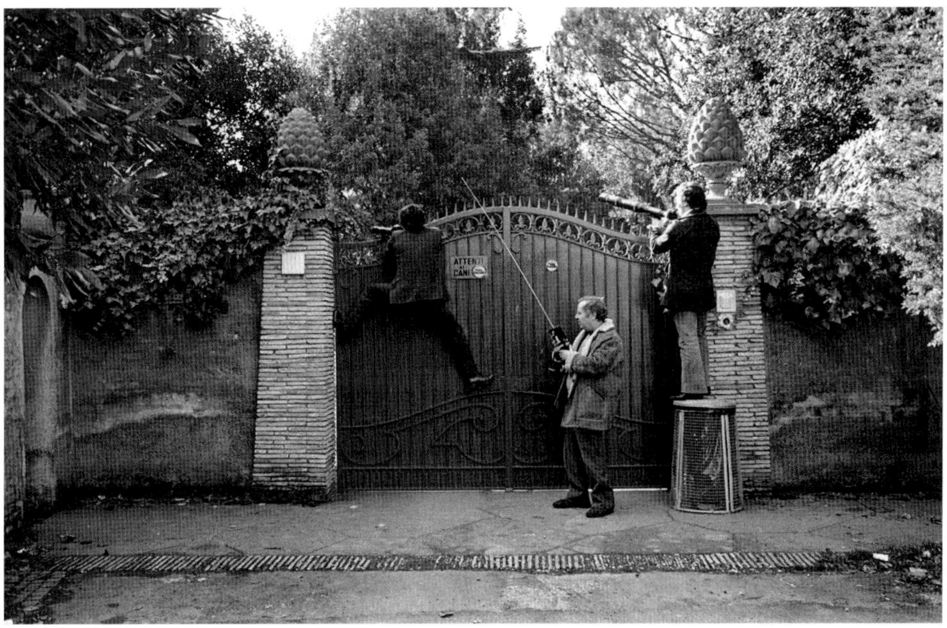

ANONYMOUS
(Reporters Associati)
Paparazzi Hiding in front of Gina Lollobrigida's House
1972

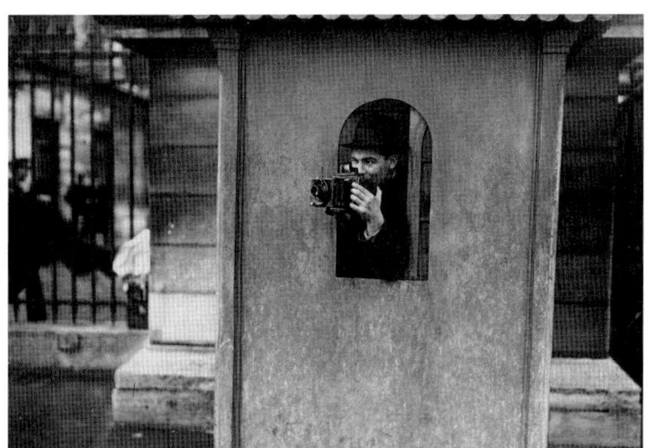

ANONYMOUS
(Service des agences françaises d'actualité et de reportage associées—Service of French Associated News and Reporting Agencies)
Photographer Hiding in a Sentry Box
c. 1938

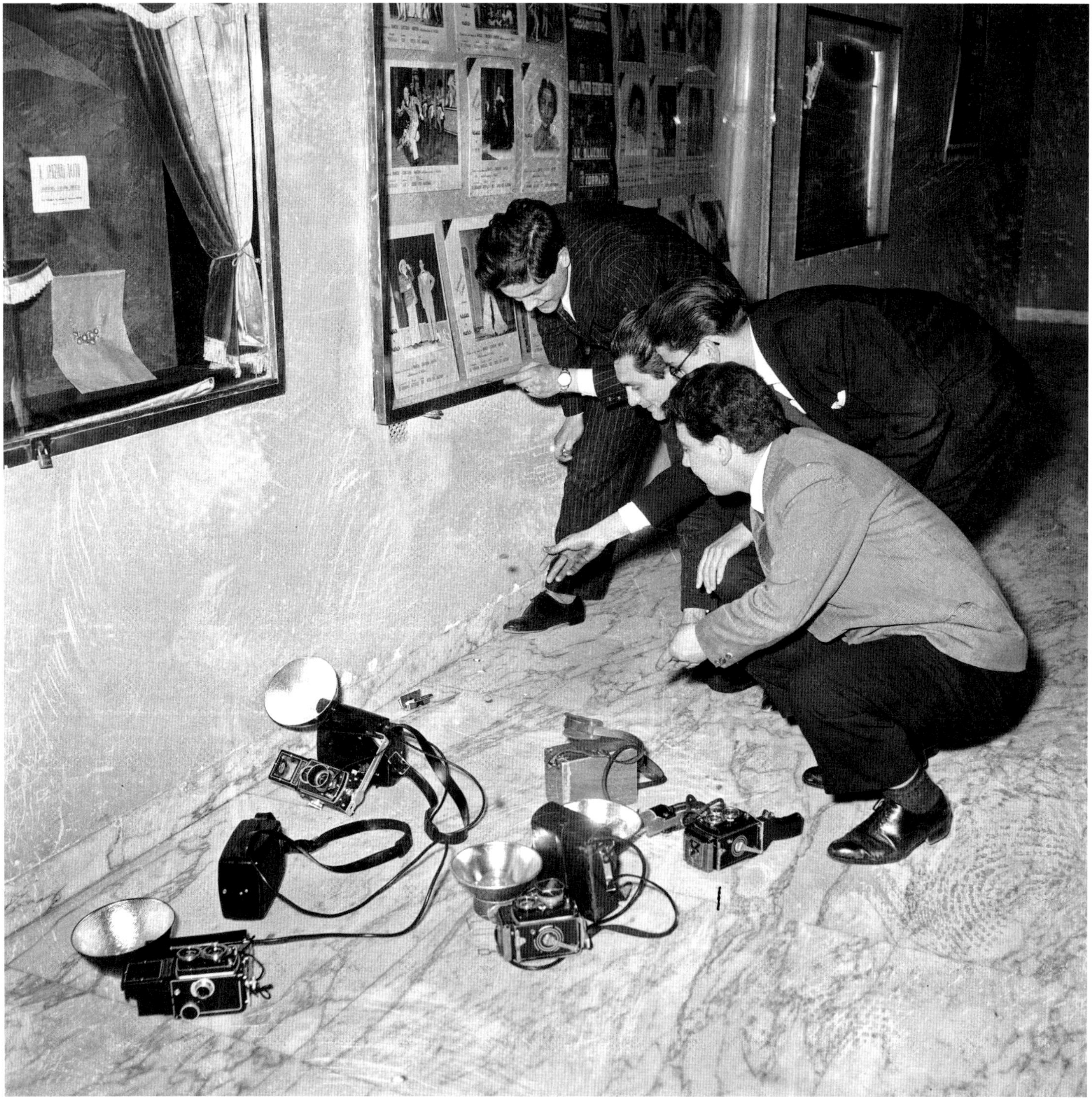

ANONYMOUS
(Reporters Associati)
Group of Photographers Playing a Game While Waiting for a Star to Leave the Theater, Rome
1954

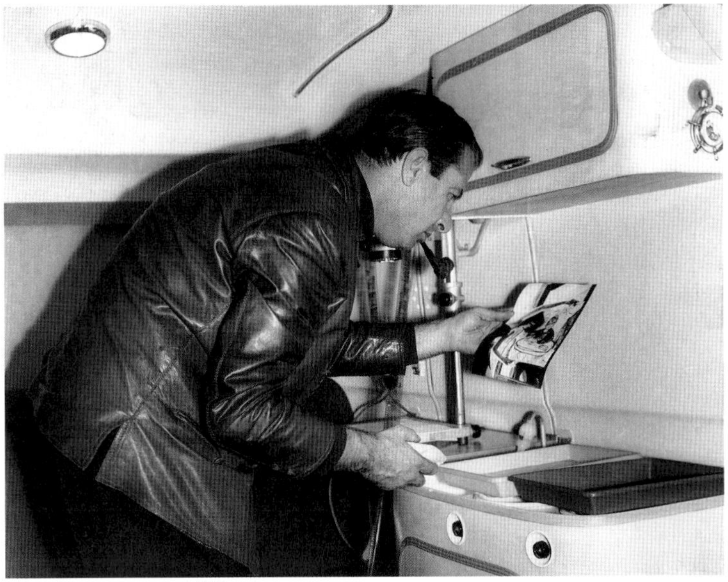

ANONYMOUS
Reportage on the Paparazzi in Rome during the Shooting of La Dolce Vita
September 24, 1959

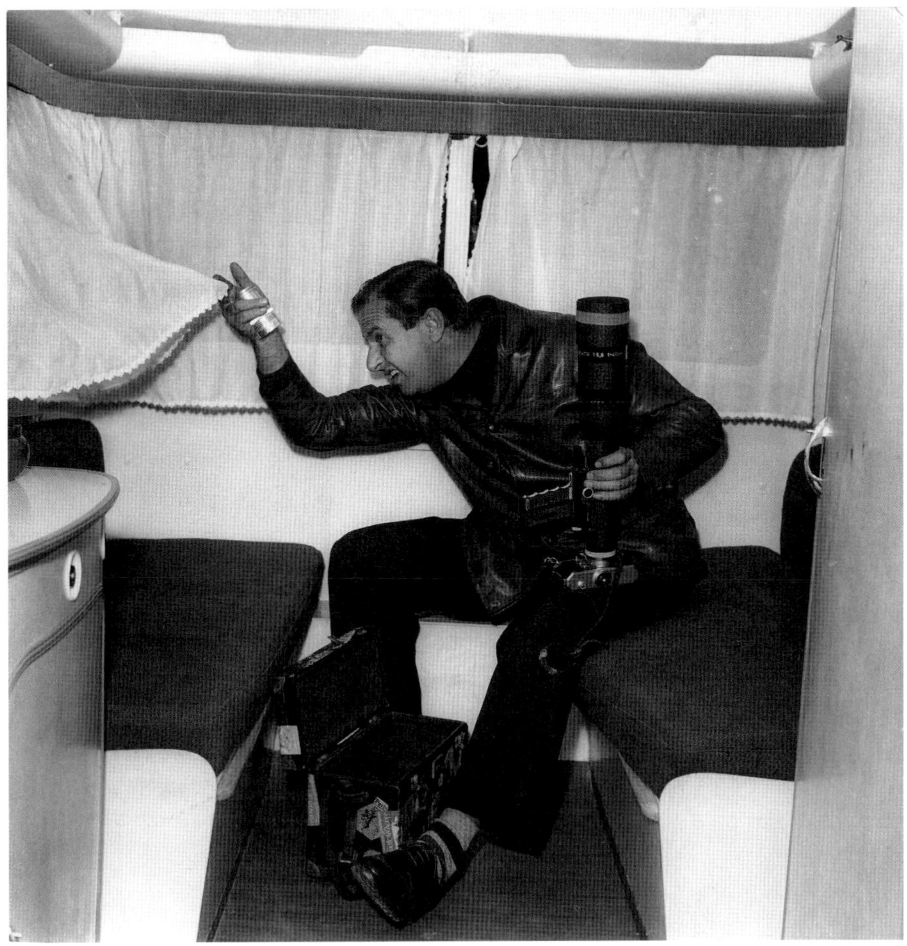

ANONYMOUS
Reportage on the Paparazzi in Rome during the Shooting of La Dolce Vita
September 24, 1959

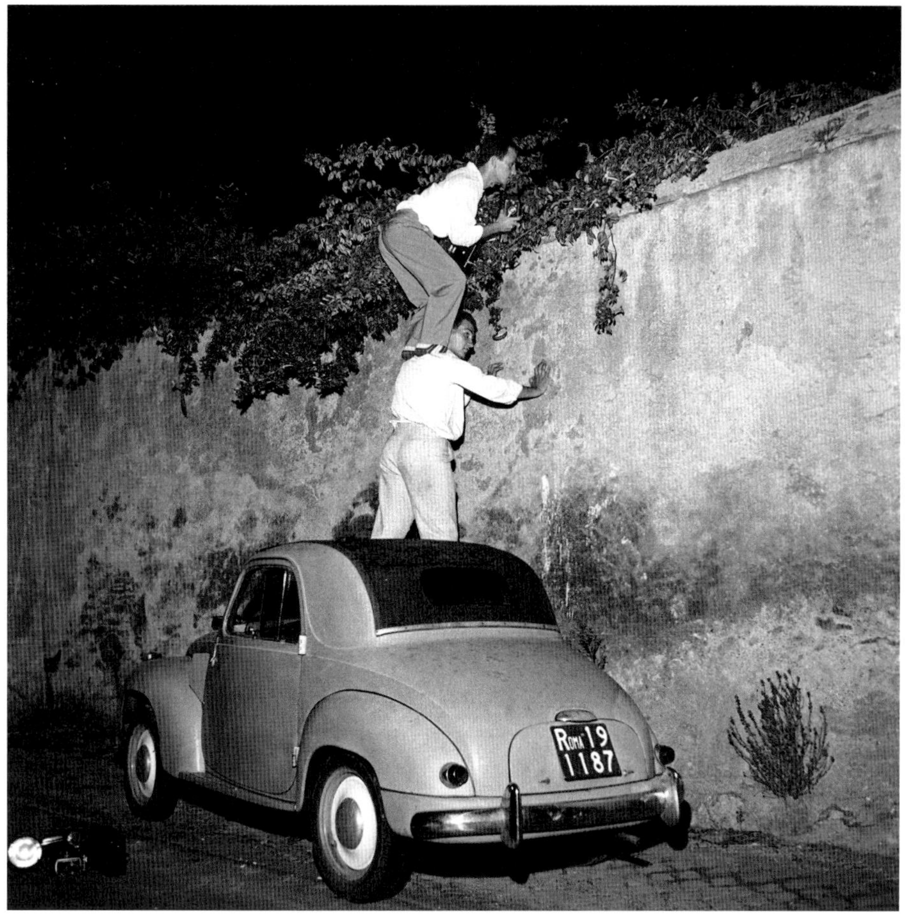

ANONYMOUS
(Reporters Associati)
Photographers Attempting to Enter Lea Padovani's Villa during a Cocktail Party
1958

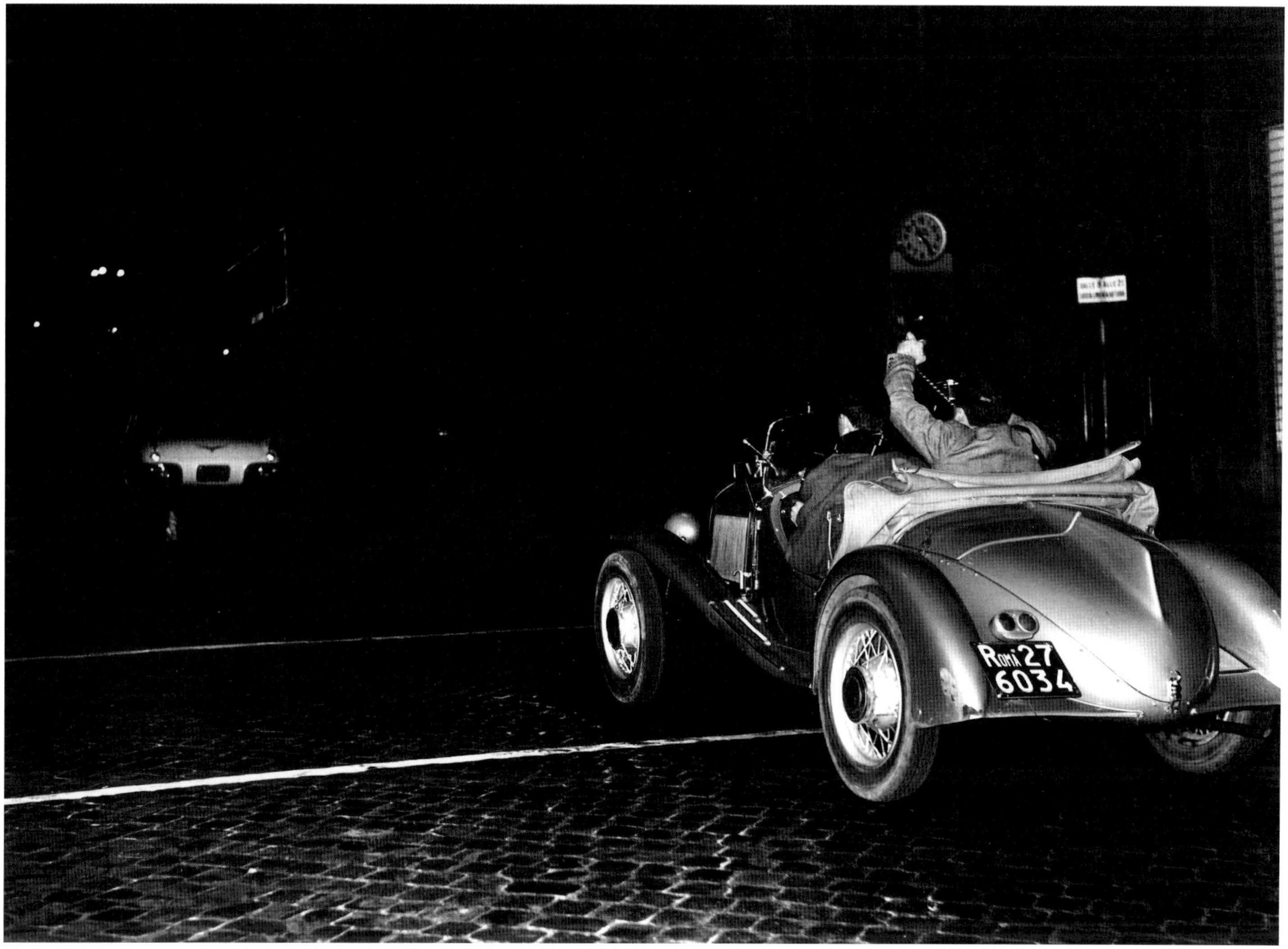

TAZIO SECCHIAROLI
Ava Gardner Chased by Paparazzi, Rome
1958

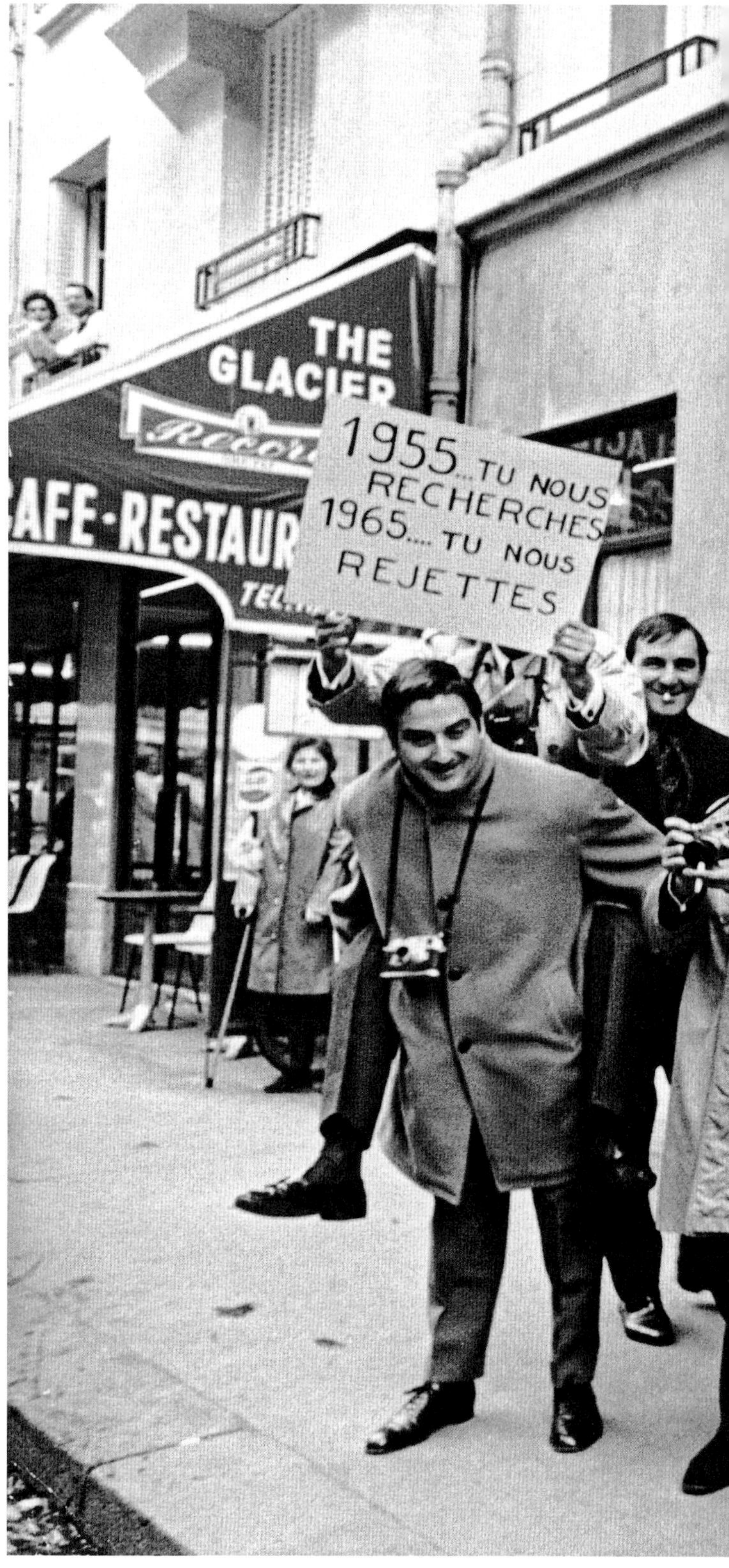

PHILIPPE D'EXEA
Paparazzi on Strike in front of Brigitte Bardot's Apartment, Avenue Paul-Doumer, Paris
1965

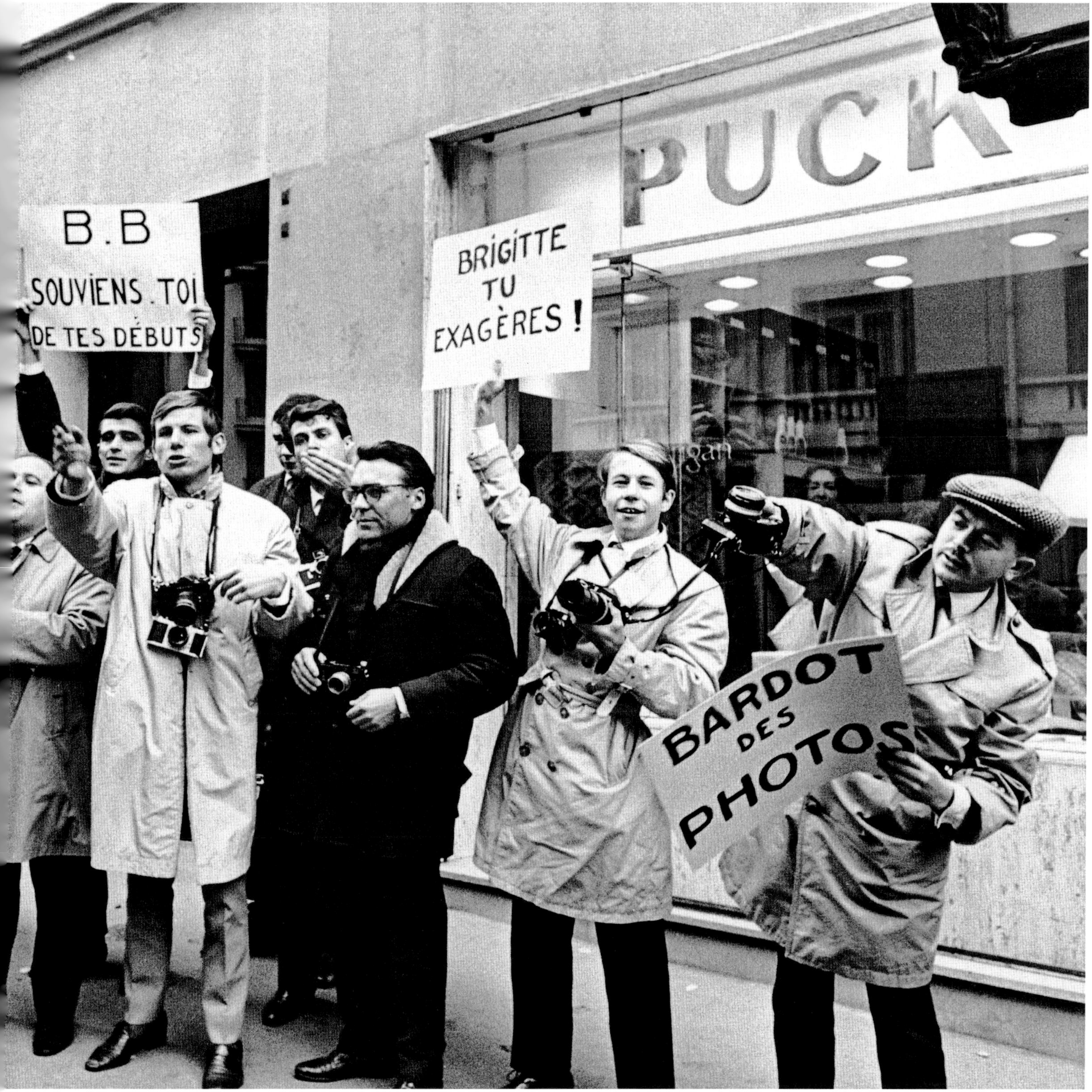

B.B
SOUVIENS.TOI
DE TES DÉBUTS
PUCK
BRIGITTE
TU
EXAGÈRES !
BARDOT
DES
PHOTOS

The Market for Paparazzi Pictures

Michel Guerrin

One of the characteristics of paparazzi photography is that it is defined not so much by aesthetics as by the market. Indeed, this visual field depends on several factors that go beyond the process of picture taking, and which are, for the most part, to do with money: the health of the planet, the state of the press and advertising, the innovations of the Internet, the development of photographic technology, the price negotiated with the distributor. Other factors include the legislation in place (the kind of pictures authorized for publication) and evolving mores (the kind of pictures the public wishes to see, or not). In the same way, almost all articles on the paparazzi focus on anecdotes about the photographers' games of hide-and-seek with their target, information on the targeted celebrities, the price paid by a newspaper to publish a picture, the scandals and lawsuits that sometimes arise, and the amount of compensation paid to the victim, but very rarely the pictures themselves or their composition.[1]

There exists, for example, a rich paparazzi "hell": images that remain unpublished—often touching upon sex or death—for reasons that are again linked to money. After the car accident in which Princess Diana died, on August 31, 1997 in Paris, a series of photographs circulated among the newspapers' editorial offices. The main picture was a portrait of the Princess of Wales, dying, with a thread of blood hanging from her mouth. Although no newspaper showed this photograph at the time, it is not because of its asking price—around €400,000, as an editor from *The Sun*, the popular British newspaper, confided to the British television channel Channel Four in November 1997. An editor from the American tabloid *The National Enquirer* confirmed that this portrait could have made a million dollars in global sales.[2] Neither is it because the image is insignificant, quite the contrary. This photograph was not published for economic reasons: its distribution would have cost more—in lawsuits, seizure of the publication, and readers' indignation—than the potential gain.

The paparazzi market, as with all markets, is a game of supply and demand, but its actors have differing interests: the photographer who takes the pictures (sometimes working in tandem, sometimes anonymously, which throws into question the notion of authorship); the model who accepts or refuses this visual game; the photographic agency that sells the photo-reportages; the newspaper that publishes them; the reader who looks at them; and the judges who condemn them. The newspapers have been at the center of this game for a long time. They pay, therefore they create a market, give many photographers a calling, impose certain pictures. If they are in bad shape, the whole field is in bad shape, and vice versa. The market has also grown because "stolen" pictures have been able to lift newspaper sales.[3] One memorable example is the November 10, 1994 issue of *Paris Match*, which revealed the existence of Mazarine Pingeot, the secret daughter of the then French President, François Mitterrand. This issue sold 1.4 million copies "instead of the usual million," confided Michel Sola, the magazine's picture editor.[4] Michel Sola also cited the example of the photograph of François Mitterrand on his deathbed, published in *Paris Match* on January 16, 1996, leading to a print run of 1.8 million copies. Not only do paparazzi photos increase sales, they can sometimes

1. See also *Paparazzi* (1998), a film by Alain Berbérian with Vincent Lindon and Patrick Timsit.

2. See Christina Khoury, "The Paparazzi Plague," on the website of the Hazel McCallion Senior Public School, in Mississauga, Ontario, http://www.snn-rdr.ca/old/may98/may/christina2.htm.

3. The magazine *Challenges* of August 30, 2007 quotes three examples taken in 2006: a *Voici* front cover of the couple Jean-Pierre Pernaut (a news broadcaster) and Nathalie Marquay (a former Miss France); a *Closer* front cover with politician Ségolène Royal in a swimsuit on the beach; and a *Public* front cover with the French pop singer Jenifer in a swimsuit.

4. Interview with Michel Sola by Michel Guerrin, "L'Homme-choc de la photo de *Paris Match*," *Le Monde 2* (April 23, 2005): 40.

5. The quotations by Jean-Denis Walter, Sébastien Valiela, Stéphane Rochon-Vollet, François Navarre, Pascal Rostain, Jean-Michel Psaila, Laurence Pieau, Paul Madalenat, and Frédéric Hervé are taken from interviews with the author from January to March 2013.

6. Information provided by Jean-Denis Walter.

7. Léna Lutaud and Thiébault Dromard, *Les dessous de la presse people* (Paris: Éditions de La Martinière, 2006).

save a newspaper. At any rate, they shaped the legend of *Hustler*, the American monthly and competitor of *Playboy*, created by the eccentric American press tycoon Larry Flynt in July 1974. In August 1975, while sales were dropping, the latter bought for $18,000 five photos of John Kennedy's widow, Jackie Onassis, then aged forty-six, who was photographed entirely naked on the Greek island of Skorpios. This issue of *Hustler* sold 1 million copies, and its print runs would reach 3 million in the following years.

The Birth and Structuring of the Market in Europe

The paparazzi profession essentially develops in cities where celebrities gather. The activity was openly acknowledged at the beginning of the 1960s in Rome, which, due to its beauty and the presence of the Cinecittà studios, attracted film stars. In the 1970s and 1980s, the paparazzi market developed in London, where popular tabloids enjoyed unequalled print runs, buoyed by uninhibited editorial lines and snatched pictures free of copyright laws. In 1997, at the peak of their success, *The Sun*, *News of the World*, *Daily Mirror*, *Daily Mail*, *Daily Express*, and *Daily Star* reached 48 million readers, and these daily newspapers needed to buy pictures every day. A leading market often depends on a leading target: photographs of Princess Diana, from her marriage to Prince Charles in 1981 until her untimely death in 1997, produced sales figures of several hundreds of millions of euros—an amount that pictures of other celebrities have yet to beat.

In France, from 1960 to 1990, paparazzi photography existed on an episodic, though sometimes significant, basis in illustrated magazines, the main one being *Paris Match*, and featured royalty and film stars as the leading subjects. The creation of the weekly magazine *Voici* in 1987 by the German Axel Ganz (Prisma Média press group) opened the way toward a visible and structured market. Initially a family magazine, in 1989 *Voici* became the first illustrated French magazine to make paparazzi photography its main editorial line. As Jean-Denis Walter, the magazine's picture editor in 1990, explained, "Insolent stars were our trademark and we were proud of this. Many celebrity magazines favor official photos of celebrities, which reveals the collusion between publication, photographer, and star, from which the reader is excluded. In *Voici*, there is complicity between the photographer and the reader, from which the star is excluded. *Voici*'s success comes from this difference."[5]

Voici has been a huge editorial success in France and achieved the highest press sales in the years 1990–2000. Its sales were around 800,000 copies with peaks in the summer, a season in which the distribution of celebrity press traditionally increases by 20 to 30 percent. *Voici* even printed 1 million copies of one or two issues. Its power is such that it can, like *Paris Match*, buy two photo reports on the same subject, made by two different photographers, and only publish one of them, with the aim of depriving other competing magazines of the pictures.[6]

The editorial and economic success of *Voici* disrupted the entire paparazzi market chain in France: it gave photographers a new vocation, incited the creation of photo and press agencies, and developed a new readership. Consequently, Hachette Filipacchi Médias (*Paris Match*) launched *Public* in 2003, while the British press group Emap created *Closer* in 2005, before handing it over the following year, along with its branch Emap France, to the Italian group Mondadori. *Voici* and *Closer* are today the two leading paparazzi magazines in France, the second having broadened its field of photographed celebrities to politicians, ever since the publication on its front cover of a photo showing Ségolène Royal on a beach in a swimsuit in 2006, at the time when she was running for French president. If we add to *Voici* and *Closer* titles such as *Paris Match*, *Public*, *Gala*, *VSD*, *France Dimanche*, *Ici Paris*, *Point de Vue*, *Oops!*, among others, one in three French people reads a celebrity magazine every week.[7] These magazines often resemble each other in form, with a chaotic cover dominated by a red, pink, or orange logo. In addition, the market is regularly disrupted by glossy magazines such as *Planète VIP*, *So People*, *Exclu*, *People Story*, and *Show Biz*, which only bring out occasional issues.

As for photographic agencies whose mission is to sell pictures to the papers, *Voici* probably instigated the creation of Sphinx, active from 1989, and Eliot Press in 1993, whereas generalist agencies such as Sipa Press established a specialized department at this time. These new players on the market joined Daniel Angeli's agency, created in 1967: it carried its founder's name, a paparazzo of note in France. Finally, *Voici* gave rise to the first generation of photographers in the early 1990s (they are often younger than thirty) who devoted themselves entirely to paparazzi work: Sébastien Valiela, Tony Fitoussi, Pierre Suu, David Ker, Fabrice Chassery, and Laurent Salmon, to name a few. "I saw the success of *Voici* increase week after week," explains Sébastien Valiela, the author of many *Voici* front covers, including Patrick Poivre d'Arvor and Claire Chazal, Gérard Depardieu and Carole Bouquet, Pierre Arditi and Jane Birkin, and Patrick Bruel, among others. He adds, "We showed love affairs, relationships, breakups, mistresses, pregnant mothers, and babies. The stars were always wondering what was going to hit them next." This generation experienced a euphoric era from 1990 to 2008. At the time, there were few paparazzi in France—about twenty or so—their range of subjects widened (TV presenters and journalists, fashion, reality shows, politics), and they earned a good living. The photographer Stéphane Rochon-Vallet explains, "I began in the profession in 1996–97 for the Angeli agency as a freelance photographer. I surprised the lawyer Arno Klarsfeld and the actress Béatrice Dalle together, and my pictures were sold for F 90,000 [French francs] to *Voici*. The agency took a third of this sum and left me with F 60,000, which is a lot of money when you are eighteen years old. I could buy the equipment of my dreams. I devoted myself 100 percent to paparazzi work. We worked a lot but we earned a good living. We published in *Voici*, but also in *Hola!* in Spain, *Bunte* in Germany, in the British press, in Italian newspapers such as *Novella 2000*, in Japan, in Australia. Only the American market did not count for much at the time."

Pricing photographs and calculating photographers' incomes are imprecise endeavors, as the parties concerned misinform and give misleading information about the market. Another difficulty is that they often only remember the first sale of a picture, whereas they should count the entire set of transactions engendered over several years and in the press globally—which it is almost impossible to calculate. All observers nevertheless confirm that the average price of a paparazzi picture has regularly and sharply risen over the last forty years due to the structuring of this market and competition in the media. Jean-Denis Walter, who bought pictures for *Voici*, confides that in the 1990s an average series cost him F 10,000 and an important series between F 30,000 and F 50,000, but that four or five sensational scoops were bought for around F 500,000 each (approximately €80,000)—prices much higher than those charged in the 1970s and 1980s.

Two memorable photographs from the Angeli agency are good examples of this increase in price. Daniel Angeli claims to have sold for only F 1,500 a black-and-white series of the Italian Giovanni Agnelli, the head of Fiat, jumping naked into the Mediterranean sea from his yacht in 1976. The photographer admitted years later, "Today, the picture would be worth twenty times more."[8] The second picture, this time in color, was taken by one of Daniel Angeli's friends. It shows Sarah Ferguson in the summer of 1992, when she was still married to Prince Andrew, Duke of York, having her toes licked by her "financial advisor," the American businessman John Bryan, near Saint-Tropez. The picture was published by the *Daily Mirror* and then by other newspapers, and remained for a long time the most expensive photo in history, making, according to Daniel Angeli, a global sales figure of close to F 10 million.[9]

The picture's price greatly depends on the surprised celebrity's degree of fame, the importance of the revelation, and its exclusive character. "There also has to be an air of the forbidden and scandalous," adds photographer Pascal Rostain. The latter cites two different scoops, which he coauthored with Bruno Mouron, that combine these ingredients, resulting in sales figures he alleges were as follows: Caroline of Monaco's relationship in 1982 with the tennis player Guillermo Vilas, caught on film on an island near Honolulu and sold for F 650,000 to the German newspaper *Bunte*; and a portrait in 1983 of Stéphanie of Monaco at eighteen years old, topless on the island of Mauritius, which made F 800,000 in worldwide sales. We could also cite Daniel Angeli, who claims to have accumulated F 2 million in sales in 1988 from a shot of Prince Charles crying over the death of a friend in an avalanche in Klosters, Switzerland.[10]

This last example should not, however, be allowed to mask the reality: prices are higher for photos of female celebrities. For its tenth anniversary, *Voici* "paid tribute" to its victims by listing those who had adorned the magazine's cover: Stéphanie of Monaco was at the top of the list with 57 front covers, then her sister Caroline (47), Johnny Hallyday (32), Princess Diana (30), Vanessa Paradis and Sarah Ferguson (31), Isabelle Adjani (10), Estelle Hallyday (9), Patrick Bruel (8), and Cindy Crawford (7).[11] In this list, women outnumber men four to one; interestingly, the same ratio is to be found in *Voici*'s readership. Moreover, the handful of celebrities who have dominated the market since 1950 are all women: Maria Callas, Jackie Onassis, Caroline and Stéphanie of Monaco, Princess Diana, and Britney Spears.

From time to time, a picture fails to realize its promise of obtaining a high price, due to factors beyond its control. Published on the cover of *Paris Match* in 1994, the photograph that revealed the existence of Mazarine, François Mitterrand's daughter—they appear side by side in front of Le Divellec restaurant in Paris—was taken by Pierre Suu and Sébastien Valiela from the Sphinx agency.[12] Sébastien Valiela explains, "The agency expected to receive F 350,000 as well as a bonus of 1 French franc for each issue over the magazine's average print run. I think the agency must have received about

8. Michel Guerrin, "Chasse à l'homme privé," *Le Monde* (September 24, 1996): 11

9. Michel Guerrin, "Daniel Angeli, l'homme qui en savait trop," *Le Monde 2* (July 1, 2006).

10. Michel Guerrin, *Profession photoreporter* (Paris: Centre Pompidou/Gallimard, 1988), 218.

11. Michel Guerrin and Alain Salles, "*Voici* fait amende honorable," *Le Monde* (March 20, 1998): 15.

12. *Paris Match*, no. 2372 (November 3, 1994).

F 500,000—40 percent for the agency, 60 percent for us, the photographers. But that is not a huge amount for such a scoop. Less interesting photos have made more money. Daniel Filipacchi [who relaunched *Paris Match* in 1976] said that he would have given a million dollars to have this picture. I think the price remained low because the subject was of little interest outside of France. And politics was a taboo subject at the time. Moreover, the image was published in a small format on the front page, and in a larger format inside." Michel Sola, the *Paris Match* picture editor at this time, was annoyed by this editorial decision: "When we get hold of a scoop, we show it!"[13]

Diana, Princess of Wales, was the object of a series of the most expensive paparazzi pictures in history. They were taken at the beginning of August 1997, one year after her divorce and a few weeks before her death, when she was the companion of the millionaire Dodi Al-Fayed. In the main picture, Dodi and Diana, both in swimsuits, embrace and kiss each other on a yacht in a cove in Sardinia. The series was taken with a telephoto lens by the Italian paparazzo Mario Brenna. It was published on the front page of the *Sunday Mirror*,[14] and then by the *Daily Mail* and *The Sun*, before being published by numerous media across the world. The global sales figures of this series, or the amount quoted most often, is purportedly £7 million, including £265,000 for the *Sunday Mirror* alone.[15]

The United States: A New Eldorado for the Paparazzi

Although the first stage of the development of the paparazzi market took place in Europe in the 1990s, the second stage took place in the United States at the beginning of the 2000s. The city that symbolized this new market was Los Angeles, for several reasons: L.A. is powerful, airy, light, summery, and Hollywood is its lighthouse—the capital of a cultural industry of global influence, with hundreds of celebrities who interest the international press. Moreover, American legislation tolerates paparazzi: all pictures taken in the public space are authorized, unless the author is too aggressive to his subject. As Sébastien Valiela comments, "Brad Pitt leaving a Starbucks in Los Angeles, that's a photo. [Gérard] Depardieu leaving a Starbucks in Paris, that's a lawsuit."

This freedom of action influences the pictures' form and content: the photographer no longer hides from his "prey," as is the tradition in Europe; he openly goes out to meet them. This paparazzo "of contact" represents a return to the profession's origins in 1960s Italy, when photographers congregated next to restaurants and cafés where film stars could be found. It is no longer a question of revealing information that the celebrity wishes to conceal (a love affair, child, etc.) but about recording their appearance—physique, clothing, attitude—when they leave their property, walk along the street, drive a car, go shopping, go to the hairdresser, relax on a beach, leave a palace, or enter an airport. The composition counts less than the revelation of a detail—a look, a slimmer body (or not), a haircut, clothes, shoes, sunglasses, jewelry, a tattoo or piercing, etc. In Los Angeles, this is not called paparazzi photography but candid celebrity photography. In the profession, the term "strolling" is used.

This "contact paparazzo" can be aggressive, but he is more often a product of the collusion between the hunter and the hunted; each party stands to gain. Since many Hollywood stars have signed contracts with one or several fashion labels for clothes and accessories, they don't grudge having their picture taken if the photos show the brand of their pants, watch, or handbag. "It's Paris Hilton on the beach with an Eres swimsuit and Gucci sunglasses," explains Jean-Michel Psaïla, director of the agency Abaca Press. "Strolling is less about information than advertising." Sometimes the photographs are driven by stakes that go well beyond a simple publication. Complicated links are established between a star, his or her agent, a photographer, a news website, a newspaper, a TV channel, a sponsor, a film producer. "That's how the entertainment industry works in Los Angeles," explains a paparazzo living in the city who wishes to remain anonymous, adding, "The producer of a film in which a famous actress was starring called me to ask me to come and take photos of her, more or less without her knowledge, in order to create a buzz before the film came out." A synergy exists, for example, between the paparazzi website TMZ, *People Magazine*, and the television channel CNN, which all belong to the Time Warner group. TMZ, which is at the forefront of "brutal" revelations of news stories as well as celebrity news, even created buses in its name that offer tourists a tour of the main villas owned by Hollywood stars.

Before 2000, the Los Angeles paparazzi market was in a rut, as were the American celebrity magazines. But from 2002, the journalist Bonnie Fuller transformed the failing publication *Us Weekly* into a rival of the successful celebrity magazine *People*, a leader on the market. The editorial formula perfected by Bonnie Fuller for *Us* is the following: "Stars are just like us." The rivalry between the two magazines was bitter and contributed to the increase in price of cover pictures from $50,000 to $75,000.[16] This competition gave a huge boost to the paparazzi market, which

13. Ibid.

14. The publication in the *Sunday Mirror*, on August 10, 1997, was accompanied by the headline "The Kiss."

15. See Alan Markham's article "The Love and Looking: Princess Diana, The Press and Us," December 2010, http://www.alanmarkham.co.uk/Essays/Diana.php.

16. David Samuels, "Shooting Britney," *The Atlantic* (April 1, 2008).

17. See their website, splashnewsonline.com.

18. Samuels, "Shooting Britney."

19. Ibid.

today is wrangled over by several newspapers and magazines: *In Touch*, *InStyle*, *Star*, *New Weekly*, *Life & Style*, *The National Enquirer*, *The New York Post*, as well as five to ten entertainment shows on TV channels that occasionally buy controversial photographs.

These publications are supplied by American agencies that are far more plentiful and powerful than in other countries: Splash, X17, Bauer-Griffin, INF, WireImage, LDP, Phil Ramey, MPG, Visual, Star Face, Pacific Coast News, and FameFlynet, to name but a few. Splash, created in 1990—probably the top paparazzi agency in Los Angeles—is present in several countries and employs thirty or so salaried photographers and around three thousand freelance photographers.[17] But the symbol of the advent of paparazzi photography in Los Angeles is the X17 agency, created in 1996 by the Frenchman François Navarre. He came up with the idea of giving cameras to dozens of people, mainly of Latin American origin (from Mexico, Brazil, Argentina, Nicaragua, El Salvador), whose main job—as gardeners, chauffeurs, restaurant waiters, barmen etc.—gave them an easier access to celebrities. Transforming themselves into photographers, whether on an occasional or regular basis, they were generally paid a fixed price for their photos. This strategy of using a plethora of operators automatically increased the chances of obtaining a scoop. This is how Paris Hilton was snapped as she was being handcuffed by the police in 2007; the picture earned $100,000 to $150,000 according to X17. This agency, followed by others, adopted a "variable geometry" sales strategy: instead of targeting an exclusive customer, it multiplied transactions for a single series of images, which would be negotiated at a lower price with magazines, television channels, and websites.[18] This strategy, which is increasingly common, has adapted to the digital revolution that, in the 2000s, led to the expansion of photographic sources and distributors.

The relative easiness of "strolling" and the promise of good earnings explain the spectacular increase in the number of paparazzi in Los Angeles. There were only thirty or so at the end of the 1990s, that is to say a handful of specialists—a few Americans, English, German, and French. In the 2000s, this number had increased to around four hundred. A two-tier profession was thus created: on the one hand, the Latin Americans, with no training, meagerly equipped, and with a somewhat precarious status; on the other hand, Europeans, owners of sophisticated equipment, recognized as journalists, drawing the benefits of a fixed salary or income, and often with a field of action that goes beyond that of the paparazzi. Frenchman Paul Madalenat, who has lived in Los Angeles for the past twelve years where he is employed by the Splash agency, belongs to the second category. He has the following expression: "We are the elite troops; the others are cannon fodder."

The evolution of prices confirms the industrialization of the paparazzi market in Los Angeles from 2000 onward. Specialists attest that the value of a good picture (and not even an exceptional one) has gone from $1,000 to $7,000 in ten years; $50,000 is not a rare occurrence, with peaks at $100,000 or more. "A minor celebrity can make $500,000 over a long period," adds Paul Madalenat. Stéphane Rochon-Vollet, active in Los Angeles from 2004 to 2010, recounts, "I was living in a villa in Malibu, with a pool and two or three cars. I was earning $15,000 a month, at other times $6,000 or $7,000, and sometimes $20,000 or $30,000. The money was flowing in, everything was selling." It is not unusual for a minor female celebrity, caught drunk by a photographer in her car, to fetch prices of around $100,000.

The main stars of this Los Angeles market are not always the same as those we admire at the movies. Alongside the Brad Pitt-Angelina Jolie couple, are, for example, Paris Hilton, Jennifer Lopez, Lindsay Lohan, Nicole Richie, and Kim Kardashian, among others. But Britney Spears best embodies this kind of close-up paparazzi photography and this period of prosperity in Los Angeles.[19] She is unbeatable in terms of the number of photographers who followed her around during the 2000s, the quantity of images that were produced and published, the revenue she generated, the stories and scandals that peppered her life and gave rise to pictures (weddings, family arguments, boyfriends, divorces, car chases, and hospitalizations). "A photographer could make a thousand dollars a day with Britney Spears," confides Paul Madalenat. She took over from Princess Diana, but flaunted herself much more. Sébastien Valiela recalls, "A circus of about forty photographers hovered around Britney Spears because she accepted being followed around everywhere. We waited every morning in front of her property. She would come out for any little thing—to go to the mall, to the beach, for gas, into public restrooms. Every time, a troupe of twenty cars formed to chase her, the aim being to get in just behind her. Then she would get out of the car, actually looking for a contact with the paparazzi, allowing us to easily photograph her from five feet (1.5 m) away, which was surprising considering her level of fame. She even had an affair with a paparazzo. Her attitude meant that hundreds of photographers could earn a living." One image from this Britney

20. Claude Soula, "Info et publicité: les liaisons dangereuses de Webedia," *Nouvel Observateur*, last modified January 11, 2013, http://tempsreel.nouvelobs.com/economie/20130111.OBS5157/info-et-publicite-les-liaisons-dangereuses-de-webedia.html.

Spears era stands out from the others: in 2007, the singer shaved her head at a hair salon in Los Angeles. The X17 agency that sold this image apparently made $300,000 to $500,000.

Photographer and journalist Olivier Mirguet, who lives in Los Angeles, explains that "there was a before-and-after Britney Spears for the paparazzi." A before-and-after 2008, one might add. A kind of photographic bubble did indeed form around the singer—a micro-phenomenon of the speculative bubble that disrupted the global economy at the same period. The paparazzi market is one of the multiple collateral victims of the 2008 stock market crash, of the economic crisis that followed, and the cascade of side effects: the fall in newspaper sales, the decrease in advertising pages, the dwindling number of paparazzi images published, and the price of photos and photographers' incomes in free fall. This domino effect is summed up in the words of François Navarre, founder of the X17 agency: "The paparazzi market is indexed to stock exchange prices."

The Internet Upheaval

The arrival of the Internet was another factor that, beyond print media, was bound to disrupt the paparazzi market, since the Net both provokes and attracts this kind of image. At the end of the 1990s, numerous websites combining celebrities and paparazzi were created that then went on to structure themselves and become serious competitors for the printed press in the 2000s. Again, the phenomenon occurred above all in the United States with three distinct types of website: those of newspapers specialized in paparazzi images that, as in all sectors of the press, extended their brand to the web (the American magazine *People* with people.com, or the British newspaper *Daily Mail* which created dailymail.co.uk early on); websites created by important online brands such as Yahoo!, or television channels such as CNN; and pure play publications, available on the Internet only, that specialize in stars and paparazzi. In the United States, the pure play publications are supported by an important distribution network and thus disrupt the global market: Popsugar.com created in the Silicon Valley; PerezHilton.com conceived by Mario Lavandeira, who borrowed his blog name from Paris Hilton; TMZ which produces and often buys aggressive pictures and texts; and Just Jared (on the Internet since 2005), considered a reference by the paparazzi. In addition, there are the American agencies such as Splash or X17, whose websites have blurred the boundaries between the providers and the distributors of pictures. Specialized websites are also behind another threat to the paparazzi press: the massive broadcasting of celebrity videos, which took off from 2005–6. For example, a video in 2007 showing the stripper, singer, and actress Anna Nicole Smith, dead, supposedly made $1 million—the most expensive video to date, according to Gary Morgan, the director of Splash, who negotiated the fee.

In France, there are still only a few pure plays. The leading website is Purepeople, launched in 2007, one of the few profitable websites on the life of celebrities. It belongs to the Webmedia group, whose activities are focused on entertainment (it owns other fashion and retail websites). Just after launching, this website published the first photograph showing Carla Bruni and Nicolas Sarkozy together, on December 15, 2007 at Disneyland.[20]

This boom of specialized websites on a global level has provoked a spectacular increase in the number of photographs produced each year, in particular of the "strolling" kind. Many of the players in the field agree that websites have rendered the paparazzi photo commonplace: "It is no longer about pictures, it is about a stream of pictures." According to François Navarre, "With the Internet, the paparazzi have become a tool of reality TV. People want to follow, hour by hour, the lives of Britney Spears or Paris Hilton." Laurence Pieau, editor in chief of *Closer* magazine, tells how "between 2005 and 2008, I received six thousand photographs a week. I could use a certain number of them. Today I receive sixty thousand a week. I can't look at everything, which changes our relationship with the image. It's turned into an avalanche where everything looks the same."

Everything looks the same, including the subjects, from the untouchable film star to the celebrity, major or minor, who is quite willing to exhibit themselves. "When the star becomes a sub-star, it is not surprising to see the paparazzi profession going downhill," comments Sébastien Valiela, who considers that it is also his role to manage rarity. The best example is Kim Kardashian, one of the most sought-after stars at the moment, not so much for her work but for the persona she has created. The daughter of a famous lawyer, in 2007 she posted a pornographic video on the web in which she appeared with her boyfriend of the time, the singer Ray-J (her friend Paris Hilton, whose path she has more or less followed, had done the same thing in 2003). This video aroused much interest, and since then she has become the heroine of a reality show, *Keeping up with the Kardashians*, which brings together most of the members of the family. The series was first broadcast on the American channel E! in 2007, before achieving success around the world. In 2013, Kim Kardashian had a daughter with the rapper Kanye West, which confirmed her status as a star who accumulates celebrity magazine covers and website homepages.

21. Guerrin and Salles, "*Voici*," 15.

22. Over a hundred sentences were given in 2012 by the courts of Nanterre and Paris. See Nicolas Maubert and Marion Varinot, "The Rights of the 'Photographers of Private Life,'" p. 153 of this book.

23. Nicole LaPorte, "Crash of the Stalker Press," *Daily Beast*, last modified November 16, 2009, http://www.thedailybeast.com/articles/2009/11/16/the-crash-of-the-britney-economy.html.

The crisis in the paparazzi market has taken hold since 2008 and the fall in sales of the printed press allows us to evaluate its scale. The circulation of *Closer* has fallen from 550,000 copies in 2007 (with a peak at 850,000 in the summer) to 375,000 copies in 2012. *Voici* sells 350,000 copies each week, while it sold 800,000 copies a week in the 1990s. Consequently, as Frédéric Hervé, the coeditor in chief of the Bestimage agency, notes, "*Voici* used to publish four paparazzi stories per issue. Today, it's two, and with fewer pictures."

Contrary to popular belief, the compensation the papers have to pay stars for breach of copyright plays a minor role in this crisis. This is an issue particularly relevant to France, which has very protective legislation, confirmed by a huge number of precedents. Civil lawsuits became a major issue with *Voici* in the 1990s, well before the economic and financial crisis. In 1994, *Voici* had to pay around F 4 million in damages. In 1997, the year of Princess Diana's death, this figure went up to nearly F 20 million, excluding legal fees.[21] Yet, *Voici* estimated that the profits from sales exceeded the costs of the lawsuits, even though some of them cost as much as F 400,000. Jean-Denis Walter, the magazine's former picture editor, confirms this: "Whether to publish or not was a question we asked ourselves every week, and it was something that was accounted for in the magazine's general budget. But at that time, sales were so high that the answer was invariably yes, we could publish."

Did Princess Diana's death on August 31, 1997 change things? Nine photographers were charged with "involuntary homicide and failing to render assistance to a person in danger," before being acquitted two years later. This tragedy, beyond the fact that it did nothing to reduce magazine sales in France (35 percent additional sales of *Voici* for the two issues following the princess's death, and sales of over 750,000 copies for the summer of 1998), did nothing to temper their contentious choice of pictures either. It was not until the 2000s and the drop in sales with the rise of the Internet that the paparazzi tabloids began to be wary of lawsuits. "The press no longer has the means to pay heavy fines, so it self-censures more than before," explains Frédéric Hervé. The press makes fewer revelations (the love affairs or breakups of celebrity couples), giving priority to "strolling" and foreign stars who are supposedly less litigious. As even "strolling" falls under French law, there are still many lawsuits in France, but the compensation has dropped sharply (an average payout of €3,800), as the judge adapts the fine to the supposed damage.[22] "The accumulation of small sums to be paid nevertheless ends up being heavy and expensive," considers Laurence Pieau, "whereas fifteen years ago, these payouts were not even taken into account."

A Profession in Crisis?

The rise of the Internet, therefore, combined with the economic crisis and tough conditions for newspapers have greatly contributed to the lowering of prices for paparazzi pictures. This is especially true for the majority of photographs taken on the streets, most of which cannot find any takers, or only at a very low price. And why is this the case? On the one hand, the web is dominated by a no-cost culture. On the other hand, these specialized websites give priority to quantity and not quality, as they do not (yet) have the means to acquire a big scoop, nor to run the risk of a lawsuit. "Four years ago, a "strolling" picture was worth €350. Today, it's €100, sometimes much less, between €20 and €60 when it's sold on the net," explains Frédéric Hervé. "Websites even buy eighty to a hundred pictures for a lump sum from agencies, each one costing about €7 or €8." The websites have also helped to cause a drop in prices for pictures published in print magazines. Why indeed would the latter buy a paparazzi photo for €350 when the same image, or almost, comes in at €7 on a pure play website? "And, in addition, the websites post the picture before us," points out Laurence Pieau, from *Closer*. Even exclusives, which usually push prices up, are weakened. "We were able to buy a portrait of the singer Rihanna in a swimsuit, and we then found out that a website was going to publish a similar picture before our issue came out," observes Pieau. "And when we do have exclusivity, it only lasts a few minutes. The websites and social networks reappropriate the pictures as quickly as possible."

Even the price of scoops—whether they are average, big, or huge—has often fallen. Pictures worth €15,000 in the 1990s are now worth on average €5,000 to €6,000, as many observers confirm. In Great Britain, notes Frédéric Hervé, picture sales that would have been worth £4,000 or £5,000 previously can be negotiated today at £100 or £200. An American website, *The Daily Beast*, looked at ten of the most lucrative pictures taken during the golden years from 2005 to 2007 by the X17 agency in Los Angeles, and tried to imagine their price in 2009, a year after the economic crisis.[23] The author of the study concluded that the price of the images had fallen by 31 percent (this drop has accelerated). Let us consider three examples. Britney Spears shaves her head: $300,000 in 2007, according to *The Daily Beast*, $100,000 in 2009. Lindsay Lohan passes out in her car: $150,000 in 2007, $60,000 in 2009. Anorexia rumors concerning Nicole Richie and Lindsay Lohan: $100,000 in 2005, $50,000 in 2009.

One final factor weighs even heavier on the lives and incomes of the paparazzi: there

24. Laurent Calixte, *Challenges*, no. 89 (August 30, 2007).

are now more of them compared to twenty years ago. "In the 1990s, in France, the pie was divided between six to eight photographers. Today, there are thirty and the pie is smaller," explains Frédéric Hervé. The photographer Pascal Rostain adds, "When I began in the 1970s, there were fifty of us in the world, that is to say less than the number of astronauts. Today, there are five hundred, and with mobile phones there are millions." Significant images, photos, or videos are now taken by amateurs equipped with a mobile phone (the photo of the model Kate Moss snorting cocaine was taken by a an ordinary eyewitness). These "snaparazzis," as they are called, sell their images to a newspaper or post them on social networks, even on specialized websites such as gawker.com or actustar.com.

This increase in the number of photographers has made the competition harder, leading to excessive methods and, as a consequence, occasionally to the intervention of a judge. It is true that in Great Britain the tabloids have been more restrained over the past year, since the revelation of the tabloid newspaper *News of the World*'s phone-hacking scandal, and its subsequent closure on July 10, 2011. In the United States, during the 2000s, the swarms of paparazzi cars in the streets of Los Angeles not only annoyed the celebrities but also the locals and certain political officials. Complaints were lodged. In 1999, François Navarre, director of the X17 agency, was ordered to pay Jennifer Aniston $550,000 for having commercialized a picture of her sunbathing topless in her courtyard—the picture represented a private property violation. The actresses Scarlett Johansson and Lindsay Lohan had their cars hit by paparazzi trying to take photos.[24] In 2010, an anti-paparazzi law came into effect in California, on the initiative of Arnold Schwarzenegger, the state governor. This law renders the photographers responsible for any damages suffered by their victims as a result of their relentless chasing. Although this law does not seem to have had much effect, it says a lot about the general feeling toward the paparazzi.

The paparazzo inevitably witnessed a drop in his income at the end of the 2000s. The most experienced still earn a reasonable income, such as Paul Madalenat: "I earn $46,000 a year, plus commissions on the sales. I must have earned $75,000 in 2012, $100,000 in 2011, $135,000 in 2010. This is a general trend. There are also huge differences in income, as some only earn $2,000 a month." The situation is the same in France, asserts Frédéric Hervé: "In the 1990s, the average monthly income of a good paparazzo was between €8,000 and €12,000, sometimes as much as €15,000. Now, it is between €4,000 and €6,000 for the best, but many of them are on minimum wage." Pascal Rostain claims that he declared an income of €100,000 per year "when it was going well." Today, he announces the same figure, but shared, with his accomplice Bruno Mouron. No one sums up the decline better than Stéphane Rochon-Vollet: "In Los Angeles I earned easy money. Today, I get income benefits in Paris."

The photographic agencies are in the same slump. In France, Daniel Angeli's agency employed twenty-four people and its turnover was €3.8 million in 2006; it filed for bankruptcy in 2012 (and most of its photographers were picked up by the Bestimage agency). The agency Eliot Press is in a fragile situation. It is difficult for small companies to hold out, and so the tendency is for the sector to consolidate. The two major global news agencies—the American agencies Corbis (Bill Gates) and Getty Images (Mark Getty)—have entered into the paparazzi market: Corbis bought Splash in 2012, and Getty bought WireImage for an estimated price of $200 million.

These two transactions show that the sector still has great potential despite the economic crisis. Although, over the past few years, websites have caused prices to drop, many observers are convinced that they will be practically the only ones to show "scandalous" images in five or ten years' time. Paul Madalenat believes that "we are in a period of transition. For every magazine that closes, ten celebrity blogs are created. Everything is moving very fast. These websites have made big investments. To begin with, they practically stole the photos and sold them at knockdown prices. Today, they buy for 50 percent less than the print media bought them during the golden era, but that is still 50 percent more than the prices three years ago. Some of them, such as PopSugar or TMZ, can already buy a 10,000- to 30,000-dollar story."

Another reassuring factor for the sector is that a paparazzi story revealing exclusive information can still make a very high price—up to "$400,000 or $600,000," says Paul Madalenat. For Frédéric Hervé, the FameFlynet agency's picture of Kristen Stewart, star of the *Twilight* films, caught in the arms of Rupert Sanders, the director of *Snow White and the Huntsman* (2012), while she was in a more-or-less official relationship with the actor Robert Pattinson must have made a sales figure of $300,000 across the world. However, to do this the reporter not only needs the stature but the network to unearth this information, the means to finance such stories—many cost several tens of thousands of dollars in transport, hotels, tailing, contacts, and so on—and a newspaper or website that can then pay to publish them. "Between the very good, expensive image and the good but less expensive image, I would take the latter, which would have been unthinkable a few years ago," admits Laurence Pieau from *Closer*.

Nevertheless, *Closer* did publish the most conspicuous and most controversial picture of 2012 in its issue of September 14: the Duchess of Cambridge, Kate Middleton, wife of Prince William, photographed topless in a villa in the south of France, during the summer of 2012. However, Frédéric Hervé adds, "That photo was a sensation, not a story; a story would be if we saw Kate with another man." The Italian magazine *Chi*, the Irish newspaper *Irish Daily Star* (whose editor in chief, Michael O'Kane, was disowned by shareholders and had to resign), the Swedish celebrity magazine *Se och Hör*, and its Danish equivalent *Se og Hoer* also published this photographic report, but not one English newspaper did. A preliminary inquiry is underway in France, further to a criminal complaint lodged by the British Crown at the Nanterre court for "breach of private life," on the grounds that the Duchess of Cambridge was photographed while on private property. *Closer* was forbidden to print a new run of its issue and had to hand over the digital files for the images. Editor in chief Laurence Pieau concedes that "over 100,000 copies more than usual" were printed of this issue, but as she refuses to reveal how much the photo report cost, it is impossible to know if this was a lucrative operation, particularly since they are still awaiting the outcome of the lawsuit and possible sentence. This operation did, however, allow *Closer* to earn global notoriety. Laurence Pieau nevertheless adds, "Four years ago, we would have sold four times as many copies, if the cover of this issue had not been scanned by websites across the world."

A final factor shows that the future does not seem completely hopeless. Prices have dropped over the past few years, but the number of media outlets potentially interested in paparazzi photos—newspapers, websites, blogs, and television channels—continues to increase across the world. For example, the American agency Splash sells pictures to 250 customers in 54 countries. Forbidden pictures have never been so widely distributed. The prices are not always high, and neither is the quality, but, as we have seen, the quality of a paparazzi photograph is a fragile concept.

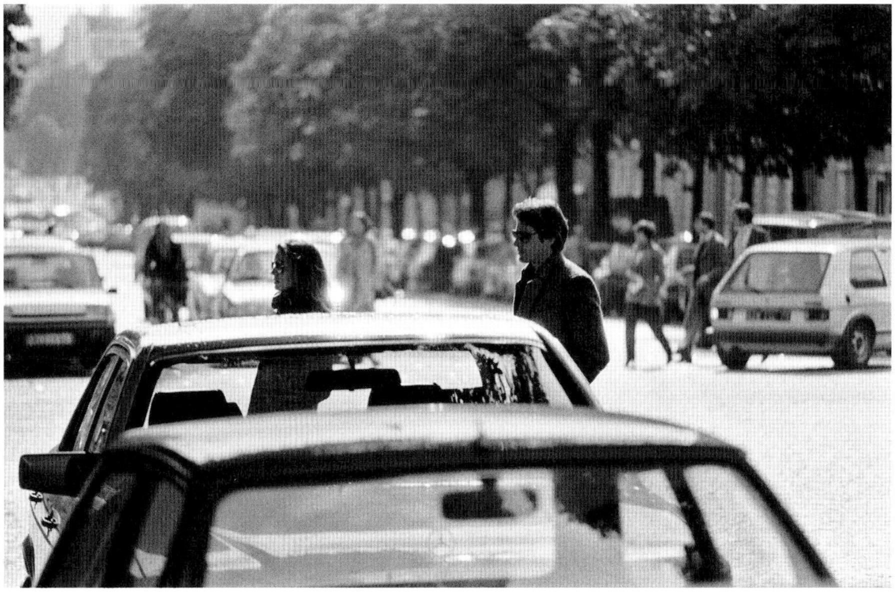

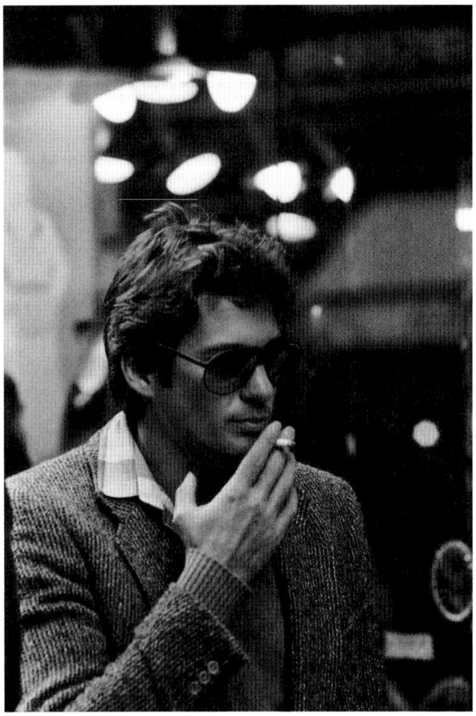

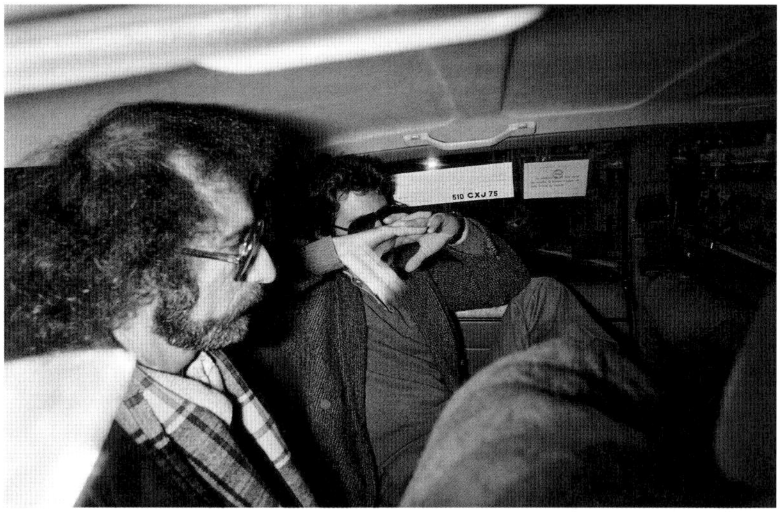

FRANCIS APESTEGUY AND PATRICK SICCOLI
(Gamma Agency)
Richard Gere
1980

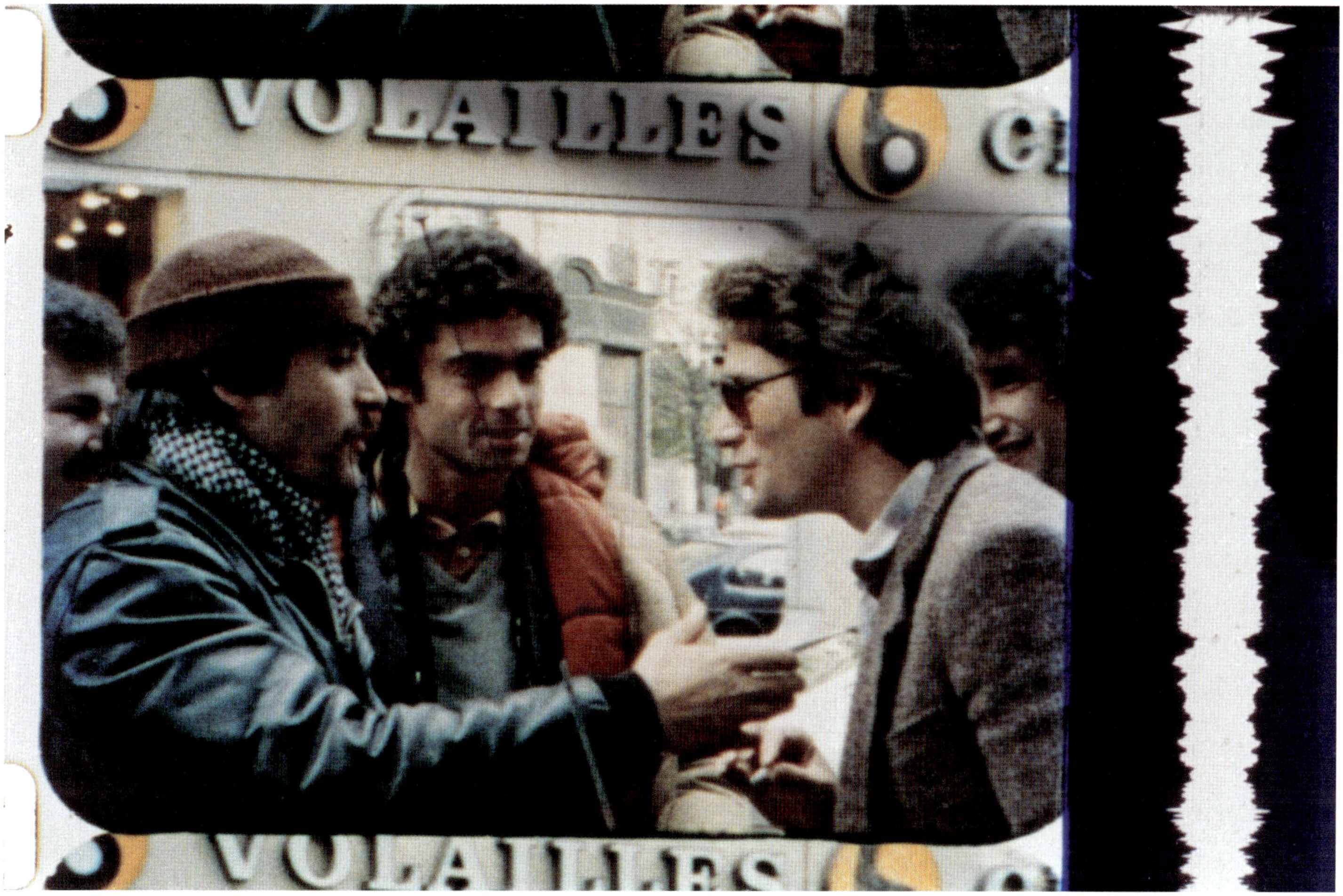

RAYMOND DEPARDON
Reporters
1981

RAYMOND DEPARDON. In 1980, Raymond Depardon filmed *Reporters*, a documentary film on Gamma, one of the largest press agencies at the time. He recorded the daily routine of photographers—shooting breaking news and special features, snapping elected officials leaving ministry meetings—and showed how the profession was evolving toward a focus on celebrity coverage. Among the photographers followed by Depardon was Francis Apesteguy, a charismatic and unorthodox reporter who specialized in tracking celebrities. One famous scene in the film shows Apesteguy and a few other reporters from the agency confronting Richard Gere. The young star, already crowned with blockbuster success in *American Gigolo*, did not wish to play the photographers' game. Pursued by reporters who blocked his car, he refused to get out or even raise his sunglasses to let them get a headshot. The showdown lasted several long minutes. But in this face-to-face confrontation between the star and the photographer, the more photogenic participant is not the man you would expect. Throughout the entire scene, it is Apesteguy who dominates the screen.

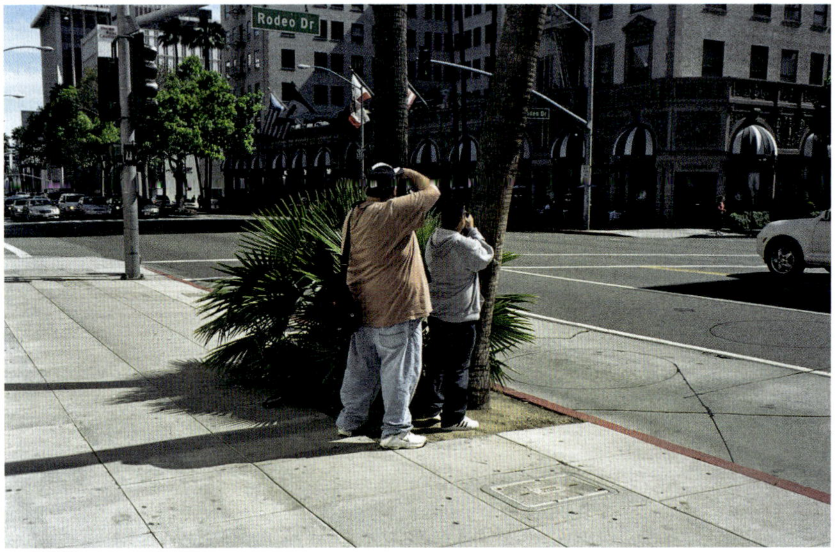

OLIVIER MIRGUET
Paparazzi #21 – Los Angeles
2009

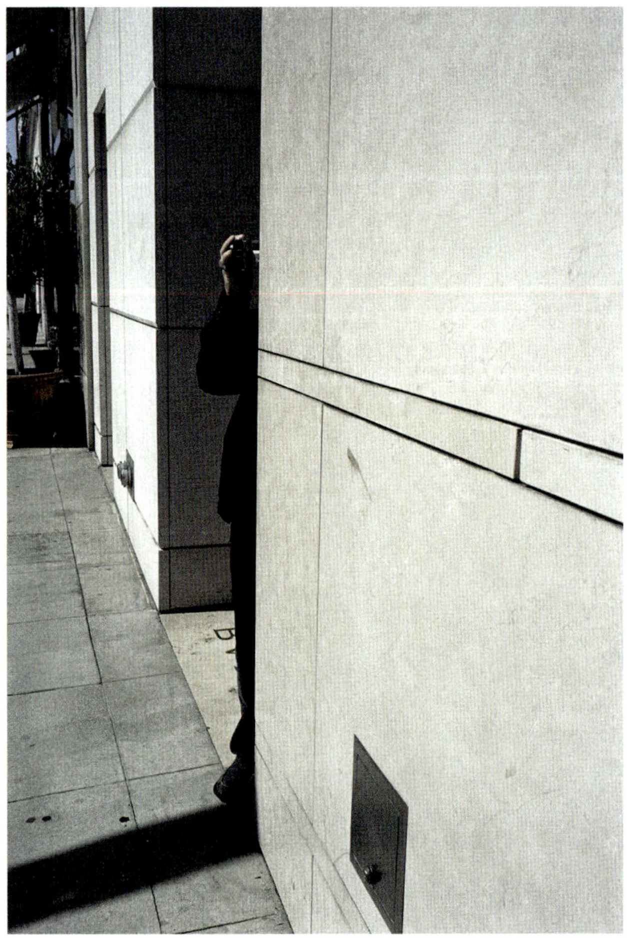

OLIVIER MIRGUET
Paparazzi #14 – Los Angeles
2009

OLIVIER MIRGUET, born in 1972, is a French journalist and photographer. He has lived in Los Angeles for several years, and tracks down manifestations of physical and symbolic surveillance in urban spaces. Whether working with architecture, monitoring cameras, or paparazzi, his interest is in "the sense of invisible omniscience." Mindful of the shifting status of images, he documents the lives of the paparazzi in Los Angeles and revisits the snapshot aesthetic by repurposing photographs that have been rejected by the agencies. This appropriation allows him to take a different stance toward traditional celebrity shots and offers a possible alternative to the all-powerful media. His images carry a new meaning and are able to reach a different audience.

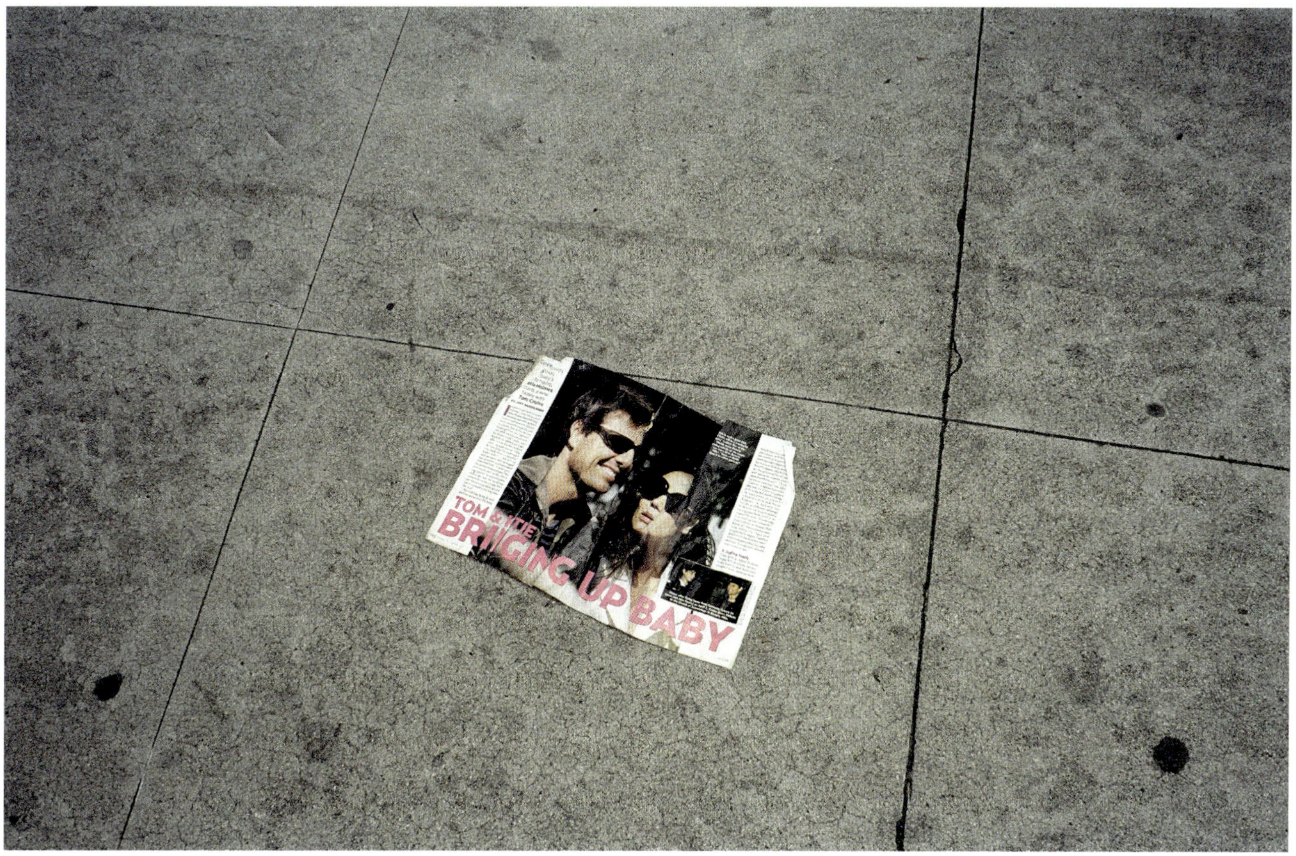

OLIVIER MIRGUET
Paparazzi #4 – Los Angeles
2009

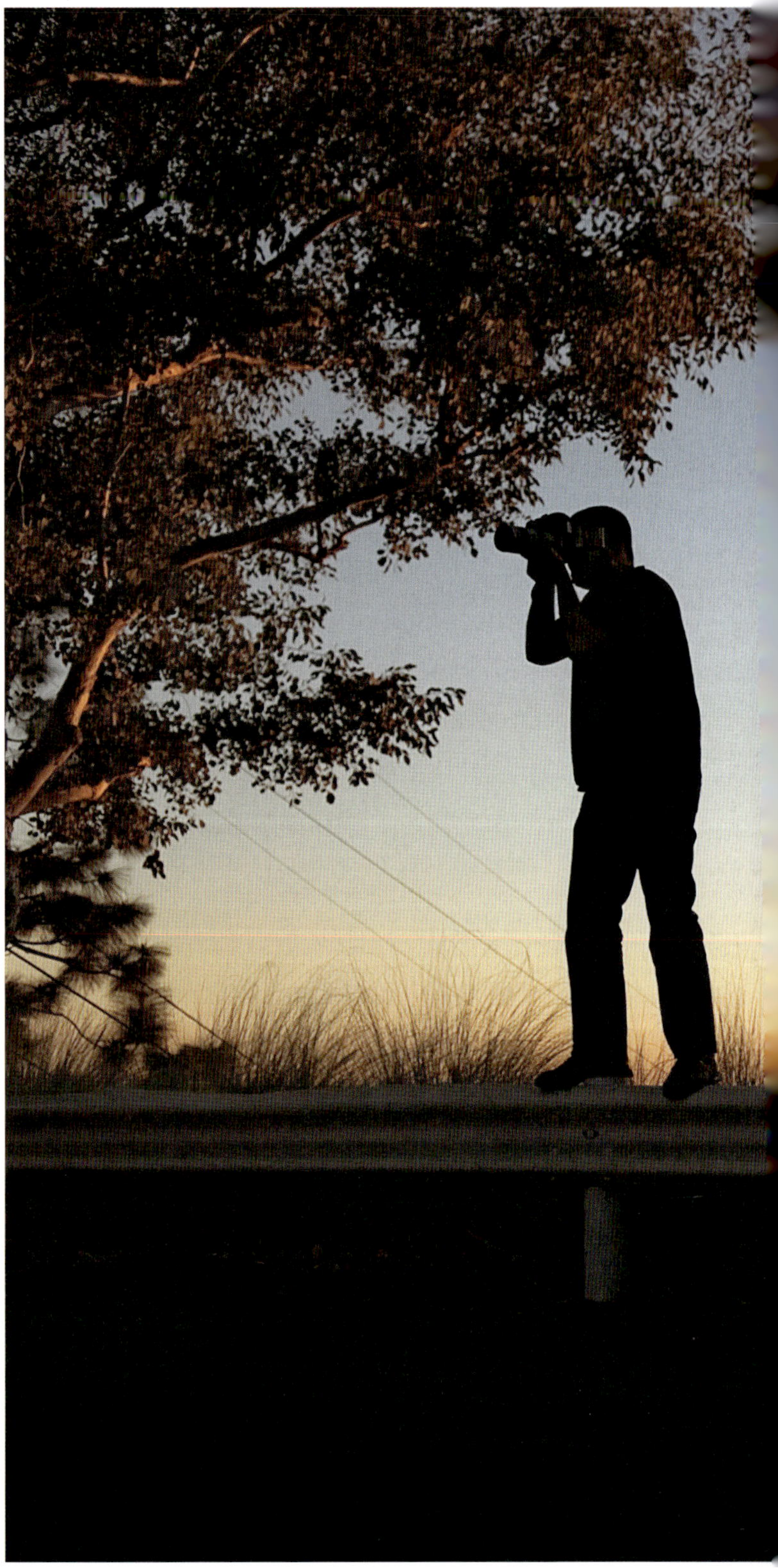

JESSICA DIMMOCK
Jessica Alba, from
the series *Paparazzi!*
2009

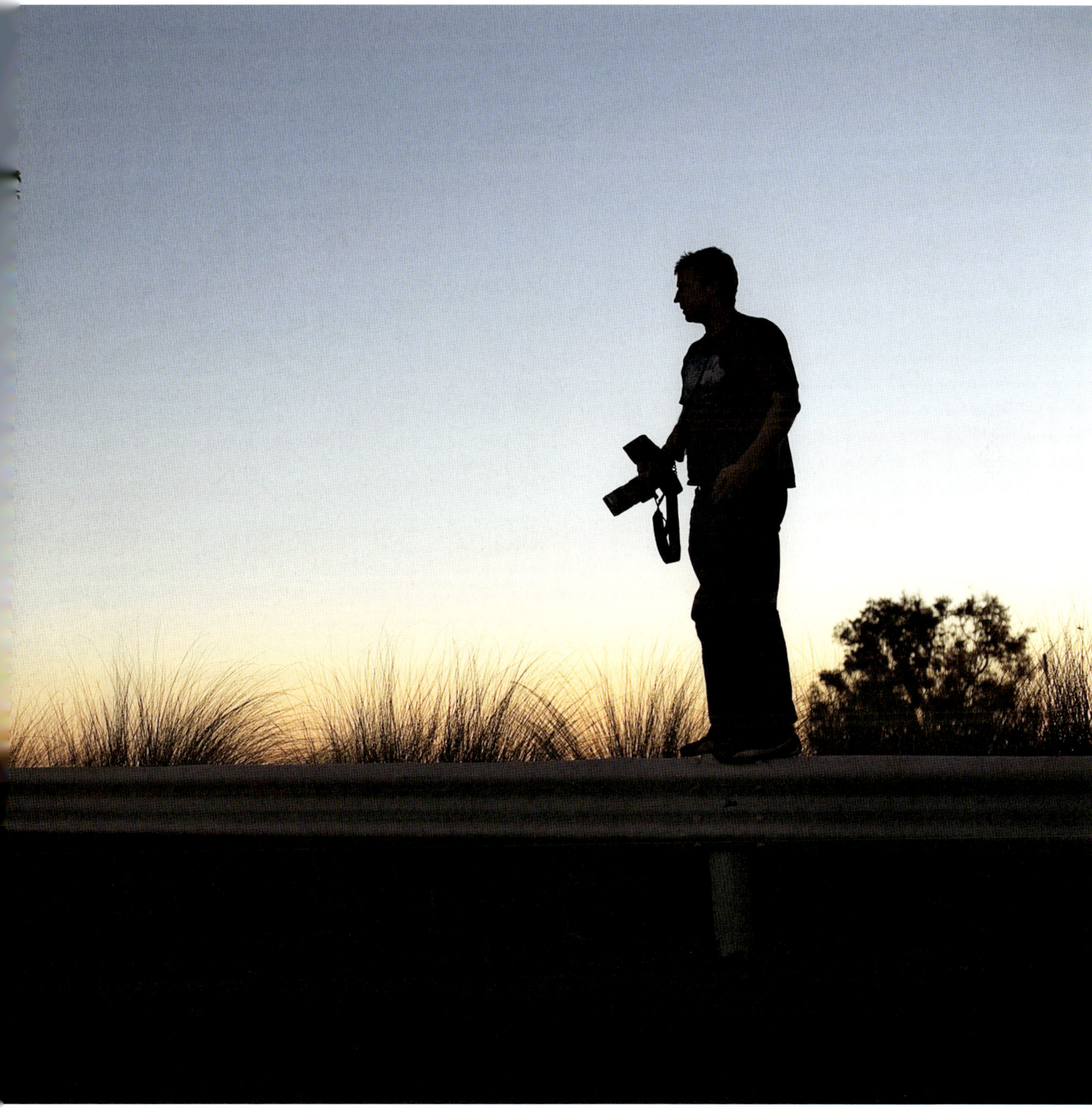

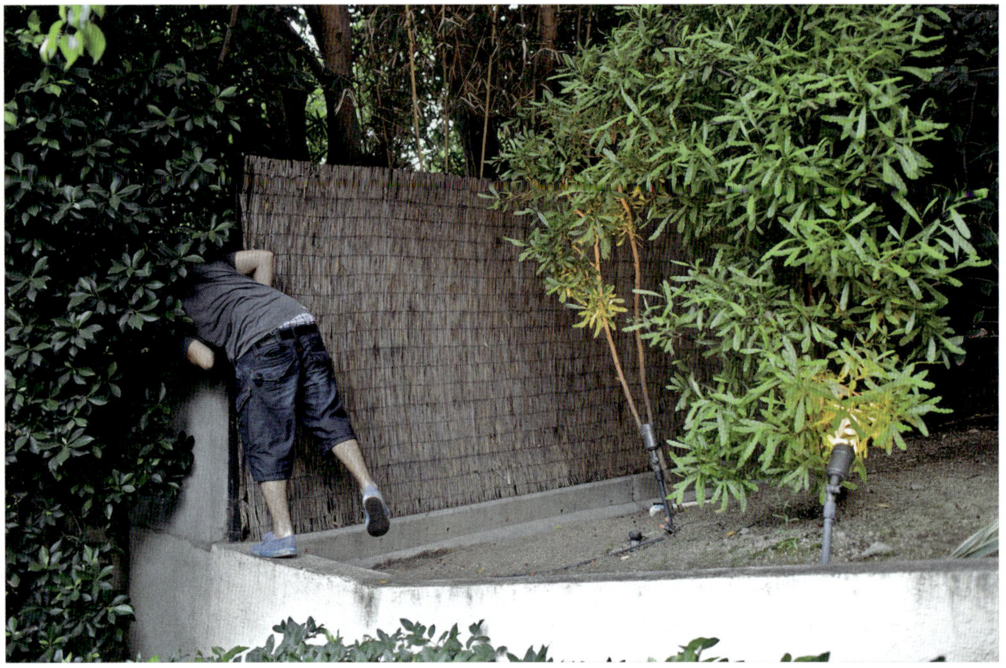

JESSICA DIMMOCK
Tom Cruise, from the series *Paparazzi!*
2009

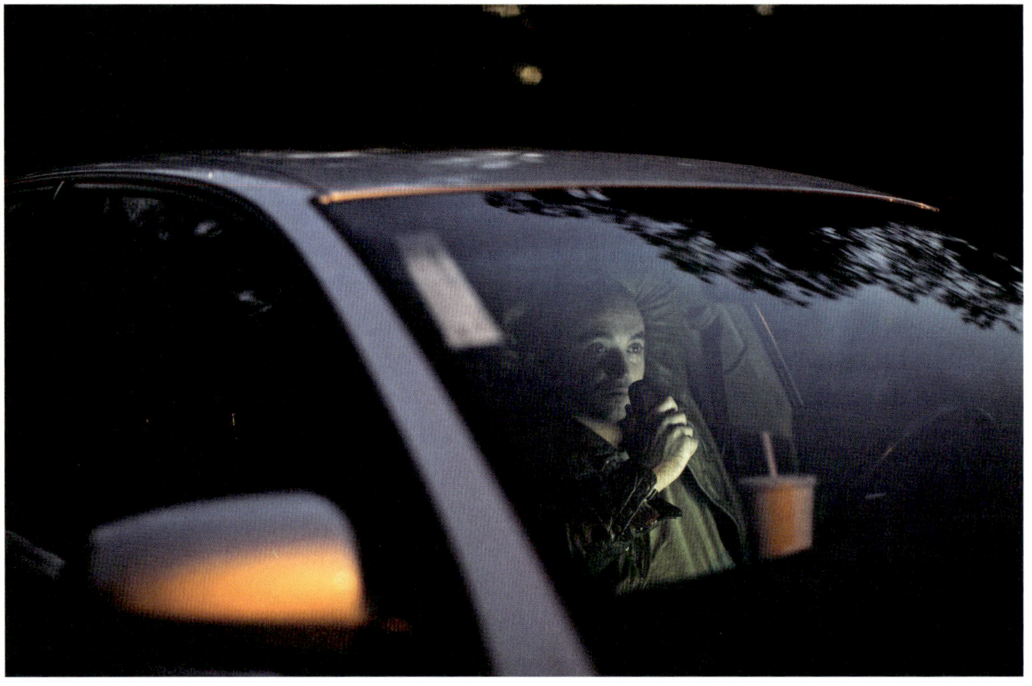

JESSICA DIMMOCK
Madonna, from the series *Paparazzi!*
2009

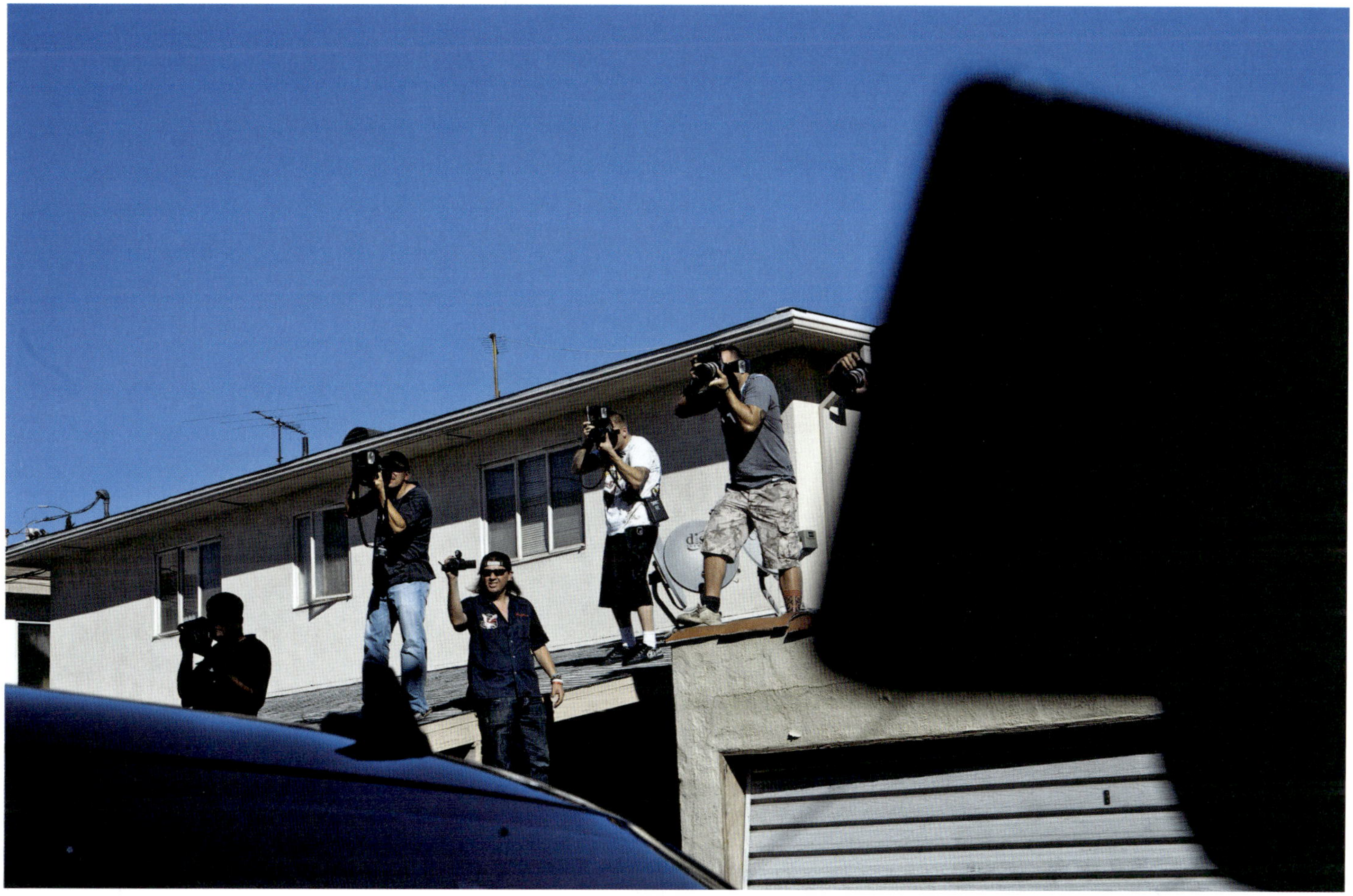

JESSICA DIMMOCK
Madonna, from the series *Paparazzi!*
2009

JESSICA DIMMOCK is an American photographer originally from New York. She worked in Los Angeles between 2008 and 2009, where she followed and photographed a group of paparazzi. Her series *Paparazzi!* conveys her immersion in a largely masculine universe, peopled by aggressive young males whose sole mission is to hunt down stars and make money from them. Her photographs document the daily routine of the paparazzi: the endless waiting, the hours spent camped out in cars parked in front of the target's door, and then the sudden mass attack when the star finally appears. With a background in photojournalism, Jessica Dimmock is intrigued by the resilience of celebrity coverage at a time when the press is in general decline. Will the paparazzi be the last surviving "journalists" capable of producing iconic images that can generate a profit? Will shots of Britney Spears shaving her head play the same role in the collective imagination as famous icons of photojournalism, such as Nick Ut's horrific image of the young girl burned by napalm?

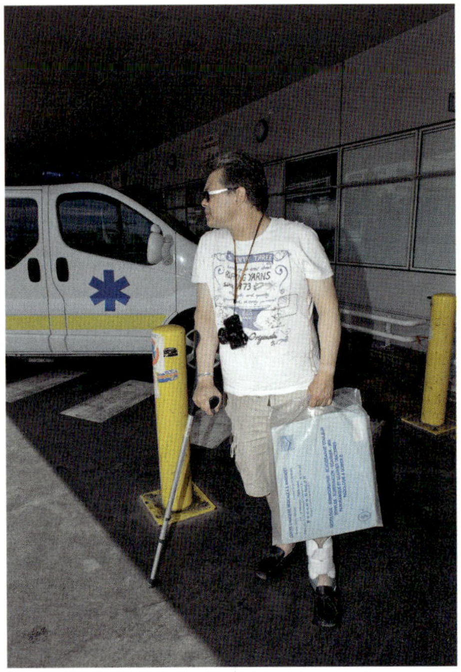

CHRISTOPHE BEAUREGARD
Hôpital Européen Georges-Pompidou, Paris, from the series *Hush … Hush*
2013

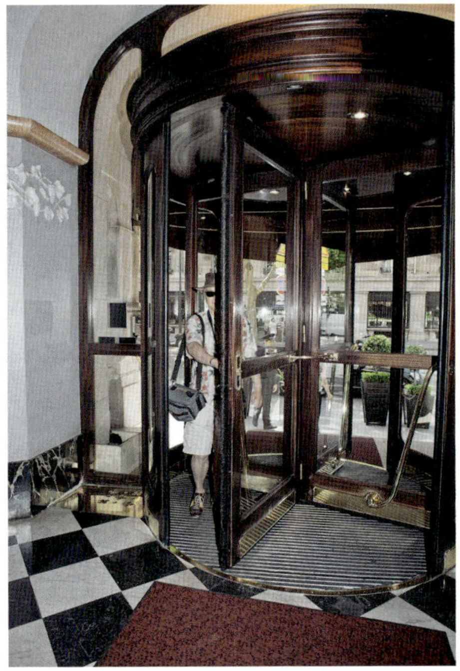

CHRISTOPHE BEAUREGARD
Hôtel Lutetia, Paris, from the series *Hush … Hush*
2013

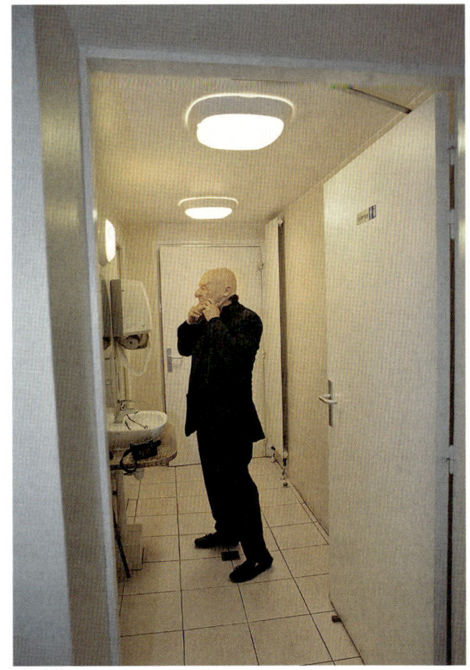

CHRISTOPHE BEAUREGARD
Town Hall, 7th Arrondissement, Paris, from the series *Hush … Hush*
2013

CHRISTOPHE BEAUREGARD is a French artist who places the issue of artifice at the forefront of his work. Known for his series of photographs of the homeless and the worlds of childhood and business life, he often employs makeup and reconstructions. He called on the services of a professional paparazzo to be photographed for *Hush … Hush*. His model wore the outfits he actually used in his stalking expeditions to demonstrate one of the job's characteristic requirements: dressing in costume. By using dissimulation as well as disguise, the photographer disappears into the background, becoming invisible in the eyes of his prey, enabling him to capture the image he covets. The art of camouflage allows him to successfully hunt down pictures to feed the insatiable appetite of celebrity magazines. Deception is put to profitable use, and is displayed in a variety of perfectly staged artificial scenarios: in a hospital, at the Hôtel Lutetia, in the Bois de Boulogne, and at the town hall in Paris's seventh arrondissement. The paparazzo's profession is oddly close to the actor's performance.

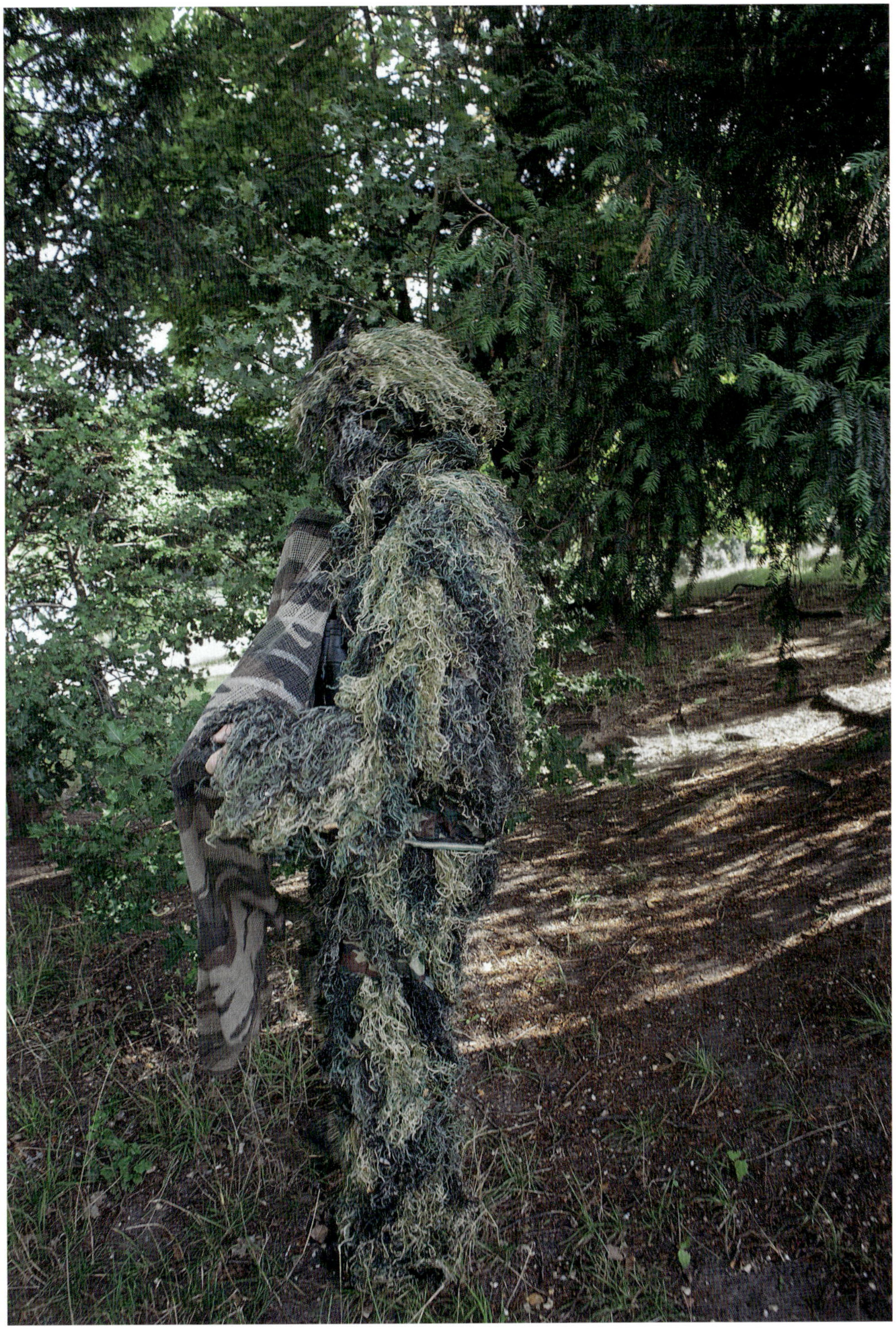

CHRISTOPHE BEAUREGARD
Bois de Boulogne, from the series *Hush … Hush*
2013

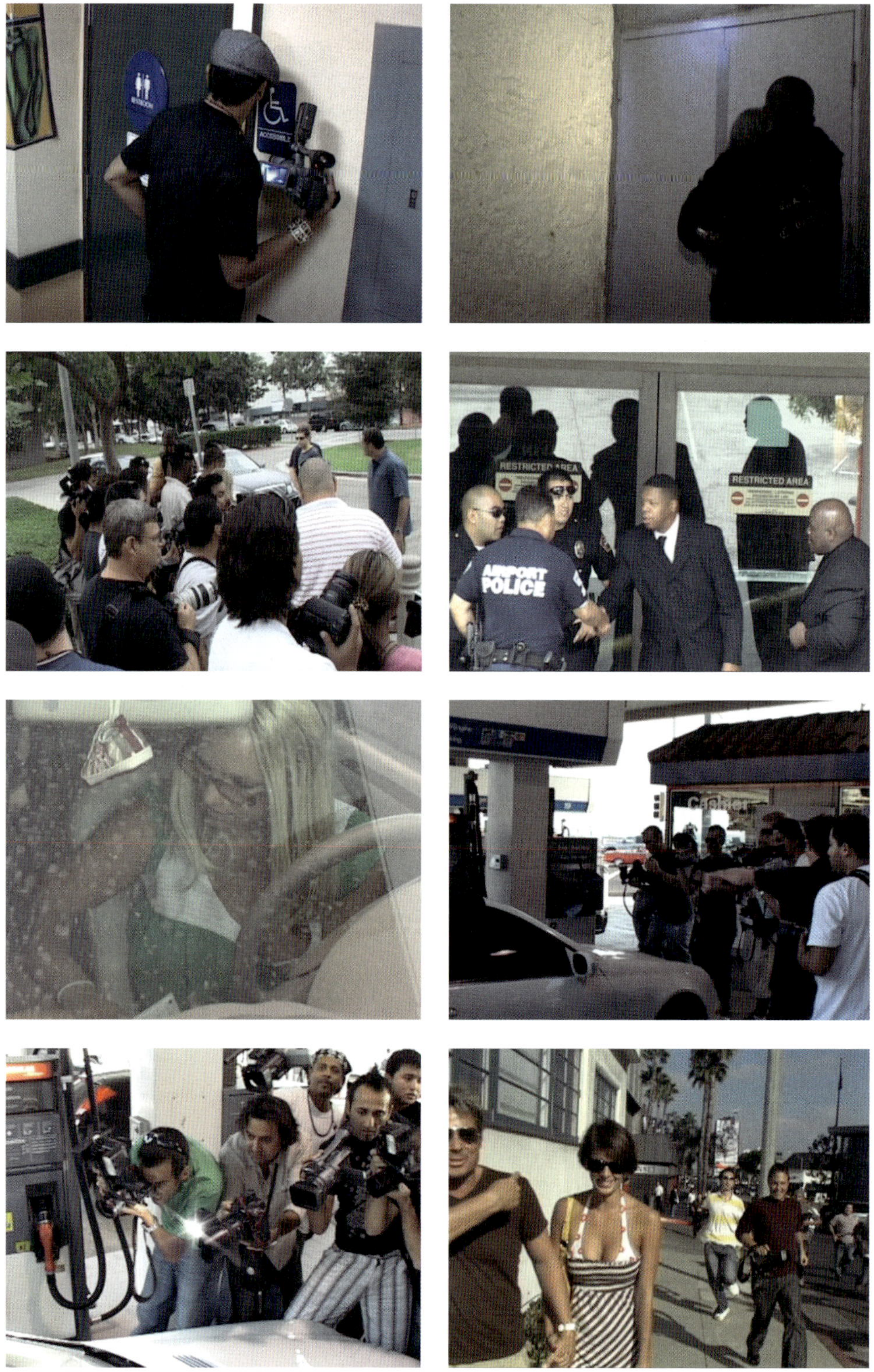

ROMAIN DUSSAULX AND BENJAMIN LALANDE
L.A. 2006
2013

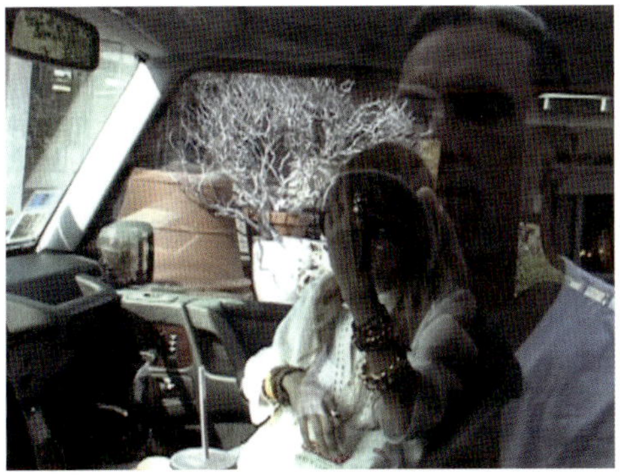
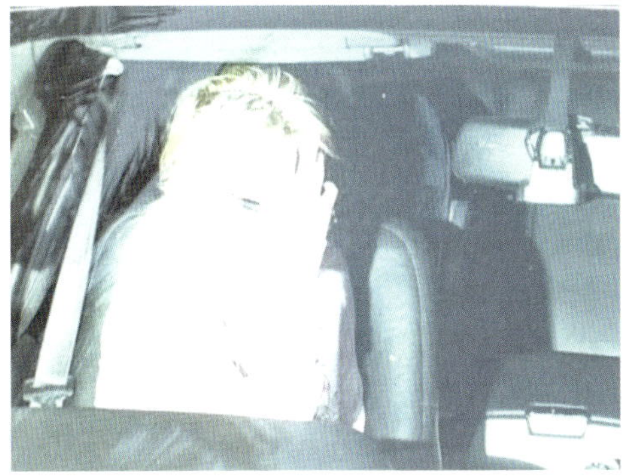
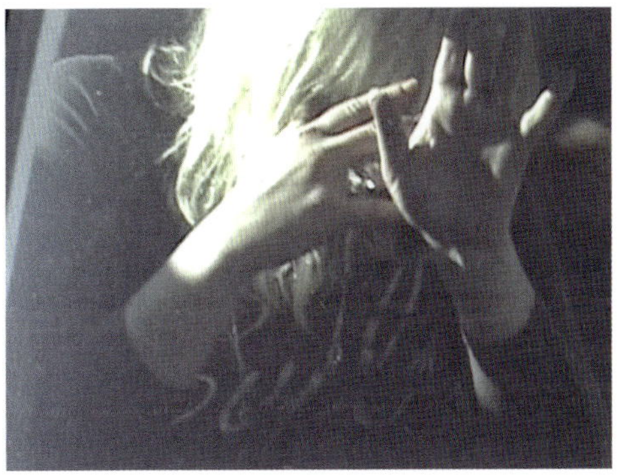
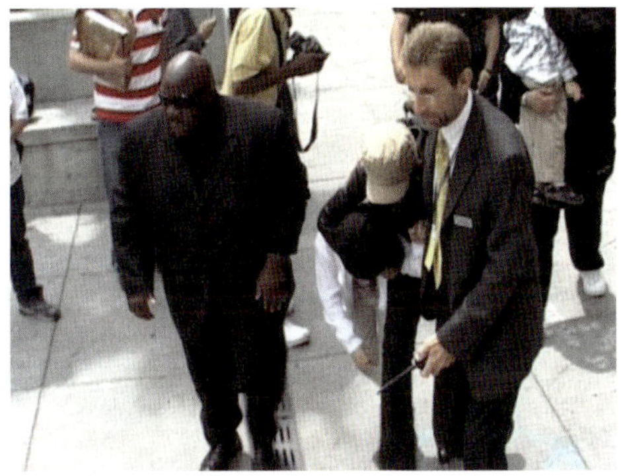
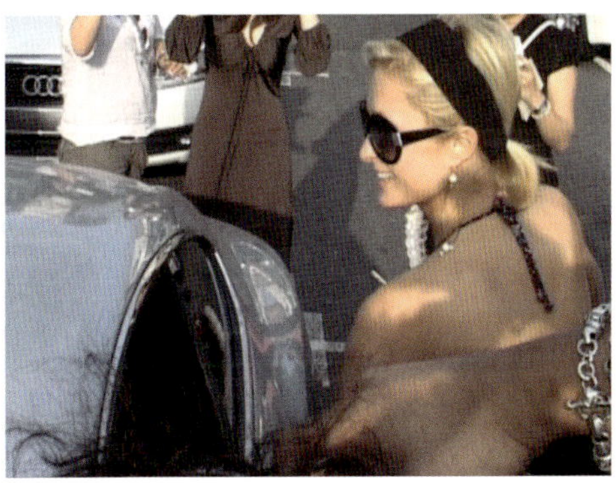
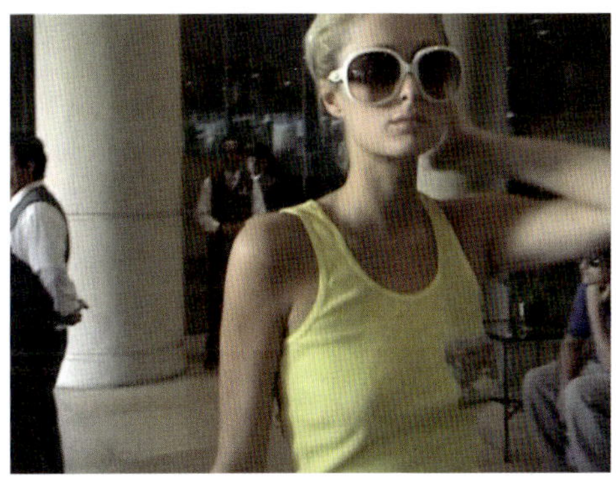

ROMAIN DUSSAULX AND BENJAMIN LALANDE. Romain Dussaulx is a French director and video-maker, born in 1979. With an educational background in sociology and ethnology, he has developed a documentary approach in his work and directed a series of stories covering the Los Angeles paparazzi. Working with Benjamin Lalande, another director and video-maker, he created a multiscreen installation that offers viewers a visual and sonic immersion into the world of the paparazzi. The video is presented in five acts: the waiting, the stalking, the hideout, the star's craving for visibility, and the culminating moment when the flashbulbs explode. Carefully edited, the work has a narrative structure that reveals the ambiguous nature of the relationship between the celebrity and the photographers. The film is a polyphonic account that articulates the essential interaction between the two protagonists, who are engaged in a strange kind of dance. It recounts this experience in a thoroughly novel fashion, deliberately leaving room for doubt over what is fact and what is fiction.

MYTHOLOGIES

The paparazzo is one of the great antiheroes of the postmodern era. At the end of the 1950s, Federico Fellini baptized this media phenomenon when he created a character named Paparazzo. This character has since become a mythical figure of popular culture that embodies all the flaws of our hypermediatized society. Focusing on *La Dolce Vita*, in addition to extracts from films by Brian De Palma, Andrzej Zulawski, William Wyler, Paul Abascal, and Dario Argento, this chapter shows how the general public perceives the paparazzo. A solitary wolf, often a loser, an altogether unpleasant character devoid of morals or pity who will stoop to anything in order to earn excessive amounts of money at celebrities' expense, he represents the opposite or double negative of the war photographer.

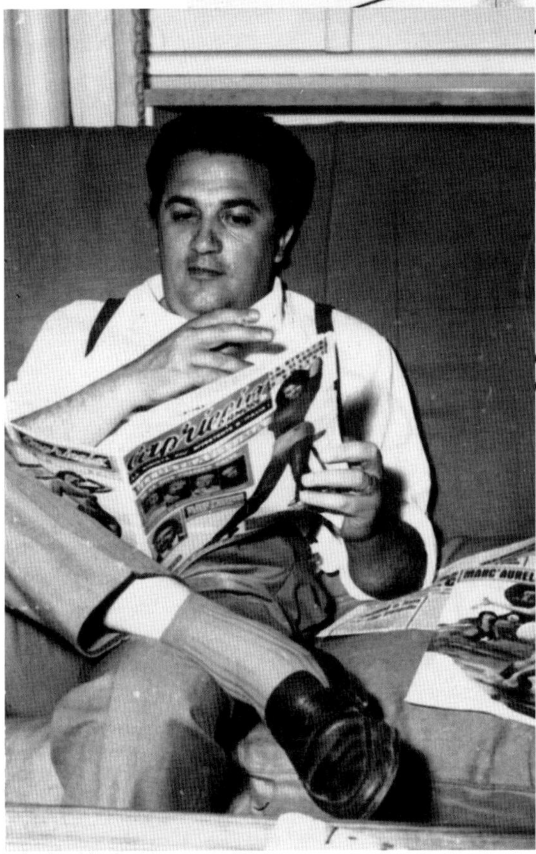

ANONYMOUS
Federico Fellini Looking at a Magazine
c. 1960

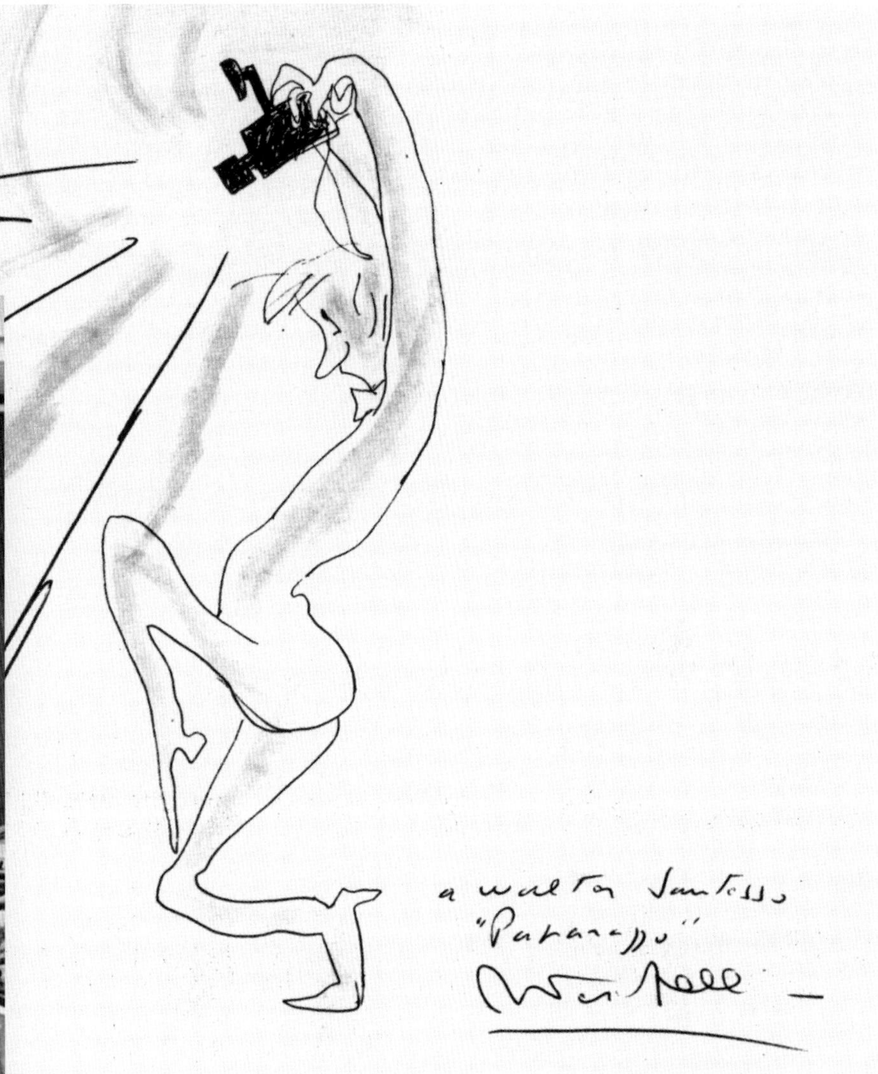

FEDERICO FELLINI
Walter Santesso, Paparazzo, the Photographer of La Dolce Vita
c. 1960

When the First Paparazzo Made a Scene

Sam Stourdzé

In the 1950s, Italy was recovering from the humiliations of war. It enthusiastically embraced the carefree spirit of the modern age. Rome discovered rock 'n' roll, and was carried away by its wild rhythms. Everything the century was producing in terms of images and frivolity could be found here, in the very cradle of antiquity. Rome—which had already taken center stage a few millennia previously, with tales of its escapades and decadence being told throughout the Empire—found itself in the spotlight once again. Like an open-air film set, it offered a show worthy of the greatest twentieth-century movie—full of intrigue and suspense, adventure and romance, with a long string of American film stars and, in the main role, these new photographers who brought scandal with them, and who would soon be known as paparazzi.

Hollywood on the Tiber

In order to understand what was happening in Rome at this time, we first have to look at Los Angeles. At the end of the 1940s, the American cinematographic industry faced the first great crisis of its history. Henceforth, the new antitrust law imposed upon major film producers the separation of their production activity from their distribution activity. Agents renegotiated an increase in the contracts of the actors they represented; and the technological developments—from talking pictures to color, and from CinemaScope to Technicolor—raised the price of productions, which struggled to make a profit. With no choice but to reinvent its model, Hollywood attempted to lower its expenses by all possible means in order to maintain its margins.

Six thousand miles (ten thousand kilometers) from the Pacific coast, Rome was enjoying a passionate relationship with cinema. The war had never prevented the development of the seventh art—quite the contrary. In the Italy of the 1930s and 1940s, all cinematographic trends coexisted side by side, from the neorealists who favored a direct contact with everyday life, without any artifice, to fascist propaganda cinema. Under Mussolini, Italy equipped itself with ultramodern studios. Inaugurated in 1937, Cinecittà, the city of cinema, was built in only fifteen months. Situated just outside Rome, it stretched across 150 acres (60 hectares), included all the trades of the industry, and boasted sophisticated infrastructures. The triumph of its first years, with close to three hundred films shot in less than six years, confirmed its clearly asserted ambition to compete with Hollywood by imposing itself as the venue for European cinematographic production. The war cooled this enthusiasm. It was not until the end of the 1940s that Californian producers started to look to Italy. The first American films shot at Cinecittà were epic films where the geographic setting apparently justified the delocalization. The real reasons were more pecuniary. In Rome, producers found high-quality infrastructures and skilled labor at an unbeatable price.

Several hundred American films were made in Rome over fifteen years. Films such as *Quo Vadis*, *Roman Holiday*, *War and Peace*, *Cleopatra*, and *Ben Hur*, among others. While shooting in Cinecittà, the Americans locked themselves away, and the studios were as

1. Quoted in the foreword by Cornell Capa, "If your pictures aren't good enough, you're not close enough," in Robert Capa, *Slightly Out of Focus* (New York: The Modern Library, 1999), xi.

inaccessible as Fort Knox. Only people with the right credentials could gain access. The curious were driven back and any information about the shooting underway was a closely guarded secret. Only a few official, accredited photographers were provided with a precious pass. The actors allowed themselves to be photographed within this framework: on the set, with good lighting, makeup, and in costume. They replayed the film's important scenes for the photographers, making sure they were immortalized in the same way as with the film camera. The photographers worked as they always had done: they documented the shooting or took portraits of the film stars against a neutral background. The negatives were sent to the production, which then chose the image that would be shown to the public. Rebaptized "Hollywood on the Tiber," the Italian capital, already shaken by the winds of change, gave its passing guests a warm welcome. During the day, the film crew worked at Cinecittà; at nightfall they flowed into the streets of Rome. In just a few years, the great cinema convoy took up residence in the Eternal City.

Everything was to be invented here: the celebrities and their escapades, the paparazzi and their knockout photos, the illustrated press and its scandalous stories. In the Mediterranean heat and an electric atmosphere, golden youths, decadent aristocracy, and American film stars kept joyful company to the wild rhythms of new music, at the wheel of convertibles or coupés, on view on café terraces or in fashionable nightclubs. The atmosphere was festive and lighthearted. Rome danced, drank, had fun, as the rest of the world was soon to discover.

The Assailant Photographers

By becoming film stars, actors began to lose control of their image. Their transformation into celebrities was indeed concomitant with the rise of the illustrated press. It is difficult to say which came first, but for the encounter to take place there was necessarily an intruder who slipped between the star and his image as a messenger of scandal. Rome offered a breeding ground for cultivating all kinds of indiscretions, rumors, and revelations. The handsome Italian males did nothing to hide their charms from the succumbing actresses, while the voluptuous Italian women never ran out of arguments. Life was consumed at high speed, in a consecration of immediacy. Roberto Rossellini left Anna Magnani for Ingrid Bergman, Ava Gardner cheated on Frank Sinatra with Walter Chiari, Anita Ekberg flaunted herself with Anthony Steel. Street photographers filled the magazine pages with pictures. As soon as they brought in a picture with a whiff of scandal, it was in the newspaper headlines. The strong demand from the press and easy money incited them to depart from their villages for Rome. Leaving behind them a probable life as painter or mason, they became photographers. With no training and rarely speaking English, they canvassed magazines to sell their photos, and when they succeeded they earned a lot of money.

Italy lived to the rhythm of the weekly publication of its magazines. *L'Espresso*, *Il Tempo*, *Le Ore*, *L'Europeo*, *Settimo Giorno*, and *Lo Specchio* had their readers spellbound. They informed them of the state of the world or of a country, of new discoveries or the conquest of space. Henceforth, it was the lives of celebrities that were spread across the glossy pages. In a flourishing market, they printed several hundreds of thousands of copies, seducing the public with the effective graphics of the *fototesto*: full-page photos accompanied by a short caption that left the pictures pride of place.

Photography itself had changed a lot over the previous decades. The democratization of light, easy-to-handle cameras, associated with the spread of flash use, which meant photographs could be taken at night with short exposure times, encouraged the emergence of a new documentary style. Robert Capa paved the way with his famous expression, "If your photos aren't good enough, you're not close enough,"[1] and encouraged war photography to develop an unbearable proximity to its subject. Weegee took things further by tuning his radio to the police frequency. Informed in real time of all the murders perpetrated in the city, he sometimes arrived at the crime scene before the police themselves. Accident, murder, or society news items became his trademark. He also positioned himself in a close face-to-face with his subject. In short, everything was ready for photographers to give film stars the same treatment in the 1950s. They had probably been spared thus far due to a concern for respectability. Indeed, only the tabloids dared to transgress the unspoken rule of respecting privacy.

The war, however, blew away any lasting resistance: the world changed and morals became freer. The illustrated press, as well as the actors, now had to contend with ruthless competition. They had to stand out from the rest, make themselves noticed.

The public was positioned as umpire. The press and the actors embarked upon the task

2. One day we should reread the history of photography from the viewpoint of the impoverishment of images. The appearance of the paparazzi aesthetic would fit perfectly into this history.

of gaining the public's attention, united by the need to seduce. Adopting the two roles of reader and viewer, the public became, in this era of mass consumerism, a target that had to be reached and an audience whose support needed to be obtained. Forming a link between the press and the film stars, the photographers echoed the escapades of those who wished to maintain or to gain the ranks of celebrity; the press took on the responsibility of relaying the information. In a Faustian foursome, the stars, the photographers, the press, and the public sealed their fate by creating a vast, interdependent network.

The desire for knowledge is a form of demand. Certainly, things have come a long way since the beginning of the twentieth century, a period when producers refused to reveal actors' names for fear of having to answer their demands. It took their relentless persuasion, along with the public's desire to know who its heroes were, before their names could at last be credited. Dissatisfied with the extent to which news was being controlled, the public, by buying these papers, now encouraged those who gave them access to the stars' private lives. Revealing yourself was the price to be paid for entering the star system; it was the ransom of success. The cultural break was coupled with an aesthetic break. These new photographers upset the codes of a photographic practice that had become too academic.[2] In the light of established standards, the photo grew poorer. It became chaotic and disorderly, its framing was random, its precision was blurred, and the foreground was regularly barred by an opposing hand or even hindered by the reflections of a car window. There was a change of paradigm, where two categories clashed in what was virtually a class struggle: the profession's aristocrats—accredited photographers with authorized access to the film sets—and the others—the proletarians of photography who awaited the arrival of a film star for hours on the sidewalk, who hunted the film star down until they succeeded in snatching his or her picture. This merry band of Romans included Vélio Cioni, Marcello Geppetti, Franco Pinna, Pierluigi Praturlon, Tazio Secchiaroli, Sergio Spinelli, Elio Sorci, Sandro Vespasiani, and Arturo Zavattini. They were wild, combative, assailant photographers. They had no photographic culture and had no real need for it. All of them had assimilated the magazines' expectations, and more often than not simply had to capture the spectacle that offered itself to them. And if they had to encourage things a little, that was no problem. They were quick, agile, and shrewd. They photographed in packs, like others hunt. Friendly with the concierges of big hotels, the waiters of chic restaurants, nightclub bouncers, and taxi drivers, at the slightest indiscretion they jumped onto their Vespas, straddled their Lambrettas, or took to the wheel of their Fiat 500s, and crossed the city like lightning so as not to miss anything. They hid out and waited for hours: in order to capture David Niven and Ava Gardner scantily clad, Tazio Secchiaroli chose to hide for five hours in a corridor cupboard in the Cinecittà! They had become true masters of surprise.

The Via Veneto served as a meeting point. Bars and clubs lined Rome's chic main street. Film stars and their entourages, high society people, other prominent figures—everyone crowded there to party and have fun for most of the night. In the early hours, they reappeared with weary faces, reeling with the effects of alcohol and fatigue. The photographers, posted on the opposite sidewalk, finally saw their patience rewarded. They went crazy, flashes popping, buzzing like mosquitoes around their prey. If an illegitimate couple had formed overnight, it was a jackpot. The photographers often worked in pairs and their routine was well rehearsed. If a bachelor appeared with a new conquest, they would try to provoke him; action was needed for a film star to fly off the handle. One of them would shout out, "Have you seen the ugly dog you picked up last night!" The reaction was immediate: the film star would chase the impertinent heckler. The second photographer, off to one side, would then rush to follow them and immortalize the scene. Their trouble would be rewarded with several pages in a magazine, or, even better, a magazine cover. Tazio Secchiaroli is said to have enraged King Farouk by supposedly coming up to him and letting slip an offensive remark about his female companions.

From the Via Veneto to *La Dolce Vita*

As a refined observer of Italian society in the full swing of change, Federico Fellini best discerned this sudden eruption of a new aesthetic into popular culture. The arrival of the modern age spared neither the economy, nor transport, nor tradition, nor customs, nor even the media and the way in which they fashioned the image of the world. *La Dolce Vita* (1960) tells this tale, and Fellini even used the film's form to represent the revolution in progress, choosing to break with

3. Interview with the author on May 19, 2009.

4. *Les Propos de Fellini* (Paris: Buchet-Chastel, 1960), 107–8.

the principle of a linear narrative. Marcello Mastrianni plays the role of a reporter in the movie, often followed by a horde of photographers. Thus begins a strange game of to-and-fro between reality and cinema, between the photographers of film stars and the filmmaker, to such an extent that it is difficult to know which inspired the other.

In *La Dolce Vita*—often described as springing straight from Fellini's imagination—many scenes are taken directly from real situations. Fellini undertook a vast operation of dissecting current events in order to extract the narrative essence. He drew his inspiration from the source of reality.

Benno Graziani, an important reporter in Rome for *Paris Match* in the 1950s, tells of his long discussions with Fellini.[3] One day the "maestro" confessed that the character of Marcello in *La Dolce Vita* owed much to him. Fellini himself wrote that the role of the photographer, Paparazzo, was inspired by Tazio Secchiaroli. It must be noted that Secchiaroli was behind the most sensational scoops during the 1950s. He alone embodied the new generation of film-star hunters: free, unabashed photographers who followed the film stars as hunters chase an animal. In a lucid analysis of the relationship that linked the photographer with the film star, Secchiaroli simply said that the day the photographer stopped following the star, the star would run after him.

At the start of his career, working in the street and taking portraits of passersby or American soldiers stationed in the city, Secchiaroli trained with Adolfo Porry-Pastorel, before founding Roma Press Photo in 1955 with Marcello Geppetti. The agency made a succession of scoops and their photos made the front pages of newspapers, including King Farouk in good company, Ava Gardner kissing her lover Tony Franciosi at a café, Anita Ekberg and her husband Anthony Steel slightly the worse for wear, and a striptease at Rugantino's nightclub. As fate would have it, he actually joined those he had spent so many years chasing. After *La Dolce Vita*, Secchiaroli was to become a renowned cinema photographer, often working with Fellini, as well as becoming Sophia Loren's official photographer. In so doing, he confirmed the importance of the paths he had forged.

In 1958, while preparing for *La Dolce Vita*, Fellini met Secchiaroli and the Via Veneto photographers. He arrived with his arms full of magazines and asked who was responsible for each photo. He wanted to understand how they operated, how they worked, and who their victims were. And was it his plan all along to cast Anita Ekberg as herself, as a film star sucked into the whirlpool of Roman life, whose every act and gesture was followed by journalists?

A photograph from October 1958 immortalizes the encounter: grouped around Fellini are the photographers Tazio Secchiaroli, Sandro Vespasiani, and Pierluigi Praturlon, the set photographer of *La Dolce Vita*. In his autobiography, Fellini recalls, "I spent many evenings with the photographers of Via Veneto, talking with Tazio Secchiaroli and the others and learning about the tricks of their trade: how they tracked down their prey, what they did to make them nervous, and how they prepared their reports to meet the requirements of the different papers."[4]

The most memorable story took place a few weeks later, one November evening in 1958, at Rugantino's, a fashionable nightclub in Trastevere. On that evening, a young man from a respectable family was celebrating his birthday. The party was lively, gathering together the city's golden youth. Among the guests were a few aristocrats, writers, starlets, and Anita Ekberg. The pinup, who had fallen under Rome's spell when she was filming *War and Peace* there, had moved to the Eternal City with the aim of participating fully in the frenzied atmosphere. Witnesses vividly described how she took off her shoes to dance barefoot. Then she threw herself into a torrid cha-cha, captivating her audience. One of the onlookers, a young Turkish actress called Aiché Nana, contemplated the performance of the older actress and decided to take up the challenge. The tables were pushed back, the musicians formed a circle, men took off their jackets and laid them on the floor to give her a stage. Everyone moved closer and Aiché Nana began her striptease. Flashes started to pop. Alerted by the clamor, the club owner, obligated to preserve the anonymity of his clients, began to worry about the trouble he would get into if word of the event got around. He collared the photographers and confiscated their films. Tazio Secchiaroli, the shrewdest of the lot, quickly understood what he could get out of the scene. He took a few photos before entrusting the film to one of his friends. It was a blank film that he gave to the club owner. His friend left the club without being bothered, and rushed to the photo laboratory to develop the photos. The next day, the pictures of Aiché Nana's striptease were on the editors' desks.

All the magazines published them, provoking an unprecedented scandal. The story even crossed the Atlantic and was published by American newspapers. In Italy, *Lo Specchio* headlined "The genteel people undress like this," or even "The Turk for dessert."[5] The photo was accompanied by a diagram identifying and naming all the celebrities present. *L'Expresso* published the story on its front page and nicknamed Aiché Nana "The Naked Turk."[6] More discreet than the others, the newspaper took care to cover the intimate parts of the young woman's body with a black band. It also took advantage of the situation to mask, in a similar fashion, the eyes of the participants. These attemps to hide the identity of the guests probably only encouraged some readers to do everything they could to try and recognize them!

When Fellini discovered the Rugantino scandal in the press, he immediately sensed the cinematographic potential of the story. It captured Rome's postwar antagonisms between the liberalization of morals and the weight of tradition. The shock of the two cultures was sometimes violent. The deep changes in society that had accompanied the economic boom shook Italy and obliged the Church and conservative parties, somewhat reluctantly, to lessen their hold.

When he finished his screenplay for *La Dolce Vita*, in the fall of 1958, Fellini decided to insert a striptease scene reminiscent of the incident at Rugantino's at the end of his film. Another event that left its mark on *La Dolce Vita* was one that played with popular beliefs. Indeed, in postwar Europe and even more so in Italy, there was an increase in the apparitions of the Virgin Mary. The Vatican adopted a reserved—even hostile—attitude toward these apparitions, while the public, driven by collective belief, greeted each miracle with enthusiasm. Thus, during the summer of 1958, the Madonna appeared to two children in the region of Terni, about an hour from Rome. The news spread immediately to the village inhabitants, and the media flocked there in droves to cover the event. Huge crowds took over the village.

The same summer Fellini wrote the script for *La Dolce Vita*, with Flaiano and Pinelli. They included the story of this apparition in the film, thereby acknowledging that they drew inspiration from current events. In the scene, the film producer emphasized the media spectacle of the event; he had grasped the full significance of modern communication. In the society of the spectacle, the press and television fashion our perception of the real. With Fellini, the place where the miracle happened became a theater of illusions transmitted live to the masses. Fellini's importance lay in his capacity to detect the cinematographic potential of any event, in order to account for the radical change disrupting society, virtually in real time. The opening scene of *La Dolce Vita* is in itself emblematic of the Fellinian construction.

Two similar helicopters—Bell 47s—hover over Rome.[7] The first one is transporting a statue of Christ suspended by a cable, arms outstretched and seemingly blessing the chaotic image of the Eternal City from the sky. The second follows the first, carrying Marcello Mastroianni as a journalist and Walter Santesso as a paparazzo. Together, they cover the event. The procession heads for the Vatican to deliver its strange cargo and in turn flies over the new suburbs, a football pitch situated alongside the ruins of a Roman aqueduct, and a modern building with two women in bikinis relaxing on its roof terrace. The soundtrack plays a jazz tune, followed by the chiming of the bells of Saint Peter. The scene is built around antagonisms, beginning with the incongruous association of the helicopter and Christ. The transportation of a symbol of tradition by one of modernity[8] served as an event in a society in which the spectacle now attracted the attention of all the media. This society had settled into its own rhythm, under the implacable gaze of the picture hunters who brought in, like trophies, damning proof of how this new way of living was being exhibited. As they were to establish themselves lastingly in the field of the media, they had to be given a name. Fellini, catching onto the significance of their emergence before everyone else, gave an entire profession, if not notoriety, at least a name. In the film, the photographer answered to the name of Paparazzo; all of these photographers, after *La Dolce Vita*, would forever be known as paparazzi![9]

5. *Lo Specchio*, November 16, 1958.

6. *L'Espresso*, November 16, 1958.

7. It is important to remember that this scene has a prior history. Indeed, in the news items of CIAK of May 1, 1956, a helicopter transported a statue of Christ from the Piazza del Duomo in Milan to the Vatican. On this subject, see Sam Stourdzé, "Le Christ en hélicoptère," in *Federico Fellini, La Dolce Vita* (Paris: Xavier Barral, 2009), 264–69.

8. The helicopter is a powerful symbol, inherent in the image of the reconstruction of postwar Italy. Indeed, the Italians claim the first civil helicopter flight, which took place in Rome in 1930. The flying machine imagined by Leonardo Da Vinci became an allegory that was constantly related by the popular press. Its exploits and its setbacks both found an echo in the media: the helicopter embodied modernity, technological excellence, and the conquest of the sky.

9. For details on the origins of the term "paparazzi"—the plural of "paparazzo"—see the text by Clément Chéroux (theory number 3) on p. 12 of this book.

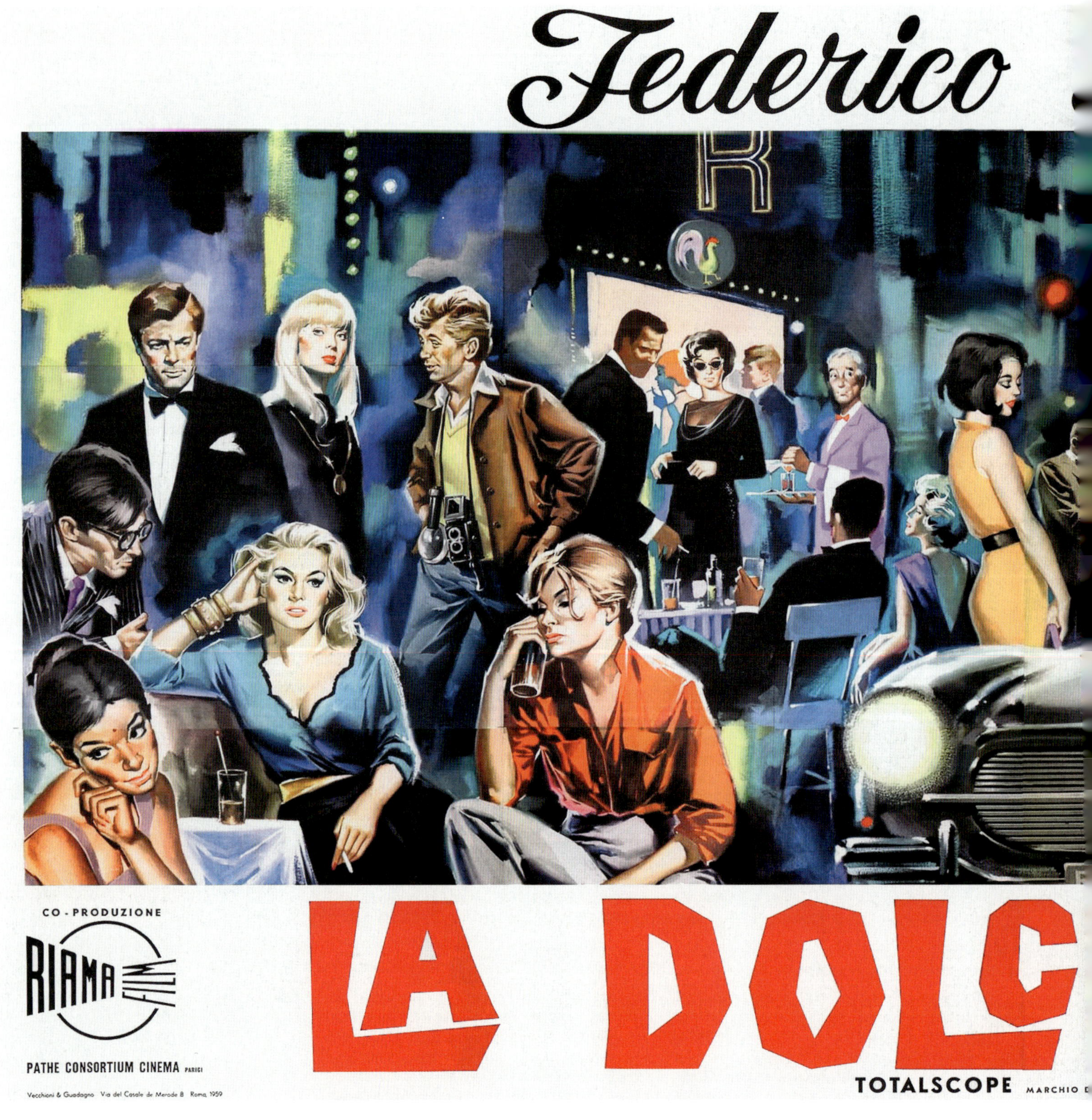
Federico
CO-PRODUZIONE
RIAMA FILM
PATHE CONSORTIUM CINEMA PARIGI
Vecchioni & Guadagno Via del Casale de Merode 8 Roma, 1959
LA DOLC
TOTALSCOPE MARCHIO D

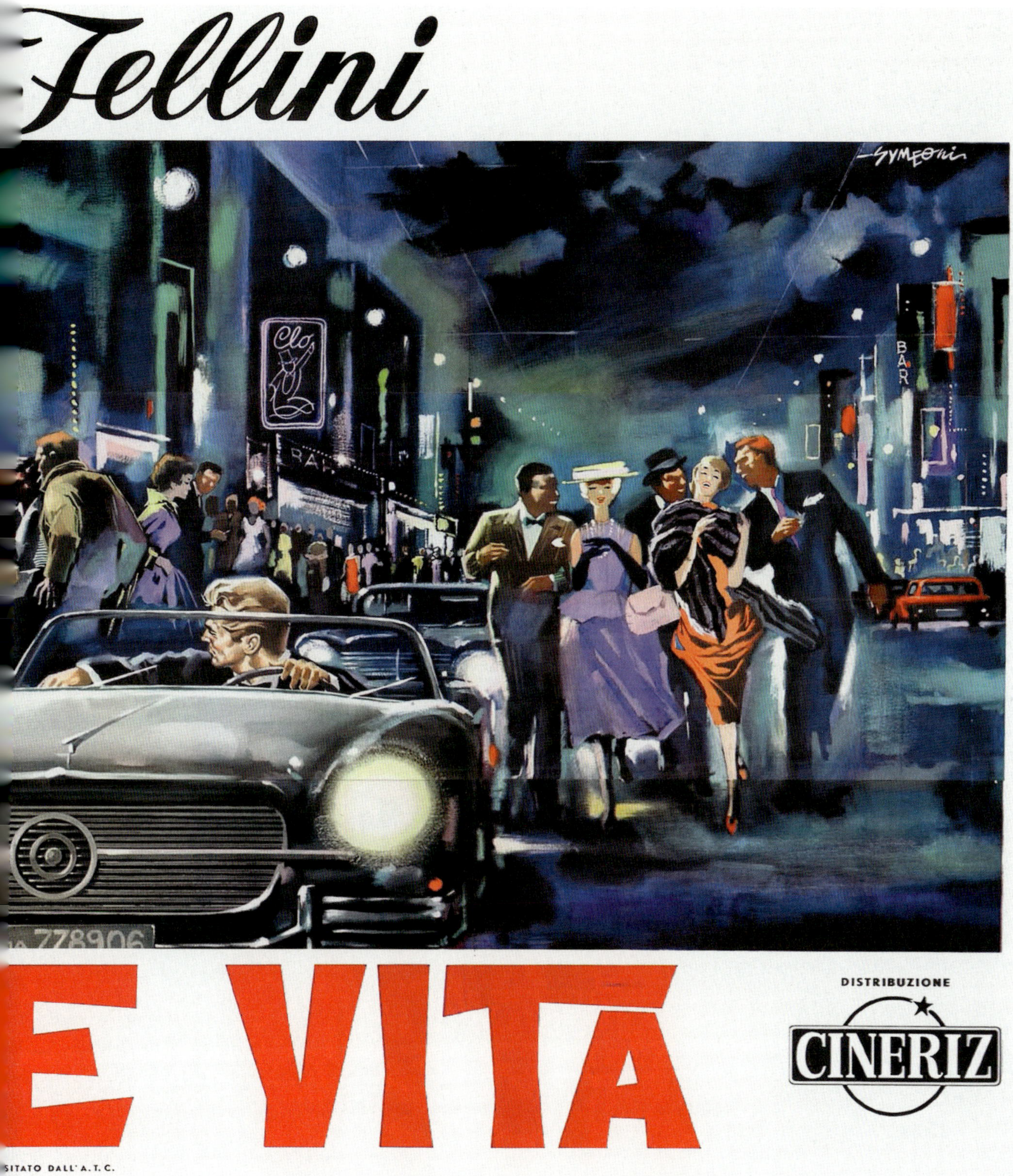

SANDRO SIMEONI
Poster for *La Dolce Vita*
1960

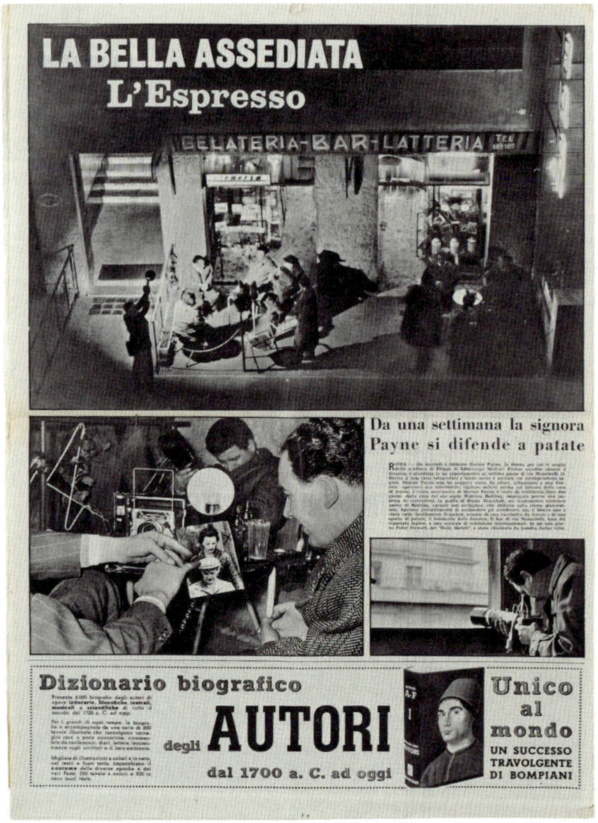

LA BELLA ASSEDIATA

L'Espresso

GELATERIA-BAR-LATTERIA

Da una settimana la signora Payne si difende a patate

Dizionario biografico degli AUTORI dal 1700 a. C. ad oggi

Unico al mondo

UN SUCCESSO TRAVOLGENTE DI BOMPIANI

"La Bella Assediata" (The Mobbed Beauty), *L'Espresso*, February 17, 1957, back cover (Photograph: anonymous)

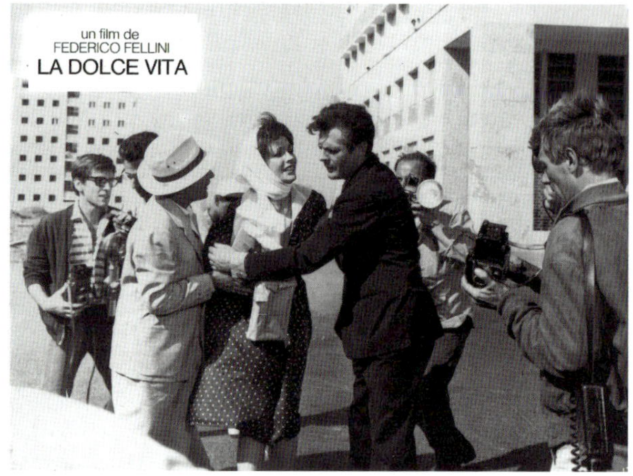

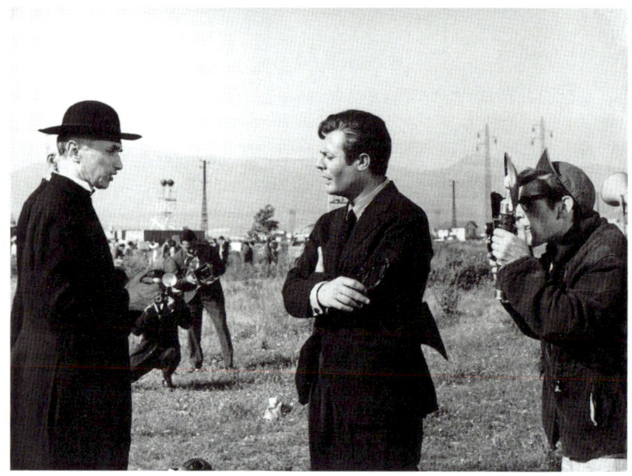

ANONYMOUS
(Pierluigi Agency)
La Dolce Vita
1960

LA DOLCE VITA. "I didn't make anything up. Just read the papers. The 1958 tabloids were my inspiration." This is how Fellini explained the origin of *La Dolce Vita*. The film, released in 1960, is a virtual synopsis of the events that mesmerized the press that year.
His scenes of rock 'n' roll and the Trevi Fountain evoked the flamboyant exploits of celebrities who were avidly covered by contemporary magazines. The striptease sequence replicated an act in a Roman nightclub that had already been extensively chronicled. In Fellini's view, Anita Ekberg, who was present at the event, was the virtual personification of this media-obsessed, decadent world. She was the muse of Roman nightlife, a sex symbol par excellence, and her exploits were abundantly documented by the celebrity press of the city aptly known as Hollywood on the Tiber. The director was primarily interested in the phenomenon of media hype and by the figure of the photographer who feeds that frenzy. He becomes one of the film's central characters. Fellini decided to call him "Paparazzo," and that became the name of the profession itself. The actual set photographer for *La Dolce Vita* was a real paparazzo named Pierluigi Praturlon. Fellini enthusiastically delivered scoops to photographers during the filming to encourage their coverage of his fictitious tale.

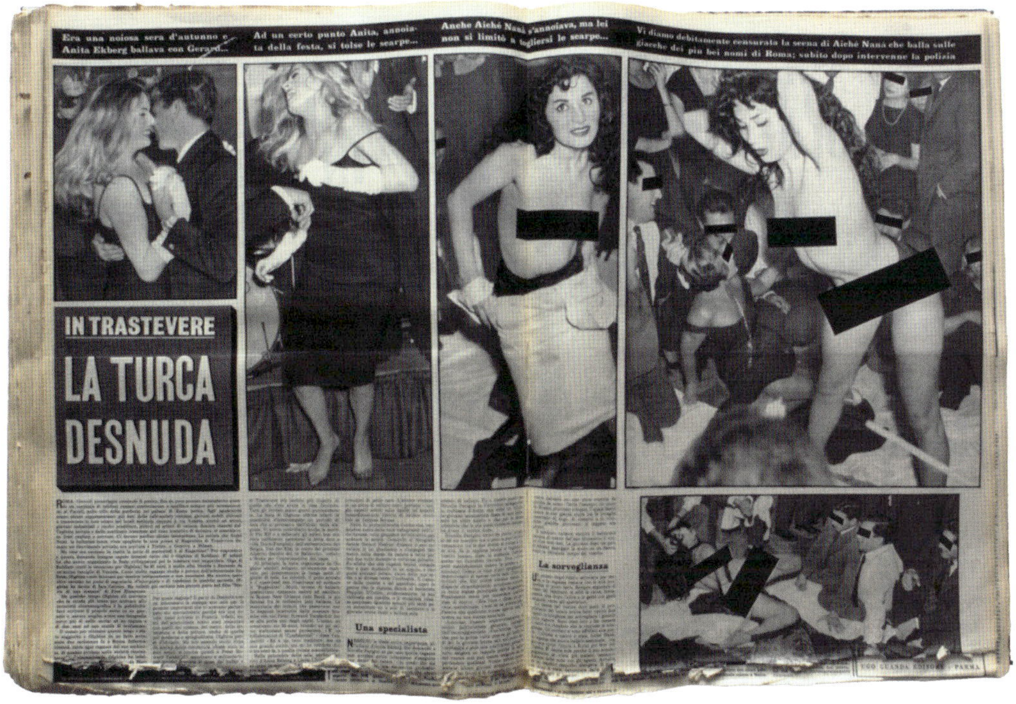

Era una noiosa sera d'autunno e Anita Ekberg ballava con Gerardo...

Ad un certo punto Anita, annoiata della festa, si tolse le scarpe...

Anche Aiché Nanà s'annoiava, ma lei non si limitò a togliersi le scarpe...

Vi diamo debitamente censurata la scena di Aiché Nanà che balla sulle giacche dei più bei nomi di Roma; subito dopo intervenne la polizia

IN TRASTEVERE

LA TURCA DESNUDA

Una specialista

La sorveglianza

UGO GUANDA EDITORE - PARMA

"In Trastevere. La Turca Desnuda" (In the Trastevere District. The Naked Turkish Woman), Aiché Nana's striptease at Rugantino's, *L'Espresso*, November 16, 1958 (Photographs: Tazio Secchiaroli)

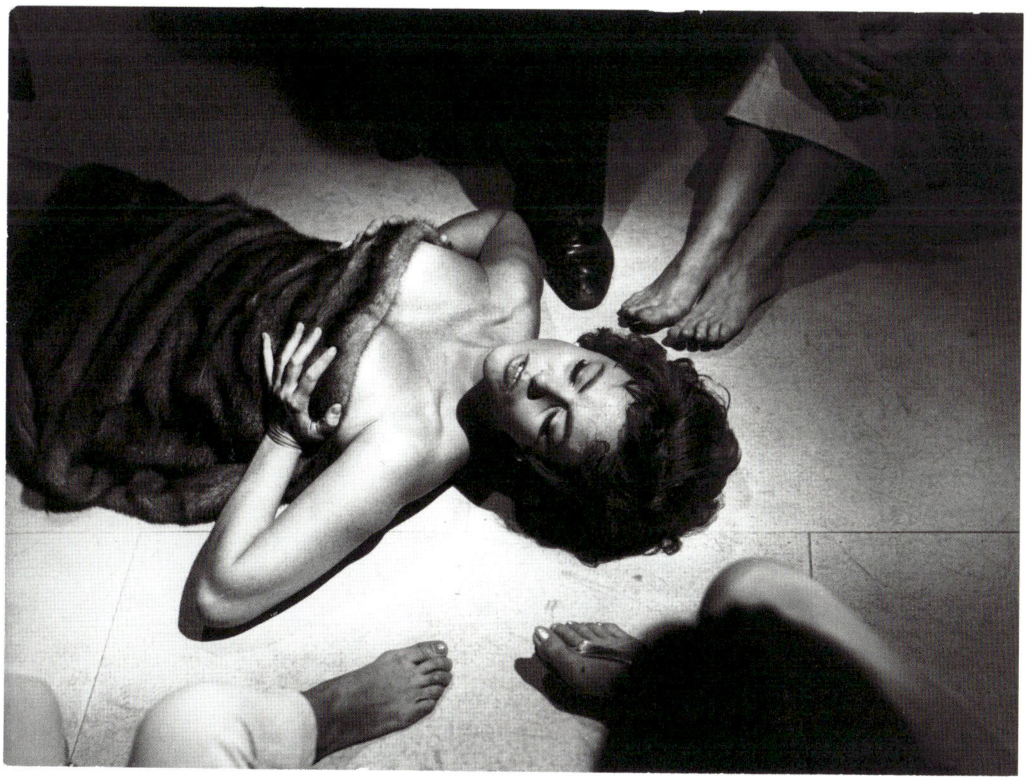

ANONYMOUS
(Pierluigi Agency)
La Dolce Vita
1960

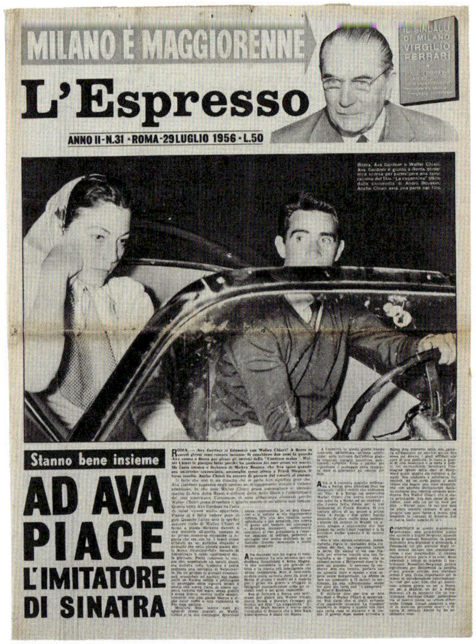
MILANO È MAGGIORENNE

L'Espresso

ANNO II - N.31 · ROMA · 29 LUGLIO 1956 · L.50

Stanno bene insieme

AD AVA PIACE L'IMITATORE DI SINATRA

"Ad Ava Piace l'Imitatore di Sinatra" (When Ava [Gardner] Appeals to a Sinatra Imitator), *L'Espresso*, July 29, 1956, cover (Photograph: anonymous)

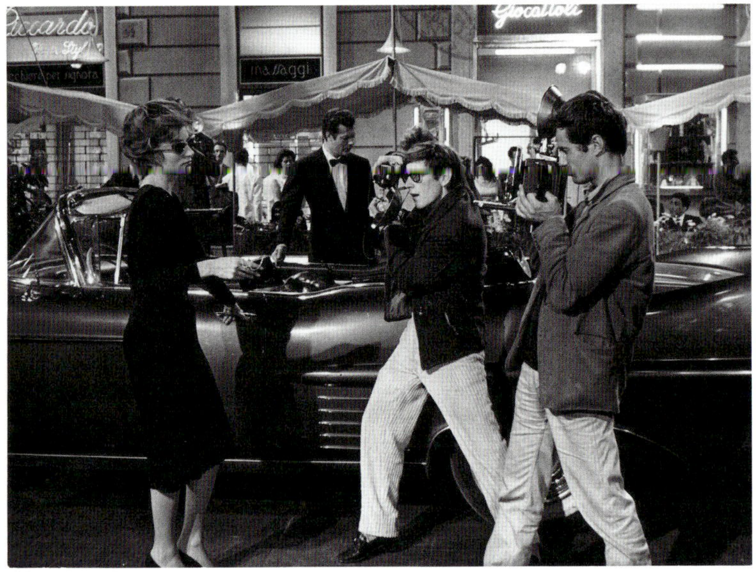

ANONYMOUS
(Pierluigi Agency)
Anouk Aimée and Two Photographers from the Via Veneto in La Dolce Vita
1960

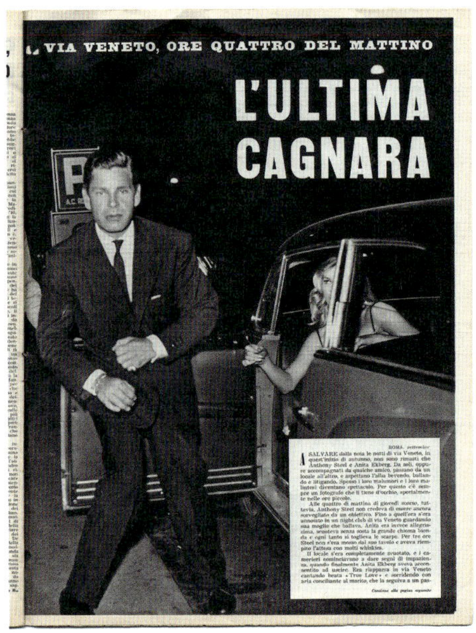
VIA VENETO, ORE QUATTRO DEL MATTINO

L'ULTIMA CAGNARA

"L'Ultima Cagnara" (The Last Uproar, Anthony Steel and Anita Ekberg), *L'Europeo*, September 28, 1958 (Photograph: Tazio Secchiaroli)

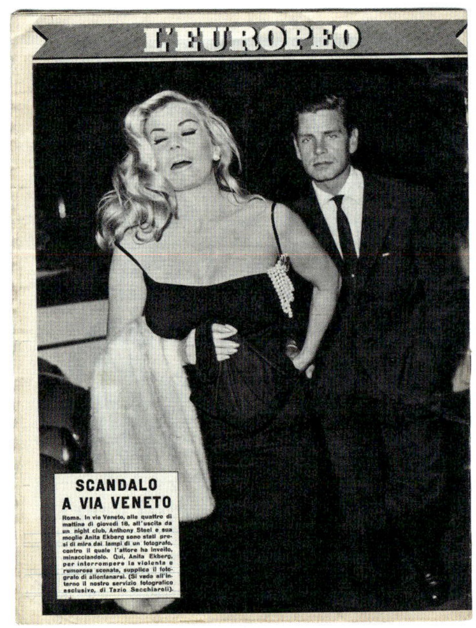
L'EUROPEO

SCANDALO A VIA VENETO

Roma. In via Veneto, alle quattro di mattina di giovedì 18, all'uscita da un night club, Anthony Steel e sua moglie Anita Ekberg sono stati presi di mira dai lampi di un fotografo, contro il quale l'attore ha inveito, minacciandolo. Qui, Anita Ekberg, per interrompere la violenta e rumorosa scenata, supplica il fotografo di allontanarsi. (Si veda all'interno il nostro servizio fotografico esclusivo, di Tazio Secchiaroli).

"Scandalo a Via Veneto" (Scandal on the Via Veneto, Anita Ekberg and Anthony Steel), *L'Europeo*, September 28, 1958, back cover (Photograph: Tazio Secchiaroli)

ANONYMOUS
(Pierluigi Agency)
Anita Ekberg,
Marcello Mastroianni,
and the Photographer
in La Dolce Vita
1960

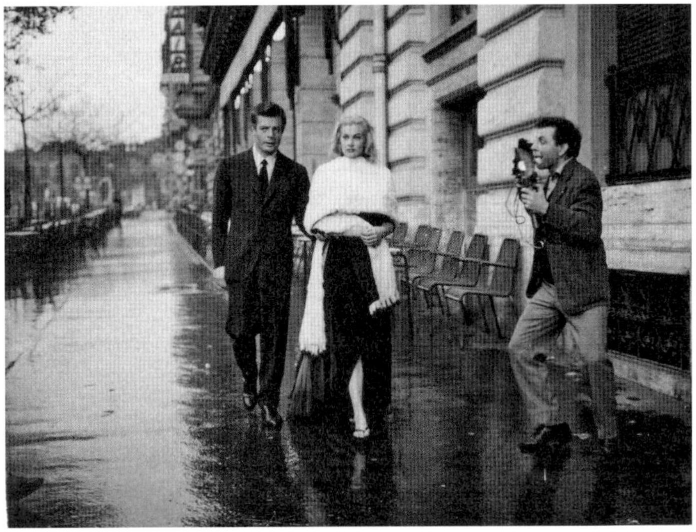

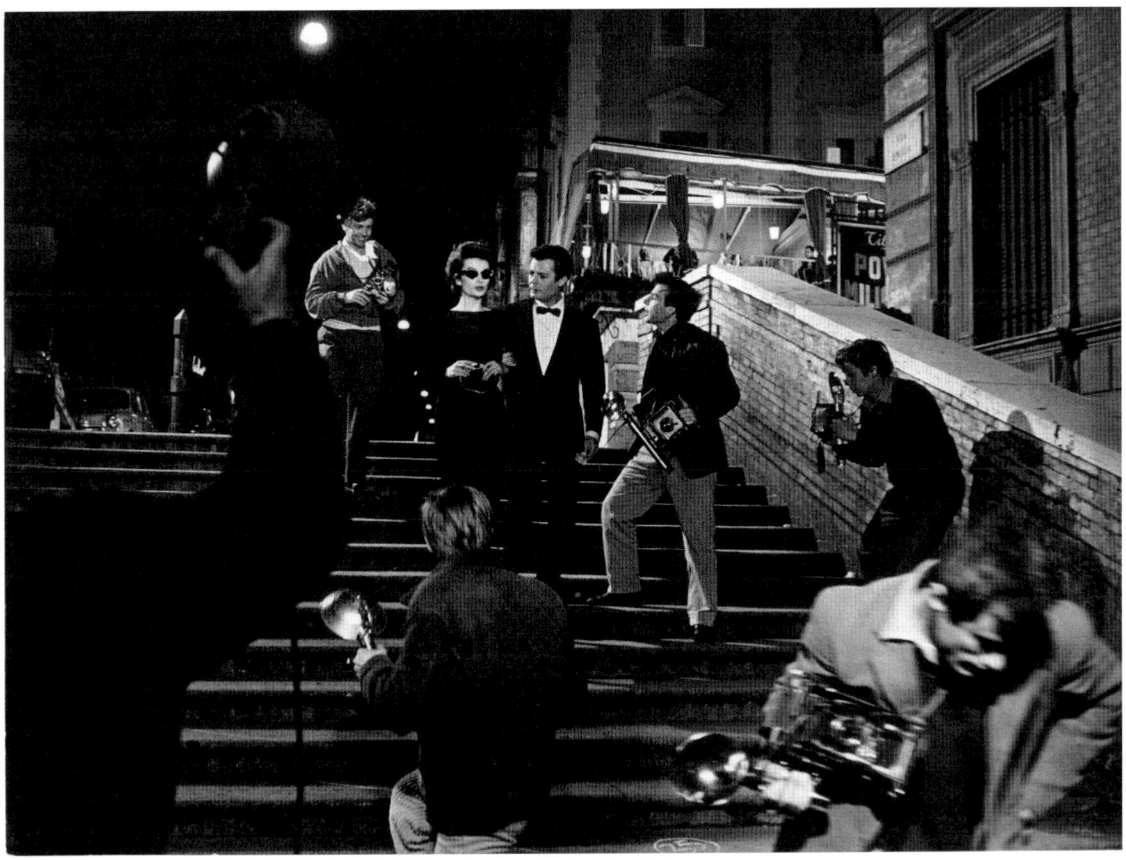

ANONYMOUS
(Pierluigi Agency)
Anouk Aimée,
Marcello Mastroianni,
and the Photographers
in La Dolce Vita
1960

The Paparazzo on Screen: The Construction of a Contemporary Myth

Aurore Fossard-De Almeida

"For while I don't know whether, as the saying goes, 'things which are repeated are pleasing,' my belief is that they are significant."[1]

The recurring figure of the paparazzo in fiction films, in particular from the end of the 1990s, is less the sign of a craze for the profession than of the construction of a "contemporary myth."[2] If paparazzi photography is the poor relative of the history of photography, it is a precious source of inspiration for film and television fiction. While the war reporter is celebrated by the history of photography, fiction finds in the paparazzo a figure to make the story exciting.[3] Subversive conditions of production—theft—a means of distribution that reaches the masses—the press—and a fascinating subject—celebrities—are the elements that define the paparazzo on screen. At the same time, these parameters create a narrative tension and raise major visual issues for cinematographic and televised fiction. The particularities of this hybrid photographic practice allow for the construction of a character that is both typical and complex: on the one hand, fiction builds a stereotype of the photographer by decking him out with recurring characteristics; on the other hand, it enriches him. By gaining access to an increasingly important position in the story, the paparazzo multiplies his "character" traits[4] and gains in subtlety.

Seducer, savior, hunter, thief? An analysis of the character allows us to understand how the paparazzo has entered our imagination. How did cinema appropriate the paparazzo, and how much did fiction determine his main characteristics? Questioning the paparazzo "within the prism of gender relations"[5] allows us to understand the hierarchy established in the community of the story's characters; studying the different forms assumed by the paparazzo in fiction reveals a strong sense of scorn toward this figure, as much on a narrative as on a visual level, that goes as far as questioning the photographer's humanity. By representing him as a deviate individual, both strange and a stranger, fiction thus legitimates the desire to make him disappear.

"Badass" but "Dumbass": An Undesirable Masculinity

"Antonio Banderas is too good-looking to be a paparazzo, it's not credible. He is a playboy, whereas there are no paparazzi playboys."[6]

As a rule, fiction creates paparazzi characters that are interpreted by men.[7] What happens to their sex appeal? Among the actors who have played this role, some of them possess a "persona"[8] that is seductive. By stepping into the shoes of a paparazzo, Vincent Lindon (Michel Verdier in *Paparazzi* by Alain Berbérian, 1998), Guillaume Canet (Nemo in *Fidelity* by Andrzej Zulawski, 2000), and Antonio Banderas (Nicolas Bardo in *Femme Fatale* by Brian De Palma, 2002) brought to the role a wealth of seduction accumulated from their previous roles.[9] Young, dark, and eager for extreme adventures—travel, fights, but also easy money—these paparazzi characters of the 2000s exert a kind of fascination over the people around them in the plot. However, this fascination is quickly counterbalanced by a social instability that jeopardizes the paparazzo. In this respect, the character of Michel Verdier in Berbérian's film is exemplary: fickle, selfish, and cowardly, this paparazzo is despised as much as he is desired by women, detested as much as he is admired by men. Clélia (played by Sophie Marceau) is attracted to Nemo in *Fidelity* which is identified as dangerous by the very poster for the film: though the body attracts, getting any closer is dangerous because the paparazzo is a tortured character.

More than just a practice, paparazzi photography is, in Berbérian's and Zulawski's films, a state that determines the individual's social position and behavior. Even if the character is endowed with sex appeal, it is never enough to allow the individual to integrate socially, and acts instead to his disadvantage. The paparazzo seems to enter the category of "lovable rogues" proposed and defined by Brian McNair. Marked by ambivalence, the relationship of the spectator with the picture snatcher generally corresponds to the feelings experienced when faced with the tabloid press, which fascinates at the same time as it makes the reader/spectator feel vaguely guilty. According to McNair, "the lovable rogue embodies this dimension of journalism that we both love and hate at the same time."[10] This ambivalence is evident in Delmas (Pierre Grasset) in *Two Men in Manhattan* (by Jean-Pierre Melville, 1959), a character who is indispensable to the affair's progress and a charmer of women, yet belittled by his peers. In comparison with Moreau (Jean-Pierre Melville), the journalist who accompanies him, seduction is clearly a distinctive character trait of the paparazzo figure. Fundamentally, McNair's analysis seems to echo the very principle of making a film about paparazzi. If fiction generally builds an argument against these contemporary photographers, it wagers nonetheless on the attraction that the subject will exert over the potential viewers.

Whereas the films of Berbérian and Zulawski create a paparazzo figure who is seductive in spite of everything, the film *Delirious* (by Tom DiCillo, 2006) and the series *Dirt* (by Matthew Carnahan, 2007–8) complicate the popular vision of paparazzi by proposing characters deprived of love affairs—even tragically alone. In *Delirious*, Les Galantine (Steve Buscemi) rejects all displays of affection from Toby (Michael Pitt) and feigns total disinterest in the feminine gender as a rule: "Don't let yourself be distracted by all the beautiful chicks, they won't be any use to us," the paparazzo advises his assistant. The absence of eroticism in his relationships with women directly contrasts with those Toby enjoys with the film's different female characters. Thus, DiCillo's photographer distinguishes himself from the one in Melville's film by a total absence of desire. In the television series *Dirt*, the way in which Carnahan treats the paparazzo's love affairs is remarkable insofar as he only authorizes them in a fantasy or metaphorical mode. These are two ways of depriving him of love. On the one hand, Don (Ian Hart), the paparazzo, sleeps with Kira (Shannyn Sossamon), the product of one of his many schizophrenic deliriums, who disappears as soon as he starts taking his medicine

1. Roland Barthes, *Mythologies* (1957), trans. Annette Lavers (New York: The Noonday Press - Farrar, Straus & Giroux, 1991), 11

2. Ibid.

3. This article is a summary of part of my doctoral thesis on the representation of paparazzi in fiction. Aurore Fossard, "Paparazzi à l'écran: Présence et disparition d'un personnage photographe dans la fiction cinématographique et télévisuelle occidentale (1940–2008)," doctoral thesis, Université Lumière Lyon 2, 2013.

4. Vincent Colonna explains that "the character is a combination of strength in action, a form of a particular kind of typification revealed as soon as the character acts and, occasionally, even before he acts." The proliferation of the paparazzo's character traits defines his "thickness" in the story, the power of his presence and action. Vincent Colonna, *L'Art des séries télé, ou Comment surpasser les Américains* (Paris: Payot, 2010), 136.

5. The expression comes from Noël Burch and Geneviève Sellier who questioned "cinema through the prism of gender relations." In my study, the character is understood as a social construct on the same level as cinema is by these two authors. Noël Burch and Geneviève Sellier, *Le Cinéma au prisme des rapports de sexe* (Paris: Vrin, 2009).

6. Interview with the paparazzo Pascal Rostain in Paris on November 16, 2011.

7. This treatment is not simply confined to the paparazzi practice but also to that of photography in general. This choice of representation echoes Sylvain Maresca's study which observes that despite a (slight) feminizing trend over the past ten years, the profession of photographer remains very masculine. Sylvain Maresca, "Photographes: sociologie d'une profession mal connue," *Culture visuelle*, last modified March 30, 2010, accessed June 10, 2012, http://culturevisuelle.org/viesociale/783.

8. Ginette Vincendeau defines the "persona" as a "trilogy: acting on screen, identity as an individual (as perceived by the media), and type of character." Ginette Vincendeau, *Les Stars et le star-système hollywoodien en France* (Paris: L'Harmattan, 2008), 10.

9. Vincent Lindon plays the role of a nice but lost seducer in *Les Victimes* by Patrick Grandperret in 1996, and his love affair with Princess Caroline of Monaco was in all of the French celebrity magazines at the time; Guillaume Canet had just played the lead romantic role alongside French actress Virginie Ledoyen in *The Beach* by Danny Boyle, which came out a little earlier in 2002; Antonio Banderas is known for his roles as a seductive hero, in *Desperado* by Roberto Rodriguez in 1995 or *The Mask of Zorro* by Martin Campbell in 1998, for example.

10. "Our relationship to the lovable rogue is, then, like our relationship to the popular media in general: ambivalent. We are attracted to him, as to the racy headlines of *The Sun* or the *New York Post*, with the feelings of guilt associated with the consumption of any kind of forbidden fruit. . . . The lovable rogue represents in human form that dimension of journalism which we both love and hate. He embodies that promise of naughtiness and transgression which is at the root of much human desire, and which so frequently gives him the mystique of a sex symbol." Brian McNair, *Journalists in Film: Heroes and Villains* (Edinburgh: Edinburgh University Press, 2010), 143–44.

again; on the other hand, the show transforms what could have been a sex scene with Abby (Tara Summers) into a childlike hoo-ha where the characters stuff themselves with cake, laugh hysterically, and play with their food instead of making love. By turning the sexual act into a sweet yet inaccessible dream for the paparazzo, or by limiting it to a metaphor in which the other characters from the series are permitted to take very explicit pleasure,[11] fiction removes any possibility for the paparazzo's sexuality.

Fiction uses the character's seduction to present him as a troubled, ambivalent being. He is fascinating and seductive, but he also represents a threat to the social balance of the other characters. Anthropological and sociological studies, and later cultural or gender studies, have shown that masculinity and femininity are not innate, but constructed.[12] In the same way that the masculine ideal is characterized by a group of physical and moral norms—strength, honor, reserve,[13] Erving Goffman reminds us that "the belief (in Western society) is that women are precious, ornamental, and fragile, uninstructed in and ill-suited for anything requiring muscular exertion ... or physical risk."[14] Because fiction applies these social constructs on the story's characters, it creates distinctions and feeds into the hierarchy between the photographer and those around him.

In *Roman Holiday* (by William Wyler, 1953), everything—both in the staging and the story—is set up so that Irving (Eddie Albert), the paparazzi photographer, is upstaged by the journalist Joe (Gregory Peck). First, the photographer's build is openly mocked, in particular when the Italians prefer shaking his hand from a distance rather than embracing him, or when his body is associated with the miniscule proportions of his car. The story then proceeds to feminize the photographer, which constitutes one of the film's comical aspects. The dynamics of the café and dance scenes rely upon the photographer's lack of discernment and his incapacity to defend the lady in distress (Audrey Hepburn), unlike the exemplary attitude of the journalist. In this way, Wyler uses the character of the picture snatcher to cast a favorable light upon another actor—Gregory Peck—and on another profession—journalism. In addition, Irving's masculinity is questioned in order to eliminate the possible threat that another male character could prove to be, in order to ensure the stability of the celebrity couple on screen: Gregory Peck and Audrey Hepburn.

Although this still remains an exception, a paparazzo can be played by a woman. In *The Philadelphia Story* (by George Cukor, 1940) and *Delirious*, two stories in which a paparazza appears, the character's treatment echoes the one identified in Wyler's film: the photographer is either given a rough time and represented in a bad light next to the story's main female character—Katharine Hepburn in Cukor's film—or she takes on exaggerated masculine physical and behavioral traits and is thus emptied of all femininity. Indeed, the violence and uncouthness of DiCillo's paparazza character contradicts the stereotyped notion of female gender that had supposedly determined the choice of this actress.[15] In both cases, the relations between the sexes work as a sanction denying the paparazzi photographer's sex appeal for the benefit of the subject, that is to say of the *star*, toward whom the photographer's—and spectator's—gaze turns systematically.

Fiction uses the relations between sexes to render this character undesirable. Whether he has, a priori, a certain sex appeal, or he is physically belittled, or whether played by an actor or an actress, tragedy seems to dominate the love lives of paparazzi characters.

From Outsider to Sick Man: The Paparazzi Practice as a Scourge

"You're a louse, you're a swine, you're filth, you're a shit!"[16]

Fiction defines the paparazzo as a "stranger" who does not belong to any group; a person with whom no one has anything in common.[17] Film is an area where the paparazzo photographer undergoes attacks through the attribution of negative characteristics that constantly put him down. In a comical fashion (*Roman Holiday*; *Paparazzi*) or in a dramatic fashion (*Two Men in Manhattan*, *Delirious*), the paparazzo is, above all, a corrupt character. Each click of the camera seems to be worth millions, as Michel's explicit comment in Berbérian's film demonstrates "[Click] twenty thousand ... [clack] fifty thousand! ... [click] Bingo! Three million!" As early as *Picture Snatcher* (by Lloyd Bacon, 1933), for the snatcher of Danny Kean's (James Cagney) pictures, the salary is a primary motivation and easy money becomes a recurring motif in the representation of the paparazzo photographer. The paparazzo is, then, often a coward, a cur. Not only does he hide in order to take his pictures, but he also avoids all responsibility for his acts by carefully preserving his anonymity when the pictures are published. On screen, this behavior generally triggers the subject's anger and

11. All the other main characters (Lucy, Holt, Julia, and McPherson) in the series are allowed to have several "hetero" or homosexual sex scenes. The comments of internet users on the *IMDb* website show that the series has been adopted or rejected for its scandalous side, which indicates that the sex is a major particularity of *Dirt*. Accessed on June 10, 2012, http://www.imdb.com/title/tt0496275/reviews?ref_=tt_ov_rt.

12. On this subject, see Françoise Héritier, *Masculin/Féminin I. La pensée de la différence* (Paris: Odile Jacob, 1996), 200. Elisabeth Badinter questions the construction of gender in *X,Y. De l'identité masculine* (Paris: Odile Jacob, 1992).

13. George L. Mosse, *The Image of Man: The Creation of Modern Masculinity* (Oxford: Oxford University Press, 1996).

14. Erving Goffman, "The Arrangement Between the Sexes," *Theory and Society* 4, no. 3 (1977): 311.

15. On this subject see Aurore Fossard, "Paparazza? Approche genrée d'un personnage photographe dans *Delirious*, Tom DiCillo, 2006," last modified May 2, 2013, http://teteschercheuses.hypotheses.org/597.

16. The character of Michel, to Franck in *Paparazzi* by Alain Berbérian (1998).

17. Definition in French from the dictionary *Le Petit Robert 2012*.

18. McNair, *Journalists in Film*, 137. We may note, moreover, that before *La Dolce Vita* (Federico Fellini, 1960) the picture snatcher was someone who revealed the truth at all cost, even against the established order, rather than being portrayed as a liar: for example, in *Two Men in Manhattan* (Jean-Pierre Melville, 1959), the picture snatcher is a figure of resistance (on this subject, see Ginette Vincendeau, *Jean-Pierre Melville: "An American in Paris"* [London: BFI, 2003], 121). Also, in *Roman Holiday* (William Wyler, 1953), although the character of Irving demonstrates the impact that a decontextualized and then commented photo can have, it is not until Fellini's film that the paparazzo transforms truth into a means of financial gain.

19. The character of Arty in *The Public Eye*, adressing Bernzy, the picture snatcher.

20. Interview with Pascal Rostain in Paris on November 16, 2011.

leads to scenes of conflict. However, the paparazzo rarely confronts his assailant and prefers to slope off when the situation deteriorates (Michel in Berbérian's *Paparazzi*) or to seek shelter in the parallel world that the story allows him to have (Don in *Dirt*). Fleeing and denying are character traits that contribute to making the paparazzo a reprehensible coward for the rest of the community—both the other characters and the audience: "Bastard paparazzo, one day I'm gonna get one, you'll see," asserts the taxi driver in Berbérian's film. Finally, from the character Paparazzo (*La Dolce Vita*) to Don (*Dirt*), the paparazzo on screen is invariably a liar: he fabricates facts and manipulates the truth, integrating the category of "nasty" journalist as defined by McNair.[18]

If verbal insult is an explicit way of denigrating the character in the plot, certain storylines push depreciation of the paparazzo further, by having him go beyond the ordinary. A veritable virus that contaminates anyone who tries it, paparazzi photography turns the photographer into a sick character. With Berbérian, the protagonists are touched by evil in turn: Michel embraces it and then abandons it, while Franck discovers and adopts it. The paparazzi photo is a kind of plague that attacks the characters. On a narrative and visual level—Franck's and Michel's physical build evolves according to their degree of implication in the practice—the story presents the paparazzi profession as a cause of social decline. The issue of contamination thus constitutes the dynamics of the film. While the story's progress makes us believe in the final recovery of the characters, the last scene, in a final twist, confirms that once the individual has been contaminated, he will never be cured.

The paparazzo from the series *Dirt* is truly suffering from a disorder: schizophrenia. The question of whether the illness is the cause or the effect of his paparazzi activities is not answered in the series' twenty episodes. However, his schizophrenia harbors narrative and visual issues that give the paparazzo a full-fledged role in the story. Firstly, the illness means the photographer has his own fantasy world in parallel to that of the diegesis: the victims of his photographic scoops inhabit him in the form of visions; his brother, mistreated in childhood, comes back to haunt him; and several animals call to him, reminding him of his multiple complexes. The disorder therefore gives form to the character's guilt, revealing a critical discourse against this kind of photography. However, at the heart of this parallel world, paparazzi photography also intervenes as a kind of protective neurosis that allows the photographer to keep a grip on reality while escaping several times from the danger and cruelty of the professional field in which he evolves. The illness is, then, presented as a reassuring refuge which allows the photographer—and the viewer—to escape from sordid, everyday life. Fundamentally, Don's illness is the image of fiction in which the spectator takes refuge, the illusion in which he likes to lose himself at the whim of characters he knows to be fleeting. By inviting the viewer to share the character's neurosis and his uncertainties in the face of reality, Carnahan makes Don into a kind of double of the cinema spectator. Finally, the disorder constitutes a useful alibi to allow the story to deal with sensitive subjects or depict violent situations by deconsecrating the representation. Through Don's gaze, the raindrops are blood red and the decapitated heads sing. In the same way that Irving's awkwardness guarantees the comedy in *Roman Holiday*, Don's neurosis is an alibi for an off-the-wall representation of the paparazzo individual and practice. By making the paparazzo into a sick character, the story underlines everything that distinguishes him from an ordinary character. And it does not stop there. In a general approach that rejects the paparazzo character, the story radicalizes its message and builds an argument that questions the paparazzo's humanity. As with the scornful doorman in *The Public Eye* (by Howard Franklin, 1993), who qualifies the picture snatcher as a "shutter bug," fiction turns the paparazzo into half-animal, half-machine.

Half-Rat, Half-Robot: A Dehumanized Character

"You are the only person in New York who thinks you are an artist and not a kind of animal."[19]

"Between ourselves, we call each other 'the rats,'" declared the paparazzo Pascal Rostain.[20] Like the nickname the photographers claim for themselves, the paparazzo appears on screen both as a creepy-crawly insect and a carnivorous animal. Described as "creatures" in *The Philadelphia Story*; as "vermin" in *The Public Eye*, or as "parasites" in *Paparazzi* (by Paul Abascal, 2004), the paparazzi are shown fleeing on all fours in *The Picture Snatcher* and rummaging through trash bins in *Paparazzi* (Berbérian) or *Paparazzi* (Abascal). When questioned about

21. Interview with Francis Apesteguy in Charançon, France, February 14, 2012.

22. On this subject, Fellini's film again marks a turning point in the representation of the picture snatcher photographer. He may work alone in earlier films (*The Philadelphia Story*, *Roman Holiday, Two Men in Manhattan*), but he is almost invariably represented in a group in *La Dolce Vita*.

23. The fact that these three popular fictional films in different languages are simply entitled *Paparazzi* reveals the semantic power of the term which suffices in itself. As François Brunet explains with the term "Kodak" in its time, the term "paparazzi" is short, playful, easy to remember, and crosses cultural borders: Francois Brunet, *La Naissance de l'idée de photographie* (Paris: PUF, 2012).

24. In popular American cinema of the 2000s, the hero/star versus evil/paparazzi dichotomy can be found regularly. It appears in *Bedtime Stories* (by Adam Shankman, 2008), or again in *The Dark Knight Rises* (by Christopher Nolan, 2012). It is also important to note the existence of a smartphone application entitled *Stars vs. Paparazzi*, that uses the war between the two parties as the dynamics for a game, accessed April 2, 2013, https://play.google.com/store/apps/details?id=com.Ama.StarsVsPaparazzi&hl=en.

his activity, the paparazzo Francis Apesteguy declared, "When I put on my jeans, my sneakers, and a rucksack with the 'tele' inside, I put on my bird-of-prey mode. I've got another one—less beautiful, but I like it too: my 'jackal' mode. A jackal sounds good, and it's crafty; it sneaks in and out, it's capable of anything, it's lousy, unscrupulous. In fact, it's the most appropriate."[21] If he is a dynamic character, the animalistic quality makes the paparazzo an instinctive figure. He reacts immediately, takes only the essential from his prey, and leaves it scandalized or wiped out behind him. As rats move beneath the sidewalks of those who orchestrate our society, the paparazzi move in the depths of the media and cultural industries brought to the cinema screen.

In fiction, the paparazzo lives and evolves, then, in obscure places, and enjoys a somewhat particular relationship with hygiene. The furnishing and lighting of Don's apartment in the series *Dirt* assimilates his living space to a bear den; in *The Public Eye*, Bernzy hides in his lair and is ashamed to receive guests because every inch of his studio's floor and wall space is covered with photos, and his last frames are drying on a washing line; in *Delirious*, whole forests are spread across Les's living room wallpaper, while stuffed animals sit imposingly on the furniture. At Les's and Bernzy's homes, spaces dedicated to the most elementary needs—eating, sleeping, washing—are taken over by their obsession with photography. It is reflected in the "Films Only" sign stuck on Les's fridge door, and the photographic dark room in Bernzy's bathroom. The paparazzo is a "photographivorous" animal.

It can be noted that in *La Dolce Vita*,[22] *Notting Hill* (by Roger Michell, 1999), *Paparazzi* (by Berbérian), *Paparazzi* (by Neri Parenti, 1998), or even *Paparazzi* (by Abascal),[23] the paparazzi characters often move in groups, thus acquiring the characteristics of a pack of dogs or wolves. This plural representation creates a threatening and oppressive presence through sheer numbers. In *Private Life* (by Louis Malle, 1961), Jill (Brigitte Bardot) is surrounded by photographers from all corners of the world, and some even seem to have fallen from the sky, like the paparazzo who jumps from a tree in which he has been hiding. In *Paparazzi* (Parenti), they emerge out of the ground. This increase in numbers gives the paparazzi a monstrous image. Bo Larami (Cole Hauser), an actor of recent and dazzling success, is attacked from all sides by Abascal's four paparazzi, like a four-headed hydra, thus triggering a power struggle between these enemy brothers of the cinematographic industry. In an extremely caricatured way, the fierce slaughter of each head, one after the other, means the star is able to achieve a heroic posture when faced with the paparazzo, the sworn enemy of the 2000s.[24] The way in which the photographers reemerge after the final confrontation does justice to the metaphor of the hydra: the undermining of the individual only reinforces the profession's aggressiveness.

Finally, while we have seen that in fiction the paparazzi's activity occasionally operates like a virus between the characters, it is also possible for the camera to contaminate the individual. Although it gives the paparazzo animalistic characteristics that contribute to our dislike of the photographer, the association of the character with his camera directly questions his humanity. In *Paparazzi* (Parenti), the filmmaker exploits the camera's anthropomorphic particularities, in a derisive tone, to represent the character's power. From Irving (*Roman Holiday*) to Michel and Franck in Berbérian's film, the paparazzo is a photographic technician and virtuoso who defines himself, in particular, by the different kinds of camera he is capable of manipulating, from the "detective camera" to the telephoto lens. However, as well as being the indispensable accessory of the paparazzo's professional success, the camera appears in the story as a constituent element of the individual. In *Two Men in Manhattan*, not only does the camera keep Delmas company, but it completes an insufficient sense of self. "Why are you taking that camera?" Moreau asks Delmas. "I hate feeling alone. A drink or a camera in my hand, and I feel like a man. Take both away from me, all that's left is me." "You wouldn't be in this mess if you were capable of expressing, let's say, three human emotions without a camera in front of your face!" Arty exclaims at Bernzy in *The Public Eye*. Hidden behind his camera, the character backs out of the emotional risks of human relationships, like Les Galantine in *Delirious* or Mark Lewis, the killer in *Peeping Tom* (by Michael Powell, 1960), who clings onto the images of death that pass before his eyes instead of living his love life to the full. On screen, the paparazzo merges with his apparatus to such an extent that the very sound of the photographic click is enough to represent—in metaphorical and spectacular fashion—the character's presence and his relentless tracking of his subject (*Notting Hill*; *Paparazzi* by Abascal). Hoisted up on a tripod and covered with a black curtain in *The Public Eye*, the camera takes on a human scale and seems to fix the spectator with its only eye.

Where the hired killer expects to flush out the photographer, he discovers a cyclops monster in place of the picture snatcher. It is no longer a metaphor for the photographer, but a veritable incarnation.

This fantasy of the paparazzo as a machine-character goes beyond the frontiers of cinema and television series. Indeed, in the music video *I Wanna Go* (2010) by the American singer Britney Spears, the heroine, surrounded and attacked on all sides by photographers, discovers with horror that not only are the paparazzi not human—crackling electrical systems break out from under their skins—but also that a paparazzo is asleep inside all of us—the mechanical red eye of the star's savior reveals that he, too, is a part of this "mechanical" congregation.[25] In short, the paparazzi are not men, they are elusive; as Delmas confirms in *Two Men in Manhattan*, once started, "the machine can no longer be stopped."

Insulting the paparazzo, making him "subhuman," throwing him into society's margins and questioning his humanity—such are the dynamics of the underlying argument of fiction, on both the big and small screen, since the paparazzo's first appearance. The recurring visual and behavioral particularities of the paparazzo in cinema build an imaginary idea of him that opposes the heroic figure of the war photographer.[26] A secondary but important character in cinema from 1940 to the 2000s, the paparazzo is turned by fiction into the figure of the subversive antihero. By representing him as dissipated and dehumanized, cinema turns this photographer into the scourge of celebrities but also of our social fabric. Yet, the "paparazzi practice" is undoubtedly one of the most widespread contemporary photographic practices, from amateurs to professionals.

Between 1998 and 2008, cinema often allowed the paparazzo a main role, but from 2010 it has tended to make him into an indefinite and elusive figure. Being a paparazzo is no longer about a role but a function that can be taken on by anybody, as with the characters in the series *Gossip Girl* (by Stephanie Savage and Josh Schwartz, 2007–13), who are by turn "paparazzo" and "paparazzi'd." The character might be disappearing but the practice is increasingly present and has become a sign of the celebration—or the denunciation—of the cult of celebrity.

It is probable that such a mythology derives from the fact that the paparazzo is perceived as working *against* his subject. Whereas, under the Harcourt studio spotlights, the actors have skin that is "smooth, sleek, pumiced by the virtue, aerated by the gentle light of [the studios],"[27] the actors caught by the paparazzo's lens have faces that are distorted by surprise or by cries of scandal, with rough skin, padded and hollowed by the thick grain of the indiscreet picture. Because the paparazzo undermines the myth of the Olympian actor, fiction has forged a kind of simplistic image of the *other* photographer. This "popular image of bright colors" is no longer "roughly engraved in wood,"[28] but is depicted in many different forms, on film and digital media, that contribute to the construction of a mythos of the *bad* photographer.

25. See Aurore Fossard, "Britney contre l'homme-machine," *Culture visuelle*, last modified February 17, 2012, http://culturevisuelle.org/paparazzi/archives/21.

26. On the mythology of the war photographer, see Clément Chéroux, "Mythologie du photographe de guerre," in *Voir/Ne pas voir la guerre. Histoire des représentations photographiques de la guerre* (Paris: BDIC/Somogy, 2001), 306–11.

27. Roland Barthes, *The Eiffel Tower and Other Mythologies* (Berkeley: University of California Press, 1997), 19.

28. Michel Mélot, "Épinal, image d'", *Encyclopædia universalis*, accessed April 1, 2013, http://www.universalis-edu.com/encyclopedie/image-d-epinal/.

BRIAN DE PALMA
Femme Fatale
2001

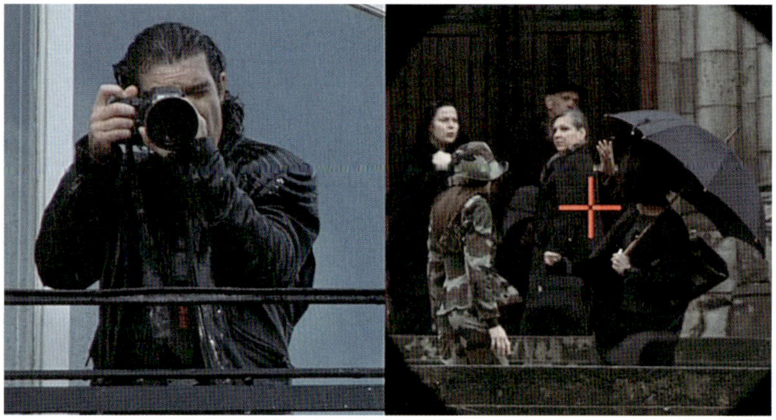

ANDRZEJ ZULAWSKI
The Most Important Thing: Love
1975

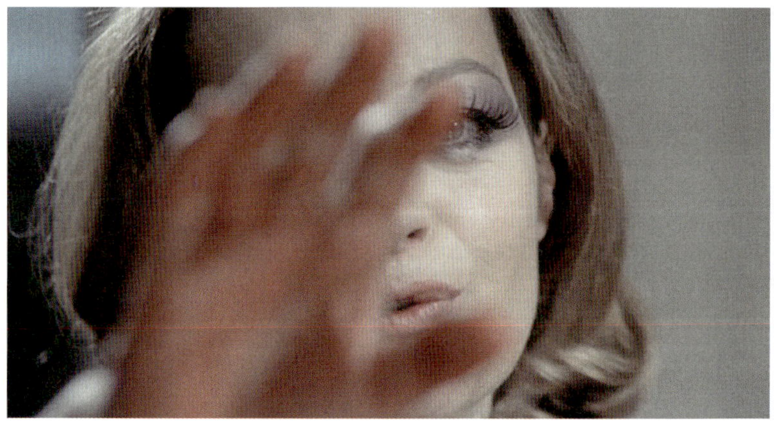

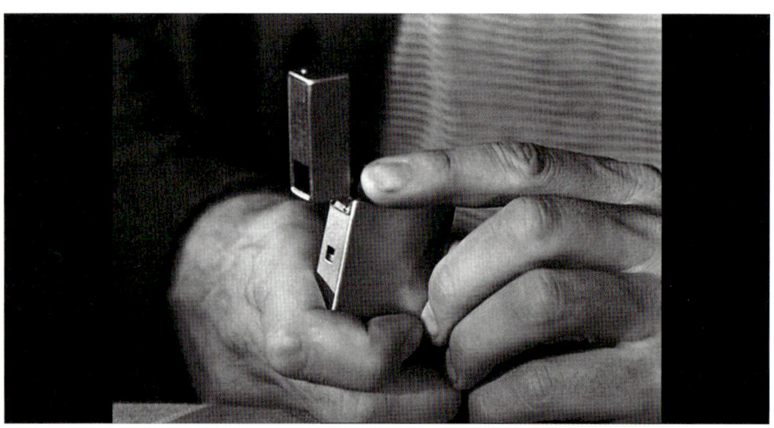

WILLIAM WYLER
Roman Holiday
1953

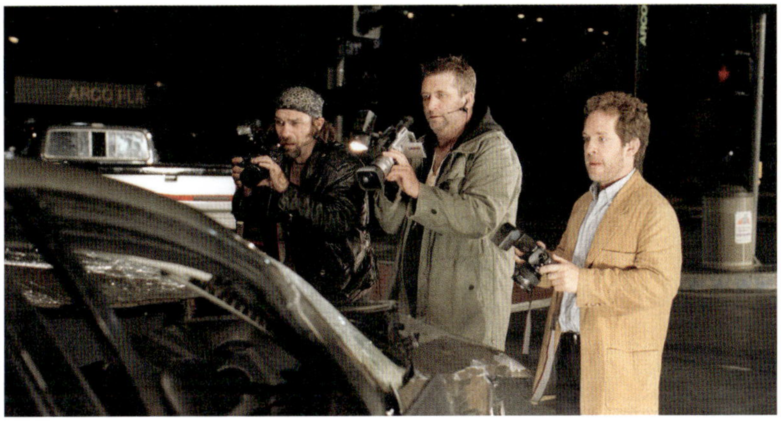

PAUL ABASCAL
Paparazzi
2007

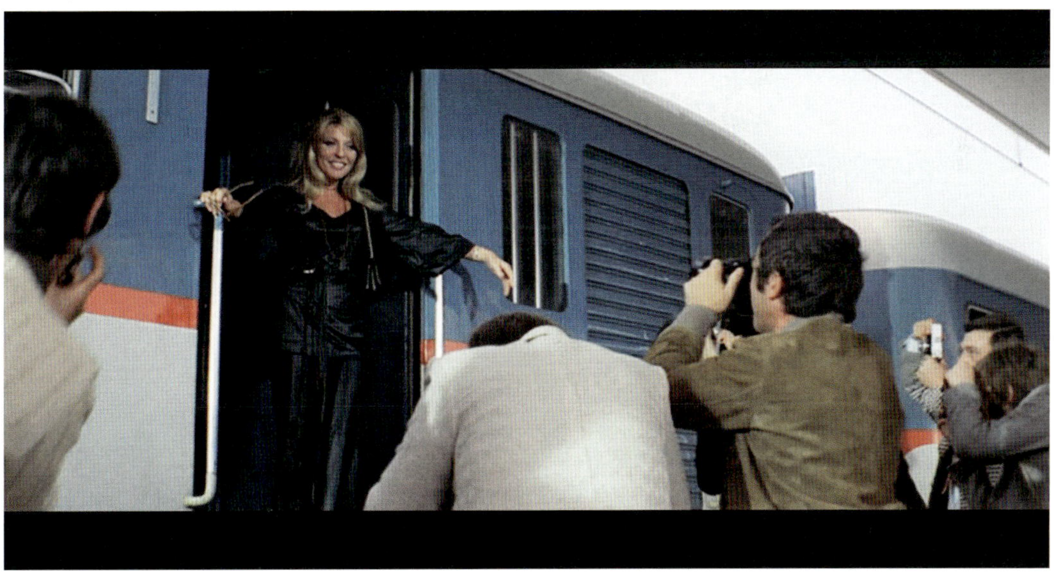

DARIO ARGENTO
Il Gatto a nove code
(*The Cat O' Nine Tails*)
1971

STARS

IN THE SPOTLIGHT

The vast majority of paparazzi photographers are male. Their "victims," on the other hand, are usually female—women who ostensibly lay proud claim to their femininity. Paparazzi photography openly flaunts the stigma of male chauvinist aggression. Beginning in the 1950s, certain stars exercised a particular fascination over these photographers: Elizabeth Taylor, Jackie Kennedy-Onassis, Brigitte Bardot, Caroline and Stéphanie of Monaco, Princess Diana, Britney Spears, and Paris Hilton. Admittedly, the paparazzi stalked them. However, these photographers played an essential role—perhaps more than anyone else—in constructing the virtual shrines that our media-obsessed society has dedicated to these celebrities. Through the stories of these women, we observe the evolution in the style of paparazzi photography and the challenges that these professionals have faced over the last fifty years.

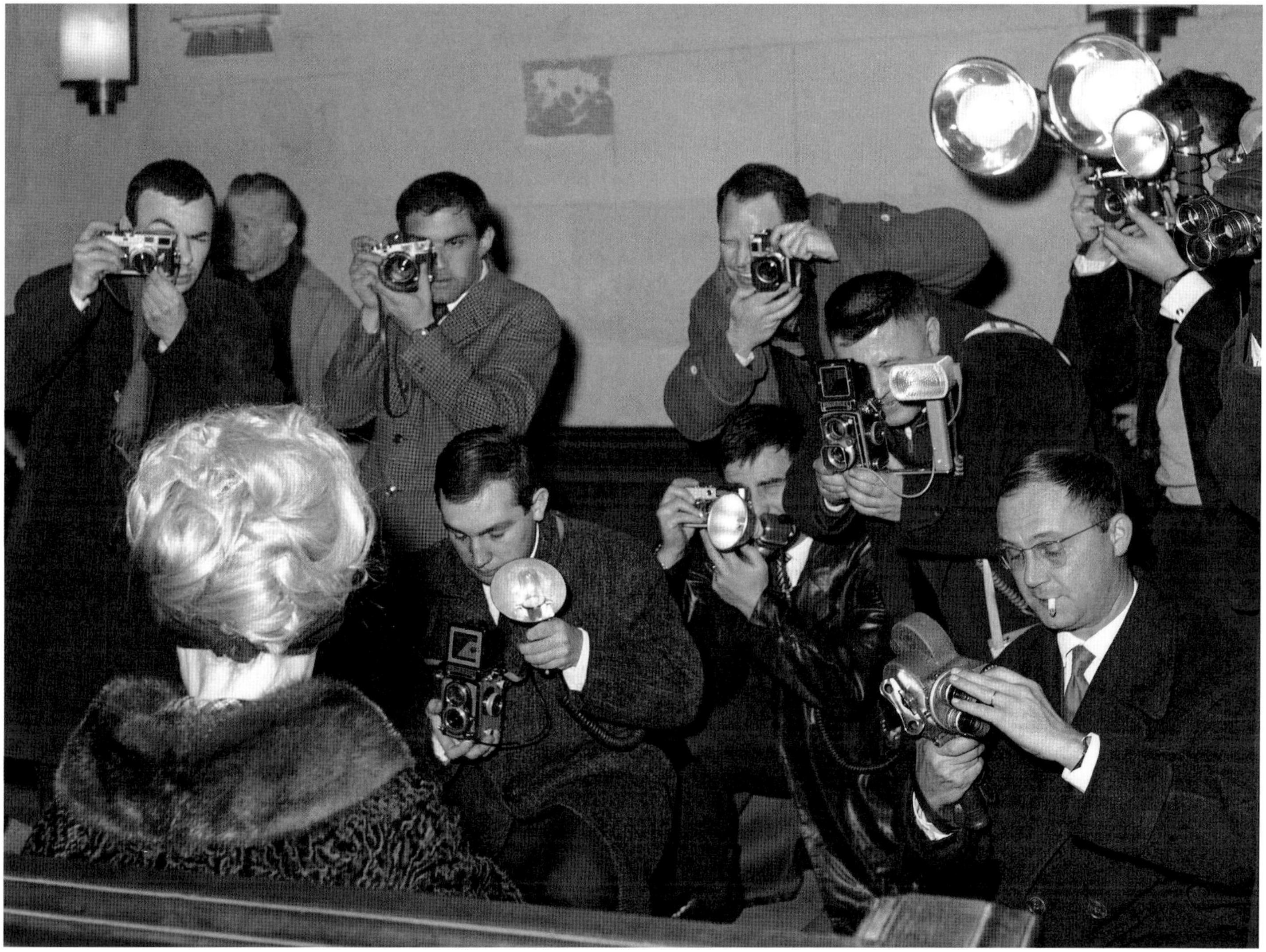

DANIEL CANDE
Brigitte Bardot Leaving Court during the Trial Opposing the Nouvelle Vague and Roger Vadim, Paris
1961

Paparazzi: Agents of Visibility Capital

Nathalie Heinich

An observer of an American movie star's arrival in Europe commented, "Her reception was worthy of a visiting political dignitary. Three taxis drew up that morning in front of the Athens Hilton where we were staying, and a lady sporting a flamboyant hat got out. She was accompanied by an entourage of six absolutely indispensable attendants: a personal photographer, a secretary, a bodyguard, a press agent, etc."[1]

The teams that coalesce around a star are made up of two distinct professional categories. First, there are the "embellishers," whose job is to maintain and enhance the star's appearance (including the stylist, makeup artist, hairdresser, and photographer). Then there are the "intermediaries," who are responsible for orchestrating and filtering her contacts with the outside world (secretary, press representative, and bodyguard). However, as we contemplate the star and her team, we should also envision the chaotic scene on the other side of this picture. It consists of a handful of heavily laden photographers "shooting" at full speed in the fervent hope of selling their snapshots to the press.

This group represents another entire cadre of people, in addition to the embellishers and intermediaries, who are effectively employed by the stars or their agents. These individuals ask nothing whatsoever in return from the stars themselves; they do not even request authorization to exploit the images they capture. This is the tribe known as the "paparazzi." The word is thought to have been coined by Federico Fellini in his film *La Dolce Vita*. The term is now a fixture in both international language and practice. So commonplace has the concept become that it has given rise to several French neologisms: the verb "*paparazzier*," the substantive noun "*paparazzade*," and the portmanteau word "*snaparazzi*."[2]

Trading on Visibility

"The sixth in line to the British throne has arrived. And it's a girl! The second daughter of Prince Andrew and the Duchess of York, Sarah Ferguson.... Thronged on the sidewalk across from the Portland clinic, some hundred photographers, perched on their stepladders, await the appearance of mother and child. There's a flock of them, like birds perched in a tree. They're known by the British term of 'Royal Watchers.' Whether they work for a paper or agency, or ply their trade as freelancers, most of them follow the royals and plenty of other targets as well. A mere handful confine their activities to royals alone. At least a third of them will succeed in selling a photo of the new royal's appearance.... The first metal stepstool was unloaded in Great Portland Street at 9:30 in the morning. The police gave the alert when they began installing barriers on the sidewalk across from the clinic. Every stepladder is clearly labeled with the name of its owner. All these photographers huddle together on the site, resigned to several long days and nights of waiting."[3]

We find ourselves in the company of a very special category of photographers. Their work is the antithesis of the carefully posed photographs and society portraits produced by the famed Studio Harcourt. The latter's works are sought after and commissioned by their subjects, who are meticulously prepared. These pictures are entirely devoted to flattering their subjects. In utter contrast, paparazzi snap their shots by stealth, often illegally. They have no interest in respecting the dignity or "face" of their subjects. In fact, their "subjects" might often be perceived as their victims.

The paparazzi constitute a category of photographers that would not exist without the phenomenon of media exposure,[4] and its offshoots. There is a desire for images that not only depict stars but also give access to their private lives, even against their will. Press outlets have become more and more expert in marketing these images to the public. Meanwhile, technical advances have produced devices that are capable of capturing images from a great distance, without the subject's knowledge, using extremely long telephoto lenses. This was the origin of a "strange type of thief," in the words of a historian of photography. "His booty is worthless unless it is displayed before all eyes."[5]

The paparazzi's work does not even have the legal status of intellectual property. In contrast to documentary photographs, the law considers paparazzi photos to be "commonplace or already widely reproduced." They are deemed "snapshots reflecting the professional, domestic, or emotional life of stars, as well as their ailments, mood swings, and misadventures." The photos "are so pointless in nature that they cannot be considered to be documents with a degree of originality sufficient to be protected as 'intellectual property' in the sense of the Law of 1957."[6]

Photos by paparazzi now go far beyond the simple "candid photographs" that began to be taken of stars in the 1910s.[7] They are visual invasions of celebrities' private lives. These photos pit subjects and photographers against each other in ceaseless combat for control of the image. This struggle is played out on both sides of the ever-shifting frontier between private and public life. As Salman Rushdie observed, "the public figure is happy to be photographed when she or he is prepared for it, 'on guard,' one might say." The paparazzo, on the other hand, is only interested in capturing the moment when the target reveals "an unguarded moment. The battle is for control; for a form of power."[8] This determination to exercise control over an image also allows the paparazzi to relegate the matter of personal privacy to the background. Instead they stress the duplicitous nature of the stars who are "ready to do anything" to get publicity when they want it, but nevertheless are determined to "control" that visibility once they have achieved it. "When those people get into show business, they sign a pact with the devil. As for me, I'm the devil's assistant," declared one paparazzo.[9]

Paparazzi At Work

Consider these photographers as they ply their trade. The profession consists of "two different families of star seekers with diametrically opposed cultures," as two investigators explain. There are independent photographers, whose modus operandi contrasts sharply with that of agency employees: "The first group wants to take a series of close-ups of the French radio and TV host Christophe Dechavanne sunbathing in the nude on a pontoon afloat in the Indian Ocean. And they want to run the most explicit shot of all on page one of the sensationalist French magazine *Choc*.... The second type tracks his prey like a hunter and will photograph the same target walking alone through the streets of Paris. Or they'll take photos that are pre-negotiated with the star willingly posing for the camera.... Obviously, the prices these photos command will be different. The first group will sell their photos for 20,000 euros. The second will pull in a maximum of 2,000 euros. Their financial return is just a tenth as much.... Nicknamed 'the lords' or 'the brains' by their colleagues, this species [the independents] is on its way to extinction; they won't get out of bed in the morning for less than 15,000 euros. These paparazzi are genuine investigative journalists—the only photo that matters to them is a big scoop. Something like a shot of Mazarine, François Mitterrand's secret daughter, or the singer Mylène Farmer bare-breasted in the Seychelles in February 2006, or Sarah Ferguson, Duchess of York, with her lover sucking on her toes in a Saint-Tropez villa, or Prince Albert and his illegitimate son Alexandre."[10]

It is hardly surprising that sexuality is at the top of the list of the most popular topics for the paparazzi and their audiences. Capturing these activities unquestionably involves the most aggressive acts of intrusion into private life. The prices that these pictures command reflect this fascination. The costs involved can admittedly be substantial. A photographer pursuing David and Victoria Beckham in the Bahamas stayed in the same hotel as they did, at 2,000 euros a night—but the payoff can be spectacular. "The morning of the next day at breakfast, I took a series of shots that sold for 20,000 euros, ten times the price of my room," he reported.[11] Incomes for the most productive paparazzi can average 15,000 euros a month, despite the percentage retained by their agencies. "For a 100,000-euro photo story, a paparazzo will pocket an average of 50,000 euros if it's sold abroad and 45,000 if it's sold in France."[12]

With the incentive of earning such lofty sums, all—or nearly all—tactics are practiced, if not permitted. These include stalking and constant surveillance. Sometimes the star's life is actually endangered. Pursuers have gone so far as to incite automobile accidents, as they did in Beverly Hills, with the complicity of Mafiosi: "A first van bumped into the star's vehicle, then two other guys arrived and took pictures of the scene. The shots were shopped around to paparazzi agencies in Los Angeles."[13] Practices are especially brazen in America, where photographers literally hurl themselves on top of stars, preventing them from moving by blasting them in the face with their flashbulbs. Coming from these experiences, it is understandable that the actor Brad Pitt, during his stay in France, was eager to thank the French paparazzi. He was grateful that they took their shots from a distance using telephoto lenses. This approach allowed him "to live almost normally," he told them.[14]

The brutal skirmishes in this war are not confined to stars alone. The struggles can be fierce among the paparazzi as well, as one of them once acknowledged; he did not hesitate to come to blows when he realized that he'd been followed for two days by a junior paparazzo who had concealed himself in the shrubbery. Younger practitioners are sometimes content to trail their elders in the hope that the more experienced professional will lead the way to a star.[15] Since the boom in mobile phones, professional paparazzi also face competition from amateurs, nicknamed "snaparazzi" (a term that combines "paparazzi" and "snapshot").[16] Paparazzi even risk serving time in jail. One received a suspended six-month prison sentence in 2006, along with a three thousand–euro fine. His wife was given a three-month suspended sentence and a two thousand–euro fine for "the crime of invading privacy" and "the crime of endangering

1. Charly Koubesserian, *De de Gaulle à Belmondo, les Mémoires d'un grand maquilleur du cinéma français* (Paris: Bayard, 2003), 81.

2. See Léna Lutaud and Thiébault Dromard, *Les Dessous de la presse people* (Paris: Éditions de La Martinière, 2006).

3. *Libération*, March 26, 1990.

4. This phenomenon was explored in Nathalie Heinich, *De la visibilité. Excellence et singularité en régime médiatique* (Paris, Gallimard, 2012), on which these observations are based.

5. André Rouillé, *La Photographie* (Paris: Gallimard, 2005), 197.

6. Roland Dumas, *La Propriété littéraire et artistique* (Paris: PUF, 1983), 73.

7. See Charles Leonard Ponce de Leon, *Self-Exposure: Human Interest Journalism and the Emergence of Celebrity in America, 1890–1940* (Chapel Hill: University of North Carolina Press, 2002), 63–64.

8. Salman Rushdie, "Diana's crash," in Marc Augé et al., *Diana crash* (Paris: Descartes et Cie, 1998), 71.

9. Quoted by Jake Halpern, *Fame Junkies: The Hidden Truths behind America's Favorite Addiction* (Boston: Houghton Mifflin, 2007), 108.

10. Lutaud and Dromard, *Dessous*, 54–56.

11. Ibid., 57.

12. Ibid., 58.

13. Ibid., 62–63.

14. Ibid., 48.

15. Ibid., 53–54.

16. Ibid., 64.

17. Ibid., 51.

18. *Le Monde*, February 14–15, 2010.

19. *Le Monde 2*, July 1, 2006.

another's life" after steering too close to Princess Caroline of Monaco's vehicle.[17]

Conversely, a paparazzo's work can sometimes—although only in exceptional cases—earn him acknowledgment and respect. Felice Quinto, known as "the king of paparazzi," may have served as Fellini's model for the character in *La Dolce Vita*. He went on to become Elizabeth Taylor's personal photographer, and his work was shown in exhibitions and museums.[18] In 1981, the photographer Raymond Depardon devoted a full-length documentary film, *Reporters*, to several of his colleagues who specialized in tracking down stars. In 2006, the venerable photography festival in Arles even officially honored Felice Quinto. At the age of sixty-two, he had become the owner of an agency bearing his name. It employed eighty people, earning revenue of 3.8 million euros a year: "I was a pal of John Lennon's, I ate with Brel and Brassens, sipped white wine with Agnelli, took nighttime strolls with Onassis, and now I'm sharing great times with Johnny Hallyday.... I adored being a paparazzo. Photographing the truth about a person without being seen. Having that image in my sights is real inner happiness."[19]

The paparazzo's trade is such an integral part of our world that we might suppose that it has always existed. However, the profession is only two generations old. Celebrity certainly existed before that, but it was not all that closely associated with visibility. If we are to understand how this formerly reviled profession has succeeded in becoming an icon of the contemporary world, we must go back in time to capture the moment when the notion of media visibility first reared its head. It was then that a widespread appetite for a sense of intimate connection with people in the spotlight emerged. Feeding this hunger is how the paparazzi earn their living.

A History of Media Visibility

For most of humanity's history, the notion of celebrity did not correspond with visibility—the dissemination of a face and name in the public arena—or at least that was rarely the case. Prominence was conveyed through a sense of respectful admiration—the communication of the names and stories associated with a great man. Until the advent of modern methods of reproducing images 150 years ago, a great man's visibility was confined to his name and his biography. Sometimes there were portrait sculptures, paintings, or engravings. Occasionally some admirers experienced his actual presence, but relatively few would have the chance to encounter him in person.

The invention and subsequent mass-market availability of photographic portraiture profoundly shook traditional concepts of celebrity. Depictions now took the form of relatively precise reproductions of facial features, which could be produced in infinite quantities. By the mid-nineteenth century, countless throngs could *recognize* an individual on paper and put a face to a well-known name. Potentially vast communities of admirers were coalescing at the same time as their objects of admiration were gaining visibility and becoming all the more singled out and valued because they were so widely recognized. This newly enhanced visibility of celebrity gave birth to the "cult of stardom" in the early twentieth century.

The invention of photography, and subsequently of film, television, and ultimately the Internet, opened up a new era in the history of our relationship with the wider world. It immeasurably expanded the presence of beings through space and time, using the medium of images that were very faithful to the original. This technical ability to fabricate ubiquitous images on a vast scale has become so commonplace for us that we are scarcely able to grasp its revolutionary implications, which would have astounded our ancestors. We also fail to understand the innumerable impacts on our relationship with the outside world and each other. Foremost among these is our extraordinary acceptance of the value of celebrity. It is a concept that has profoundly altered social life in its hierarchical, professional, economic, legal, psychological, political, and moral spheres.

When we consider traditional manifestations of fame, this expansion of the scope of celebrity through techniques that enhance visibility is not an inevitable sequence of events. In fact, it represents a doubly abrupt break—both hierarchical and axiological—in the preexisting relationship between privacy and publicity. In the past, the renown of great men continued into posterity, long after the end of their earthly lives. Within just a few generations, the situation was reversed. Celebrities now had visibility in space, which promoted media coverage of stars that ranged far beyond their actual physical presence. At the same time, this reversal of the relationship between time and space and the old ways and the new was coupled with a hierarchical shift in the perception of high and low culture, vulgarity and dignity. Different values were now attributed to public depictions of individuals. In the past, public exposure of an individual's image represented an assault on that person's dignity; now such visibility had become a means of self-aggrandizement, even among those who had traditionally been resistant to such coverage. Publicity had become a tool for self-promotion.

The new phenomenon brought with it a new terminology. To genuinely consider the specificities of modern forms of celebrity, we must seriously ponder its dimension of "visibility" in

20. See Walter Benjamin, "The Work of Art in the Age of Mechanical Reproduction," in Hannah Arendt, ed., *Illuminations* (London: Fontana, 1968), 214–18.

the most literal sense of the term. (This notion is also present in the etymology of *vedette*, a French word for "star" or "celebrity." *Vedette* comes from an Italian word meaning "observatory.") "Visibility" is the only appropriate word to employ when we are no longer dealing with an intemporal world of celebrity, where names mattered above all else. We are now in a new world where faces matter at least as much, if not more, than names, although those names do remain essential.

Exploiting Visibility Capital

In addition to the notion of "visibility," it is essential to emphasize how easily images can be reproduced now. *Because* they are reproduced, they arouse a sense of being in the midst of "the here and now of the work of art," to recall Walter Benjamin's definition of "authenticity."[20] The high visibility of technical reproductions creates a fundamental breach between the referent and its sign, between the model and its image, between the real and the representation. This disparity is the source of our yearning to be allowed into the presence of the original, although we are only familiar with the copy. This expectation engenders considerable emotional commitment. A similar expectation was once prevalent during the era when authenticity had not yet become "the substitute for cultural value." This devotion was applied to religious apparitions or, in their absence, to holy relics. Such tokens were substitutes for the presence of a saint.

Chamfort defined celebrity as being "the advantage of being known by those you don't know." This definition opens the way to two fundamental and inseparable concepts. On one hand, there is the familiarity or rather the "recognition" by which we match a name with a face. On the other hand, there is a certain asymmetry, based on the numerical disparity between the number of the "recognized" and the "recognizers." With heightened visibility, the countlessly reproduced image takes on power and summons recognition/identification, which in turn allows, in some situations, recognition/confirmation and recognition/deference, and even recognition/gratitude when the idol appears in person and *makes a gift* of their presence. According to the dictates of the media, the distinguishing feature of stardom is its close association with every connotation of the word "recognition": cognitive, interactional, hierarchical, and emotional. It suffices to be "recognized" once to be triply "recognized." Identification becomes confirmation, deference, and gratitude, all in one.

The second major criterion of visibility, coming immediately after the mass dissemination of the subject's image, is asymmetry. There is asymmetry between the one who is seen and those who see him, between the one who is identified and those who identify him, between the one who is recognized and those who recognize him, and between the one whose actual presence, in addition to his image, is perceived as a blessing by those who in turn render him their admiring homage. The multiplicity of images—the first criterion—is echoed by the multiplicity of people capable of identifying these many images of a single individual—the second criterion. The asymmetry in identification indicates and creates a disparity in the nature of celebrity. It is a kind of fame that hinges above all on the number of people capable of matching a name with a face, rather than with personal characteristics. The disparity between the multiplicity of those who "recognize" and the individuality of the one "recognized" extends the bond that unites them in the sphere of collective admiration. In sum, this inequality of interrecognition is one of the simplest and most fundamental types of inequality—too simple and obvious even to be noticed, perhaps.

Why is it essential to take the issue of asymmetry, apparently trivial and self-evident, so seriously? The answer is that this asymmetry creates a major differential in the resources available to celebrities and unknowns, resources that can be employed to build a genuine type of capital. This ability conveys prestige, power, relationships, and money to its possessor. However, it cannot be reduced to any other form of capital, not even "social capital," because that concept measures only the scope and quality of "connections" or relationships, not the degree of reciprocity. We can demonstrate that we are dealing with genuine "capital" in the literal sense of the word. Visibility capital possesses all of the characteristics of capital in the traditional (economic) sense of the term: it really is a resource that is *measurable*, *accumulable*, *transferable*, *income yielding*, and *convertible*.

Visibility capital has brought about a major transformation of the traditional hierarchy, creating a new social category. As it developed over the twentieth century, this transformation was scarcely recognized for what it really was. Visibility is handed down like a legacy, negotiated like a dowry, and treasured like a generous patron. The issues at stake go beyond defending the boundary between famous figures and ordinary people; the preservation of privilege itself is in play. This close association between the existence of a social category entirely apart, and its privileged position, adds another criterion. We have already mentioned three criteria that define the phenomenon of visibility—the technical reproduction of images, asymmetry, and a new social category. The fourth factor is the hierarchical criterion, which transforms this category into a new elite.

Visibility now seems to be a contemporary version of aristocracy, based on many similar characteristics. However, visibility is not actually identified as aristocracy's equivalent, despite the ubiquity of celebrities in the public arena. Paradoxically, there is a hidden aristocracy among figures who are in the public eye. This modern elite combines a position of prominence with a break from traditional forms of domination (power, birth, fortune). This new paradigm serves to mitigate, if not resolve, a conflict. There is a demand for equality that is typical of democratic societies, on the one hand. On the other is the aspiration to an orderly ranking of the social hierarchy, creating a sense of consensual sharing between the humble and the great. This structure offers the common man models to emulate, or at least admire. In the nineteenth century, the new artistic elite was relegated to society's margins. This marginalization allowed them to link the democratic rejection of aristocratic values with the aspiration to acknowledged excellence in their art. Similarly, the new elite of visibility that emerged in the twentieth century commingled individuality with popularity, combining traditional forms of excellence with the values of meritocracy.

Several criteria define visibility in this media-obsessed era. The first is the technical capability of reproducing images on a massive scale. Another is the asymmetry that exists between objects and subjects in the public eye, opening a vast gulf in visibility capital. This disparity has inaugurated a special social category for those in the limelight, who find themselves situated at the summit of a hierarchy whose very structure has been profoundly altered by the rapid emergence of this new elite. This is the visibility capital that the paparazzi exploit for their own purposes. They remind us of the poachers who once crept onto aristocratic properties to collect—sometimes clandestinely, but sometimes under the property holder's nose—a few scattered gleanings. For the paparazzi, these gleanings take the form of images that can be worth far more than their weight in gold. The question arises: why do these images command such a high price?

The Consumer Psychosociology of Purloined Images

Historians of film date back to the 1920s, as does news coverage of the private lives of movie stars and the development of the star system. Henceforth, great actors were not only perceived as the fictional *characters* they represented, nor merely as public *figures*. Now they were also *individuals*, who existed in a private world that was closed to the gaze of their admirers. Those admirers strove to penetrate that barrier of privacy. It was as if *public* display created a parallel awareness and desire for a glimpse of *private* life. This awareness generates a continuing appetite for the paparazzi's work. They in turn exploit this desire by profiting from what makes it possible—the images themselves.

When admirers approach their idols, even if only trailing in their footsteps, they are not satisfied by emulating the pattern of a romantic relationship. Theirs is a form of attachment that is inevitably asymmetrical, unreciprocated, and essentially imaginary. These admirers attempt to differentiate themselves from the anonymous masses, and distinguish themselves from the hordes of other fans, by striving to establish a unique relationship. This partnership between the observer and the object of his fascination nevertheless remains a fiction. The observer *is* well aware that he is not the only passionate admirer, but nevertheless, he can derive comfort by telling himself an imaginary tale of closeness, or even of intimacy—if not an exclusive relationship—with the object of his fascination.

Far from being face to face with the star individually, he is surrounded by a crowd of other fans, and he can identify with them by participating in the feelings they share toward the idol. It is a multilateral rather than binary relationship, and it continues to multiply, practically to an infinite extent. A relationship with an idol attracts other admirers, and even communities of admirers. Some are preestablished, such as fan clubs or readers of celebrity magazines. Others are gathered especially for an occasion, like the crowds that assemble for a funeral ceremony, a special event, or a performance. We are certainly never really alone with a celebrity, even and especially when we have a face-to-face encounter. And when we study the celebrity's image, we are inevitably in the presence of a third party: the photographer, who may be authorized or not, official or surreptitious, possessed of a distinctive signature or anonymous. Of course, we refer here to the paparazzi.

The actual experience of being in the idol's presence would not generate such a surge of emotion without the prior existence of the image, or rather images. The images, in turn, carry an even more powerful emotional charge when there exists the possibility, however remote, of the idol's presence or the lingering reality of his former presence. Just as the fascination finds its source in the back-and-forth between the singularity of the star and the multiplicity of his admirers, it takes on substance from the back-and-forth between presence and absence, proximity and distance. This is the "referential effect." In principle, the possessor of visibility capital is inaccessible in person. At the same time, he is limitlessly available through his images. This is the essence of someone who possesses visibility capital. This effect is created by the work of photographers, and foremost among them the paparazzi. Acting on our behalf, they insinuate themselves into the hidden nooks and crannies of the private lives of public personalities, and come back bearing trophies. Constantly admired and observed, a celebrity is simultaneously, in the words of the poet Paul Valéry, "a man who is *watched*, and who senses it."

Idolaters and Iconoclasts

Visibility is a fundamentally ambivalent concept considered from an axiological perspective. It wavers between being a moral right and an undue privilege, not only in the minds of philosophers but also for the man in the street. The diatribes against "celebrification" are legion, but this criticism does not deter millions of readers from buying the weekly magazines that feed on this obsession. The fans themselves vacillate between admiration and envy, devotion and resentment, disappointment and jubilation when their idol falls. This profound ambivalence takes us back to a very old conflict in the history of the Western world.

The iconoclast controversy originated in the Middle Ages and continued into the Renaissance. This conflict raged between those who accepted and even venerated images, believing that they had a positive role and acted as intermediaries with the divine. On the opposing side were those who rejected and even destroyed such images, judging their intermediation to have a negative effect, creating an obstruction to the divine presence. A similar reasoning exists behind the type of visibility that is accepted and even yearned for, and the type of visibility that is rejected and even held in contempt. This logic is founded on the ambiguous role attributed to intermediation. Is it seen as something that brings us closer to or pushes us further away from the object of our admiration, love, or simply respect? This ambivalence toward intermediation seems quite comparable to the ambivalence felt toward visibility itself, which is decried for its lack of authenticity (its "spectacle") and praised for its ability to reveal, disclose a secret, and tell all (as in the French reality TV show *Loft Story*). In sum, it is not visibility itself that is inauthentic, and hence pernicious; rather it is visibility's role as intermediary through the process of media overexposure.

Finally, visibility has the property of being an eminently *public* condition, because it can only exist through the display of a person in the media-intensive public arena; however, it also has a value—to the extent that it has an actual value—that is fundamentally *private*. The attachment to celebrities tends to be felt and practiced more than is explicitly acknowledged. From this perspective, visibility is closely related to beauty, which is also a value that derives far more from the "private" than the "public" domain. Furthermore, visibility is also a value closely attuned to femininity. Visibility does more than give women the opportunity to achieve positions of prominence. It also promotes a kind of admiration for stars that derives from a positive notion of love and recognition that is traditionally embraced by popular culture, and particularly by women.

All these factors explain why intellectuals find the concept an ideal target for their polemics. The "world of fame," to use the terminology of Luc Boltanski and Laurent Thévenot,[21] is particularly vulnerable to harsh criticism in contemporary Western culture. Visibility, and the extreme manifestations it gives rise to, exacerbate this scorn for what is stigmatized as vulgarity, publicity-mongering, inauthenticity, marketing hype, alienation, and irrationality. Philosophy, law, morality, politics, and concern about hierarchical differentiation join forces in opposition. They scorn the ever-growing appetite for celebrity. The intellectuals of the world condemn practices they see as fundamentally vulgar, iconophilic, and idolatrous. They survey contemporary idols who are fabricated using modernized techniques that are not so dissimilar from those once used to produce icons. These critics are replaying the millenary tensions that the cult of saints generated in late Antiquity.

A fundamental change occurred in our relationship with "great singular men"[22] between the early years of Christianity and our entry into the age of media. As Peter Brown explained, "these protecting figures are now human beings."[23] Today these human beings have their own intercessors, equipped with complex technologies unknown to those makers of icons long ago. With this technology, we are free to go exactly where we dream of going, through images and beyond images. We can enter into the private sphere of these eminent figures. We owe this access to an invisible, anonymous being who flashes by, capturing the idol for a fleeting instant—that mysterious figure, both powerful and reviled, known by the curious name of "paparazzo."

21. See Luc Boltanski and Laurent Thévenot, *De la justification. Les économies de la grandeur* (Paris: Gallimard, 1991).

22. See Nathalie Heinich, *La Gloire de Van Gogh. Essai d'anthropologie de l'admiration* (Paris: Éditions de Minuit, 1991).

23. Peter Brown, *The Cult of Saints: Its Rise and Function in Latin Christianity* (Chicago: University of Chicago Press, 2009), 58.

LIZ

While *Cleopatra* was being filmed in Rome in 1961, Elizabeth Taylor and Richard Burton embarked on a steamy affair, although both were married at the time. The press caught wind of the scandal and photographed them locked in a passionate embrace on a boat. Reminiscent of the amorous infatuation they acted out in the film, the image became iconic. It was said to be the first photo of an adulterous couple kissing to be published in the Italian press. The shot was all the more famous for rousing the ire of the pope, who raised his voice, along with the Hollywood studios, to condemn this shocking relationship. The public, of course, was mesmerized by the couple, who seemingly personified in real life the fantasy conveyed by their screen presence: gorgeous, rich, and rapt in erotic passion. With their careers buoyed by this irresistible story and the media coverage provided by the paparazzi, Elizabeth Taylor and Richard Burton made eight films together. Ron Galella, who constantly photographed the couple, gave a very prosaic explanation for the omnipresent paparazzi surrounding the pair: the exceptionally high price that their photos commanded in the media marketplace.

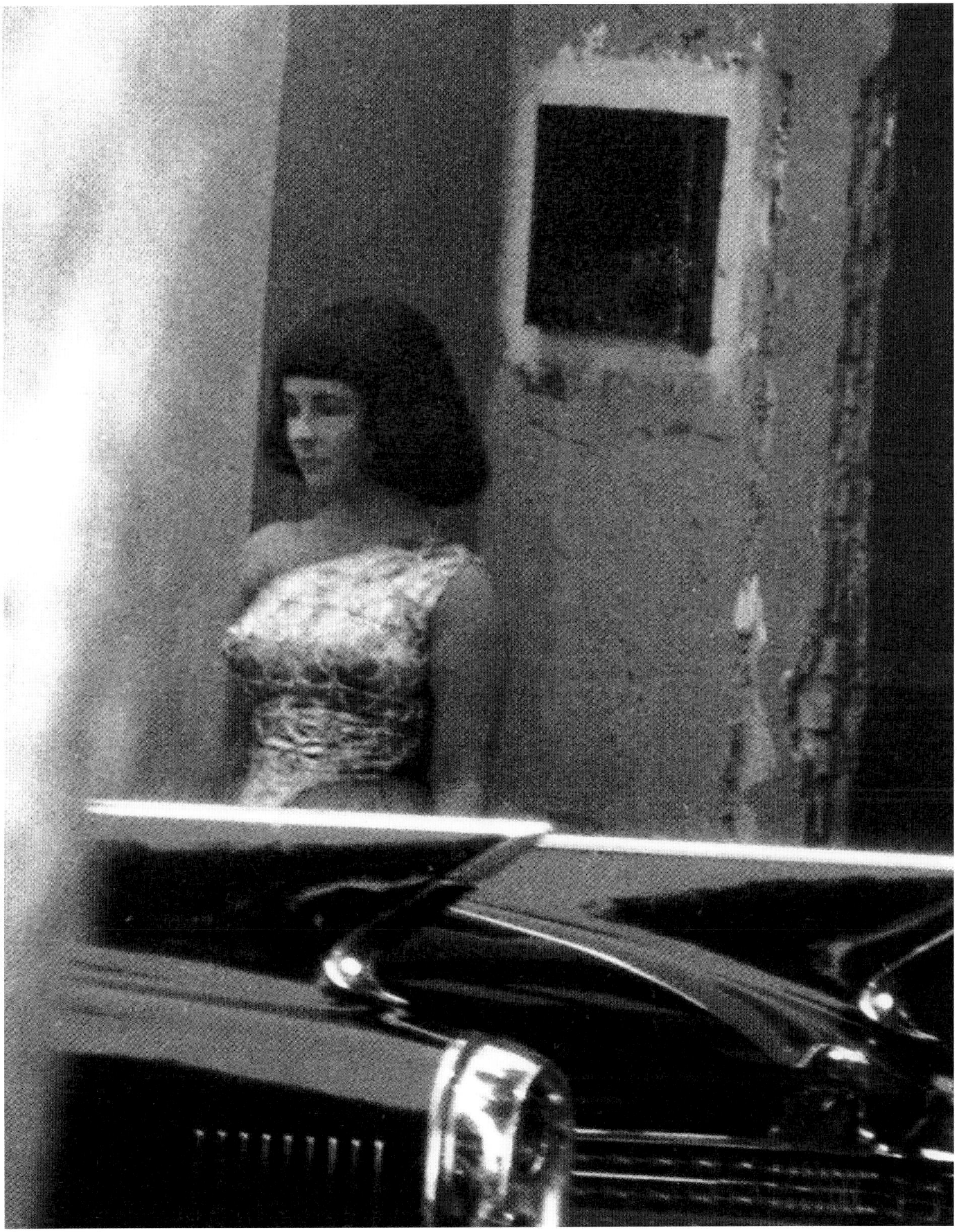

MARCELLO GEPPETTI
Elizabeth Taylor Tries on Her Cleopatra Costume in the Cinecittà Studios
September 1961

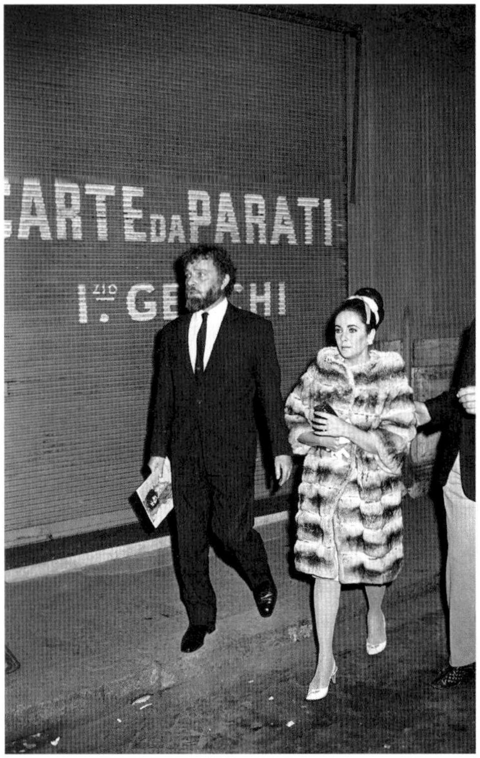

MARCELLO GEPPETTI
Elizabeth Taylor and Richard Burton Going to the Teatro Quirino, Rome
1966

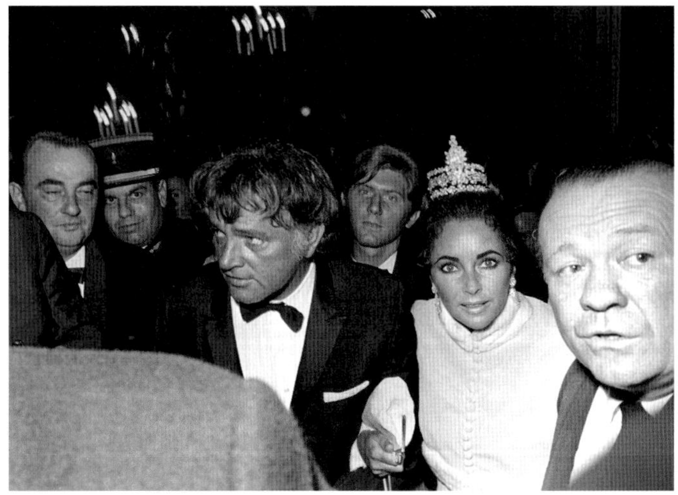

ANONYMOUS
Elizabeth Taylor and Richard Burton
March 16, 1961

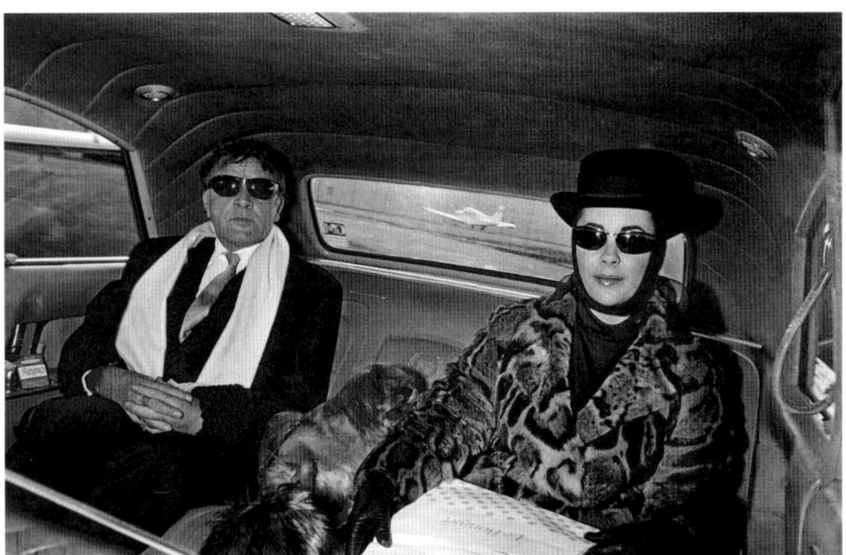

JACK BURLOT
Elizabeth Taylor and Richard Burton, Le Bourget Airport
January 22, 1968

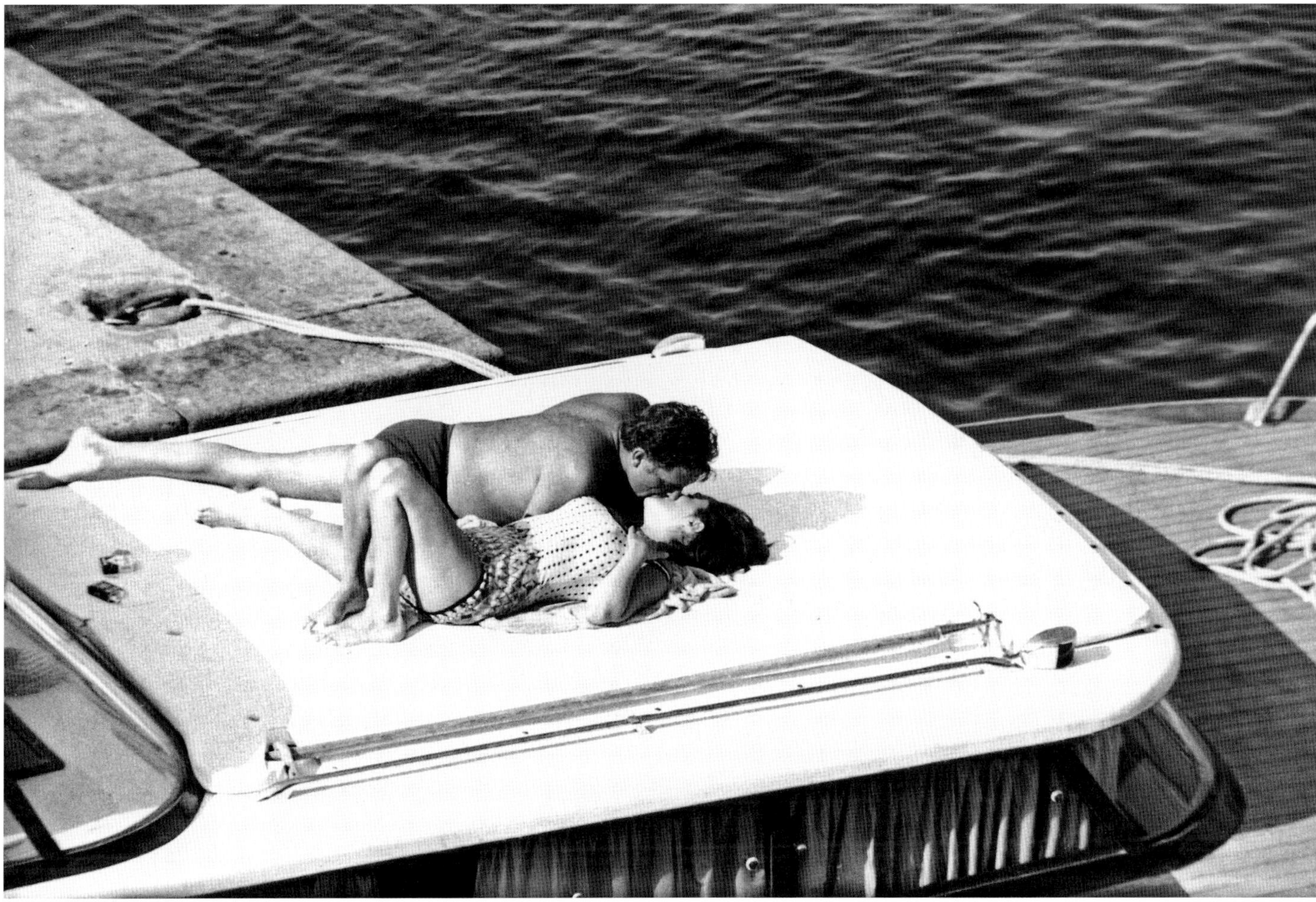

MARCELLO GEPPETTI
Elizabeth Taylor and Richard Burton Kissing on the Island of Ischia
June 18, 1962

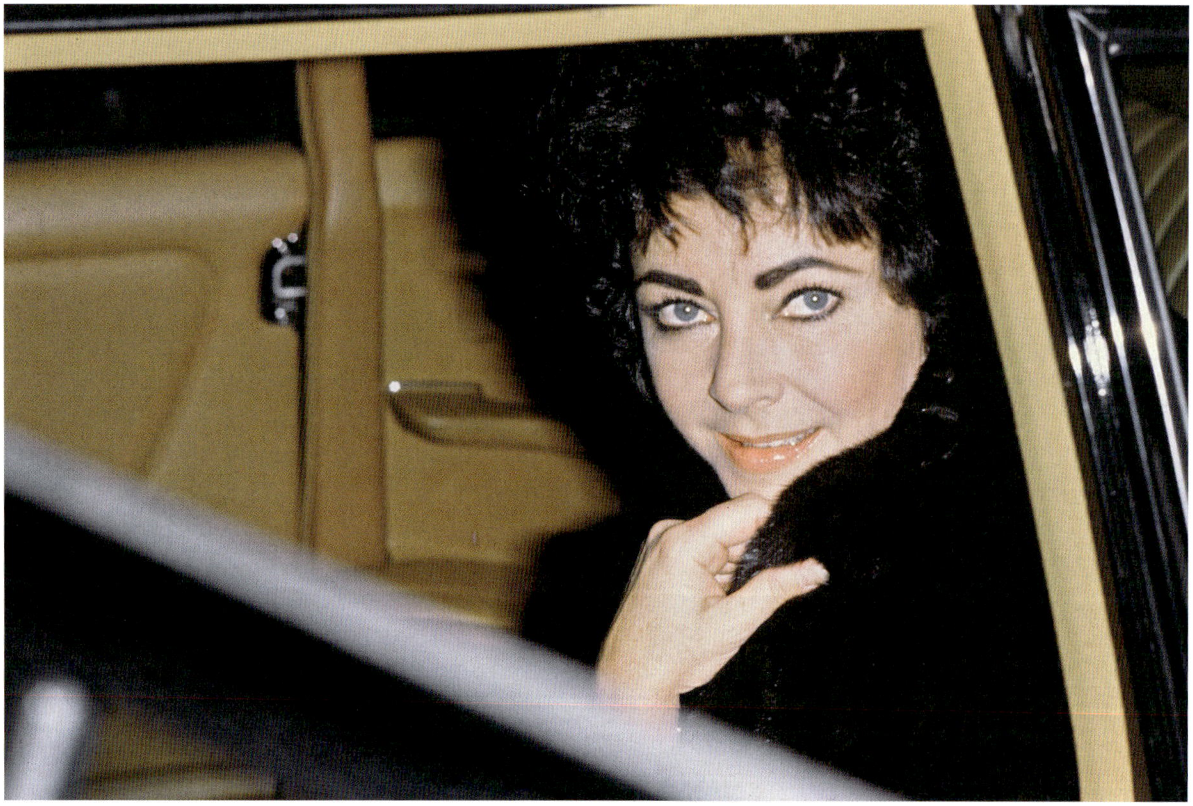

DANIEL ANGELI
Elizabeth Taylor in Gstaad
December 24, 1979

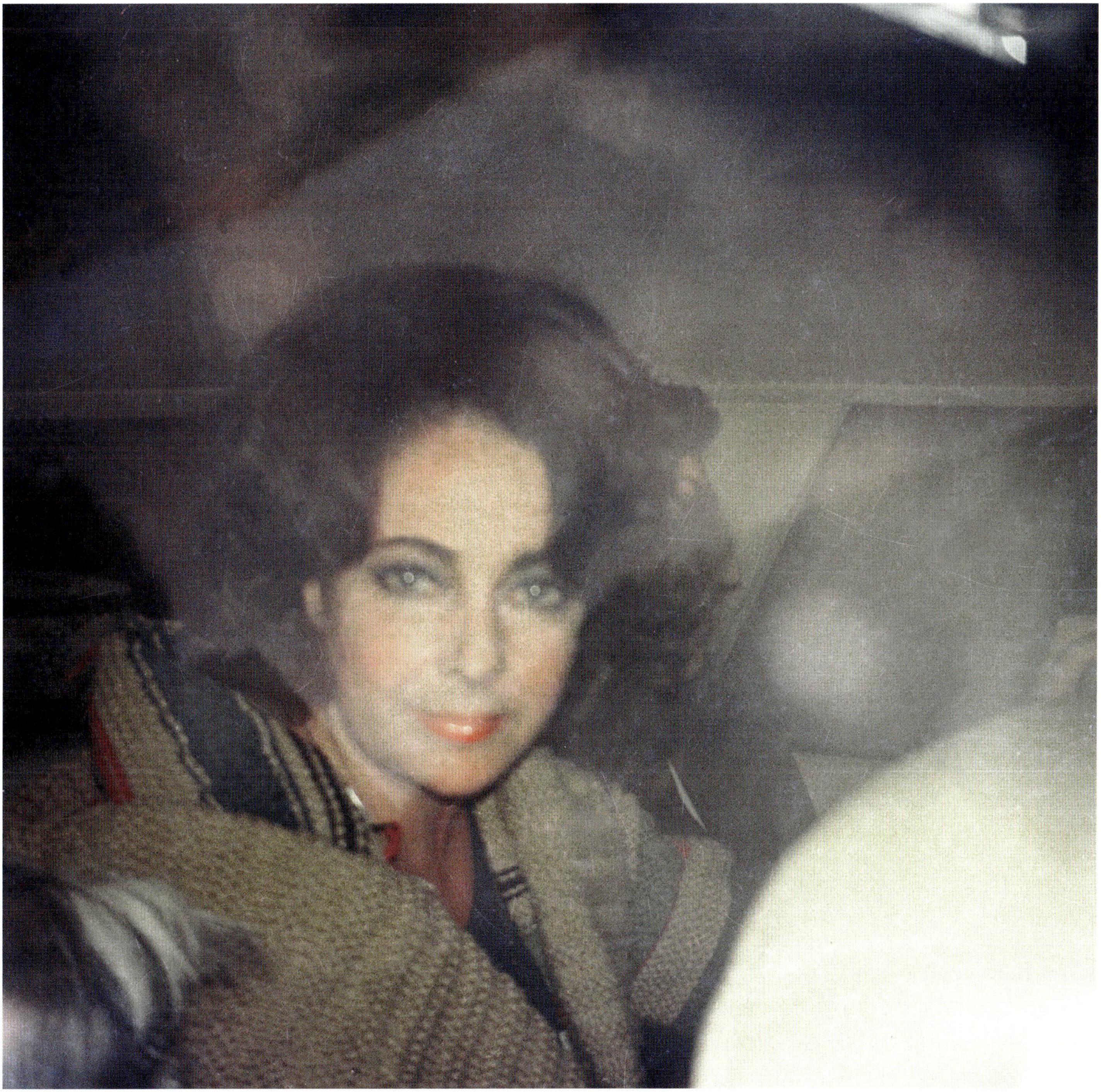

GARY LEE BOAS
Elizabeth Taylor at the Lombardy Hotel, New York
February 24, 1976

Brigitte

By 1956, Brigitte Bardot had become "the most photographed girl in the world," a role she played with increasing reluctance. The paparazzi were everywhere during the filming of Jean-Luc Godard's *Contempt* in 1963, staking her out by land and by sea. By 1965, the break was absolute. Bardot attacked the entire profession. Deploying their telephoto lenses, the paparazzi photographed the interior of her villa, La Madrague, and then set up shop in her garden. Courts granted the star the right to build defensive walls around her property extending all the way down to the waterfront. Brigitte Bardot's relationship with the paparazzi involved a series of strategic skirmishes on both sides. During the filming of *Contempt*, photographers publicized the difficulties they faced due to the star's rejection of their advances. The paparazzi felt she was betraying the fundamental principles of their profession: the right of access to locales and celebrities. This conflict became a topic of interest in its own right, as well as a new photographic challenge. The photographers deployed a variety of tactics, from disclosing the star's hideouts to staging fictional events. They managed to offer glimpses into Bardot's life, while playing up the challenges they encountered in their tireless efforts to waylay her.

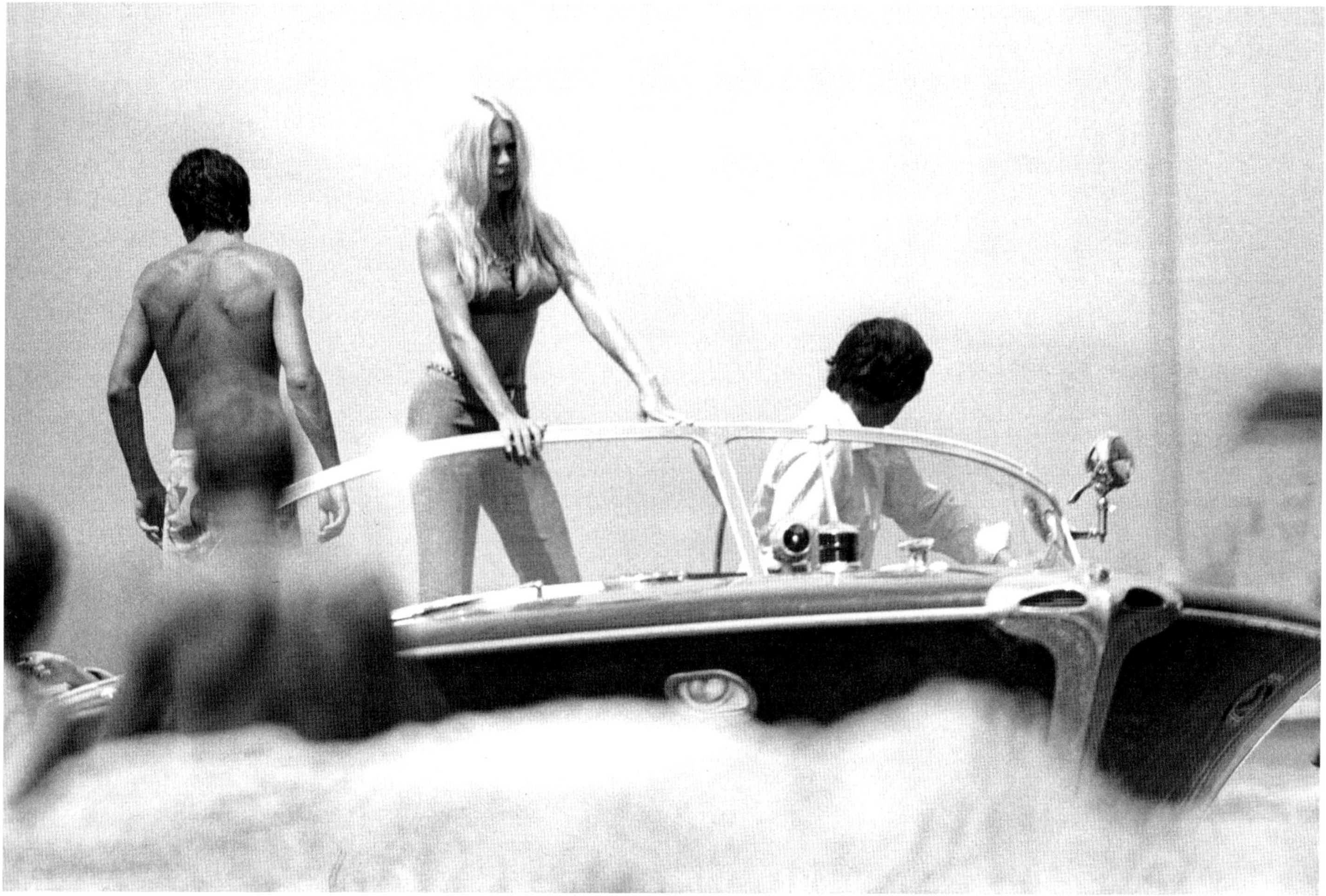

ANONYMOUS
Brigitte Bardot with Gunter Sachs at La Madrague, Saint-Tropez
1967

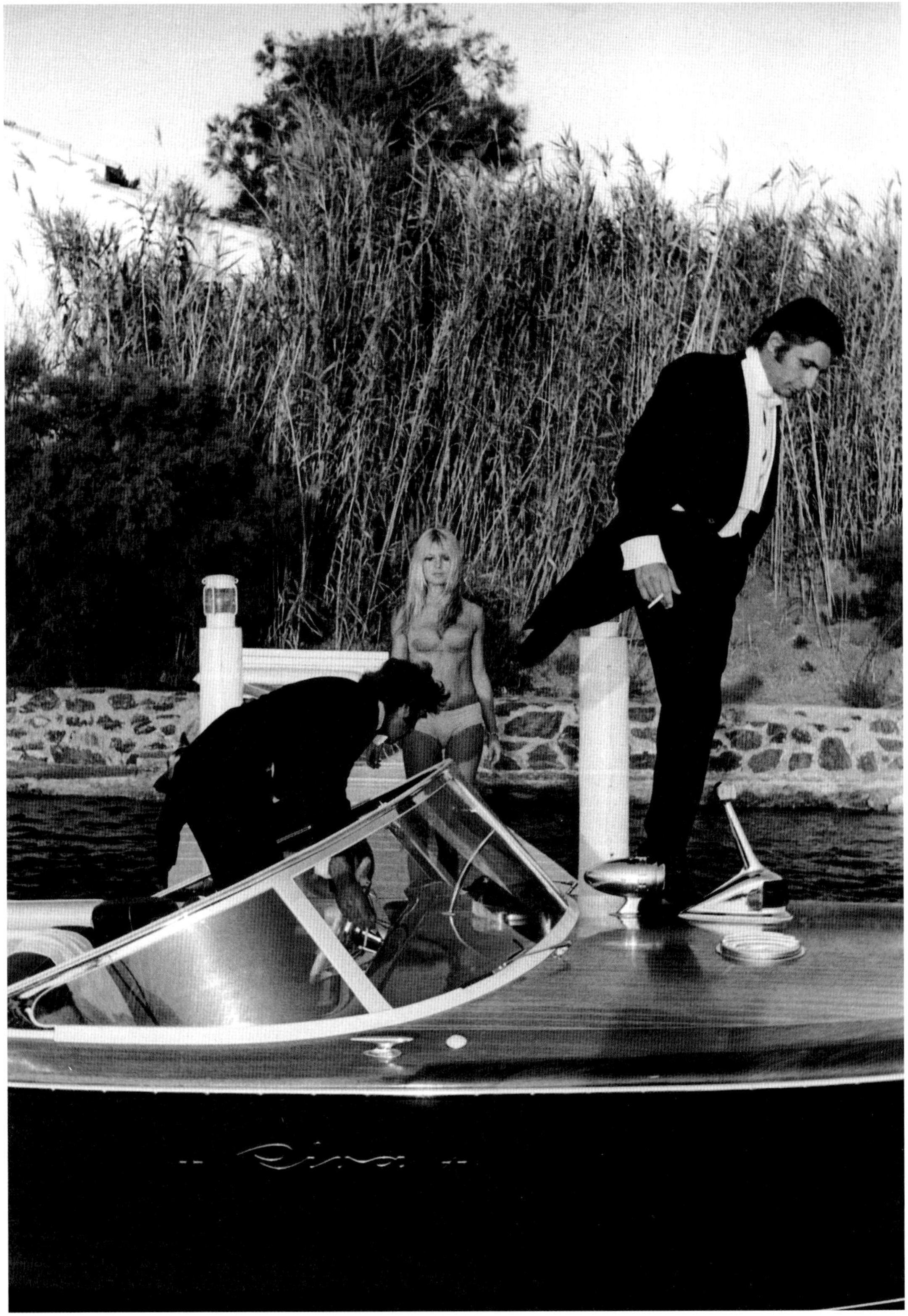

PHILIPPE D'EXEA
Brigitte Bardot and Gunter Sachs at La Madrague, Saint-Tropez
1966

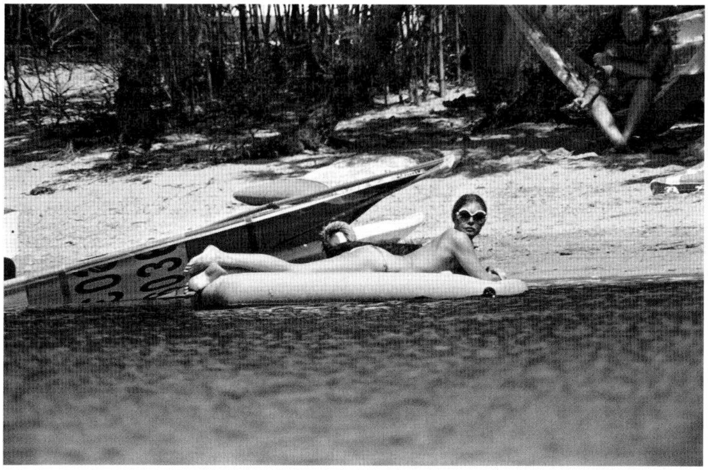

DANIEL ANGELI
Brigitte Bardot at La Madrague, Saint-Tropez
July 6, 1981

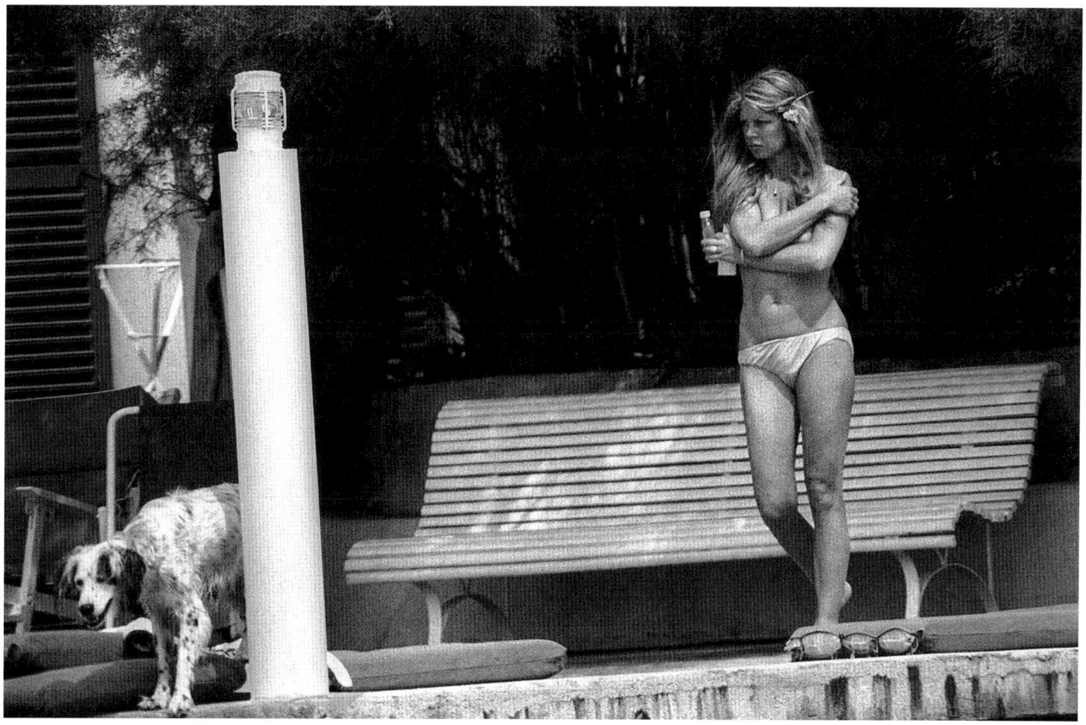

FRANCIS APESTEGUY
Brigitte Bardot on the Pontoon at La Madrague, Saint-Tropez
June 14, 1976

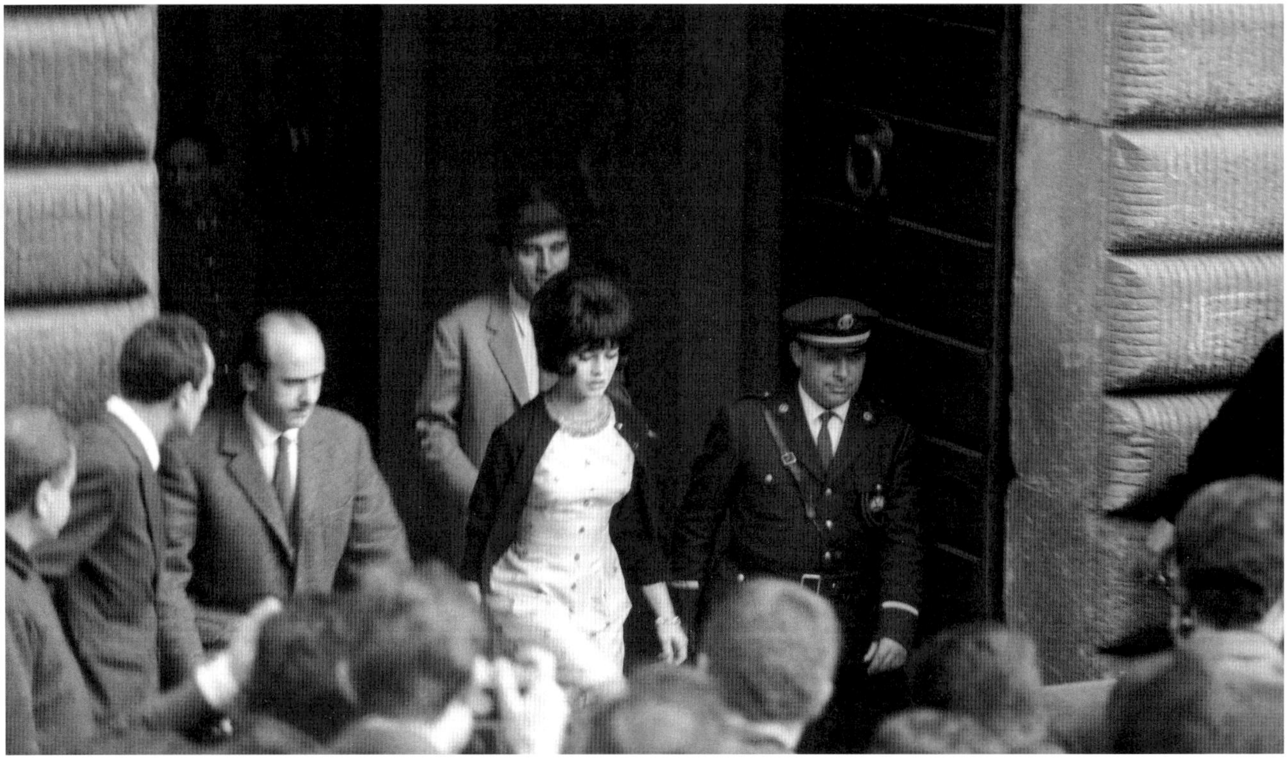

MARCELLO GEPPETTI
Brigitte Bardot Leaving the Set of the Film
Le Mépris (Contempt), *Rome*
1963

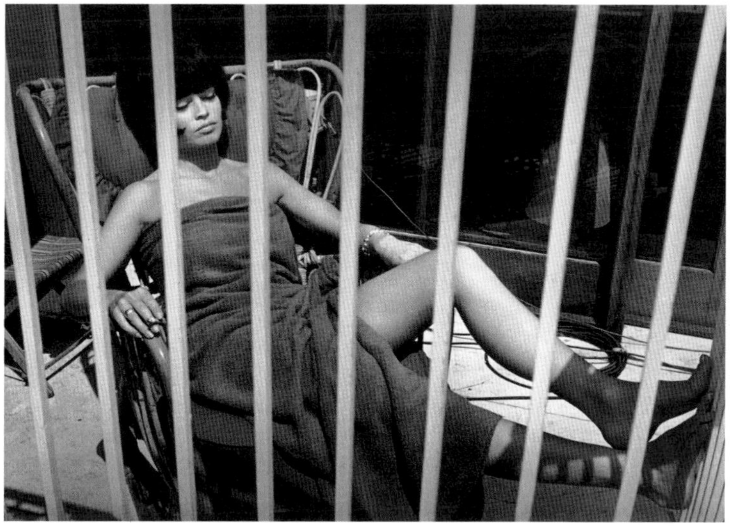

TAZIO SECCHIAROLI
Brigitte Bardot on the Set of Le Mépris (Contempt)
1963

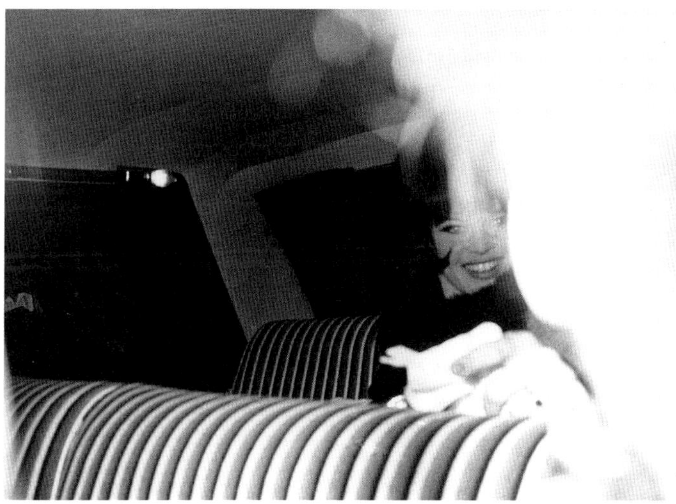

PATRICK MORIN
Brigitte Bardot during the Shooting of Le Mépris (Contempt), *Rome*
1963

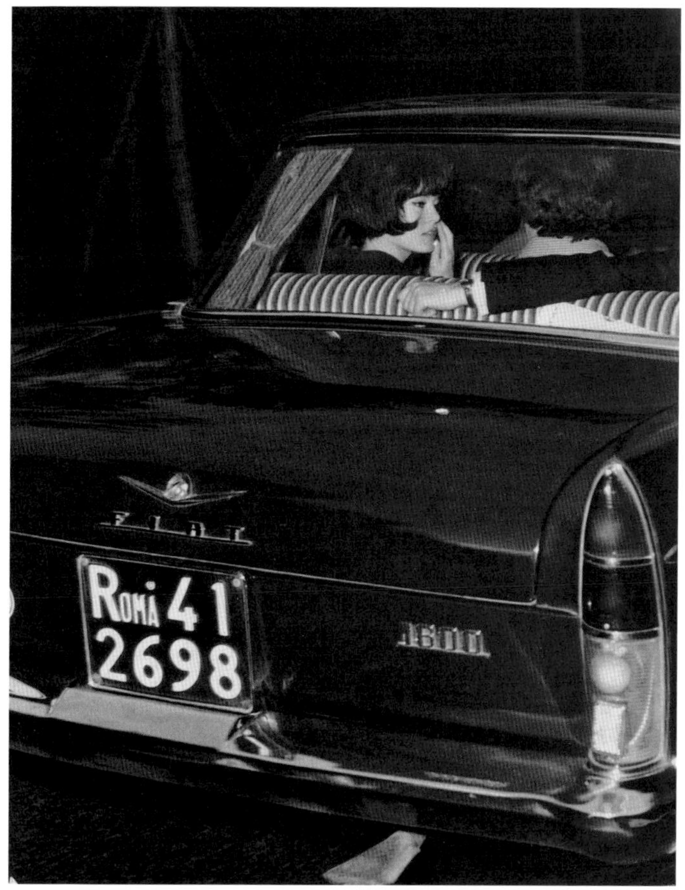

ANONYMOUS
(Keystone)
Brigitte Bardot during the Shooting of Le Mépris (Contempt), *Rome*
April 18, 1963

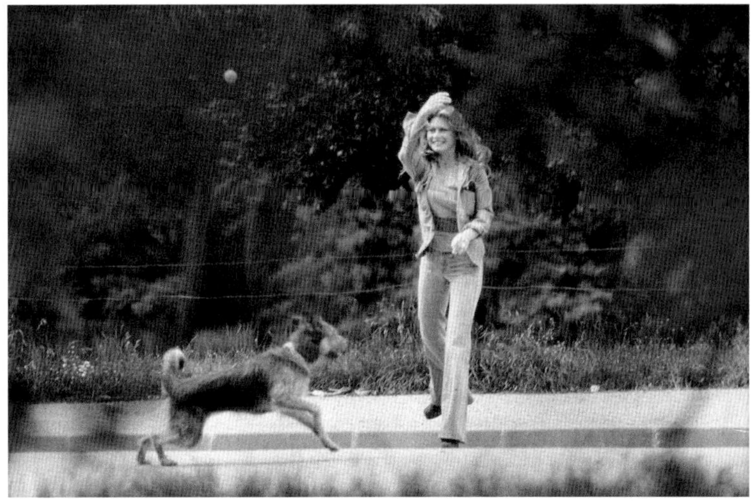

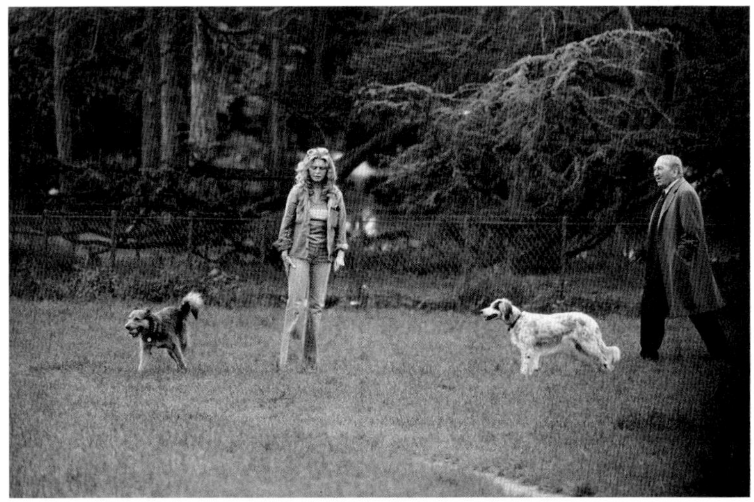

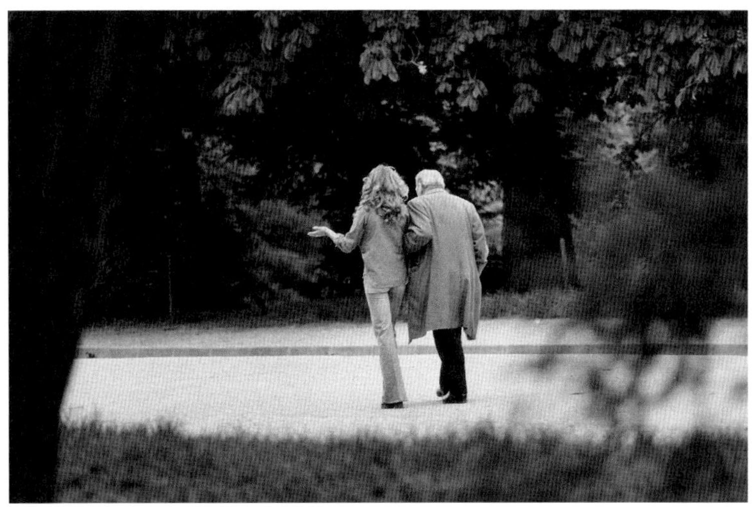

MICHEL GINIÈS
Brigitte Bardot Walking Her Dogs in the Bois de Boulogne
June 4, 1975

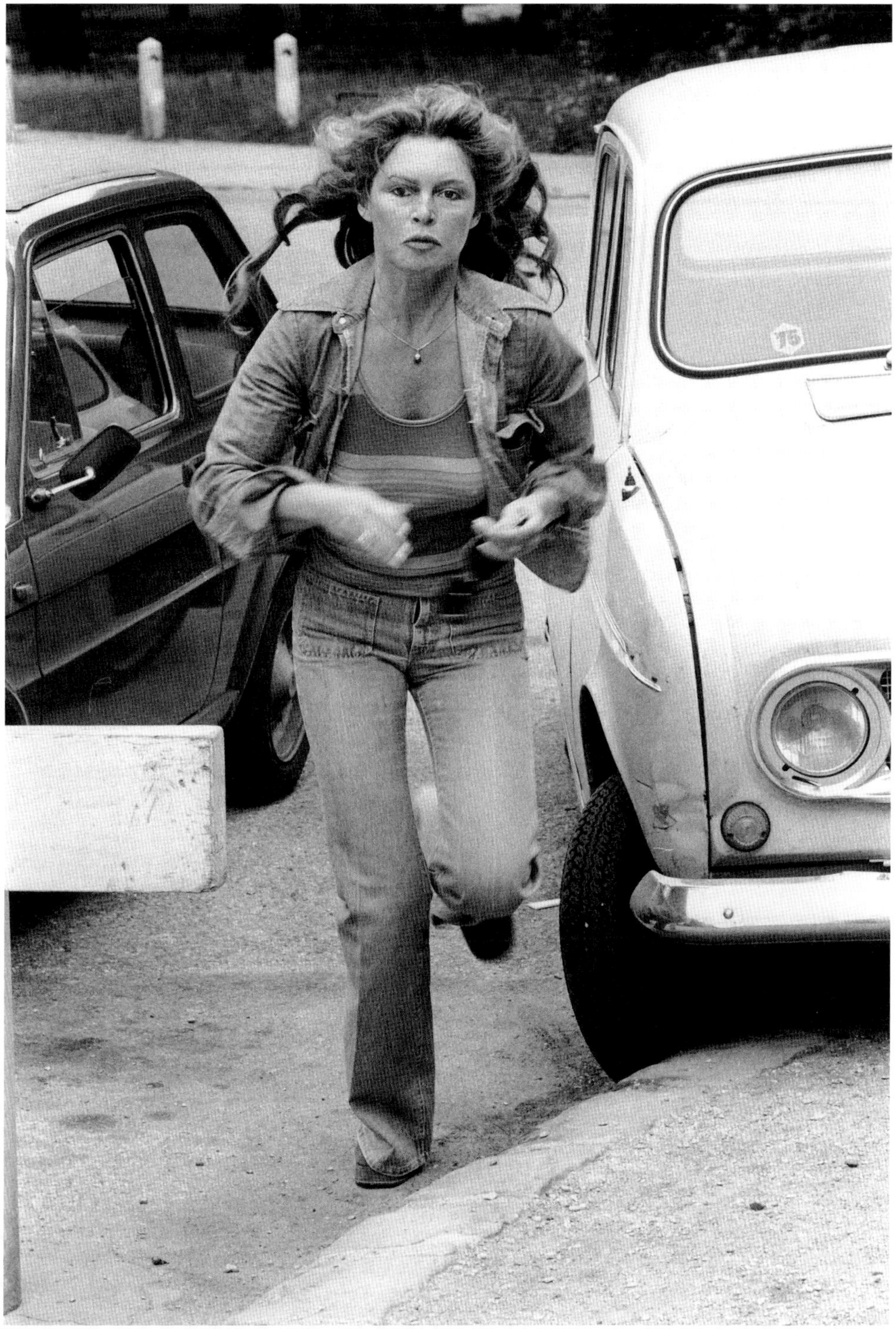

MICHEL GINIÈS
Brigitte Bardot Rushing in Anger at the Photographer
June 4, 1975

JACKIE

Jacqueline Lee Bouvier was the wife of the thirty-fifth president of the United States, John Fitzgerald Kennedy, and subsequently married the Greek shipping magnate Aristotle Onassis. She was one of the world's most photographed women in the 1960s and 1970s. The legendary American paparazzo Ron Galella began to follow her when she moved to New York in 1964. Eight years later he was hauled into court for a highly publicized trial that was featured on the cover of *Life* magazine. Jackie accused him of stalking and aggressive intrusion into her private life and asked that he be prohibited from coming within fifty to seventy-five feet of her and her children. Galella in turn accused her of preventing him from making a living and sued for $1.3 million in damages, about fifty times his annual earnings. The court ruled in Jackie's favor, setting a significant legal precedent: henceforth, paparazzi could not claim any right of access to celebrities. In contrast to the case of Bardot, it was not Jackie Kennedy's responsibility to conceal herself from prying eyes; it was the paparazzo's job to keep his distance.

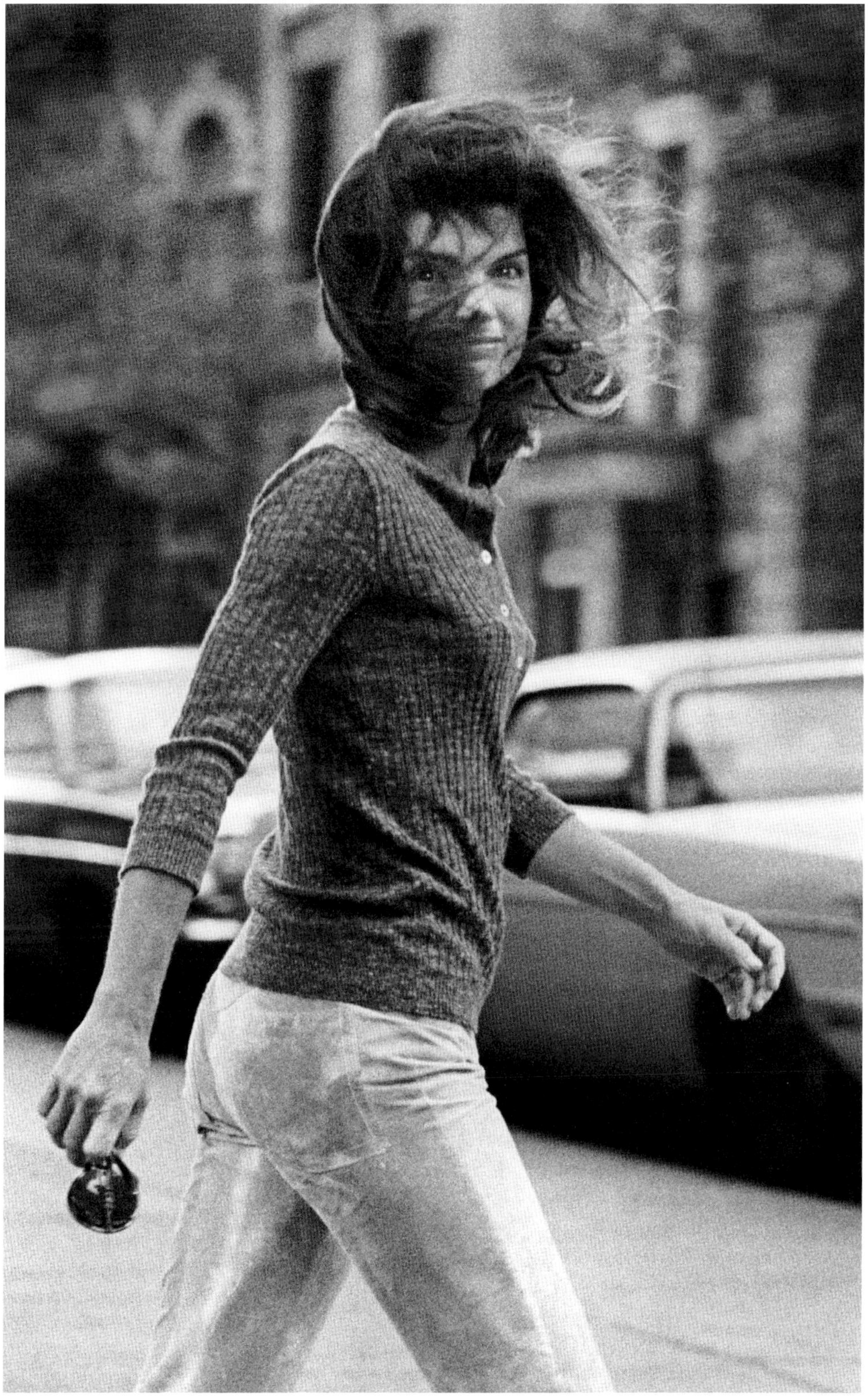

RON GALELLA
"Windblown Jackie": Jackie Onassis, on the Corner of 91st Street and Madison Avenue, New York
October 4, 1971

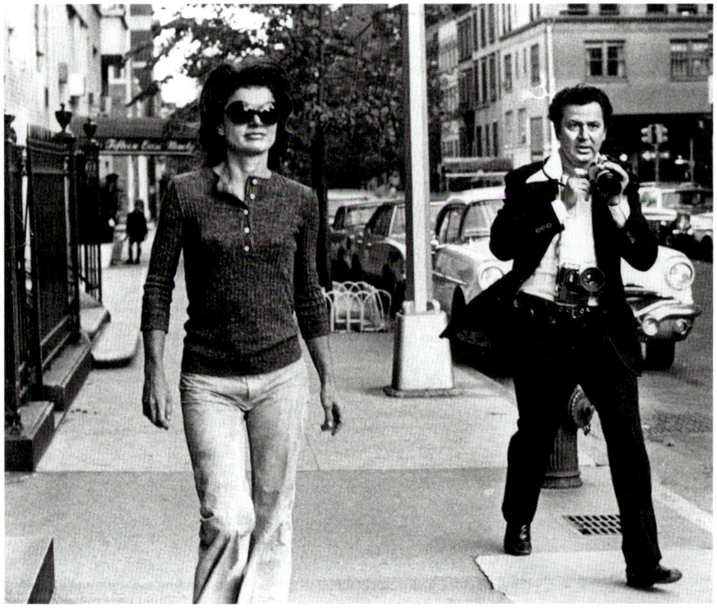

RON GALELLA (attributed to)
Jackie Onassis and Ron Galella on Madison Avenue, New York
October 7, 1971

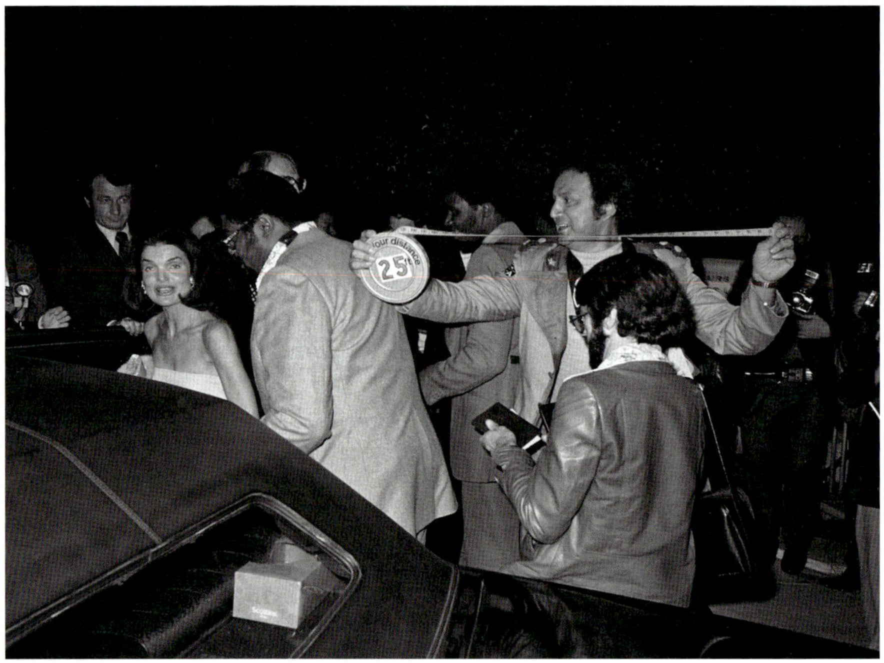

BRAD ELTERMAN
The Tape Measure
(Jacqueline Onassis and Ron Galella)
1976

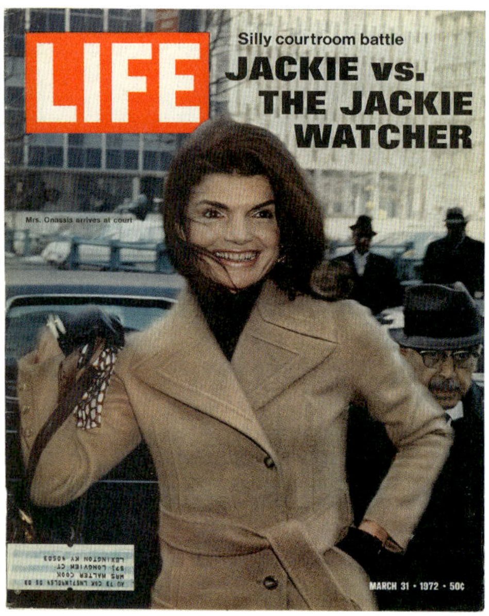

LIFE, vol. 72, no. 12, March 31, 1972, cover (Photograph: Art Zelin)

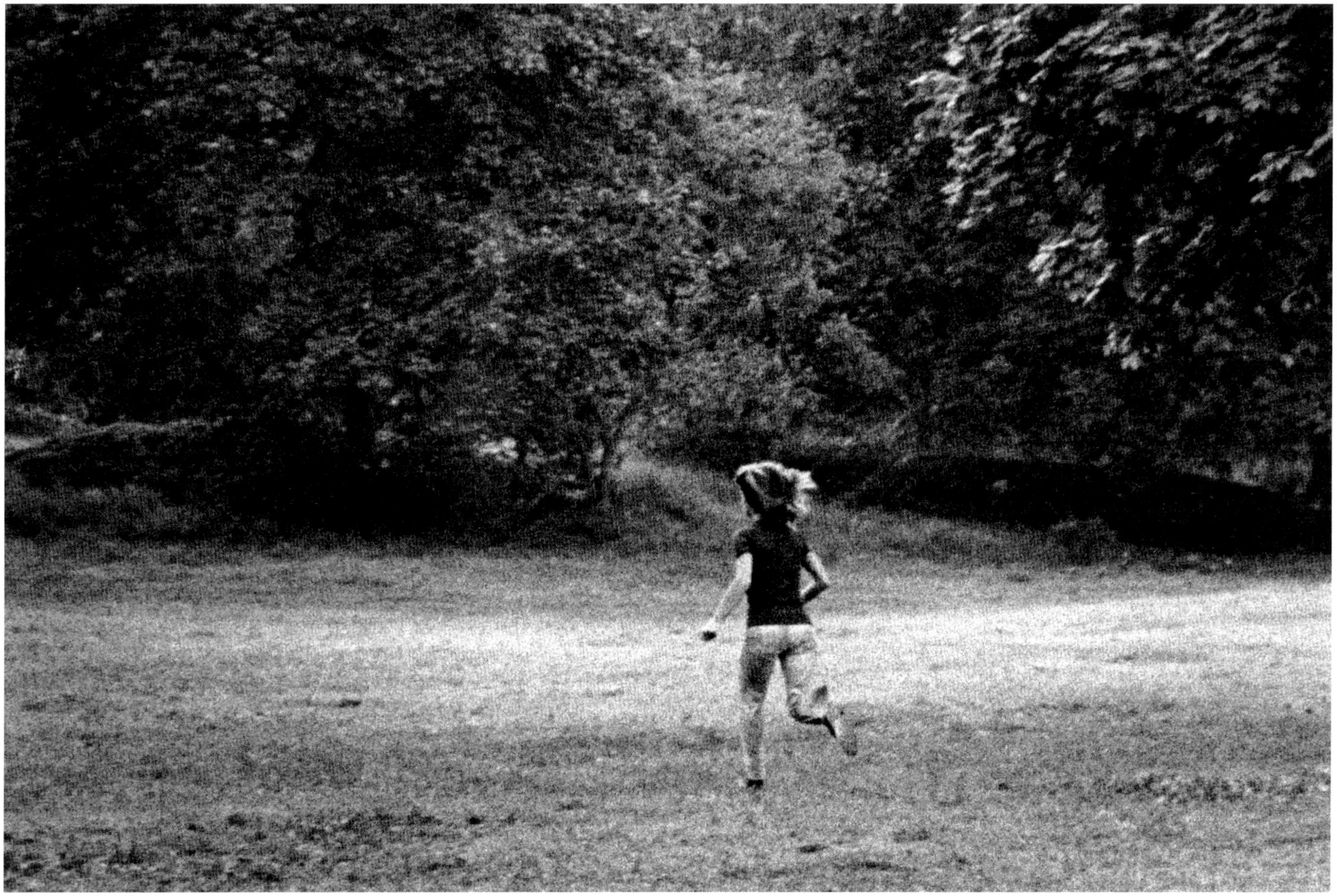

RON GALELLA
Jackie Onassis Glimpsed in Central Park, New York
October 4, 1971

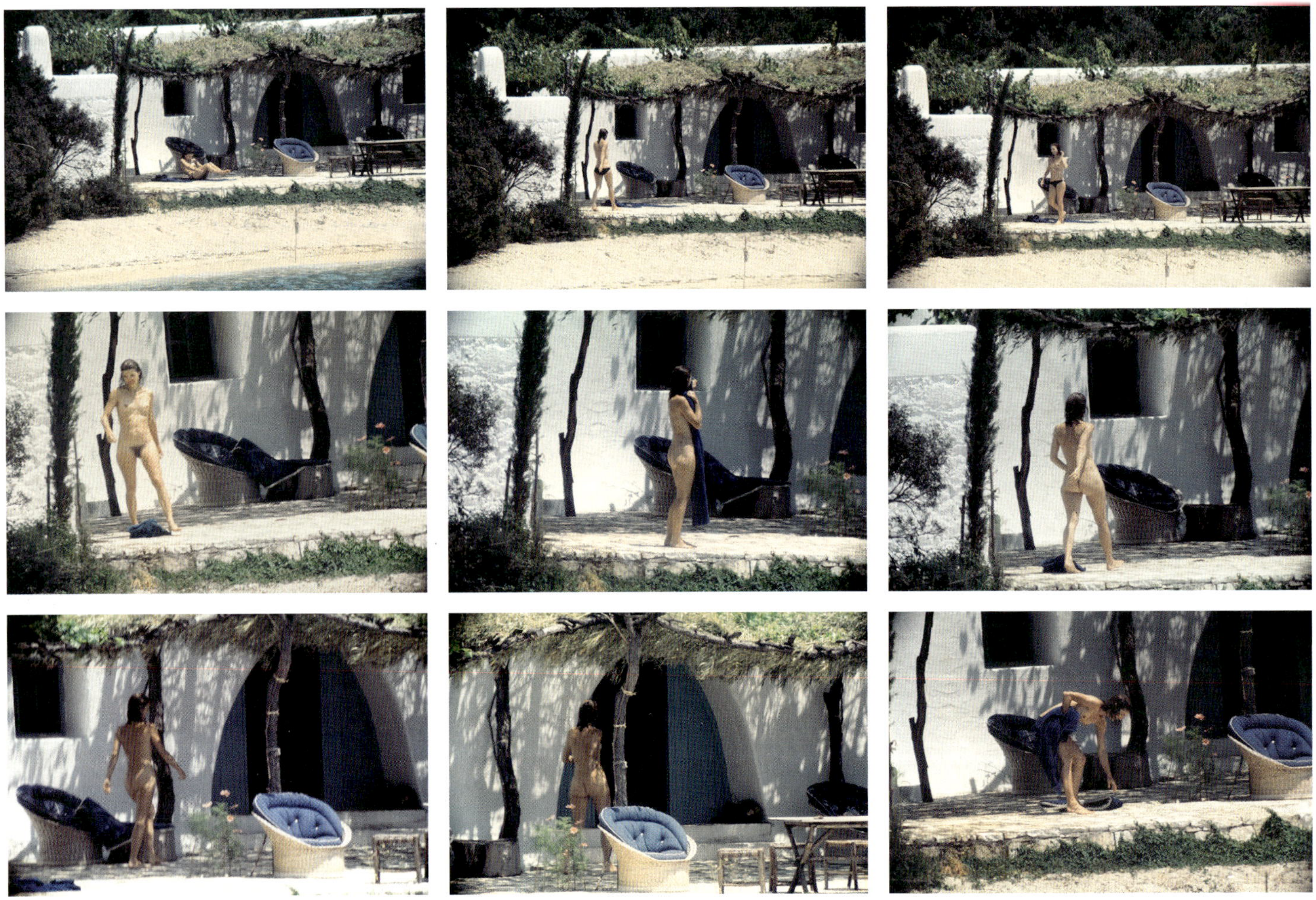

SETTIMIO GARRITANO
Jacqueline Onassis Naked, Skorpios
1972

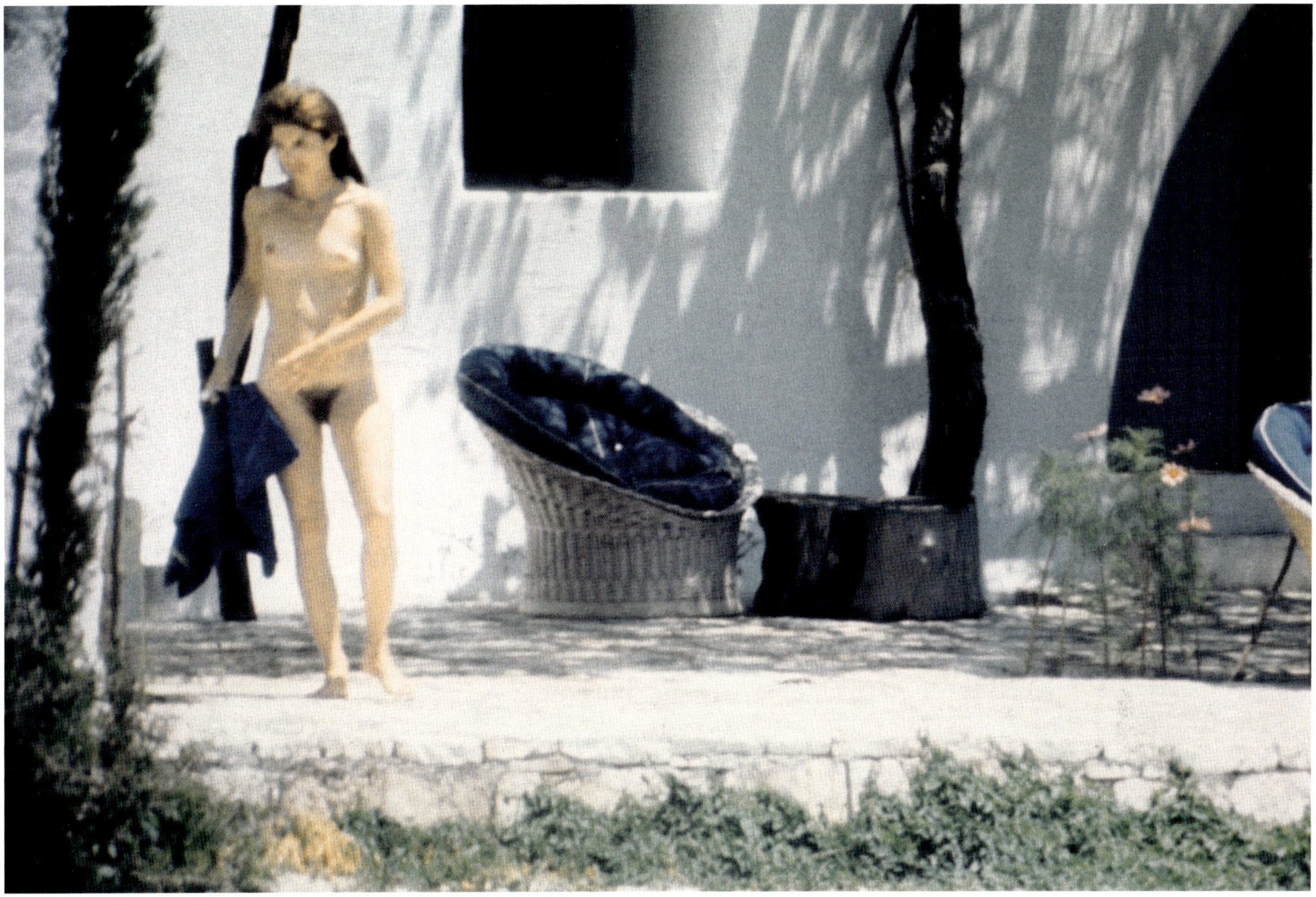

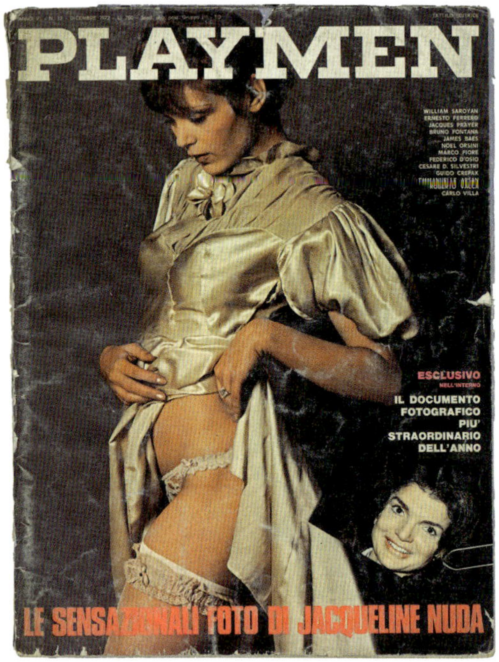

Playmen, vol. 6, no. 12,
December 1972

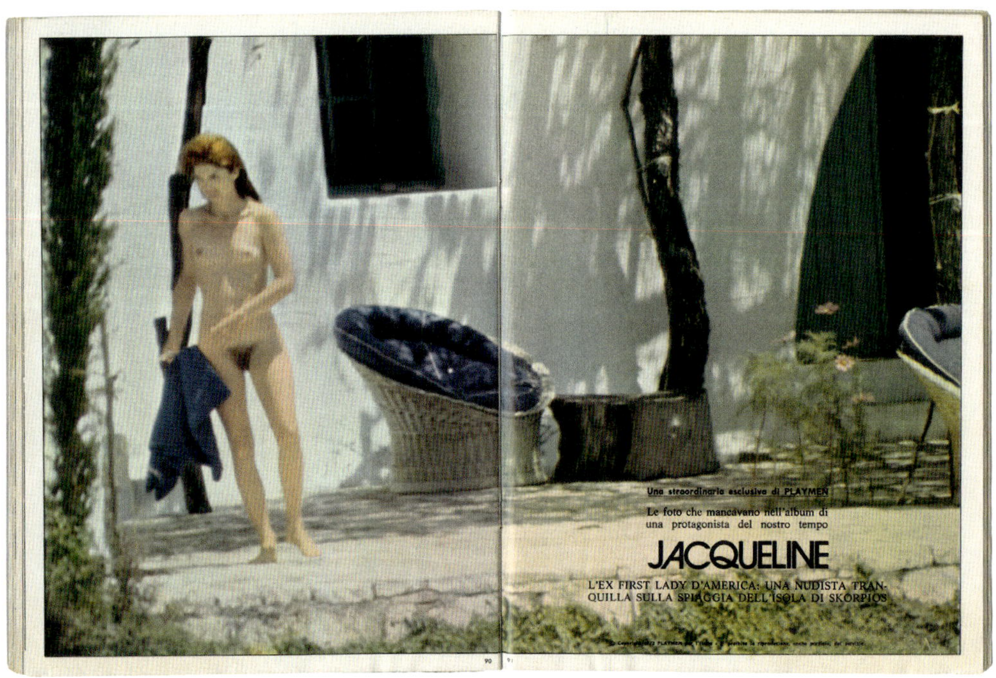

Playmen, vol. 6,
no. 12,
December 1972
(Photograph:
Settimio Garritano)

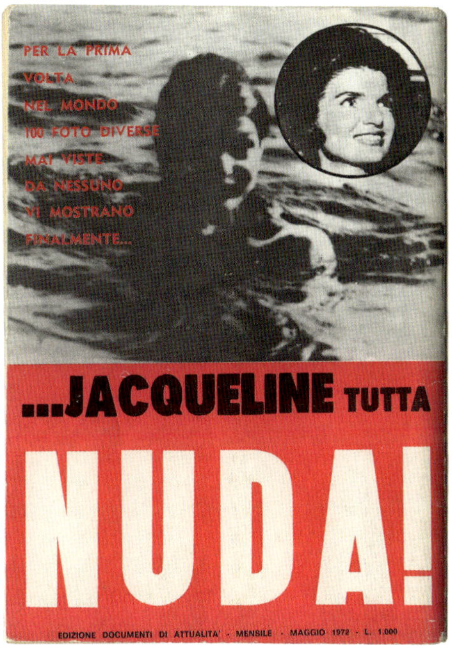

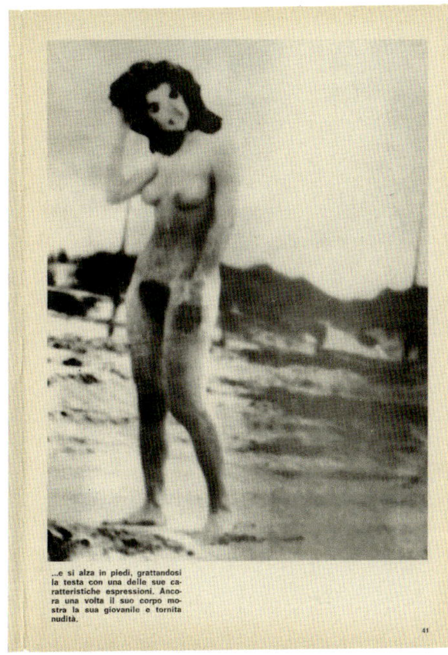

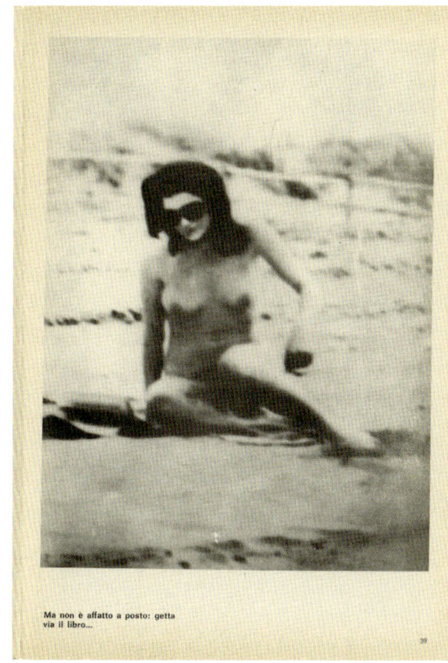

Documenti di Attualità', "Jacqueline tutta nuda!", May 1972, cover, pp. 39 and 41 (Photomontage: anonymous)

CLANDESTINE PUBLICATIONS. In the summer of 1971, Jackie Kennedy-Onassis was photographed in the nude on the private island of Skorpios. Settimio Garritano, who managed to remain anonymous for many years, took the shots. Although he was not actually a member of the league of paparazzi—he was actually a reporter and portrait photographer—he followed Jackie for three years. The photographs were not published immediately. A number of magazines turned them down out of respect for the former first lady of the United States. Perhaps their reluctance was also due to fear of reprisals from the era's two most powerful families, the Kennedys and the Onassises. The existence of the photos was, however, a matter of public knowledge. Unscrupulous publications ran stories entirely composed of fabricated shots cobbled together using the techniques of photomontage. The genuine photographs ultimately appeared in the December 1972 issue of *Playmen*, the Italian competitor of *Playboy*. They were subsequently published by the notorious American magazine Hustler. Helmut Newton called them "some of the most disturbing photos of the century."

Caroline & Stéphanie

The wedding of Prince Rainier and the Hollywood actress Grace Kelly in 1956 marked the arrival of paparazzi in the principality. Caroline and Stéphanie of Monaco were photographed as children, adolescents, and in all their rites of passage, joyful or otherwise. The family album was an open book. It is worth noting that Prince Rainier disseminated photographs of his daughters, as if to introduce a new kind of celebrity that encouraged "paparazzism." One might almost say that it was the prince's legacy to his children. As adults, the princesses brought a number of court cases in an effort to protect their privacy. In a ruling of 1999, the German constitutional court ruled that Caroline was "inarguably a public figure of our era" and that she should tolerate the publication of images showing her in public places, even if she was not engaged in public functions at the time. Five years later, the European Court ruled the opposite, deeming that the public does not have "a legitimate interest" in knowing the details of her private life. These conflicting rulings speak volumes about the absence of clear legislation in this area on an international level.

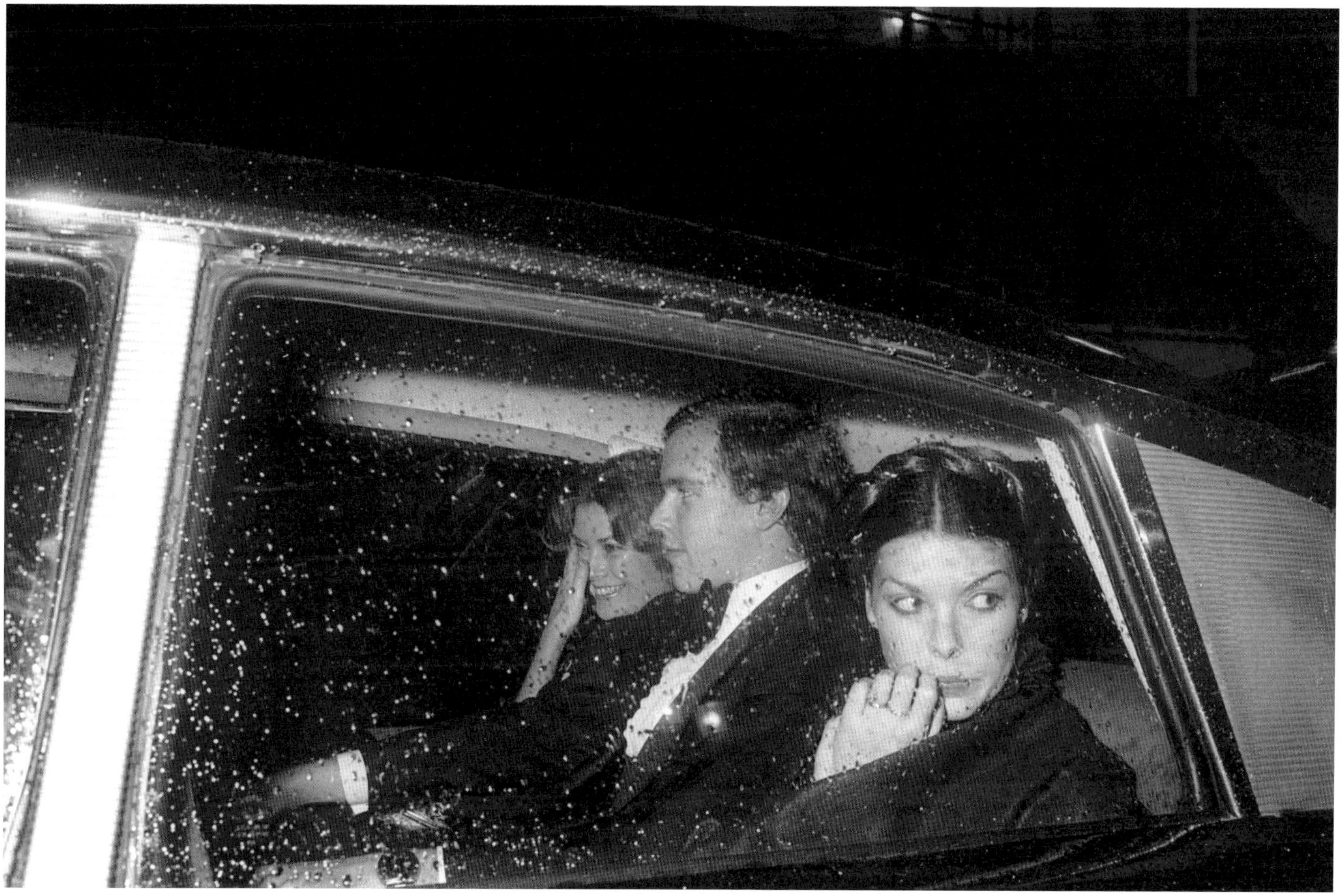

PATRICK SICCOLI
Grace, Albert, and Caroline of Monaco in a Car
1976

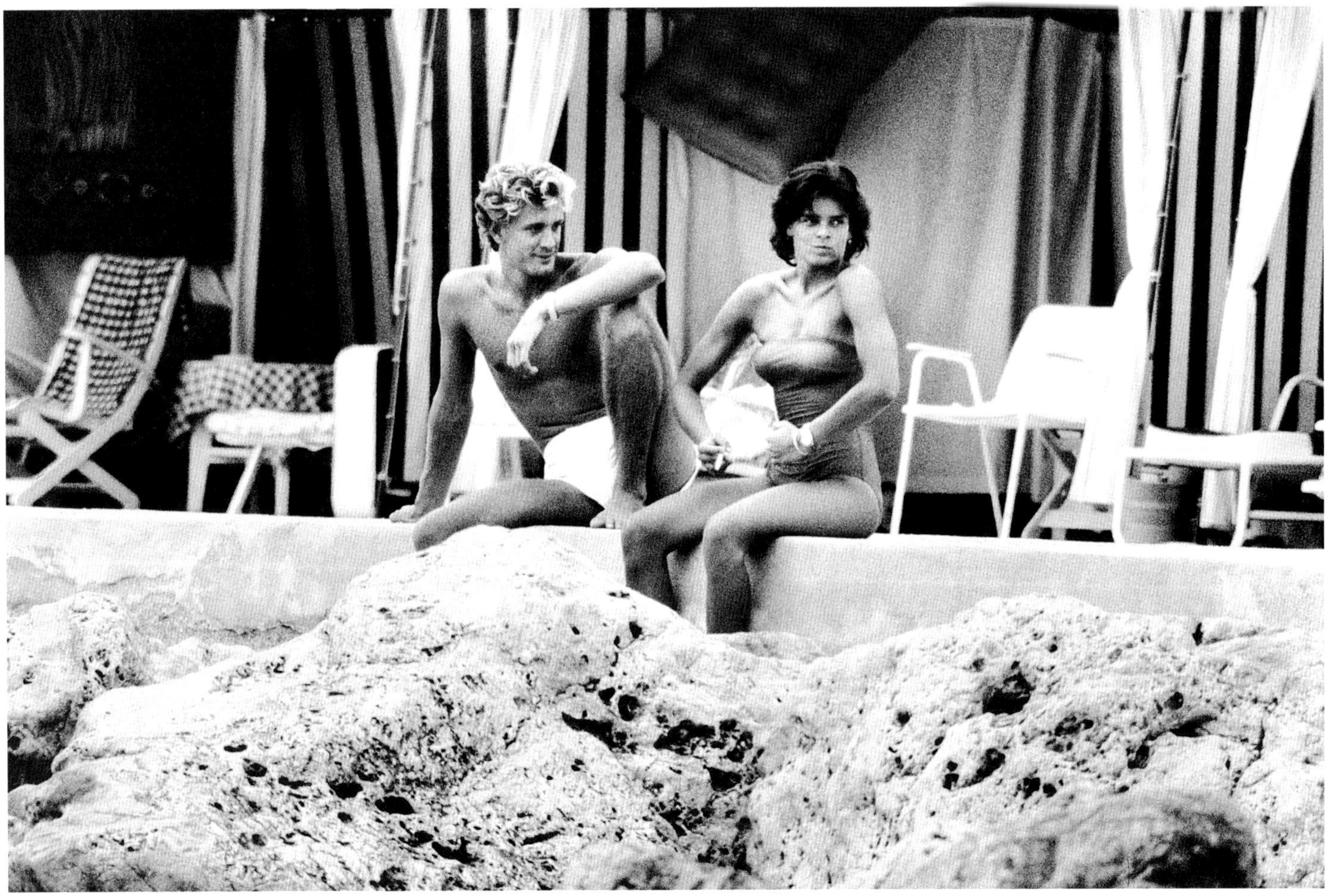

BRUNO MOURON
Stéphanie of Monaco at the Beach with a Friend
June 10, 1981

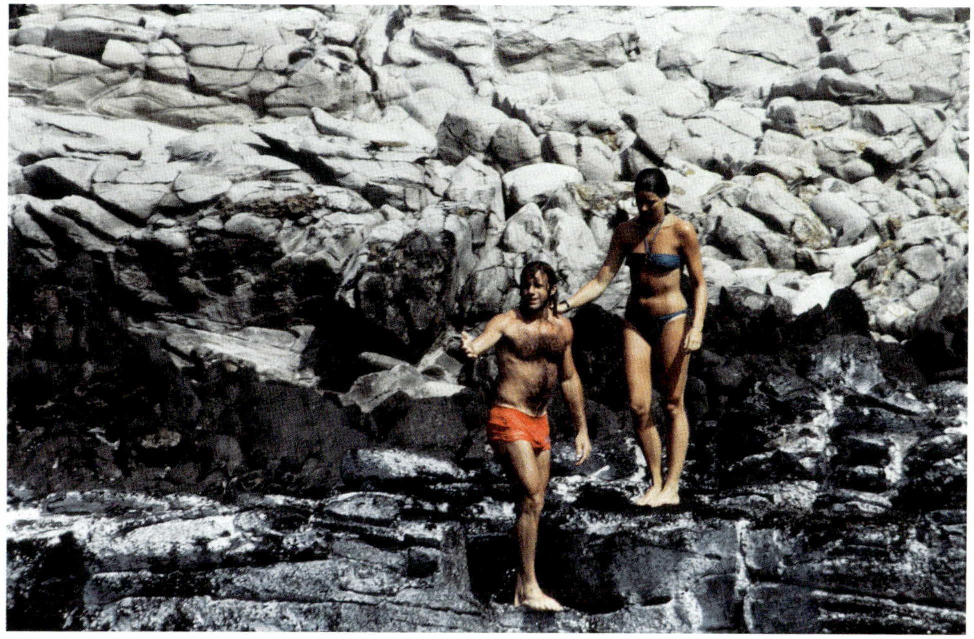

PASCAL ROSTAIN
Caroline and Guillermo Vilas on the Island of Maui in Hawaii
June 1982

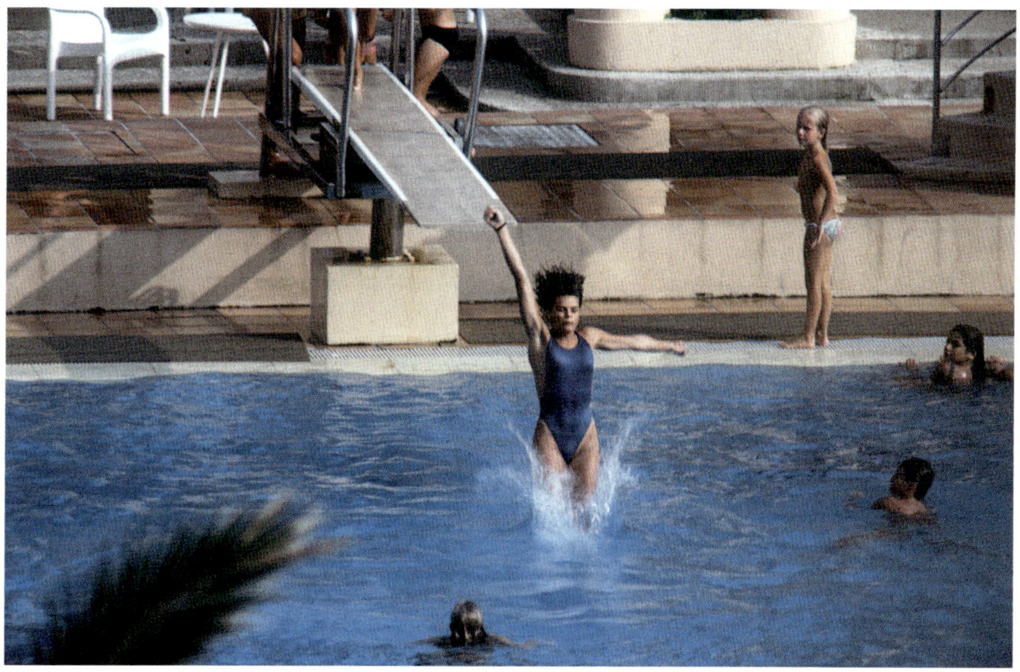

PATRICK SICCOLI
Stéphanie of Monaco Jumping into a Pool
c. 1984

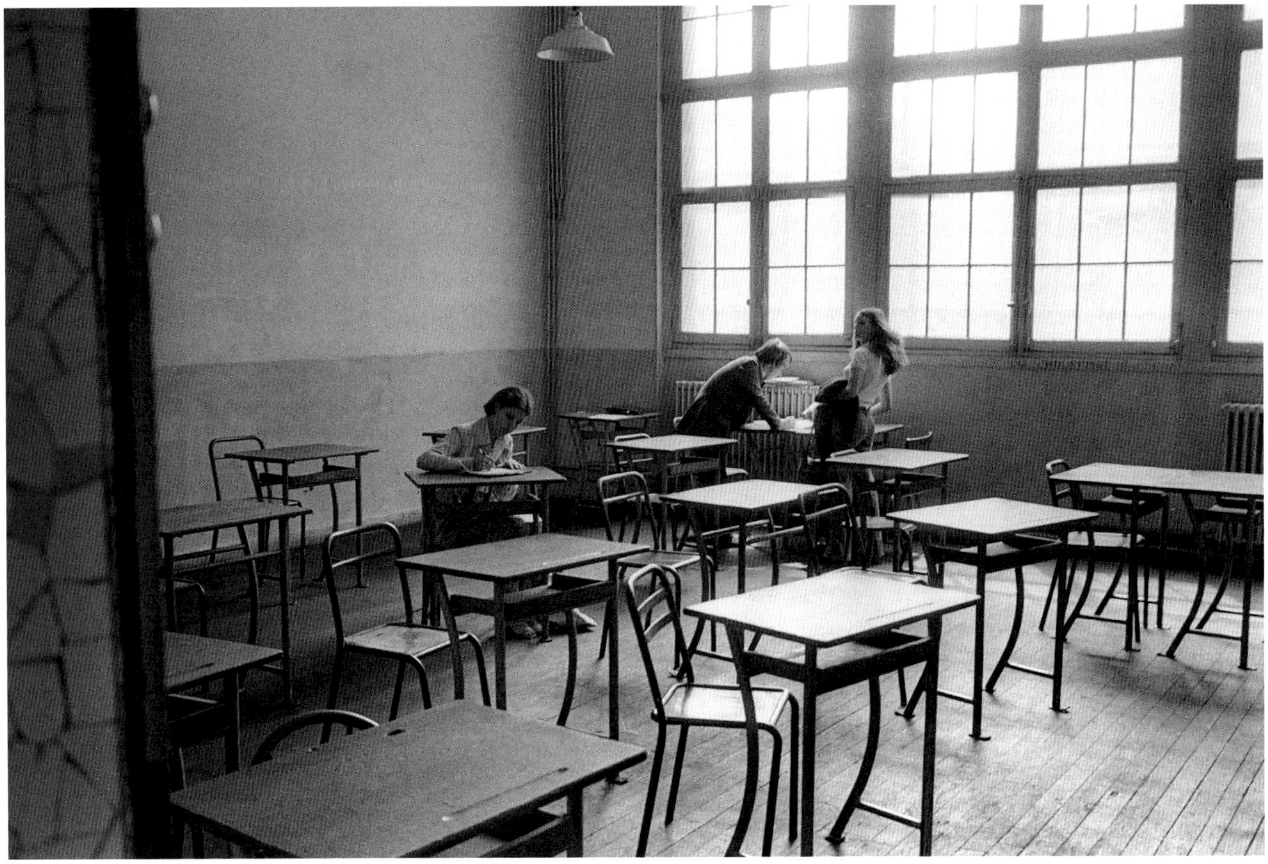

FRANCIS APESTEGUY
Caroline of Monaco Taking Her Baccalauréat Exam in a High School in the West Suburbs of Paris
June 10, 1975

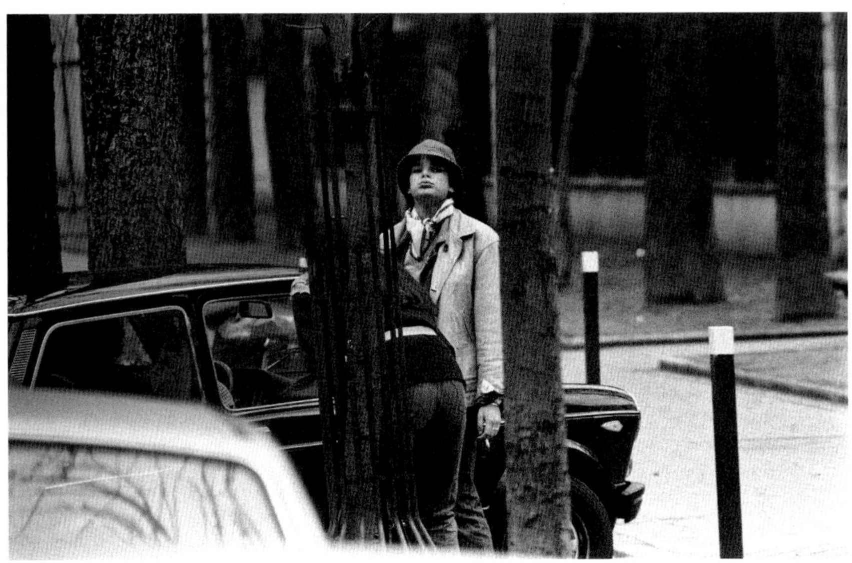

PASCAL ROSTAIN AND BRUNO MOURON
Stéphanie of Monaco, First Cigarette after School, Paris
February 9, 1981

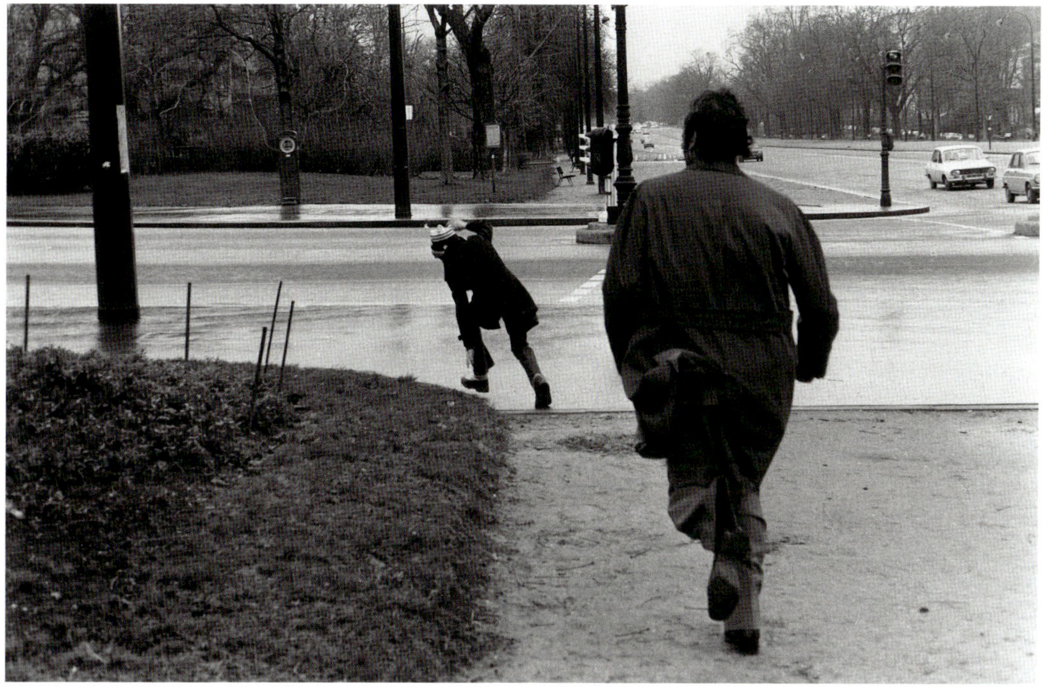

MICHEL GINIÈS
Stéphanie of Monaco Refusing to Pose for the Photographer, Followed by Her Bodyguard
1974

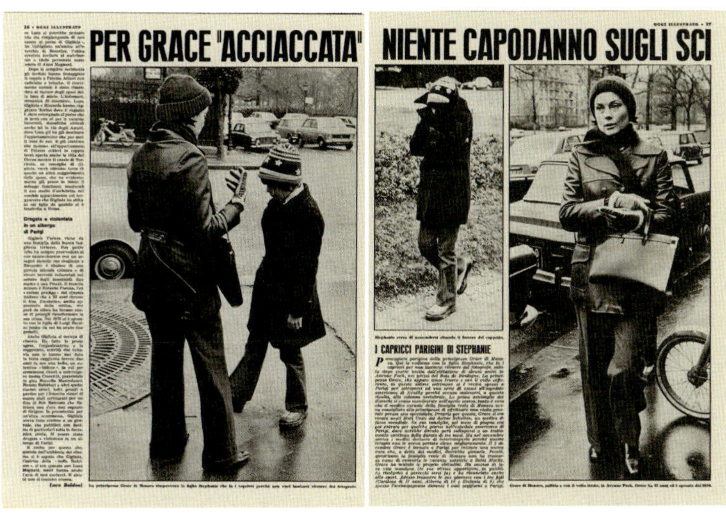

PER GRACE "ACCIACCATA"

NIENTE CAPODANNO SUGLI SCI

I CAPRICCI PARIGINI DI STEPHANIE

Oggi, January 2, 1975,
(Photographs: Michel Giniès)

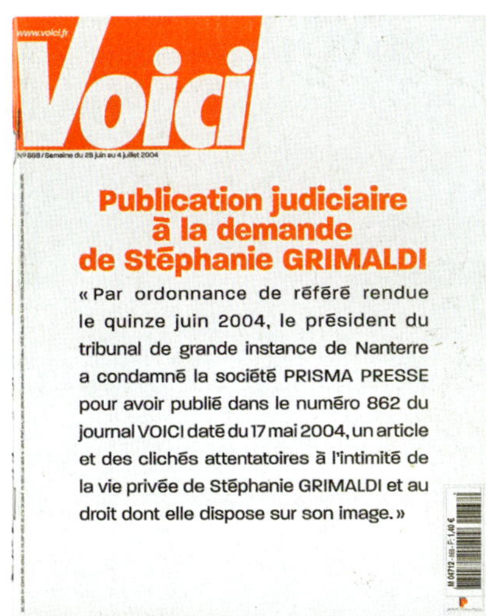

www.voici.fr

Voici

N°868 / Semaine du 28 juin au 4 juillet 2004

Publication judiciaire
à la demande
de Stéphanie GRIMALDI

« Par ordonnance de référé rendue le quinze juin 2004, le président du tribunal de grande instance de Nanterre a condamné la société PRISMA PRESSE pour avoir publié dans le numéro 862 du journal VOICI daté du 17 mai 2004, un article et des clichés attentatoires à l'intimité de la vie privée de Stéphanie GRIMALDI et au droit dont elle dispose sur son image. »

Voici, no. 868
June 28, 2004

Diana

When Diana joined the royal family in 1981, the Windsors were facing declining popularity, and she was perceived as a godsend. British tabloids deployed a force that came to be known as the "Royal Pack," a gang of photographers and journalists tasked with tracking the princess. By 1985, rumors were circulating about the royal couple's marital difficulties, and the press intensified their presence in and around her life, even in its most private aspects. A turning point occurred with the separation of Charles and Diana in December 1992. The breakup made the front pages of the British press. The paparazzi were hungry for details of the princess's every movement. Her relationship with the press was ambivalent. She used it for her own purposes to document her public appearances, while simultaneously decrying its intrusiveness. "The press is ferocious. It pardons nothing, it only hunts for mistakes," she told the daily newspaper *Le Monde*. It is true that the aggressive attitude of some British press coverage conflicted with Diana's widespread popularity with the public at large.

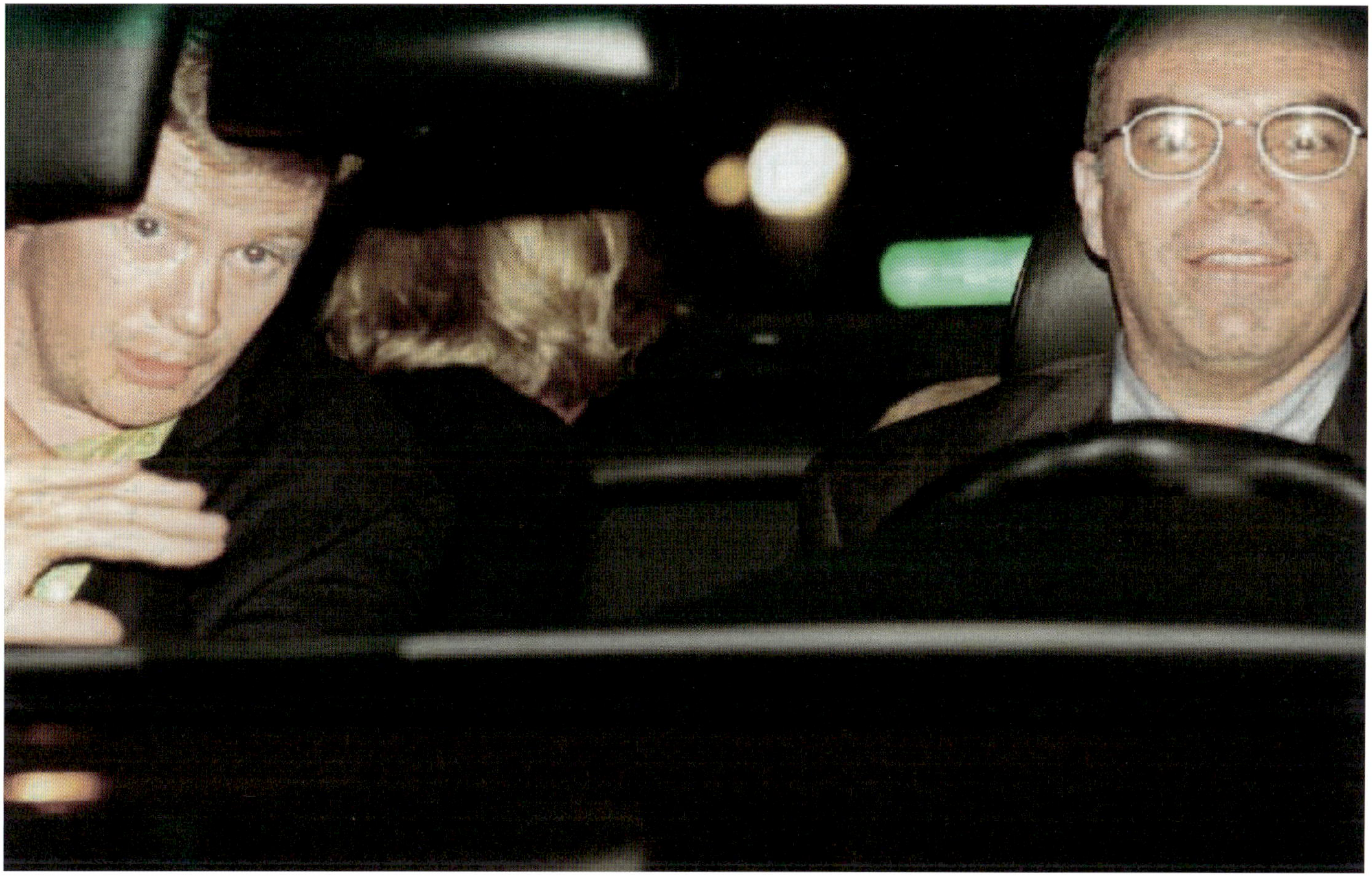

JACQUES LANGEVIN
Last Photograph of Princess Diana
August 31, 1997

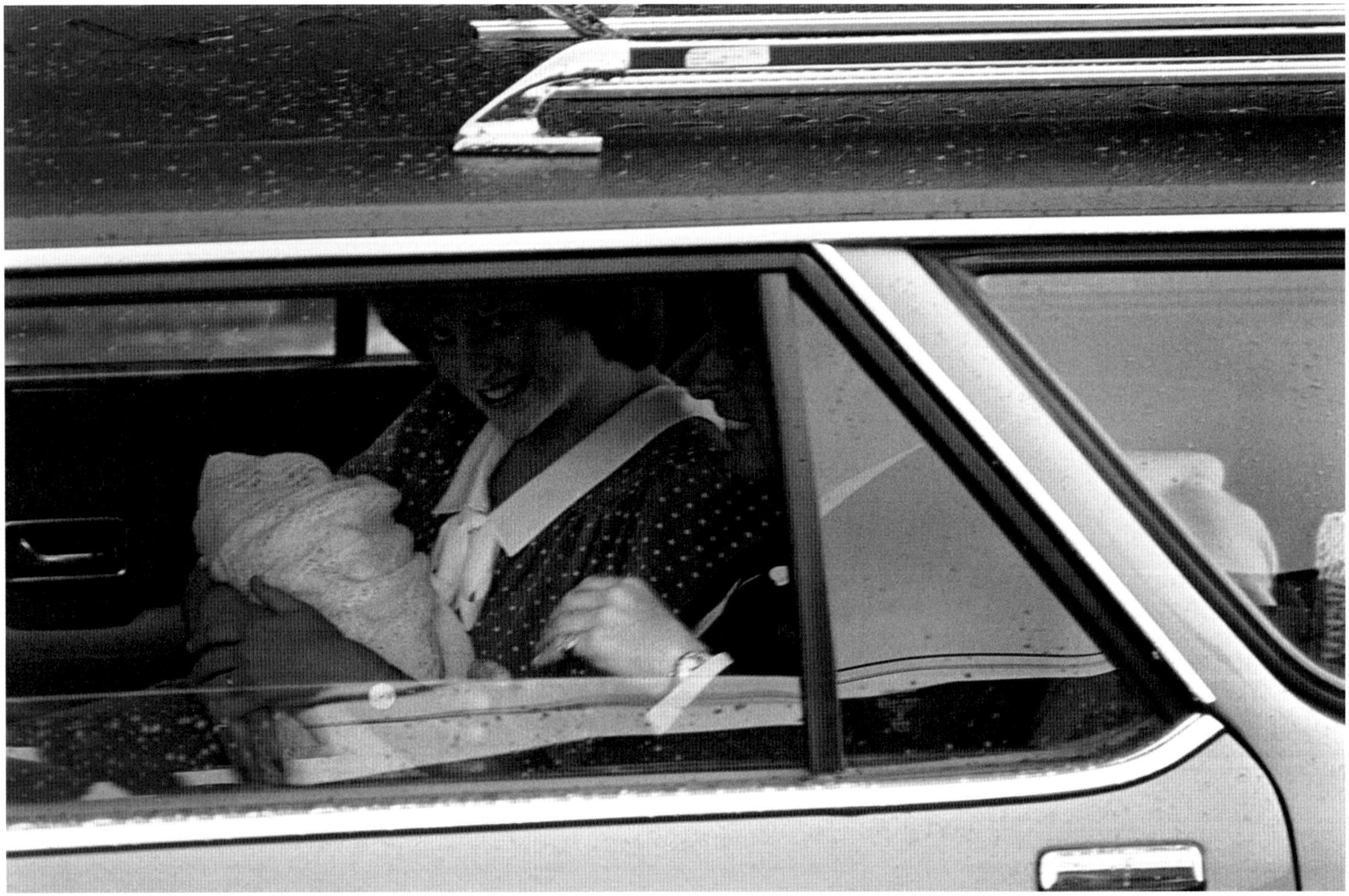

BRUNO MOURON
Princess Diana, Prince Charles, and William, Leaving St. Mary's Hospital, London
June 27, 1982

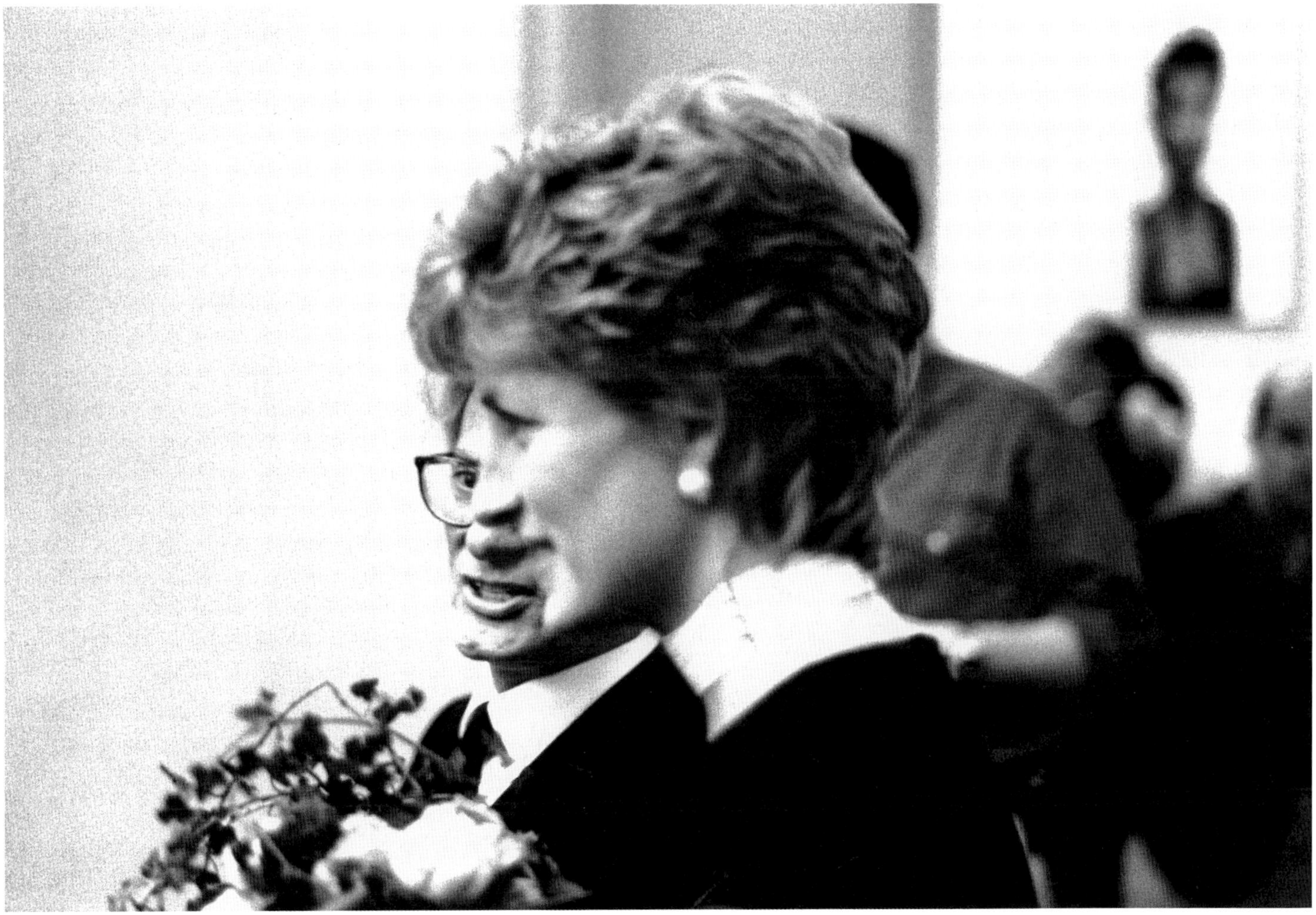

PHILIPPE GARNER
Richard Avedon and Princess Diana at a Private Opening at the National Portrait Gallery, London
March 21, 1995

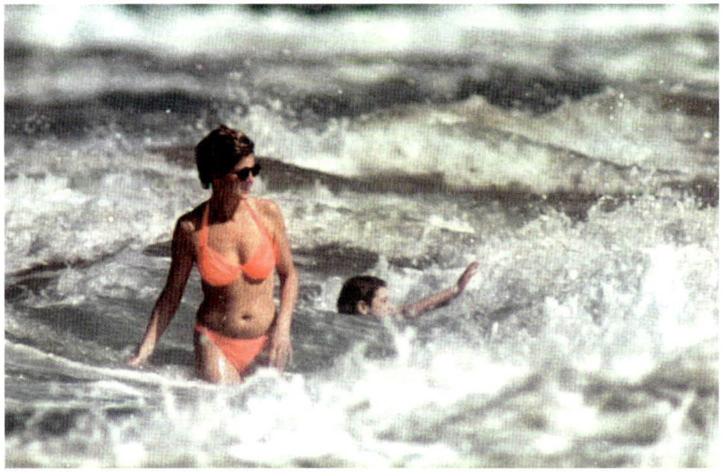

PAUL J. RICHARDS
Princess Diana Swimming
January 4, 1993

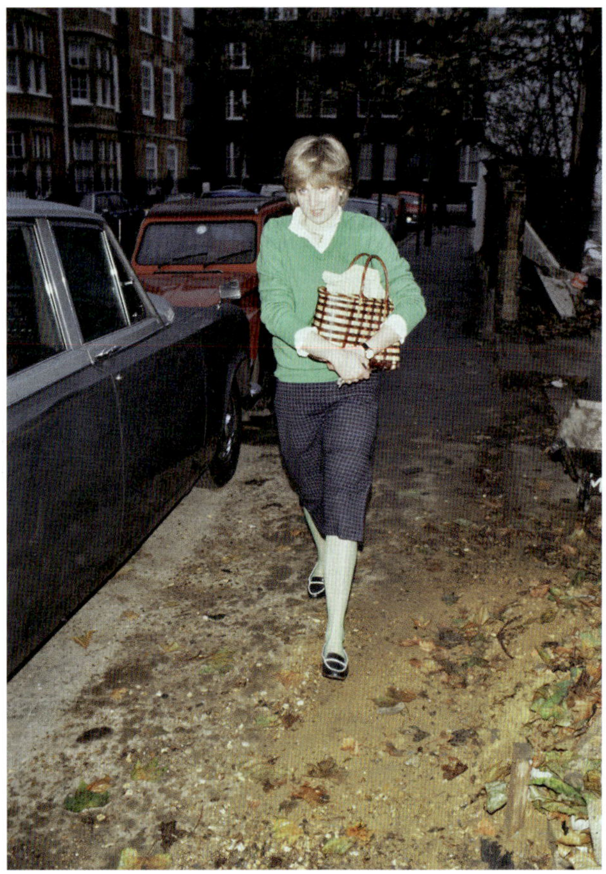

ANONYMOUS
(Bettmann Collection)
Lady Diana Spencer
Walking in Kensington, London
November 22, 1980

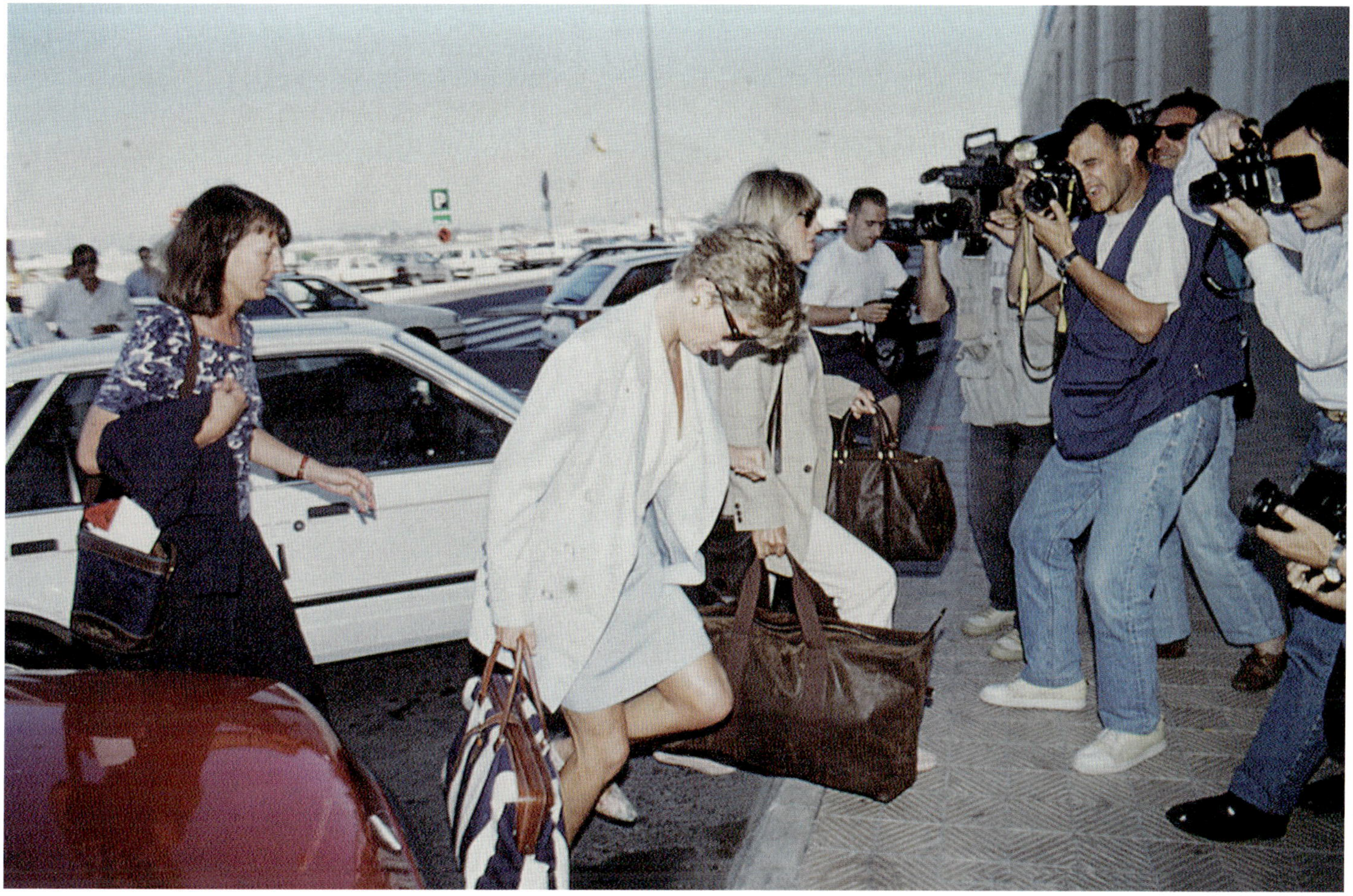

DUSKO DESPOTOVIC
Princess Diana in Malaga
May 2, 1994

PARIS

Paris Hilton gained international notoriety with the 2004 Internet release of a sextape depicting her *in flagrante delicto* with her companion of the moment. Her ex-boyfriend had sold the video and she brought legal action, obtaining 400,000 dollars in damages and interest, but also—no mean feat—a percentage of the profits! The video received several adult video awards, including one for “Best-Selling Video of the Year” and “Best Promotional Campaign—Individual Project.” Paris Hilton is an archetypal figure. She is a public personality, embroiled in numerous legal tangles, with a deep interest in media coverage. She has created her own website and Twitter account, defying the traditional boundaries between the public and private spheres. The case of Paris Hilton is symptomatic of a new era in media iconography. Images of this young woman are no longer confined to the printed press. They are omnipresent on multiple blogs, demonstrating the growing role of the Internet and amateur photographers in the distribution of celebrity images.

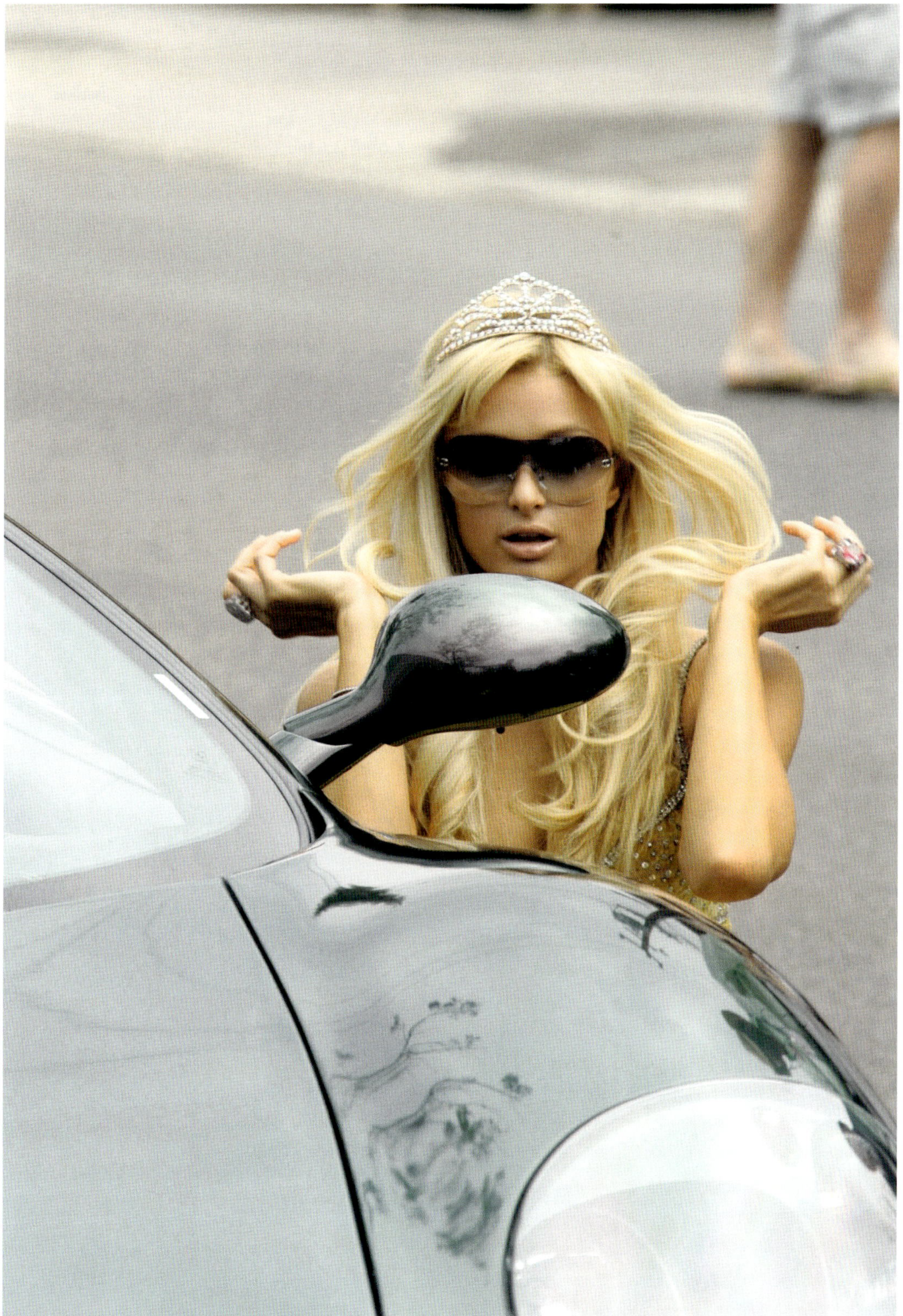

JIM SMEAL
(BEImages)
Paris Hilton at the Gay Pride Parade, West Hollywood, Los Angeles
June 12, 2005

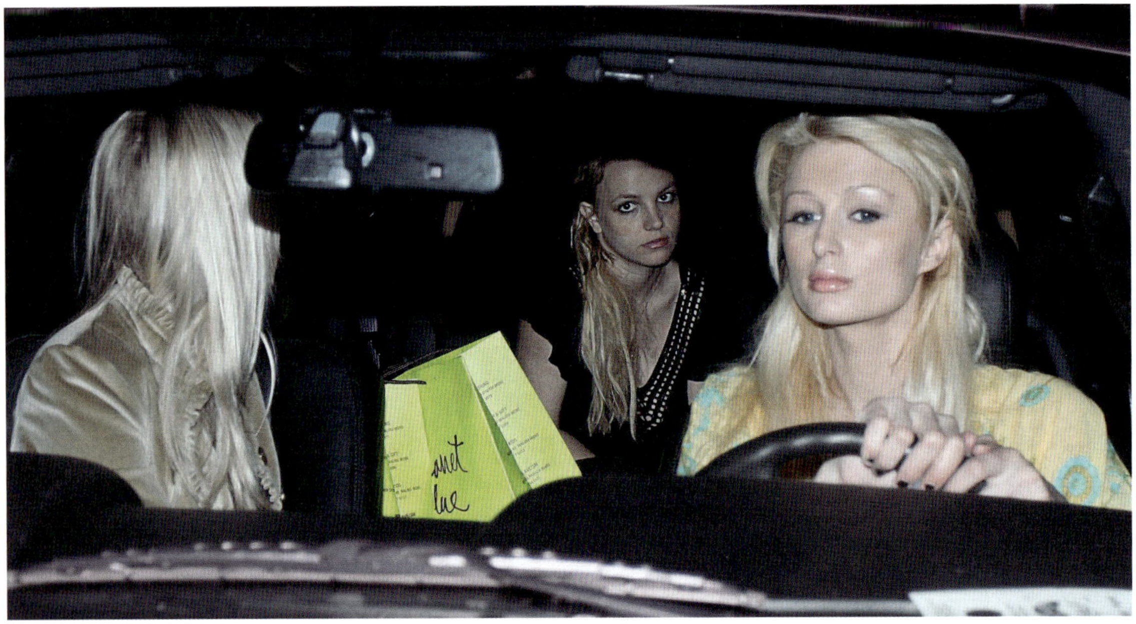

SÉBASTIEN VALIELA
Paris Hilton and Britney Spears Shopping
November 26, 2006

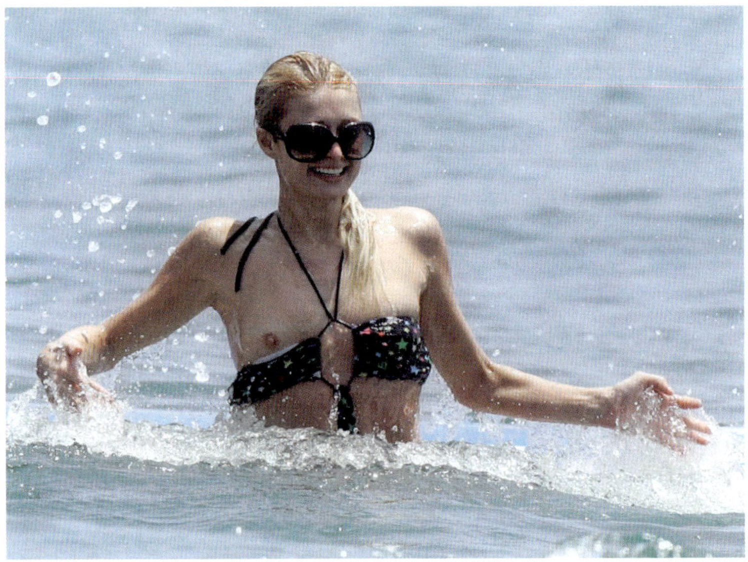

ANONYMOUS
Paris Hilton in a Bikini, Malibu
July 16, 2007

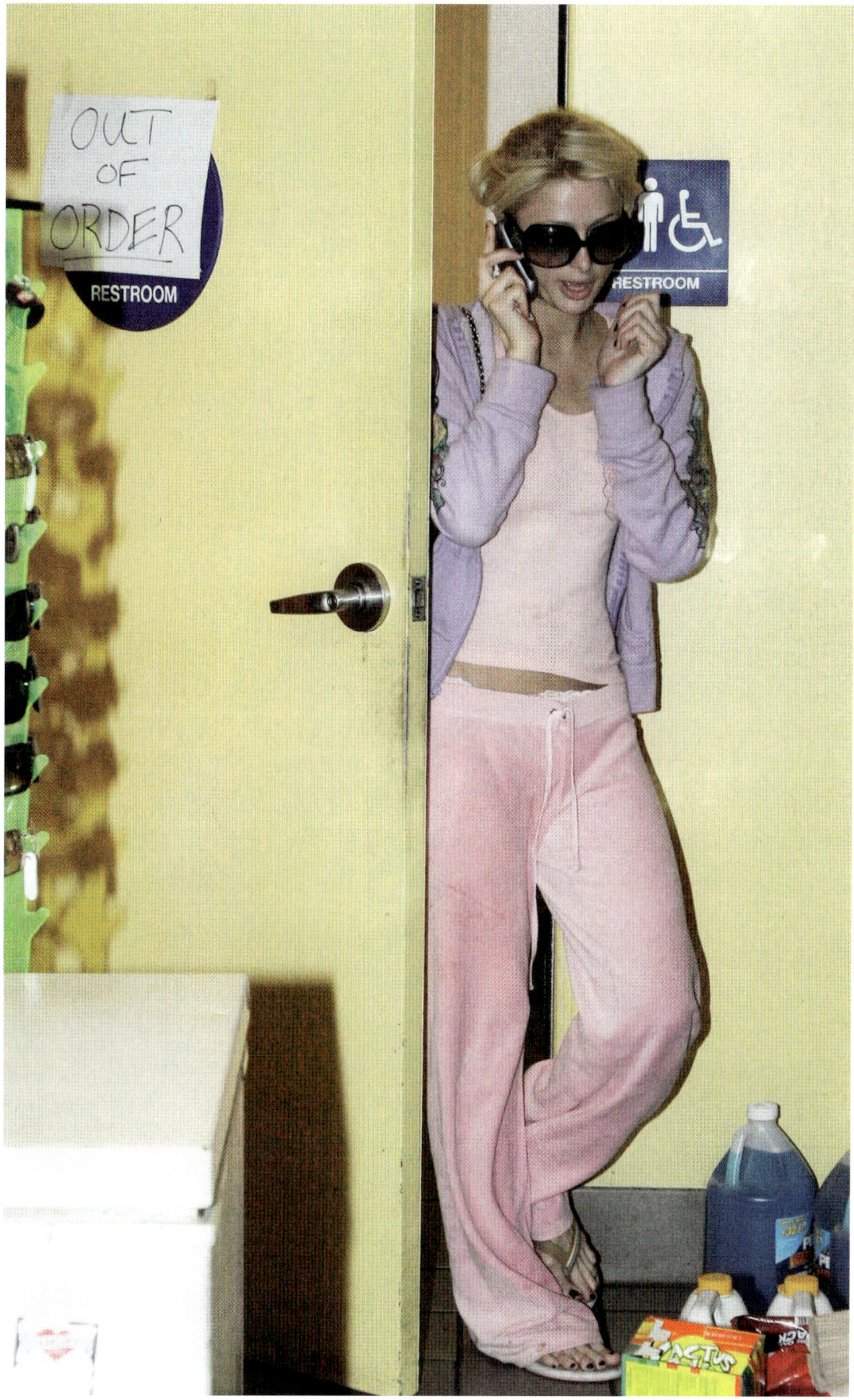

SÉBASTIEN VALIELA
Paris Hilton Out of Order
November 27, 2006

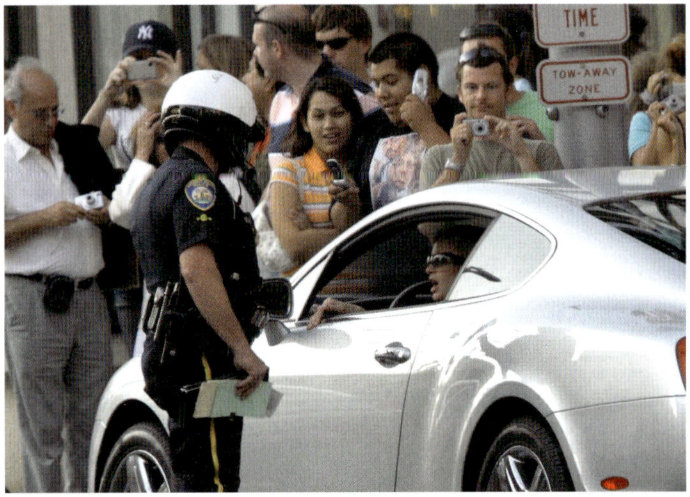

SÉBASTIEN VALIELA AND JULIEN DOORNAERT
Paris Hilton Arrested for Speeding
September 20, 2005

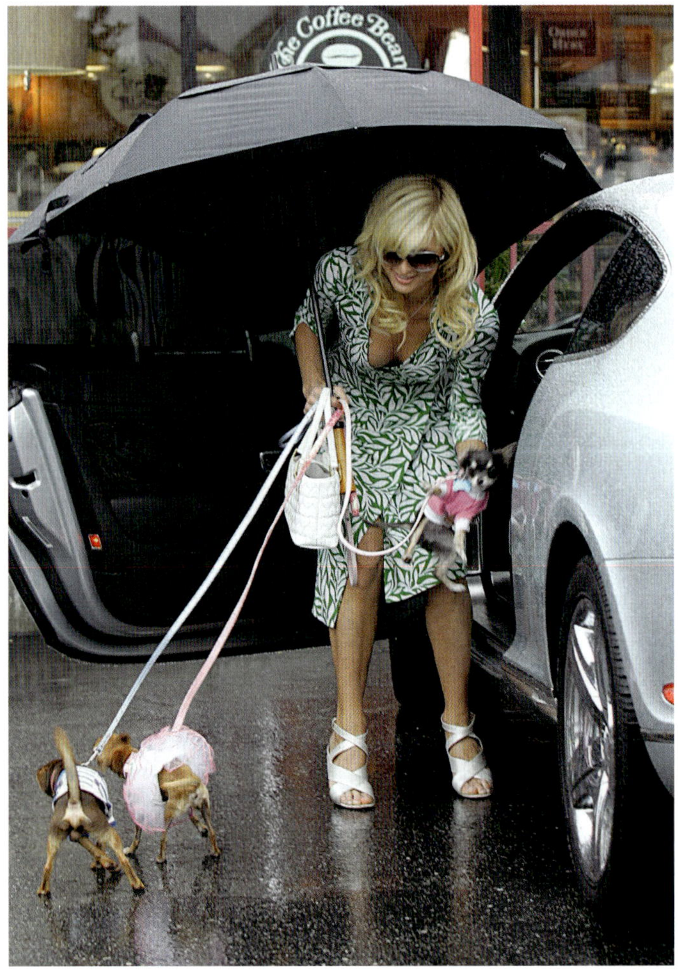

SÉBASTIEN VALIELA
Paris Hilton during the Shooting of the Fourth Season of the TV Show The Simple Life
February 27, 2006

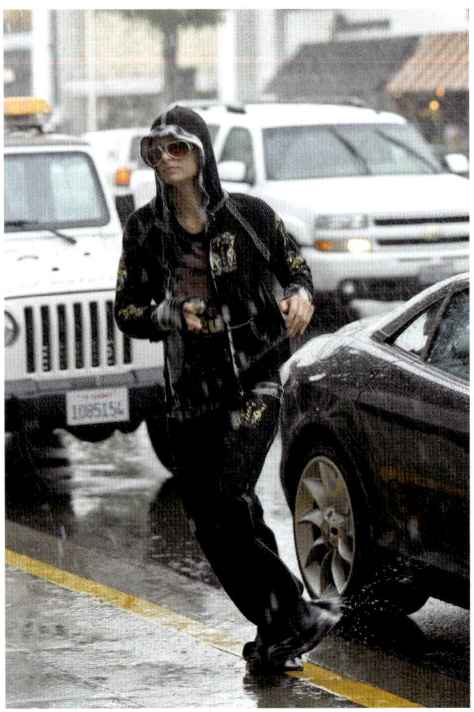

SÉBASTIEN VALIELA AND VINCENT LEPRESLE
Paris Hilton Running in the Rain
April 5, 2006

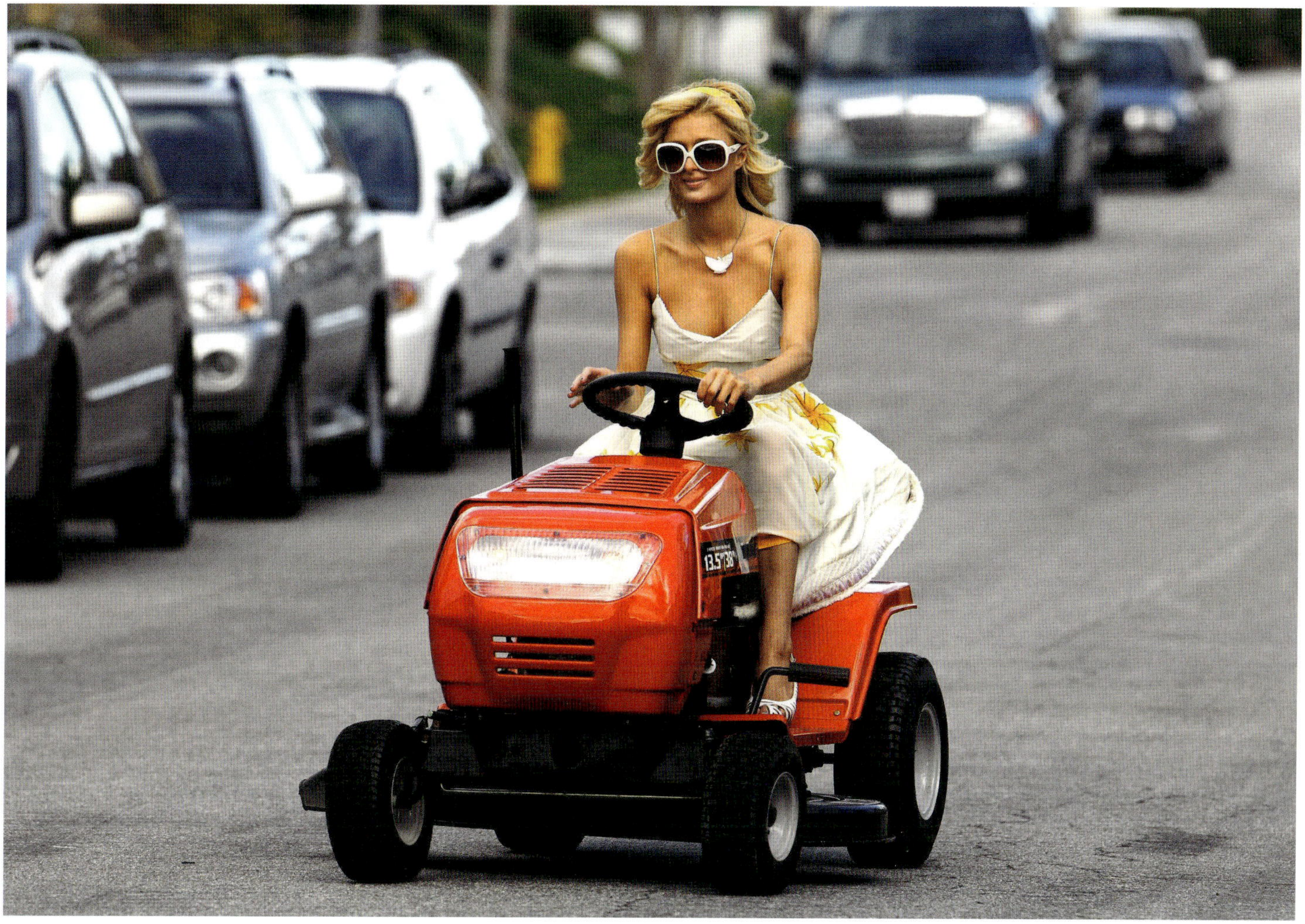

SÉBASTIEN VALIELA
Paris Hilton on a Lawn Mower
March 21, 2006

Britney

Britney Spears was undergoing a personal crisis at the end of 2006, and every detail was on display for the paparazzi. She had already opened the floodgates. In 2005, she had willingly participated in a television reality show that followed her daily routine. In 2007, she drove her Mercedes over a paparazzo's foot. He sued for $220,000 in damages before auctioning his sock, which bore those distinctive tire marks, on eBay. The fetishism surrounding Britney Spears was nothing new. The owner of the hair salon where she had her head shaved had sold her hair on the same website. This is an interesting case where the paparazzo, generally perceived as the aggressor, becomes the victim. Following an out-of-court settlement, Britney Spears paid him a substantial amount of money. It was a reminder of the good old days of the 1950s and 1960s, when the photographer found himself in the foreground, an actor in his own right. Britney Spears has also made the paparazzo a central figure in her songs and videos. In her 2007 hit "Piece of Me," she sang about the omnipresence of paparazzi in her life.

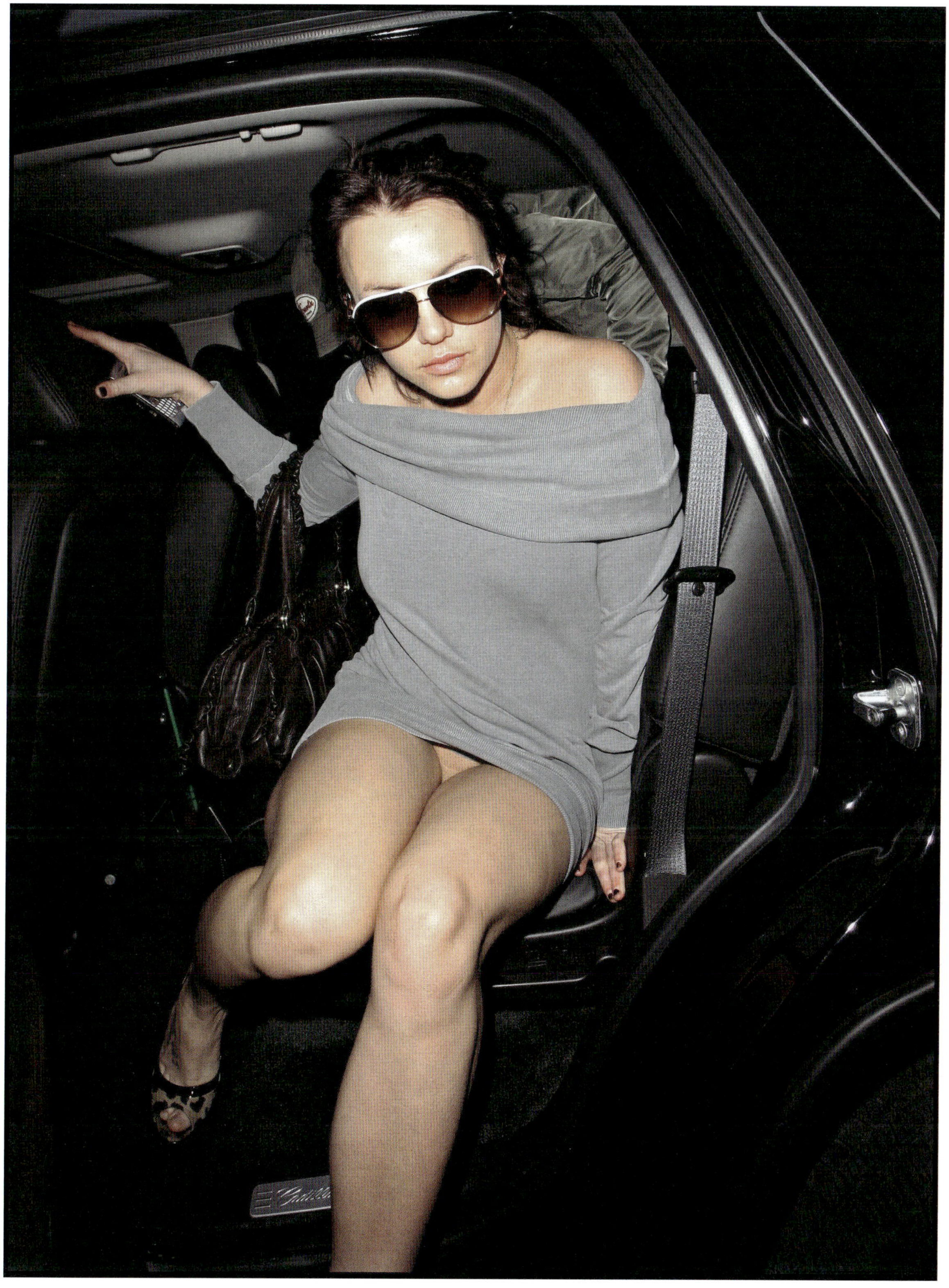

ANONYMOUS
Britney Spears with No Panties
February 19, 2008

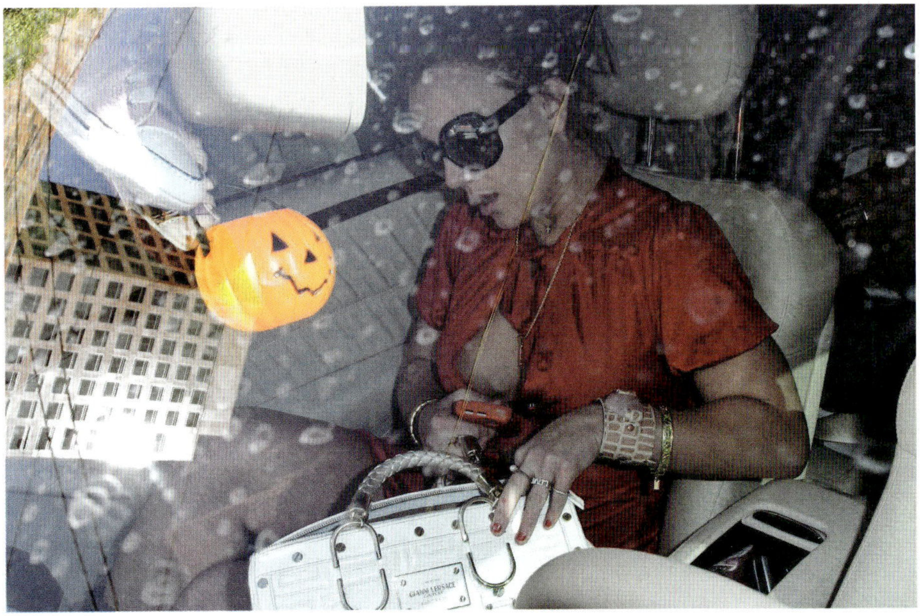

SÉBASTIEN VALIELA
Britney Spears Decides to Go Shopping
October 10, 2007

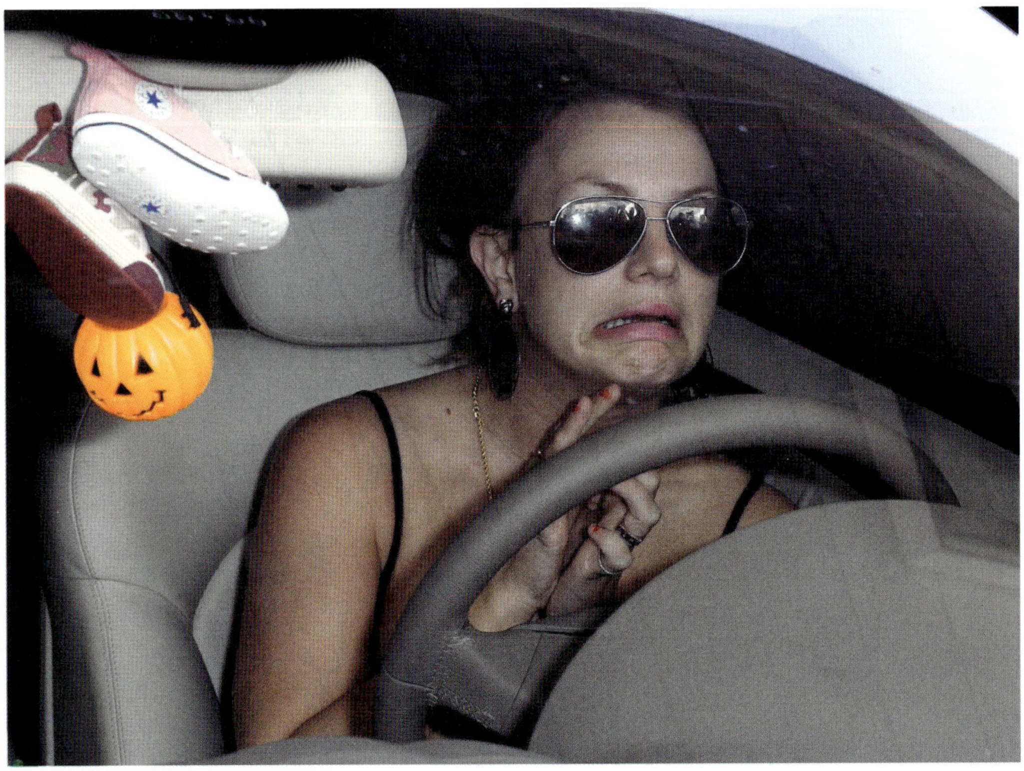

SÉBASTIEN VALIELA
Britney Spears Pulls a Face while We Take Photographs
October 12, 2007

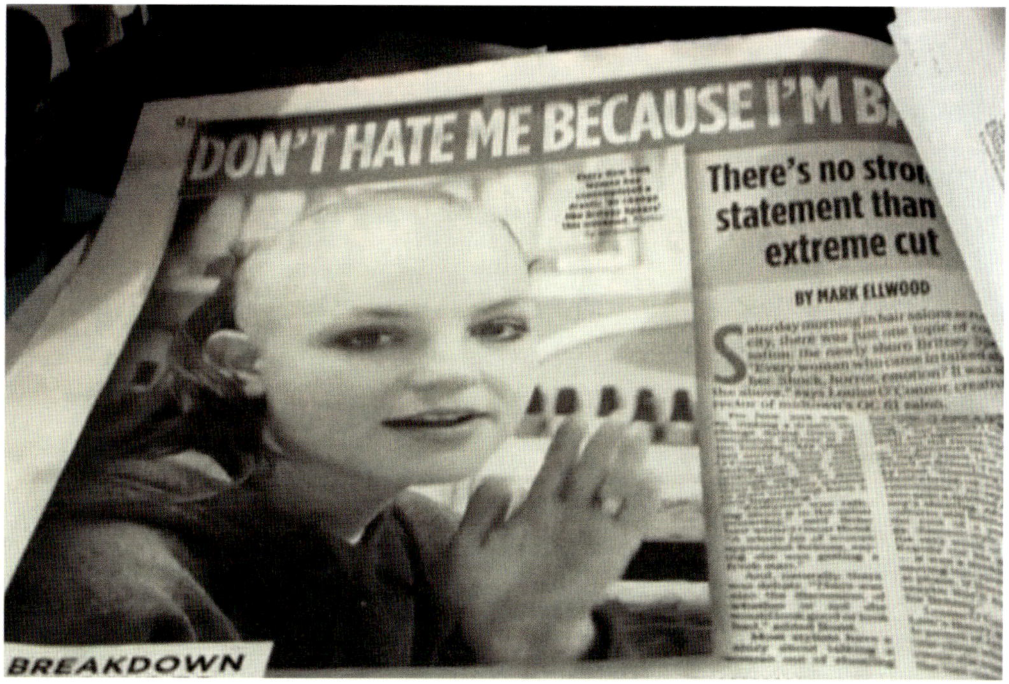

JONAS MEKAS
Shaving Her Head, from the series
365 Day Project
February 21, 2007

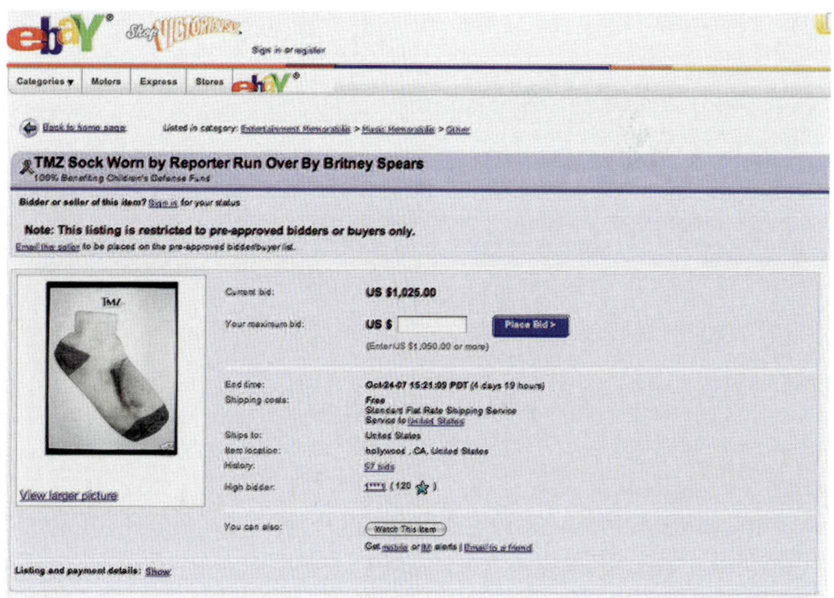

PHIL RAMEY AND
SÉBASTIEN VALIELA
Paparazzo Phil Ramey's
Sock, Driven Over
by Britney Spears,
for Sale on eBay
October 19, 2007

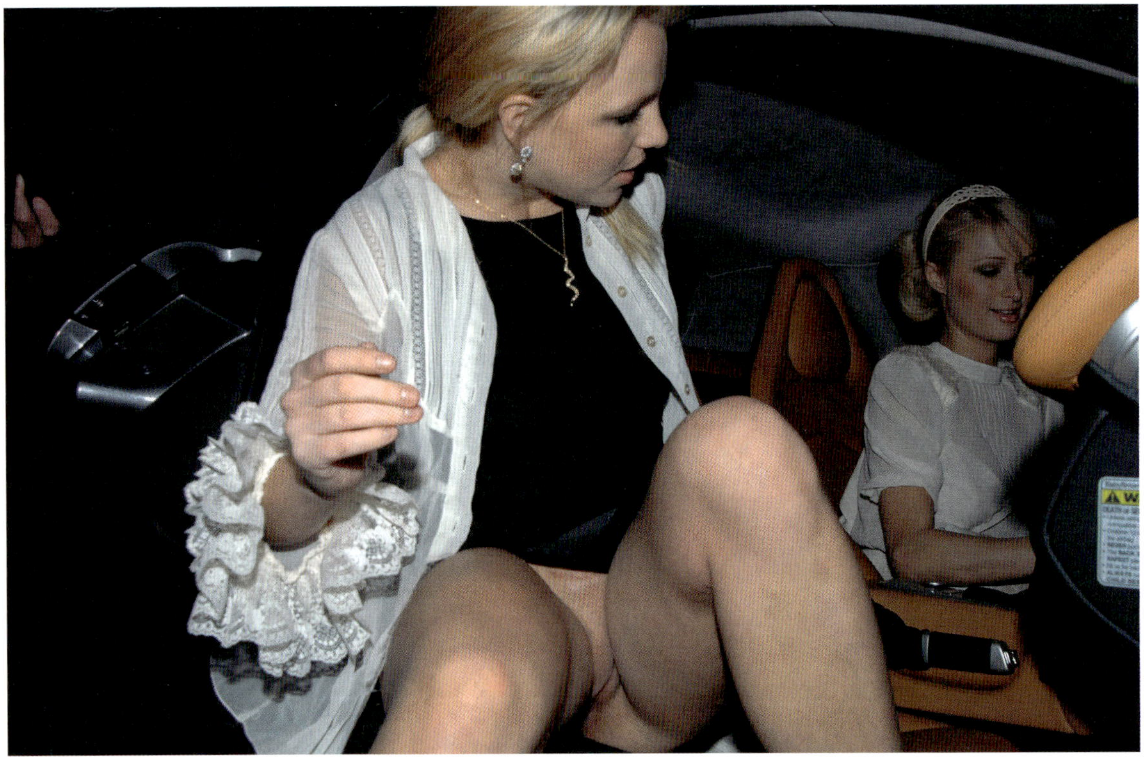

ANONYMOUS
Britney Spears with No Panties
2008

The origin of the world. A single image that was mass distributed in the press and on the web exemplified Britney Spears's period of crisis: the notorious shot of the star exiting her car, wearing a miniskirt, sans underpants. The paparazzi now circulated an image that was the antithesis of what the star had formerly stood for. She had built her success, at least partially, on her supposed virginity in the context of a puritanical American society. When she lost custody of her children, her former persona of nurturing mother morphed into that of a lascivious seductress. This was not the first time her image had shifted. Back in 2001, she had tried to transform herself, releasing an album with overtly sexual content. The shots of the singer without her panties became ubiquitous, liberally reproduced and quoted by artists. The images these artists created vacillated between echoes of high culture—the reference to Gustave Courbet's famous painting *The Origin of the World* is clear enough—and the pornographic vocabulary so prevalent on the web.

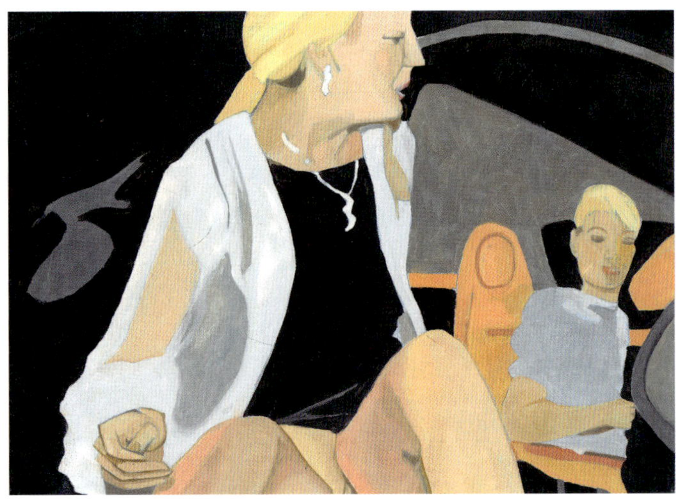

JEREMIAH PALECEK
Britney Spears Upskirt
2008

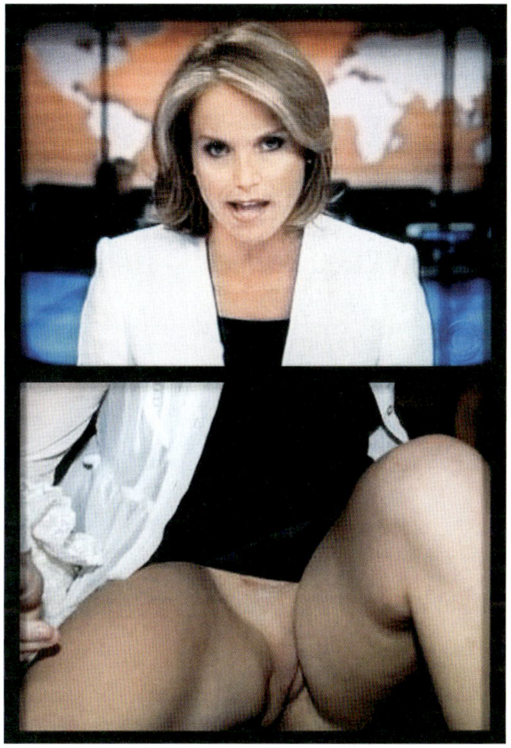

JONATHAN HOROWITZ
CBS Evening News/
www.britneycrotch.org
2008

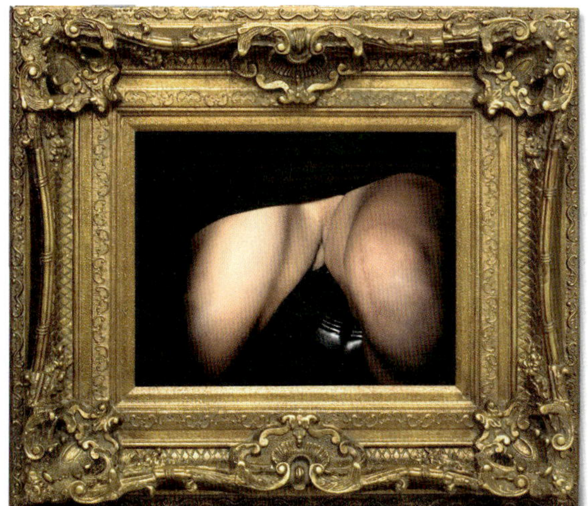

ALICIA ROSS
The Origin of the World
(Britney)
2010

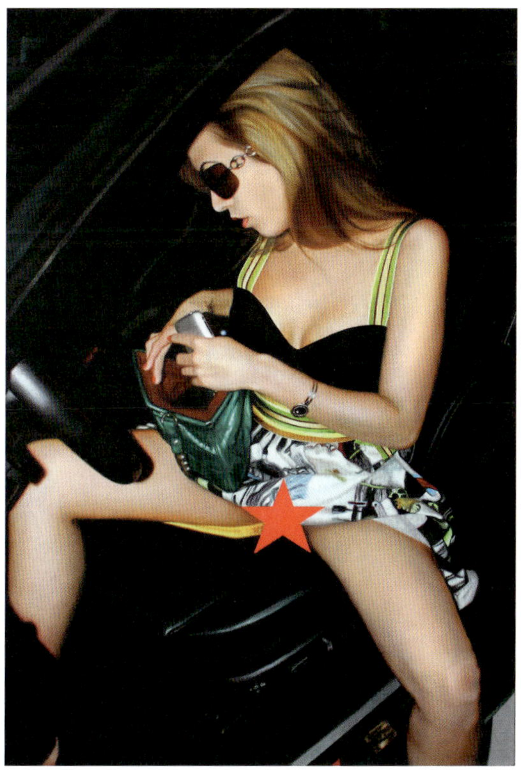

JACLYN SANTOS
Super Star
2009

BEHIND THE SCENES

Stars do not always allow themselves to be passive victims when confronted with the intrusive lenses of the paparazzi. When spotted by these stalkers, celebrities have the option of cooperating and allowing themselves to be photographed or adopting the reverse tactic of evasive action. Their responses may range from a simple polite refusal to outright aggression. Some develop their own tricks and strategies to elude the "star system" that condemns them to live perpetually in the limelight. This chapter reveals photographs by the twentieth century's most famed paparazzi: Erich Salomon, Weegee, Marcello Geppetti, Tazio Secchiaroli, Sébastien Valiela, Daniel Angeli, Ron Galella, Francis Apesteguy, Bruno Mouron, and Pascal Rostain, among others. The photos demonstrate the wide range of reactions from celebrities when faced with these photographers.

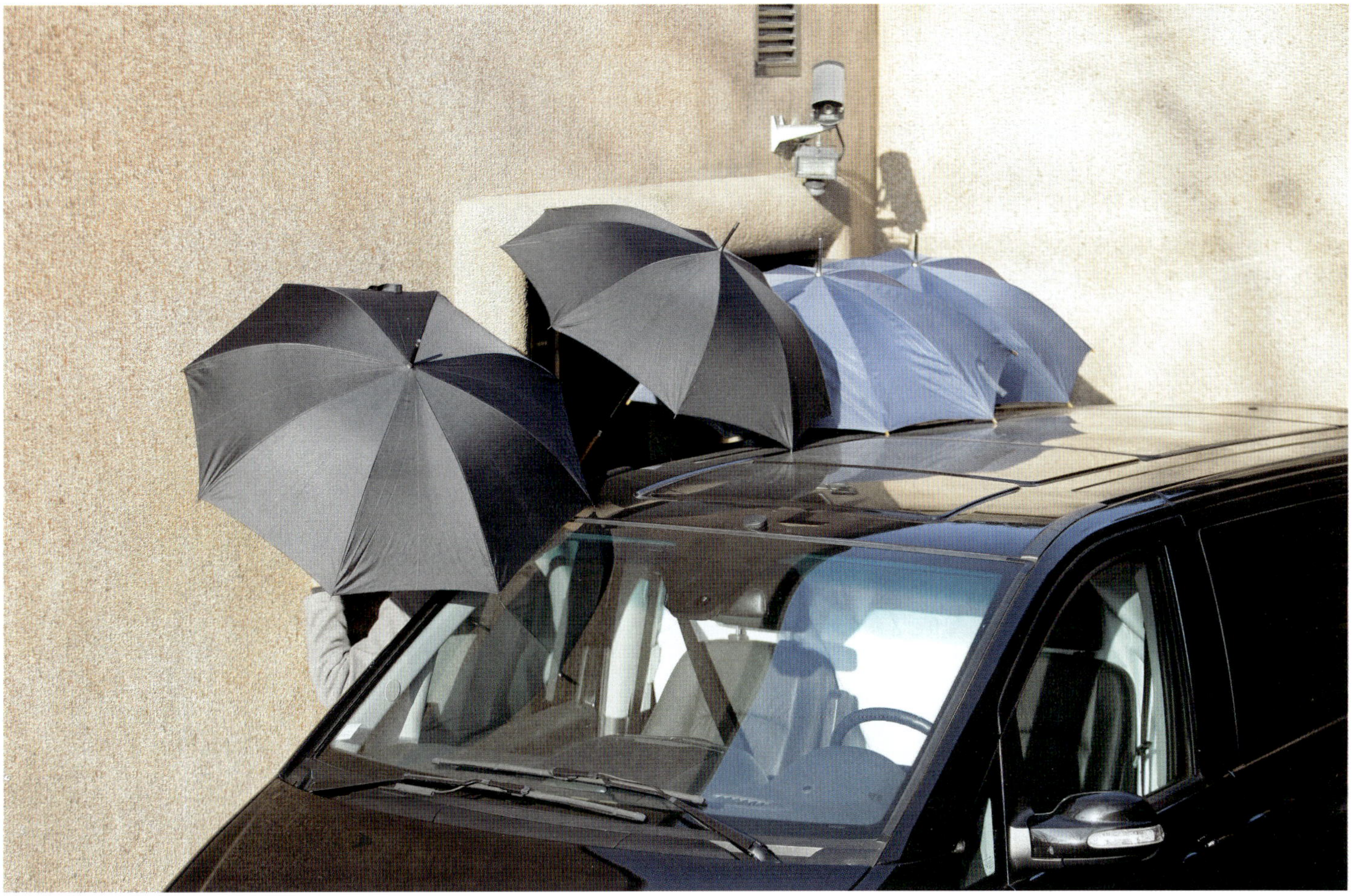

PHILIPPE BLET
Brangelina (Brad Pitt and Angelina Jolie) in Paris
2010

The Rights of the "Photographers of Private Life"

Marion Varinot and Nicolas Maubert[1]

"Liberty has limits that are imposed by justice."
—Jules Renard

Paparazzi are not like other photographers. Indeed, the work of these "photographers of private life" touches on fundamental and contradictory questions, whichever the applicable legal system. On the one hand, there is a need for the private sphere of those who are unwittingly photographed to be respected, and, on the other, the need for information to be disseminated by a free press. The legislature and the courts, according to different criteria depending on the country, establish a delicate balance between these fundamental social freedoms. In Anglo-Saxon legal systems, the penalties incurred by the paparazzi or the press—when these practices are condemnable, which is not always the case—may include punitive damages, whose primary purpose is to severely penalize the guilty party. France, on the contrary, which condemns fairly systematically those who infringe image rights and/or the right to privacy, does not recognize punitive damages on the grounds that the penalty should have for sole purpose to repair the damage actually suffered by the victim. Thus, the frequent convictions of celebrity magazines rarely result in the allocation of large sums in France.

At a time when there are more and more paparazzi, and information and images are instantly disseminated, the rules governing the rights and freedoms of the individual must be precisely defined. In France, judges' protection of privacy leads to the internationalization of legal disputes, as many celebrities choose the French courts for the redress of injury subsequent to the publication of photographs also published in other jurisdictions offering fewer guarantees for the protection of privacy. This essay aims to present the current legal framework applicable to paparazzi photographers in France.

***

Paparazzi in the Eyes of the Law

The law, a true mirror of our society, generally reflects sociological developments. Although the French legal system strives to protect private life and an individual's image rights, it is disturbing to observe the growing quantity of headlines and websites devoted to celebrity topics. These publications largely derive their success from stealthily captured photographs, although some of these shots may simply be the product of set pieces craftily staged with the willing complicity of their subjects.

Whatever the case, the practices of the paparazzi are frequently denounced. Consider the numerous debates spurred by the circumstances surrounding the death of Princess Diana. In this case, the paparazzi were potentially implicated in a French criminal investigation, although the case was eventually dismissed. In the collective imagination, paparazzi remain closely associated with activities that are underhand, verging on the illegal. Armed with zooms and telephoto lenses, these photographers can impose themselves in the private lives of celebrities. It is thus no surprise that the law frowns upon the profession. Its practitioners, at least in France, often operate "underground."

A Paparazzo Is No Ordinary Photographer . . .

Under French law, a photograph constitutes a work of intellectual property protected by copyright law so long as it presents material of an original nature. Until 1985, only photographs of an artistic or documentary type were recognized as achieving the status of

1. Attorneys-at-law with the firm Rivedroit. The authors wish to thank Agathe Michel for her invaluable research.

2. Cour de cassation, 1st civil chamber, [October 20, 2011], 10-21.251.

3. Cour d'appel de Paris, [November 26, 2008], 07/99.57.

4. In this domain, the judges have ruled that "it is unimportant that these shots are intended to provide an image of an athletic, political, or cultural event or that they were taken on the spot, so long as the choices made by the photographer bear the distinctive mark of his artistic eye and are representative of his initiative and intentions" (Cour d'appel de Paris, February 26, 2010).

5. Cour d'appel de Paris, [December 5, 2007], 06/15.937.

6. Cour d'appel de Paris, [February 24, 2012], 10/10.583.

intellectual property works. The law of July 3, 1985 eliminated this condition: henceforth, all types of photograph could qualify as protected work so long as they were characterized by a certain degree of originality. Originality is the necessary and determining condition: without it, the photographer cannot claim copyright protection. Originality is a subjective concept that judges evaluate on a case-by-case basis.

In order to assess originality, judges rely on a variety of indicators to verify whether the personality of the photographer is expressed in the photos. The term generally used is the "the imprint of the artist's personality." The criteria most frequently employed are the choice of pose, the point of view, the framing, the play of light and shadow, the selection of clothing and accessories, the facial expression, the subject's surroundings, the timing of the shot, the quality of the contrasts of color and depth, the choice of a printing technique adapted to the effective expression of the intended style, etc. In addition, recognition of the work's originality hinges on the degree of the photographer's personal involvement, as well as his freedom in executing his photographs, and his range of choice with regard to subjects and their compositional possibilities. A photographer who limits himself to merely developing technical expertise is therefore regarded as a technician and not as a creative artist.

The Supreme Court in France (Cour de cassation) has already dismissed the case of a professional photographer who laid claim to the status of a creative artist for a photograph depicting two red mullets on a plate. (This photograph had been partially reproduced, without his permission, in both a magazine and on an advertising poster.) The court ruled that "the photograph in question does not exhibit any aesthetic effort in the various elements of its composition, and represents no more than the simple provision of a technical service that does not translate into genuine professional expertise."[2]

In the realm of documentary photography, judges have recognized the artistic originality of photographs representing the blossoming of a flower.[3] The courts generally consider that photojournalists (whatever their status) have copyright privileges on their work.[4] Finally, fashion and advertising photographs featuring celebrities and models quite consistently benefit from protection under copyright law. Patrick Demarchelier, Mario Testino, and Peter Lindbergh—to cite a few examples—inarguably benefit from the status of creative artist when they photograph familiar stars in their own distinctive styles.

Ultimately, the criterion of originality appears to be an eminently subjective judgment in the realm of press photography. It remains subject to the court's own discretion, leaving considerable uncertainty as to the legal outcome from one photograph to another. An informed eye can discern without much difficulty "the brushstroke" that distinguishes the work of one painter from another, expressing his artistic personality. However, identifying creativity in a press photograph is a more delicate matter.

While paparazzi may occasionally be compared to photojournalists and benefit from the status of creative artist, judges generally refuse to recognize any originality in their work, depriving them of the protection conveyed by copyright. The terms employed by the courts in rejecting the protected status of copyright are often without the right of appeal. In 2007, the Paris Court of Appeals (Cour d'appel de Paris) ruled on a case that had been brought regarding photographs showing Prince William and Kate Middleton. These shots showed the couple "using telemark skis side by side with one hand on the axial bar of the apparatus and the other holding their ski poles."[5] The judges deemed that the disputed photographs were limited to depicting "a very commonplace scene and do not display the photographer's artistic sensibility or his professional competence." Furthermore, the court of appeals deemed that these photographs did not demonstrate "any selection of point of view, and still less any choice of timing. The photographs in question were taken at the moment when [the photographers] deployed their equipment; their activity was solely dictated by the momentary appearance of the individuals targeted for a photo." (In this regard, the judges noted that the paparazzo had used the technique of continuous high speed or "burst" photography.) The timing of the shot and the point of view were dictated primarily by the momentary appearance of the individuals targeted. The judges refused to consider that the paparazzo had exercised any personal discretion, even deeming that "the photographer's conduct was purely passive, typical of the behavior of all paparazzi when on the lookout for a shot, and had nothing to do with any concept of composition." The same fate is reserved for photographs taken at sporting events using the "burst" technique. In a ruling dated February 24, 2012,[6] the Paris Court of Appeals refused to recognize any originality whatsoever in several photographs taken during soccer and tennis tournaments, including most prominently a shot of soccer

7. Tribunal de grande instance de Paris, [June 2, 2004], M. Bensalah vs. L. Delahaye Magnum, Éditions Phaidon Presse Limited and SA Mk2.

8. Law no. 70-643 of July 17, 1970 – art. 22 JORF July 19, 1970.

player Zinedine Zidane, who had actually posed for the photographer.

These decisions clearly demonstrate a harsh attitude with regard to the work of sports photographers and paparazzi. The courts refuse to acknowledge any originality in their work, although they base these judgments on criteria that are actually quite vague. Does a photographer really behave in a "purely passive" manner when he watchfully aims his lens from his hideout? He carefully selects this discreetly located site to target the subject but also chooses it for the background and lighting effects it offers. Surely a photographer is engaged in planning the setting for the subject when he meticulously plots the photo's framing, selecting which lens to use and setting the exposure time. Does the ephemeral appearance of the subject imply a complete absence of originality in the work? Would a judge adopt the same attitude toward a nature photographer who finally succeeds, after a lengthy vigil, in capturing a hummingbird about to dip its beak deep into the corolla of a flower? Such a judicial ruling seems highly unlikely.

It is interesting to note that, even without the protection afforded by copyright, a number of paparazzi photographs have fetched several thousand euros in the marketplace. Admittedly, the asking price for these transactions seems to have dropped considerably (largely due to the advent of smartphones and their users, who do their own paparazzi improvisations when they chance to encounter a celebrity). However, a number of shots have commanded top prices quite recently. For example, according to the French magazine *Entrevue* (no. 219, October 2010), photos of Prince Albert of Monaco in the company of his illegitimate son earned 250,000 euros for the photographer at the time. Wedding photos of basketball player Tony Parker and actress Eva Longoria apparently sold for over 100,000 euros, and shots of French journalist Laurence Ferrari and violinist Renaud Capuçon brought in over 70,000 euros in July 2009. Obviously, if press groups are prepared to pay such sums for these photos, it is because these shots are the sine qua non for the commercial success of their publications. The paparazzi thus depend on the press groups that buy their shots, while these press groups cannot hope to succeed without the collaboration of the paparazzi. This interdependence is clearly an essential factor in the competitive and relentless escalation of photographic intrusion into the private lives of celebrities.

Although a paparazzo does not generally view his photos as elevated to the rank of an original work, an artist who derives inspiration from the "paparazzi aesthetic" (blurry effects, subjects making protective gestures showing their reluctance to be photographed, etc.) do benefit from the protection of copyright. This ruling holds true not only for artists who give the false impression of shooting "stolen" photographs, when their shots are actually produced from meticulously studied poses—Helmut Newton embraced this approach in his era—but it has also been applied to some photographs actually taken without the subject's knowledge. For example, in 1999, the photographer Luc Delahaye from the Magnum agency published ninety photographs of anonymous individuals whom he had secretly photographed in a collection entitled *L'Autre*. The Paris District Court (Tribunal de grande instance) ruled that this opus was "incontestably an artistic work by virtue of the originality of the artist's intention, a photographer putting his artistic skills at the service of sociological observation,… the manner in which he has been able to convey the expression of his subjects and the quality of the images is owed in part to the way he has framed their figures and captured their gaze."[7] In other words, when a "full-fledged" artist entertains himself by playing the role of a paparazzo, judges include the work in the category of intellectual property and grant the photos the protection conferred by copyright. This differentiated treatment seems to simply reflect the negative image surrounding paparazzi. The majority of observers (including those who read the celebrity press!) consider them to be "thieves of images and intimacy."

… Because Paparazzi Intrude Into Private Lives …

In France, the laws regarding the right to privacy protect all individuals against any intrusion into private life. Endorsed by French legislation in 1970 in Article 9 of the Civil Code,[8] the law on respect for privacy applies to all individuals, whatever their social status, origins, or functions they exercise in society. The concept of private life embraces both its non-financial aspects (information regarding an individual's private concerns, family life, love interests, image, or state of health) and its financial aspects (information regarding a person's financial situation). An infringement of an individual's image rights may result in penalties that are distinct from those resulting from an infringement of rights to personal privacy. This right is absolute and applicable to all individuals, including public figures, independently of any intrusion into their private lives. The mere fact that an image of an individual has been reproduced without consent, regardless of the facts that may justify such an act, potentially gives the right to compensation.

An individual's right to privacy is extinguished with his death, and it is not transferable because of death. Heirs or relatives cannot in principle request damages for any attack on the private life of the deceased. Such a claim can only be based upon protecting the memory of the deceased or the privacy of his immediate family circle.[9] The publication by *Paris Match* of a photograph of François Mitterrand on his deathbed led to the lodging of a complaint by Danielle Mitterrand and his children. In a ruling of October 20, 1998,[10] the Supreme Court upheld the conviction of the editor of the magazine *Paris Match* for the crime of intrusion into private life of a third party, ruling that "the act of taking photographs of someone's mortal remains is indisputably an invasion of another's privacy, and violates the respect that is due to a human being, whether living or dead, and whatever the individual's status." Regarding a photograph of the French film actor Jean Gabin on his deathbed, the civil judge adopted the same position, ruling that "no one may, without the consent of the family, reproduce and make public the features of a person on his deathbed, however great the celebrity of the deceased."[11]

The distinction between private and public life has given rise to an abundance of case law whose nuances are sometimes difficult to grasp. In fact, there is no decisive boundary between the two concepts, and rulings in this area are frequently contradictory. Furthermore, this distinction has been subject to diverging interpretations between civil and criminal jurisdictions. The "invasion of the privacy of another" does indeed constitute a violation based on the terms of Article 226-1 2 of the Criminal Code, but the criminal concept of an "invasion of privacy" is far more restrictive than an infringement on private life as recognized by the Civil Code. In this regard, the criminal chamber of the Supreme Court has permitted the release of three photographs that were claimed to represent an invasion of private life. The case concerned photographs of Princess Diana and her companion Dodi Al-Fayed, pictured in a vehicle at the exit of the Hôtel Ritz Paris shortly before the accident that took their lives. In this case, Mohamed Al-Fayed, Dodi's father, brought the case and was recognized as the plaintiff. In its decision of April 12, 2005,[12] the Supreme Court ruled that even if these pictures had been taken inside a private space (in this case the vehicle), they showed no behavior that could be associated with the private sphere of the lives of those concerned.[13] Furthermore, the criminal court judges qualified as private only a space that was open to no one without the permission of those occupying it. This is not the case for a house of worship; the publication of photographs taken during the marriage of singer Patrick Bruel in a public ceremony held in a synagogue does not therefore constitute the crime of invading the privacy of the married couple.[14] These criminal court rulings clearly explain why most victims prefer to initiate an action before civil courts rather than take their case to criminal authorities.

Civil courts do not limit themselves to basing decisions on this dichotomy between private space and public space when characterizing an invasion of privacy. In addition to consistently condemning the publication of photographs taken in private spaces (interpreted in the broad sense of the term), they also condemn the use of an image representing a person within a public space if the image's setting infringes upon the individual's peace of mind. Thus, an invasion of privacy was deemed to have occurred when photographs of the son of French journalists Claire Chazal and Patrick Poivre d'Arvor were taken with a telephoto lens during a tennis tournament, without his knowledge. These shots were accompanied by captions related to the private life of those concerned.[15] The same reasoning applies to individuals who are not celebrities. The Supreme Court of Appeals has already recognized that the publication of photographs taken in the street (a public place) represented an invasion of the privacy of several young women. In this case, the subjects were easily identifiable, in poses that are typical of prostitutes. The court ruled that these images made public the prostitution in which these women were engaged, whereas their personal contacts or neighbors might be unaware of the existence of these activities.[16] In conclusion, the fact that the pictures were taken in a public place, i.e., a place where a person is exposed to the view of others, does not justify the publication of these images.

Every individual has the right to privacy and to their image rights, and is entitled to obtain protection for those rights. People can establish their own limits for what may be published. The issue at stake is whether consent has been given by the party concerned for the publication of a certain photograph or information. With regard to the right to privacy, it has been held that any prior

9. The same holds true for the right to an image. Recently the Paris District Court convicted a well-known jeweler on the Place Vendôme for using a photo of violinist Mstislav Rostropovitch, who died in 2007, in an advertising campaign. (The case was brought by the musician's heirs.) In this instance, the dignity of the deceased had not been impugned, but the judges ruled that the company had erred in "appropriating the image of Mstislav Rostropovitch for its own purely commercial purposes, and had removed it from its historic context and deprived it of the meaning, import, and spirit of the message that a man of conviction and a great artist had wished to convey to the world." (Tribunal de grande instance de Paris, [March 14, 2012], 10/16.659).

10. Cour de cassation, criminal chamber, [October 20, 1998], 97-84.621.

11. Tribunal de grande instance de Paris, [January 11, 1977], JCP G 1977, II, 18711, obs. D. Ferrier; D. 1977, p. 83, note R. Lindon. – Confirmation on appeal, CA Paris, November 12, 1979: D. 1981, p. 72, note R. Lindon.

12. Cour de cassation, criminal chamber, [April 12, 2005], 04-85.637.

13. However, in this decision, the Cour de cassation recognized that the photographs were an infraction of civil law, representing an intrusion into Dodi Al-Fayed's private life without any consent on his part. See also Agathe Lepage, "Le Paparazzi et l'ami de la princesse," e-commerce communication no. 3, March 2008, comm. 43.

14. Cour de cassation, criminal chamber, [October 25, 2011], 11-80.266.

15. Cour de cassation, 2nd civil chamber, [March 18, 2004], 02-12.981.

16. Cour de cassation, 1st civil chamber, [September 18, 2008], 07-16.471.

17. Tribunal de grande instance de Paris, [June 17, 1998], Grimaldi vs. Hachette Filipacchi.

18. Cour d'appel de Versailles, [September 20, 2007], 06/05517.

19. Cour d'appel de Paris, [January 20, 1998], 96/16089.

20. Tribunal de grande instance de Nanterre, [December 20, 2000], C. Chazal vs. Hachette Filipacchi.

21. Tribunal de grande instance de Nanterre, [March 14, 2000], M. Gauthier (known as Mylène Farmer) vs. Hachette Filipacchi et associés.

22. Cour de cassation, 1st civil chamber, [February 20, 2001], 98-23.471.

23. Tribunal de grande instance de Nanterre, [September 17, 2009], O. Bonamy.

acquiescence does not justify a subsequent invasion of privacy. For example, just because a person confides his romantic misadventures to the press on one occasion, he does not lose all protection for the secrets of his emotional life in the future.

An individual's right to privacy and his own image can be affected when another right or another freedom intervenes. Generally, it is not considered to be an invasion of privacy if the information divulged is routine or already public knowledge (even if it is of a private nature). Also, if there is a justification for revealing these facts that involves the public's interest, either by informing the public of a current event or making a contribution to a debate of issues in the public interest, the right to privacy is superseded by the right to freedom of information. However, confusion reigns over the notion of "public interest." The courts rule on a case-by-case basis whether there is a necessity to inform the public of one fact or another. Additionally, the right to an image may be superseded when the photograph is a relevant illustration of a current event, a general debate on various societal phenomena, or a historical topic.

In order to satisfy the public's legitimate need for information in matters of major importance in private life, an interesting decision was made in a case involving Princess Stéphanie of Monaco. "Although pregnancy generally represents an aspect of private life, it becomes a current event of which the public should be informed when the future mother belongs, as in this case, to a highly publicized royal family. Furthermore she has not tried to conceal her pregnancy since she has continued to make public appearances."[17] Similarly, it was judged that there was not an infringement of the right of Princess Stéphanie of Monaco to an image of her taken during the funeral services held for her father Prince Rainier. The court ruled that "these services were organized in the context of public life and reports on the figures who were in attendance, or not in attendance, represent information that the paper could legitimately bring to the attention of the public."[18] Conversely, certain events were deemed to be private in nature, raising no legitimate need for informing the public. These included the baptism of the children of Princess Stéphanie of Monaco,[19] the marriage of the journalist Claire Chazal,[20] and the burial of the brother of singer Mylène Farmer.[21]

In any case, even when the disputed information pertains to matters of general interest and the public's right to information, the images released must still respect the dignity of the individual. This is a prevailing value in our judicial system, but one that is very difficult to define precisely. On this point, judges have already refused to recognize an infringement of the dignity of an individual when the photographs of victims of terrorist attacks (RER B line at the Saint-Michel station in Paris in 1995 and the AZF factory in Toulouse in 2001) were published in the press. They ruled that there existed a legitimate right to information in these cases and that the disputed photographs had been devoid of sensationalism and indecency.[22]

Photographs taken by paparazzi are quite consistently held to be infringements of privacy under tort law. This is the case even when the party concerned may have decided to communicate details of his private life in the past.

... And the Exploitation of Paparazzi Photographs Is a Subject of Contention

Although the photographs taken by paparazzi are the source of a multitude of disputes, the actual photographers of these invasive shots are rarely challenged directly (unless their approach puts the life of the subject in danger, for example in the case of a car chase). The explanation is simple: it is not the taking of the photo that creates the disturbance but rather its publication and distribution at the instigation of scandalmongering press groups. In this case, the mere recognition of an invasion of privacy or a breach of image rights is enough to engage the responsibility of the magazine that was behind the publication of the photo in question. Once this responsibility has been recognized, the judge may order a variety of measures: seizure of the contested publication, judicial edicts, prohibition of publishing or republishing contested photographs, return of negatives (or destruction of digital files) and, of course, payment of damages. The French Civil Code does not provide any standard reference levels for financial penalties: the amount of fines varies considerably from one judge to another.

Regarding the objective criteria applied in these cases, the methods of distribution and the publication's content may both influence the assessment of the damages incurred. Judges consider the quantity of printings of contested magazines as well as the size of the publication's audience "that reinforce the impact of matters that the plaintiffs wish to keep within the protected sphere of their private lives."[23] A variety of factors pertaining to the actual conditions of the publication of the photos may also influence the assessment of the damages incurred. For example, the place given to the contested photograph in the publication (the visibility of the invasion of privacy is considerably greater if the photograph appears on the cover page), or the associated descriptive material pertaining to the subject's private life. Judges can take into account aggravating behavior, such as car pursuits or media harassment. They often refer to the methods used to capture "stolen photos"[24] or "stalking shots"[25] to raise the issue of aggravated damages. Similarly, the Paris District Court took into consideration the fact that the actress Virginie Efira was the victim of "constant surveillance ... that was so pervasive that the plaintiff had the sense of being constantly spied upon"[26] to evaluate the increase in damages awarded to her.

Among the subjective criteria used, judges review the victim's general comportment with the media to assess the degree of harm incurred; the plaintiff's conduct is not taken into account to determinine whether a civil crime has occurred, but only for setting the amount of the damages awarded. It is interesting to note one further point: the fact that a victim is not a famous person tends to increase the amount of damages and interest that are granted. Thus in a decision of August 29, 2012, the Paris District Court sentenced a magazine to pay 15,000 euros—a record amount for 2012—to a student whose photograph had been published on a magazine cover. (It was a photograph featuring the plaintiff next to a competitor in a television reality show at a nightclub.)[27] The judges based their decision on the fact that the plaintiff, who was completely unknown to the public, found herself on the cover and interior pages of a very widely distributed magazine. This exposure caused her significant harm. Similarly, the involuntary media exposure of a private person and her relationship with a celebrity may represent a case of aggravated harm. Thus we have seen a number of examples of companions of prominent individuals initiating legal actions against magazines that have published their photographs without permission, following the examples of cases brought by Madonna's companion or actress Laura Smet's boyfriend.[28]

Judges may also consider the victim's attitude toward the media to evaluate the harm incurred. For example, the Paris District Court noted the "particularly discreet attitude [of singer Jean-Jacques Goldman] regarding his private life. The defendant was fully aware of his feelings and mentioned the fact that he rarely granted interviews to the press in the disputed article." On this basis, the court ruled that the damages were aggravated.[29] The plaintiff's wish for privacy can also be determined if a vacation spot is selected because it is particularly distant and remote.[30] Judges assess the harm incurred based on an individual's explicitly expressed and repeated desire to avoid any commingling of his private and public lives. Thus the Nanterre District Court noted "the desire [of comedian Gad Elmaleh] to remain in control of what he intended to divulge to the public by the numerous proceedings he instigated ... demonstrating his opposition to any unauthorized intrusion into his private life."[31]

In contrast, a demonstrated tolerance for media exposure or a figure's cooperation can reduce the penalty incurred. In this context, the judges in Nanterre made reference to the numerous interviews granted by Patrick Bruel during which he conveyed "various and numerous aspects of his private life." They concluded that "the allusion, without his approval, to his emotional life and his presence in the Parc des Princes did not cause him the harm that a person who had never agreed to publications on his private life would have experienced."[32] At the extreme, they consider matters such as "the deliberate posting by the plaintiff [the notorious lingerie designer Zahia Dehar] of numerous photographs on the Internet, particularly on her Twitter account, where she exploits her image as a seductive young woman; this behavior is manifestly intended to attract the attention of the public and the media." This led the judges to reduce their assessment of alleged harm.[33]

An exhaustive analysis of the decisions handed down in 2012 by the district courts in Paris and Nanterre shows that compensation of victims for violations of their privacy rights and image is based on a form of reasoning that is difficult to pin down with precision. It is interesting to review the decisions handed down in 2012 by the 17th chamber of the Paris District Court in two cases pertaining to the same photographs. The two rulings resulted in the award of differing amounts of damages.[34] In this case, photographs taken of the entertainment personality and producer Nagui during his family vacation were published in two different magazines (which explains why the victim brought two court cases). In a decision of April 11, 2012, the victim received a payment of 6,000 euros in damages, while in a decision of August 29, 2012 he was awarded 2,000 euros. This disparity can be explained

24. Tribunal de grande instance de Nanterre, [April 5, 2012], 11/13842, M. Cotillard vs. SAS G.-K. Engineering.

25. Tribunal de grande instance de Paris, [September 21, 2009], 08/11635, A. Bent vs. SAS Mondadori Magazines France (publisher of *Closer*).

26. Tribunal de grande instance de Paris, [March 29, 2010], 09/08881, V. Efira vs. SNC Hachette Filipacchi associés (publisher of *Ici Paris*).

27. Tribunal de grande instance de Paris, [August 29, 2012], 11/16974, C. Couprie vs. SAS Mondadori Magazines France (publisher of *Closer*).

28. Tribunal de grande instance de Nanterre, [April 5, 2012], 11/11801, A. Alexandroff vs. SNC Prisma Presse (publisher of *Voici*).

29. Tribunal de grande instance de Paris, [March 29, 2010], 09/04020, J.-J. Goldman vs. SNC Prisma Presse (publisher of *Gala*).

30. Tribunal de grande instance de Paris, [September 21, 2009], 08/14737, M. Chedid, known as "M" vs. SNC Hachette Filipacchi associés (publisher of *Public*).

31. Tribunal de grande instance de Nanterre, [May 10, 2012], 12/02147, SNC Prisma Media (publisher of *Voici*) vs. G. Elmaleh.

32. Tribunal de grande instance de Nanterre, [February 16, 2012], 11/06965, P. Bruel vs. SAS Mondadori Magazines France associés (publisher of *Closer*).

33. Tribunal de grande instance de Nanterre, [January 5, 2012], 10/11654, Z. Dehar vs. SAS Mondadori Magazines France (publisher of *Closer*).

34. Tribunal de grande instance de Paris, [April 11, 2012], 11/12192, Nagui vs. SNC Prisma Presse (publisher of *Voici*), and no. 11/12193, August 29, 2012, Nagui vs. Société Hachette Filipacchi Associés (publisher of *Public*).

35. In *Les Dessous de la presse people* (Paris: Éditions de la Martinière, 2006).

by the fact that the company that produced the magazine cited in the decision of April 11, 2012 had already been sentenced fourteen times for having published photographs showing the victim. Despite these sentences, the said company "persist[ed] in ignoring the individual rights of the plaintiff, inevitably crea[ting] a sense of powerlessness, a factor further aggravating the harm incurred." These two decisions emphasize the relatively random nature of the means of evaluating the harm experienced by the plaintiff.

Over two hundred decisions were handed down during 2012 by lower courts in Nanterre and Paris in the area of infringements of image rights and the right to privacy. The amounts awarded by magistrates as damages in these cases were sometimes as minimal as the symbolic single euro. This was the amount requested, for example, by Prince William and Kate Middleton for the publication by the magazine *Closer* of photographs of the couple relaxing around a swimming pool in the Lubéron at the end of the summer of 2012. The largest award was 15,000 euros, with the average amount coming to around 3,800 euros per plaintiff. This is far below the sometimes very substantial sums granted several years ago by the same jurisdictions. According to Léna Lutaud and Thiébault Dromard,[35] the singer Patrick Bruel and his former wife, Amanda Sthers, were awarded amounts as large as 170,501 euros in 2005, while members of the Monegasque royal family received a total of 525,503 euros in the same year.

A number of public figures nevertheless continue to systematically combat publications infringing on their privacy or image rights, despite the negligible amount of damages and interest awarded by the courts. For example, the name of Brahim Zaibat (Madonna's companion) appears in over twenty judicial decisions handed down in 2012 in Nanterre and Paris; in total, these yielded him only 45,000 euros in damages and interest (or an average of 1,800 euros of damages and interest per case). The actress Marion Cotillard received a total of 25,000 euros from fifteen cases (scarcely more than 1,500 euros per trial) that she pursued during the same year. While some plaintiffs may be suspected of acting for mercenary gain, others in contrast seem to be motivated by a genuine determination to put an end to practices that they believe to be abusive. However, this wish will remain no more than a pious hope so long as the French courts continue to hand down minimal fines against scandalmongering press groups. There seems to be a growing gap between the generally consistent recognition that the publication of paparazzi photographs is a criminal action on the one hand, and the assessment of the harm incurred on the other. This imbalance is no doubt attributable to the growing ubiquity of celebrity photographs in this era of multimedia exposure and the development of a society based on "image." It may also result from the findings of certain judges who minimize the moral harm, which is by its nature difficult to quantify, incurred by an individual whose professional life is at least partially reliant on public visibility. It is undoubtedly for this reason that the record fine of 2012 (totaling 15,000 euros) involved the case of a student who was a complete unknown. Finally, these decisions can be explained by the fact that in French law the payment of damages is intended solely to compensate for the harm caused. The payments are not punitive in nature, in contrast to the principles of Anglo-Saxon law; under the common law system, judges can (and do) grant punitive damages.

The minimal amounts of damages currently being awarded by French courts constitute a kind of carte blanche for the scandalmongering press groups, who can thus continue to publish these contested photographs. There is really no correlation between the revenues generated by a publication and the compensation for the harm incurred by the plaintiff. Legislation could be written to establish guidelines, following the precedent set by rulings applicable to violations of an author's copyright or the counterfeiting of a brand. In these cases, fines are based on the income derived by the counterfeiter. In conclusion, as long as a publication remains profitable for its publisher, there is no incentive for paparazzi photographers to cease their activities. This conclusion illustrates the pertinence of the opinion voiced by the author and popular philosopher Jules Renard. The celebrity tabloid press enjoys great freedom in France, despite repeated sentences, for the simple and logical reason that the judicial system ultimately condones very porous barriers against invasions of personal privacy and the breaches of image rights. The paparazzi can apparently anticipate good times ahead for themselves, to the delight of millions of readers and the dismay of a number of their subjects!

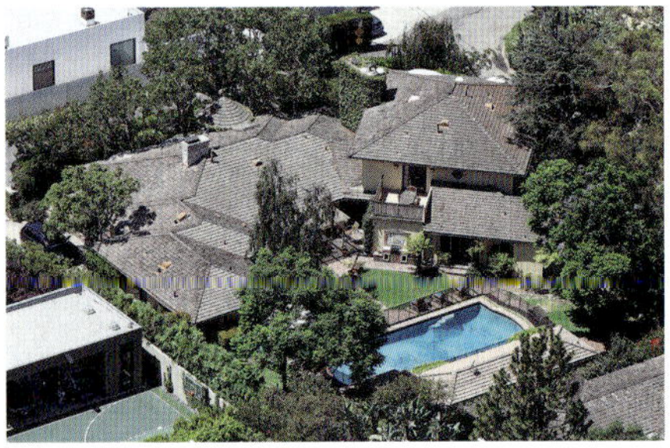

TOBEY MAGUIRE
Hollywood Hills

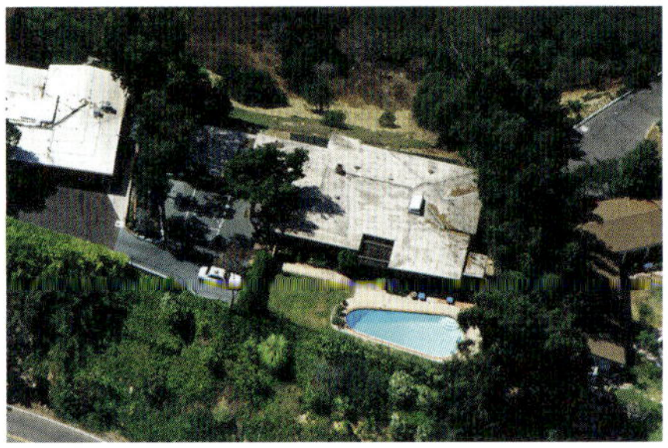

MARLON BRANDO
Los Angeles

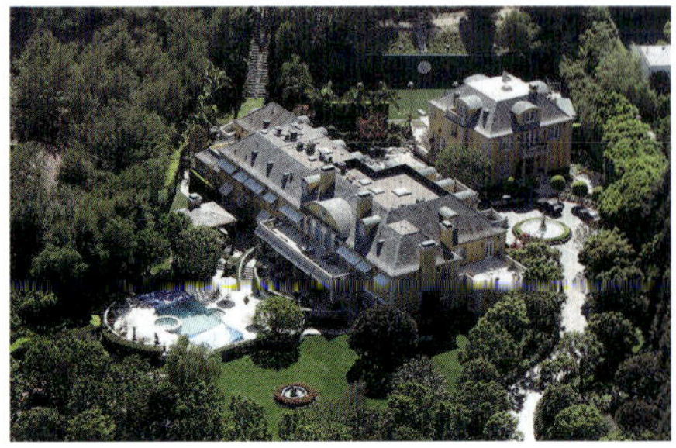

ROD STEWART
Beverly Hills

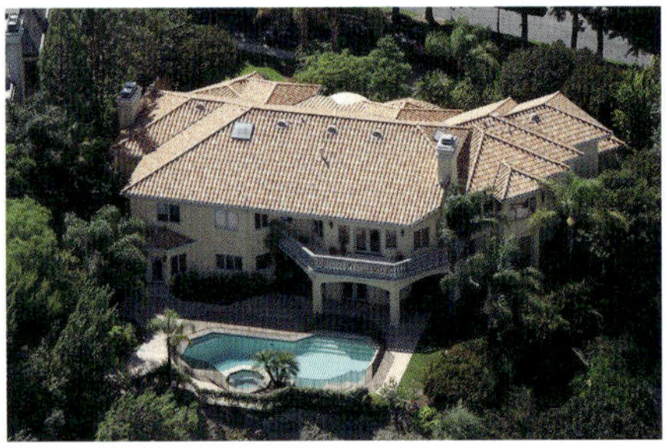

PARIS HILTON
Beverly Hills

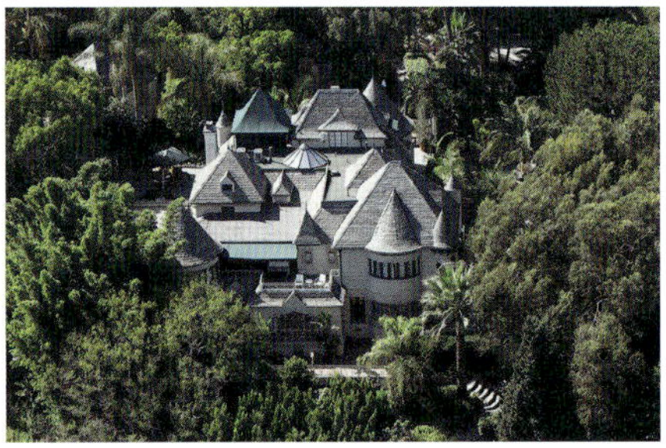

JOHNNY DEPP
Hollywood

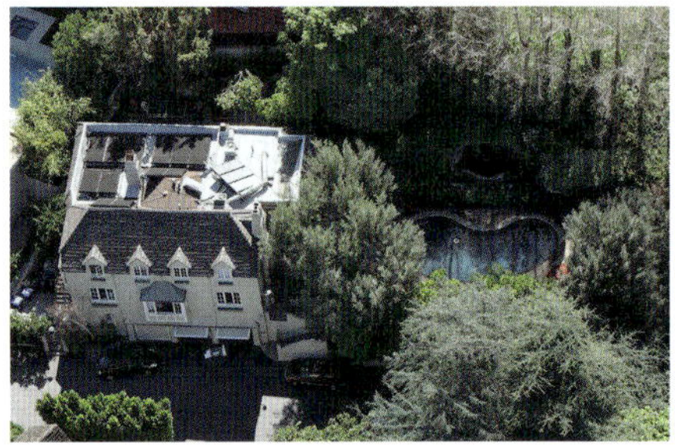

CASEY AFFLECK
Los Feliz

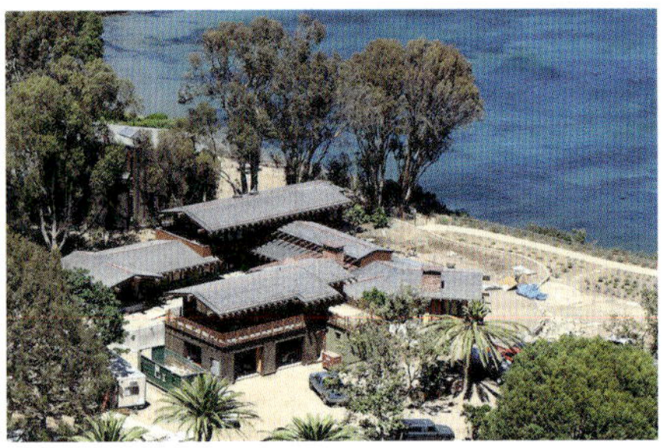

JULIA ROBERTS
Malibu

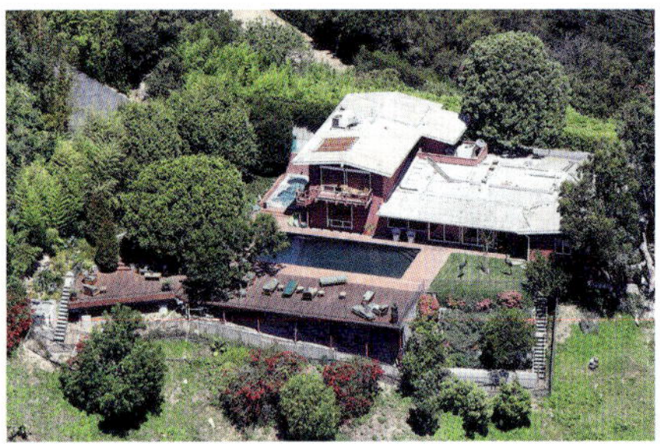

JACK NICHOLSON
Mulholland Drive

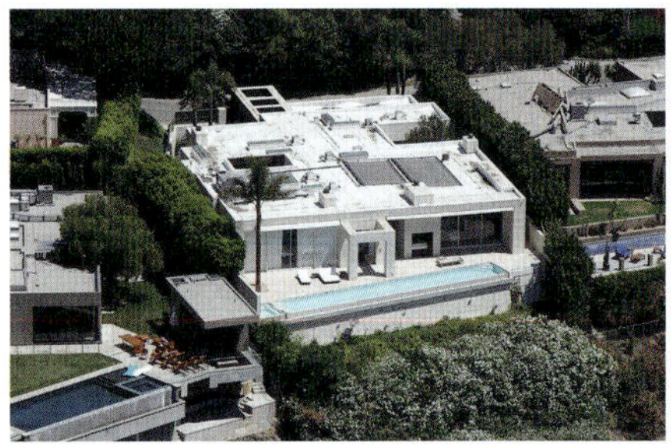

KEANU REEVES
Hollywood Hills

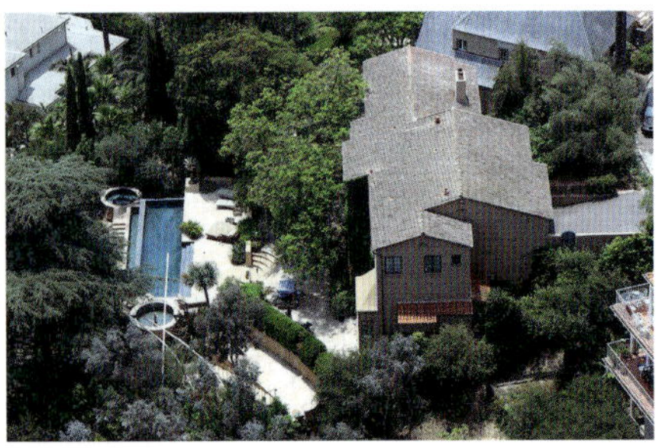

COLIN FARRELL
Los Feliz

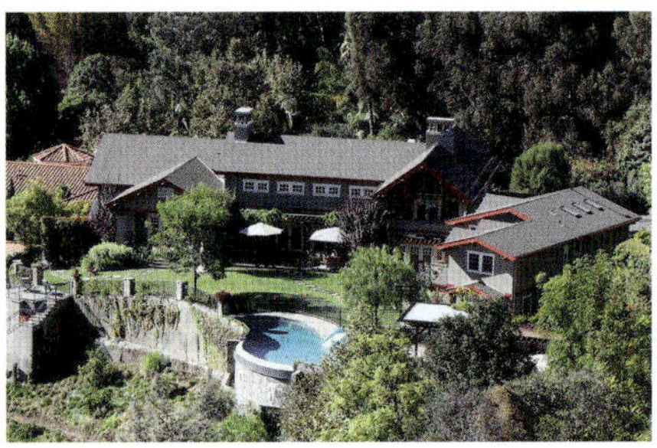

FELICITY HUFFMAN
Beverly Hills

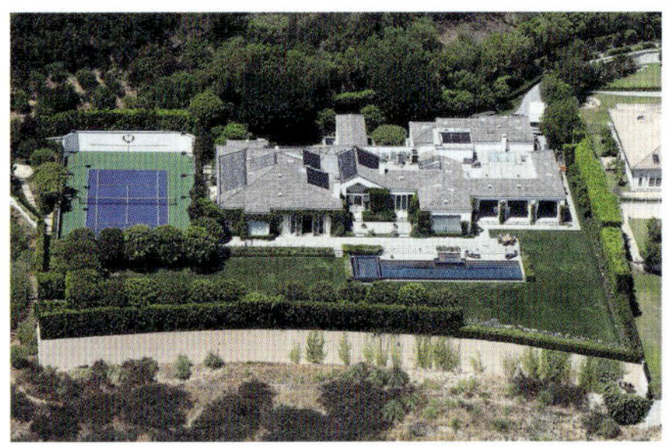

GWEN STEFANI
Los Angeles

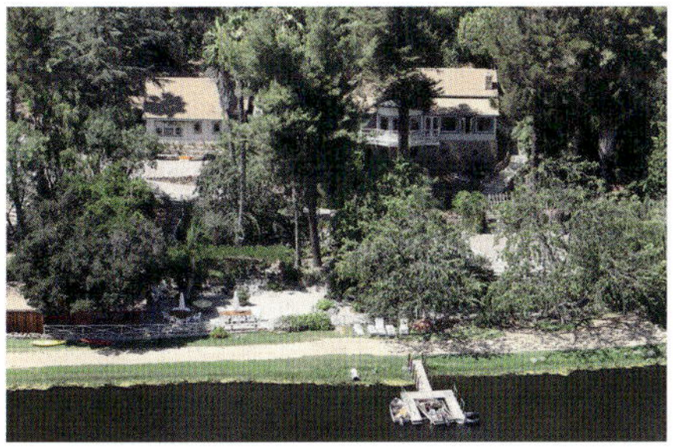

SYLVESTER STALLONE
Thousand Oaks

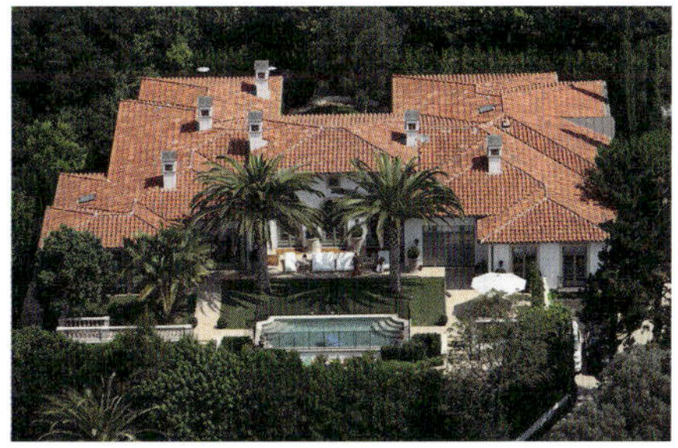

DAVID AND VICTORIA BECKHAM
Beverly Hills

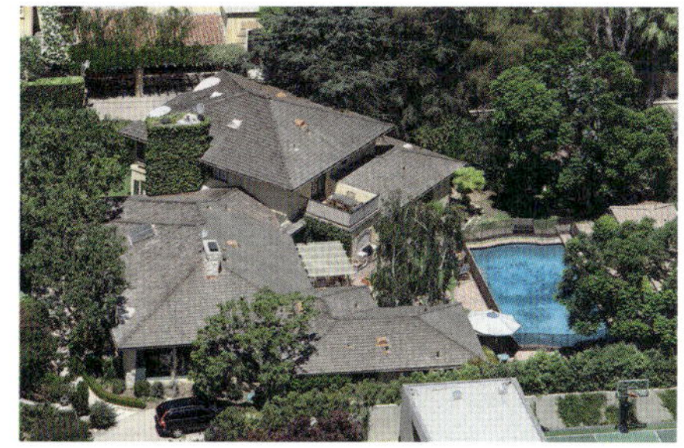

LEONARDO DICAPRIO
Hollywood Hills

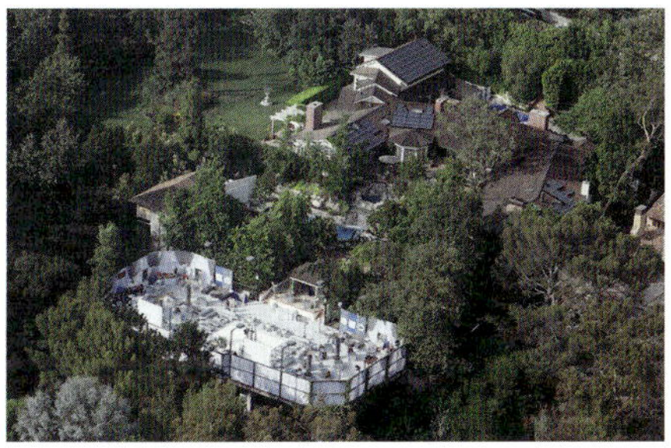

JIM CARREY
Brentwood

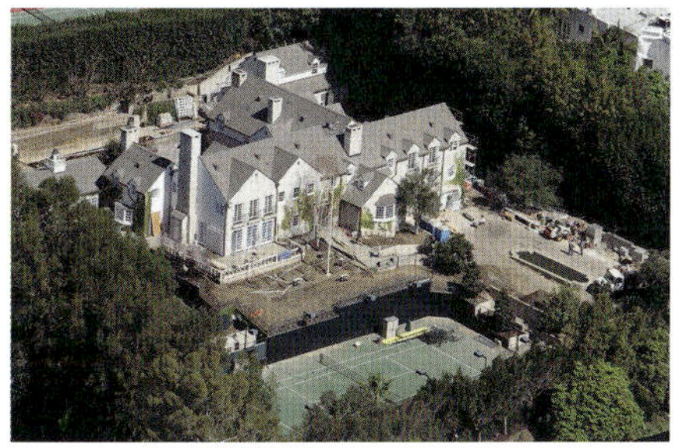

TOM CRUISE
Beverly Hills

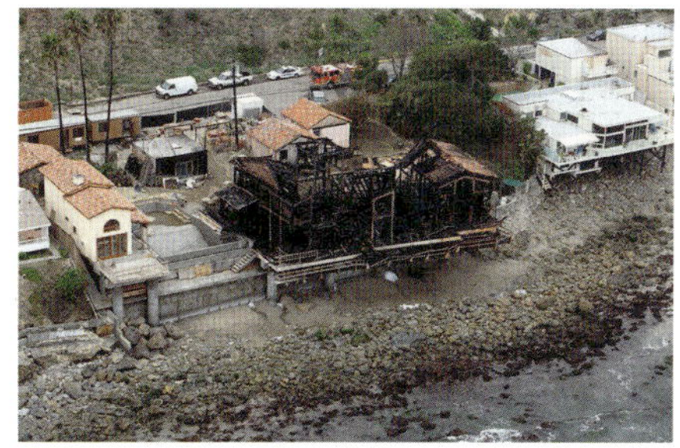

LILLY LAWRENCE
Malibu

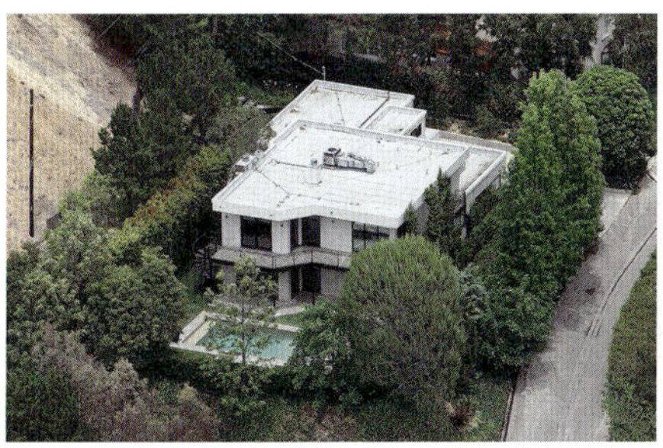

NICOLE KIDMAN
Beverly Hills

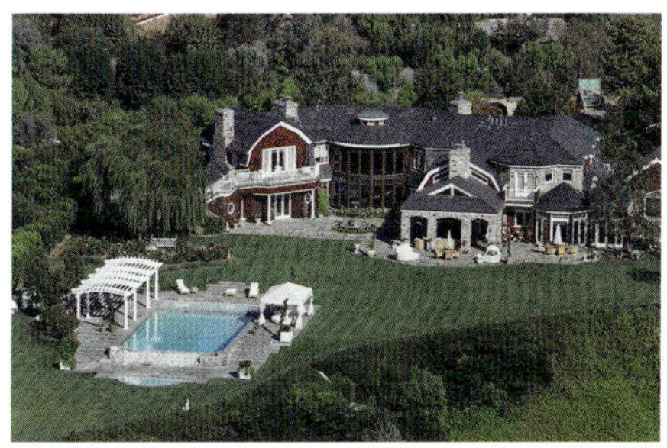

OZZY OSBOURNE
Hidden Hills

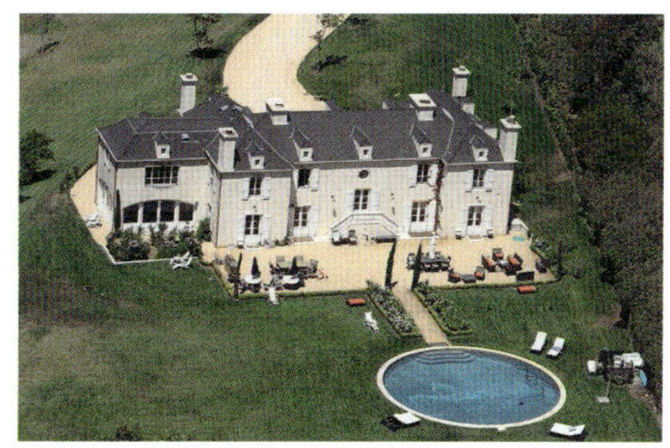

PAMELA ANDERSON
Malibu

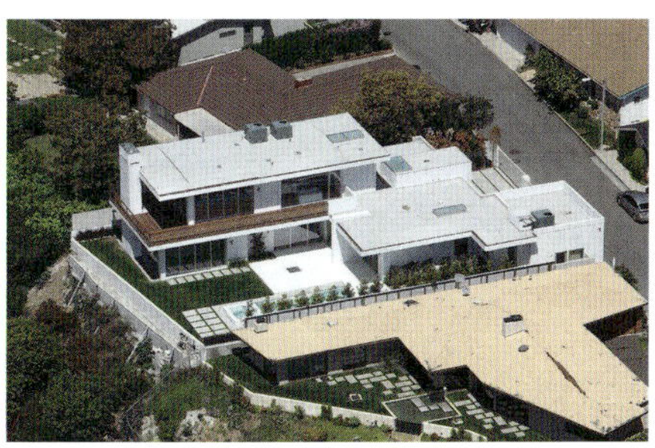

MATT PERRY
Hollywood Hills

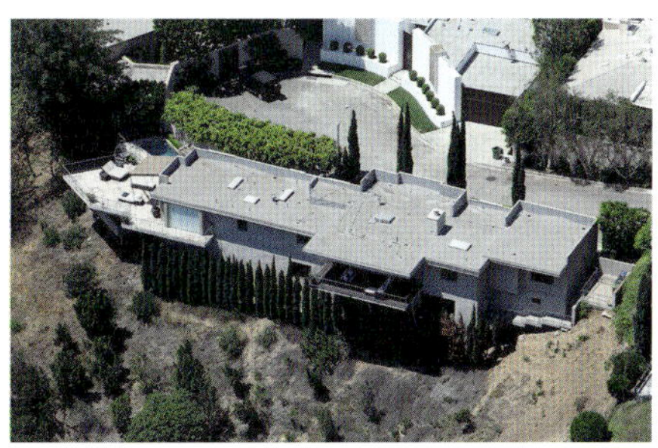

MICHEL POLNAREFF
Los Angeles

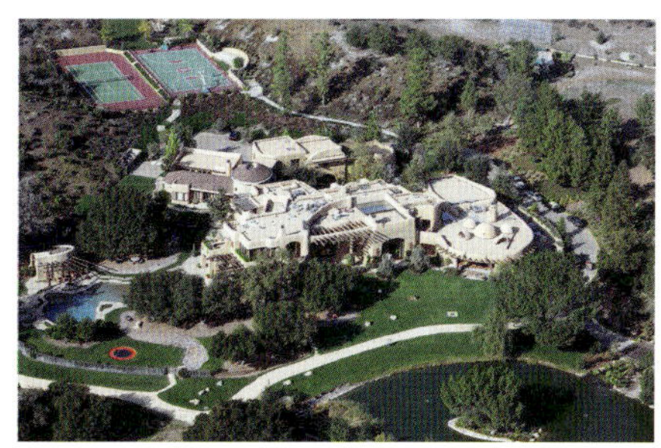

WILL SMITH
Los Angeles

SÉBASTIEN VALIELA
Stars' Houses in California
2005–8

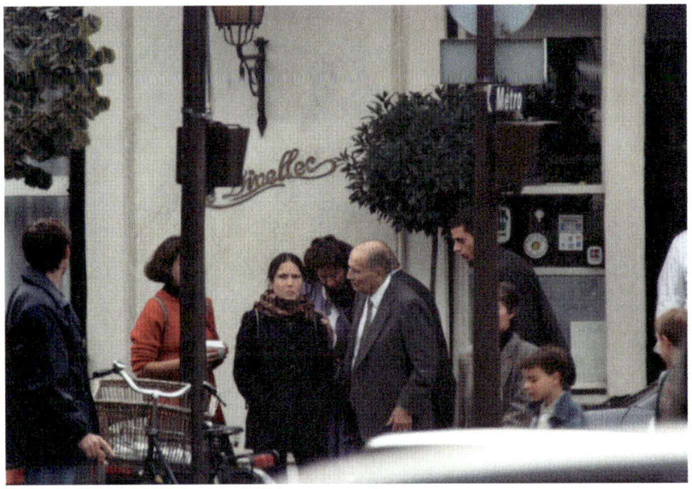

SÉBASTIEN VALIELA AND PIERRE SUU
Mazarine Pingeot and Her Father, François Mitterrand, in front of Le Divellec Restaurant, Paris
September 21, 1994

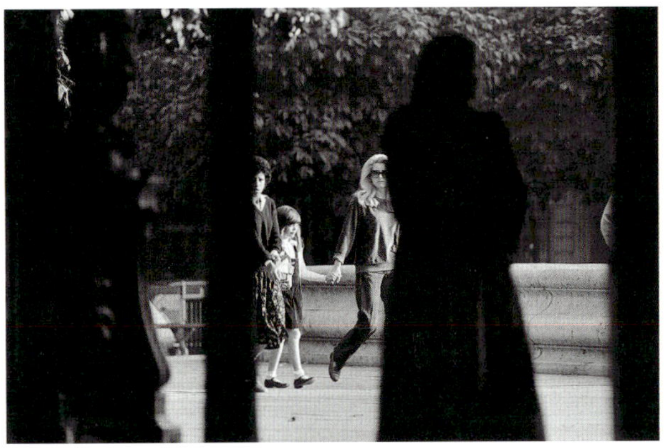

BRUNO MOURON
Catherine Deneuve and Her Daughter Chiara Mastroianni, Going Back to School, Paris
September 16, 1980

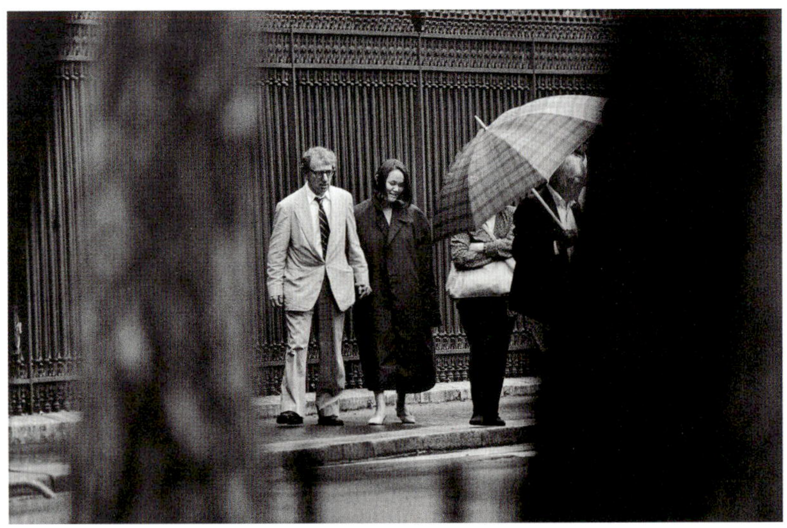

PASCAL ROSTAIN AND BRUNO MOURON
Woody Allen and Soon-Yi at the Tuileries Gardens, Paris
October 1994

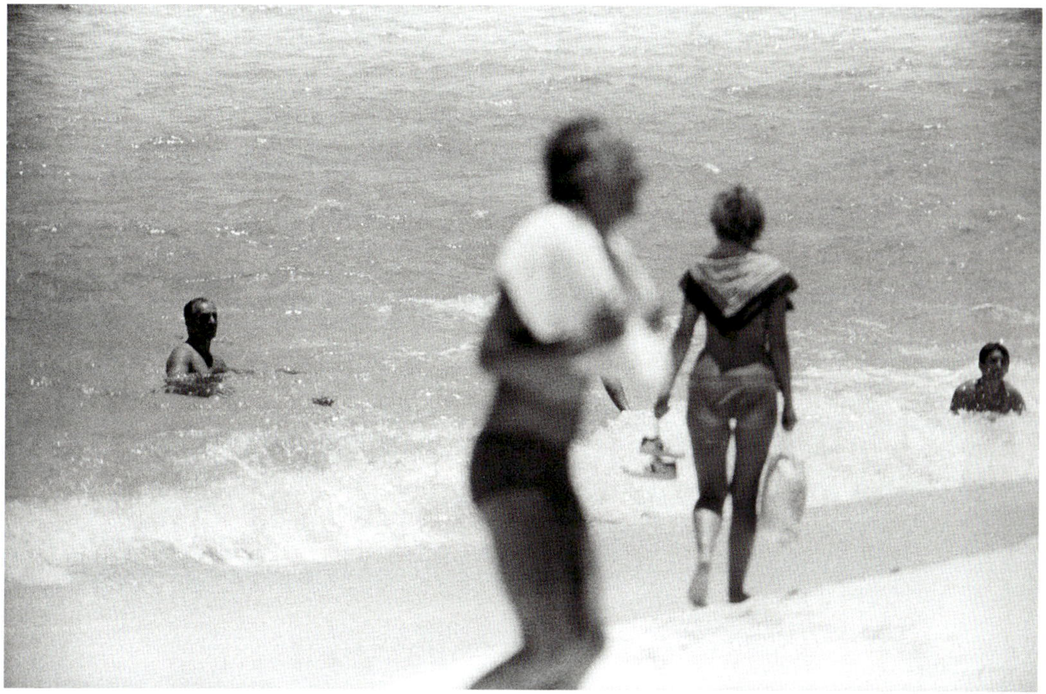

FRANCIS APESTEGUY
Reza Pahlavi, the Exiled Iranian Shah, Bathing in the Sea among Tourists at Nassau, in the Bahamas
May 20, 1979

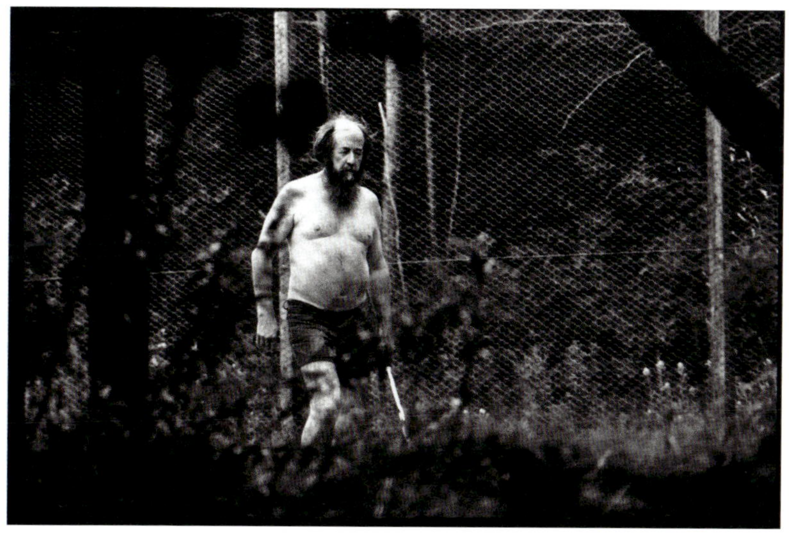

PASCAL ROSTAIN
Alexandre Solzhenitsyn Playing Tennis at His Vermont Property in the United States
August 1981

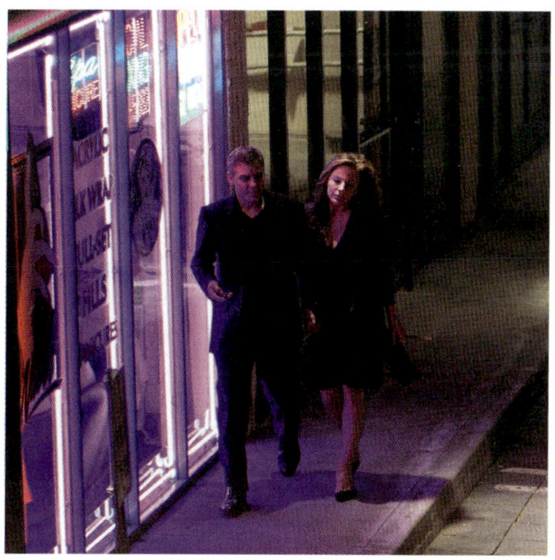

SÉBASTIEN VALIELA AND VINCENT LEPRESLE
George Clooney and Krista Allen, Holding Hands in front of a Sushi Restaurant, Beverly Hills
March 4, 2006

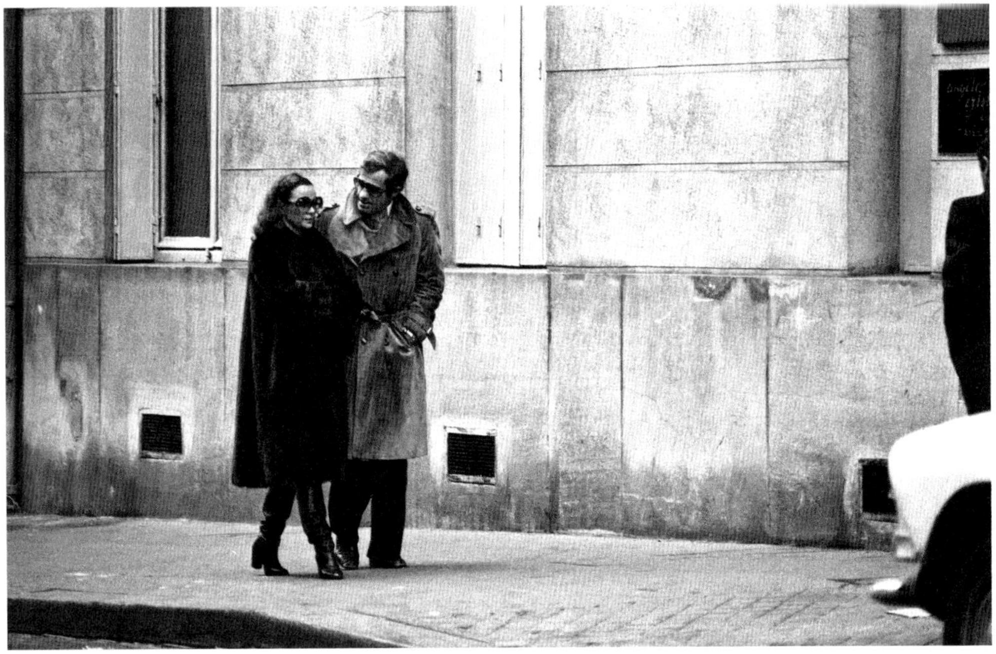

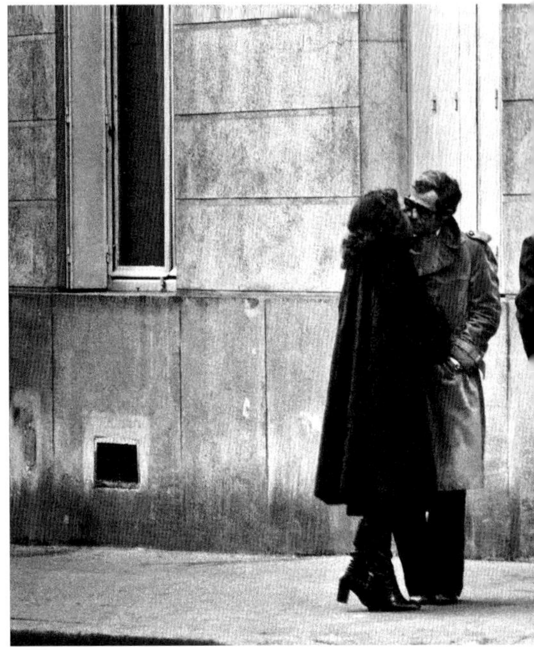

XAVIER MARTIN
Jean-Paul Belmondo and Laura Antonelli: The Kiss, Paris
1976

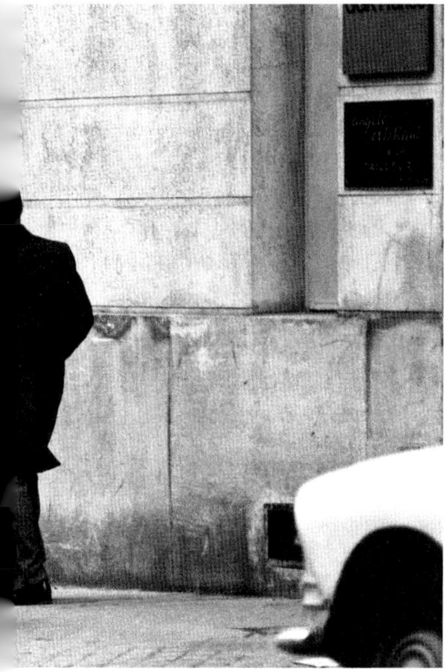

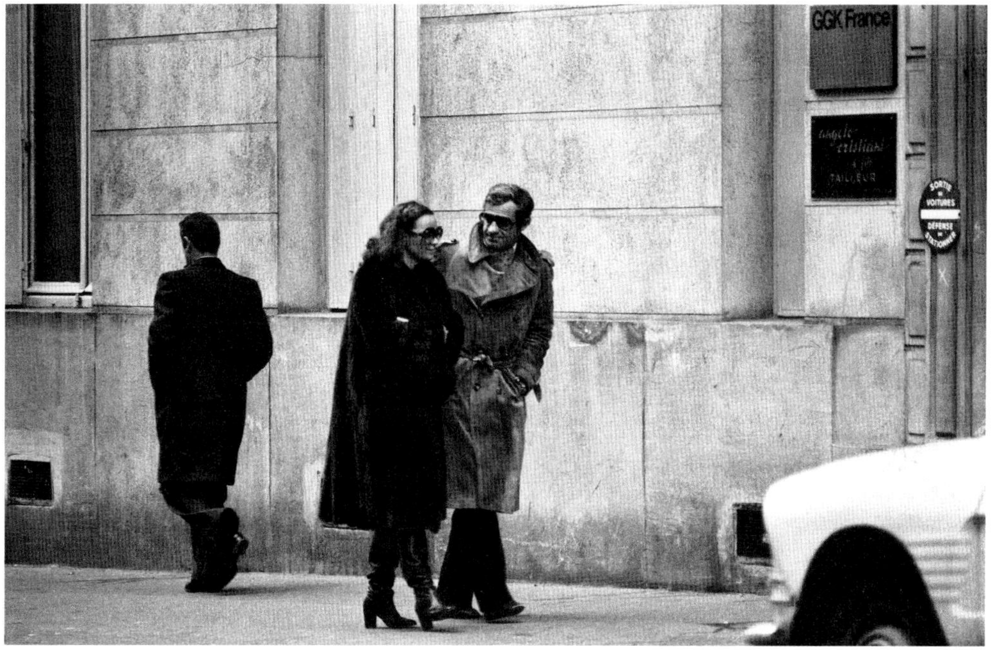

IT'S PERFECTLY INNOCENT. Paparazzi images most often capture their subjects unawares, using telephoto lenses that compress the distance between the subject and the photographer, raising the issue of voyeurism. All the photos shown here are proof of the desire to surprise celebrities in private moments. Aided by modern optical devices, paparazzi can observe without being observed. They act behind a protective screen, free to penetrate the intimate lives of stars without risking discovery themselves. They can record the most minute details of their chosen subject's daily life, in shots taken on a beach, through a hedge, or over a fence. In contrast to wide-angle lenses, which tend to expand the sense of space, telephoto lenses have the effect of flattening and compressing the image's foreground and background. Viewed by the paparazzi from a distance, stars seem to inhabit a strangely one-dimensional universe.

Paris Match, no. 1727,
July 2, 1982,
front cover
(Photograph: anonymous)

Paris Match, no. 1775,
June 3, 1983,
front cover
(Photograph: anonymous)

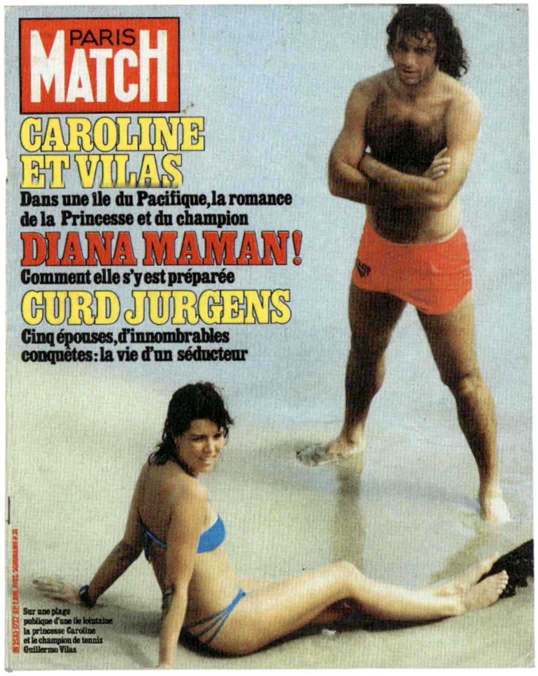

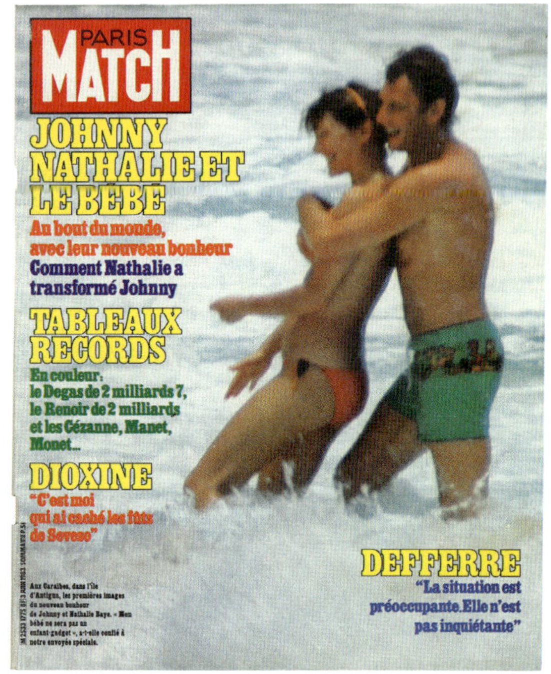

Paris Match, no. 1769,
April 22, 1983,
front cover
(Photograph: anonymous)

Paris Match, no. 2936,
August 25, 2005,
front cover
(Photograph: anonymous)

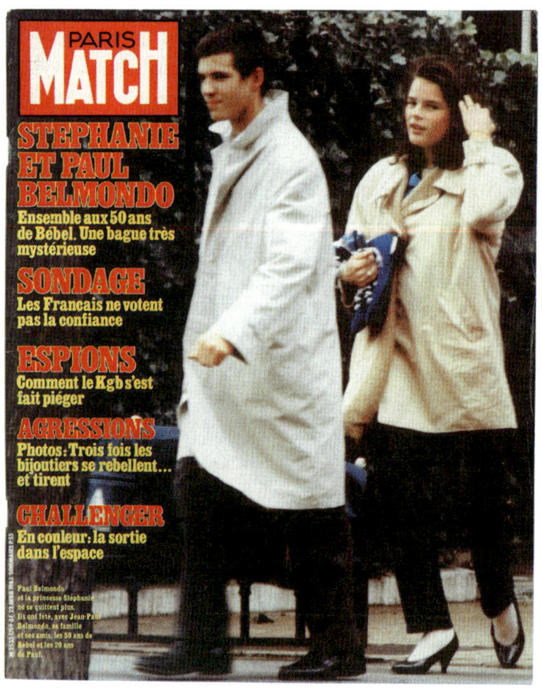

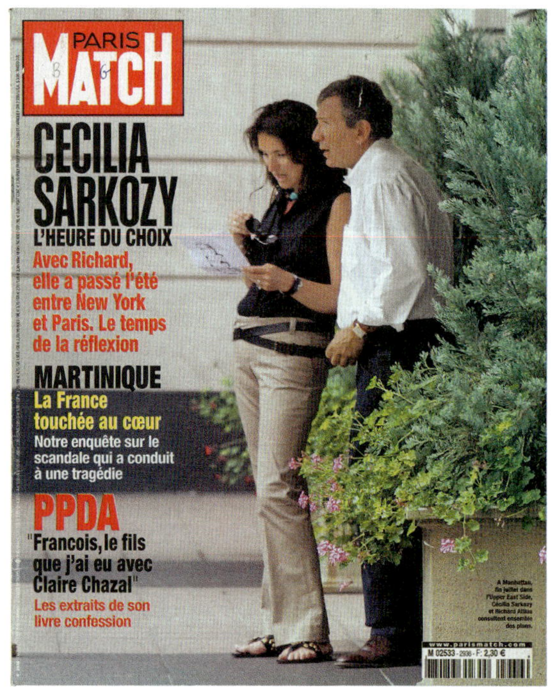

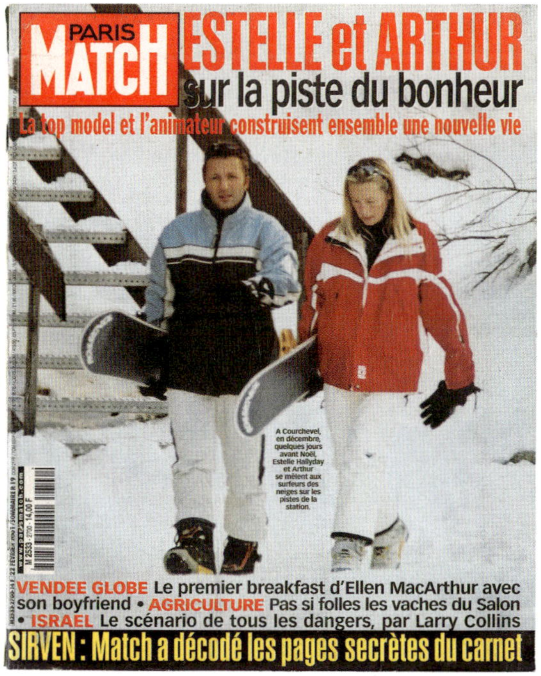

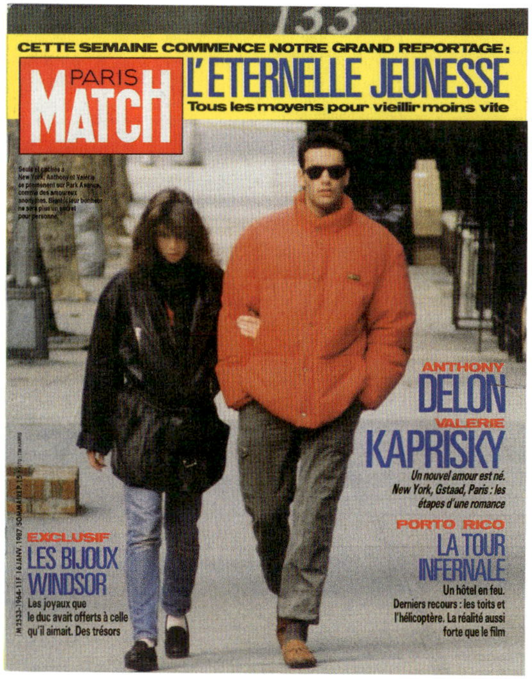

Paris Match, no. 2700, February 22, 2001, front cover (Photograph: anonymous)

Paris Match, no. 1964, January 16, 1987, front cover (Photograph: anonymous)

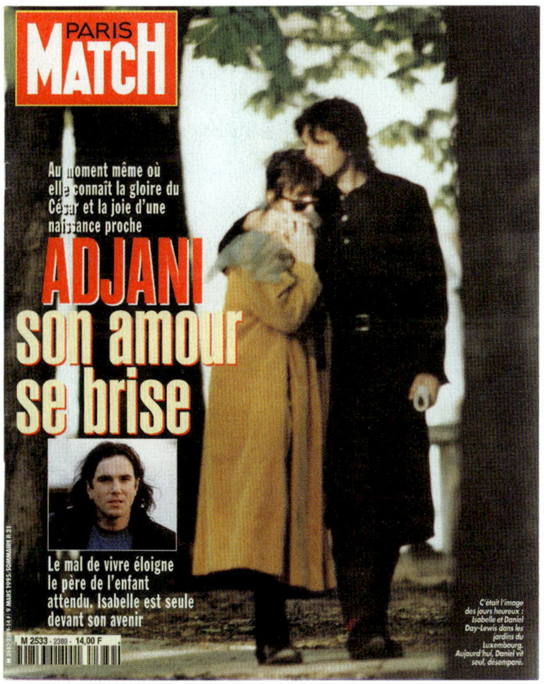

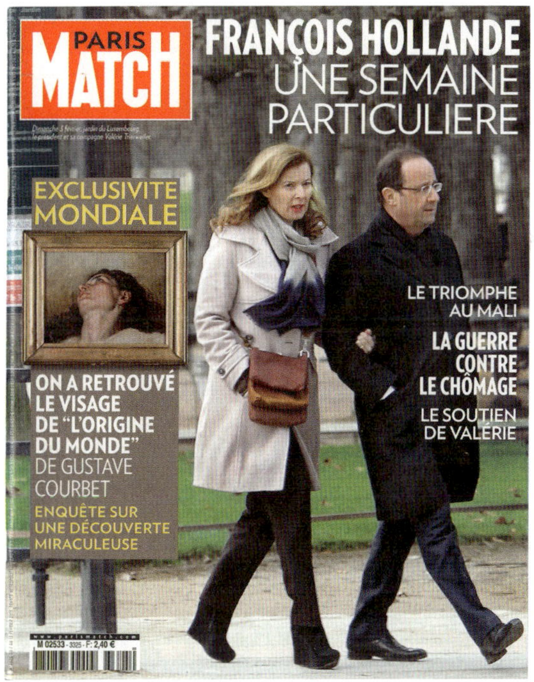

Paris Match, no. 2389, March 9, 1995, front cover (Photograph: anonymous)

Paris Match, no. 3325, February 7, 2013, front cover (Photograph: anonymous)

DISCREET ARRANGEMENTS. The star is not always a victim of the paparazzi. She may also initiate the photos. In this case, the images are not stolen; they are the product of a prenegotiated agreement. The shots Tazio Secchiaroli took of Sofia Loren in 1968 are a perfect illustration of this role reversal. When her son Carlo Jr. was born, the actress asked the legendary Italian paparazzo to photograph her pushing his baby carriage through the park. In "breaking" this scoop, the publication of these preplanned images assured the actress's peace and quiet. More recently, the French reality TV star Loana has frequently organized fabricated paparazzi events to boost her career or convey a message to her audience. She publicizes herself in photographic shoots where she appears leaving the hospital, visiting the gym, or frolicking on the beach with her companion of the moment. However, there is a real risk to the star's relationship with her audience if the subterfuge is revealed.

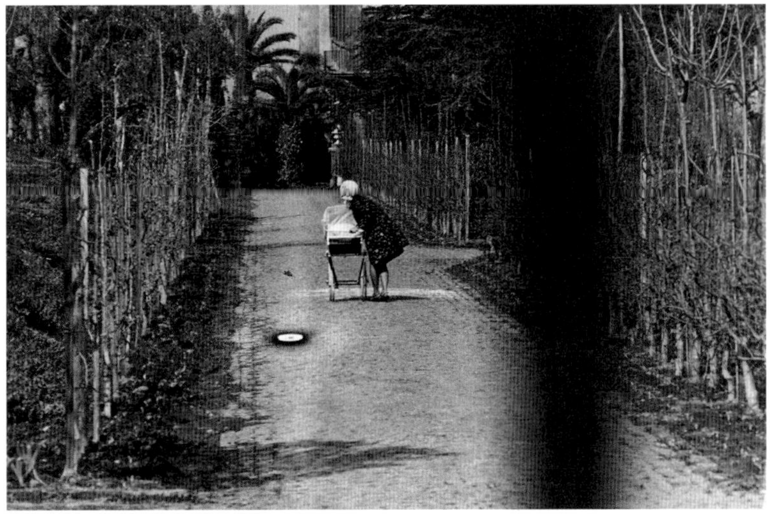

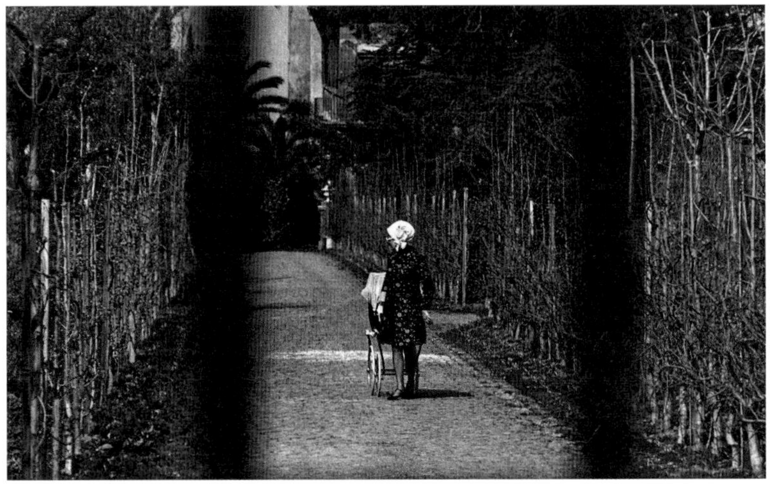

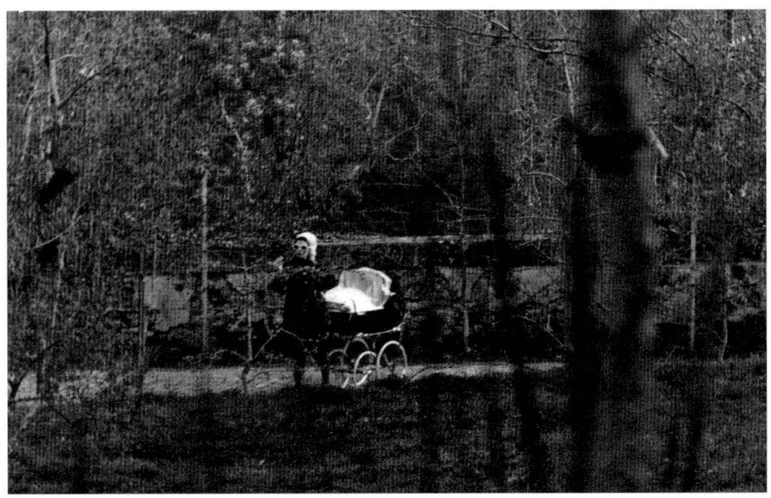

TAZIO SECCHIAROLI
Sophia Loren with Her Son Carlo Jr. in a Pram, in the Gardens of Her Villa in Marino, near Rome
1968

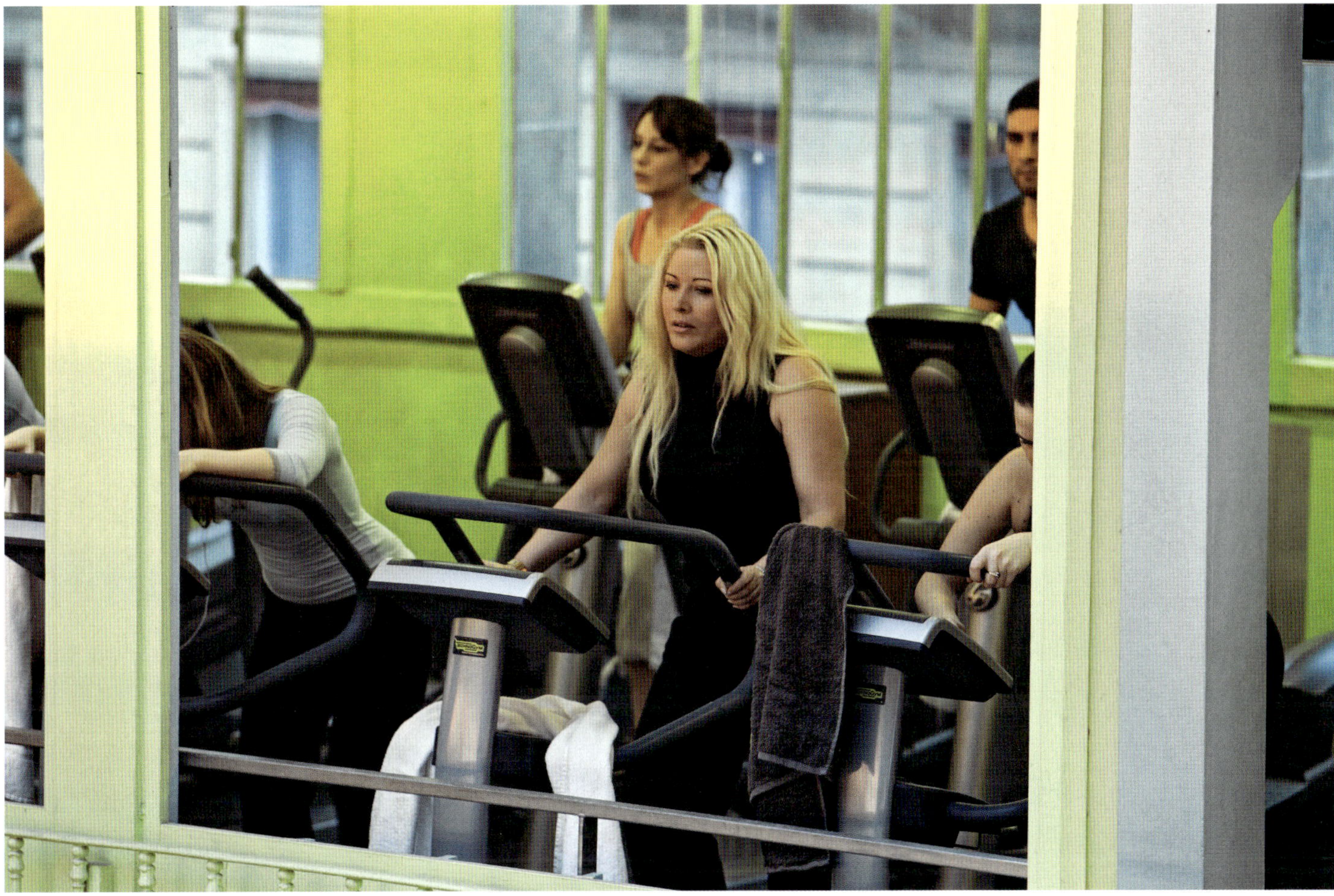

SÉBASTIEN VALIELA
Loana Working Out
February 25, 2011

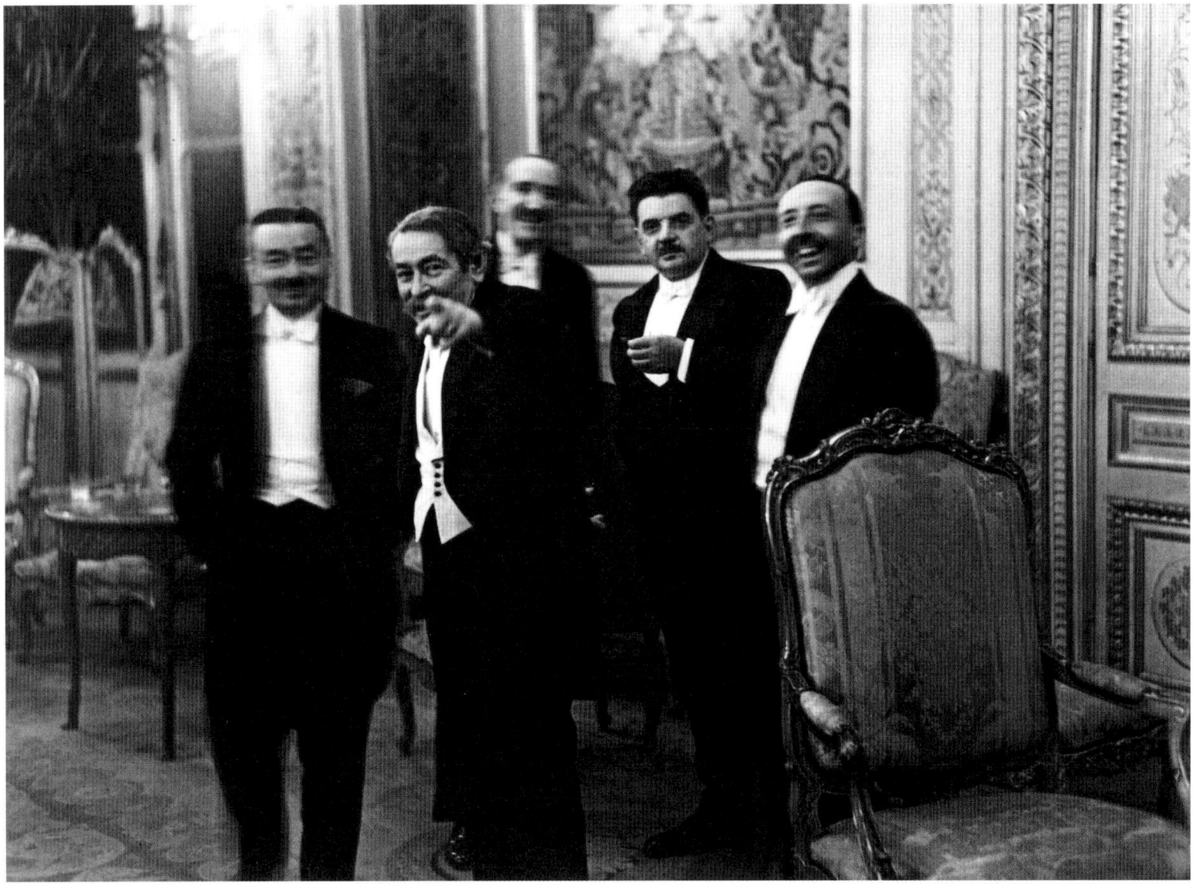

ERICH SALOMON
Aristide Briand Pointing At Erich Salomon, Quai d'Orsay, Paris
August 1931

PLAYING THE GAME. While usually hidden, the paparazzo is sometimes revealed. A legendary photograph by Erich Salomon, taken in a ministry on the Quai d'Orsay in Paris in 1931, recorded the very moment that the Minister of Foreign Affairs, Aristide Briand, pointed his index finger at the man he had dubbed "the king of indiscretion." When the prey reveals the predator, an entirely different relationship is established between the parties. It is expressed in a codified set of gestures. Once revealed, the paparazzo is identified with a pointed finger. The exasperated celebrity makes an obscene gesture, threatens him with a clenched fist, sticks out his tongue, or moons him. Behind this apparently aggressive language of signs peculiar to the star system there often lurks a kind of connivance or amused complicity. The celebrity knows perfectly well that these excessive reactions are a bonanza for the paparazzi. They are sure to capture images that are especially revealing and original, commanding a high price in the media marketplace.

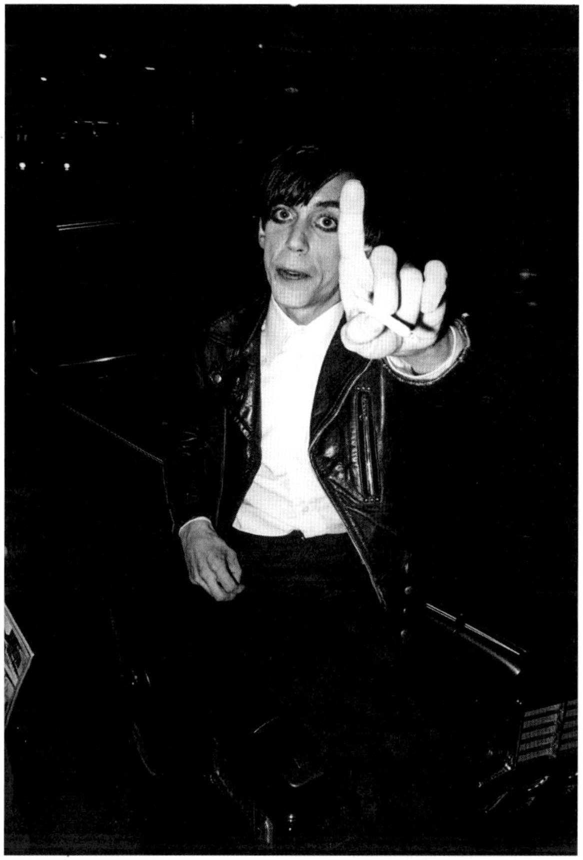

BRAD ELTERMAN
Iggy "No Photos" Pop
1978

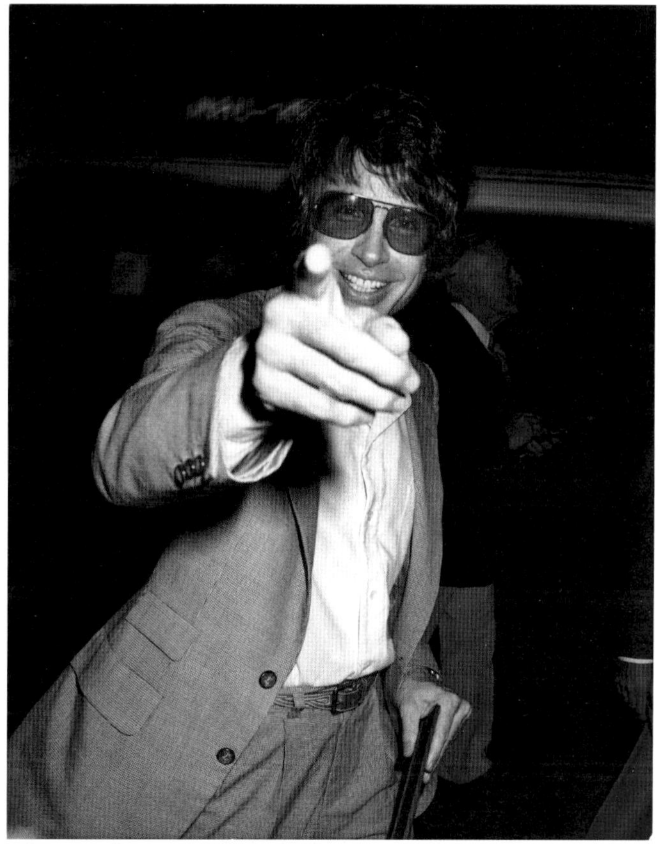

RON GALELLA
Warren Beatty at the 31st Writers Guild of America Awards at the Beverly Hilton Hotel, Beverly Hills
April 5, 1979

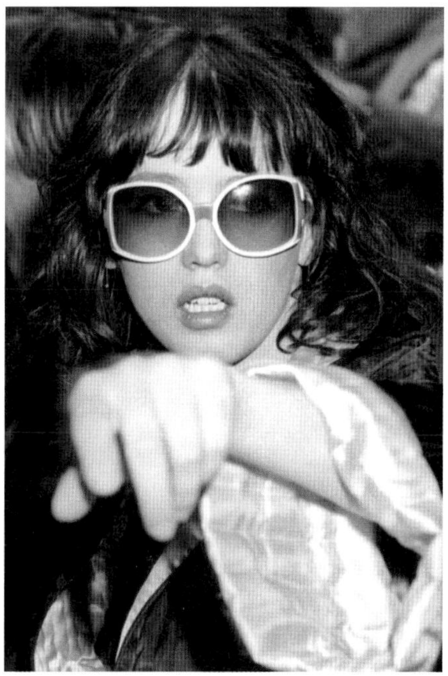

PATRICK SICCOLI
Isabelle Adjani Pointing Her Finger
1976

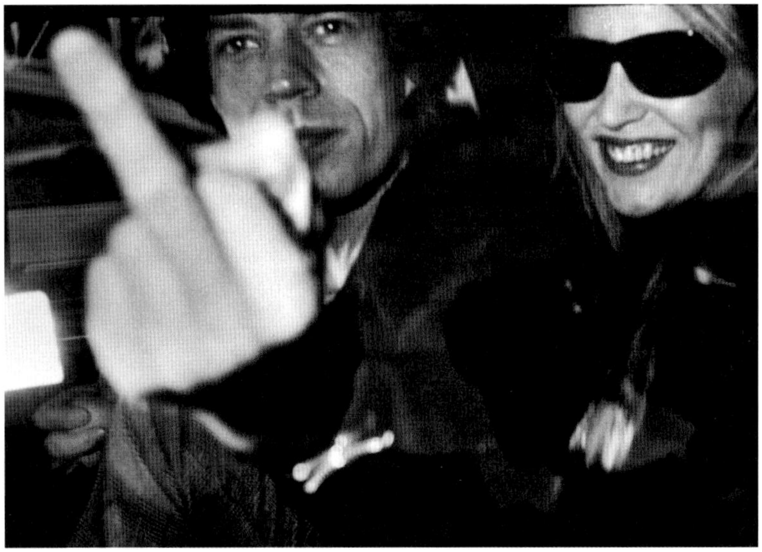

RON GALELLA
Mick Jagger and Jerry Hall Leaving the Mizuno Gallery, Beverly Hills
January 16, 1983

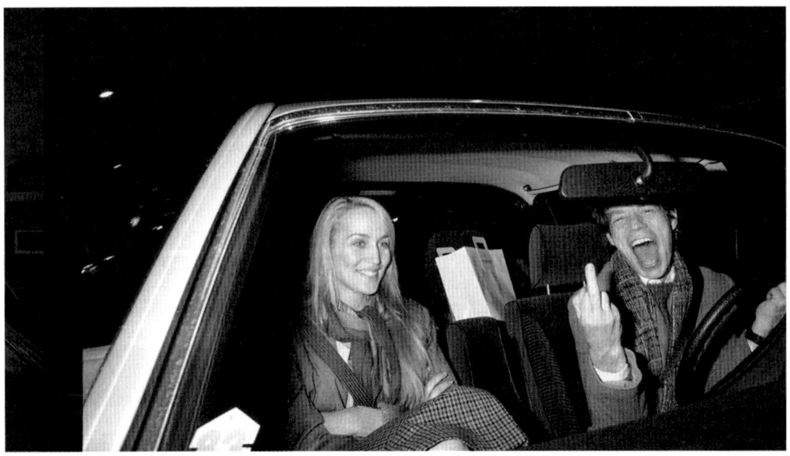

PATRICK SICCOLI
Jerry Hall with Mick Jagger at the Wheel, Giving the Finger
1982

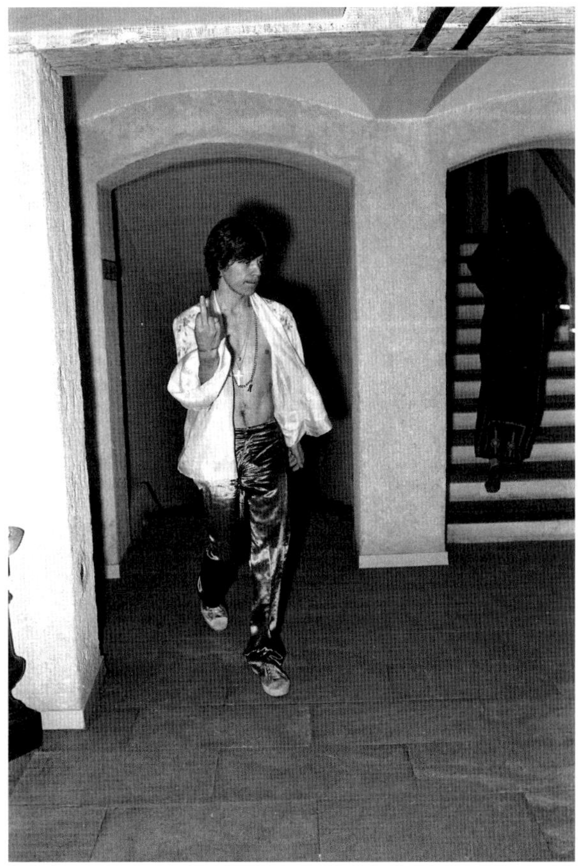

DANIEL ANGELI
Mick's Opinion: Mick Jagger at the Byblos Hotel after His Wedding with Bianca Moreno in Saint-Tropez
May 12, 1971

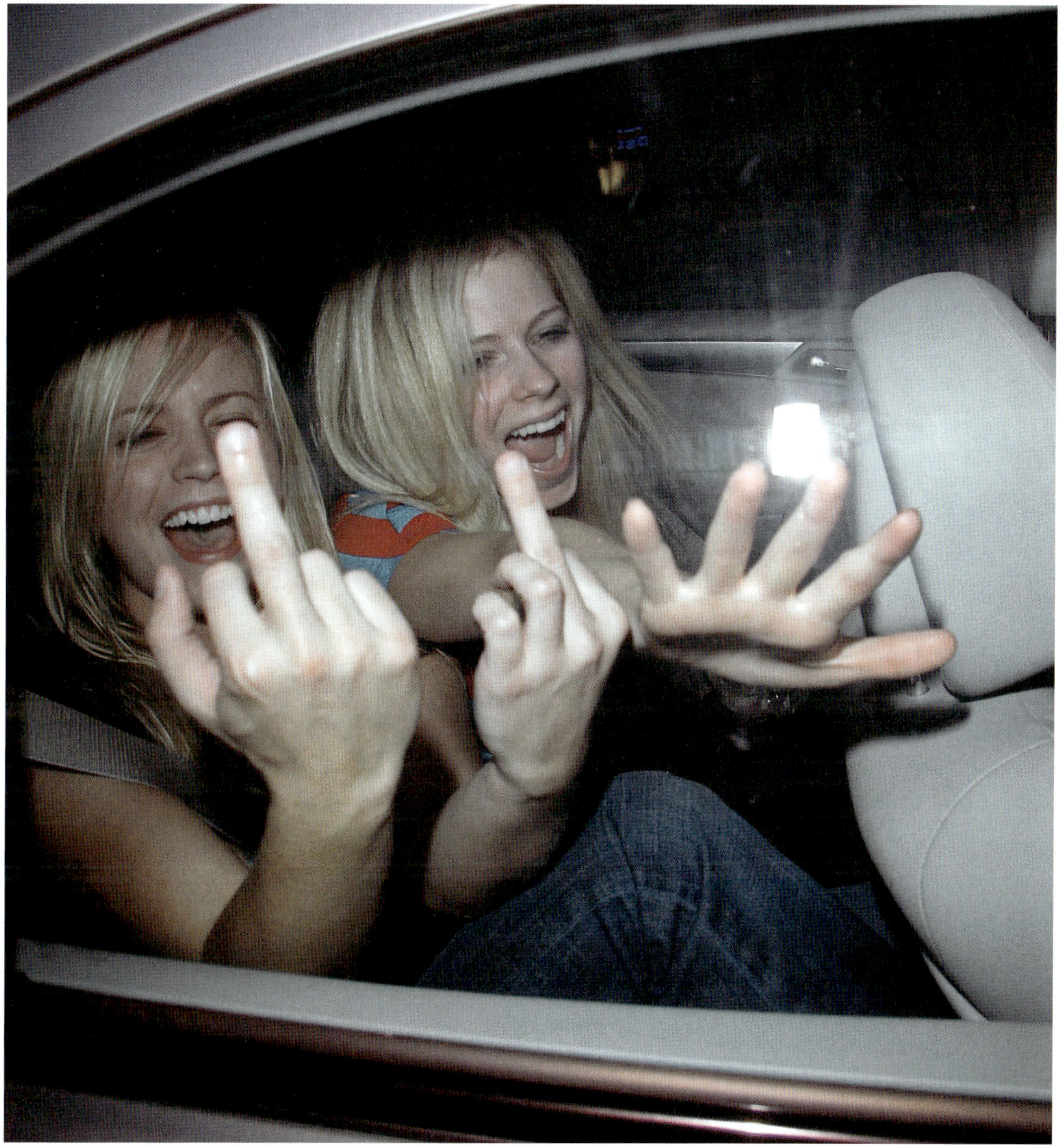

HENRY FLORES
Avril Lavigne and a Friend
2011

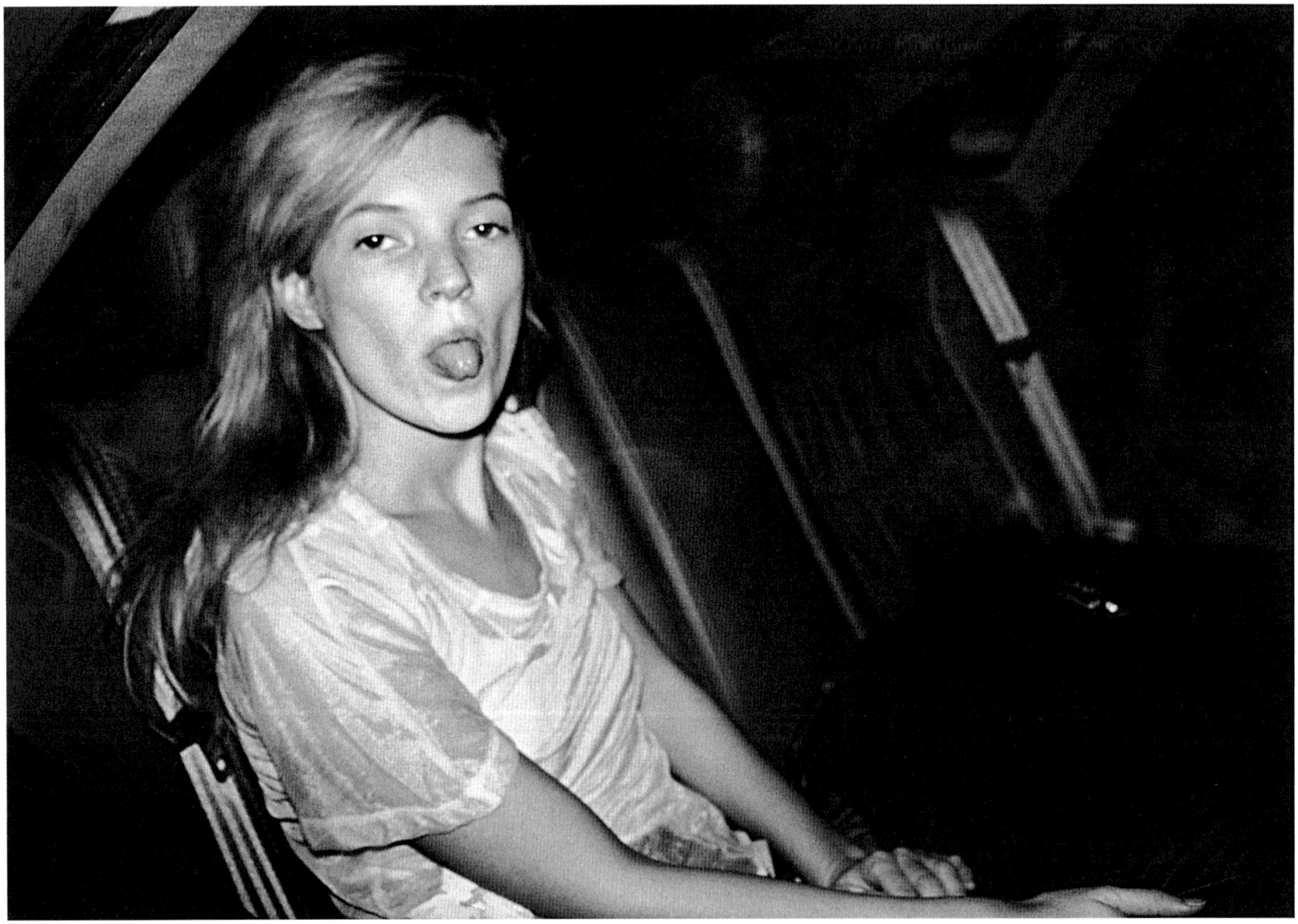

BRUNO MOURON
Kate Moss during
Fashion Week, Paris
1992

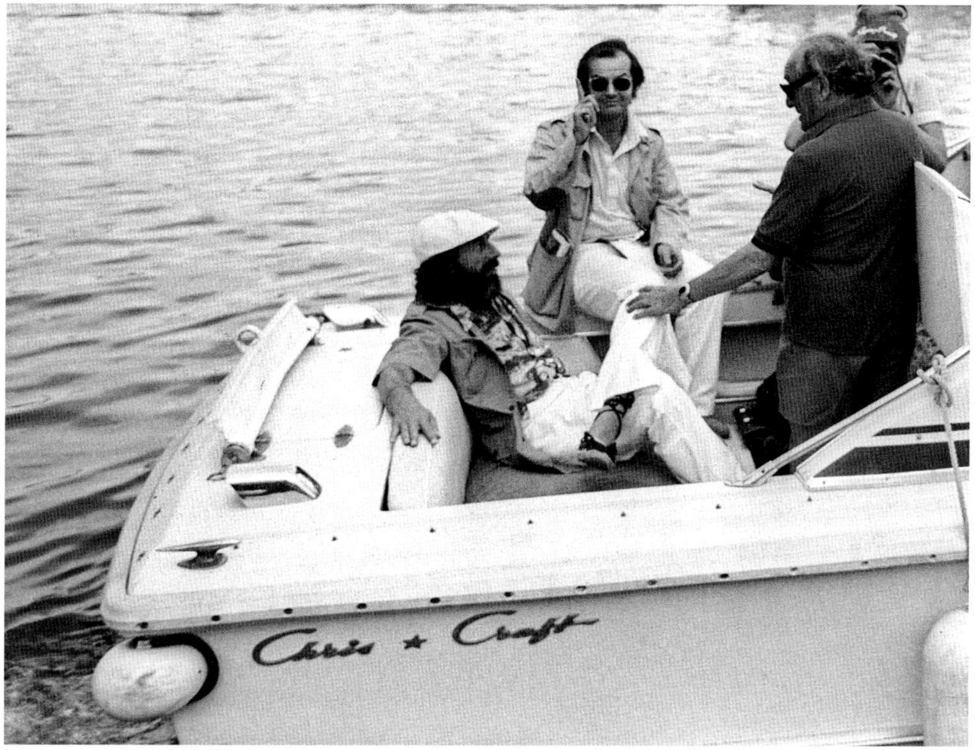

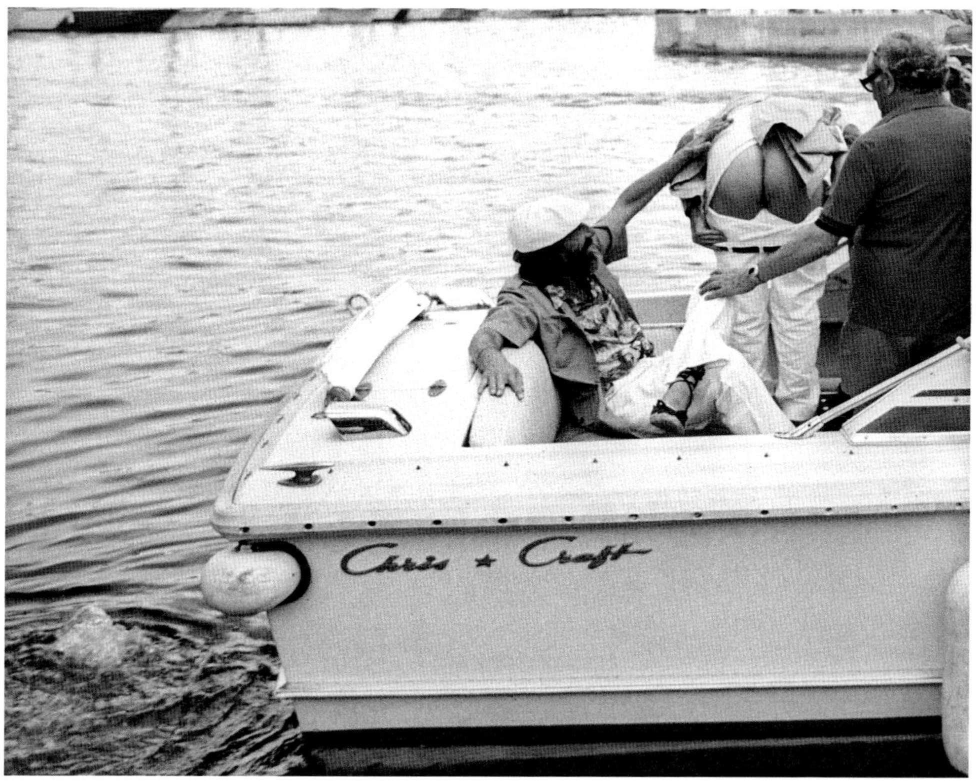

XAVIER MARTIN
Jack Nicholson Showing His Buttocks, Saint-Tropez
July 1976

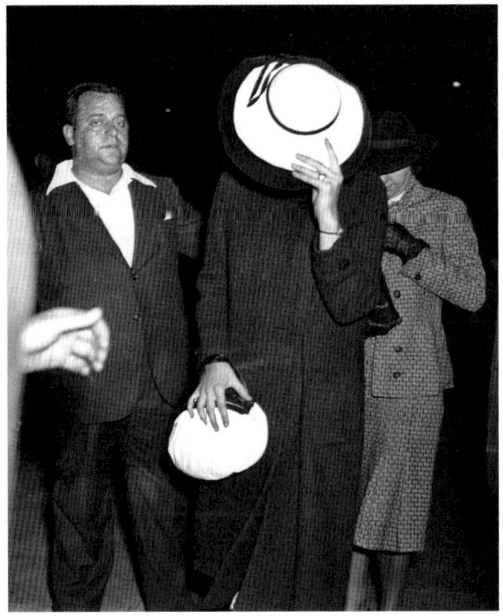

WEEGEE
Young Women Arrested at Anna Swift's after a Vice Squad Raid
1941

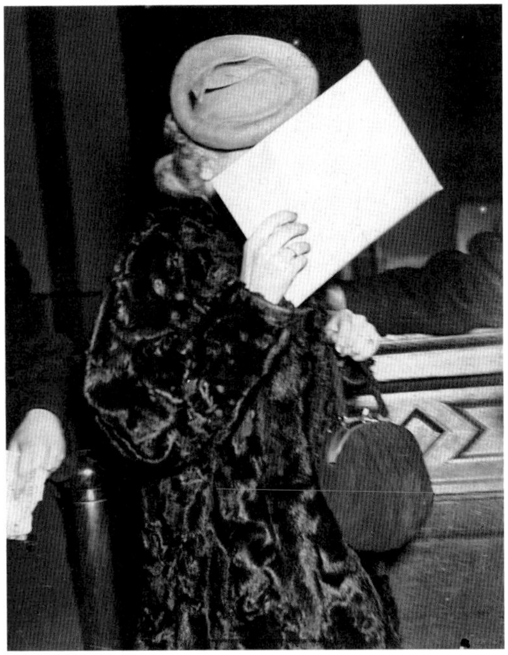

WEEGEE
Maxine Tursen
c. 1938

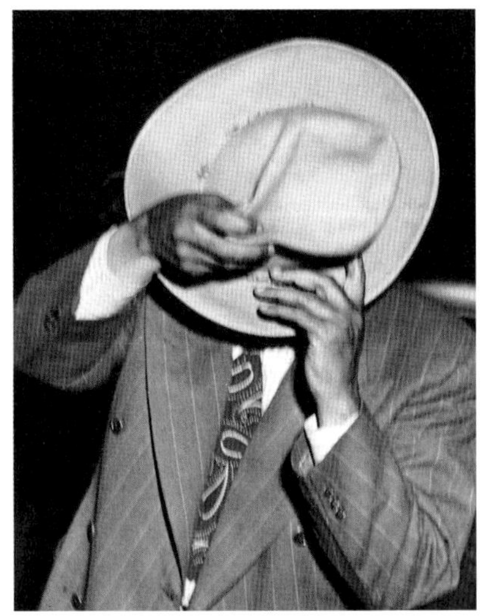

WEEGEE
Robert Redwing Is Taken for Questioning by the New York Police as Part of the Inquiry into the Murder of Albert Langford
June 1945

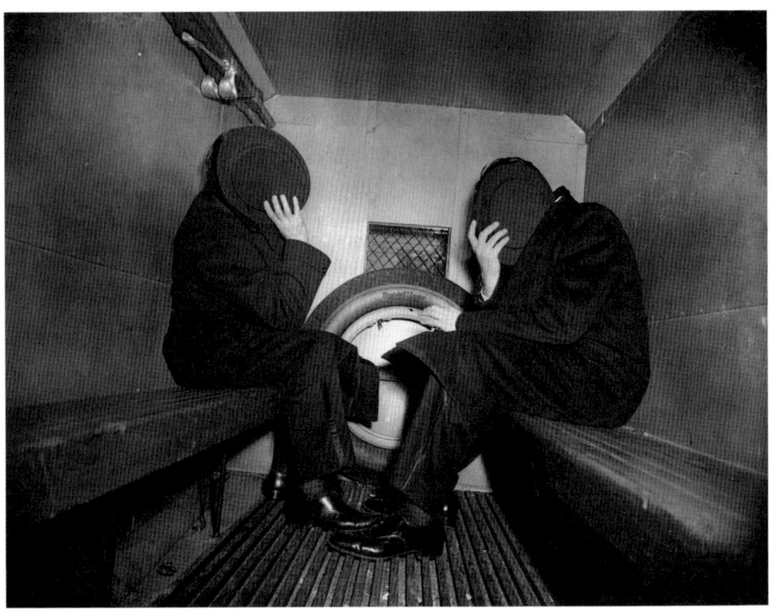

WEEGEE
Charles Sodokoff and Arthur Webber Using Their Hats to Hide Their Faces, New York
January 27, 1942

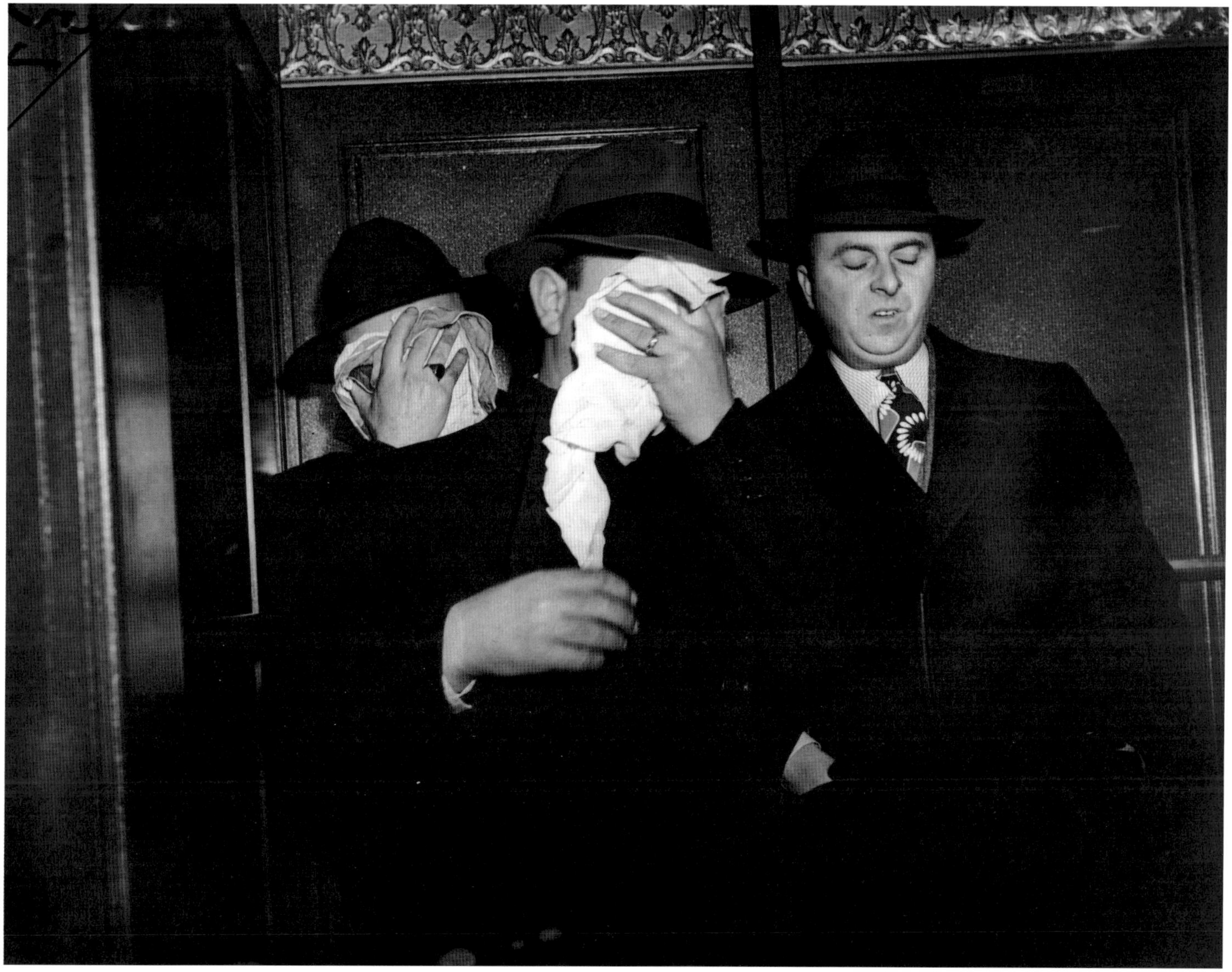

WEEGEE
Henry Rosen and Harvey Stemmer Are Arrested for Having Bribed Brooklyn University Basketball Players, New York
July 25, 1945

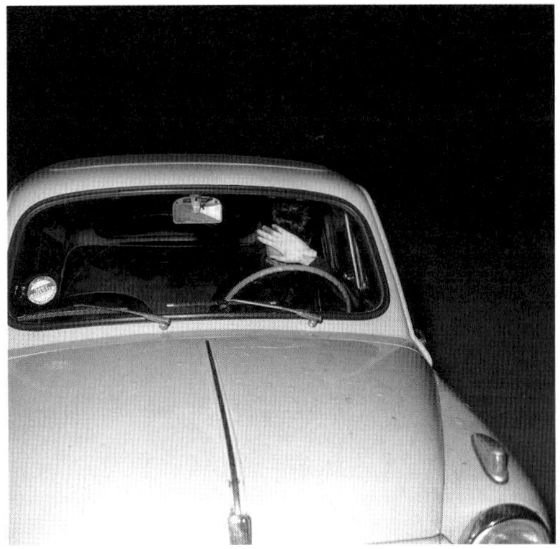

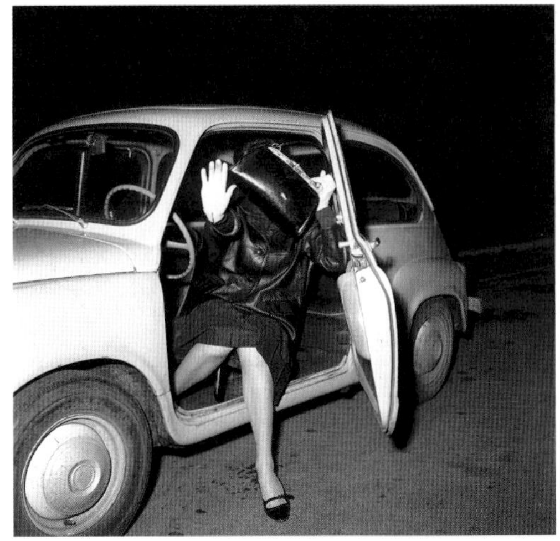

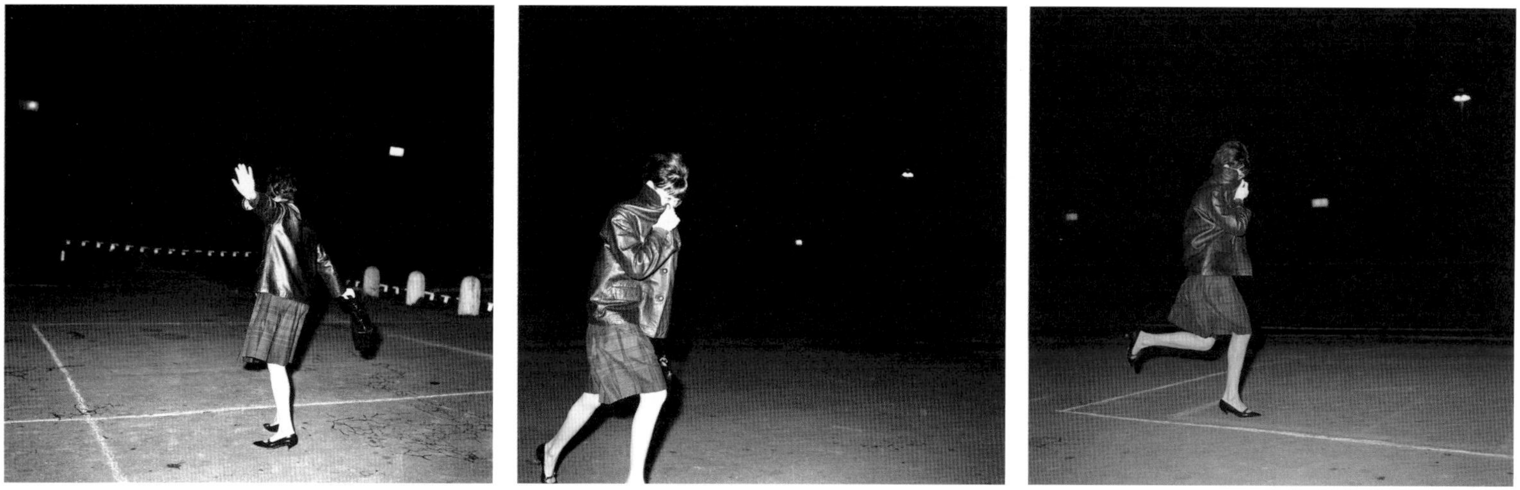

MARCELLO GEPPETTI
Hanna Rasmussen after the Call-Girls Scandal
January 1962

NO PHOTOS! Dark glasses, hoods, umbrellas. There is an entire typology of accessories that celebrities deploy when trying to avoid being photographed. But the most efficient tool for concealment—the one that can be instantly interposed between the face and the paparazzo's inquisitive lens to interfere with the shot and the legibility of the image—is the human hand. Since the 1940s, when Weegee took his photos of subjects exiting police stations and courtrooms, countless photographs have been taken showing celebrities ostensibly refusing to allow themselves to be photographed. Over time, this gesture of refusal, a kind of visual veto, has become a leitmotif of the paparazzo's trade. It has come to signify the stolen moment, captured in a snapshot. Most books on the topic—and this one is no exception—have covers featuring the image of a star with their hand raised in a universally recognized gesture that signifies "No photos!" in international sign language.

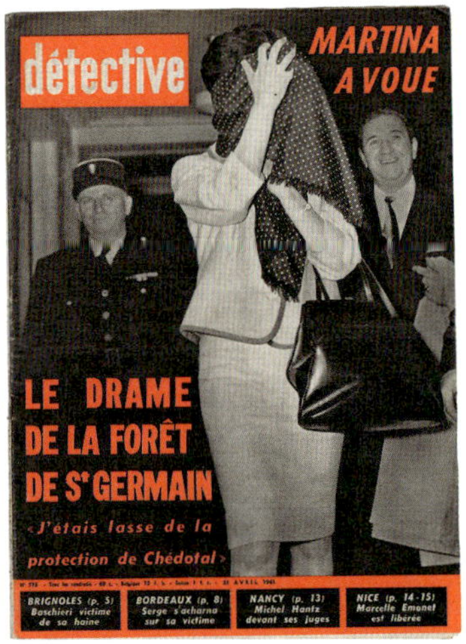

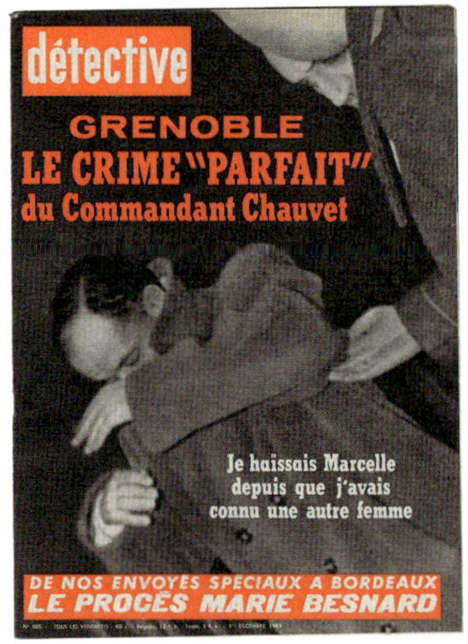

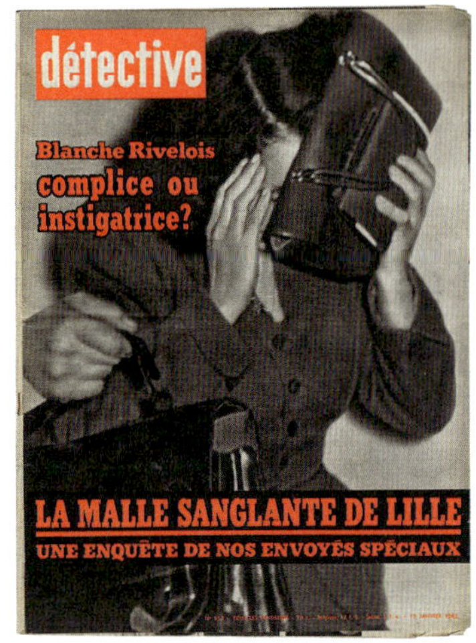

Détective, no. 773, April 21, 1961, front cover (Photograph: anonymous)

Détective, no. 805, December 1, 1961, front cover (Photograph: anonymous)

Détective, no. 812, January 19, 1962, front cover (Photograph: anonymous)

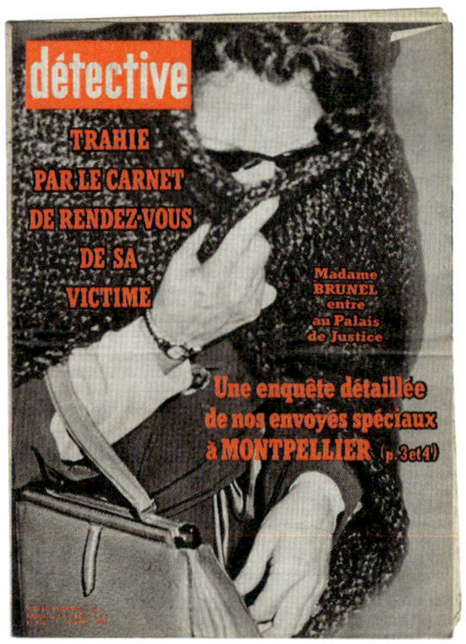

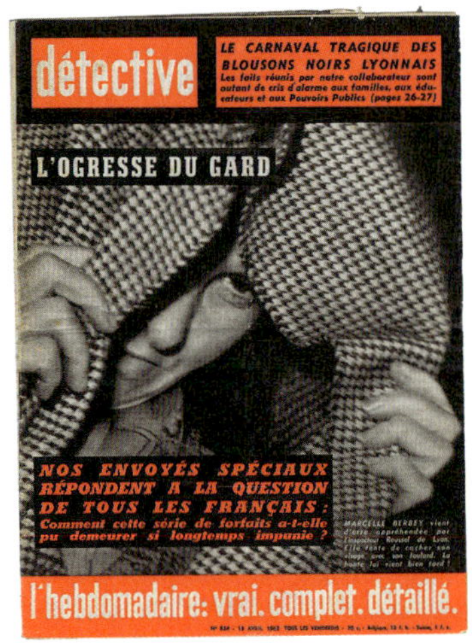

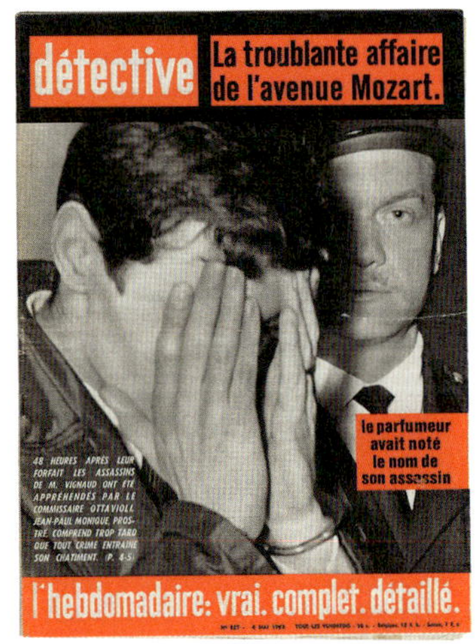

Détective, no. 814, February 2, 1962, front cover (Photograph: anonymous)

Détective, no. 824, April 13, 1962, front cover (Photograph: anonymous)

Détective, no. 827, May 4, 1962, front cover (Photograph: anonymous)

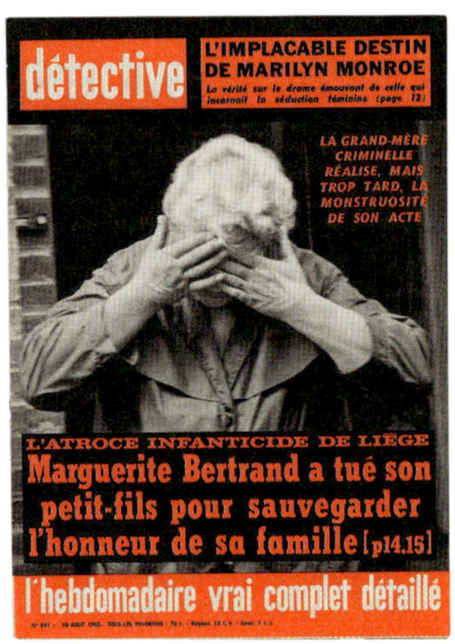

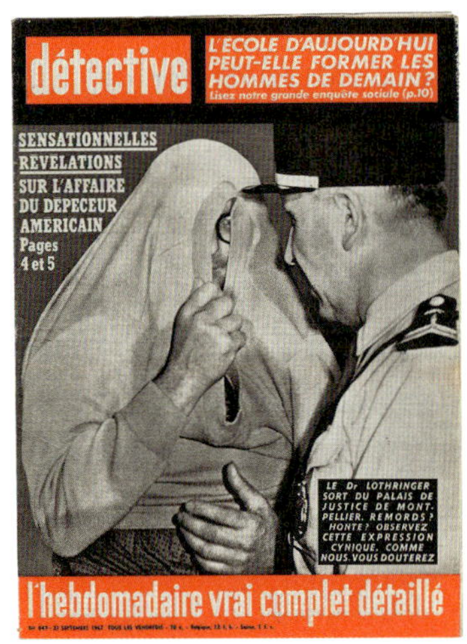

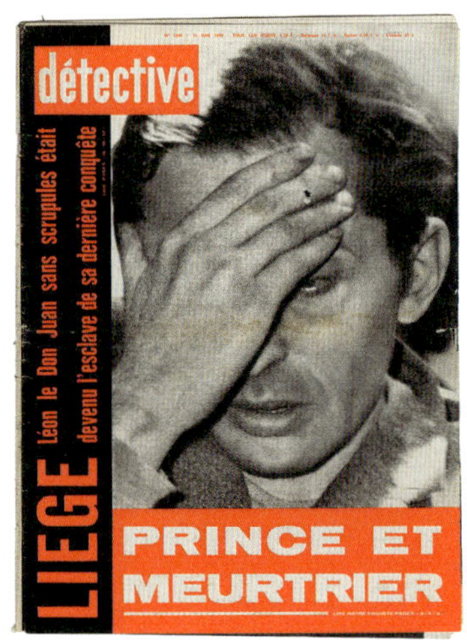

Détective, no. 841, August 10, 1962, front cover (Photograph: anonymous)

Détective, no. 847, September 21, 1962, front cover (Photograph: anonymous)

Détective, no. 1244, June 11, 1970, front cover (Photograph: anonymous)

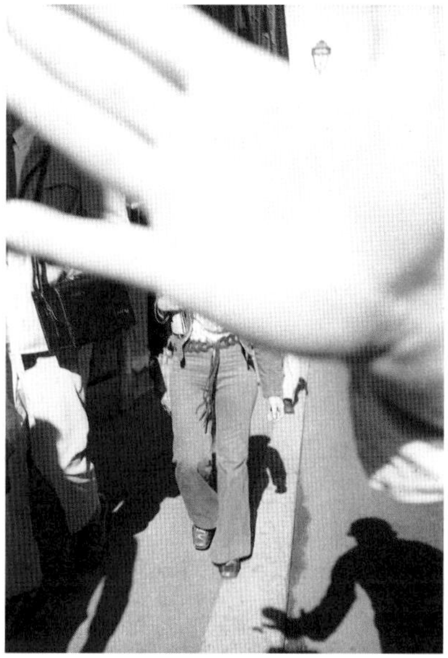

MARCELLO GEPPETTI
Rita Pavone, Via Condotti, Rome
1972

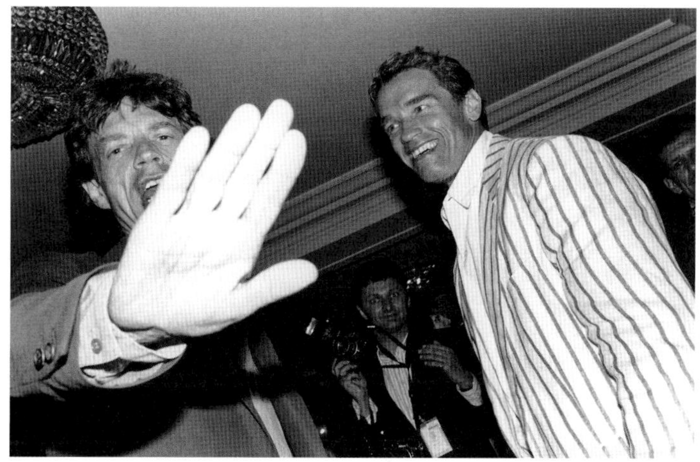

JEAN PIGOZZI
Mick Jagger and
Arnold Schwarzenegger,
Hôtel du Cap, Antibes
1990

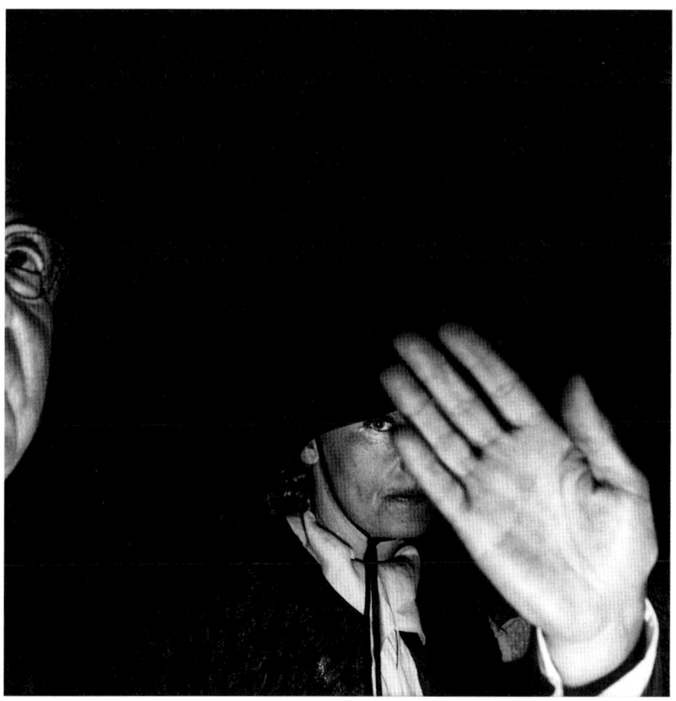

GEORGES DUDOGNON
Greta Garbo at the Club
Saint-Germain, Paris
c. 1952

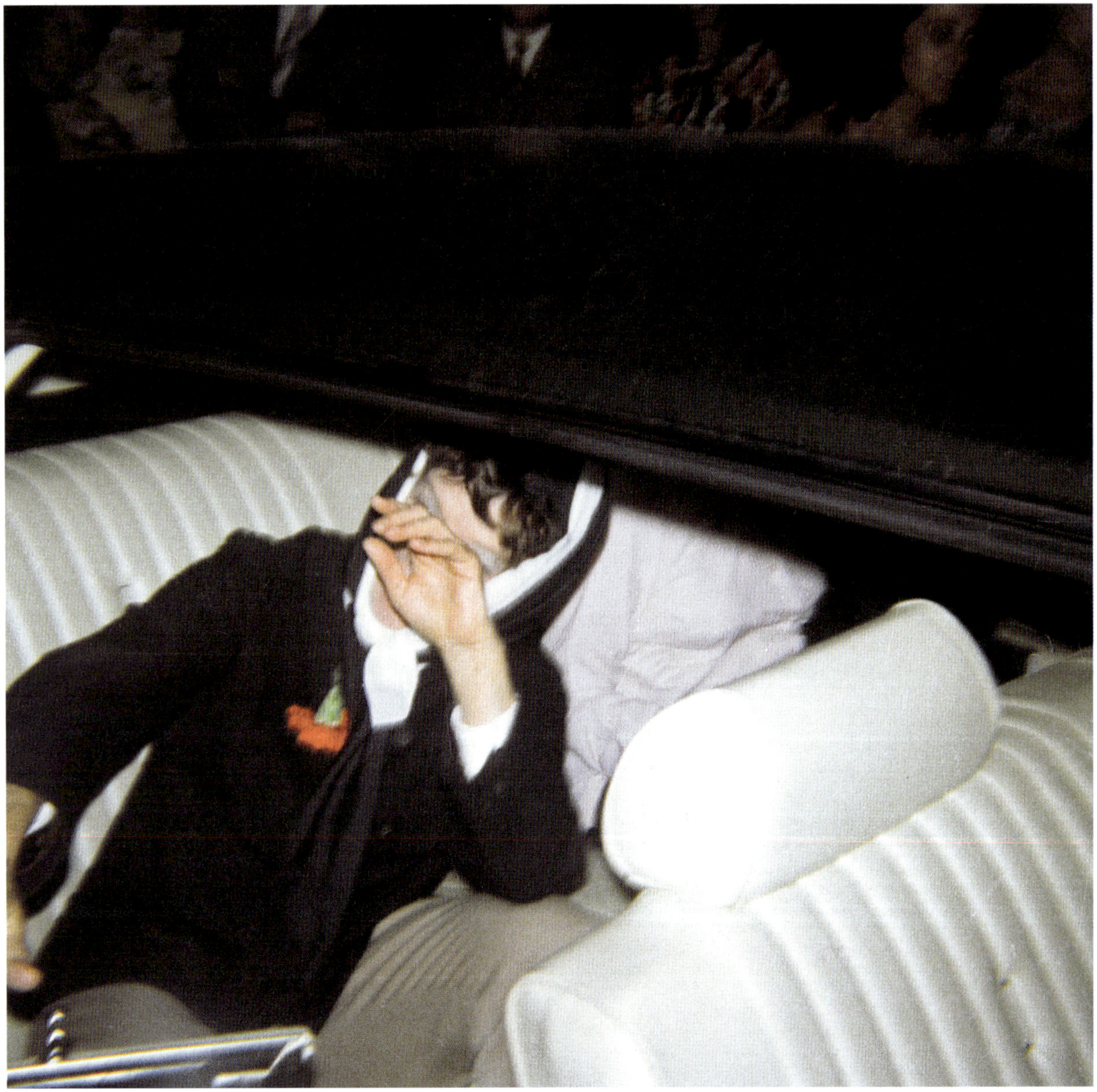

GARY LEE BOAS
Katharine Hepburn,
Mark Hellinger Theater,
Broadway
January 31, 1970

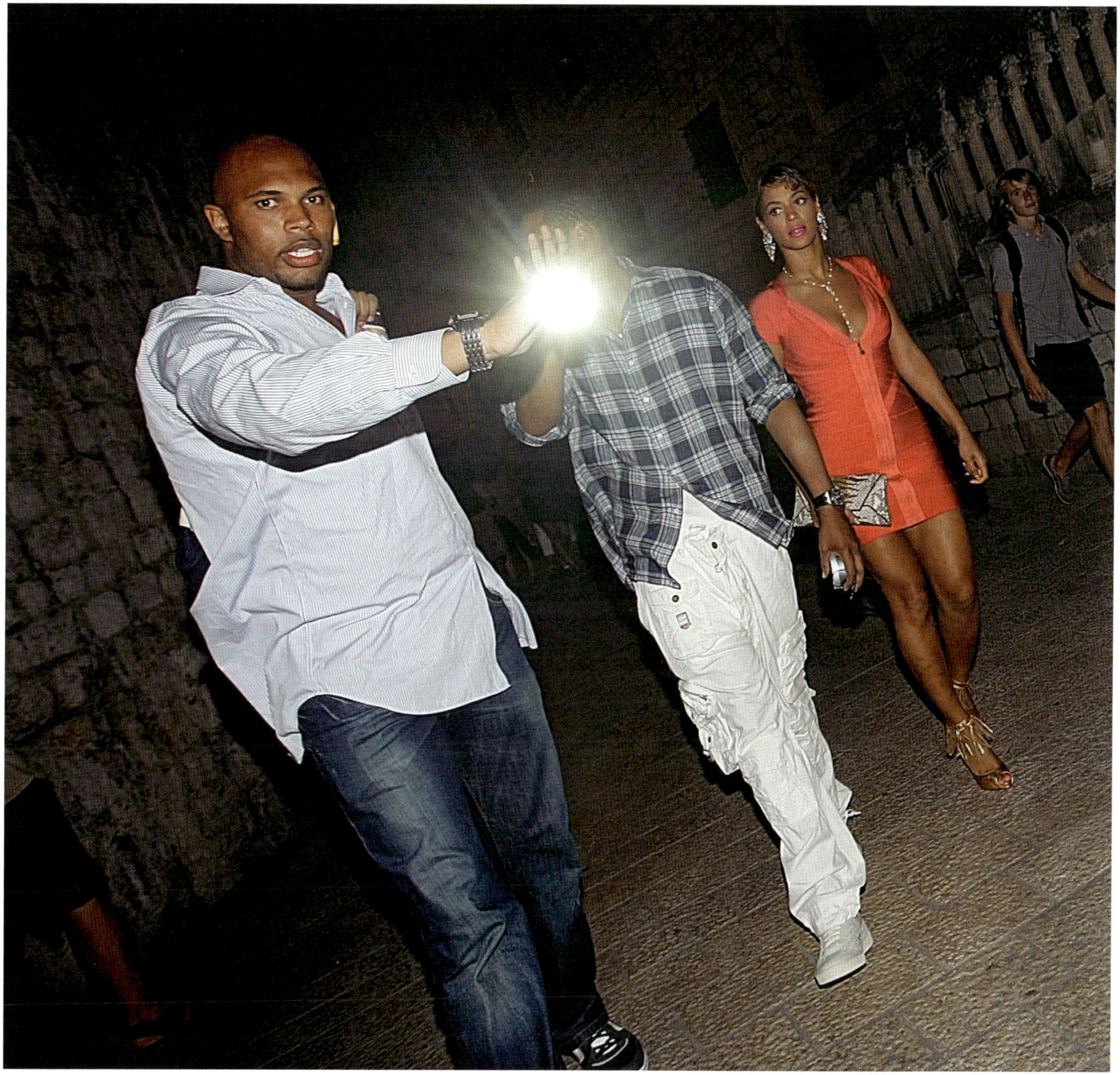

BRANIMIR KVARTUC
Beyoncé and Jay-Z, on Vacation in Dubrovnik, Leaving a Restaurant Protected by Their Bodyguards
August 18, 2009

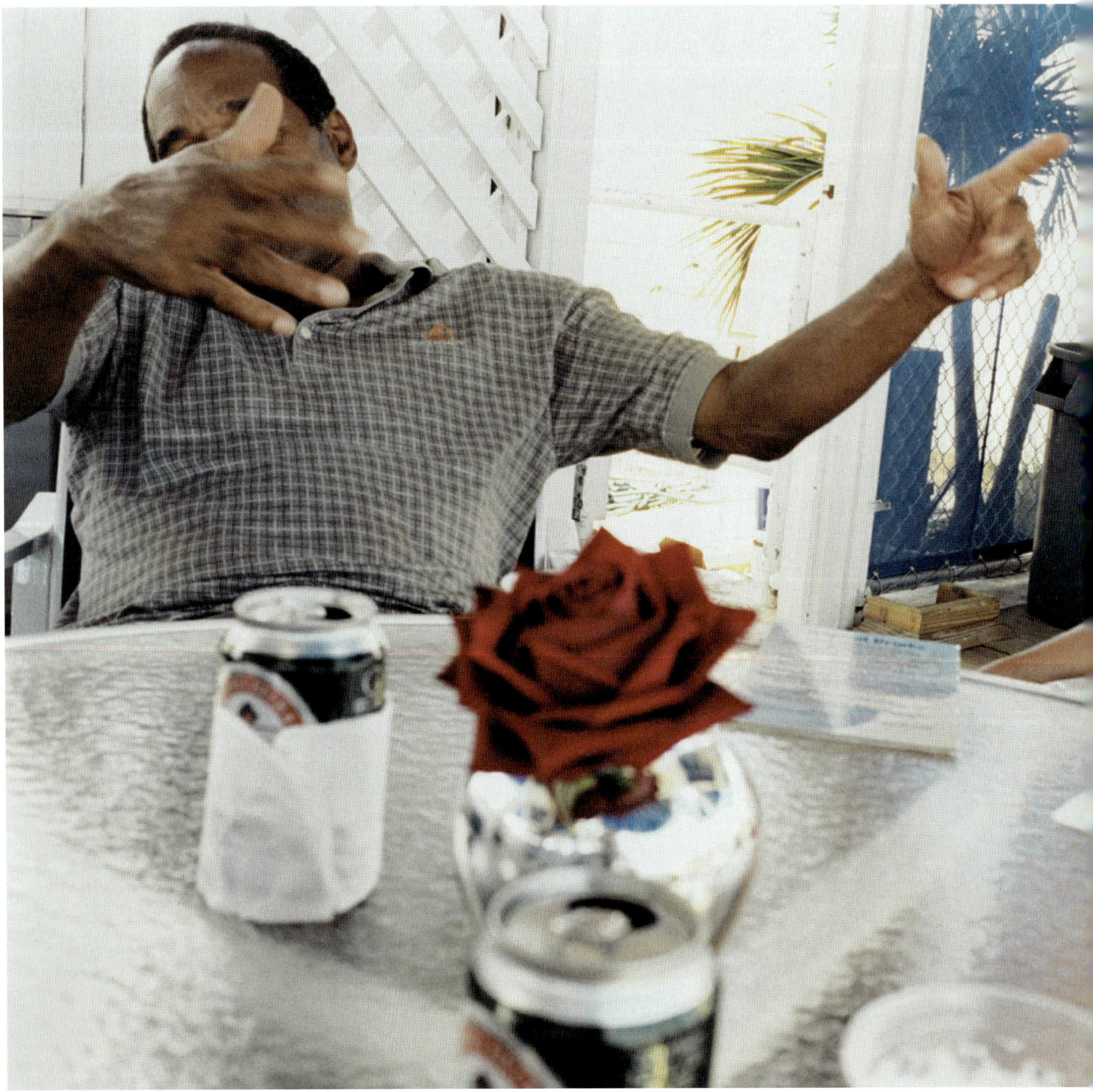

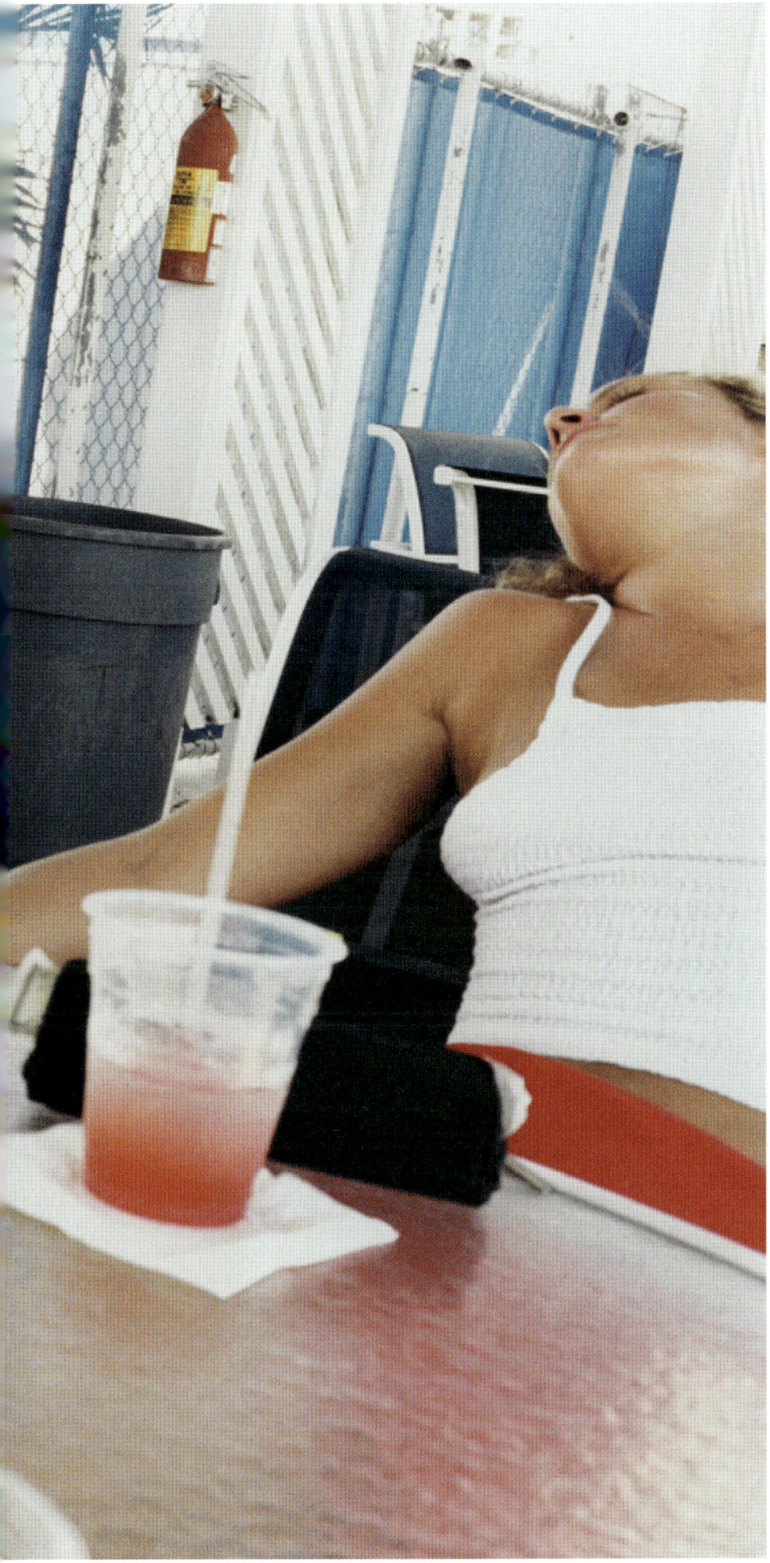

JUERGEN TELLER
OJ Simpson, Miami
2000

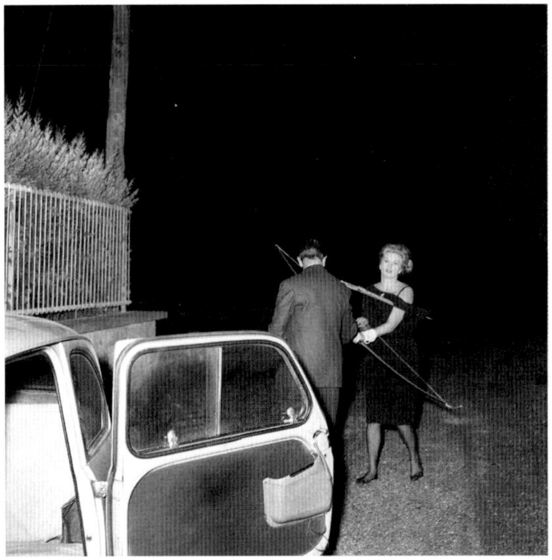

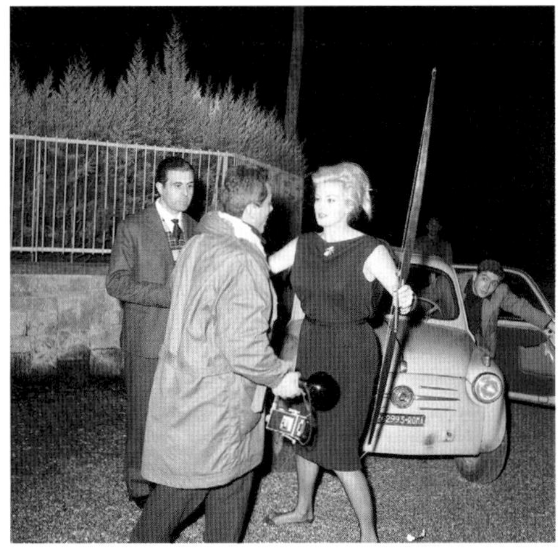

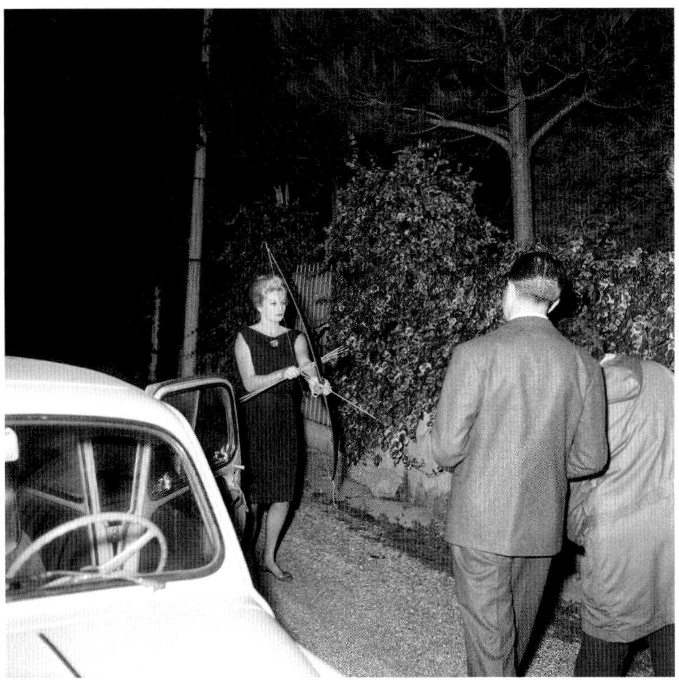

MARCELLO GEPPETTI
Anita Ekberg with Bow and Arrows
October 20, 1960

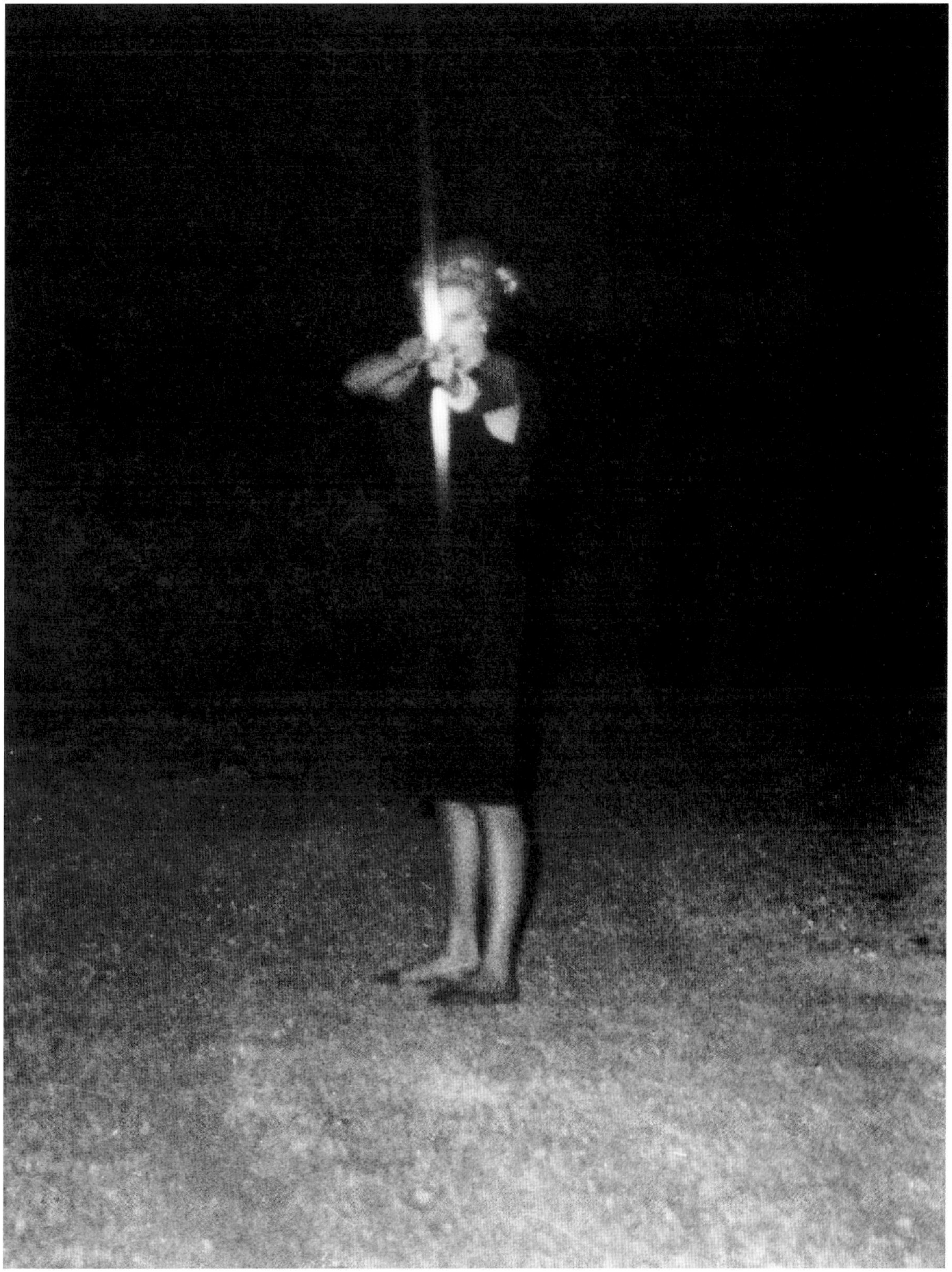

MARCELLO GEPPETTI
Anita Ekberg Threatens Photographers with Her Bow and Arrow
October 20, 1960

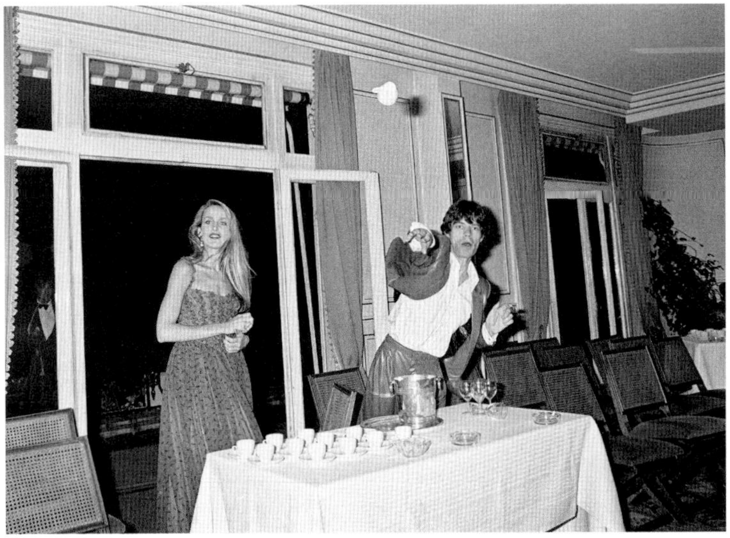

PASCAL ROSTAIN
Mick Jagger and Jerry Hall at the Pré Catelan, Paris
June 19, 1980

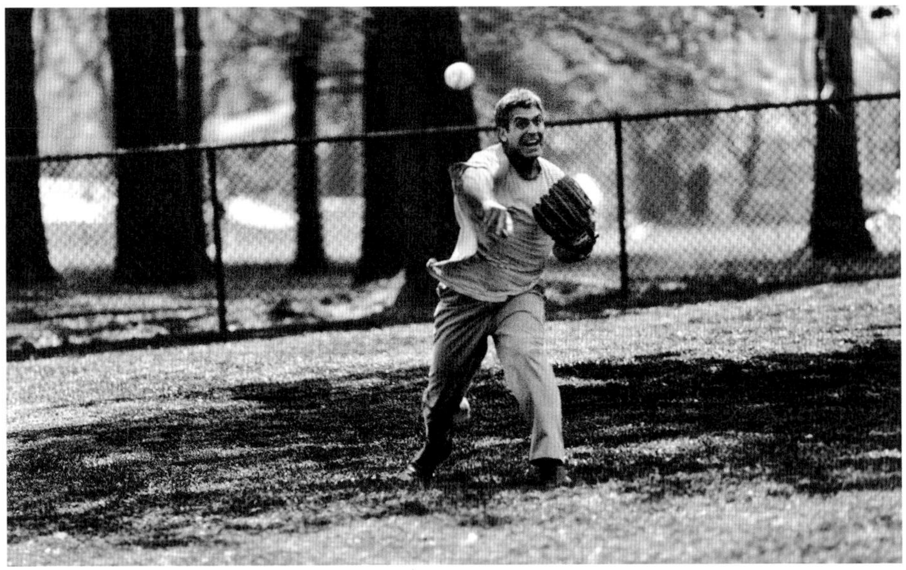

PASCAL ROSTAIN AND BRUNO MOURON
George Clooney Playing Softball in Santa Monica, California
1996

RESORTING TO VIOLENCE. When celebrities are disturbed in private moments, stalked, and even attacked, there inevitably comes a time when the star becomes enraged with the paparazzi, and the aggression is reciprocated. The infuriated star insults the photographer, hurling whatever he is carrying and sometimes even going on the attack. A few unforgettable images exemplify these moments: Anita Ekberg demonstrating her wrath by pointing a bow and arrow at the paparazzi; Sean Penn knocking out a photographer with a powerful punch; Ron Galella sporting a football helmet to protect himself from Marlon Brando, who had already broken his jaw. Some paparazzi go so far as to initiate these altercations, operating in pairs. One provokes the star while his accomplice immortalizes the resulting scene. The shot is well worth a few bruises. It's sure to sell for considerably more than a routine photo of a cheerfully smiling celebrity.

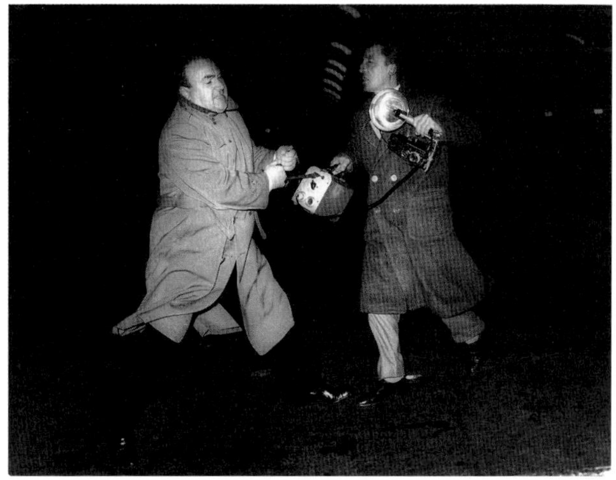

ANONYMOUS
Don Gussoni and
Marcello Geppetti
1959

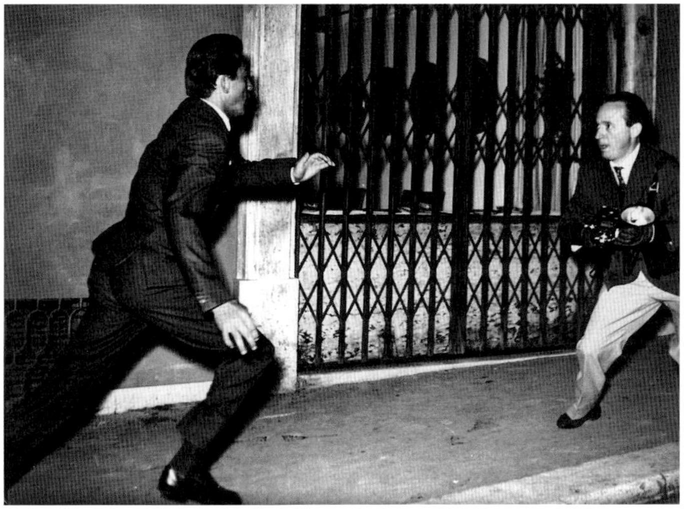

ELIO SORCI
Walter Chiari and
Tazio Secchiaroli, Rome
1958

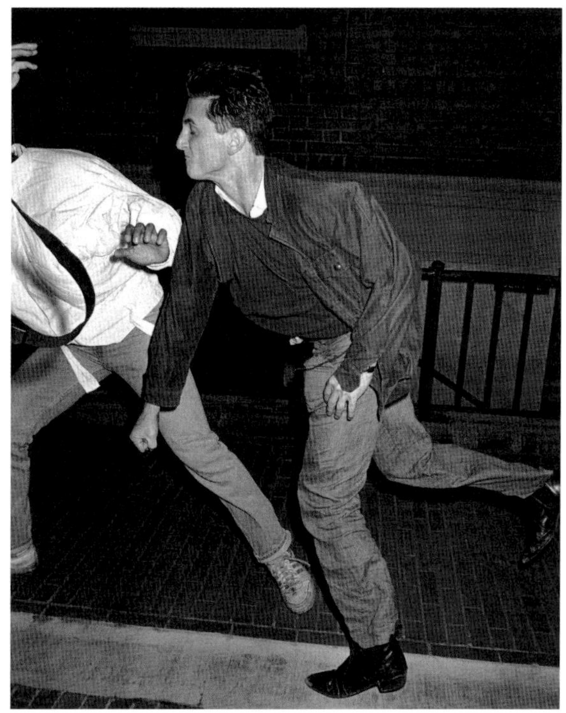

RON GALELLA
After a Showing of Goose and TomTom *at the Mitzi Newhouse Theater, Sean Penn Punches and Throws the Photographer Anthony Savignano Out of His Home on 64th West Street, New York*
August 29, 1986

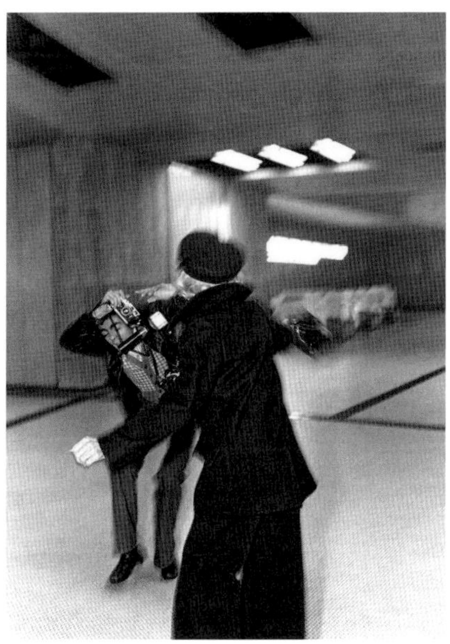

DANIEL ANGELI
Marlene Dietrich Attacks a Photographer [Francis Apesteguy] at Orly Airport
1975

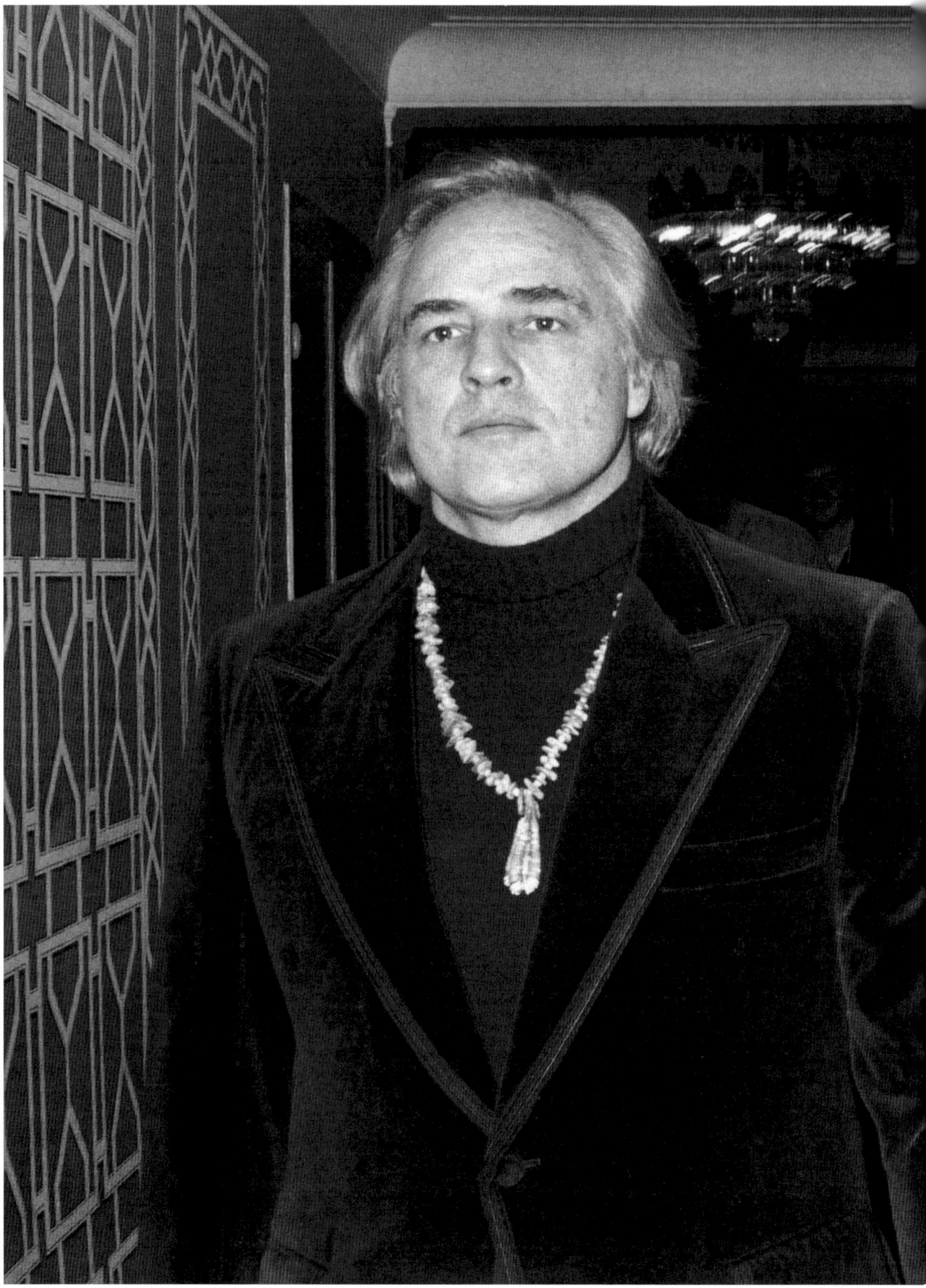

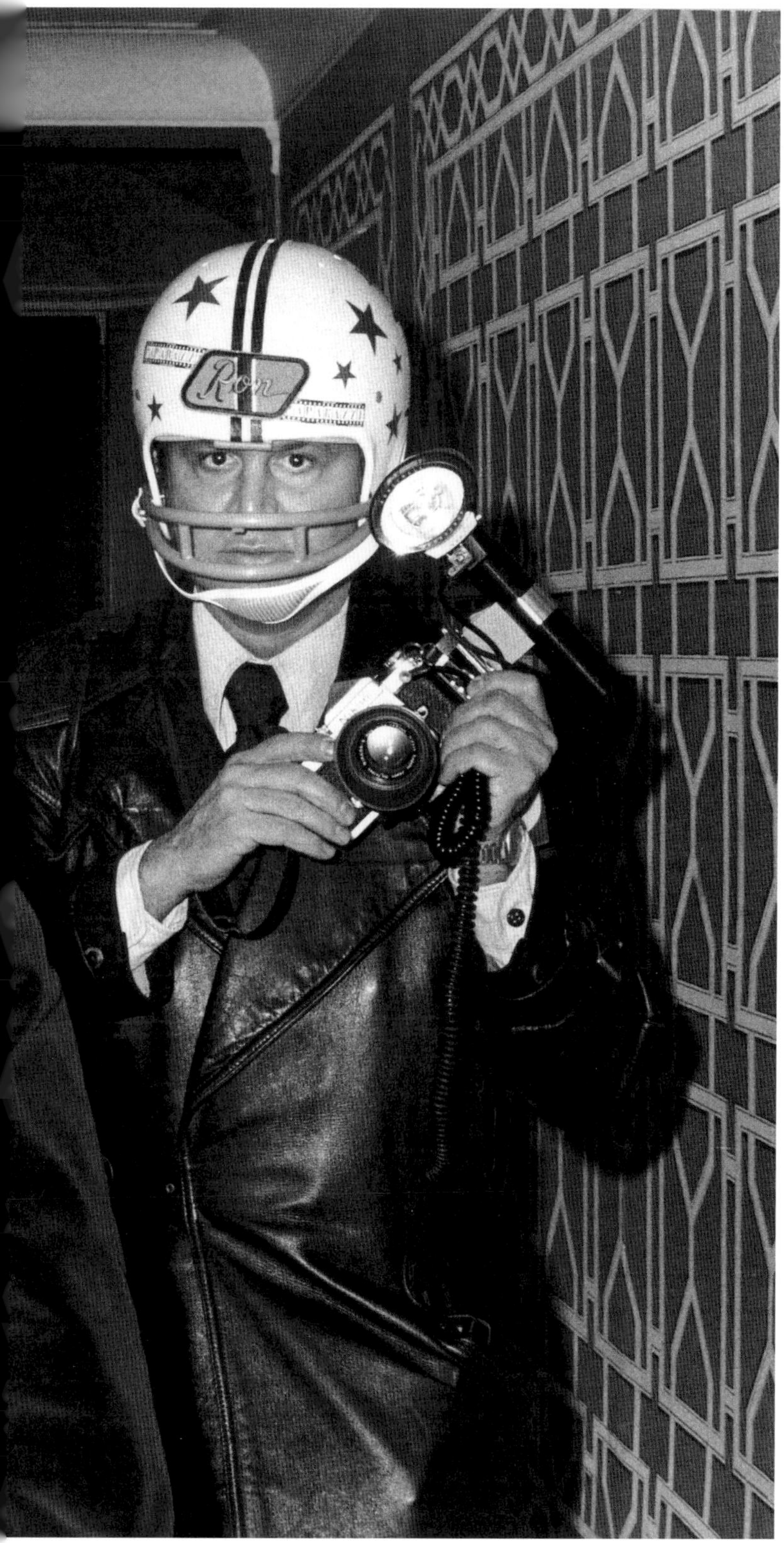

PAUL SCHMULBACH
Marlon Brando and Ron Galella at the Charity Ball for the American Indians Development Association at the Waldorf Astoria Hotel, New York
November 26, 1974

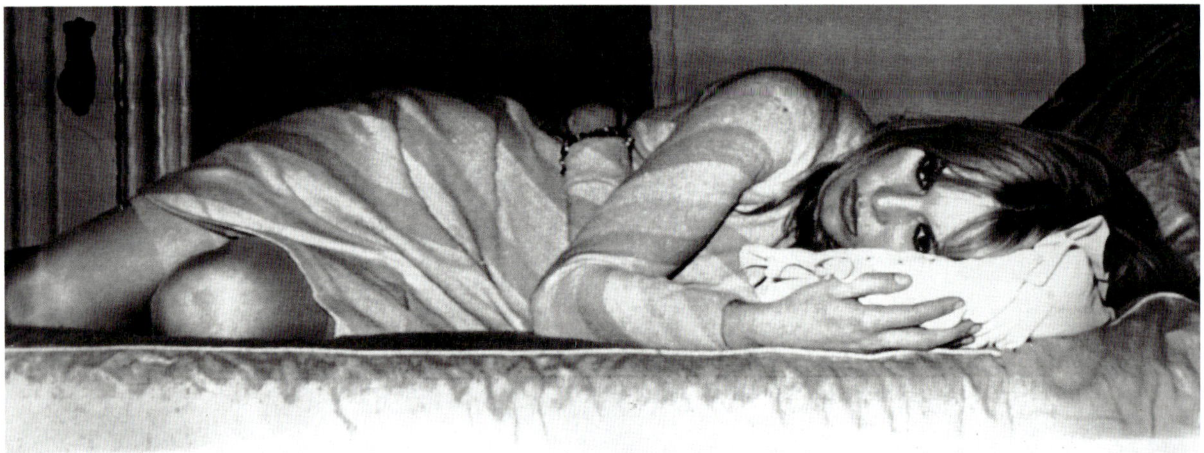

ANONYMOUS
(United Press International Photo)
Brigitte Bardot Resting at Her Hotel after Having Been Slightly Wounded in the Eye by the Explosion of a Photographer's Flash, New York
December 20, 1965

THE OTHER SIDE OF THE COIN.
In December 1965, Brigitte Bardot was photographed curled up in her bed, apparently in a state of shock. She had just been wounded in the eye by a paparazzo's flash. As the star system evolved, celebrities were no longer shown solely on their good days. They now appeared in the prosaic interludes of their daily lives, at moments when they were definitely not at their best. In response to promotional or stylized portraits where stars appeared serene and happy in a flattering light, a very different iconography developed that was bleak, even belittling—the antithesis of the glamorous facade. In May 2007, Paris Hilton was photographed weeping in her car after being convicted of speeding. The shot was taken by none other than Nick Ut, the Vietnam War photographer who took the unforgettable picture of a young girl fleeing her napalmed village in 1972. Thirty-five years had elapsed between these two images of suffering. The magazines of earlier decades had gradually abandoned traditional photojournalism, embracing the celebrity press in its stead.

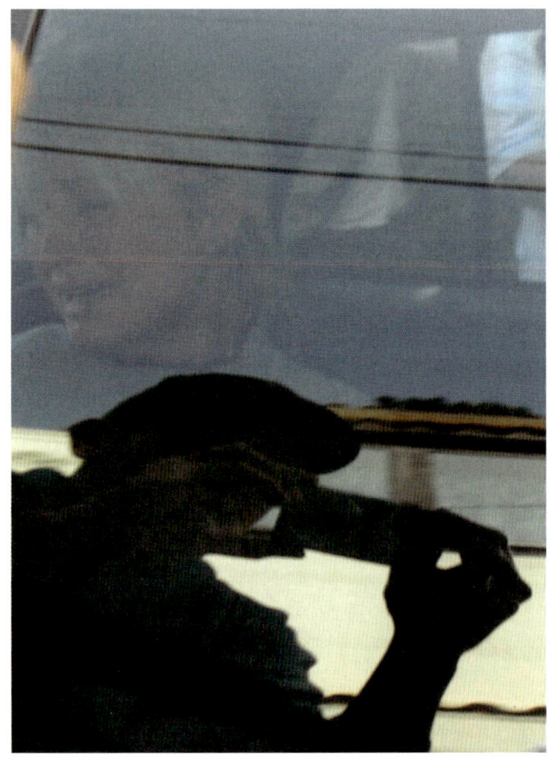

NICK UT
Paris Hilton Seen through a Police Car Window before Appearing in Court
2007

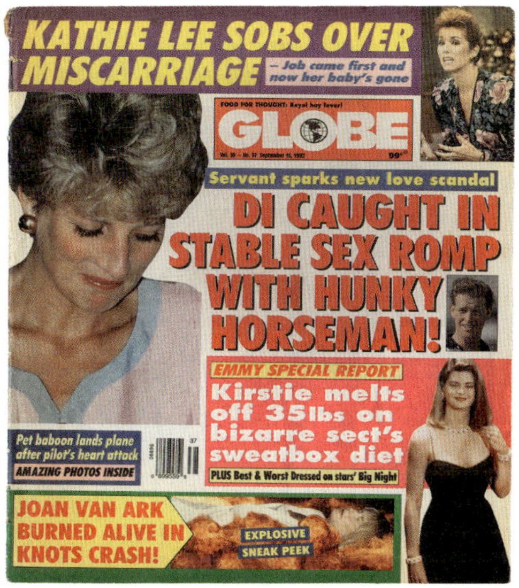

Globe, vol. 39, no. 37,
September 15, 1992,
front cover
(Photograph: anonymous)

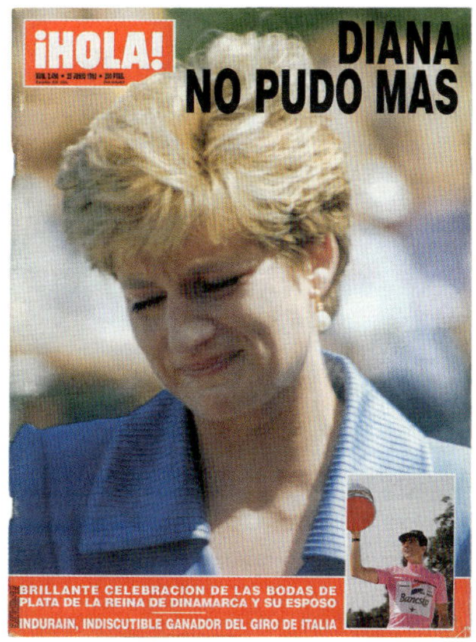

¡Hola!, no. 2498,
June 25, 1992,
front cover
(Photograph: anonymous)

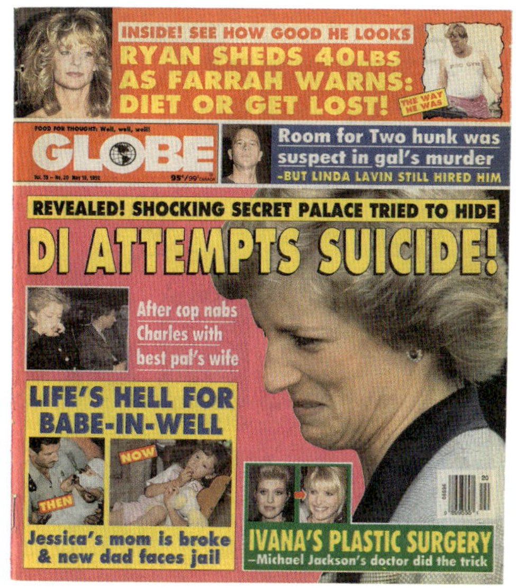

Globe, vol. 39, no. 20,
May 19, 1992,
front cover
(Photograph: anonymous)

The Night of the Hunters

André Rouillé

Princess Diana's tragic death in 1997 elicited a profound emotional response worldwide. It also drew tremendous attention to the field of photojournalism and the decline of genuine news reporting, to the benefit of sensationalist celebrity photographs and the ascendency of the paparazzi.

Symptoms of this decline were already evident throughout the 1990s. Photography had been virtually absent in press coverage of the Gulf War, although that war was one of journalists' primary topics. Photography had been accused of deliberate deception on several occasions, particularly with regard to the pseudo-discovery of a falsified mass grave in Timisoara in Romania. Now photography was held responsible for the accident and premature death of Princess Diana. Absence, lies, and even murder. These accusations revealed a crisis in the field of photojournalism, and there was an added financial aspect to be considered. A scoop in the celebrity press could command astronomical prices, dwarfing any comparison with photos taken by the news press, and the international competition was formidable.

News reportage retreated before the surge in celebrity photographs: film stars, singers, princes and princesses, kings, television anchormen, and sports champions were now the focus of attention. The French press agencies Sipa, Gamma, and Sygma had occupied the most prominent positions in photojournalism during the last quarter of the twentieth century, but their attempts to assume a role in the celebrity press proved unsuccessful.

The Celebrity Photojournalism Machine

The celebrity photojournalism machine has its very own mechanisms, materials, and production methods, as well as its own set of ethical standards. Stars of all kinds, including the short-lived heroes of random events, constitute the primary material. The paparazzi photographers and their agencies are the artisans of this trade. Printed magazines, which are part of the intensely competitive corporate structures directed by press barons, form a close-knit circle of producers-investors. Finally, the clientele consists of those countless buyers and readers in search of emotional experiences and dreams. Selling emotion and happiness, tears and laughter—and making profits from sensation and sentiment: these are the raisons d'être of celebrity photojournalism.

Although the ephemeral stars of trivial news stories are sometimes disturbed or even overwhelmed by the voracity of this photojournalism machine, genuine celebrities have learned how to harness it and put it to work in their own best interests. They also attempt to manage—and sometimes put a price tag on—their image. But they do so with varying degrees of success and do not always escape the fate of being reduced to mere images of themselves. Stars sometimes become overexposed symbols of simplified externalities, without any interiority, individuality, or privacy. They become entirely public beings, whose private lives are relentlessly threatened with the overwhelming appetite of popular culture. Famous stars cease to be genuine subjects or human beings. Stars become objects, products of consumerism and envy, particularly in the eyes of the paparazzi.

1. *Libération*, September 5, 1997: 6.

2. Henri Cartier-Bresson, "The Decisive Moment," preface to *The Decisive Moment* (New York: Simon & Schuster, 1952).

3. Gilles Deleuze, *Proust et les signes* (Paris: Quadrige / PUF, 1996), 218.

The term "star"—which has entered other foreign languages, including French—reminds us that stars are indeed luminous beings. Unlike the stars of the cosmos, however, the stars of the celebrity world do not sparkle without being illuminated by an artificial source. They are reflective surfaces rather than emitters of light. What is the nature of the light that makes them glitter so brilliantly and sometimes consumes them, giving them visibility and liberating them from obscurity? It is none other than the vast machine of celebrity promotion, casting a light that is both intense and capricious. This communications behemoth encompasses photography, magazines, advertising, television, and film—all the media combined.

This media machine is both a lens and a source of illumination. It creates visibility, brilliance, and sparkle for those beings so aptly called "stars." Any star becomes more brilliant if she understands how to capture, modulate, and reflect this light that gives her life. It was in this realm—as every paparazzo acknowledged—that Princess Diana truly excelled.

The Paparazzo's Role

In the last quarter of the twentieth century, sensational celebrity photojournalism made its fortune by capturing scoops. Its iconic figure was the paparazzo armed with a powerful telephoto lens, who was endowed with both patience and tenacity. The scoop's value did not reside so much in its aesthetic merits as in the feat of capturing some aspect of the hidden side of a star who was already highly overexposed. The goal was to create a breach in the wall erected around the star's private life. The paparazzi were always on the brink of illegitimacy, invading private life, probing the forbidden, violating intimate details. The success and market value of their shots were based on this perverse ethic. The paparazzi earned their living at the expense of their "prey" and often against the victim's will.

Photojournalist news reporters walk the streets and travel the world to shoot "the decisive moment" (to echo the English translation of the title of Henri Cartier-Bresson's book *Images à la sauvette*), and then continue on their way. However, the paparazzo lurks, observes, and stalks his prey. Stalking, "spin," and voyeurism are his tools. He practices the spider's stratagem. As the spider spins its web, the paparazzo weaves a network of observations on his prey. He is poised to leap at the slightest indication, the tiniest movement. Seemingly eyeless and brainless, he responds in a quasi-reflexive fashion to stimuli. Eyeless? Consider the shots taken blind in the midst of the bustling hordes that appear the moment a star appears. Brainless? Remember the paparazzo who arrived on location just moments after Princess Diana's accident. He proclaimed, "It's true that Diana was still alive, she was still moving. OK, we took the photos without thinking. But what was I supposed to do? My job is to take pictures."[1]

The ethic of the paparazzi, who operate through the vast machine of celebrity journalism, is based on the exploitation of horrific events. Their behavior is justified by calling such photos a "job." The paparazzo is an automaton. ("We took pictures without thinking.") He shuns individual responsibility. Cartier-Bresson viewed reporting as "a joint operation of the brain, the eye, and the heart." His camera's only purpose, he said, was to "register upon film the decision made by the eye."[2] In contrast, paparazzi seem incapable of making use of their eyes, their hearts, or their brains. Theirs are involuntary feelings, involuntary memories, involuntary thoughts: the paparazzo is no more than a tracking machine. He resembles a soulless agent within a nerveless body, reacting mindlessly to the stimuli of a communications network.[3]

His approach is an aggressive version of the fundamental assumption underlying the film version of a photographic document. There is a presumption that truth is always more or less hidden away within the secret heart of things and beings. This truth must be uncovered and brought to light by reporters, or, if absolutely necessary, by the paparazzi's extreme methods. Both approaches are rooted in the (very ideological) notion of a "decisive moment," which supposedly conveys the densest burden of truth, and is endowed with the greatest power of revelation.

In this spirit, light reveals, illuminates, and brings the star into being. If she retreats into the shadows of the private, intimate side of her life that is hidden from view, the paparazzo's role is to use photography to forcibly and sensationally reveal this shadowy zone where she is suspected of harboring secrets.

Based on this binary notion that contrasts light and shadow, public life and private life, truth and lies, paparazzi make it their mission to penetrate and expose the sequestered personal domain of the stars to public view. After all, there must be something dark and scandalous in these zones that are kept out of the limelight. Of course, the real motive is to satisfy the avid curiosity of the mass audience. In short, a paparazzo's celebrity photo is the outcome of the sensational confrontation between illusory photographic truth and the brilliant falsity of superficial appearances.

The Digital Watershed

But all this is history. The whole structure is in the process of collapsing with the advent of a new era and the explosion of digital images and networks. This shift is attributable to the meteoric rise of smartphones, which are capable of capturing digital images and distributing them instantly and without charge on social networks and the Internet. Now a new actor has burst upon the stage of celebrity photography: the audience itself. In the broadest sense, this includes anyone equipped with a smartphone.

This vast, globalized community of smartphone owners has expanded at vertiginous speed since the initial introduction of the iPhone (first marketed in the US in late June 2007). It far exceeds the community of actual photographers who have a certain degree of interest, however modest, in photographic images and practices. They pay at least a minimum of attention to the framing and composition of their shots.

The paparazzi are a dying breed; the celebrity press for whom they were once heroes and the stars they hunt down are constantly transforming, keeping pace with vast societal changes. Yesterday's hunters are now the prey. They are falling victim to the immense conflagration of digital, computer, and web networks. The few remaining paparazzi, who are professional photographers, are now faced with brutal competition from a horde of random picture-takers. These new players have the formidable capacity to provide blanket coverage, and the hitherto unheard of ability to capture and display any event, however trivial, in real time.

The paparazzo has been cast adrift in this anonymous tide of non-photographers. For these new participants, photographic equipment is no longer a tool reserved for a skilled practitioner to use in creating a documentary record. It has no need of a culturally informed eye. Today's photographic device is a kind of prosthesis inseparably attached to the user's body. It is almost a "natural" organ for recording and communicating, with little regard for meaningful content or any formal considerations.

This current situation erodes the fundamentally binary structure of canonical celebrity photography, abolishing the interaction that has always been predicated on a paradoxical conflict and bond between the paparazzo and the star. She is no longer faced with the relentless surveillance of an individual photographer. Now she confronts a multitude of non-photographers, who are more reactive than active, shooting at random. Previously, intensive surveillance was carried out at a distance by a professional equipped with his iconic telephoto lens. Now, the star is constantly monitored on her doorstep by a random mass of anonymous actors in constant motion, with a variety of motivations. Their smartphones give them the power to discreetly and efficiently record and disseminate images instantaneously.

Whatever they do, and wherever they go, stars are now trapped in the midst of a media labyrinth. They are besieged by digital recording devices in virtually continuous operation. A tremendous flood of images from a multitude of unattributable sources emanates from these devices almost automatically. Their output is effectively stripped of any of the drama associated with the discovery of hidden truths, and the pathos associated with a violation of someone's private life.

The flood of pictures generated by this horde of non-photographers using their super-smartphones resembles a modern form of the mythological hydra with thousands of voracious heads. It spares no one, not even those living the most ordinary lives. Under these conditions, every private detail of each individual life can be ceaselessly captured from every angle. The concepts of privacy and personal life have lost value, becoming illusory. Meanwhile, the "heroism" of the paparazzi and the booty they once gleaned seem completely inconsequential.

This is an era of digital convergence, where the photo and telephone networks are merging. Now, "truths" about each individual are no longer revealed by snapshots of ephemeral moments heroically captured by the targeted actions of kamikaze-paparazzi. These realities are now rooted in the continuous, automatic recording of data generated by the masses, often unwittingly. The most mundane activities of daily life—making a phone call, using a credit card, or taking a subway or plane—are recorded.

The most detailed images of private moments and ordinary life are no longer conveyed in photographs; they are digital and not necessarily figurative or even visual. They are no longer discontinuous; they are constant. They no longer result from individual initiatives; they are generated by automated systems.

The community of non-photographers engaged in photographic activities is the visual version of a new informational model.

These non-visual images of individual lives may actually be coupled with increased visibility, however fleeting it may be. "In the future, everybody will be world famous for fifteen minutes," Andy Warhol asserted in 1968. It was a sentiment that was still just a matter of conjecture for the media of that "celebrity society" era. Now, in today's "information society," this fame can be achieved in a different way, where photography and digital networks intersect. Instagram is one example.

Instagram, Or How to Become a Paparazzo Yourself

Many reacted with incredulity when the giant Facebook purchased the little start-up Instagram in April 2012 for the modest sum of 1 billion dollars. Why would anyone pay so much for a small company whose claim to fame was the creation of a humble application designed to create photos and videos to be shared on social networks using smartphones? Because this application, basic as it may have been, concealed a powerful strategic potential in the ultra-competitive and lucrative universe of social networks.

Mark Zuckerberg, Facebook's founder and chairman, quickly grasped the fact that Instagram would enable him to enhance and broaden the objective he had resolutely pursued: using Facebook to gain closer access to people's lives. The goal was not motivated by solicitude for people's well-being, of course. The intent was to collect—and store—the maximum possible amount of data on individuals. Viewed from this perspective, the combination of Facebook and Instagram had the potential to connect, diversify, and enhance the methods and means of access to this proximity. In our information society, "people's lives" have become the foundation for maximizing profits. Detailed data on ordinary daily lives are also the key to great power and finely tuned control. The most successful Internet companies know exactly how to gather and exploit this information for their own gain.

In no time, Facebook's acquisition fundamentally altered the general terms of use of the Instagram application. The new owner arrogated to itself the right to commercially exploit the users' photos, notably for marketing and publicity purposes, as well as the right to cross the personal data of users of the two services. In case any doubts remain as to the motivations of the Instagram-Facebook enterprise, just create an account and follow the requests for authorization that punctuate each step of user registration. Again and again, a very significant message appears beginning with "Instagram would like to access," revealing that the service may be free but it comes with plenty of demands. So, we read how Instagram would like to access the photos that are stored in our smartphone's gallery, as well as accessing its microphone. Most of all, Instagram would like to access our contacts. This final request is sufficiently strategic and sensitive to be accompanied by an attempt at explanation and justification. It is explained that you have to send the information in your address book to Instagram's servers (with a secure connection) to allow you to find your friends. The assurance of a "secure connection" is risible in this case, because it is not really protecting the user's personal addresses—they are transmitted to servers to be stored, crossed, and exploited. It is the hoard of data plundered in this way that Instagram-Facebook is actually protecting.

Besides this mass of valuable information that it collects upon entry, Instagram tries to gather a continuous stream of data as its service is used. There is a localization option, to share where you have taken your photos, followed by an invitation to identify the people in them ("tagging" them), before sending the photos to Facebook. This process entails entering their first and last names in a box after touching the zone in which they appear on the photo. Facial recognition software is then able to associate a person's first and last names with every photograph of that individual circulating on the networks.

To summarize, the free Instagram service for "sharing" digital photos involves connecting the users, via their smartphones, to a tightly knit network that is capable of gathering a constant flow of information on them and their followers. These data include their images, their first and last names, and all of their movements, gathered through the use of localization software. Most importantly, it includes their "contacts." In contrast to the more traditional pseudo-"friends" of social networks, these names are referenced in users' own address books and "identified" by them directly on their photos by using the "tag people" function.

This is a business that operates by controlling information at the intersection of social networks, smartphones, and digital photographs. It functions with the passive acquiescence and active collaboration of its users.

It is a company whose business plan is massive and global in scope (by the third quarter of 2013, Instagram alone—without counting Facebook—had 100 million active users posting more than 40 million photos a day).

Instagram's servers access, collect, store, cross, and handle the information flows, but smartphones provide the data. Digital photos are instantly available on smartphone screens, and on all the digital devices in the network. Smartphones allow users to take countless photos without any forethought, reacting rather than reflecting. It is a reflexive impulse to aim, snap, and share a scene without really seeing, framing, or composing it. The photo is little more than a random glance. For all these reasons, and many other motives influenced by our contemporary culture, an entirely new approach to creating photographs has evolved over the last few years. This capability has generated a frenzy among users. They now flood the network with photos and compete with each other to document the most random, banal, and apparently inconsequential details of their lives.

The myriad spur-of-the-moment shots of random happenings and micro-events in the daily lives of ordinary people would eventually have been consigned to oblivion in prior decades. However, they have now become the focus of vastly heightened attention. Software tools have an almost unimaginable power to capture, collect, and process these images, while linking them to other digital information, visual or otherwise. The enormous quantity of dynamic micro-data accumulated on people's lives contributes to enlarging and sustaining immense sources of power, and has profound economic influences.

The collaboration of Instagram and Facebook, at the nexus of smartphones, digital photos, and computer networks, represents a decisive step forward in the information society. This advance comes at the expense of the former society of celebrity and the paparazzi who nourished it. The nature of knowledge and power is in a state of flux. The field is no longer dominated by a select few stars and celebrities, as it was in the era of the paparazzi. Now the subject is merely "people." They are no longer captured by paparazzi from a distance, in a series of discontinuous instants, in shots of "decisive moments" assumed to theatrically reveal a hidden secret. These photos were the end result of a lengthy and complicated process of stalking, "spinning," and voyeurism. Now, they emanate from a highly sophisticated array of devices that record automatically and continuously, compiling digital information of all kinds, both visual and nonvisual. They are produced by "the people" themselves simply using their smartphones.

Anyone can play the role of paparazzo at will by photographing and disseminating the image of a star in an embarrassing or unusual situation, via a smartphone. The shot will assuredly be linked with very similar photos taken and shared simultaneously by others. What's more, our smartphones transmit—without our knowledge—an abundance of invisible personal data on ourselves: the date, time, location, and even the full names of those present with us at an event. This information is captured by the interface of facial recognition software and its preexisting identifications. We have become paparazzi of our own lives.

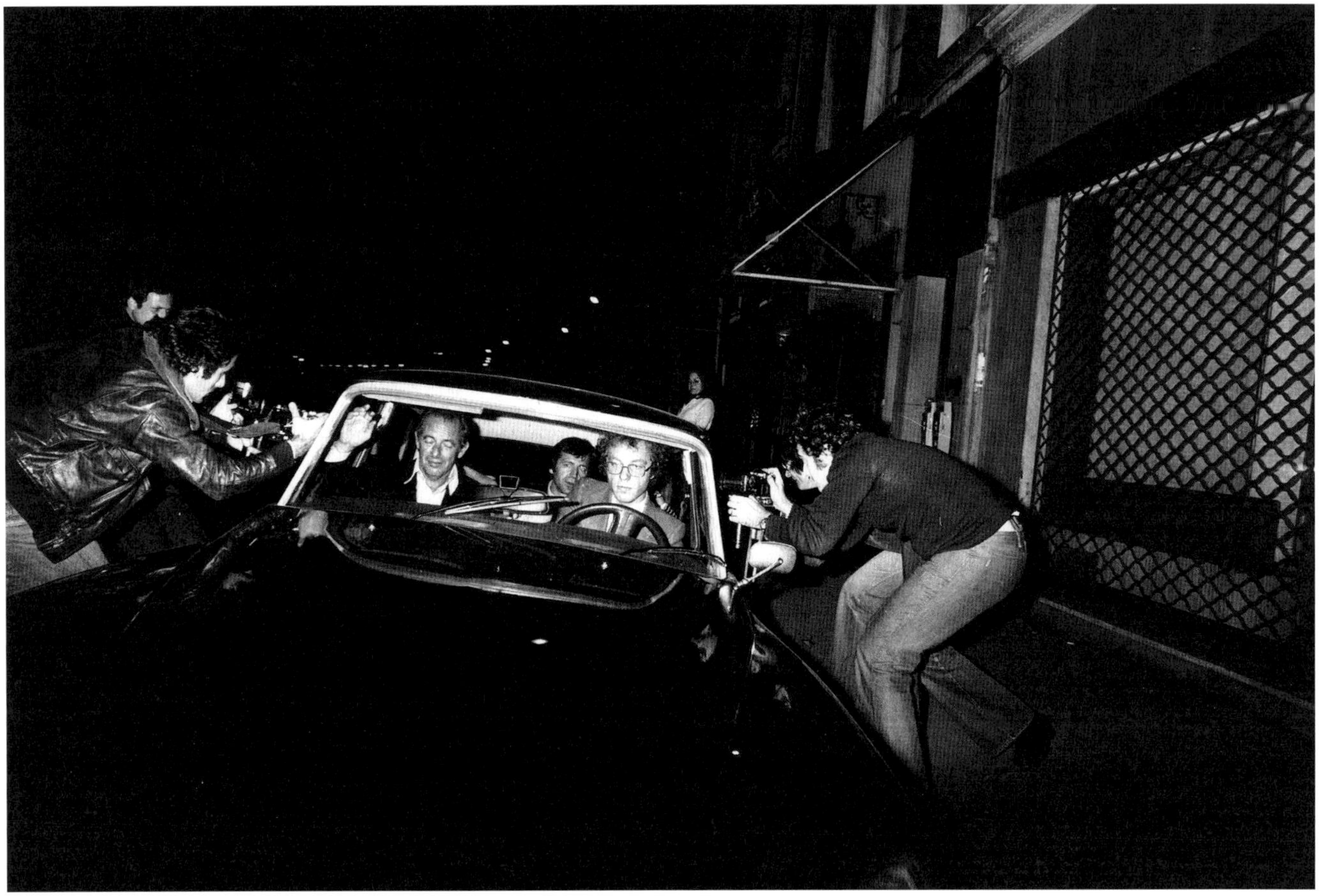

MICHEL GINIÈS
Actor Robert Redford, in the Company of Costa-Gavras, Leaving the Lapérouse Restaurant, Paris
September 1976

NO ESCAPE. Paparazzi love to photograph stars in their cars. Once inside, they are effectively immobilized and entirely at the mercy of the photographers, who can circle around their prey and shoot to their heart's content from every angle. This multidimensional and almost prison-like situation creates unique visual effects. The vehicle's windows are shiny surfaces that capture reflections. There is a play of transparency, double images, and rainbow bursts of light from flashbulbs. Snapshots of John Travolta, Marlene Dietrich, Catherine Deneuve, Claude François, and Johnny Hallyday trapped in their cars display the unique pictorial possibilities of this situation. It is at moments like these that the aesthetic of paparazzi photography is most evident. For the celebrity, of course, the situation is considerably less comfortable: the vehicle becomes a trap. The tragic death of Diana, Princess of Wales is the climactic illustration of their vulnerability.

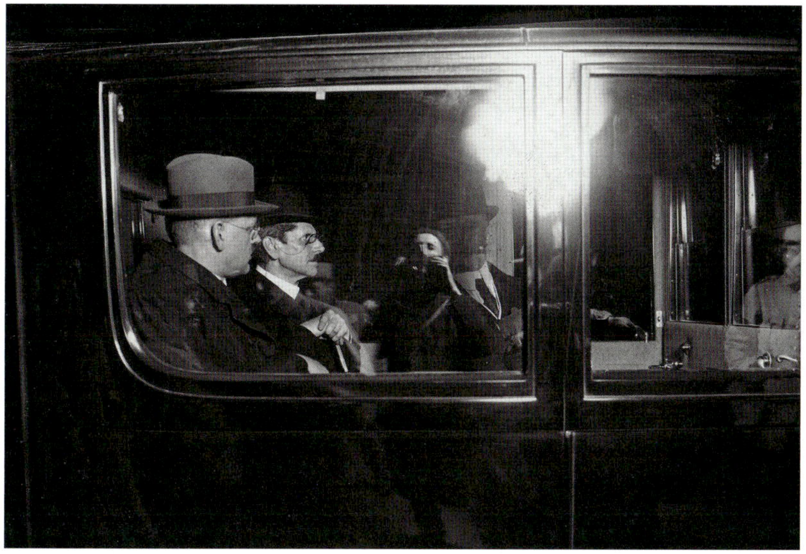

ANONYMOUS
(Underwood & Underwood)
The German Delegates Mueller and Bell, Leaving Versailles after Having Signed the Peace Treaty
1919

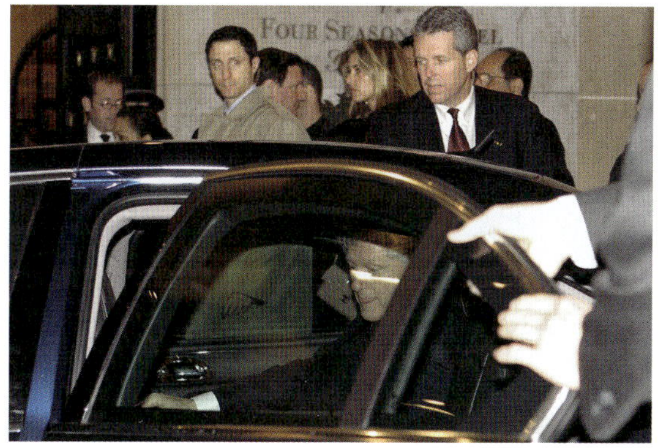

SÉBASTIEN VALIELA
Bill Clinton
March 11, 2004

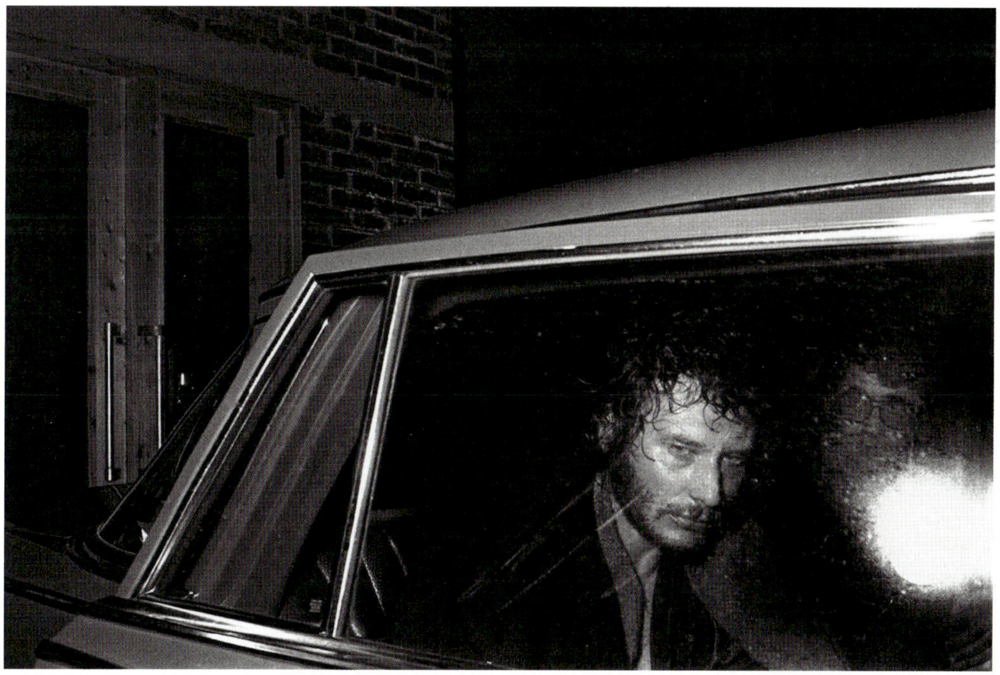

DANIEL ANGELI
Johnny Hallyday, Leaving a Concert
1972

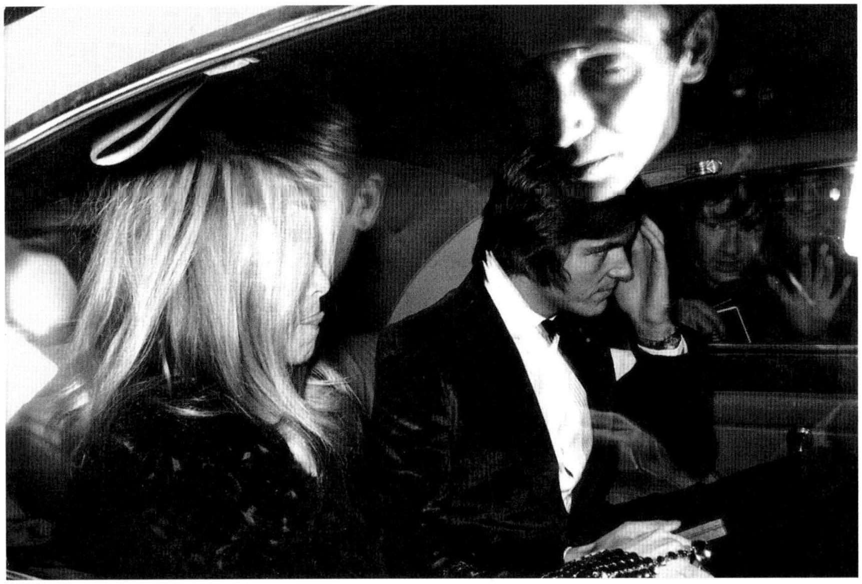

DANIEL ANGELI
Brigitte Bardot and Gunter Sachs
c. 1967

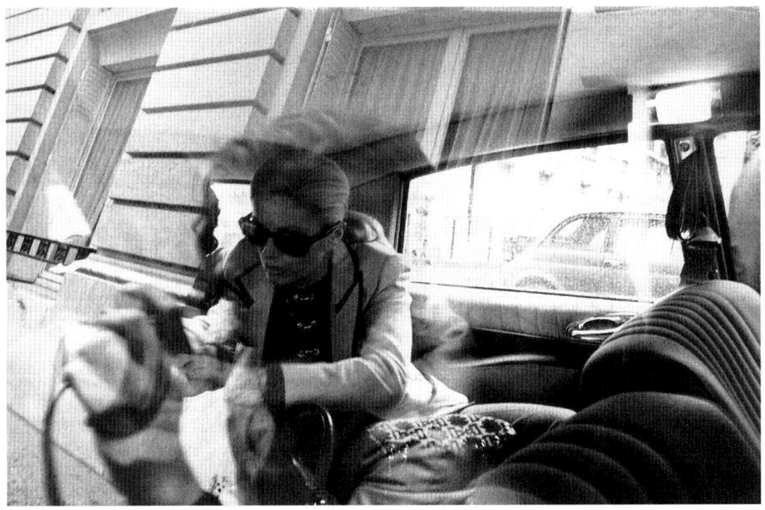

MICHEL GINIÈS
Birth of Chiara Mastroianni, Paris
May 1972

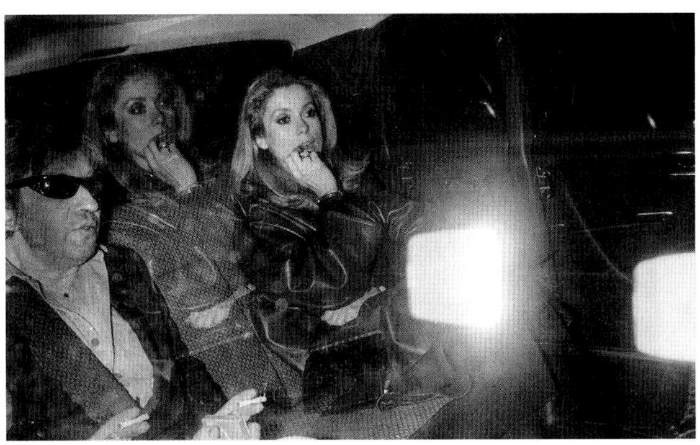

PATRICK SICCOLI
Serge Gainsbourg and Catherine Deneuve
1982

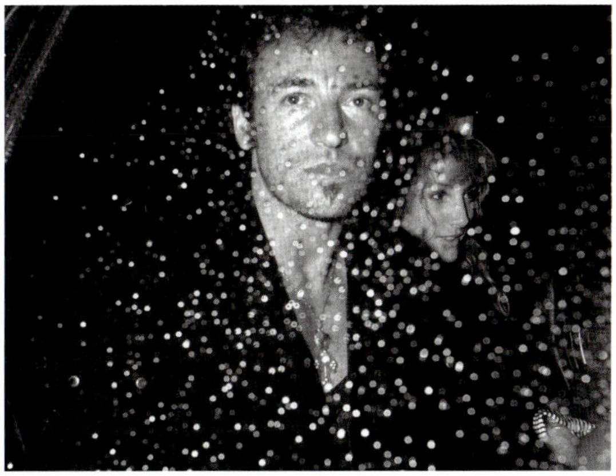

RON GALELLA
Bruce Springsteen Makes an Entrance at the Party Held after a Sting Concert at the Canal Bar, New York
August 24, 1988

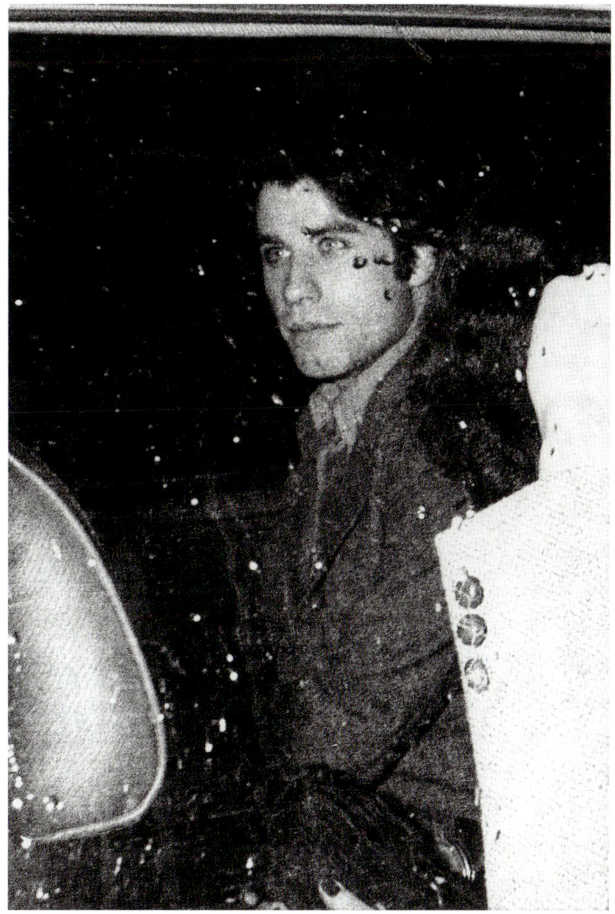

MICHEL GINIÈS
John Travolta Going to the Premiere of Grease
1978

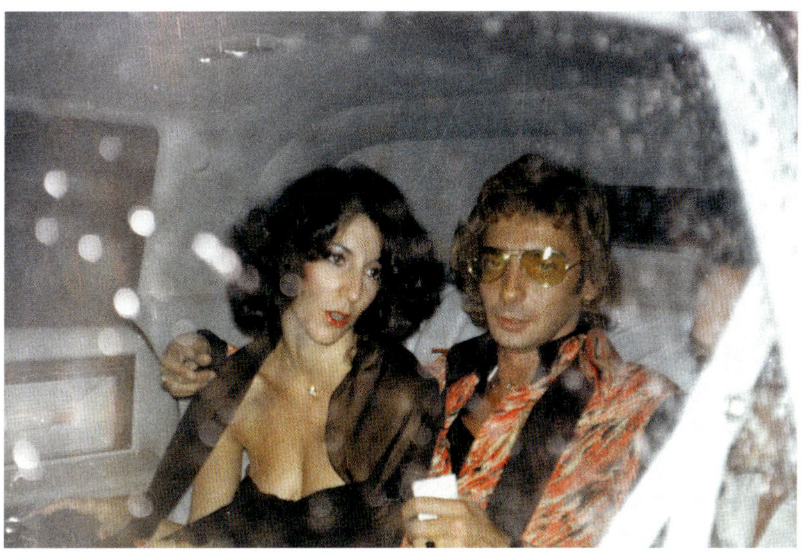

GARY LEE BOAS
Barry Manilow at the St. Regis Hotel, New York (detail)
July 26, 1978

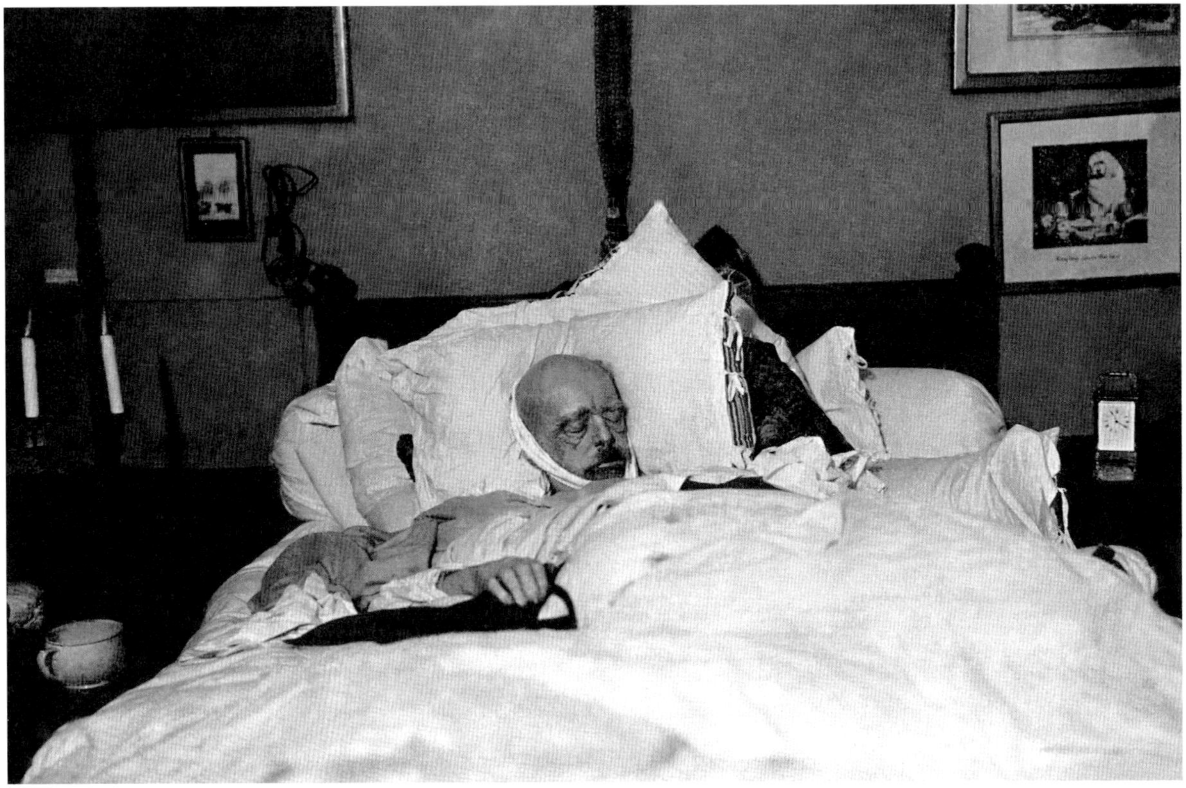

MAX CHRISTIAN PRIESTER AND WILLY WILCKE
Otto von Bismarck on His Deathbed
July 31, 1898

THE LAST PORTRAIT. When paparazzi steal an image of a celebrity on his deathbed, they are at the extreme limit of voyeurism. From a historical perspective, this type of image goes back to the portrait of Otto von Bismarck taken in 1898 by Willy Wilcke and Max Christian Priester after they were smuggled into the dead man's bedroom. The intrusion of the photographers, and their lack of respect for the mourners, stirred outrage, which was further aggravated by the exorbitant amounts of money at stake. The photograph showed the chancellor with a sunken face, a frail shadow of the authoritarian image he projected while living. It was not published at the time; instead, the photo was replaced by a considerably more presentable engraved version of the original. By the twentieth century, such stolen photographs were published with increasing frequency, nevertheless arousing controversy on each occasion. Examples include Jean Gabin, Elvis Presley, François Mitterrand, and of course Princess Diana photographed entangled in the wreckage of her car beneath the pont de l'Alma.

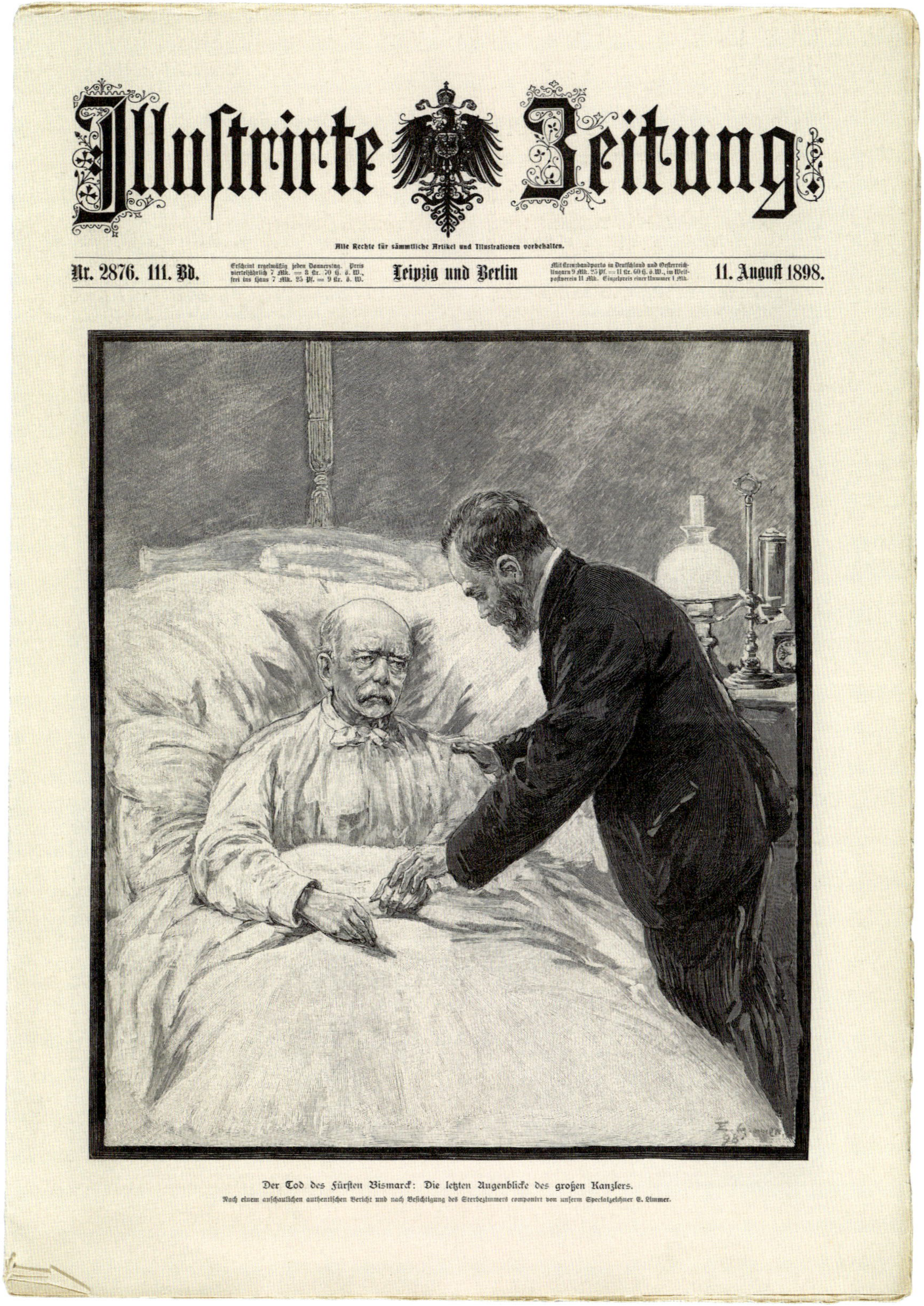

Illustrirte Zeitung

Alle Rechte für sämmtliche Artikel und Illustrationen vorbehalten.

Nr. 2876. 111. Bd. | Erscheint regelmäßig jeden Donnerstag. Preis vierteljährlich 7 Mk. = 8 Kr. 70 H. ö. W., frei ins Haus 7 Mk. 25 Pf. = 9 Kr. ö. W. | Leipzig und Berlin | Mit Kreuzbandporto in Deutschland und Oesterreich-Ungarn 9 Mk. 25 Pf. = 11 Kr. 60 H. ö. W., im Weltpostverein 11 Mk. Einzelpreis einer Nummer 1 Mk. | 11. August 1898.

Der Tod des Fürsten Bismarck: Die letzten Augenblicke des großen Kanzlers.

Nach einem anschaulichen authentischen Bericht und nach Besichtigung des Sterbezimmers componirt von unserm Specialzeichner E. Limmer.

[Otto von Bismarck],
Illustrirte Zeitung, no. 2876,
August 11, 1898, front cover

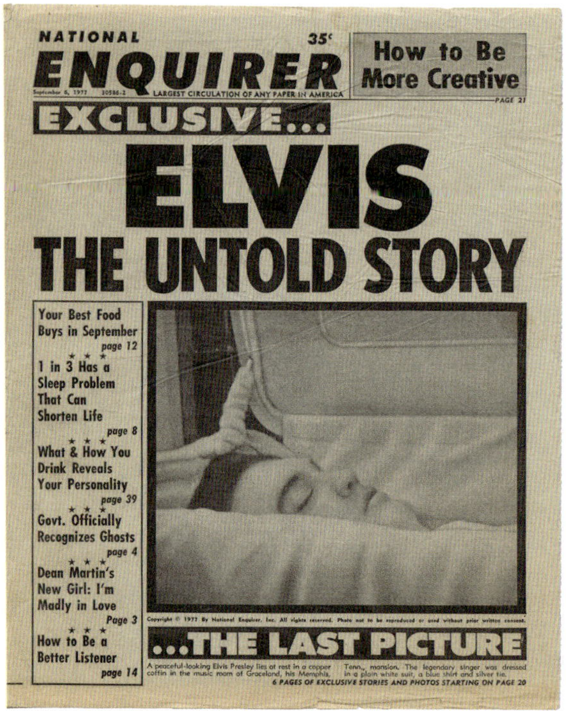
NATIONAL
ENQUIRER
35¢
LARGEST CIRCULATION OF ANY PAPER IN AMERICA
How to Be More Creative
PAGE 21
EXCLUSIVE...
ELVIS
THE UNTOLD STORY
Your Best Food Buys in September page 12
1 in 3 Has a Sleep Problem That Can Shorten Life page 8
What & How You Drink Reveals Your Personality page 39
Govt. Officially Recognizes Ghosts page 4
Dean Martin's New Girl: I'm Madly in Love Page 3
How to Be a Better Listener page 14
Copyright © 1977 By National Enquirer, Inc. All rights reserved. Photo not to be reproduced or used without prior written consent.
...THE LAST PICTURE
A peaceful-looking Elvis Presley lies at rest in a copper coffin in the music room of Graceland, his Memphis, Tenn., mansion. The legendary singer was dressed in a plain white suit, a blue shirt and silver tie.
6 PAGES OF EXCLUSIVE STORIES AND PHOTOS STARTING ON PAGE 20

[Elvis Presley]
National Enquirer,
vol. 52, no. 4,
September 6, 1977
front page
(Photograph: anonymous)

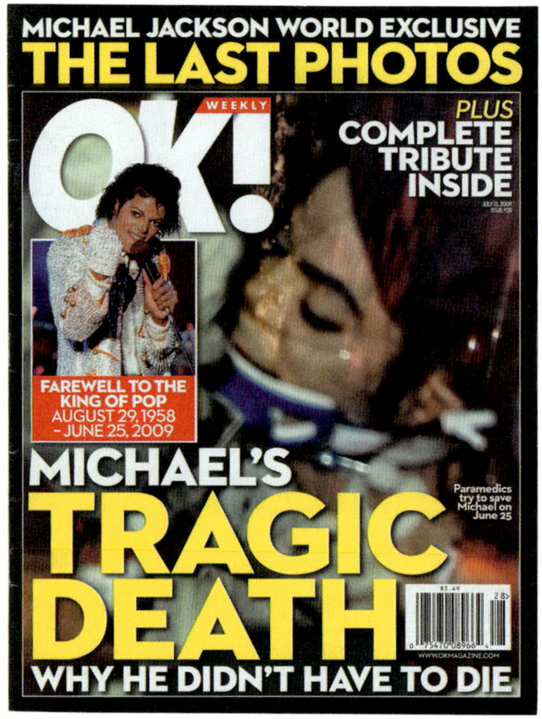
MICHAEL JACKSON WORLD EXCLUSIVE
THE LAST PHOTOS
OK! WEEKLY
PLUS COMPLETE TRIBUTE INSIDE
FAREWELL TO THE KING OF POP
AUGUST 29, 1958 – JUNE 25, 2009
MICHAEL'S
TRAGIC DEATH
Paramedics try to save Michael on June 25
WHY HE DIDN'T HAVE TO DIE
WWW.OKMAGAZINE.COM

[Michael Jackson],
OK!, vol. 5, no. 28,
July 13, 2009, front cover
(Photograph: anonymous)

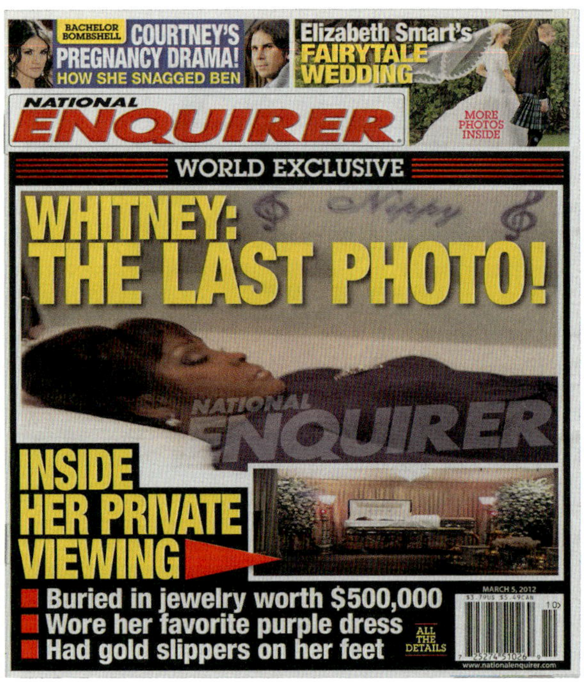
BACHELOR BOMBSHELL
COURTNEY'S PREGNANCY DRAMA!
HOW SHE SNAGGED BEN
Elizabeth Smart's FAIRYTALE WEDDING
MORE PHOTOS INSIDE
NATIONAL ENQUIRER
WORLD EXCLUSIVE
WHITNEY: THE LAST PHOTO!
INSIDE HER PRIVATE VIEWING
■ Buried in jewelry worth $500,000
■ Wore her favorite purple dress
■ Had gold slippers on her feet
ALL THE DETAILS
MARCH 5, 2012
www.nationalenquirer.com

[Whitney Houston],
National Enquirer,
vol. 87, no. 10,
March 5, 2012,
front cover and pp. 30–31
(Photograph: anonymous)

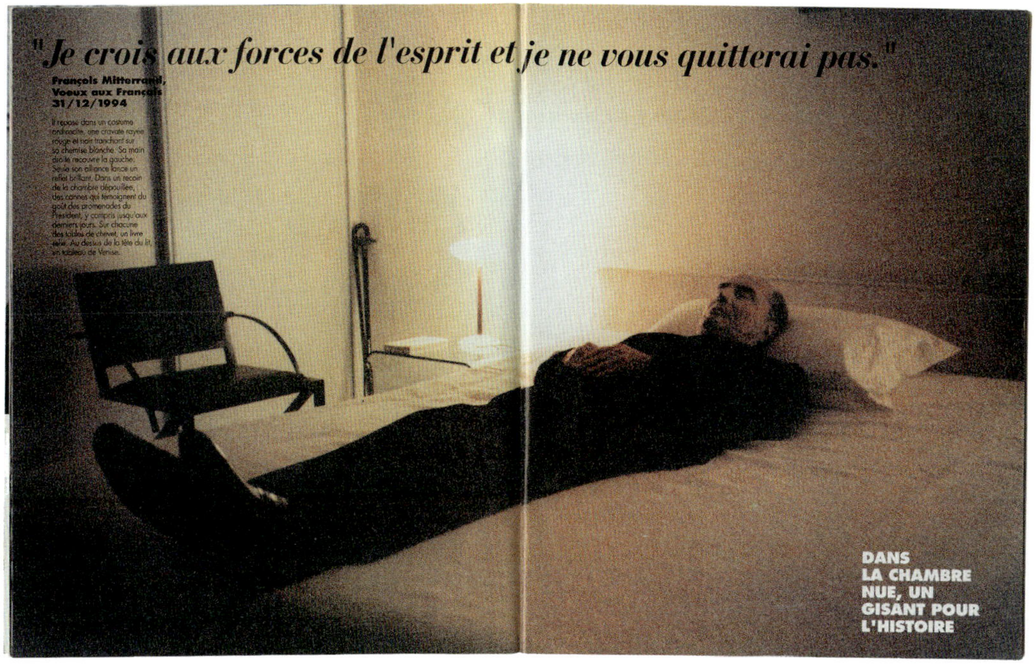

[François Mitterrand],
Paris Match, no. 2435,
January 25, 1996, pp. 36–37
(Photograph: anonymous)

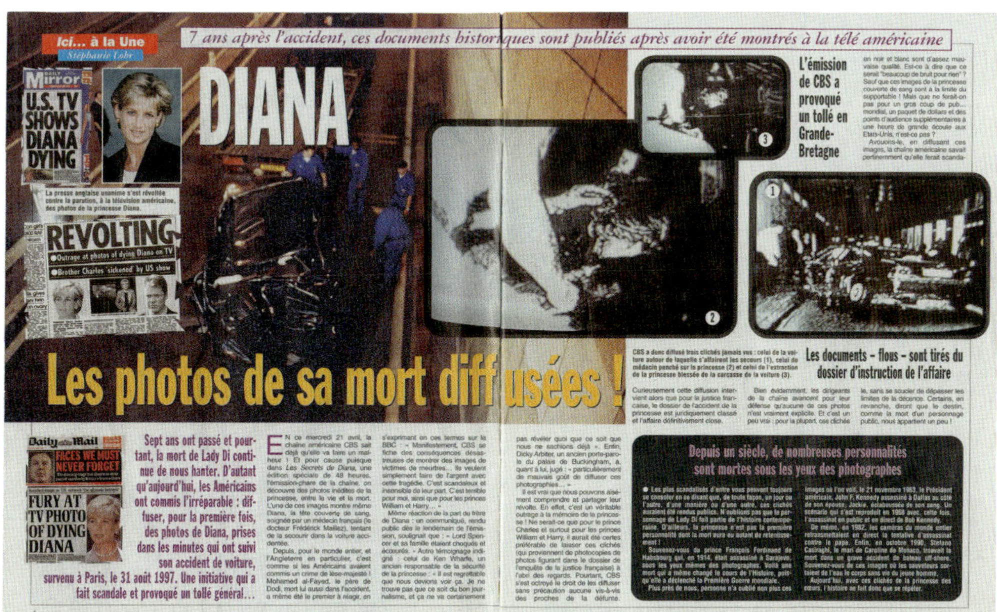

[Diana, Princess of Wales]
Ici Paris, no. 3069,
May 27, 2004, pp. 4–5
(Photograph: anonymous)

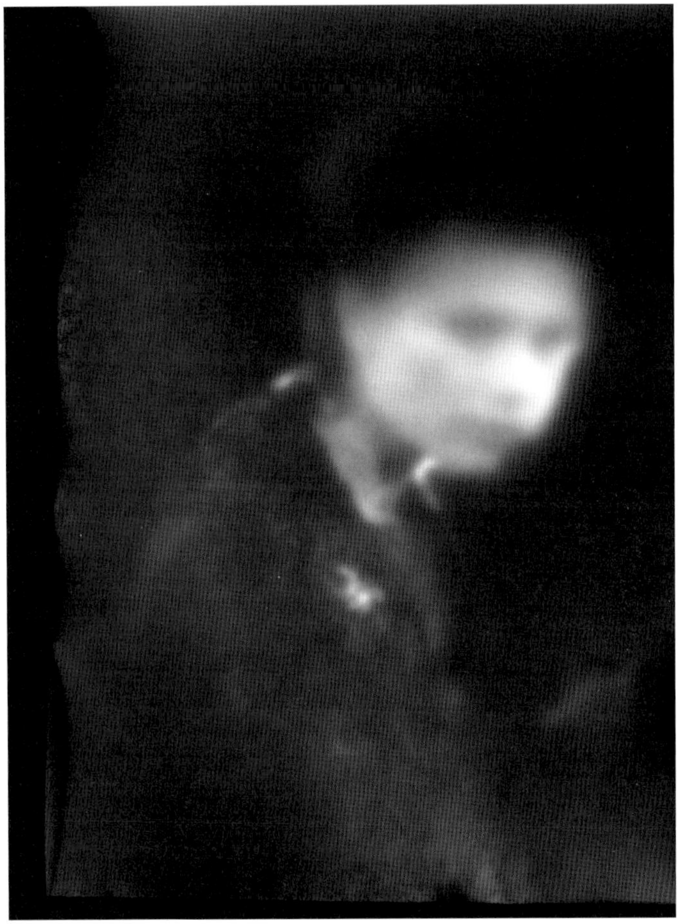

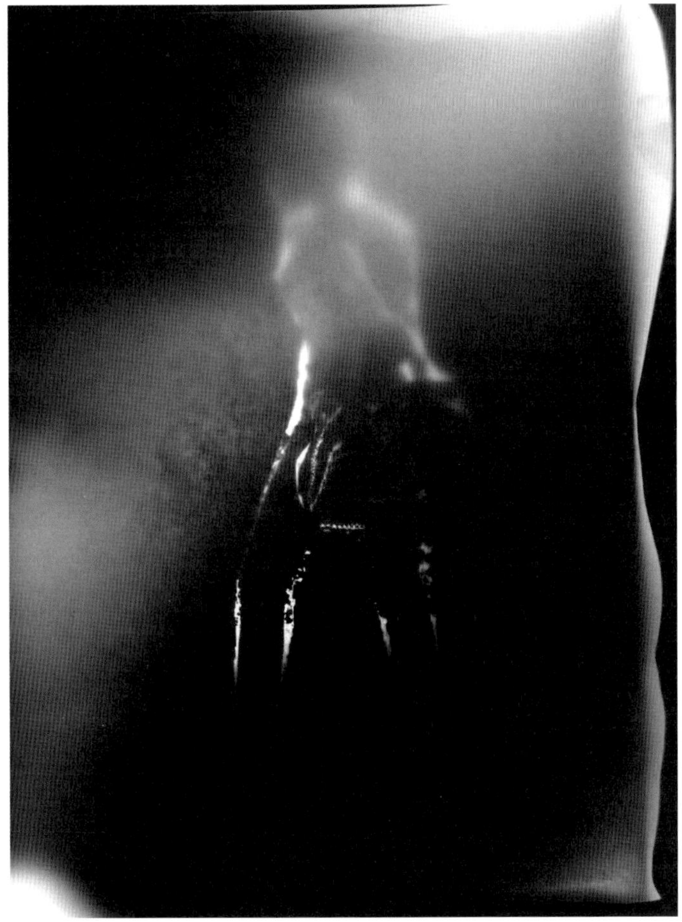

KATHRIN GÜNTER
Star Shots 2012, The Go-Between:
Double "Victoria Beckham" 07, 09, and *05*
2012

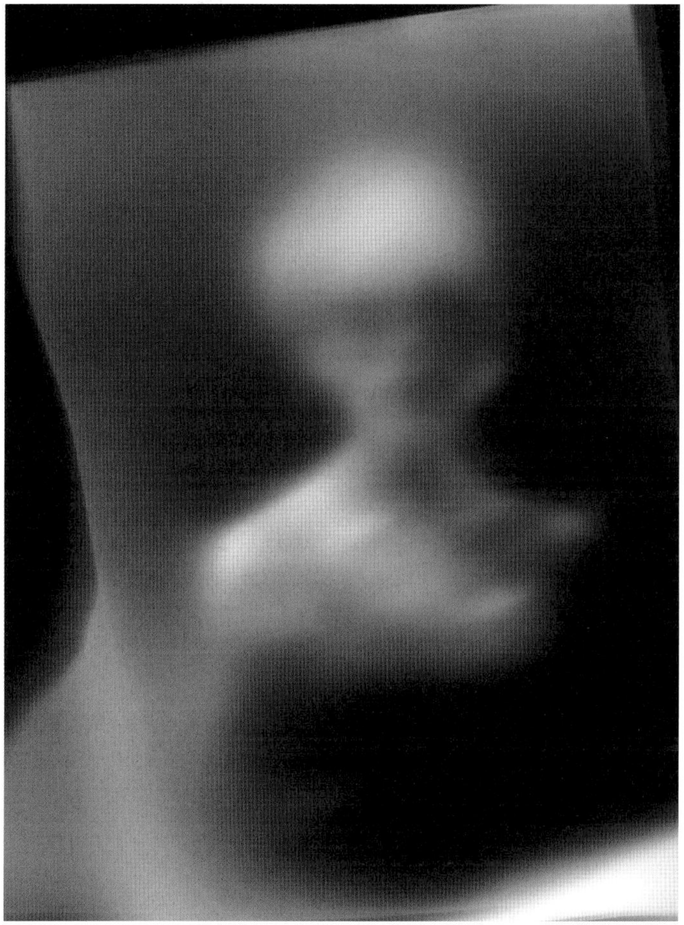

THE PHANTOM THEORY. Honoré de Balzac had a curious notion about photography. He believed that every photo stripped away an infinitesimal layer of the subject's being to be deposited on the film. Allowing oneself to be photographed excessively risked being very gradually peeled, like layers of an onion, until one disappeared entirely. Several contemporary thinkers have revived the "phantom theory" and applied it to the overexposed media celebrities of our era. Under the repeated assaults of photographers, stars lose their materiality and reality. They become no more than shadows of themselves and end up as virtual ghosts. This is exactly the process that Kathrin Günter wished to show in her series *The Go-Between: Double*. In the great tradition of nineteenth-century spirit photography, the German artist rephotographs tabloid images, with the successive reproductions layered on, one after another. She creates evanescent presences of disincarnated phantoms, who truly seem to be their own ghosts.

ARTISTS

FORMS OF APPROPRIATION

The conditions under which paparazzi take their photographs have aesthetic consequences. Haste and improvisation play essential roles in the composition of their pictures. The telephoto lens from afar and the close-up flash have a tendency to flatten the image. The star's immediate reaction—shielding their face with a raised hand—has become a leitmotif of paparazzi iconography. Since the 1960s, these stereotyped forms have provided inspiration to numerous artists: Richard Hamilton, Gerhard Richter, Valerio Adami, Paul McCarthy, and Thomas Demand have all appropriated images culled from press coverage. François-Marie Banier, Ulf Lundin, Viktoria Binschtok, Julián Barón, and Barbara Probst refer to the visual effects that are typical of paparazzi photography in their work. They all acknowledge the existence of a genuine paparazzi aesthetic.

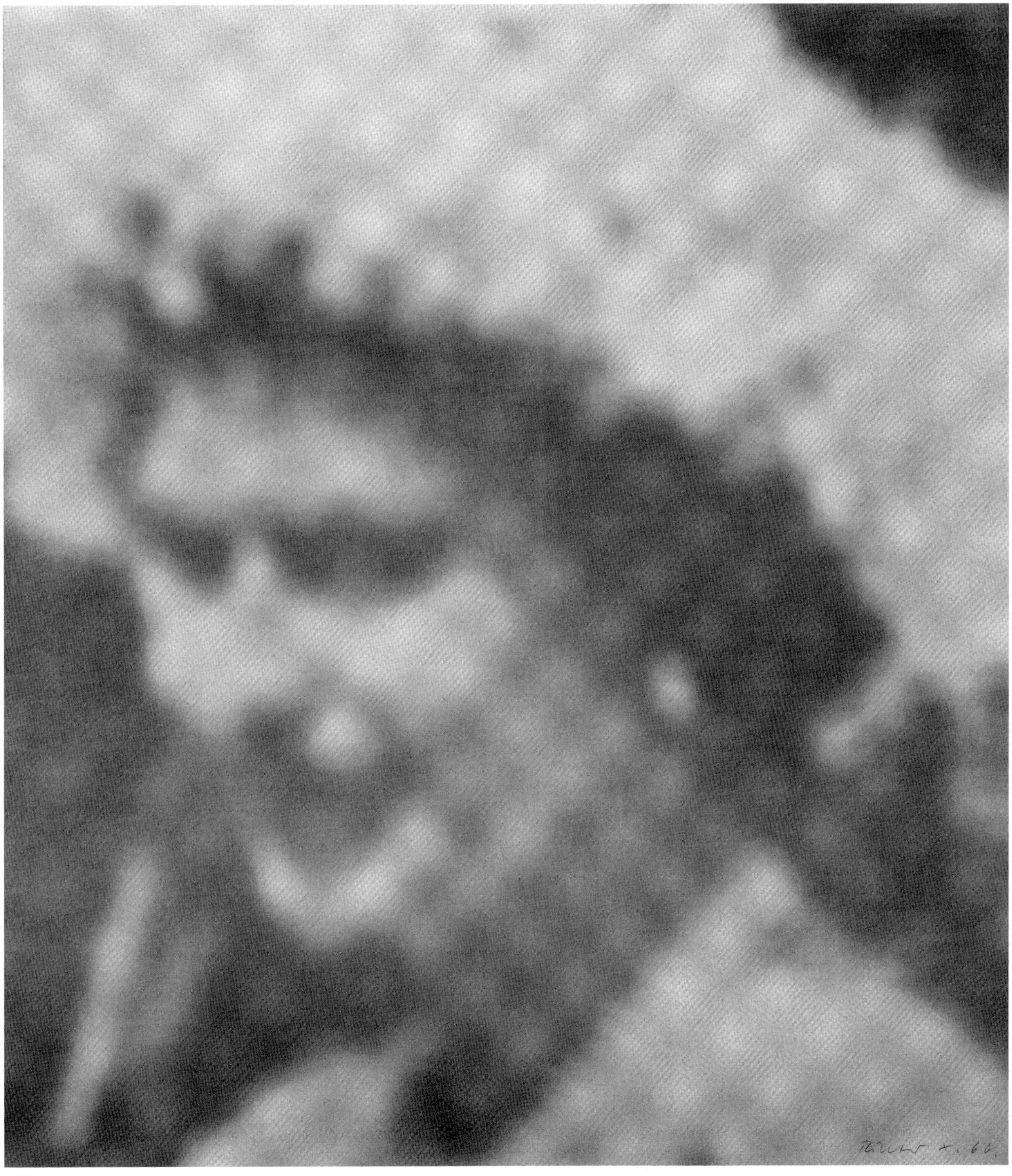

GERHARD RICHTER
Elizabeth II
1966

Migrations and Appropriations: Artists and the Paparazzi Aesthetic

Quentin Bajac

When did the phenomenon of paparazzi images begin to attract the attention of artists and *other* photographers? Why did a photographic genre that had been relegated exclusively to publications of the popular press throughout the 1950s migrate to other spaces and other distribution channels, particularly in the art world? And exactly how did this migration occur? Raising these questions requires a study of the process by which this body of work—once regarded as being of minimal cultural and artistic significance—gained recognition and achieved a certain degree of legitimacy. An important aspect of the history of art includes the canonization of genres formerly deemed "vulgar"; these forms gradually substitute or superimpose themselves on ancient and revered genres. This is one of the credos of Russian and Soviet formalism. Photography often seems to obey similar rules, from the amateur snapshot taken at the end of the nineteenth century being transformed into the aesthetic of Cartier-Bresson's "decisive moment" fifty years later, to artists adopting the use of color photography, once considered common and trivial, in the 1960s and 1970s. Although there were pockets of resistance and hesitation, a large part of the history of photography followed this principle. It was legitimized by the auteur photography of *other* genres and *other* practices, flourishing outside its own domain. Seen from this perspective, the canonization of paparazzi photography offers an even more interesting example of this tendency. It was, after all, a genre that had been very severely stigmatized. Furthermore, its modes of production and distribution had developed totally independently of the recognized art world.

The Origins: Allusions to Photojournalism

This background no doubt partially explains why the process was relatively slow and gradual. Two generations passed between the explosion of paparazzi photography in Italy in the 1950s and the fruition of its genuine recognition by the worlds of art and auteur photography at the very end of the twentieth century. Although it is difficult to set an authoritative or clearly determined date for the beginning of the process, we should consider the "reportage" published by Richard Avedon in September 1962 in the pages of *Harper's Bazaar* as representing one of the essential first steps. This double-page spread, which he created with the collaboration of Suzy Parker and Mike Nichols, was executed under the art direction of Marvin Israel. He was himself a photographer in training, and initiated the project, acting as the magazine's artistic director at the time. This publication seems to mark the first instance of borrowing from the paparazzi aesthetic by a photographer who had evolved outside of this realm. Avedon's reportage rode the wave stirred up by *La Dolce Vita*, whose release in the American market in April 1961 alerted a broad audience to the activities of the paparazzi, giving the phenomenon a face and a name. The same month that the film was released in America, the weekly news magazine *Time* devoted an article to it entitled "Paparazzi on the Prowl"[1] in its Press section. This was one of the very first mentions of the word in the American mass media. It was for this reason that Avedon's faux reportage situates the "event" in Europe, at Maxim's in Paris. The paparazzi phenomenon was still unfamiliar in the United States at that time.

Directly inspired by the highly publicized brawls of Elizabeth Taylor and Richard Burton on the set of *Cleopatra* in Rome, the reportage by Richard Avedon and Marvin Israel was elevated beyond mere pastiche. It combined a certain humorous distance

1. *Time*, US edition, April 14, 1961.

2. Daniel J. Boorstin, *The Image: A Guide to Pseudo-Events in America* (New York: Vintage Books, 1961).

3. On these questions, see Nathalie Heinich, *De la visibilité. Excellence et singularité en régime médiatique* (Paris: Gallimard, 2012).

4. On this matter, see the essay by Frédéric Monneyron in this catalog, pp. 243–44.

from the subjects, which is inherent in the genre, with a degree of empathy for its models. The project was neither satire nor true parody. Instead, the work appears to be more of a purely stylistic exercise, whose success lies in the delicate handling of a sense of distance from the subject depicted. We are neither too close nor too far away; there is a gap in our perceptions that raises the shadow of a doubt. It is said that the fabricated nature of the reportage escaped the notice of a number of readers. More generally, Avedon's faux paparazzi photographs emphasize—through their images and even more in the accompanying text—the fabricated, media-driven aspect of the event depicted. His photos were received in the United States at a time when more and more attention was being given to various media phenomena. The book published by sociologist Daniel J. Boorstin, *The Image: A Guide to Pseudo-Events in America*,[2] perfectly conveys this awareness. In the 1950s, reflections on this new celebrity culture went far beyond the American market, and could also be found in other Western contexts, as demonstrated by the publication of *Les Stars* by Edgar Morin in 1957. The importance attributed by Boorstin to a new type of celebrity, the "person who is known for his well-knownness,"[3] as well as to the role played by image in the process, is an accurate reflection of a typically American attitude, represented by the unprecedented explosive growth in the media industry. The scenes so cleverly staged by Avedon and Israel clearly form one of those "pseudo-events," to use the term coined by Boorstin, that so frequently occur in front of the lenses of the paparazzi. In fact, they actually sometimes incite and provoke such staged occurrences.

Gradual Emergence in the 1960s

In the mid-1930s, Martin Munkácsi undertook a campaign to revitalize and modernize the image of fashion, working for the prominent magazine *Harper's Bazaar*. He wished to transpose fashion, which hitherto had been dominated by studio photography, to the vocabulary of contemporary photojournalism, working en plein air and using 35-mm film. Avedon borrowed vocabulary from the mass-market press that was so familiar to him, particularly the pages of *Paris Match*. He launched the paparazzi fashion shoot, a genre that was to attract numerous imitators and followers ranging from Helmut Newton in the 1970s to William Klein. Although he was initially unfamiliar with the paparazzi phenomenon, Klein was photographing in their aggressive style as early as the mid-1950s, before he even went to Rome with Federico Fellini. More recent followers include Terry Richardson and Steven Meisel.[4] In this regard, Klein was an isolated instance of a precursor in a field—fashion photography—that was peripheral to the art world, even more so at that time than it is today. However, this same decade of the 1960s was also the moment when a generation of artists who were almost contemporaries of Avedon came to the fore. They included Andy Warhol, Gerhard Richter, and Richard Hamilton. Grouped together under the rather lame appellation of "pop art," they advocated a return to figurative painting, a commitment to rendering the modern world, and a marked interest in nonartistic photography—whether amateur, press, or advertising. Paparazzi imagery was particularly trivial, totally remote from artistic conventions. It was linked to the contemporary cult of celebrity, and sometimes possessed a powerful iconic value. Paparazzi photos seem to correspond in every detail to pop art's basic subject matter. However, a closer analysis reveals that these artists' borrowings from paparazzi imagery are fewer than might be expected. Perhaps it is this relative absence that should really be investigated.

Even among artists who, like Warhol, had made the media event and the star system the basis of their oeuvre, specific examples of reusing paparazzi photos are not all that common. Admittedly, the canvasses Warhol painted in the early 1960s made abundant use of press photography. Reportage (*Race Riot*, 1964), current events (the *Death* and *Disasters* series), and sports (*Baseball*, 1962) have a prominent place. In contrast, there is no trace of paparazzi shots. The artist wanted to create a portrait of contemporary America, and the paparazzi phenomenon was still a very new concept there. Furthermore, the typical paparazzi photo frequently features a demythologizing dimension and a confused, random composition. These aspects were in conflict with the Warhol aesthetic. His countless portraits of stars during these years invariably took as their point of departure images that idealized their subject and were immediately recognizable. The renderings are static and carefully posed, and usually frontal. They are very close to the aesthetic of studio photography, advertising, or film stills, even though they are sometimes drawn from "fanzines" (*Teen Stars*, 1962). These images had a much greater influence than paparazzi shots on Warhol's process of "iconization" through repetition, an approach that was dear to him. The simpler the motif, the more effective its repetition. Even his paintings of Jackie Kennedy at her husband's funeral ceremony in 1963 are based on "official" photographs taken in Arlington

5. Gerhard Richter, *Text* (London: Thames & Hudson, 2009), 21.

6. Or, according to some sources, Princess Soraya.

7. Paul B. Jaskot, "Gerhard Richter and Adolf Eichmann," *Oxford Art Journal* 28, no. 3 (2005): 459–78.

8. Pierre Bourdieu (ed.), *Un art moyen* (Paris: Éditions de Minuit, 1965).

National Cemetery by authorized photographers. In 1961, Warhol began his *Headlines* series, based on front pages from the American popular tabloid press. He continued to paint these works throughout his life, and we do find indirect references to paparazzi photos here. We use the term "indirect" because the artist shows more interest in the newspaper as object, and the relationship between the text and the image, mingling the trivial and tragic, than in the photo itself. However, beginning with the *Daily News* in 1962, with its front page featuring the marital strife of Eddie Fisher and Liz Taylor, the tabloid press became one of Warhol's major sources of inspiration. The works he created during the 1980s, sometimes executed in collaboration, only served to reinforce this tendency.

Gerhard Richter is an interesting case. Beginning in 1961, he consistently painted figurative works based on photography, and acknowledges that his first painting of this type was modeled on a snapshot of Brigitte Bardot.[5] If we consider the photo-paintings that Richter executed between 1961 and 1966, we find very little that is directly drawn from an image printed in the celebrity press. *Woman Descending a Staircase*, a canvas painted in 1965, takes a snapshot of Maria Callas as its point of departure.[6] She is shown in an evening gown, descending a staircase. The photo was consigned to Richter's photographic archives (*Atlas*, sheet 13, 1964). It is, however, interesting to note that in transposing the photograph to the canvas, Richter deliberately made a dual effort to put a distance between the two works, eradicating what gave value to the initial photo: its clarity and the identity of the model. By obscuring the model's identity, with his blurred pictorial treatment and the choice of a neutral title (which is also a distant echo of Duchamp's *Nude Descending a Staircase*), the artist demonstrates that he wishes to remove his canvas from any of the anecdotal or narrative functions contained in the photographic source. *Herr Heyde* is another example dating from the same year. Here the picture is not merely executed based on a photograph; it actually *represents* a press photo taken from the German weekly news magazine *Der Spiegel*, accompanied by its caption. It shows Werner Heyde, one of the doctors responsible for the Nazi regime's euthanasia policies, in 1959. He had recently been arrested and later hanged himself in his cell in 1964 while awaiting trial. The composition of the image, which shows the subject caught in passing, not looking at the camera and half hidden by the back of a police officer in the foreground, recalls countless images of criminals exiting the courthouse. Such images were captured on the fly by avid paparazzi. Like these often undistinguished photos, Richter's image is difficult to read and understand on its own. Without a caption, it would mean nothing to the observer. It is worth noting that *Herr Heyde* was the third painting devoted to Germany's Nazi past that Richter painted in 1965.[7] The first two, *Uncle Rudi* and *Aunt Marianne*, represent Richter's uncle wearing the uniform of a Wehrmacht officer, and his aunt, Marianne, who died under the Reich in a psychiatric institution. Both are based on family photographs. Such images are derived from a variety of sources: some from family albums, others from the mass-market press. But they are all historic images in some sense, unified by Richter in his pictorial style of that time whereby he systematically blurred the subject. Richter did not want to convey a "photographic" quality to his paintings. Instead he consistently short-circuited or evaded the questions of style inherent in his pictorial technique. In this case, his approach helps to reinforce the appearance of a (poor quality) press photo, with the caption remaining legible (history painting requires factual content, after all). A similar effect, obtained in a very different fashion with no pictorial intervention, is observable in *Elizabeth II*, an offset lithograph executed the following year in 1966. The selection of this commercial printing technique combined with enlargement emphasized the framing of the original press photograph; this effect is more pronounced in the second version than in the first (*Elizabeth I*, 1966). The British sovereign appears here as a spectral being, very far removed from the glossy imagery of official portraits and from the painted version executed the following year.

Beyond these examples, there is little evidence in this work of paparazzi influence, even if we scan the 783 sheets in Richter's *Atlas*, his work in progress, and the collections in his archives, as well as his photographic output since 1962. Sheet 5 alludes to a large number of photographic genres that were commonplace in the period's mass-market West German press (fashion, advertising, tourism, soft porn). Many of these images served as the basis for photo-paintings, but the genre is never defined as such. If a celebrity press shot (it would be difficult to really describe it as a paparazzi image in these two cases) made its way into Richter's body of work, it did so in a fairly limited and marginal fashion. Like many artists of his generation, particularly German painters (Sigmar Polke and Hans-Peter Feldmann, for example), Richter seems to have been more interested in "middle-brow" photographic art, to recall the title of the work edited by the sociologist Pierre Bourdieu during that same period.[8] "I collect photographs (nowadays,

9. Richter, *Text*, 21.

10. Ibid.

11. For details, see the caption on p. 223 of this book.

12. On this work, refer to Andrew Wilson, *Richard Hamilton: Swingeing London 67* (London: Afterall Publishing, 2011).

I also get a lot given to me) and I am always looking at them. Not 'art' photographs, but ones taken by lay people, or by ordinary newspaper photographers," commented Richter in 1964.[9] These are generic images, whose special quality is to have no special qualities, works by both amateurs and professionals who constructed a portrait of a certain type of banality that pervaded West German society following the war. In Richter's own words, they are images with "no style"[10] that he could easily keep at a distance, investing no emotion in them whatsoever. They are images without "punctum," to employ Roland Barthes's vocabulary, where there is nothing to catch the eye. Thus the absence of actual paparazzi shots in Richter's work can be explained by cultural factors. In West Germany, paparazzi were a virtually unknown phenomenon in the early 1960s. There is also another significant aspect: paparazzi photography would have certainly represented an iconography that was too sensational in its effects and too narrative in its content to match the description of a "middle-brow" photograph. These photos are both too blatant and too suggestive, and very rarely offer the potential for suspension of meaning. Richter's exceptional choice of such a photograph to serve as the basis for his painting *Herr Heyde* and his decision to neutralize the principal motif in his *Woman Descending a Staircase* reinforce this interpretation. We can thus propose the following hypothesis: for reasons that are both cultural (paparazzi were still a very Italian phenomenon) and stylistic (their iconography was too narrative and anecdotal), pop art painters of the period had difficulty in appropriating paparazzi shots and incorporating them into their art.

A famous counter-example of work that was very much inspired by paparazzi shots is the series executed between 1967 and 1972 by the British painter Richard Hamilton. These works were based on a photograph published in the popular conservative paper *Daily Sketch*, on June 29, 1967. Taken the day before its publication by John Twine, a photographer for the *Daily Mirror*, it shows Mick Jagger and Hamilton's art dealer, Robert Fraser, handcuffed to one another inside a police car during their trial for illegal drug possession.[11] For Richard Hamilton it was the starting point for a series of works in the form of variations, executed over a period of several years using a variety of techniques: individual collage and posters printed from this collage (*Swingeing London 67—source material*, 1968), acrylic on canvas and aluminum (*Swingeing London, 1967*, seven canvases executed between 1968 and 1969), finally followed by the lithographic series (*Release* and *Swingeing London III*, 1972).[12] Initially conceived as a protest in support of Hamilton's art dealer, the works became a condemnation of the British judicial and policing system. They were subsequently used to provide financial assistance to an association offering support services to former criminals and the National Council for Civil Liberties. The *Swingeing London 1967* series is indeed a political project that takes its place as a double "*détournement*" (hijacking), in the exact sense of this term that the situationists had been using since 1958. Firstly, *détournement* of the title: the fashionable slogan of "Swinging London" was taken up like a chorus by the media. The previous year, the American magazine *Time* had used the expression for one of its cover stories. It was now transformed into "Swingeing London," referring to the words of one of the magistrates in the case who had declared that in certain cases, "a harsh ['swingeing'] sentence could have a strong deterrent effect." Next came the hijacking of the image itself: a commercial photo taken from the conservative mass-market press, exactly corresponding to the canonical caricature of a paparazzi image (scandalous context, an international star, an image obviously taken against the subject's wishes) became a propagandistic image opposing the very system it depicted. Hamilton was playing on the power of both the slogan and the icon, turning the weapons of the mass-market press against itself and employing both words and images to do so. Hamilton was always very attentive to techniques and processes. He worked from a poorly focused print that he purchased from the offices of the *Daily Sketch,* and not from the image that had actually been published. This enhanced the visual impact of items such as the effect of the flash on the handcuffs. Sometimes the backdrop of the police premises was erased in the published image. The original snapshot was subjected to a treatment that actually restored a greater degree of truth to the situation depicted, emphasizing the violence inflicted on the subjects. Enlarged, colorized, and monumentalized, current events became history.

The 1970s: The Market Becomes Institutionalized

The overall role of the paparazzi influence on the pop generation of the 1960s is surprisingly modest. These artists were often intrigued by more commonplace press images. Examples of appropriation of celebrity photos are ultimately quite rare and marginal in their work, whether they assume historic meaning in Richter's paintings, political concerns for Hamilton, or cultural aspects for Warhol. It was not until the two decades between 1980 and 2000 that interest crystallized around the paparazzi phenomenon in the eyes of institutions and artists. Beginning in the late 1980s, a few Italian art historians took an interest in the Italian origins of the genre. In 1988, the Palazzo Fortuny in Venice devoted an exhibition to the topic, which was accompanied by the first in-depth study on the issue.[13] Six years later, Germano Celant organized a major exhibition at the Guggenheim Museum in New York. Its subject was the postwar art scene in Italy. The show included several paparazzi shots in the photography section, combining the genres for the first time in a straightforward fashion,[14] although the exhibition envisaged this more as a cultural phenomenon than a simple artistic expression. The process accelerated in the 2000s. It was a sign of the times, and the probable corollary of the emergence of a contemporary "media elitism."[15] There were unanticipated consequences to Princess Diana's fatal accident in 1997. The paparazzi phenomenon was now subjected to increasingly intense scrutiny, going beyond its traditional purview to be studied in its most recent developments. Exhibitions gave a certain prominence to the subject from a cultural perspective (*Fame after Photography*, New York, Museum of Modern Art, 1999, was explicitly conceived as a follow-up to the "Lady Di affair") and the artistic angle (*Exposed: Voyeurism, Surveillance, and the Camera*, San Francisco Museum of Modern Art and London, Tate Modern, 2010). Some exhibitions focused exclusively on the subject itself (*A Flash of Art: Action Photography in Rome, 1953–1973*, Rome, Palazzo Venezia, 2004); a sign of the times, this show was mounted at the instigation of art historian and critic Achille Bonito Oliva. *Pigozzi and the Paparazzi* (Berlin, Helmut Newton Foundation, 2008) gathered 350 images based on photos taken by Jean Pigozzi, who was actually more of a traditional photographer than an authentic paparazzo. The first book to provide a synthesis that went beyond the historic frame of reference of postwar Italy was published: it dealt with contemporary issues and photography (Peter Howe, *Paparazzi* [New York: Artisan Books, 2005]). Finally, there were one-man shows on some of the most remarkable of these "historic" figures: *Tazio Secchiaroli, Paparazzo* (Chalon-sur-Saône, Musée Nicéphore-Niépce, 2003), *Daniel Angeli* (Arles, Rencontres de la photographie, 2006), and *Ron Galella: Paparazzo Extraordinaire!* (C/O Berlin, 2011–12). These exhibitions were rapidly followed—and sometimes preceded—by acceptance into galleries and the first hesitant stirrings of interest in the art market. In 2000, the Deitch Project Gallery began to show the photographs of Gary Lee Boas, an authentic fan who became a quasi-paparazzo himself (Gary Lee Boas, *Starstruck: Photographs from a Fan*, New York, Deitch Project, 2000). Taking the opposite tack, Bruno Mouron and Pascal Rostain had originally been paparazzi stars; with the change in format and approach in their *Trash* series, which they began in 1990 and exhibited in 2007 at the Maison Européenne de la Photographie in Paris, they migrated toward the artistic scene. We should add that the figure of the paparazzo himself was increasingly becoming a focal point during these years. This fascination took a variety of forms, ranging from film, of course,[16] to song ("Piece of Me" by Britney Spears [2007] about media hype, "Paparazzi" by Lady Gaga [2009] and its accompanying video), and fiction (Jean Rolin, *Le Ravissement de Britney Spears*, 2011).

The 1980s: Appropriation and *Détournement*

If we were compelled to assign a date to the revival of interest in paparazzi photography in artistic circles, it would be tempting to take the late 1970s as the starting point. In 1979, Andy Warhol first published snapshots, taken with a small Minox camera that he had discovered in 1976, in his collection *Exposures*. These images of the jet set and the artistic circles he frequented were executed with no concern whatsoever for composition. They are midway between the work of paparazzi and that of conventional photographers. This series was exhibited in 1980 at the Museum Ludwig in Cologne and the Stedelijk Museum in Amsterdam. It was followed obsessively and marked the beginning of Warhol's recognition as a photographer. Speaking of his work, Warhol asserted that a good photograph is a photo that is "clear, showing a public figure engaged in private acts."[17] This deliberately anti-artistic definition of photography is not so different from the one offered in the late 1950s by the paparazzo Rino Barillari: "Whenever there's a star, nothing else counts, because a documentary photo that shows the event—even if it's ugly—is worth a lot more than an artistically composed image."[18]

In the United States at this time, a group of artists revived an interest in representational art, showing a critical interest in media, film, and advertising. This "pictures generation" was more reserved with regard to these phenomena than the pop generation had been in the early 1960s. However, they could not remain completely oblivious to the paparazzi's body of work, particularly in the American context of the 1980s, with the explosive growth of the celebrity press. This generation of artists frequently used

13. *Paparazzi Fotografie 1953–1964*, Venice, Palazzo Fortuny, November 1–December 4, 1988; catalog by Paolo Costantini et al., *Paparazzi* (Florence: Alinari Idea, 1988).

14. Germano Celant, *The Italian Metamorphosis, 1943–1968* (New York: Guggenheim Museum/Rizzoli, 1994).

15. Heinich, *De la visibilité*.

16. Since 1997, a significant number of films have featured the figure of the paparazzo in various guises. On this question, see the essay by Aurore Fossard-De Almeida in this book, p. 86

17. Raphaela Platow, Synne Genzmer, and Joseph D. Ketner (eds.), *Image Machine: Andy Warhol and Photography* (Nuremberg: Institut für Moderne Kunst, 2013), 47.

18. Francesca Taroni, *Paparazzi* (Paris: Assouline, 1998), 11.

quotations and reappropriations, direct and indirect, of images as well as styles. They were less interested in the unilateral migration of images from the popular domain to the artistic realm, although this had been the credo of the earlier pop generation. This contemporary group was more intrigued by the ever-increasing porosity between these worlds—the domains of art, stars, and the press. This fluidity could be described as the general hybridization of representational works of all types and genres. There was incessant movement among them, with various genres commingling and "contaminating" each other. In her series *Untitled Film Stills* (1977–80), Cindy Sherman intermingled references to film and photography, setting up a panorama of female stereotypes and film genres and the photography associated with them. Using a telephoto lens (*Untitled Film Still #45*, 1979, and *Untitled Film Still #83*, 1980), a flashbulb at night (*Untitled Film Still #54*, 1980), and stolen images (*Untitled Film Still #7*, 1978, and *Untitled Film Still #27*, 1979), these works are subterfuges that play on the narrative and suggestive power of the paparazzi aesthetic. In the mid-1980s, Richard Prince occupied a place at the intersection of a fan's passion and an artist's work of appropriation. He collected photos of every kind of celebrity, sometimes establishing a typology of the representations by motifs and genres, and sometimes reintegrating these images into the media cycle by having them autographed by their subjects. Extending the vogue for galleries of celebrities that dated back to the nineteenth century, Prince produced a very contemporary "anti-pantheon" where the determining factor was now merely access to visibility, trumping merit and talent (*Criminals and Celebrities*, 1986).

Closer to our own era and coming from the West Coast, Paul McCarthy combined stories and genres in *Heidi* (2000). His version of the children's tale from the last century mixes news headlines with images of Alpine peaks and Hollywood hills, the innocent with the sordid. Summoning up the child and the adult who coexist simultaneously within himself, he uses the medium of collage to create glaring juxtapositions of bland images from the story and "trash" photos from the celebrity press. It is an incongruous visual graft of two profoundly alien universes: *Heidi* set in Beverly Hills. At the same time, the Austrian collective G.R.A.M. extended this generalized porosity between different worlds to their own practices, as well as to their representational work. In 1987–88, G.R.A.M. decided to move to Los Angeles for a while. It had become *the* city for paparazzi. For almost a decade, G.R.A.M. dedicated its efforts to the paparazzi phenomenon and the new culture of visibility, employing the weapons and the strategies of the paparazzi themselves—pursuit, flash, zoom, etc. Juxtaposing stars with complete unknowns, their images quickly created the portrait of a society divided between the preoccupations of voyeurism and surveillance, well before the widespread availability of the Internet or portable devices.

Princess Diana's fatal accident in 1997 focused attention on the role of the paparazzo as never before. The paparazzo now became an extreme figure, half cynical muckraker and half antiestablishment hero. His conduct and illicit photographic activities aroused both condemnation and fascination. Now we are at the beginning of a new century, at a time when the Internet will fundamentally redefine the boundaries between the public and private spheres. A new generation—mostly born during the 1970s—will endeavor to make this language its own. They will question the relationship—our relationship—with this kind of image. They will take various directions. Consider Olivier Mirguet and his *mise en abyme*, which falls between a documentary and an artistic approach to studying the paparazzi phenomenon; Viktoria Binschtok exploring the boundaries between abstraction and representation with her flashbulb aesthetic; Kathrin Günter, a paparazza of her own private life, toying with the incongruous alliance between the introverted practice of self-portraiture and a certain sense of media-inspired voyeurism; and Alison Jackson, whose impossible photos challenge both photographic veracity and our unhealthy appetite for spectacle. All these artists are participants in this phenomenon. It has reached the point where the paparazzi aesthetic has become domesticated, and its style of photographic expression, once marginal, has become our society's common currency. "Are we all paparazzi?"[19] This was the question pondered by attendees of round table sessions organized by the Getty Center in 2012. The topic was photography of contemporary celebrities. Now, thanks to a company established in America just last fall, anyone can rent the services of faux paparazzi (and faux fans and security guards) to be a star for a day. Andy Warhol's prophecy has become a reality. Now we might be tempted to raise another question: "Are we all celebrities?"

19. "Are We All Paparazzi?", round table, Getty Center, May 16, 2012.

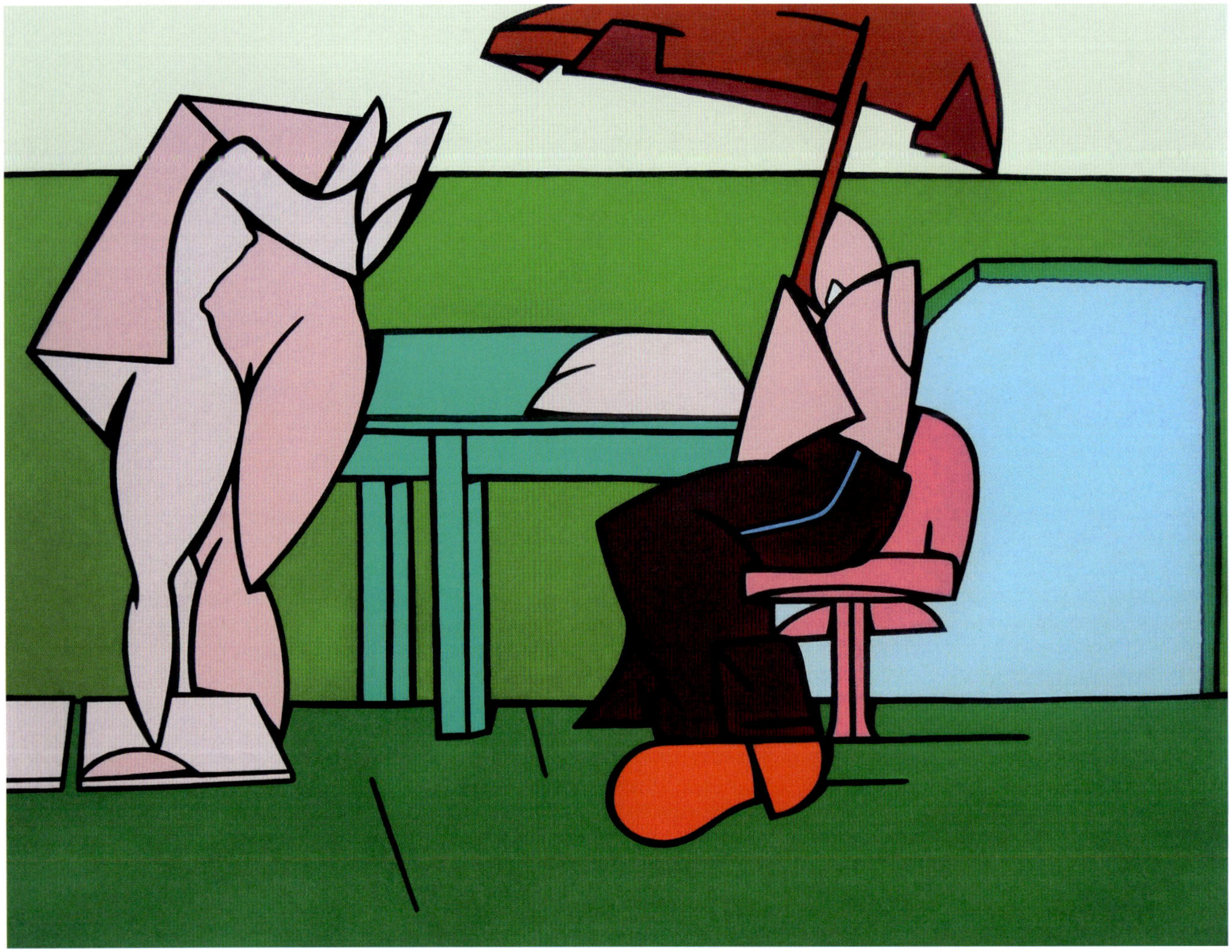

VALERIO ADAMI
Il Vecchio Timido e l'Adulterio in Piscina
1966

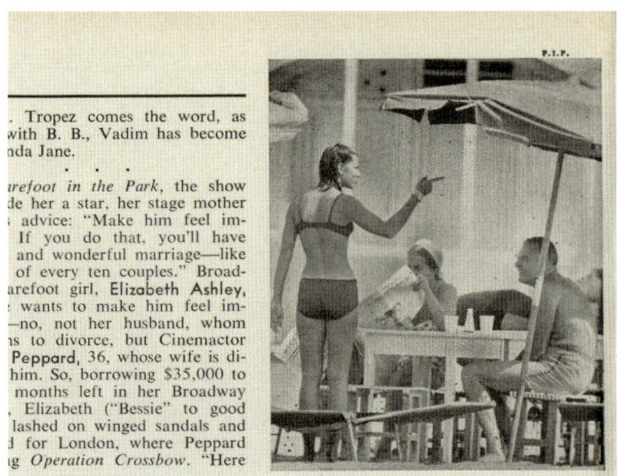

. Tropez comes the word, as with B. B., Vadim has become nda Jane.

. . .

arefoot in the Park, the show de her a star, her stage mother advice: "Make him feel im- If you do that, you'll have and wonderful marriage—like of every ten couples." Broad- arefoot girl, **Elizabeth Ashley,** wants to make him feel im- —no, not her husband, whom ns to divorce, but Cinemactor **Peppard,** 36, whose wife is di- him. So, borrowing $35,000 to months left in her Broadway , Elizabeth ("Bessie" to good lashed on winged sandals and d for London, where Peppard ng *Operation Crossbow*. "Here

P.I.P.

Time, vol. 88, no. 10, September 2, 1966, p. 46 (Photograph: anonymous)

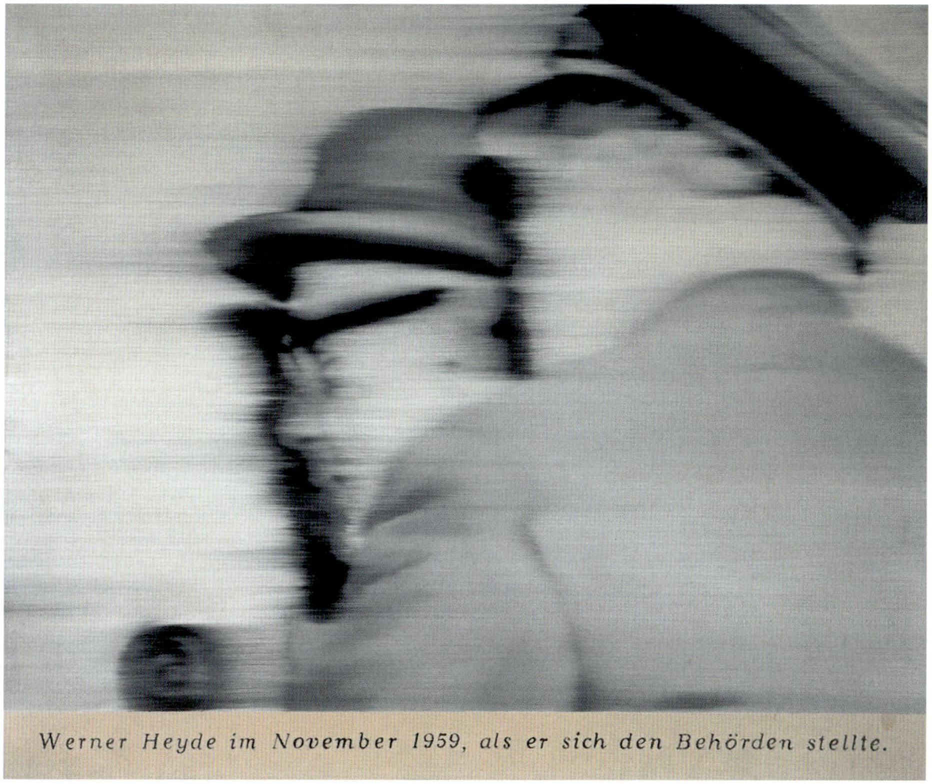

GERHARD RICHTER
Herr Heyde
1965

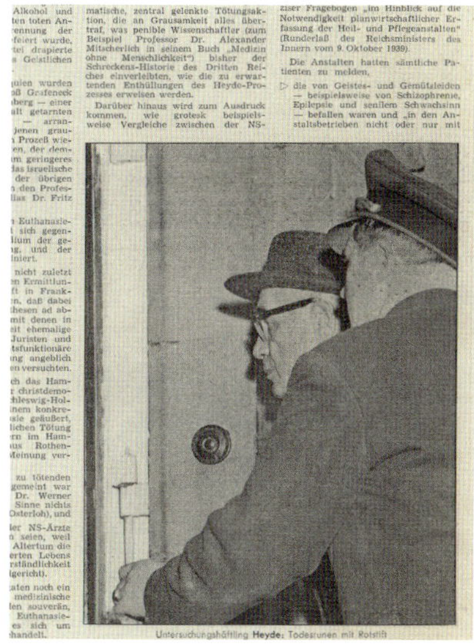

matische, zentral gelenkte Tötungsaktion, die an Grausamkeit alles übertraf, was penible Wissenschaftler (zum Beispiel Professor Dr. Alexander Mitscherlich in seinem Buch „Medizin ohne Menschlichkeit") bisher der Schreckens-Historie des Dritten Reiches einverleibten, wie die zu erwartenden Enthüllungen des Heyde-Prozesses erweisen werden.

Darüber hinaus wird zum Ausdruck kommen, wie grotesk beispielsweise Vergleiche zwischen der NS-

ziser Fragebogen „im Hinblick auf die Notwendigkeit planwirtschaftlicher Erfassung der Heil- und Pflegeanstalten" (Runderlaß des Reichsministers des Innern vom 9. Oktober 1939).

Die Anstalten hatten sämtliche Patienten zu melden,

▷ die von Geistes- und Gemütsleiden — beispielsweise von Schizophrenie, Epilepsie und senilem Schwachsinn — befallen waren und „in den Anstaltsbetrieben nicht oder nur mit

Untersuchungshäftling **Heyde**: Todesrunen mit Rotstift

Der Spiegel, no. 19,
May 3, 1961, p. 35
(Photograph: anonymous)

GERHARD RICHTER. During the 1960s, Gerhard Richter created paintings based on photographs he found in the press. The image that served as the model for *Herr Heyde* came from the magazine *Der Spiegel*. It shows Werner Heyde, one of the principal organizers of *Aktion T4*. This was the notorious euthanasia program implemented by the Nazis in the late 1930s to eliminate the physically and mentally handicapped with the goal of "enhancing racial purity." Snapped surreptitiously as the doctor exited the courthouse, the photograph presents all the features typical of paparazzi iconography: the close-up of the main subject, his partial obstruction by another person, and the glare of the flashbulb casting the faces into deep shadow. However, Richter greatly exaggerated the blurred effects of movement in his painting, a recurrent feature in his work during this period. Another type of blurred effect is at play in Richter's *Elizabeth II*. This time he addresses the use of a telephoto lens and enlargement. Working in an era dominated by mass media, Richter questions systems of representation imposed by what he calls "capitalist realism," the Europeanized version of pop art.

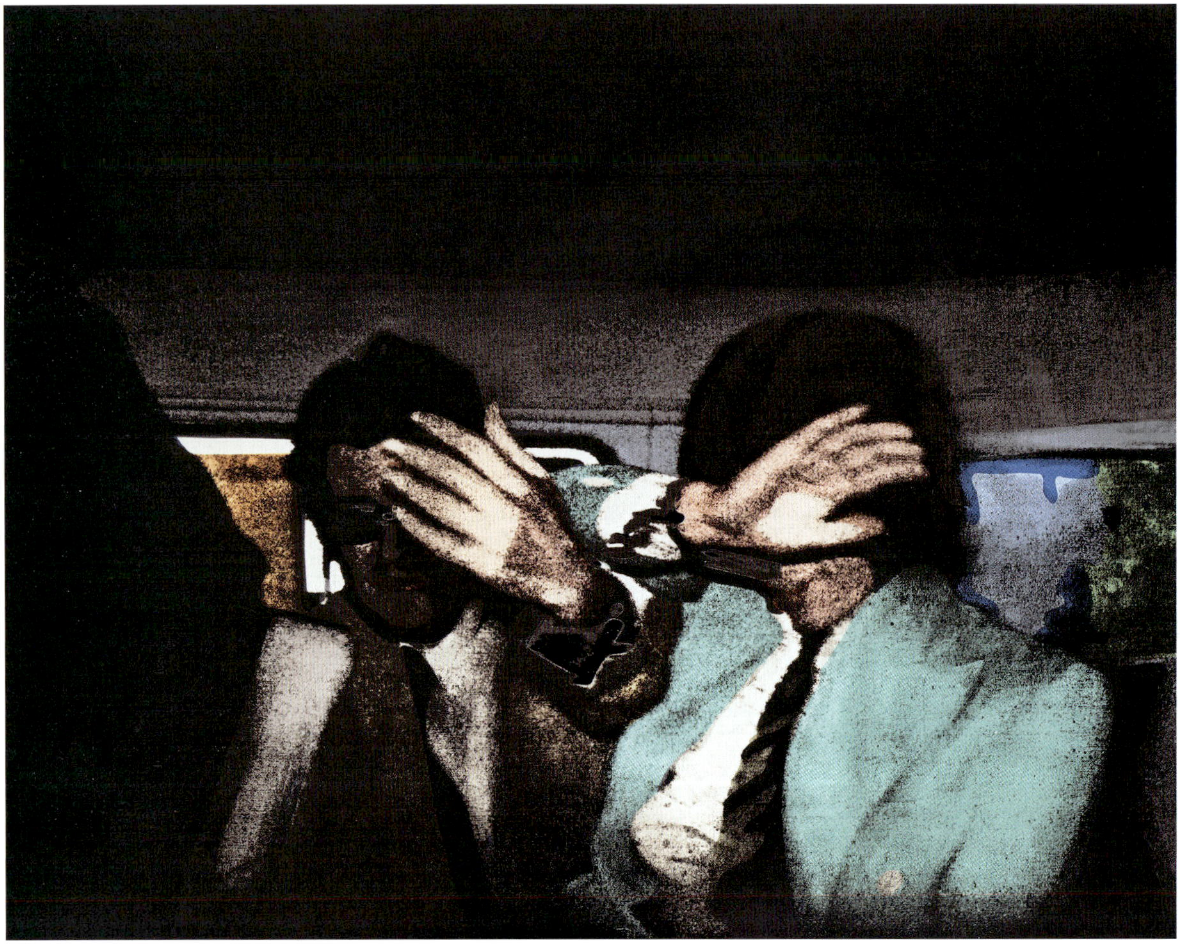

RICHARD HAMILTON
Release
1972

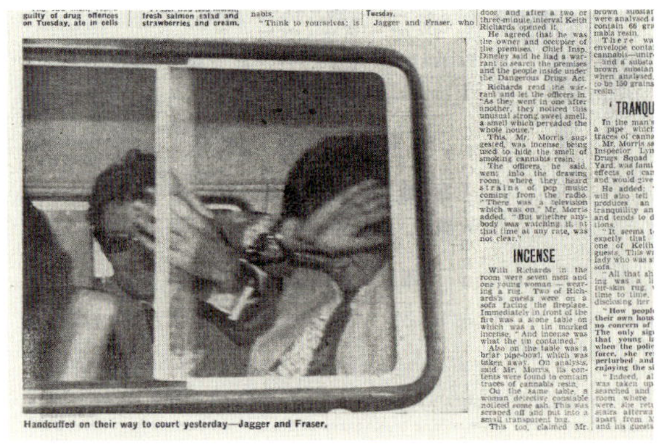

doon and after a two or three-minute interval Keith Richards opened it.

He agreed that he was the owner and occupier of the premises. Chief Insp. Dineley said he had a warrant to search the premises and the people inside under the Dangerous Drugs Act.

Richards read the warrant and let the officers in. "As they went in one after another, they noticed this unusual strong sweet smell, a smell which pervaded the whole house."

This, Mr. Morris suggested, was incense being used to hide the smell of smoking cannabis resin.

The officers, he said, went into the drawing room, where they heard strains of pop music coming from the radio. "There was a television which was on," Mr. Morris added. "But whether anybody was watching it, at that time at any rate, was not clear."

INCENSE

With Richards in the room were seven men and one young woman — wearing a rug. Two of Richards's guests were on a sofa facing the fireplace. Immediately in front of the fire was a stone table on which was a tin marked incense. "And incense was what the tin contained."

Also on the table was a briar pipe-bowl, which was taken away. On analysis, said Mr. Morris, its contents were found to contain traces of cannabis resin.

On the same table a woman detective constable noticed some ash. This was scraped off and put into a small transparent bag.

This too, claimed Mr.

Handcuffed on their way to court yesterday—Jagger and Fraser.

The Daily Sketch
June 29, 1967, p. 10
(Photograph: John Twine)

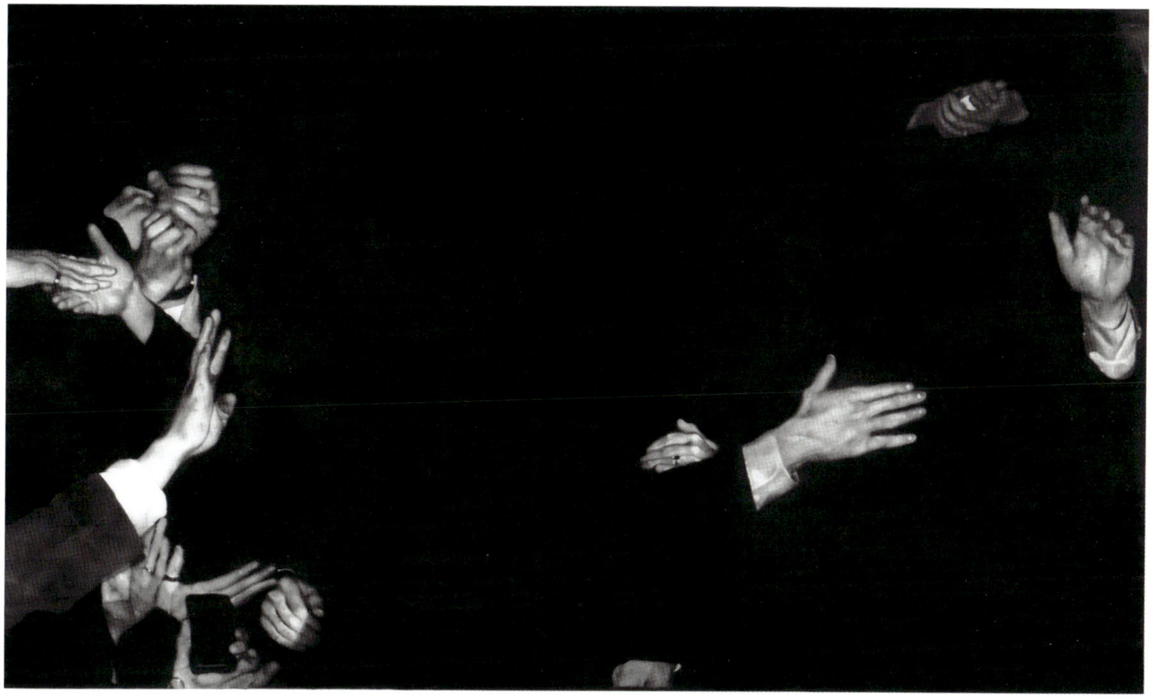

JOHANNES KAHRS
I Finally Accept Fate
2002

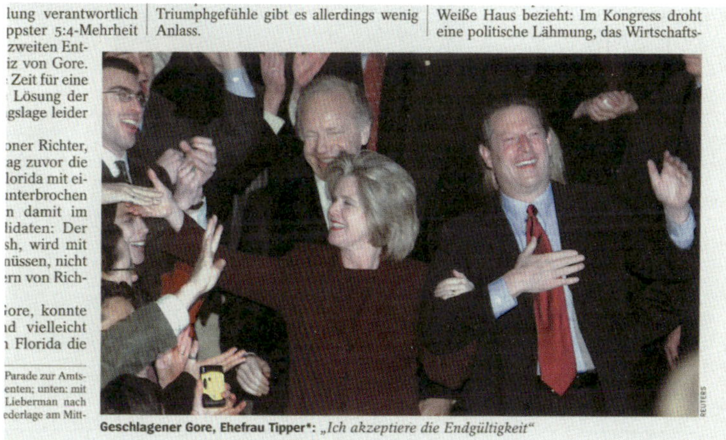

lung verantwortlich | Triumphgefühle gibt es allerdings wenig | Weiße Haus bezieht: Im Kongress droht
ppster 5:4-Mehrheit | Anlass. | eine politische Lähmung, das Wirtschafts-
zweiten Ent-
iz von Gore.
Zeit für eine
Lösung der
gslage leider

oner Richter,
ag zuvor die
lorida mit ei-
nterbrochen
n damit im
lidaten: Der
sh, wird mit
nüssen, nicht
rn von Rich-

ore, konnte
ıd vielleicht
ı Florida die

Parade zur Amts-
enten; unten: mit
Lieberman nach
ederlage am Mitt-

Geschlagener Gore, Ehefrau Tipper*: *„Ich akzeptiere die Endgültigkeit"*

Der Spiegel, no. 51,
December 18, 2000, p. 165
(Photograph: anonymous)

RICHARD HAMILTON. A leading figure in British pop art from the founding of the Independent Group in the mid-1950s, Richard Hamilton painted *Swingeing London 67* against the backdrop of London's "summer of love" in 1967. Sex, drugs, rock 'n' roll, and the counterculture were a few of the essential ingredients at this intensely liberating moment in the hippy youth movement. These trends were harshly criticized and censured by the British establishment, whence the play on words between "swinging" (dancing) and "swingeing" (crushing). On June 28, 1967, Mick Jagger and the art dealer Robert Fraser were arrested and found guilty of drug possession. A photograph by John Twine shows them handcuffed in the back seat of a police car, attempting to shield their faces with raised hands. The shot was published the following day in the *Daily Sketch*. Hamilton appropriated this photo and used it as the basis for a series of paintings and silk screens. By emphasizing the gesture so characteristic of stars attempting to protect themselves from the aggressive intrusion of photographers, these works contributed to the recognition of the paparazzi aesthetic.

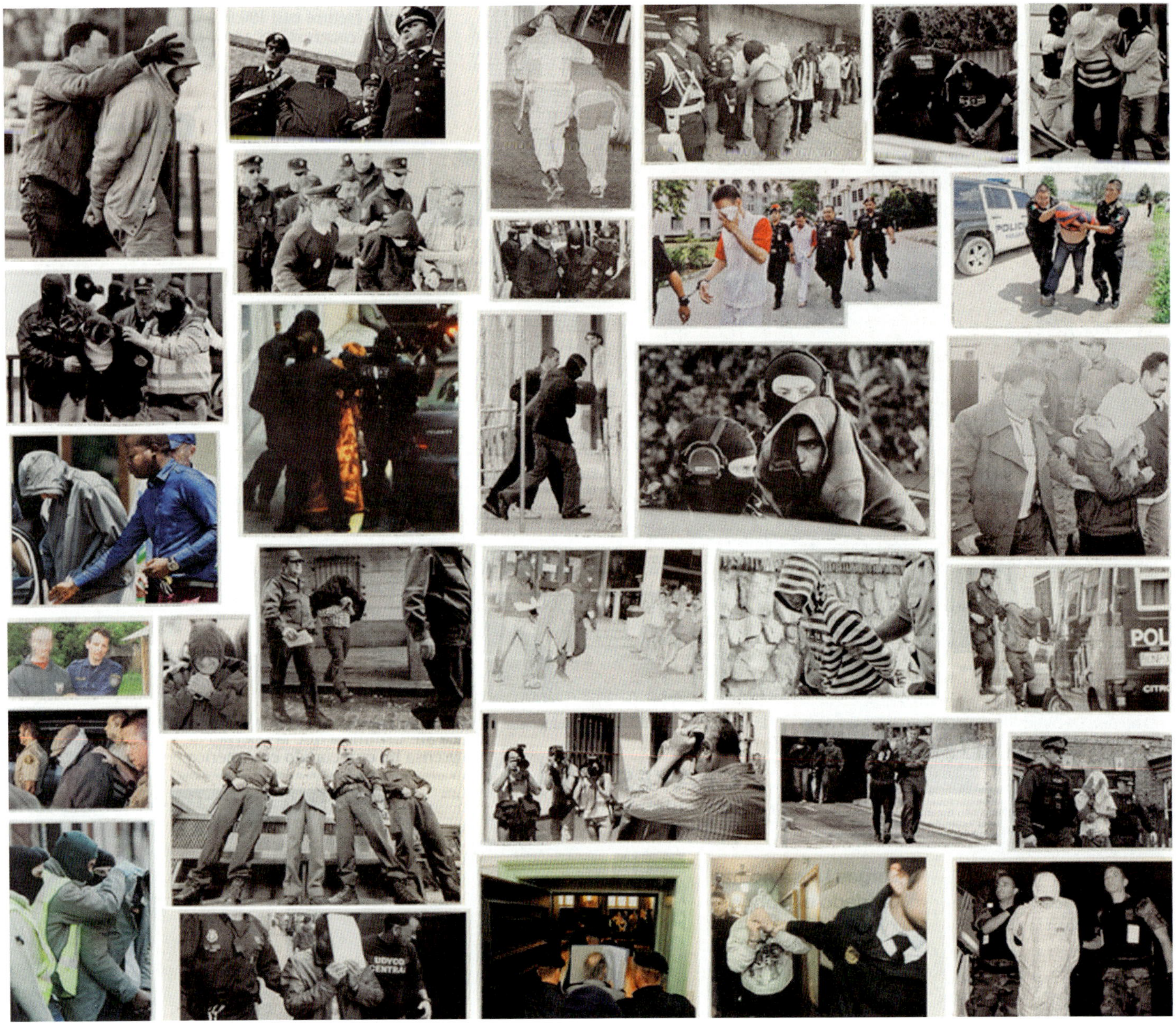

JONATHAN HERNÁNDEZ
Vulnerabilia (Covers Under Arrest)
2011–13

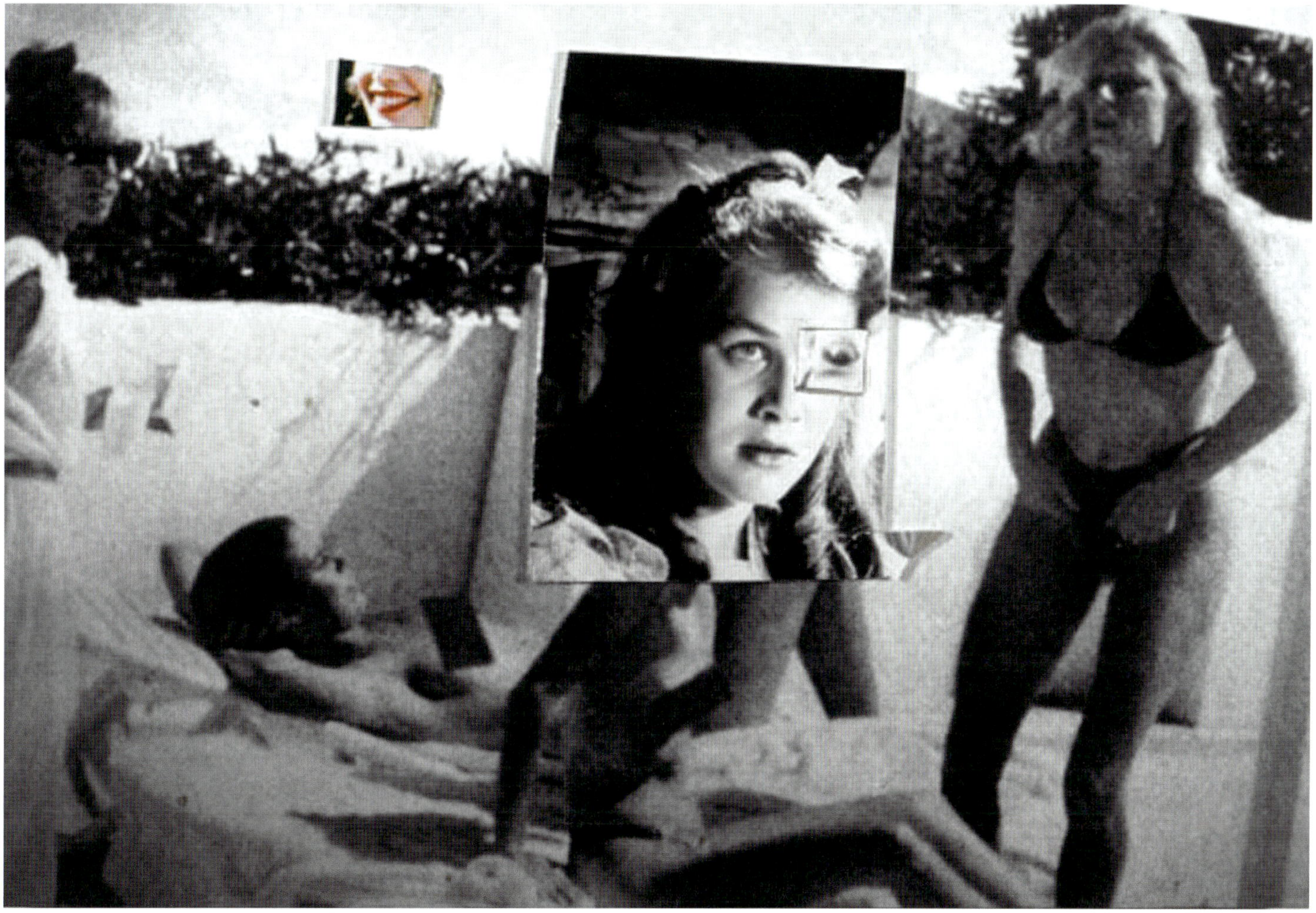

PAUL MCCARTHY
Girls 2
2000

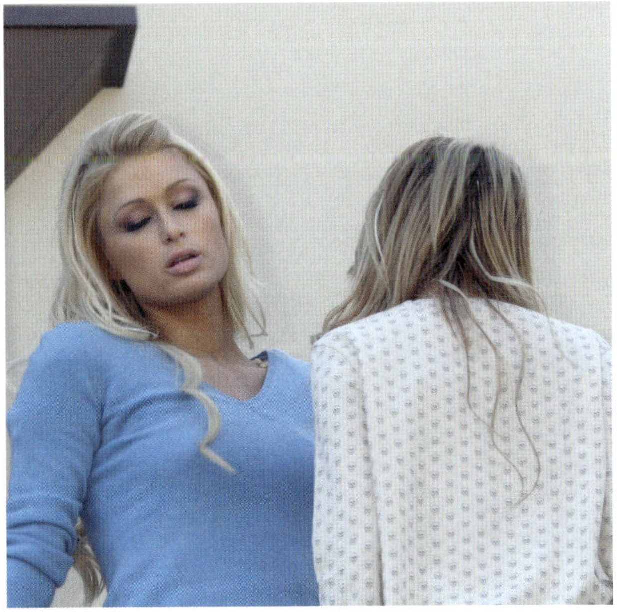

OLIVIER MIRGUET
Trash #0049
2009

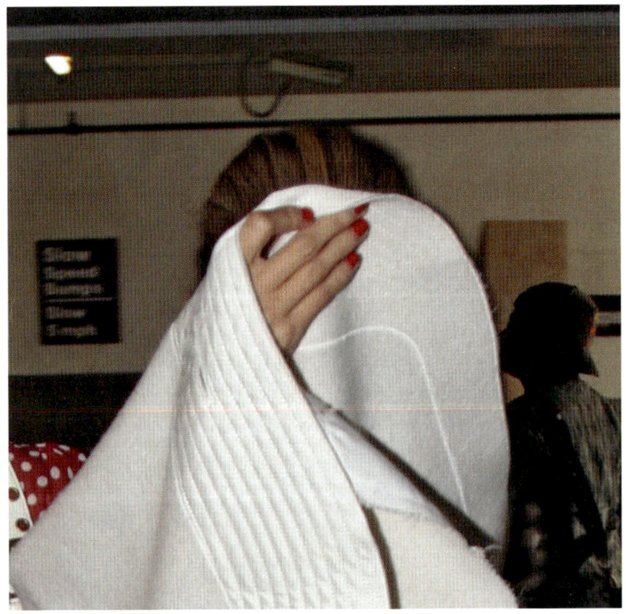

OLIVIER MIRGUET
Trash #0067
2009

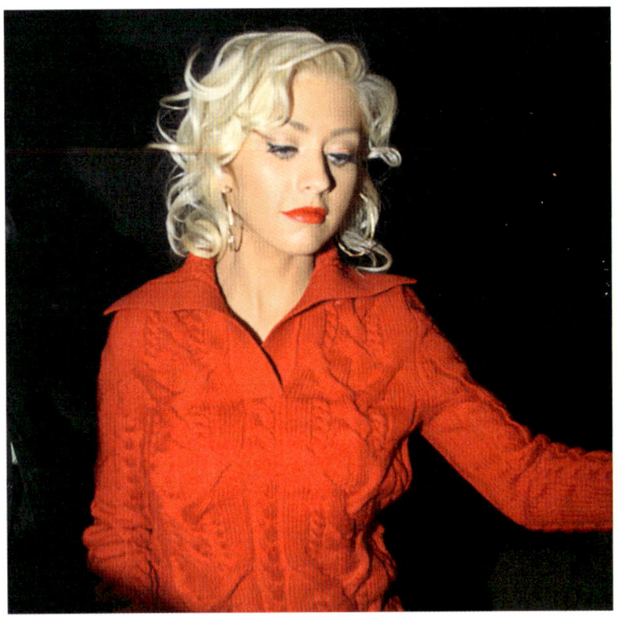

OLIVIER MIRGUET
Trash #6024
2009

THOMAS DEMAND is a German artist who originally trained as a sculptor, and later studied with Bernd and Hilla Becher at the Düsseldorf Academy in the 1990s. He recreates scenes gleaned from images found in the press in vast three-dimensional installations in paper, which he then rephotographs. The basis of his work *Junior Suite* was a photograph showing Whitney Houston in the process of eating her last meal in her bedroom in the Beverly Hilton Hotel, just before her death from a drug overdose. The artist has created a new kind of dramaturgy that celebrates the power of falsity. It emphasizes the links of the image to its simulacrum through the self-referential technique of *mise en abyme*. Varying interpretations of temporality, the effects of recognition, and techniques of distancing are juxtaposed to challenge our relationship with the creation of contemporary myths. Just as Olivier Mirguet employs snapshots that have been rejected by the paparazzi as ruined or unusable, Demand draws on some of the visual codes belonging to the media world. He challenges the notion of archival records and current events through his carefully researched and nuanced work.

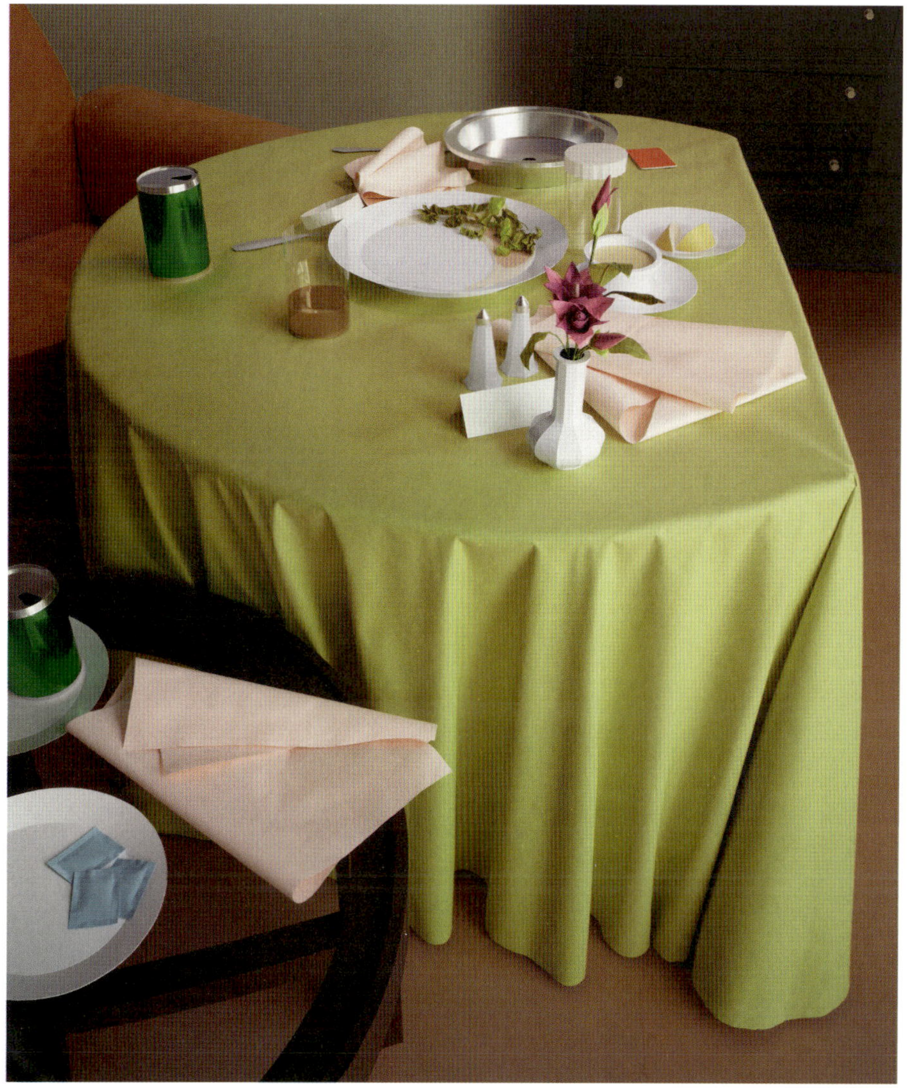

THOMAS DEMAND
Junior Suite
2012

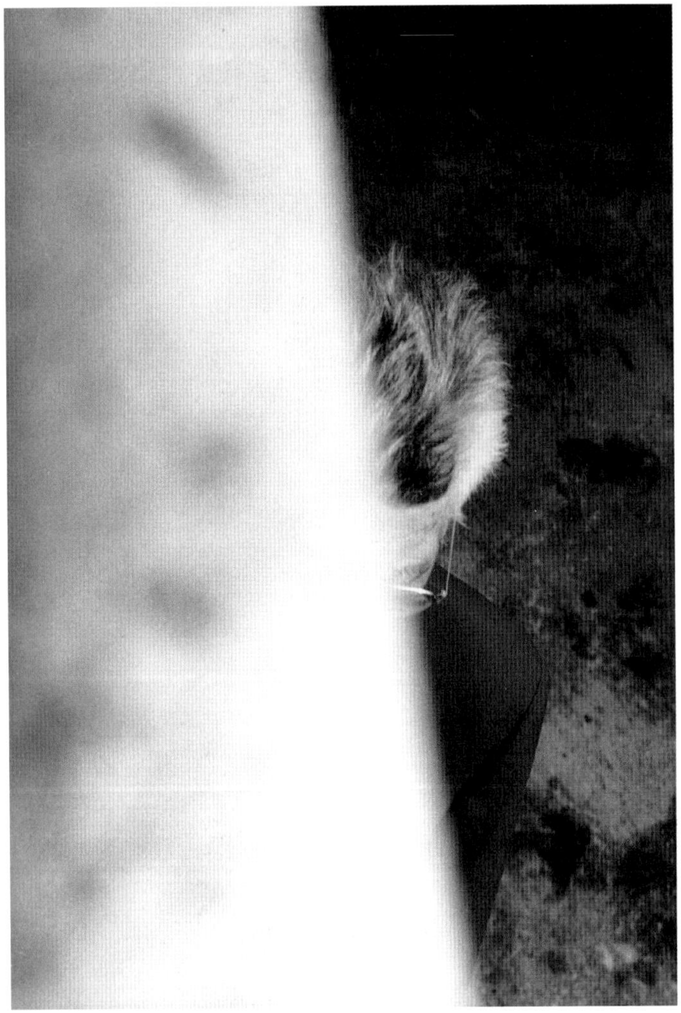

FRANÇOIS-MARIE BANIER
Samuel Beckett, Paris
September 1989

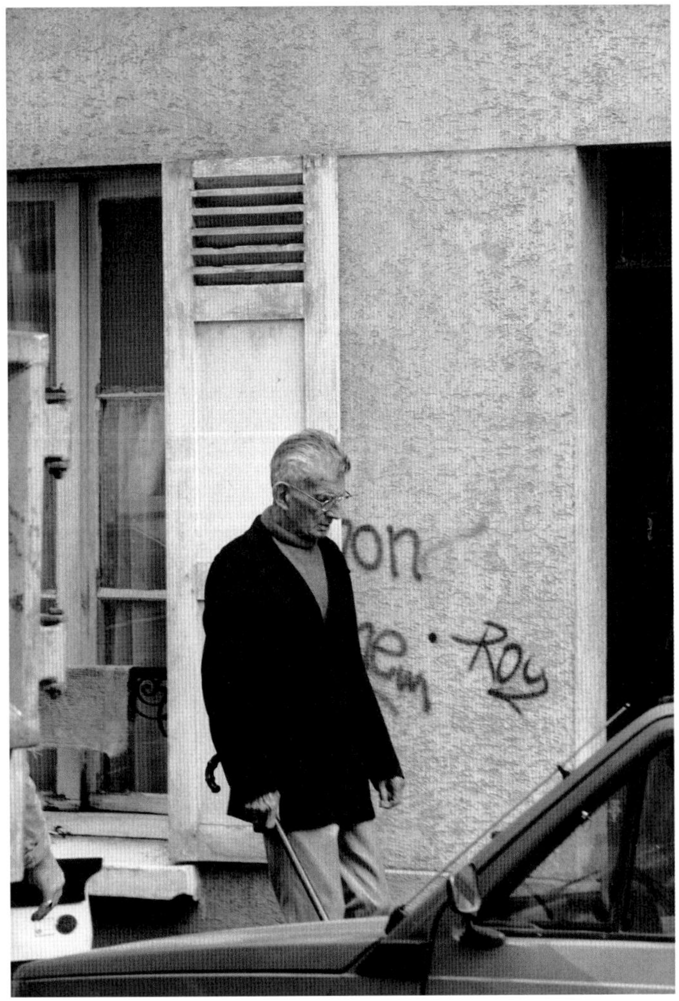

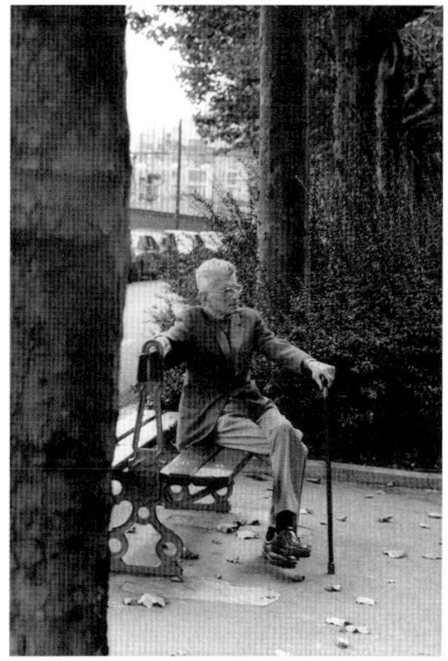

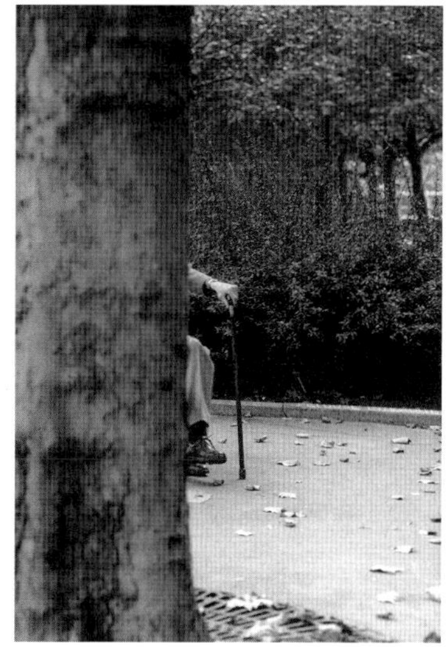

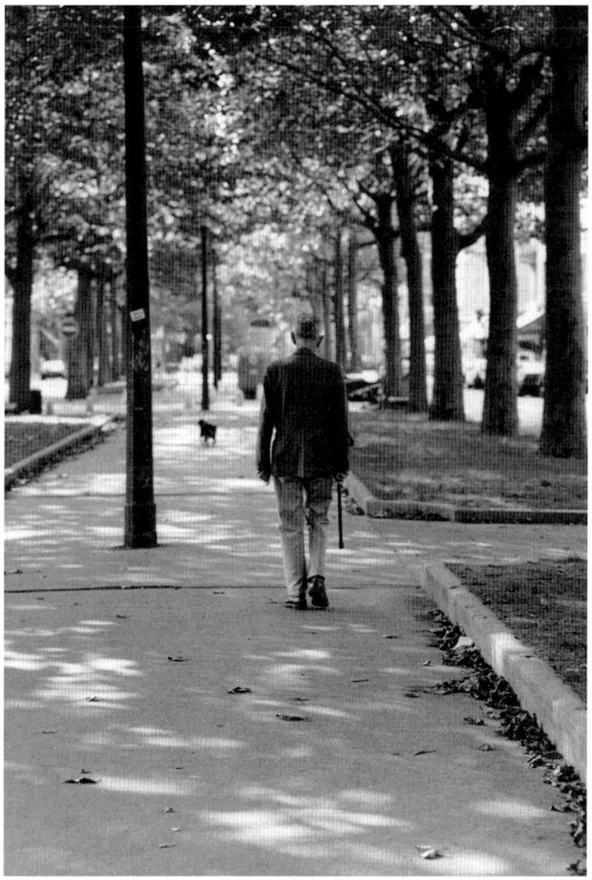

FRANÇOIS-MARIE BANIER. A writer, painter, and collector, François-Marie Banier began to photograph in the early 1970s. He always resisted being described as a celebrity photographer, but he moved in those circles and produced some moving portraits of Salvador Dalí, François Mitterrand, Marcello Mastroianni, Caroline of Monaco, and Isabelle Adjani. He photographed just as many anonymous subjects, demonstrating a particular interest in the body's expressive movements. His series on Samuel Beckett began in Tangier in the summer of 1978 and continued in the streets of Paris until 1989, slightly before the writer's death. Although he knew Beckett well, Banier chose to photograph him from a distance, using a telephoto lens. His images play with the aesthetic of "stolen" shots. They use blurred effects, distancing, and obstructions to the visual field, sometimes only revealing small details: a strand of hair, a hand gripping a cane, an attenuated profile. They are attempts, as Banier explained, to "capture every dimension of this curious figure."

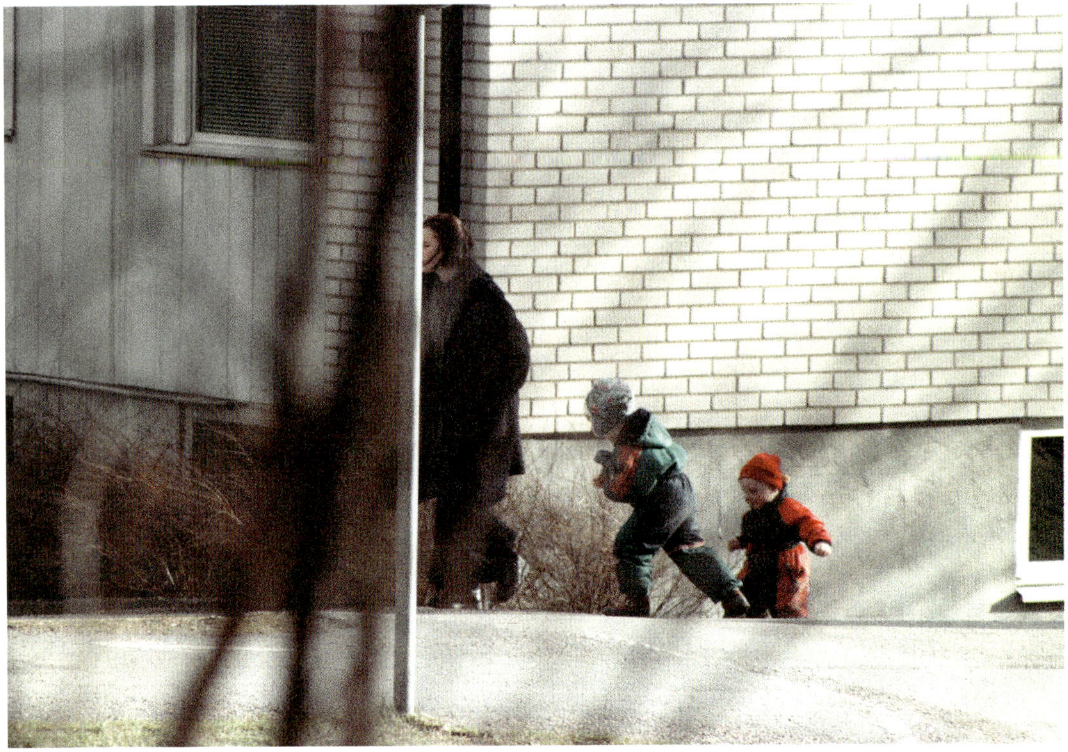

ULF LUNDIN
Pictures of a Family
1996

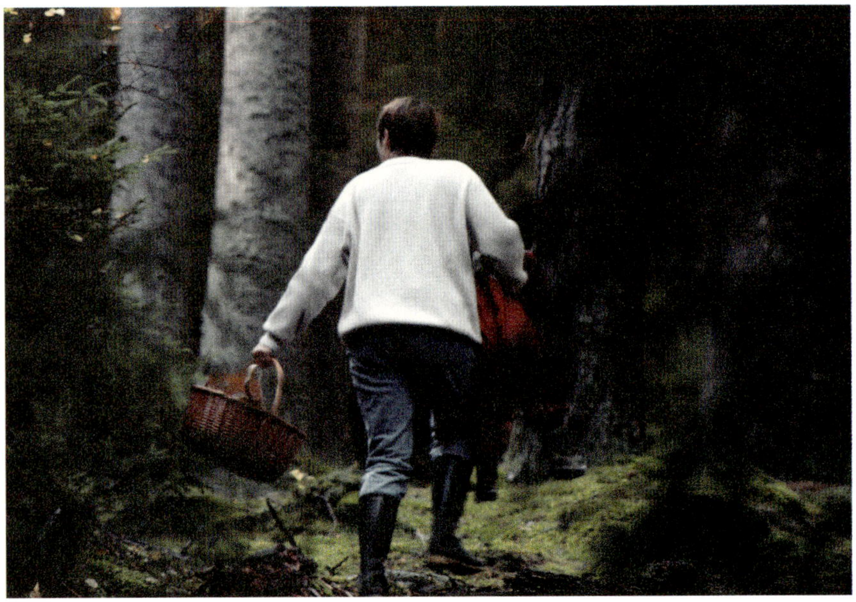

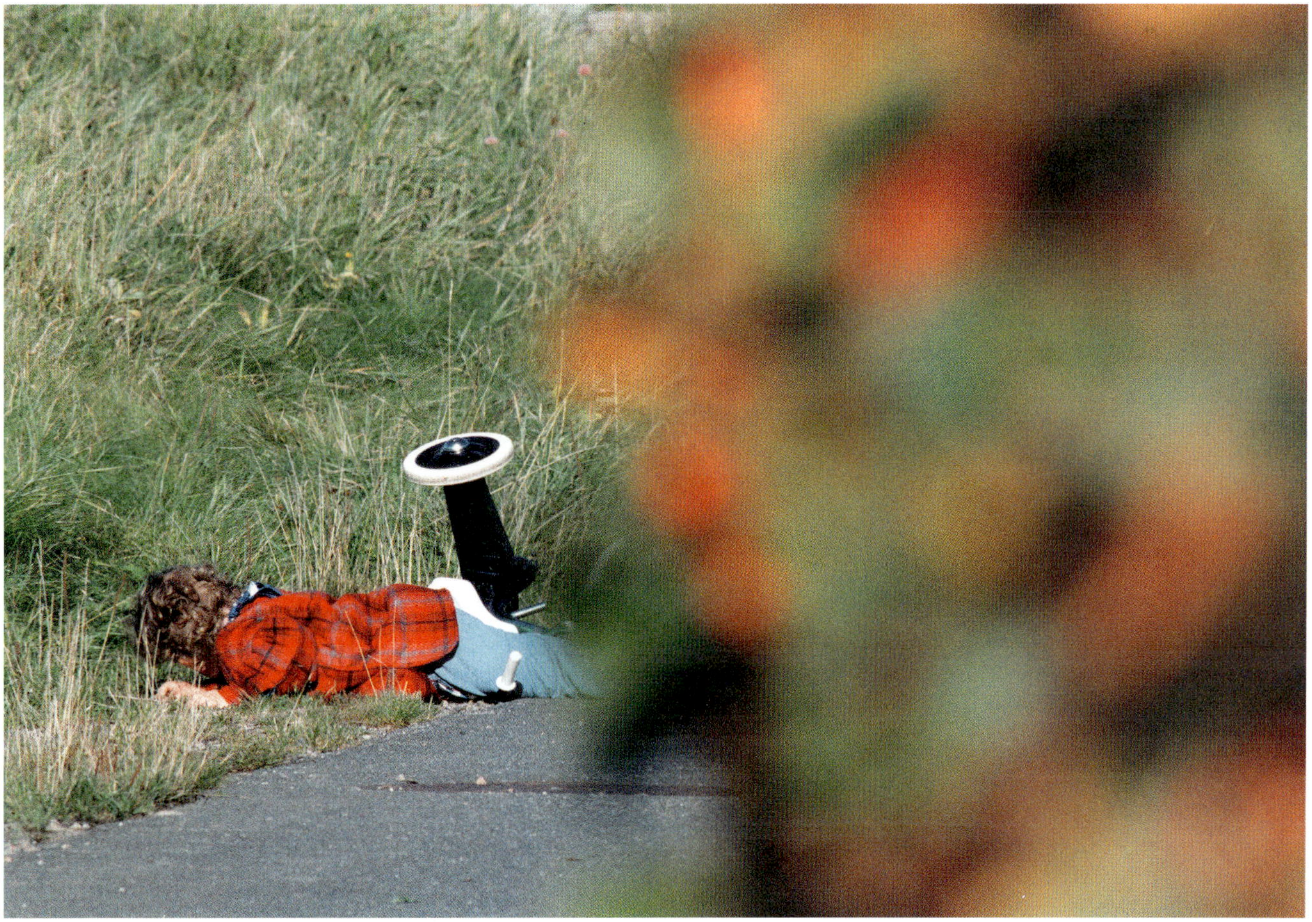

ULF LUNDIN. A Swedish artist born in 1965, Ulf Lundin lives in Stockholm. Trained at the School of Photography and Film at Göteborg University, he has been directing his efforts to photography, video, and installations in recent years. *Pictures of a Family* is a collection of snapshots of a family the artist selected for its apparent perfection and stability. For an entire year, family members cooperated in playing a "false paparazzi" game, allowing themselves to be tracked and photographed by the artist at all times. Although the work was based on Lundin's desire to project himself into this ideal family and experience its daily life from a distance, the overall impression is paradoxically a sense of unease. Viewed through a camera's lens, the most anodyne scenes take on ominous overtones.
The paparazzi style is the source of these tensions, transforming each and every one of us into a potential voyeur.

15.10.08 14:16

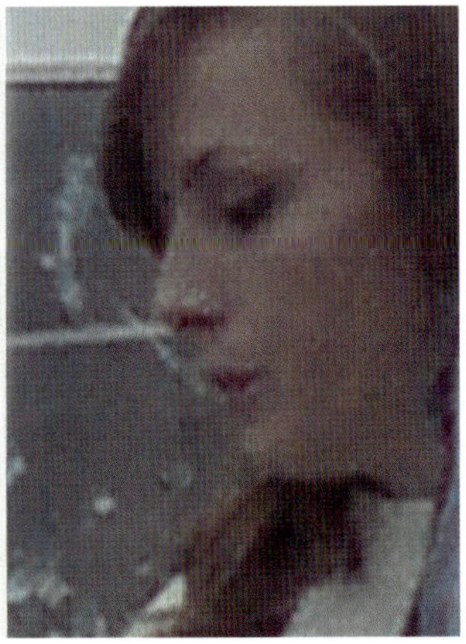

15.10.08 15:02

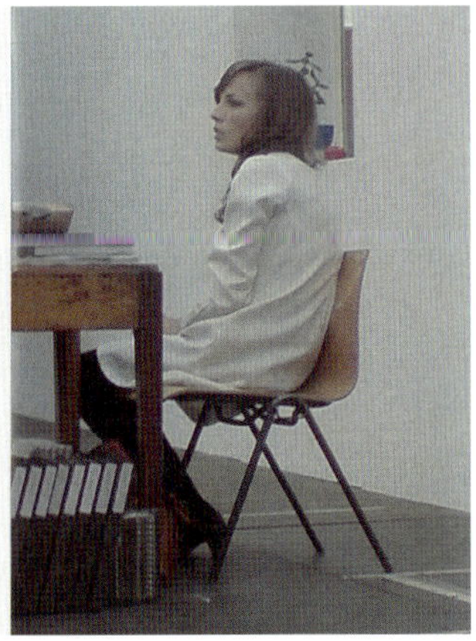

15.10.08 15:44

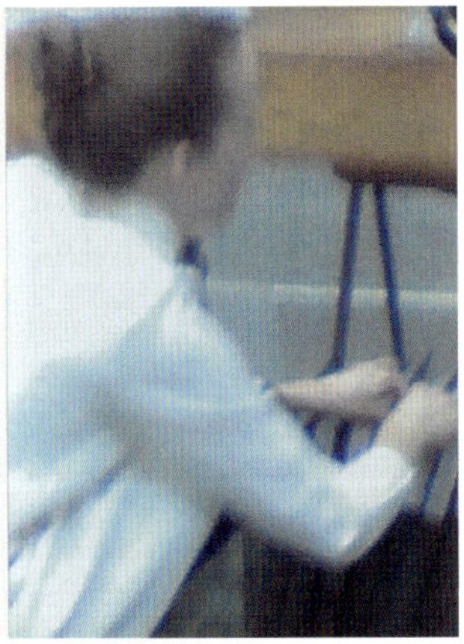

15.10.08 22:06

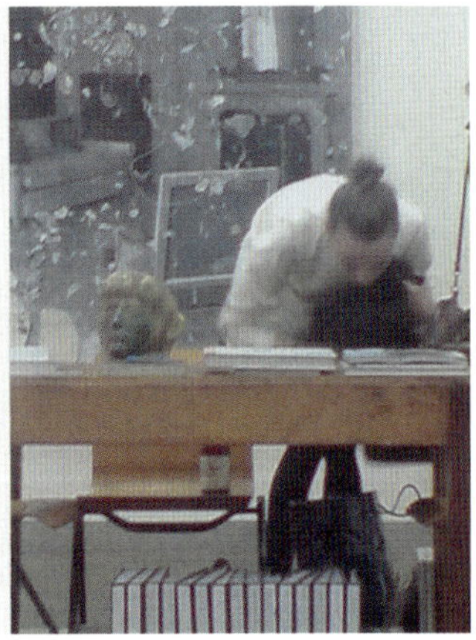

16.10.08 12:16

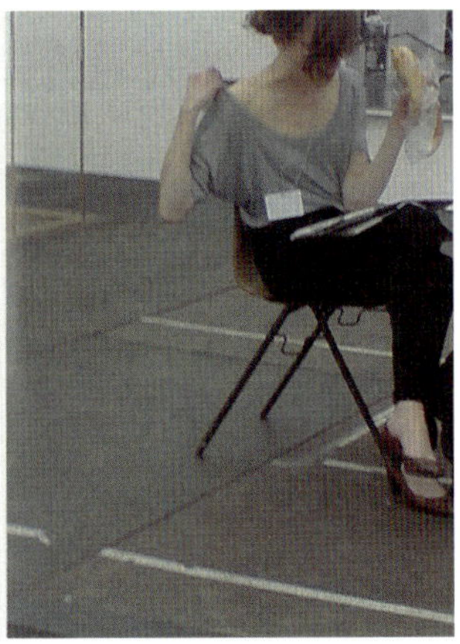

16.10.08 12:41

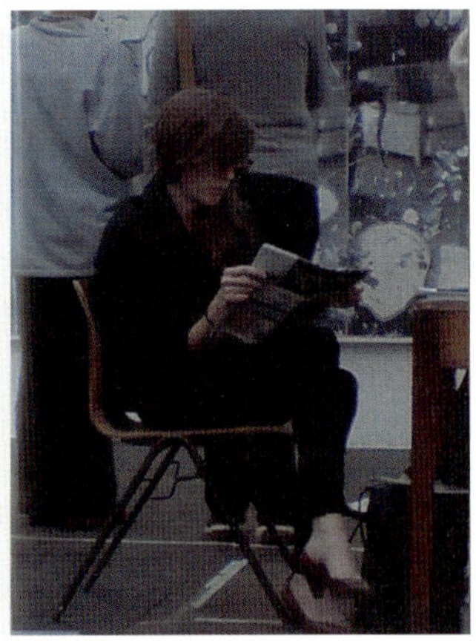

LIAM TICKNER
London
2008

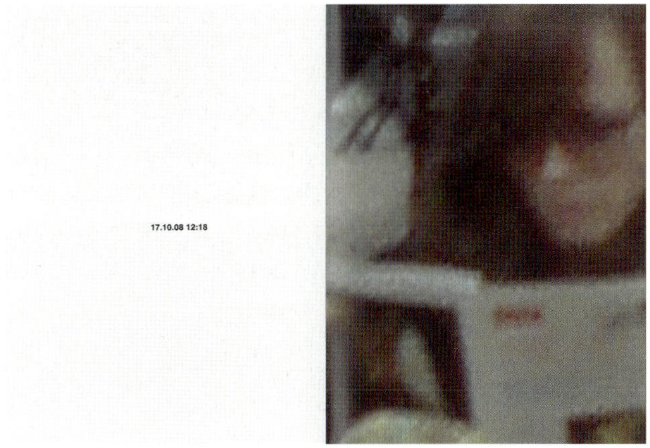

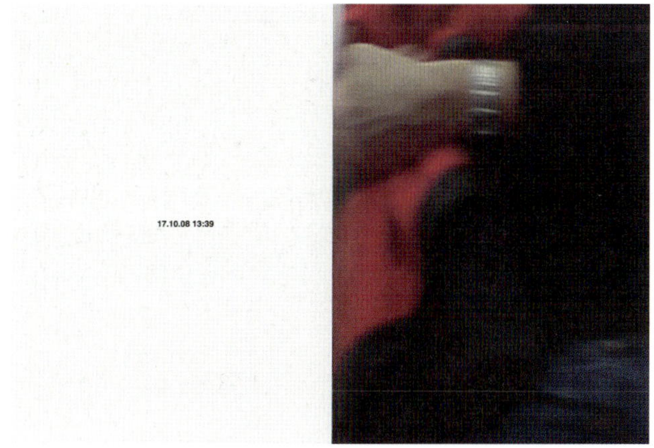

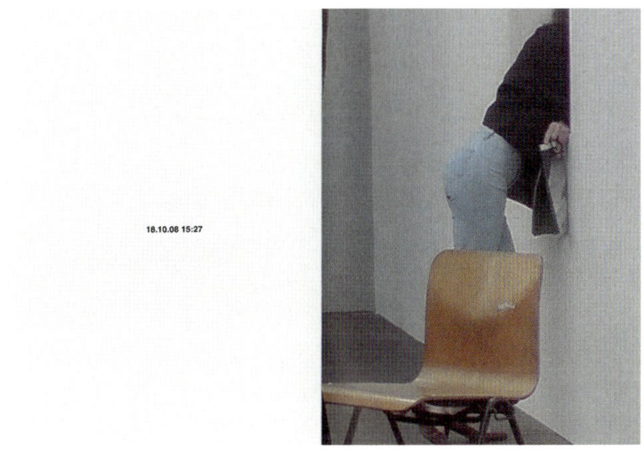

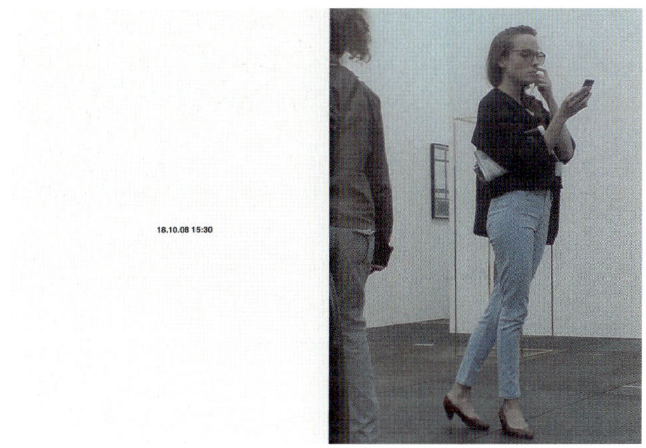

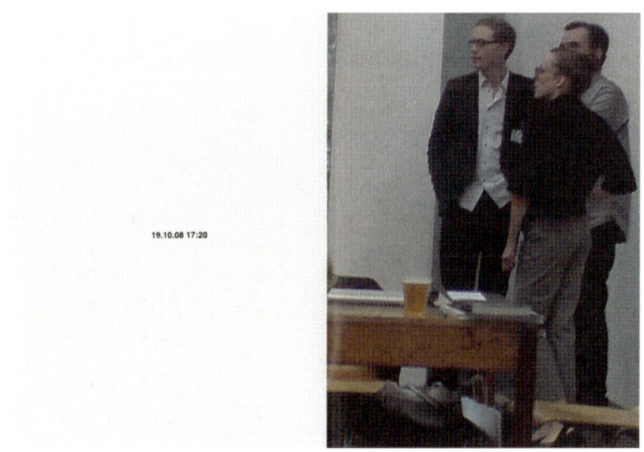

LIAM TICKNER. In 2008, an artist's book simply entitled *London* was printed in an edition of thirty copies, signed by its creator Liam Tickner. The work was a collection of photographs taken by the artist at a contemporary art fair while he was working as a gallery assistant. Over a four-day period, he meticulously captured the actions and gestures of the art dealer in the booth across from him. The spontaneity of the poses, the obstruction of portions of the visual field, and the attention given to certain details with the use of close-ups and pixelization all demonstrate that the artist has fully grasped the codes of paparazzi photography and appropriated them for his own creative purposes. He uses a series of precise chronological indicators (date and time) that appear on each facing page across from the image. Evoking the protocols of conceptual art, he demonstrates the systematic nature of his artistic approach or, we might say, of his obsession.

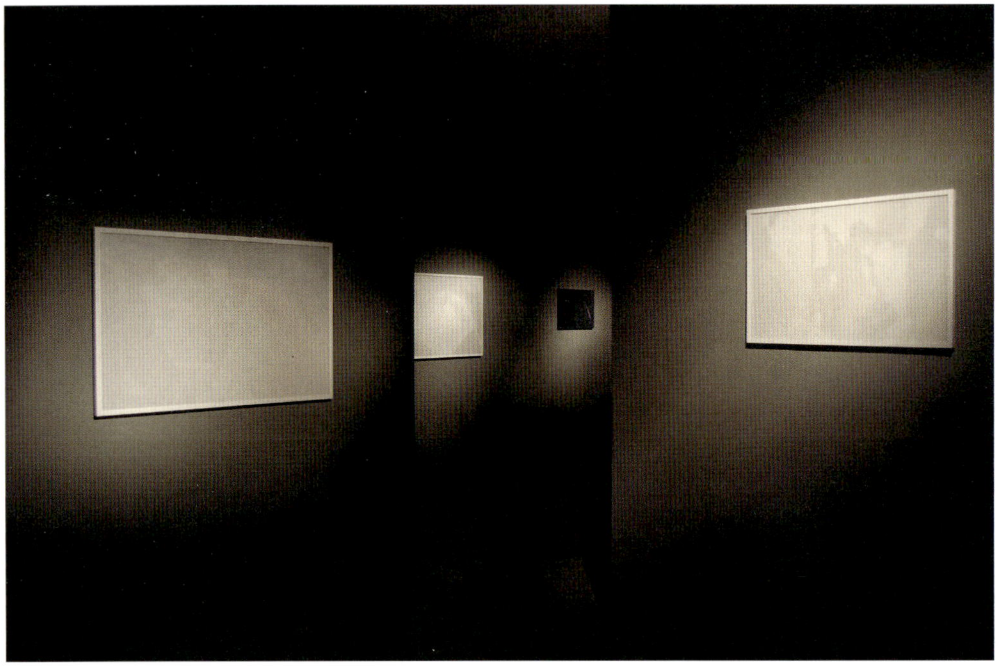

Installation view of the *Flash* series by Viktoria Binschtok at Klemm's, Berlin, 2008

OVEREXPOSURE. When discussing paparazzi photography, the ambiguity of the term "overexposure" applies in its fullest sense. It may refer to a subject who is excessively photographed and hyped in the media. It may also allude to a photo that is spoiled by improper exposure techniques. The burst of light from a flash is the instant when the two meanings converge. It is the culmination of the paparazzo's hunt—the second when the image is stolen—when the star is displayed at her most unguarded. This is the moment that is thought to be the most authentic. According to this mythology, the onslaught of the flash allows us to penetrate beyond the star's carefully contrived pose, compelling her to display a natural protective reaction by the violence of its intrusion. The flash was originally intended to provide adequate lighting, but its figurative overuse in the media has proved to be counterproductive. As Champfleury pointed out in 1863 in *La Légende du daguerréotype*, when a person has himself photographed, the real man ends up disappearing. From its earliest beginnings, photography was predicated on a society greedy for spectacle. The paparazzi photo has now elevated this hunger to a feeding frenzy.

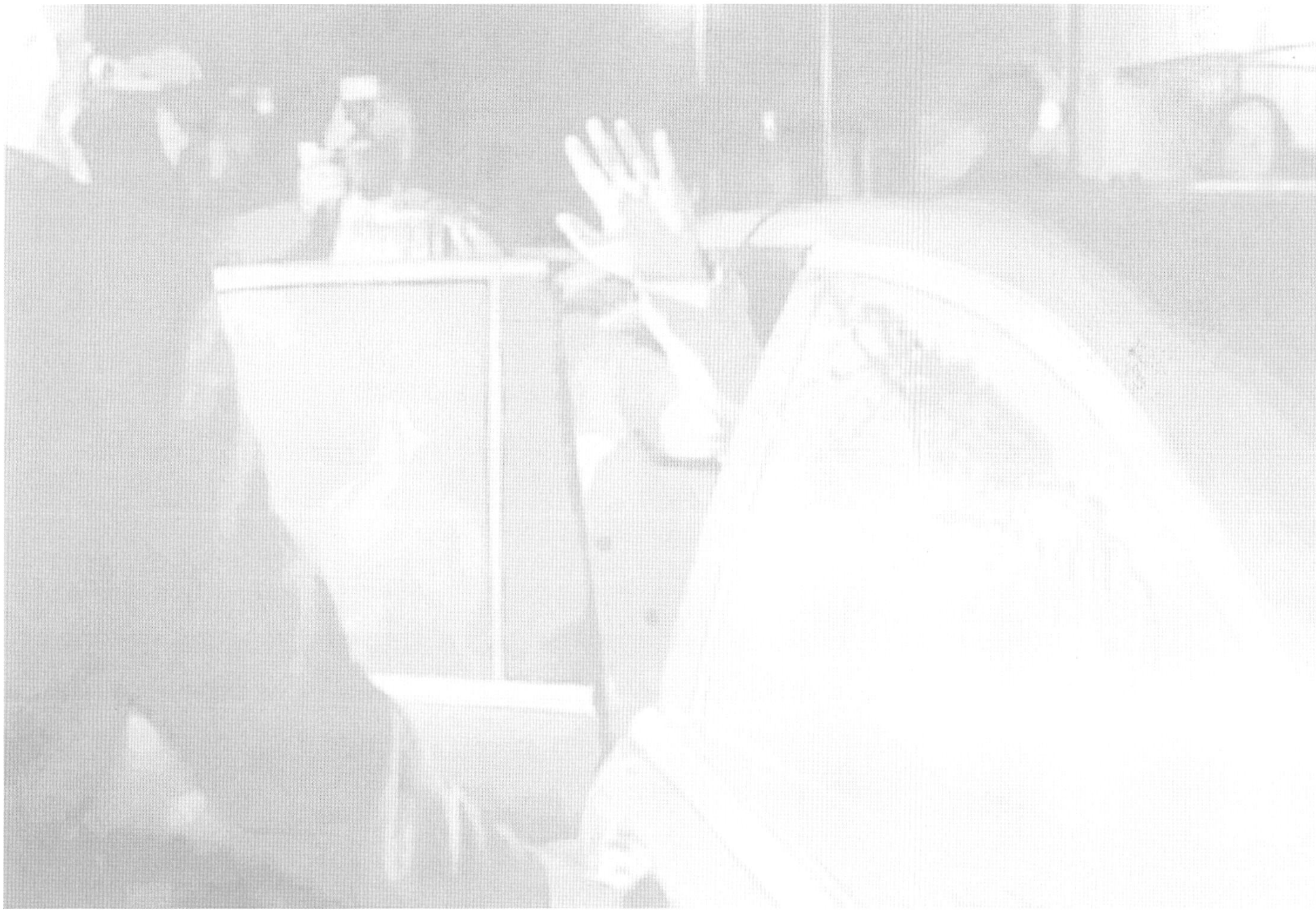

VIKTORIA BINSCHTOK
Flash #6
2008

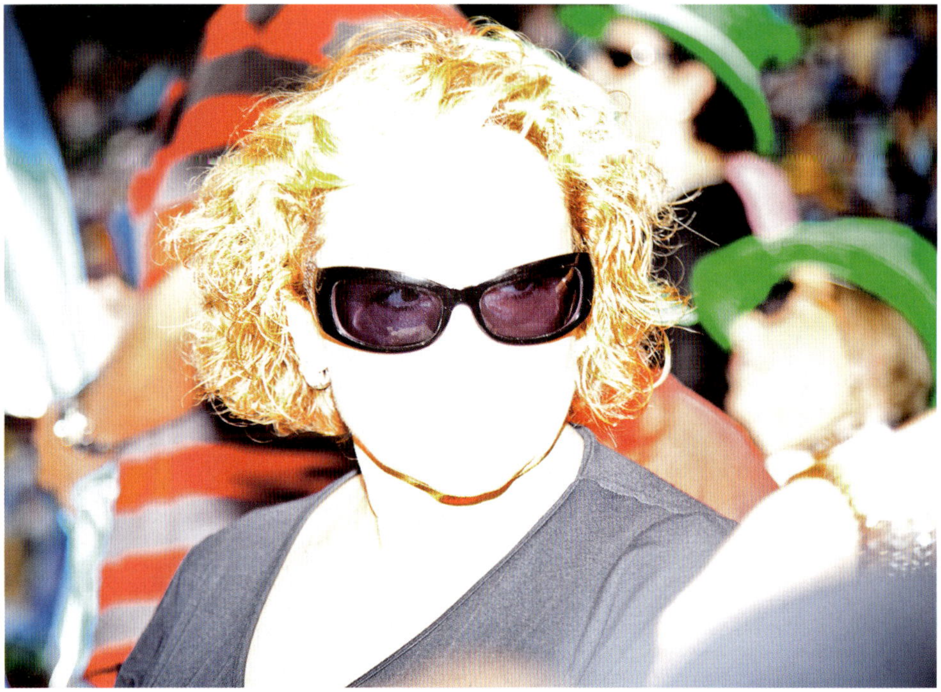

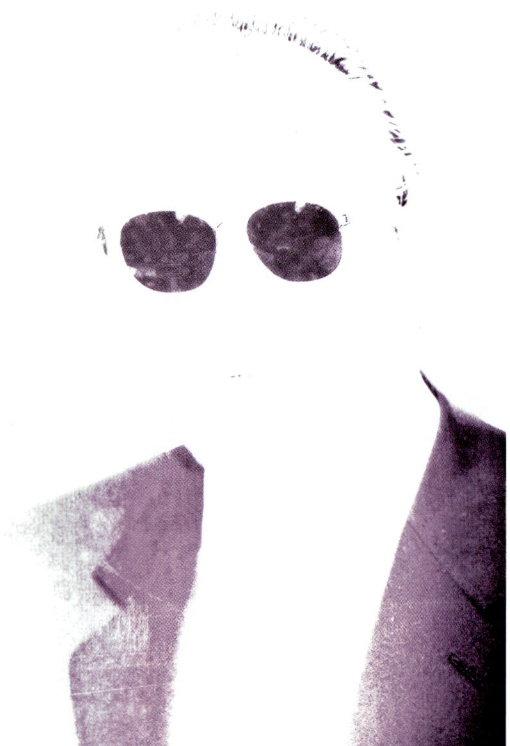

JULIÁN BARÓN
C.E.N.S.U.R.A.,
Spain
November 2011

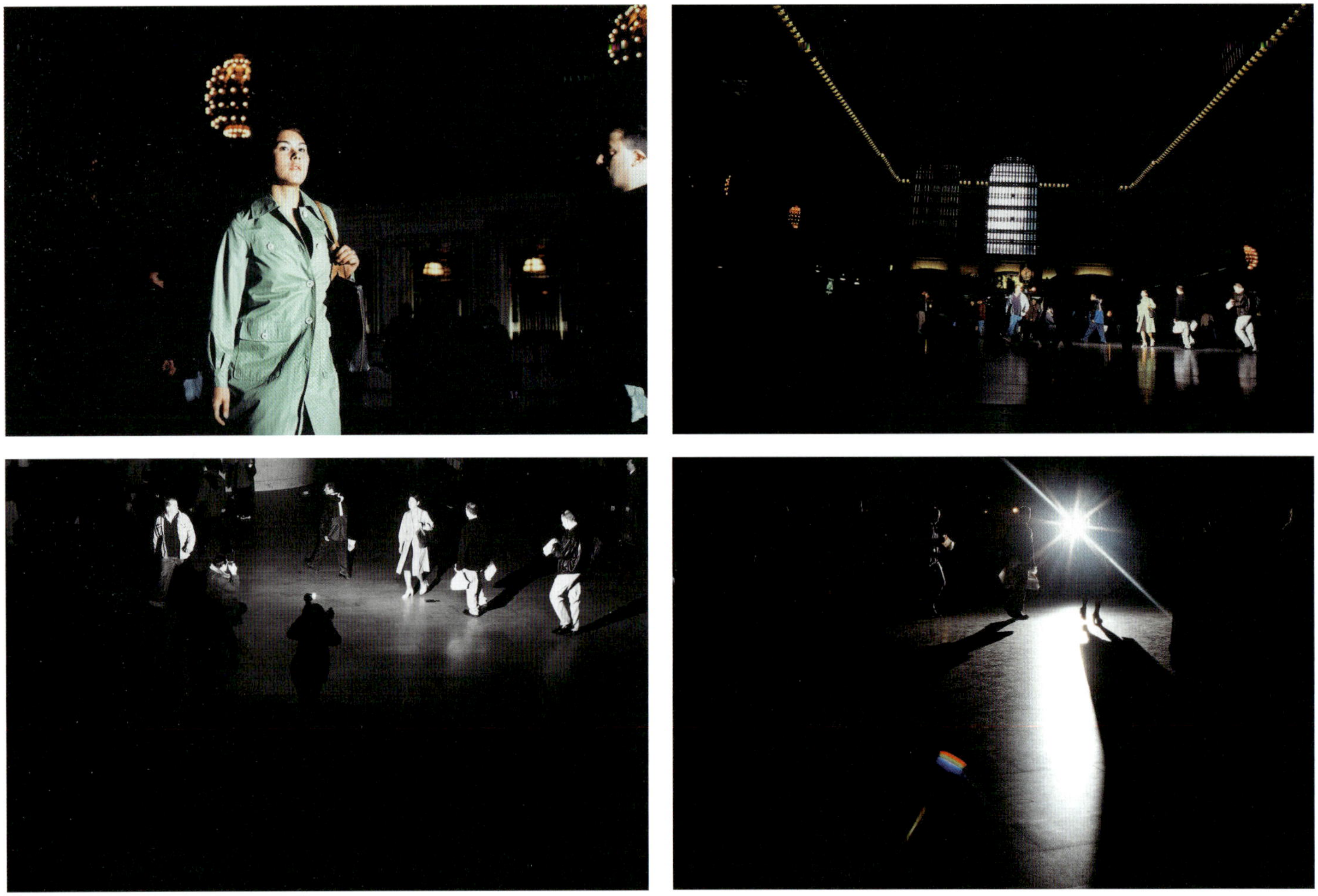

BARBARA PROBST
Exposure #9: N.Y.C.,
Grand Central Station,
12.18.01, 1:21 p.m.
2001

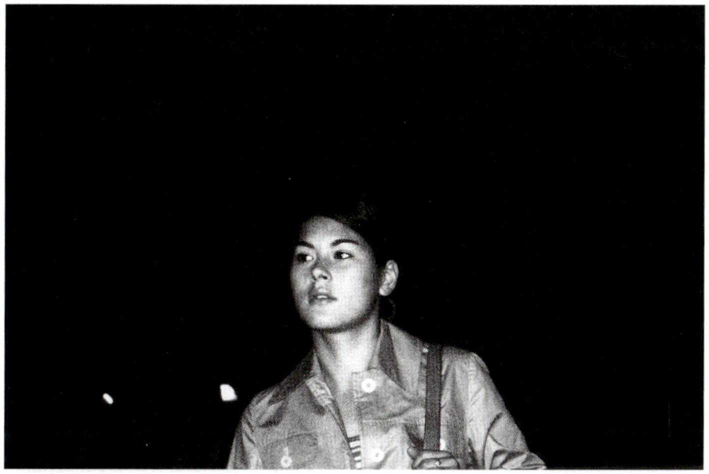

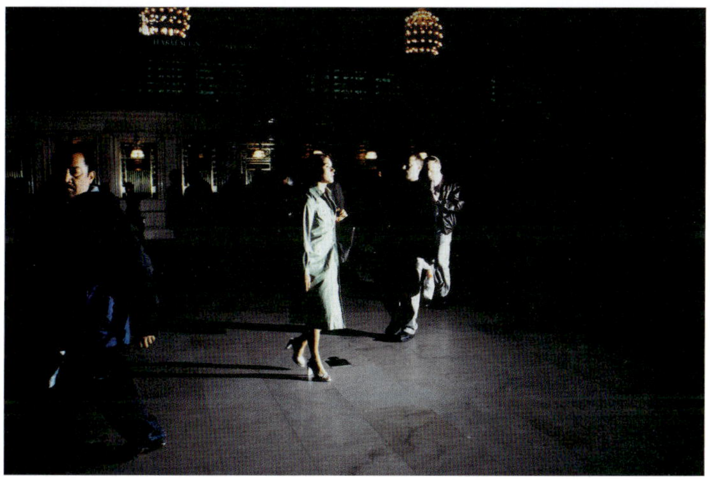

IN THE SKIN OF A PAPARAZZO

Over the last few decades, the paparazzi style has fascinated numerous artists and photographers. Those working in the field of fashion—including Richard Avedon, William Klein and, more recently, Alexi Lubomirski and Christian Lesemann—were among the first to transform themselves into paparazzi as part of a photo shoot. More recently, many artists, including the American Gary Lee Boas, the British Alison Jackson, and the Austrians of the G.R.A.M. collective, have also "collected" stars, following the lead of the paparazzi. In their photography, these artists raise questions about the power of the media, the implications of a society transfixed by sensationalism, and the ubiquitous access to celebrity. Since the 1980s, a number of women, including Cindy Sherman, Malin Arnesson, and Kathrin Günter, have raised their own provocative questions on the future of an artist who is assuming the role of star in her own right.

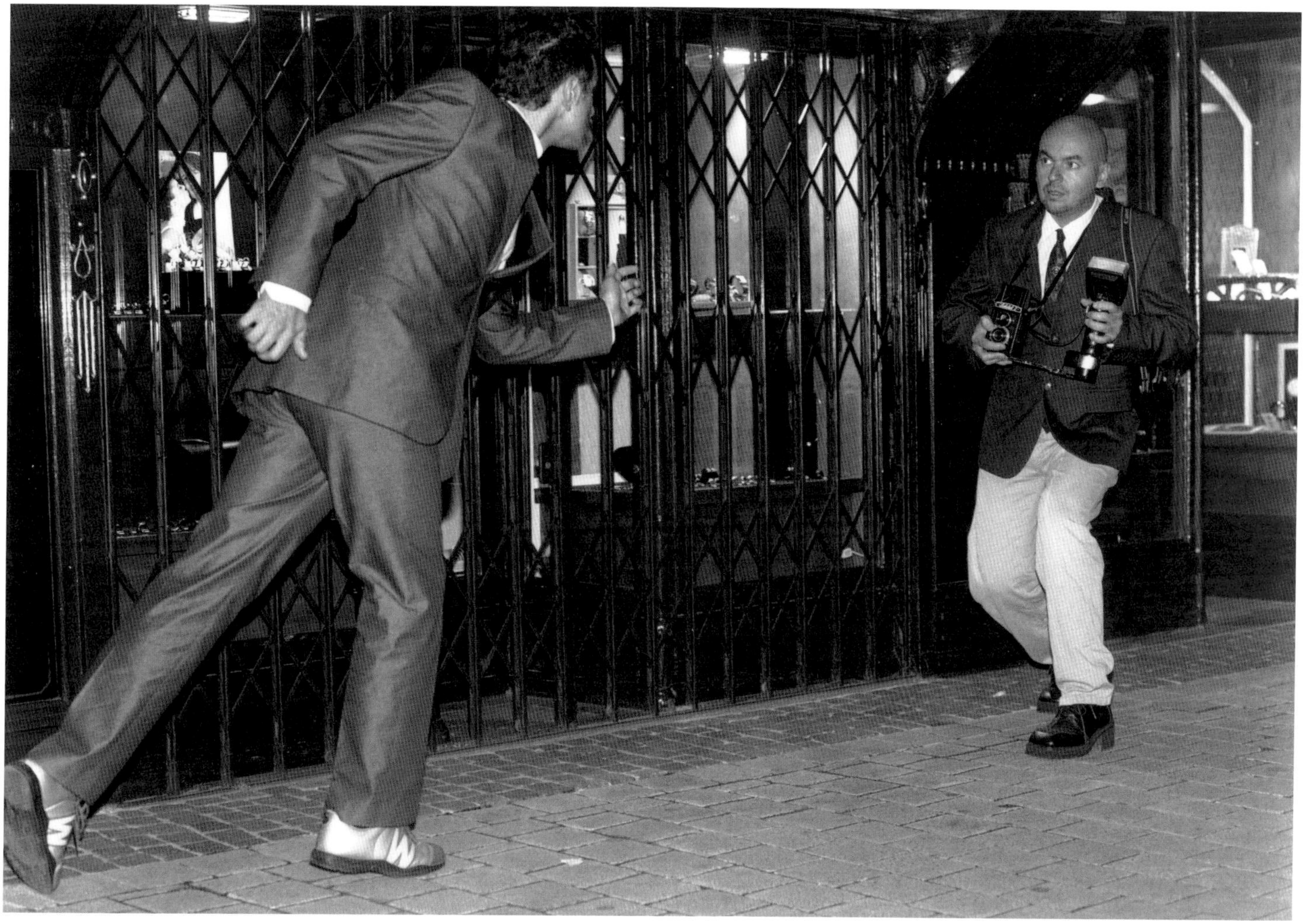

G.R.A.M.
Nach Motiven von …
2001

Fashion Photography and the Paparazzi Aesthetic

Frédéric Monneyron

In contemporary societies, it has been, indisputably, a long struggle for photography to gain acknowledgment as an art in its own right. It has also taken time to recognize that it performs all the roles generally associated with art just as well if not better than any other discipline. Photography has been engaged in a process of historic mediation. It has fashioned its own history to acquire the definitions generally attributed to art. This implies that photography is now considered as a thought process, a mode of self-expression, or a view of society; it has even been able to achieve a far-reaching independence from marketplace constraints. First and foremost, however, it has been imperative to overcome the notion that photography is fated to be limited to mere imitation, representing nothing more than the simple recording of a preexisting reality. Although photography has demonstrably participated in the important movements in contemporary art—abstraction, surrealism, conceptualism—these dismissive concepts still prevail among certain audiences today. There is real reason to be concerned that the Centre Pompidou–Metz's exhibition of a very specialized photographic genre—paparazzi photography—may be viewed as the lowliest example of the mere recording of a preexisting reality. Judged in this way, the works displayed could reactivate or strengthen these derogatory assumptions.

Fashion photographers have long confronted these disparaging attitudes. Considered minor players in an art form that is itself traditionally deemed as minor, they have struggled against these preconceptions, striving to reduce the perceived differences between the fields of fashion photography and fine art photography. In fact, fashion photographers feared that this new photographic genre of paparazzi photography would detract from the artistic respect that they themselves had so recently and arduously achieved; many viewed the paparazzi's work with a wary and skeptical eye.

Caught Between Attraction and Repulsion: Two Converging Aesthetics

It is generally acknowledged that the paparazzi phenomenon was christened, if not created, in Federico Fellini's *La Dolce Vita* in 1960: the character of the young photographer who accompanies Marcello in his Roman escapades is named Paparazzo. This idea was suggested to the director by his wife, Giulietta Masina, or perhaps by his scriptwriter, Ennio Flaiano (opinions diverge on this point). The concept of the paparazzo took shape over the next decade to become firmly established in the contemporary social landscape. Indeed, this development of the phenomenon that had been inaugurated with the naming of the paparazzo corresponded exactly with the artistic recognition of fashion photography in the 1960s—the culmination of a gradual process of acknowledgment dating back to the 1950s. In the public's perception, photographers in general became one with fashion photographers. However, it was fashion photographers who were able to climb the ranks to become photographer–heroes in their own right. The audience attributed an entire ensemble of qualities to them that no other artist could hope to combine. Accordingly, it is not surprising that a fashion photographer as well known as Richard Avedon in the 1960s would embrace the paparazzi aesthetic in a series of photographs that maintains a sense of distance that we may be tempted to consider ironic. He borrowed some of the most conspicuous features of paparazzi shots—celebrities photographed in their private lives—with the spontaneity and sketchy quality of a snapshot. He drew inspiration from Richard Burton and Elizabeth Taylor—classic paparazzi targets of the era—using his models, Mike Nichols and Suzie Parker, to play their roles. A number of these shots approach caricature, such as the pictures showing the couple absorbed in reading newspapers that apparently feature paparazzi photographs!

This spirit of mockery and caricaturization can be found in more recent fashion photographs. Their references to the paparazzi phenomenon, however ambiguous their motivation, are even more overt. One example is Alexi Lubomirski's series for *H&M Magazine* entitled *Achtung: Paparazzi!*, where the title, taken literally, appears to be a general warning. However, it can also be interpreted as a threat that would pit paparazzi photography against fashion photography as an art form. This is also the case with Christian Lesemann's photograph of a bag bearing the inscription "Famous when dead." It seems to be an exaltation of celebrity in its own right as well as an expression of the photographer's art—an art that has succumbed to the stylistic influence of paparazzi photography.

The mockery and caricaturization evident in the work of a number of photographers originates in and derives its force from the compulsion these photographers feel to differentiate themselves from the paparazzi aesthetic. Nevertheless, both groups share many aspects of this aesthetic. Despite the distanced and ironic gaze that the fashion photographer often casts on the work of the paparazzi, there are undoubtedly a number of aesthetic overlaps between the two. The paparazzi aesthetic is definitely not in opposition to the primary aesthetic functions of fashion photography; in fact it embraces many of the same concepts. When we observe trends in paparazzi photographs with hindsight, it is clear that they have closely coincided with the dominant tendencies in fashion photography over the last several decades.

The Essential Has Become a Mere Accessory

The primary function of fashion photography has traditionally been commercial: to sell, or sell more effectively, or at least somehow contribute to selling an article of clothing. Fashion photography was devoted to promotional activities from its earliest days. The garment was the focal point. The model existed only for the clothing she was wearing. The background was almost nonexistent, reduced to a simplified setting in a studio that was sometimes artfully draped, and in the best of cases perhaps enhanced by a bouquet of flowers. Since the observer's attention was focused almost exclusively on the clothing, the photographer's goal was to emphasize the garment's cut and details. It is reasonable to assume that the photographer had organized the composition based on and around the garment alone.

It is true that fashion photography can still be perceived this way today. However, if we consider the genre with a degree of objectivity, it is apparent that the clothing has lost its central role. It has now been reduced to just one aspect of the image's composition. Sometimes, the garment is no more than a decorative element that has little influence on the photo's general meaning and impact. The photographer's traditional relationship with the clothing is completely reversed. The photographer is no longer at the service of the clothing; now the clothing does the bidding of the photographer. Generally speaking, fashion photography has clearly evolved to express a personal aesthetic rather than a fashion trend, at least since the second half of the 1970s. This aesthetic approach has allowed the fashion photographer to be perceived as an artist. The photographer no longer promotes the garment: it is now the garment that promotes the photographer. It is by no means the exception for a fashion photographer to become as famous as the couturier for whom he works. In fact, the photographer often receives more publicity. The designer's name appears on the labels, but the photographer's name often figures more prominently in magazines, where it is featured beside his shots of the designer's creations.

Logically enough, this distancing from the original primary function of promoting a garment allows us to observe how fashion photographs appropriate aspects of the paparazzi aesthetic, which has never considered clothing to have anything other than accessory significance. Richard Avedon's series is an excellent early example. In an era when this distancing had not yet affected most fashion photography, his work made it difficult to identify the labels of the clothing presented in his spreads. Sometimes even the clothing's distinguishing features and brand were unclear in his pictures; it was necessary to read the captions printed next to the photographs to understand the subject matter.

1. Harriet Quick, *Catwalking: A History of the Fashion Model* (London: Todtri Book Publishers, 2001), 86.

2. See Martin Harrison, *Appearances: Fashion Photography since 1945* (New York: Rizzoli International Publications, 1991).

3. See Frédéric Monneyron, *La Photographie de mode. Un art souverain* (Paris: PUF, 2010), 122–23.

Shots taken by Christian Lesemann and Alexi Lubomirski, in a more recent period when clothing is decidedly no longer the focal point of fashion photography, push this logic to the limit. When the garment is virtually absent, superseded by a bared, blurry figure in a work by Christian Lesemann, it no longer plays any role whatsoever in defining the image. This is no longer an example of "fashion photography" in the traditional understanding of the term. These are simply the works of photographers who have been identified as specialists in this genre or who have been published in fashion magazines.

The aesthetic of fashion photography has found justification in the aesthetic of the paparazzi for its dismissive treatment of clothing. The two genres also agree on a second fundamental aspect of the composition: the model who wears the garment. Without the model, the clothing almost ceases to exist. The role and the meaning assumed by the model in fashion photography is somewhat equivalent to the role and meaning assumed by the celebrity in paparazzi photography.

The Model's Representative Role

Fashion photographers would not exist without models; indeed, they are inextricably linked, and one cannot be imagined without the other. However, the aesthetic relationship between the two far exceeds any interpersonal relationship they may have, and it assumes a much broader role. The interaction between photographer and model gives rise to images that define an era. No doubt, the fashion photographer, like the painter of old, finds the primary source of his inspiration in his model. But even more than the painter, who can always transform the image provided by the model with his brushstrokes, the selection of the model is decisive for the photographer, because that choice determines in advance the image he will ultimately produce. This decision is a defining moment for most photographers. Not only must the model who is chosen match the fashion image that the photographer already has in mind and intends to convey on film, but the model may also determine the image of the female type that is closely associated with a given era. In the selection of the model—and numerous photographers confirm this theory—it is not the model herself who is significant, but rather what the photographer is inspired to show in his work. It is clear that the most famous models represent a particular type of woman who embodies a specific type of society. Consider, for example, how Barbara Goalen, seen through the lens of John French, came to evoke the stately mansions of England and fashionable Belgravia in the 1950s.[1]

It must be acknowledged that models who play the representational role traditionally assigned to them in fashion photography have a certain commonality with the subjects of paparazzi photographers. The paparazzi aesthetic has much to do with the superficialities of life and what they can reveal. By definition, this aesthetic is obsessed with stars and only with stars. It is an approach that effectively drains the star of all interiority, leaving behind a mere figure in the public eye, if not necessarily a fashionable one, who may be representative of a society at a moment in time. It is similar to the self-referential approach that sometimes characterizes fashion photography. Although it may no longer be the society of English stately mansions and fashionable Belgravia that is represented by the paparazzi aesthetic in its more contemporary manifestations, it is certainly a society of spectacle, show business, and celebrities. Numerous works by fashion photographers aspiring to the paparazzi style are clear evidence of this transition. They range from the photos taken by William Klein for *Vogue* in 1962, which take us back to the early days of the trend, to more recent series that illustrate the shift toward sensationalism.

The similarity of the model's role in the two photographic genres is also echoed in more recent developments in fashion photography. Admittedly, most fashion photographers, until recently, have used the model to present a certain feminine type, or going beyond that to indicate the kind of society that she represents. However, some photographers have been able to distinguish themselves from this general trend and charted a different course. Beginning in the late 1960s, Bob Richardson, who valued the model in her own right,[2] opened the way for other photographers, including Helmut Newton and Guy Bourdin, and more recently Juergen Teller and Mario Testino. It was Steven Meisel who went farthest down this path. In searching for the real woman behind the model's façade, and trying to reveal her interiority (perhaps making her into a star along the way),[3] fashion photographers also make common cause with the paparazzi approach, on a slightly different level. After all, the very basis of the paparazzi initiative is for the photographer to inject himself into the private life of celebrities, revealing to the public a few glimpses of their intimate moments, their joys and sorrows. It

4. See the discussion with Helmut Newton in Frank Horvat, *Entre vues* (Paris: Nathan, 1991).

5. See Régis Durand, *Le Regard pensif. Lieux et objets de la photographie* (Paris: La Différence, 1988), 107.

certainly appears that several photographers featured in the exhibition *Paparazzi!* and in this accompanying catalog have experimented with this equivalence, capturing their models in what are perceived to be private moments—walking on the street, exiting a car, at home. Terry Richardson, Bob's son, plays an even more sophisticated game where the equivalence becomes a fusion of functions, as he has dedicated a series of shots to exposing the private moments of Laetitia Casta, who is herself a celebrity model!

In addition to treating models and celebrities comparably in various aesthetic functions, fashion photographers and paparazzi are sometimes of the same mind on a final point: the photographic context. This third constituent of a fashion image has now become in many ways the decisive element in narrating a story. Fashion photographers share views on photography's new direction with the paparazzi when it comes to settings.

Choosing the Setting: Spontaneity and Staging

Leaving aside a few practical impediments, the fashion photographer's freedom in selecting a backdrop is practically infinite. Interior or exterior; an urban, mountainous, or seaside setting; a mundane or exotic landscape; abstract or virtual spaces created by technical manipulations—almost anything is possible. Nevertheless, photographers make use of this freedom in very different ways. The selection of the photographic context does indeed vary considerably from one photographer to the next, based on an array of diverse considerations. Some may practice the art of photography under various technical and marketing constraints. Others are completely in control of all aspects of the creative process, whatever it may involve.

In an initial analysis, it is possible to establish two divergent approaches to fashion photography. On one side of this divide stand those who wish to control every detail; on the other are those who adapt to events as they occur and follow the inspiration of the moment. There does indeed seem to be a great disparity between a photographer who has arranged every aspect of an interior or exterior setting in advance, down to the last detail, and another who wanders at random through city streets, followed by his model, deciding to focus his lens wherever the light is best and the settings most intriguing. This perception seems to establish a sharp divide between the two approaches, which may sometimes be traced to the photographers' contrasting career paths. The second type would likely be a man who began his career as a photojournalist before making the transition to fashion. Consequently, he does not seek to exercise control. Used to capturing scenes on the fly, he leaves events to unfold on their own. In contrast, the first type might be a photographer who has devoted his entire career to the world of fashion. As a result, he has become accustomed to being in full control and has managed to place the constraints imposed by reality within parentheses. But this divide is no more than a generality, which can as easily be contradicted as asserted. In reality, things are much more complex. It is not uncommon for a photographer who is generally guided by inspiration to wish to control all aspects of a shoot under certain circumstances. Conversely, a photographer who ordinarily insists on controlling every detail may indulge in improvisation on occasion. In any case, there are many intermediary levels between the extremes of the all-controlling and the freewheeling photographer. It should also be added that the control-obsessed photographers are not necessarily the ones we might suppose, and the reverse holds true as well.[4]

The considerations that guide the choice of photographic settings are diverse and difficult to classify with precision. It must also be recognized that these concerns pale into insignificance when we observe the completed result. The debate should be raised on a different level and in other terms. The questions should be considered not from an outsider's perspective, but rather from within the act of photography—not in terms of control and improvisation, but in terms of composition and spontaneity. Admittedly, the dividing line between spontaneity and composition is not always clear. The concern that a setting will be so totally contrived that it excludes any element of the unexpected, or that the composition will take absolute precedence over any sense of the moment, does not stand up to sustained analysis. In one way or another, the unexpected will always intrude; rather than detracting from the composition, the unforeseen will become integrated into the setting that has been planned so carefully. It could be objected that the photographer who yields to the inspiration of the moment is nevertheless creating his own scenario. There is equal justification to believe that, when the unexpected occurs, it is immediately transformed and incorporated into the preexisting setting.[5]

If we were to compare the role played by the setting in the history of fashion photography and paparazzi photography, there would be agreement on two points. On the one hand, it is indisputable that the paparazzi enjoy almost equally great freedom in choosing a setting, given the diverse and contrasting spaces where a celebrity may be surreptitiously photographed and their private life revealed. On the other hand, and whatever the terms used to identify the photographer's inspiration—control/improvisation or composition/spontaneity—it will be readily conceded that the paparazzo's work is performed with a degree of improvisation and spontaneity that is imposed by outside circumstances.

Fashion photographers who borrow from paparazzi photography clearly follow its style, sometimes to the point of provocation. They indulge in a multitude of different backdrops: interiors and exteriors; urban, rustic, or seaside settings; cars, boats, airplanes, helicopters—all the spots where a celebrity might be sighted in the course of professional or personal life. However, in the face of such diversity, photographers who take their inspiration from the paparazzi seem impelled to adopt a particular attitude. They enjoy playing the role of an artist who acts more like a photojournalist than a fashion photographer. Ostensibly without any control of unfolding events, the fashion photographer reacts according to his own impulses. He improvises like a photojournalist who does not have the luxury of careful composition, which is sacrificed for the spontaneity of actual events. In the choice of his locations, as well as in the shooting technique used, this photographer makes a conscious effort to give the impression of a spur-of-the-moment shot. However, while they establish the framework and the limits of their paparazzi-like pose, fashion photographers are not beyond playing with it or inscribing it into an aesthetic that approaches that of photography in general. Indeed, because their approach entails *imitating* the specific photographic practices of the paparazzi, they often reverse the sense, subvert it, appearing to be in complete control of the situation and creating the most sophisticated of compositions. In other words, mimicking improvisation and spontaneity necessarily implies the exercise of control and composition. Whatever the initial intent, the paparazzi aesthetic emanates from an imaginary world that is really not so very different from that of fashion photography in general. It is an imaginary world that reflects both the personal history of the photographer and the realities of society.

The fascination that paparazzi photography has exerted over fashion photography for fifty years and the caricatures it has sometimes inspired are instructive. They have the merit of allowing us to define the basis of the paparazzi aesthetic. We also see how, contrary to expectations, the aesthetic borrowed from paparazzi work—one of the most socially and artistically reviled areas of photographic activity—has often been integrated into the well-established aesthetic functions of fashion photography. Furthermore, this aesthetic now seems to be perceived as, if not respected, then perfectly natural at least. This proximity is certainly one of the most obvious manifestations of the unifying trend among the various fields of photography, which may now be considered the preeminent art form of contemporary postmodernity.

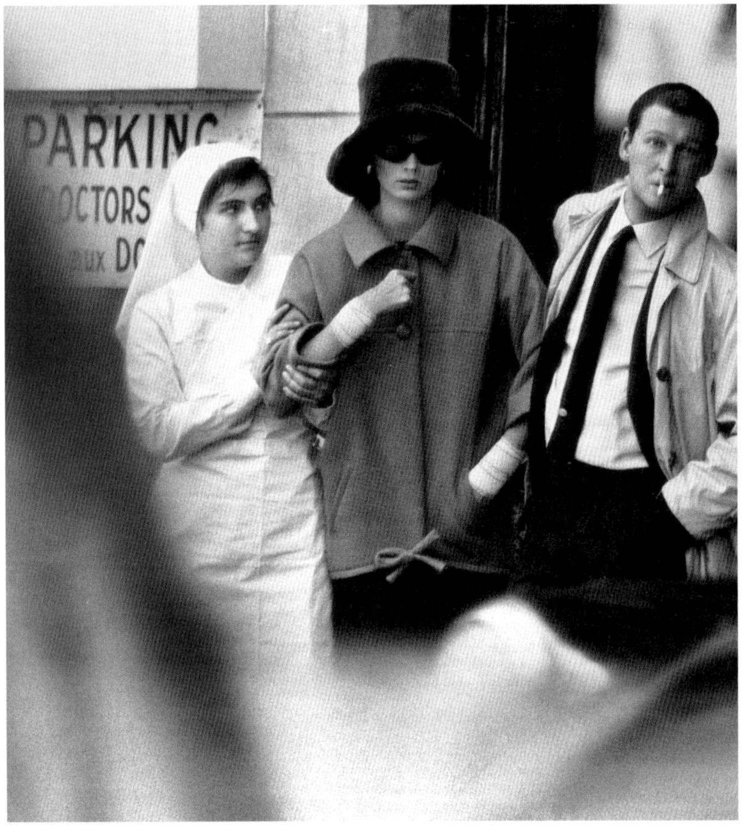

RICHARD AVEDON. In 1962, Richard Avedon traveled to Paris to photograph the new fashion collections for *Harper's Bazaar.* The series he delivered to the magazine a few weeks later was entirely inspired by paparazzi photography. He shot a pastiche of Liz Taylor and Richard Burton's highly publicized liaison. All the necessary ingredients were there: the stolen kiss, the brawl with photographers, the car surrounded by fans, and even the cinematographic setting. He just replaced the set for *Cleopatra*, where Burton and Taylor first met, with a film about Napoleon and Josephine. Avedon even went as far as to create mock magazines featuring these fictional actors. He also alerted authentic paparazzi that a celebrity couple was planning to dine at Maxim's, to get those photographers included in his own shots, and he willingly deceived an actual nurse. While the actors portrayed a falsified exit from a hospital, she assisted them, believing she was aiding genuine convalescents. The barriers between fiction and reality had been demolished.

RICHARD AVEDON
Suzy Parker and Mike Nichols,
Coat by Yves Saint Laurent,
American Hospital of Paris,
Neuilly-sur-Seine
July 31, 1962

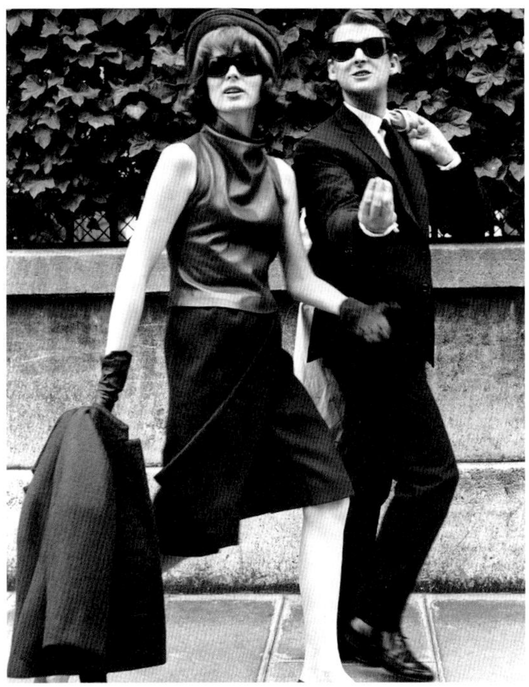

RICHARD AVEDON
Suzy Parker and Mike Nichols,
Ladies' Suit by Simonetta-Fabiani,
Rue François-Ier, Paris
July 30, 1962

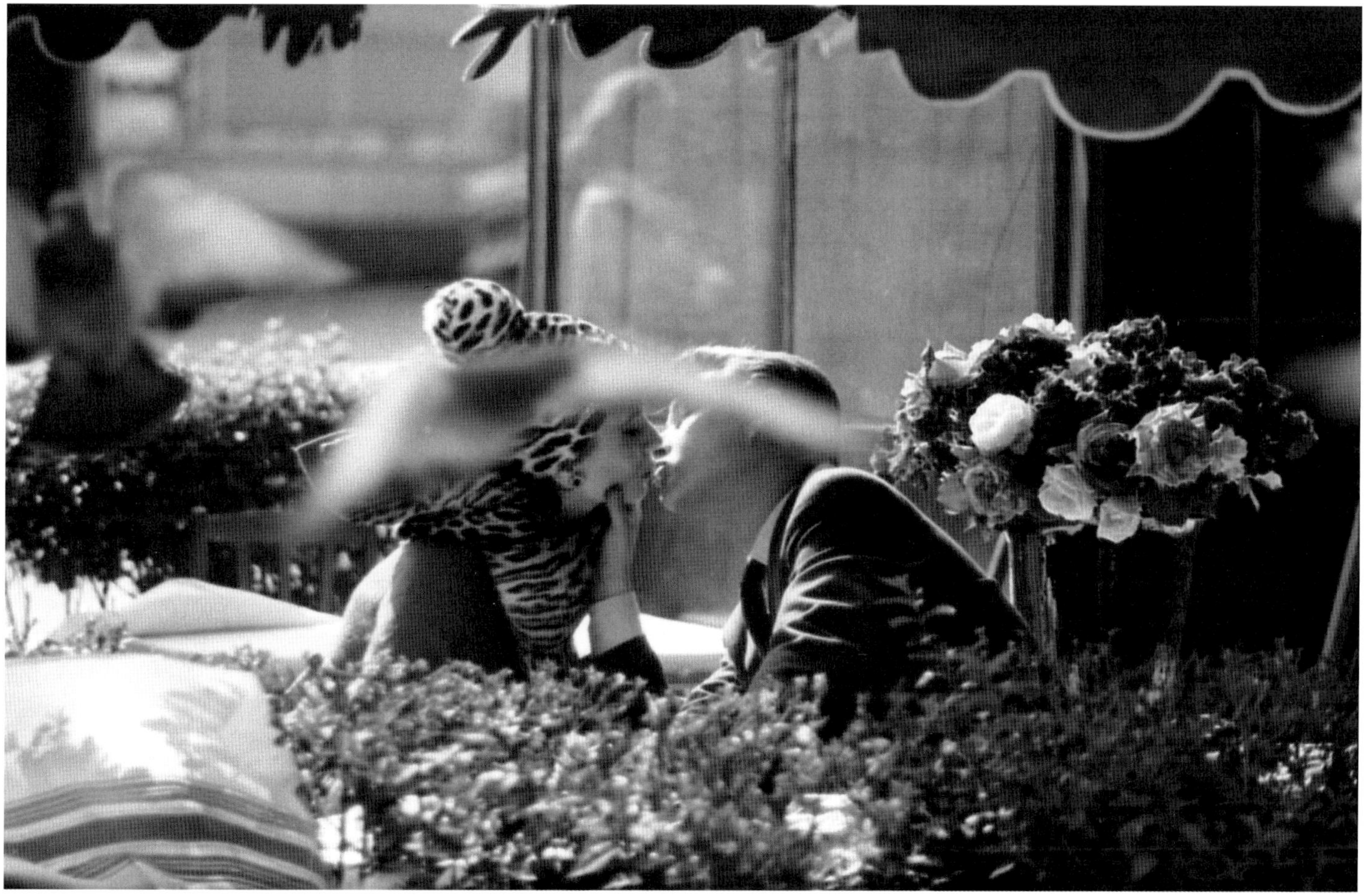

RICHARD AVEDON
Mike Nichols and Suzy Parker, Hat by Dior, Chez Anna, Paris
July 29, 1962

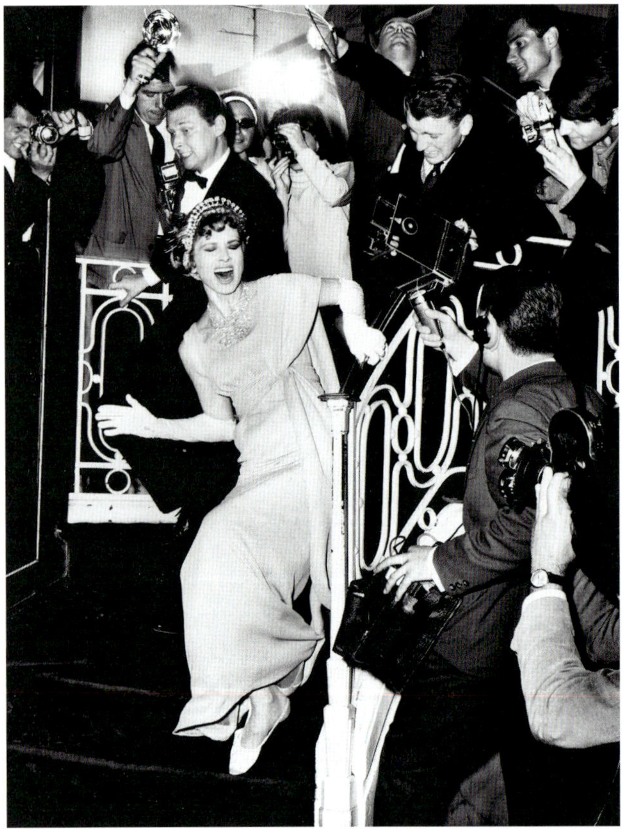

RICHARD AVEDON
Suzy Parker and Mike Nichols,
Dress by Lanvin-Castillo,
Maxim's, Paris
July 28, 1962

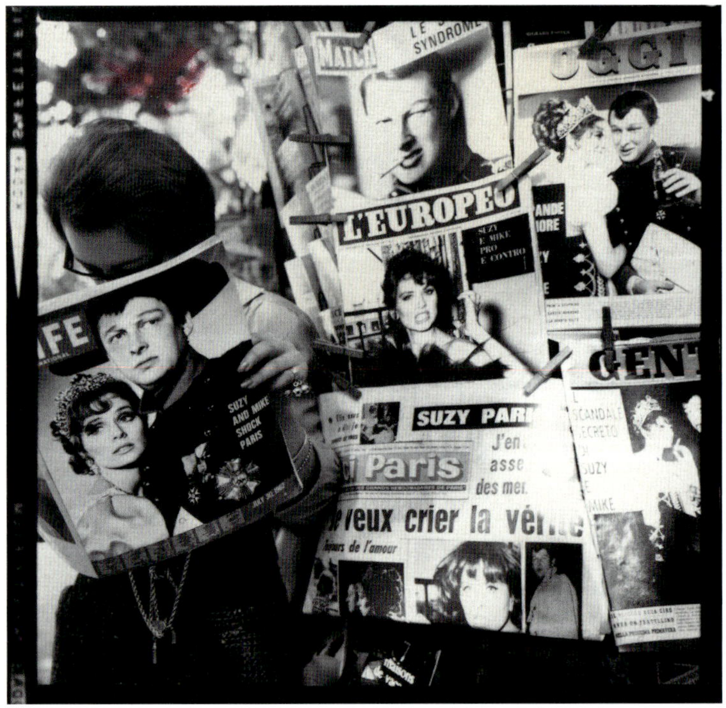

RICHARD AVEDON
Mike Nichols and Suzy Parker
Rock Europe, Paris
(detail from a contact sheet)
July 31, 1962

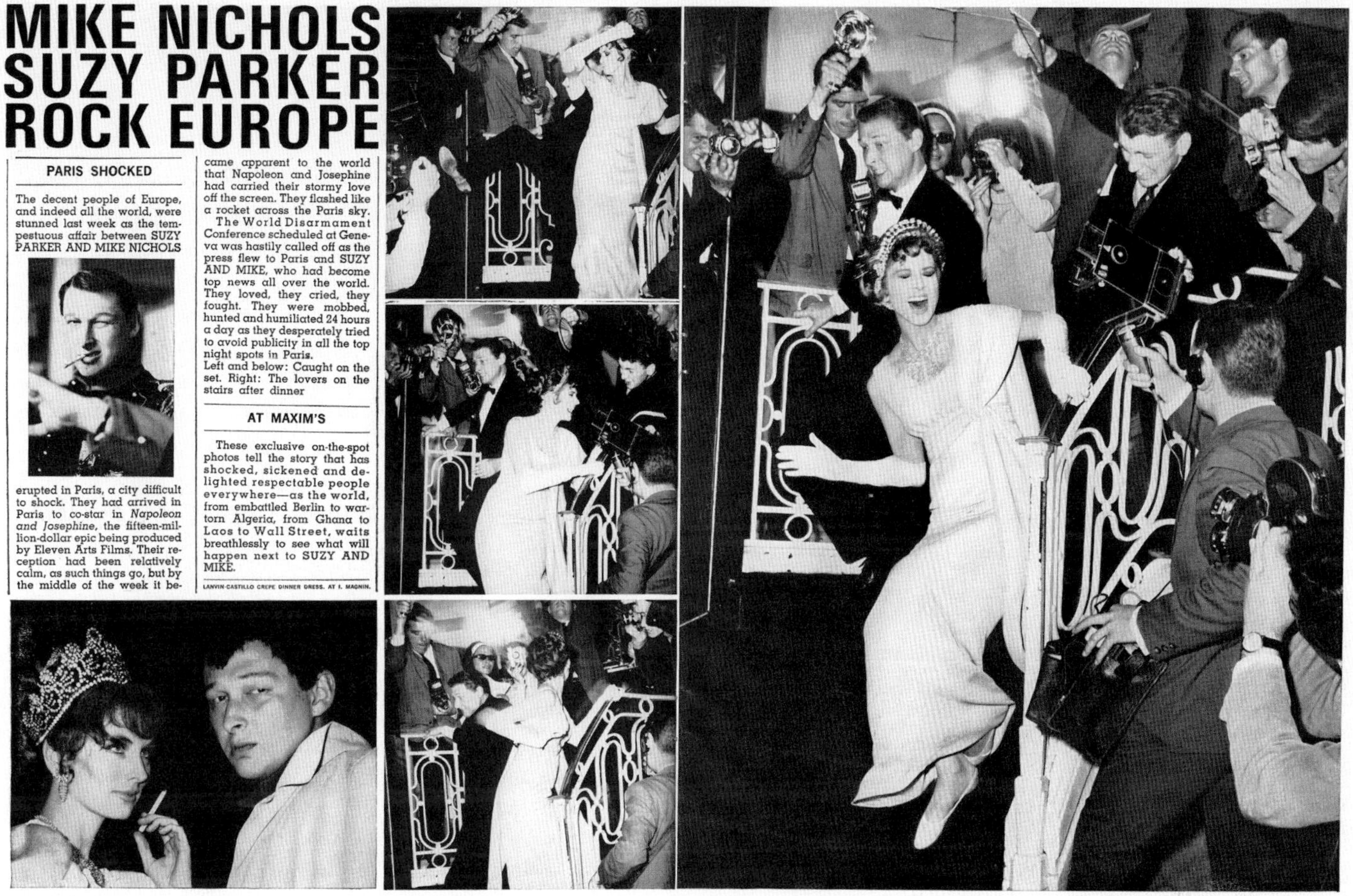

MIKE NICHOLS SUZY PARKER ROCK EUROPE

PARIS SHOCKED

The decent people of Europe, and indeed all the world, were stunned last week as the tempestuous affair between SUZY PARKER AND MIKE NICHOLS erupted in Paris, a city difficult to shock. They had arrived in Paris to co-star in *Napoleon and Josephine*, the fifteen-million-dollar epic being produced by Eleven Arts Films. Their reception had been relatively calm, as such things go, but by the middle of the week it became apparent to the world that Napoleon and Josephine had carried their stormy love off the screen. They flashed like a rocket across the Paris sky.

The World Disarmament Conference scheduled at Geneva was hastily called off as the press flew to Paris and SUZY AND MIKE, who had become top news all over the world. They loved, they cried, they fought. They were mobbed, hunted and humiliated 24 hours a day as they desperately tried to avoid publicity in all the top night spots in Paris.

Left and below: Caught on the set. Right: The lovers on the stairs after dinner

AT MAXIM'S

These exclusive on-the-spot photos tell the story that has shocked, sickened and delighted respectable people everywhere—as the world, from embattled Berlin to war-torn Algeria, from Ghana to Laos to Wall Street, waits breathlessly to see what will happen next to SUZY AND MIKE.

LANVIN-CASTILLO CREPE DINNER DRESS. AT I. MAGNIN.

"Mike Nichols and Suzy Parker Rock Europe," layout for *Harper's Bazaar*, September 1962 (Photographs: Richard Avedon)

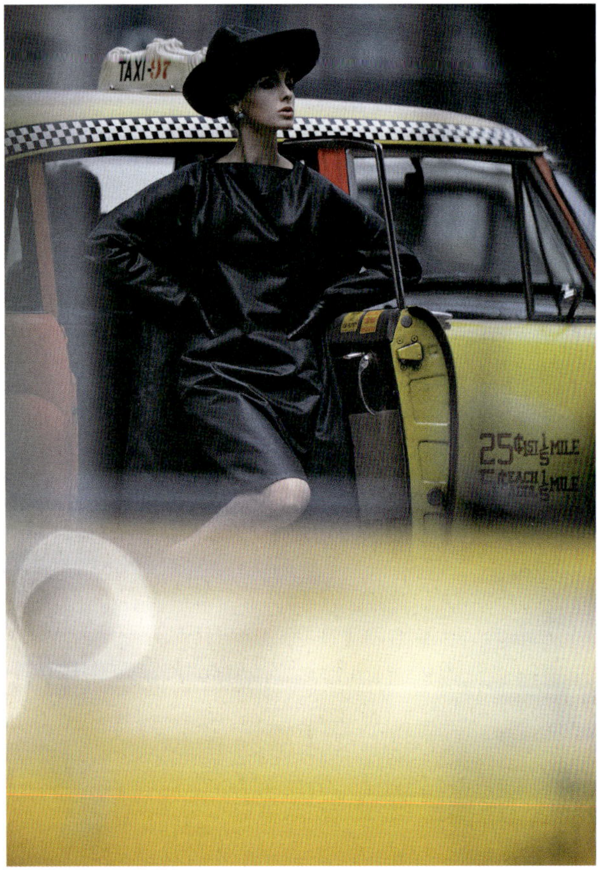

WILLIAM KLEIN
Antonia + Yellow Taxi,
fashion photograph
for *Vogue*, New York
1962

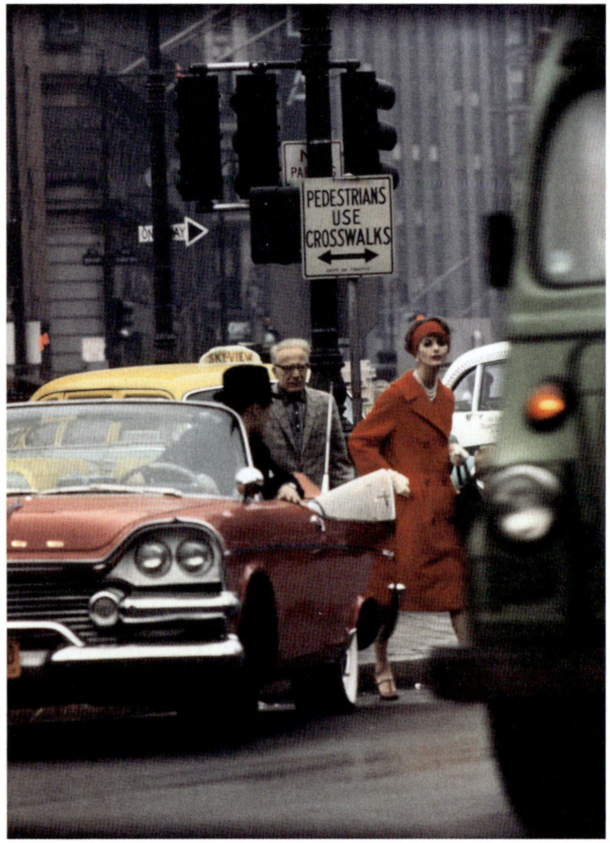

WILLIAM KLEIN
Anne Sainte Marie + Cruiser,
fashion photograph for *Vogue*,
New York
1962

WILLIAM KLEIN. Born in New York in 1928, William Klein studied in Fernand Léger's studio in the late 1940s. He was active in painting, photography, and film. By the 1960s, he was receiving regular commissions for fashion magazine spreads. His innovative approach disrupted the prevailing codes of the discipline. He had his models go down into the streets and photographed them surrounded by crowds of vehicles and pedestrians. He enjoyed creating situations beyond his control that provided opportunities for random events and dynamic compositions. When photographing from a distance, he willingly used a telephoto lens. For close-ups, he favored a wide-angle lens and flashbulbs. His in-your-face images were a perfect illustration of the violent nature of predatory photography. The intensity of his photos often recalls the stolen snapshots of the paparazzi. Klein was undoubtedly one of the very first photographers to systematically exploit the paparazzi aesthetic in the realm of fashion photography.

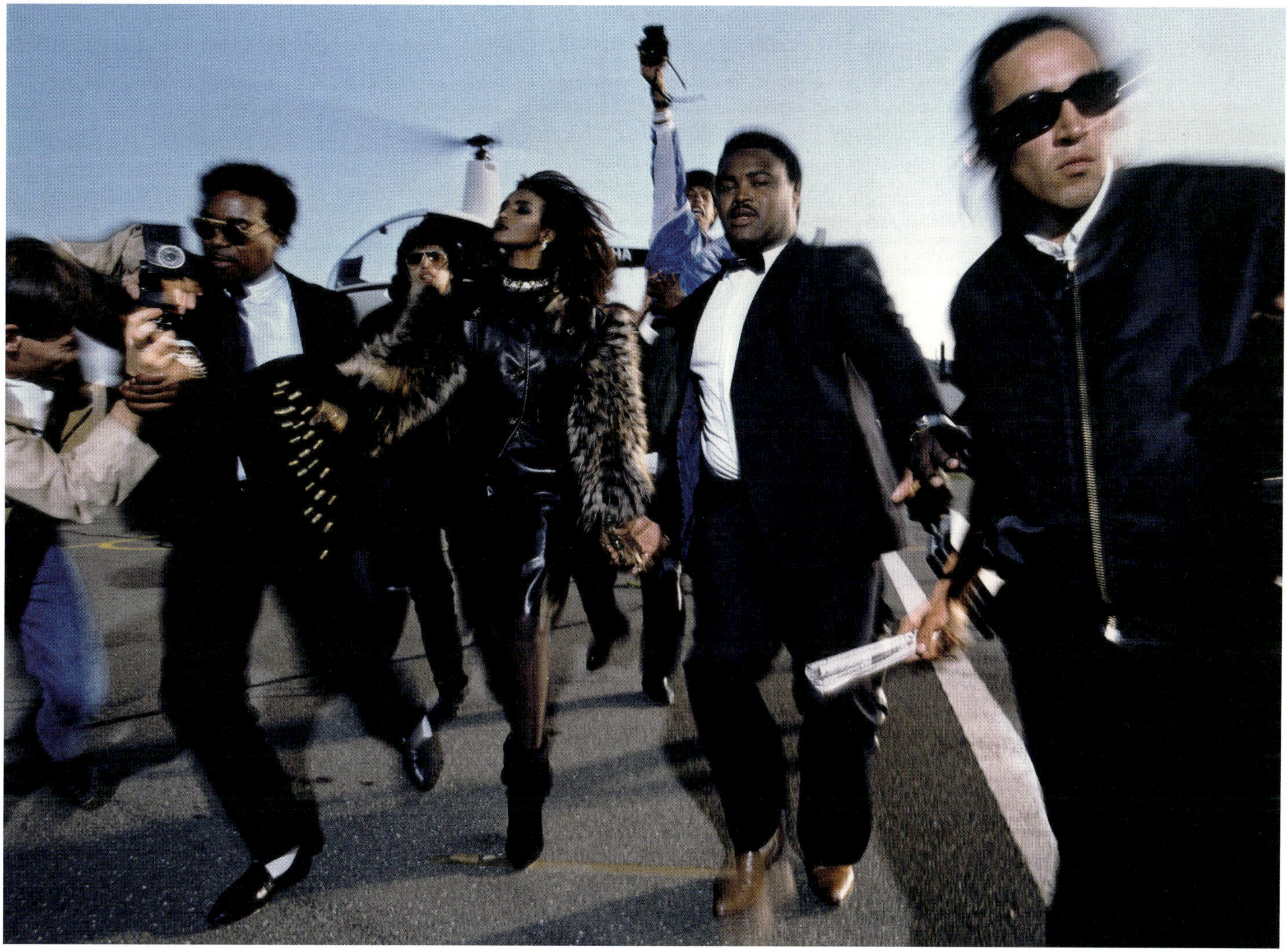

WILLIAM KLEIN
Kadidjah, "Exile" fashion series for *Vanity Fair*, Paris 1988

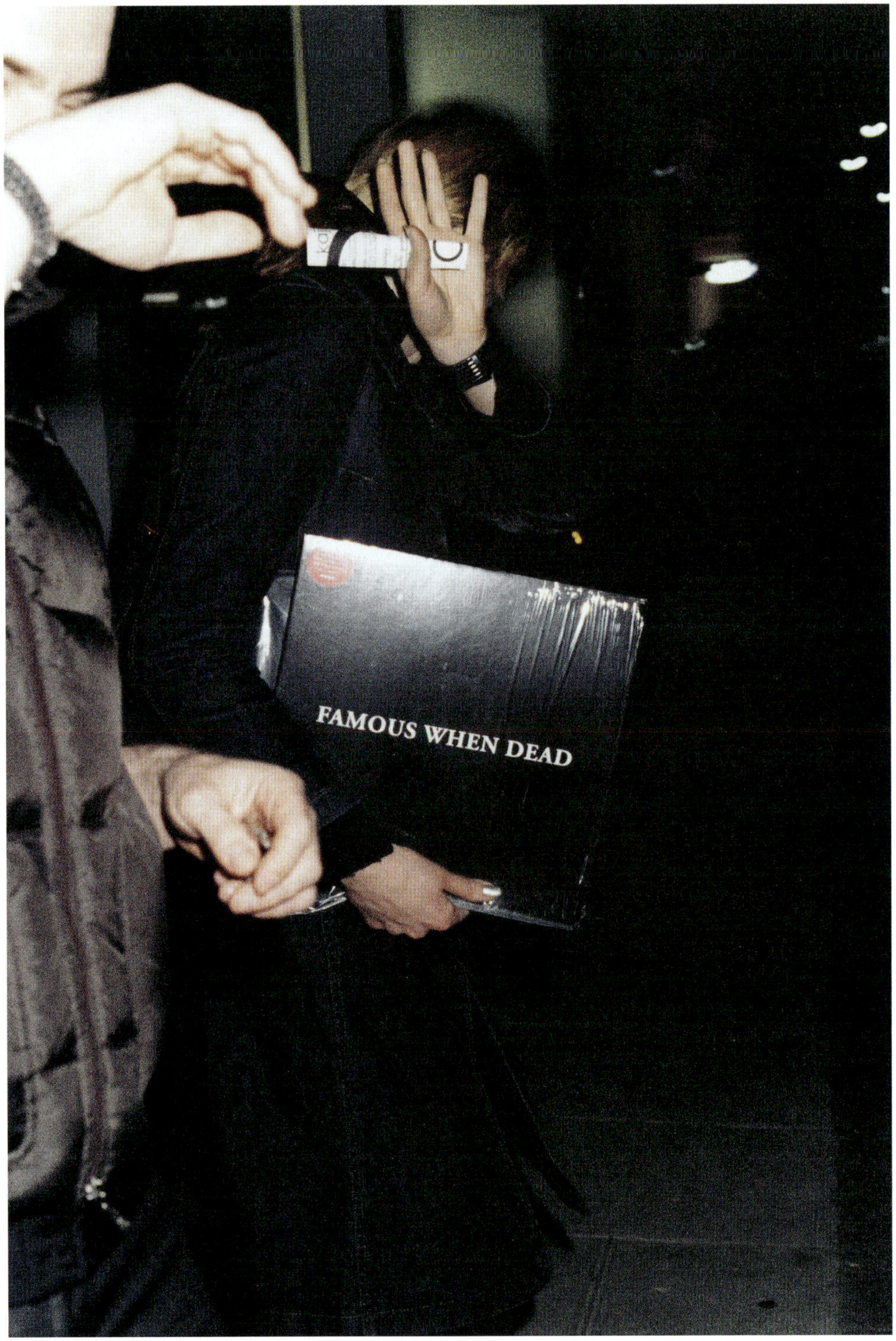

CHRISTIAN LESEMANN
Famous When Dead
2001

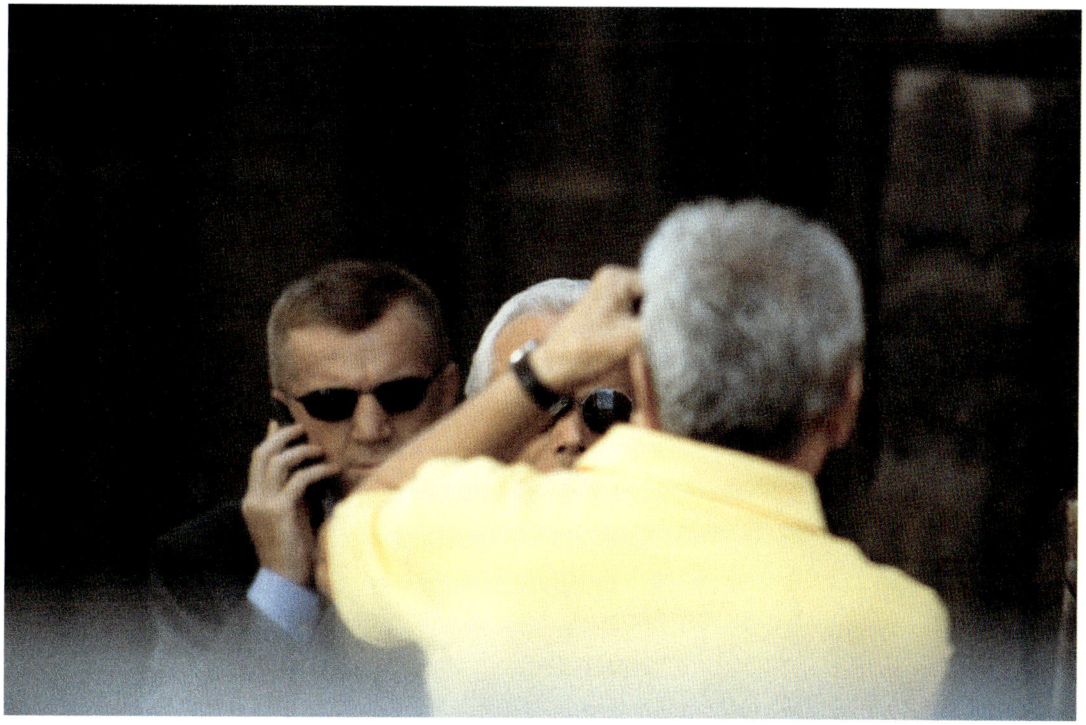

CHRISTIAN LESEMANN
Giorgio Armani
2001

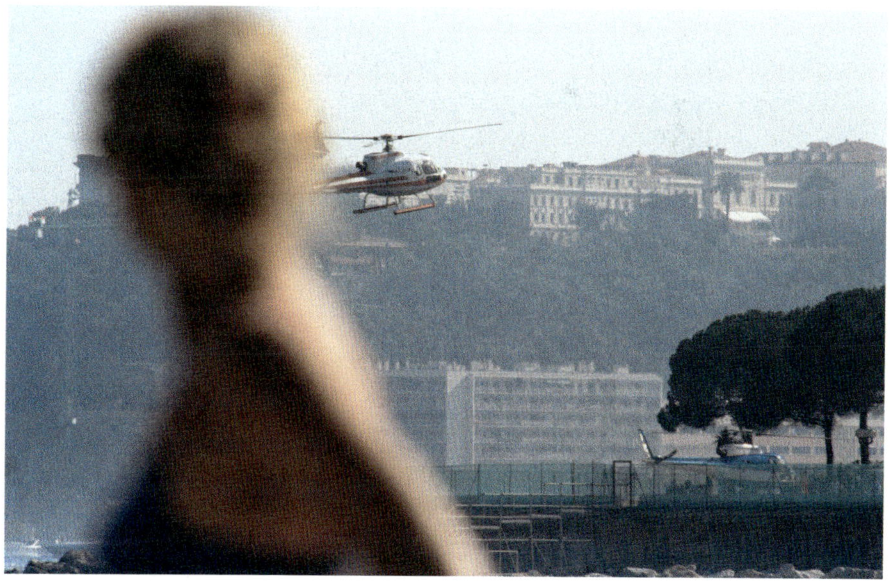

CHRISTIAN LESEMANN
Monaco Grand Prix
2001

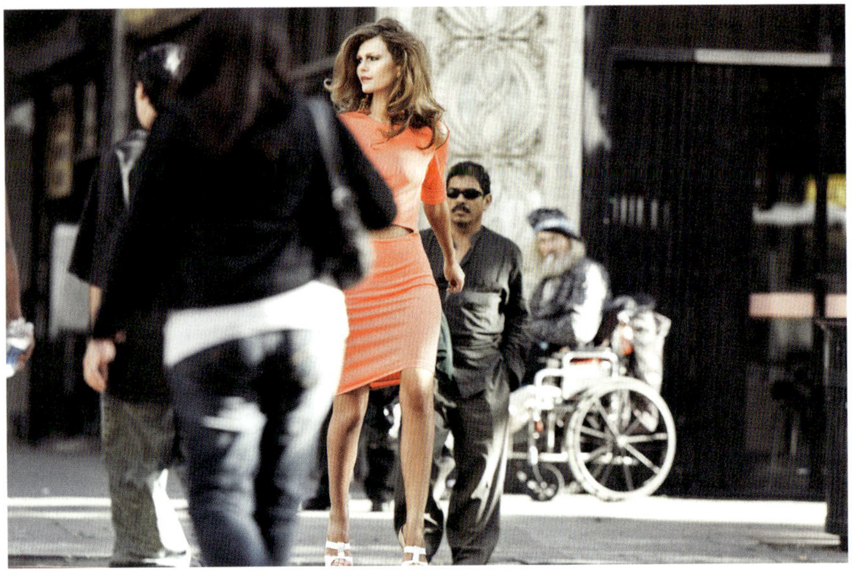

ALEXI LUBOMIRSKI
Downtown LA
2007

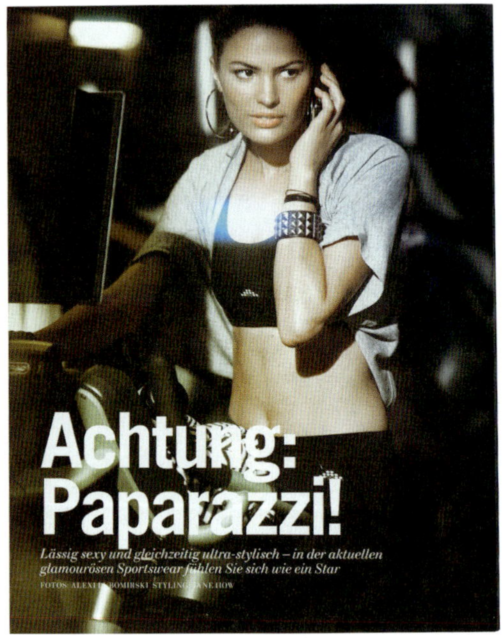

"Achtung: Paparazzi!"
H&M Magazine Germany,
Fall 2010, p. 60
(Photograph: Alexi Lubomirski)

PAPARAZZI STYLE. The work of fashion photographers and the practices of paparazzi have certain features in common. Both are intended for the press, and both play on the phenomena of identification when confronted with an idealized model. It is therefore hardly surprising that a number of fashion photographers have delved into the visual vocabulary of the paparazzi. The transformation of a model into a star confers a newly mythic aspect to their images. The iconography of the paparazzi has its roots in the mass-market press. Its vibrancy contributed to the revitalization of fashion photography, distancing it from the canonical conventions of haute couture where it had originated. In the 1960s and 1970s, fashion photographers who adopted the celebrity press aesthetic often depicted paparazzi in action in their shots, swarming around the model. As the paparazzi style came to be universally recognized, these figures were eliminated from the images. Mimicking the paparazzi also allowed the fashion photographer to assert a sort of personal stake in his work, emphasizing the importance of his own creative role. Having achieved recognition, he could freely borrow from the stereotypes of the paparazzi style with no fear of being confused with his lowly brethren.

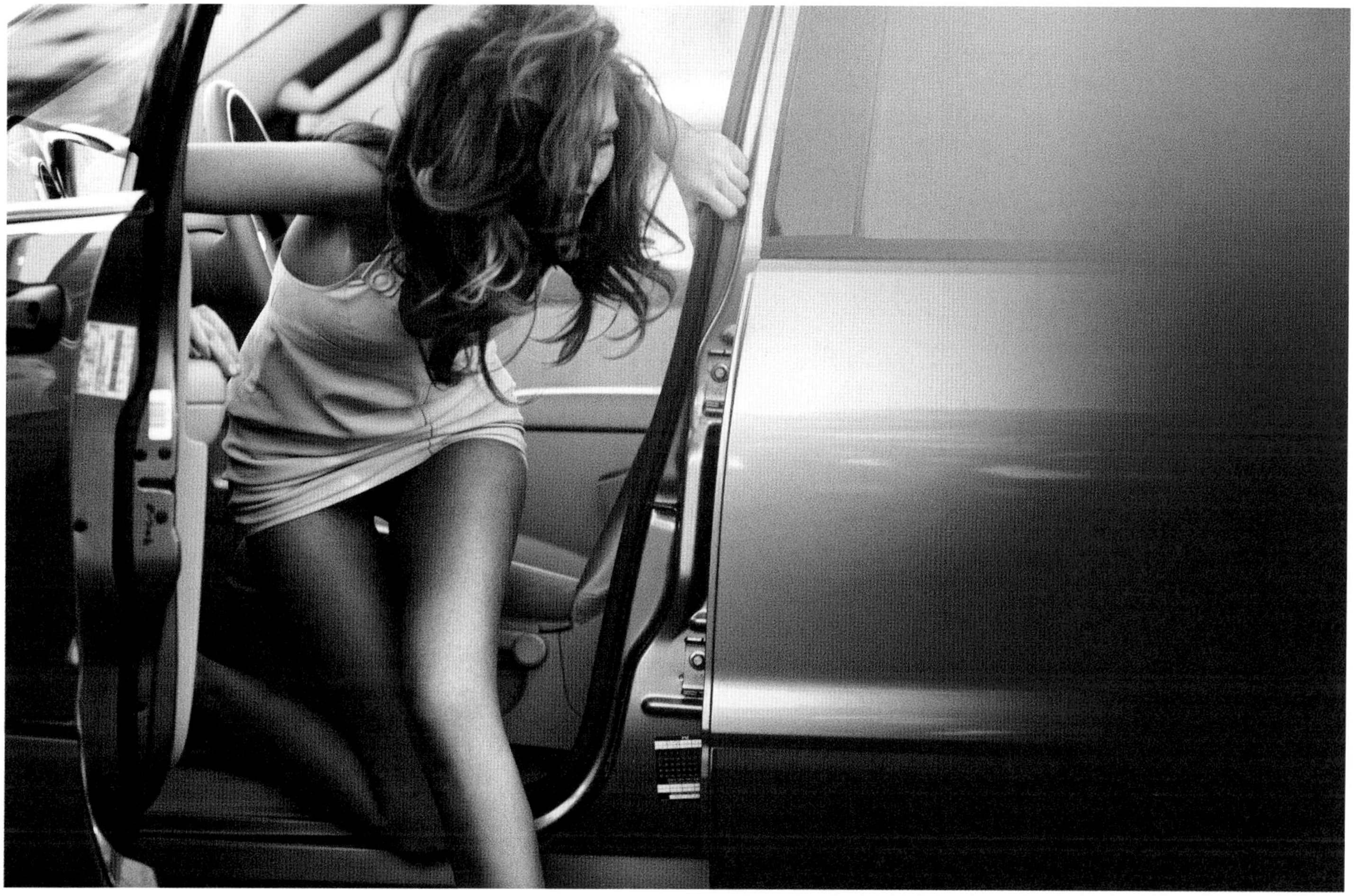

ALEXI LUBOMIRSKI
Downtown LA
2007

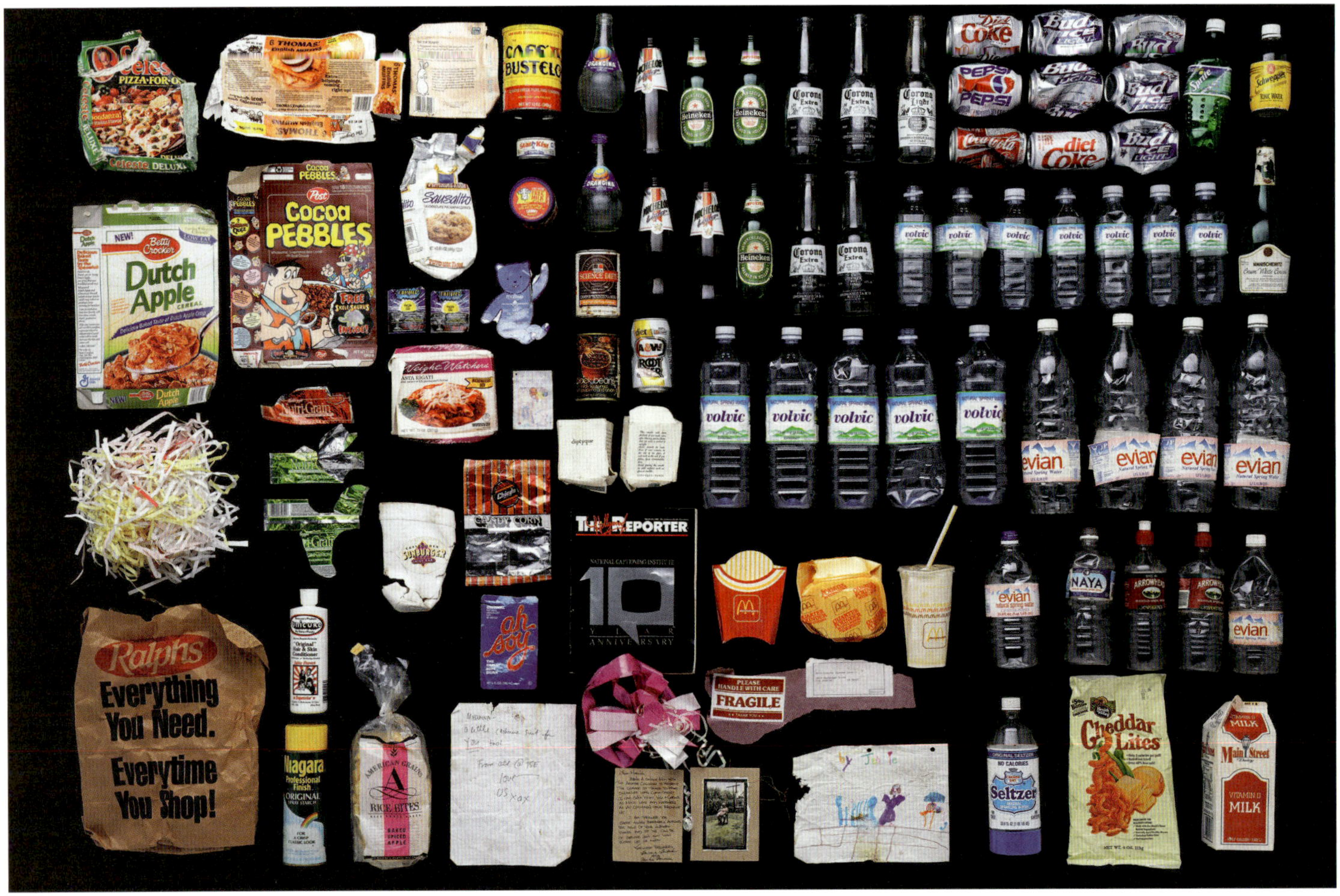

PASCAL ROSTAIN
AND BRUNO MOURON
Madonna 2
March 1990

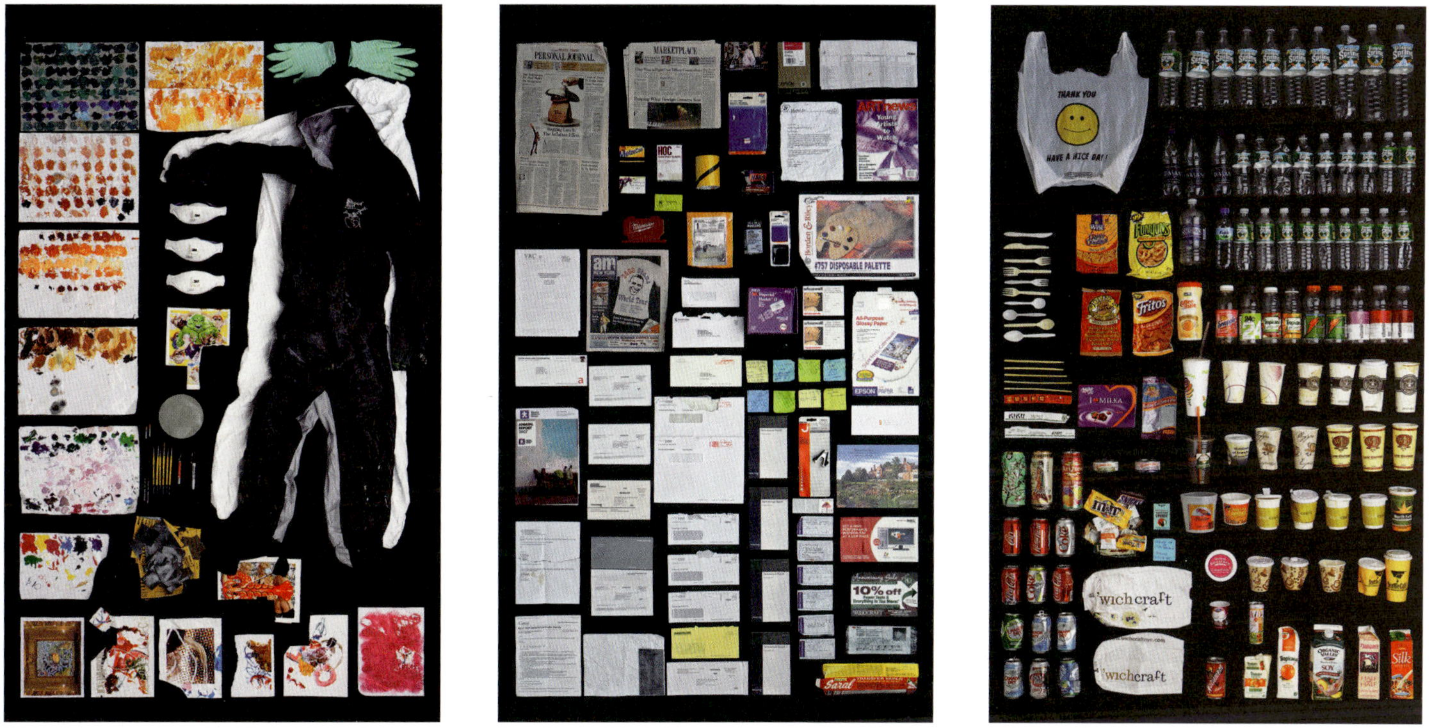

PASCAL ROSTAIN
AND BRUNO MOURON
Jeff Koons
July 15, 2008

ROSTAIN & MOURON. Pascal Rostain and Bruno Mouron are the most famous duo in the French paparazzi world. They collaborated for almost thirty years and worked together at a number of magazines before founding their own agency, Sphinx. At its peak, it employed half a dozen photographers. They have frequently exhibited their work in galleries and museums in recent years. This incursion into the art world, traditionally closed to the paparazzi, has considerably altered their business practices. Although they continue to purloin images of stars using their telephoto lenses, they have also embarked on a more consciously calculated oeuvre that involves photographing the contents of the trash cans of a few select celebrities. In these works, they employ a large format and elaborate lighting, as a fine art photographer might use for shooting a still life. These images depict an array of garbage meticulously arranged according to a taxonomical logic that casts light on the star's private life. The work also provides a perfect illustration of the widespread contemptuous charge that accuses paparazzi of "digging through the garbage."

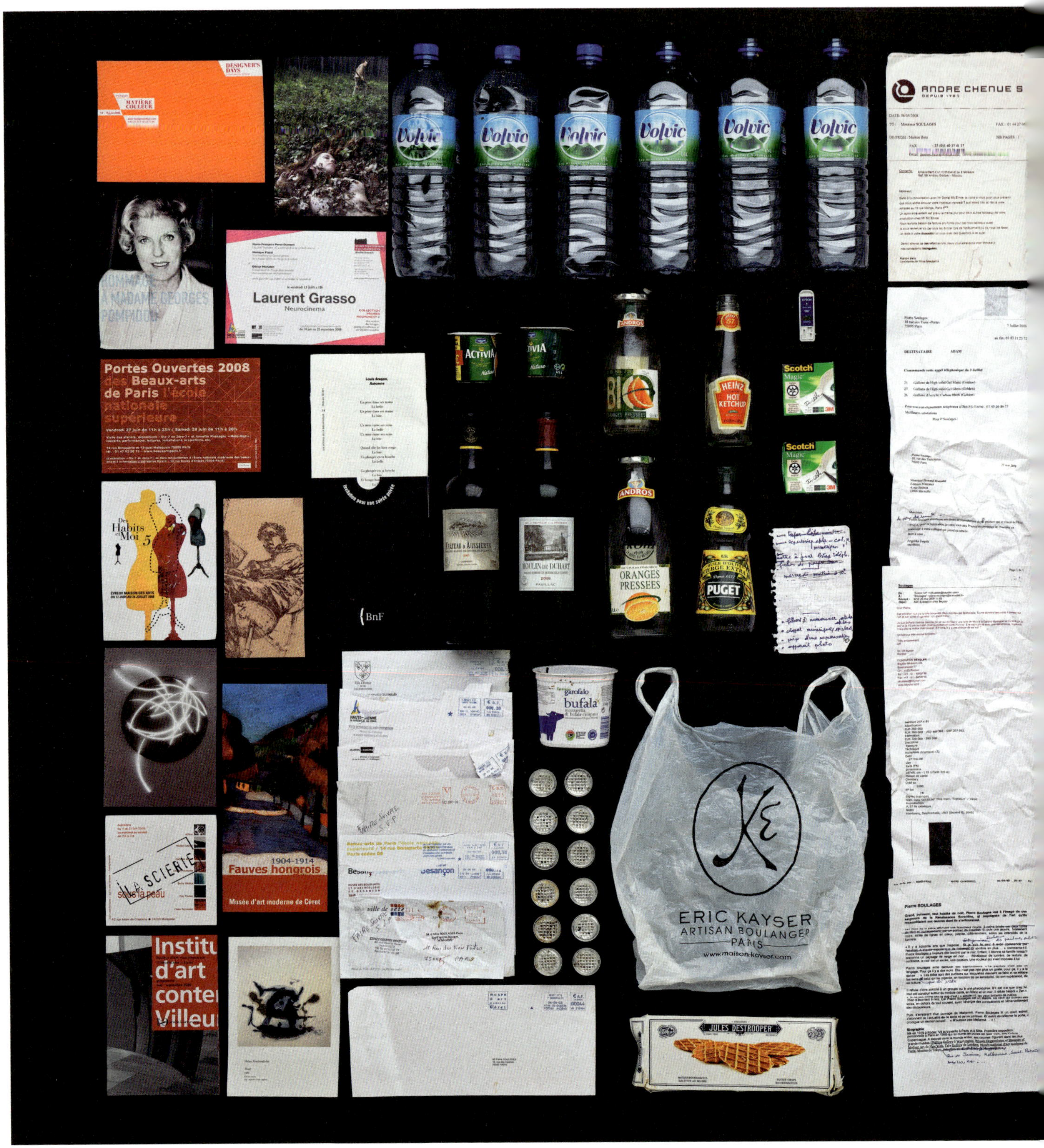
DESIGNER'S DAYS
MATIÈRE COULEUR
HOMMAGE À MADAME GEORGES POMPIDOU
Laurent Grasso
Neurocinema
Portes Ouvertes 2008 des Beaux-arts de Paris l'école nationale supérieure
Volvic
ANDRE CHENUE S
ACTIVIA
ANDROS
BIO
HEINZ
HOT KETCHUP
Scotch Magic
Des Habits et Moi 5
BnF
ORANGES PRESSEES
PUGET
MOULIN DE DUHART
garofalo
bufala
1904-1914
Fauves hongrois
Musée d'art moderne de Céret
LA SCIERIE
sous la peau
Institu
d'art
conter
Villeur
ERIC KAYSER
ARTISAN BOULANGER
PARIS
www.maison-kayser.com
JULES DESTROOPER

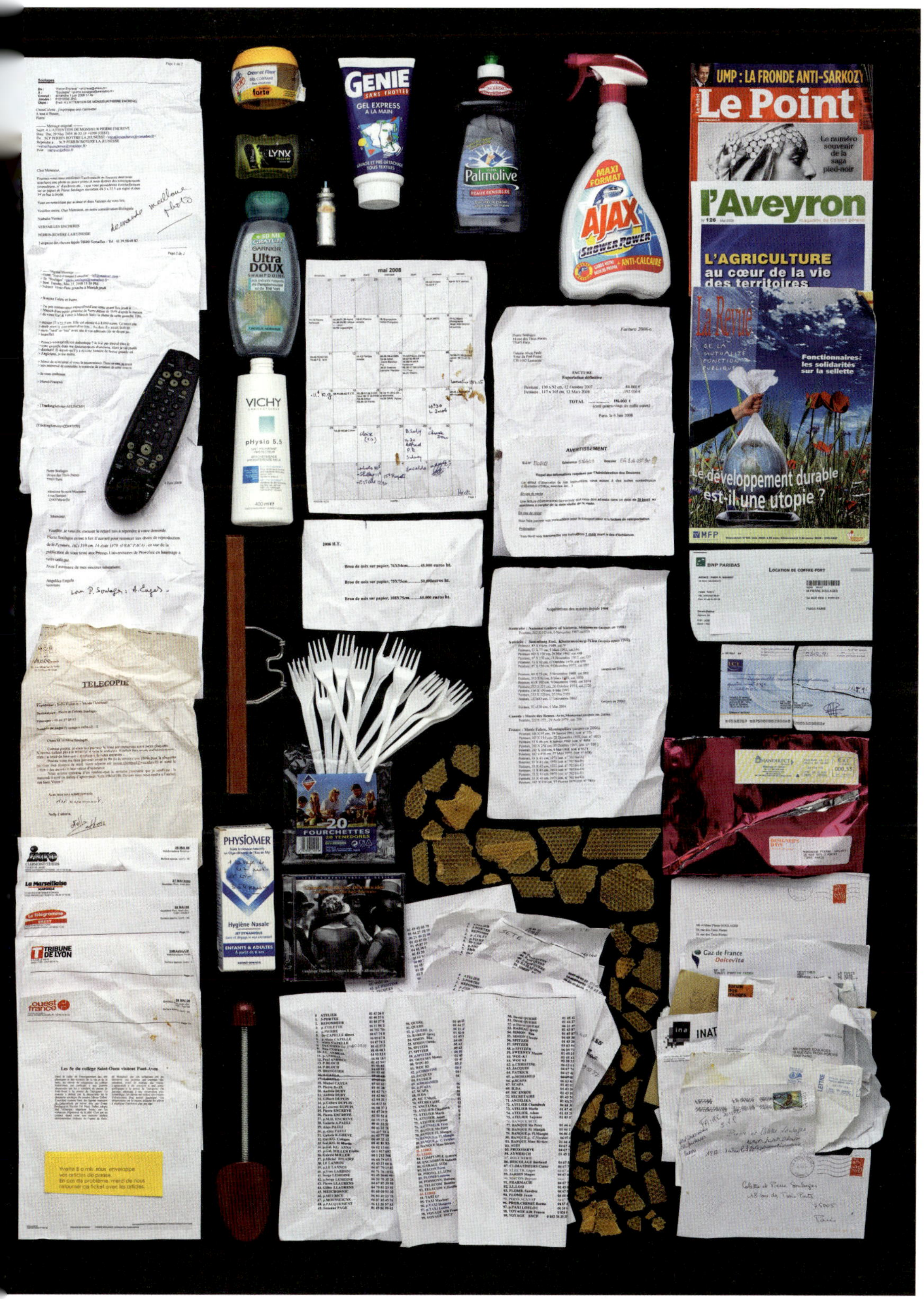

PASCAL ROSTAIN
AND BRUNO MOURON
Pierre Soulages
June 2008

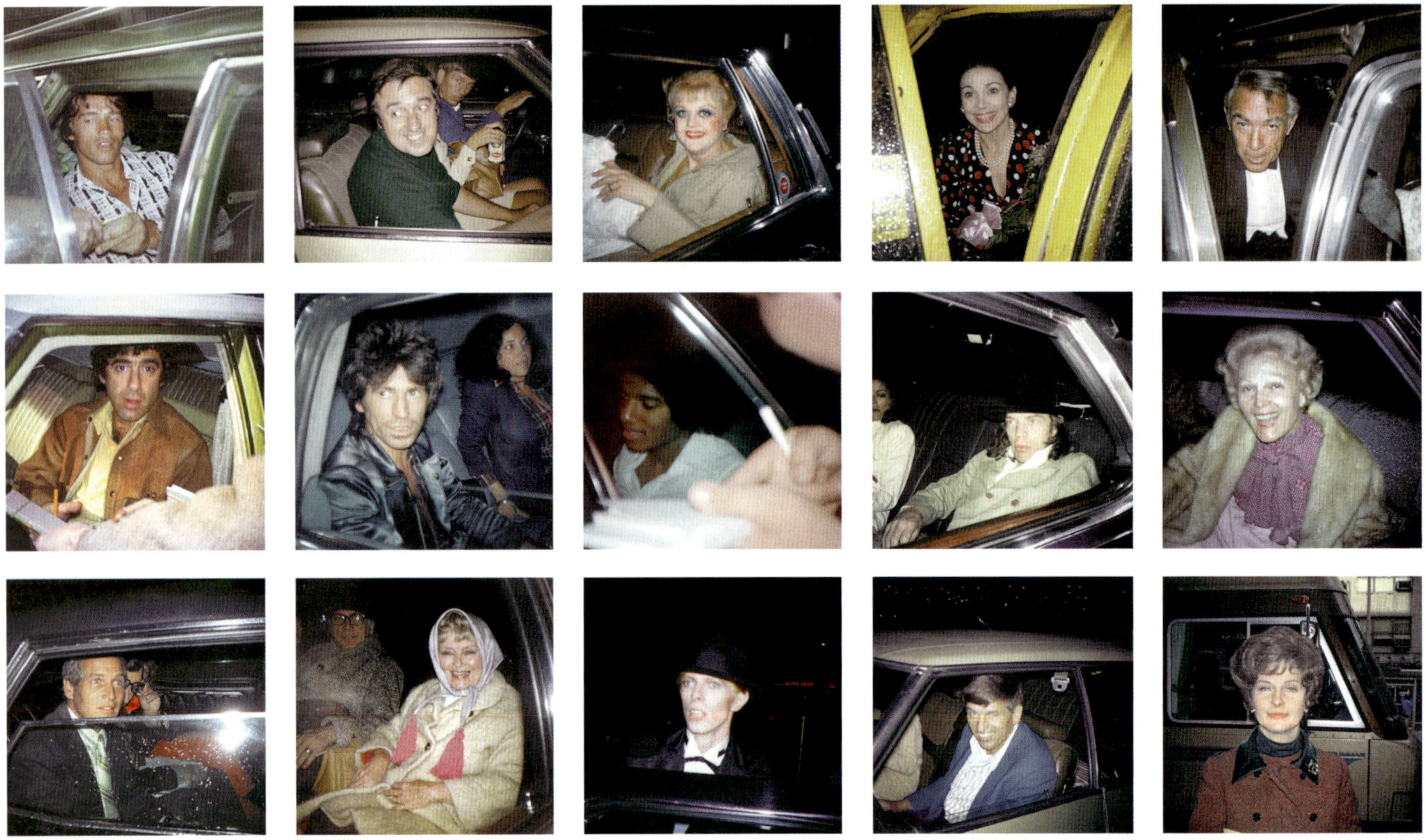

GARY LEE BOAS. Born in 1951, Gary Lee Boas has been fascinated by the world of stardom since the age of fourteen. For almost fifty years, he has compulsively documented the lives of celebrities. He stands in wait for them outside restaurants, theaters, and nightclubs to request their autographs and take photographs. He also likes to have himself photographed at their side. His personal archives now boast almost eighty thousand snapshots, autographs, and letters. First displayed in 1999 with the publication of his book *Starstruck: Photographs From a Fan*, his work on the celebrity world of the 1960s and 1970s is now internationally recognized. We see how the collection of an avid, persistent fan can suddenly change its status to assume the rank of an artistic oeuvre. This recognition represents a genuine shift in the criteria of judgment in the art world. Critics are now able to recognize obsessive practices as genuine aesthetic offerings.

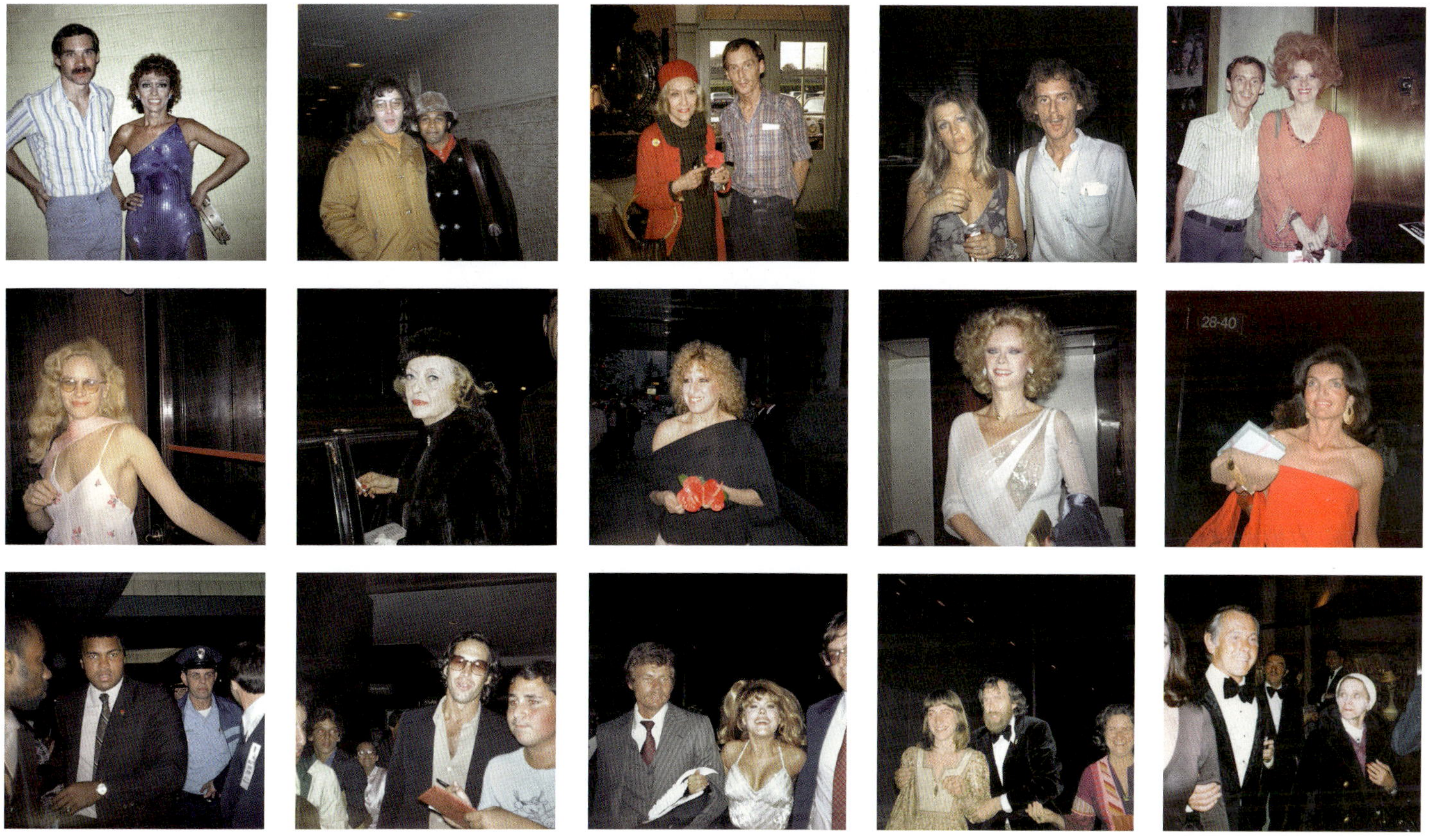

GARY LEE BOAS
A Moment Caught
1966–79

Facing page, from top left:
Arnold Schwarzenegger, Jim Nabors, Angela Lansbury, Dame Margot Fonteyn, Anthony Quinn, Elliott Gould, Keith Richards, Michael Jackson, Mick Jagger, Pat Nixon, Paul Newman, Janet Gaynor, David Bowie, Johnny Unitas, Joanne Woodward.

Above, from top left:
Rita Moreno, Raúl Juliá, Gloria Swanson and Gary Lee Boas, Julie Christie (drunk) and Gary Lee Boas, Geraldine Paige and Gary Lee Boas, Karen Black, Bette Davis, Bette Midler, Monique van Vooren, Jackie Onassis, Mohamed Ali, Chevy Chase, Charo, Jim Henson, Johnny Carson.

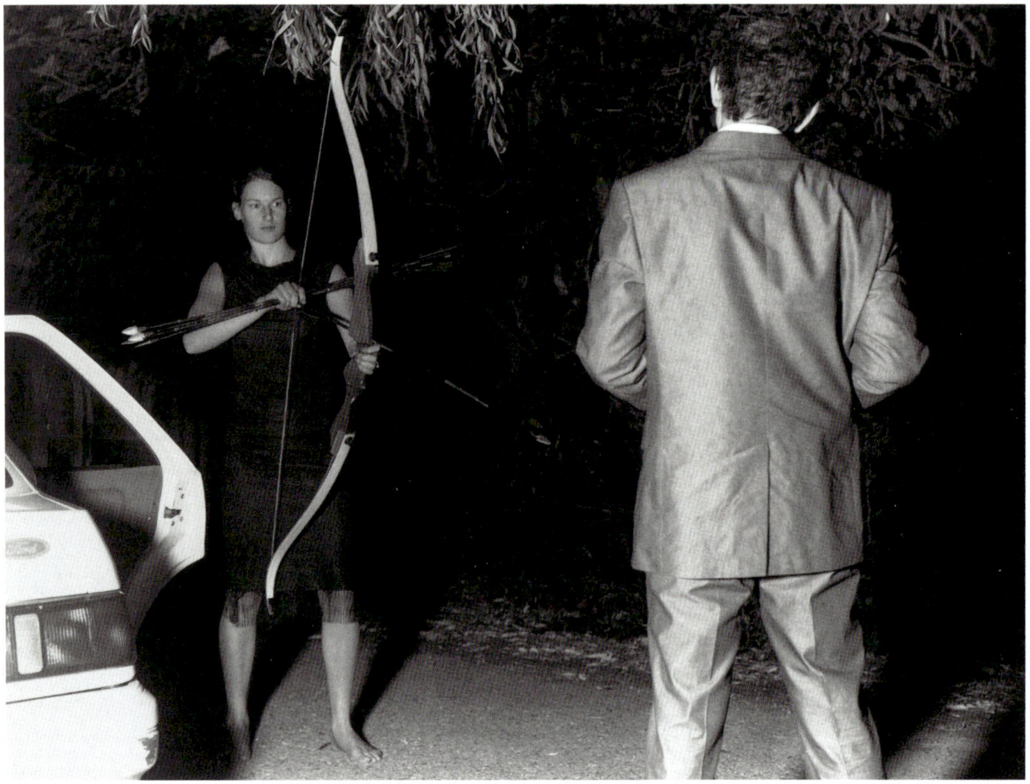

G.R.A.M.
Nach Motiven von ...
2001

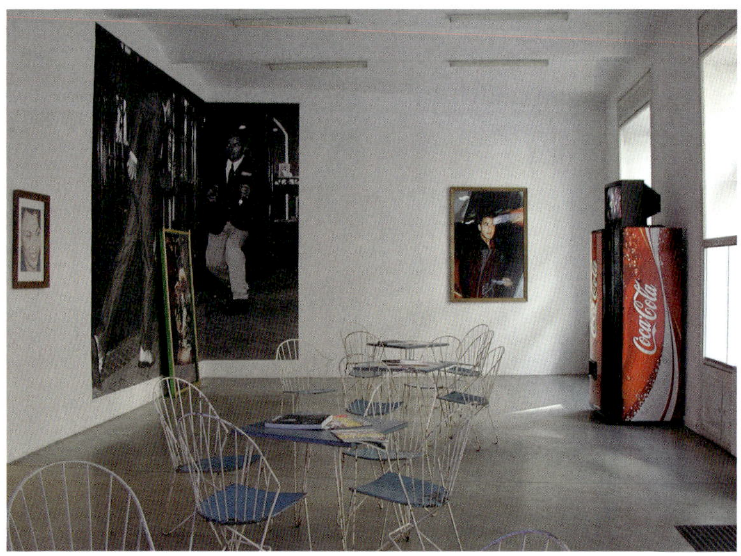

Installation view of *Café Paparazzi* by G.R.A.M. at the Christine König Galerie, Vienna, 2009

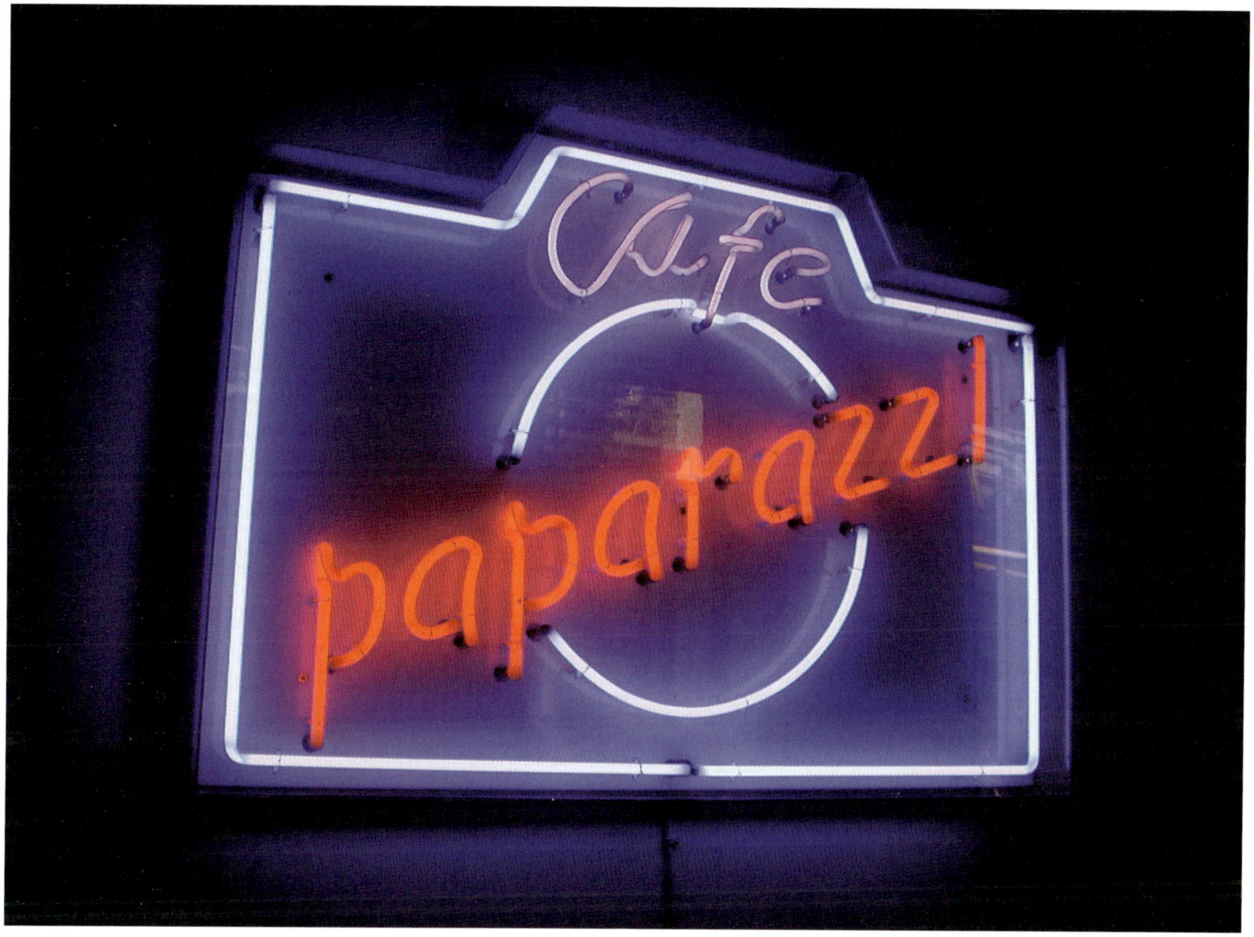

G.R.A.M.
Café Paparazzi
Neon Sign
2009

G.R.A.M. is an Austrian artists' collective established by Günther Holler Schuster, Ronald Walter, Armin Ranner, and Martin Behr. Since 1987, they have been working in the fields of photography, video, film, painting, and performance art, basing their creations on the popular iconography disseminated by the illustrated press. In 1997, they initiated a project on paparazzi imagery. Fanning out to cover the various haunts frequented by celebrities—ranging from Los Angeles to Switzerland and the Côte d'Azur—they tracked the stars down and took pictures of them just like authentic paparazzi. The project was extended a few years later with an overtly postmodern approach. G.R.A.M. staged an exhibition of famous snapshots from the history of paparazzi photography. These works were gathered together in an installation entitled *Café Paparazzi*, the café traditionally being the favored Austrian venue for catching up on the paparazzi press.

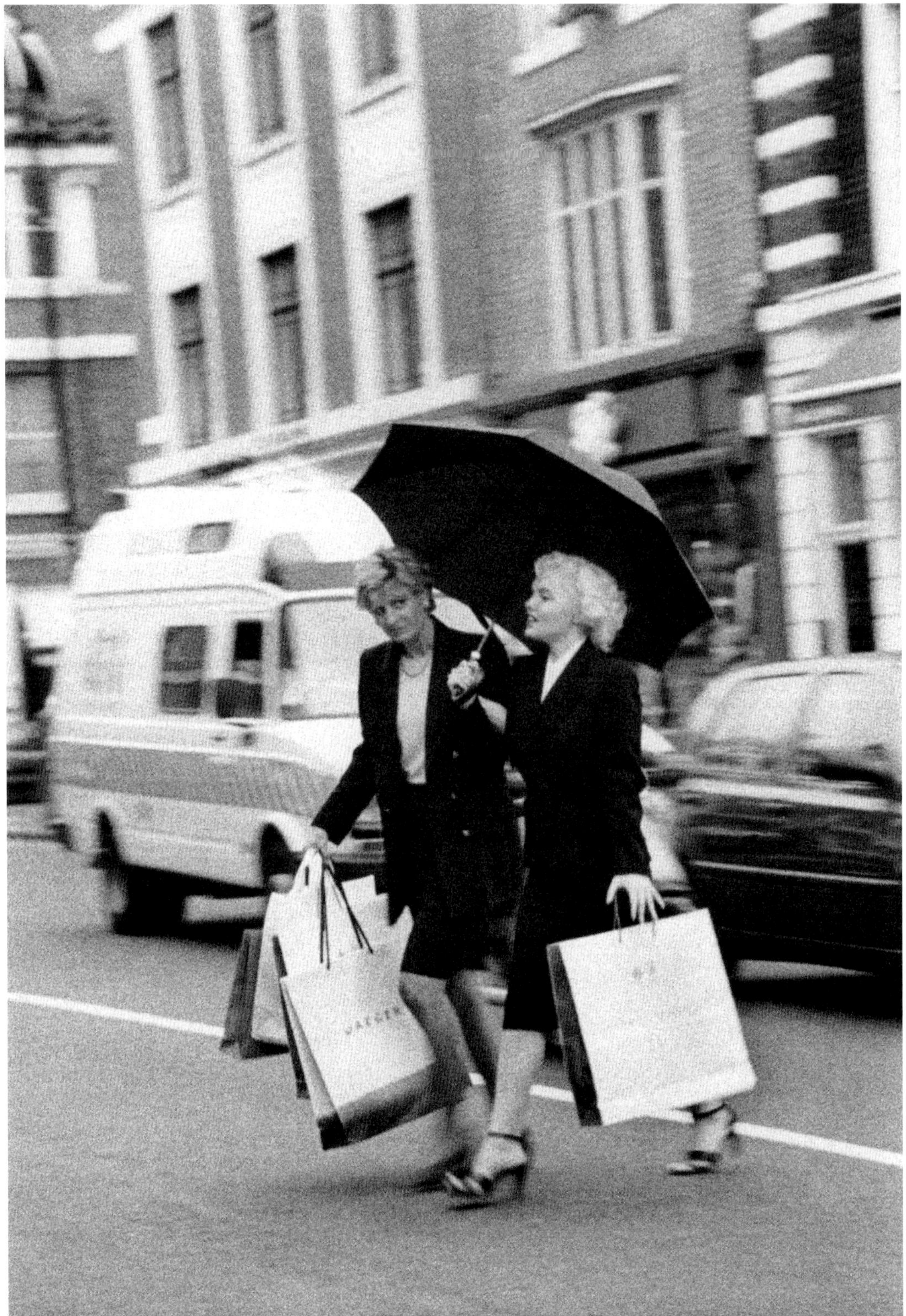

ALISON JACKSON
Diana and Marilyn Shopping
2000

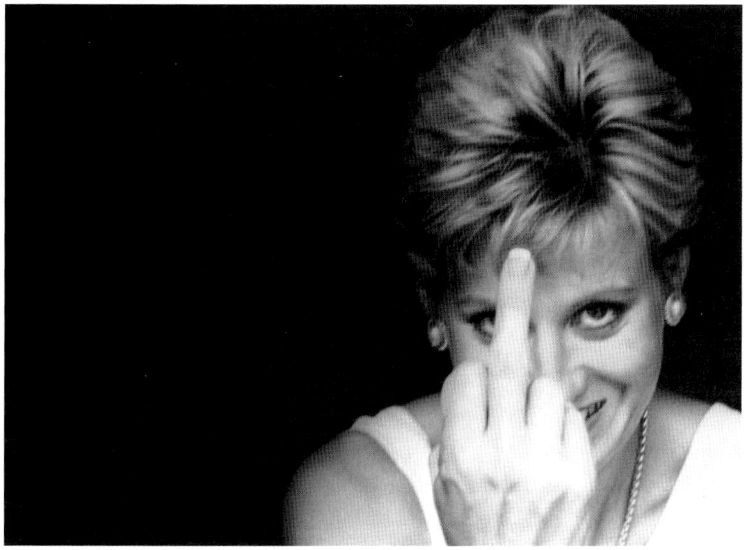

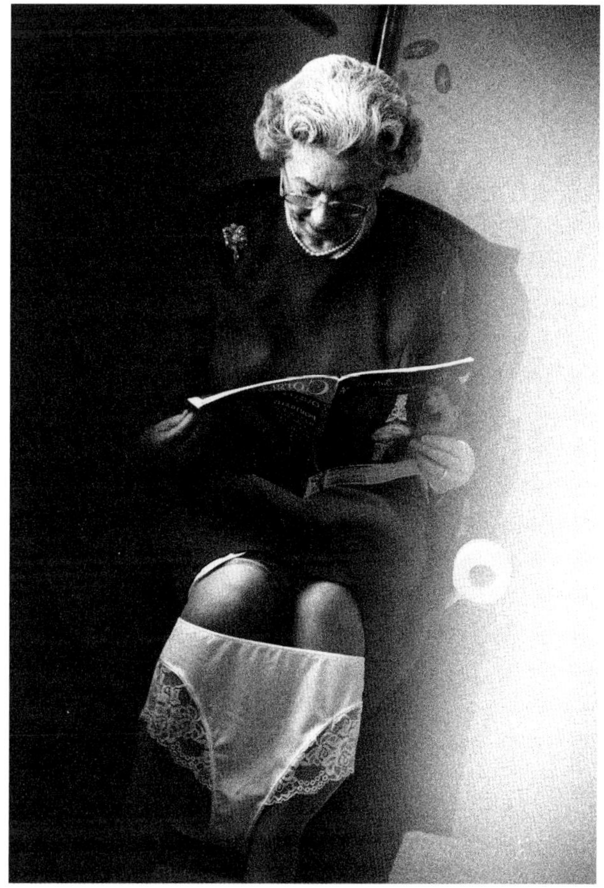

ALISON JACKSON
Diana Finger-Up
2000

ALISON JACKSON
Queen on the Loo
2003

ALISON JACKSON. A British artist born in 1960 who studied at the Royal College of Art in London, Alison Jackson has been exploring the fascination exerted by celebrities for almost twenty years. She has used photographs, videos, and, more recently, sculptures in her work. Employing impersonators hired through specialized agencies, she portrays celebrities in improbable situations—Queen Elizabeth on her "throne," Mick Jagger gripping a clothes iron, George Bush playing with a Rubik's Cube. She then photographs them paparazzi style. Rich in humorous potential, her photographs toy with a variety of notions—what we know, what we fear, what rumors the celebrity press is mongering, and what we've never seen that plenty of us would very much like to see. These fantastical—and wholly imaginary—"exclusives" speak volumes about the irresistible attractions of voyeurism. Alison Jackson truly makes the images of our media-driven fantasies into a reality.

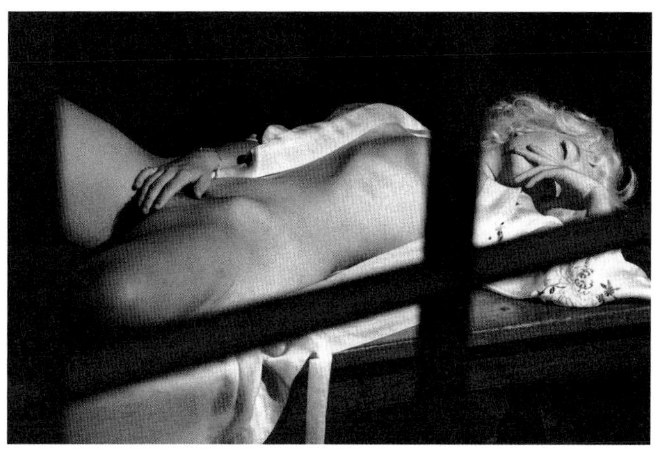

ALISON JACKSON
Marilyn Wank Window Bars
2002

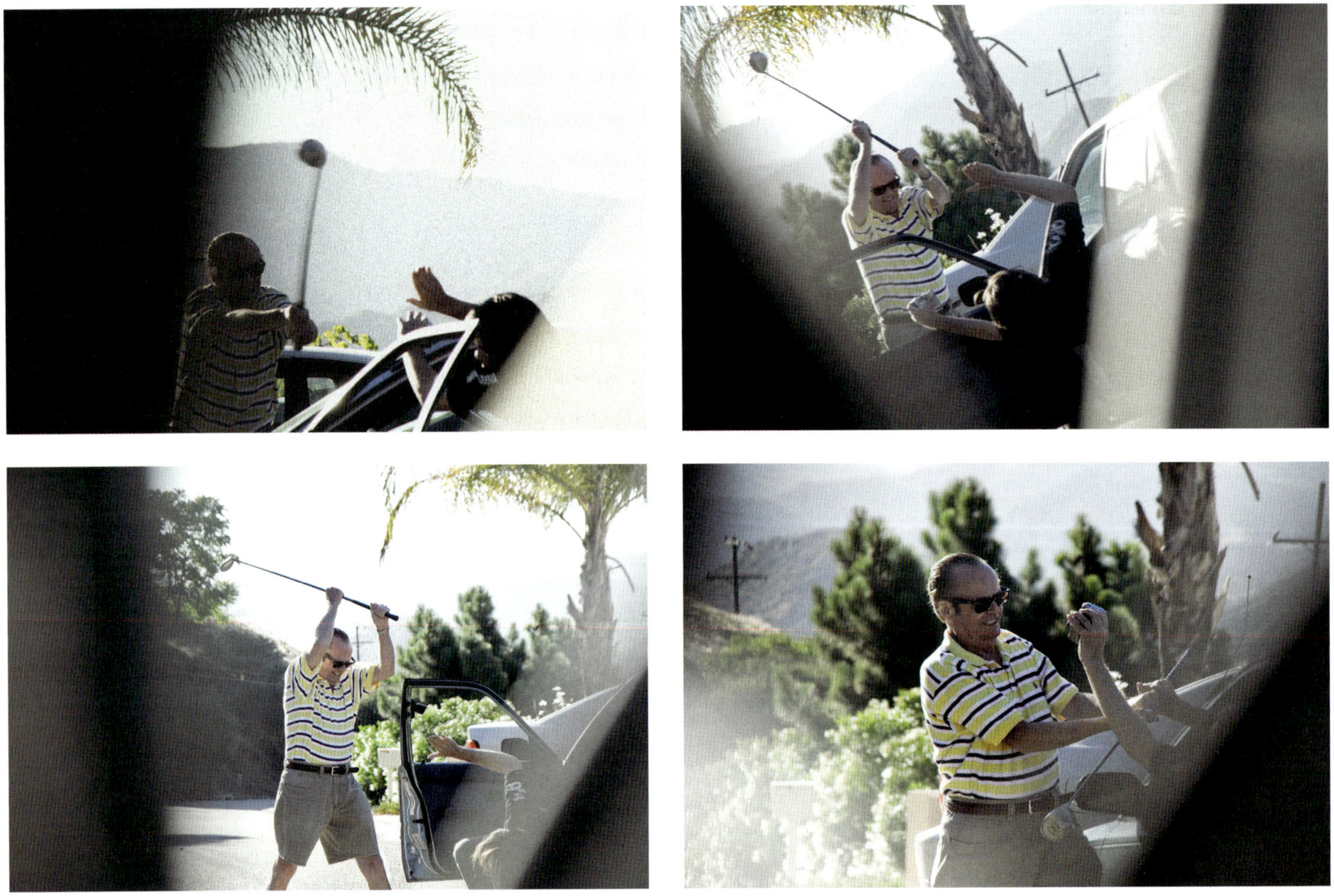

ALISON JACKSON
Nicholson Rage
2007

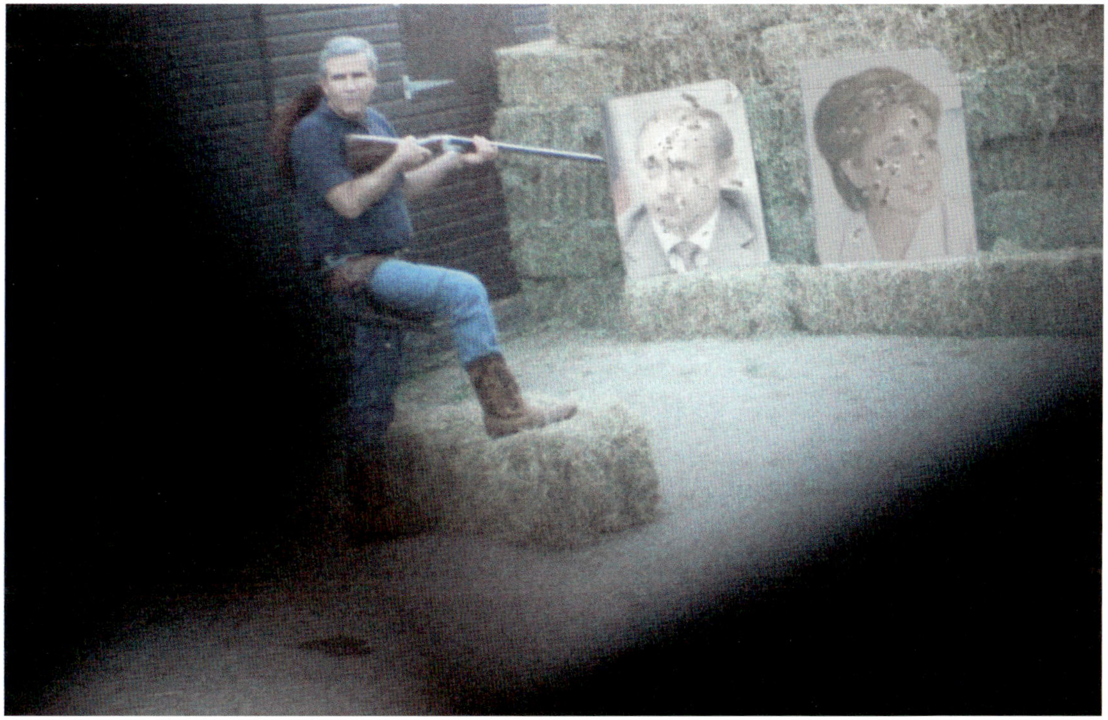

ALISON JACKSON
Bush Target Practice
2007

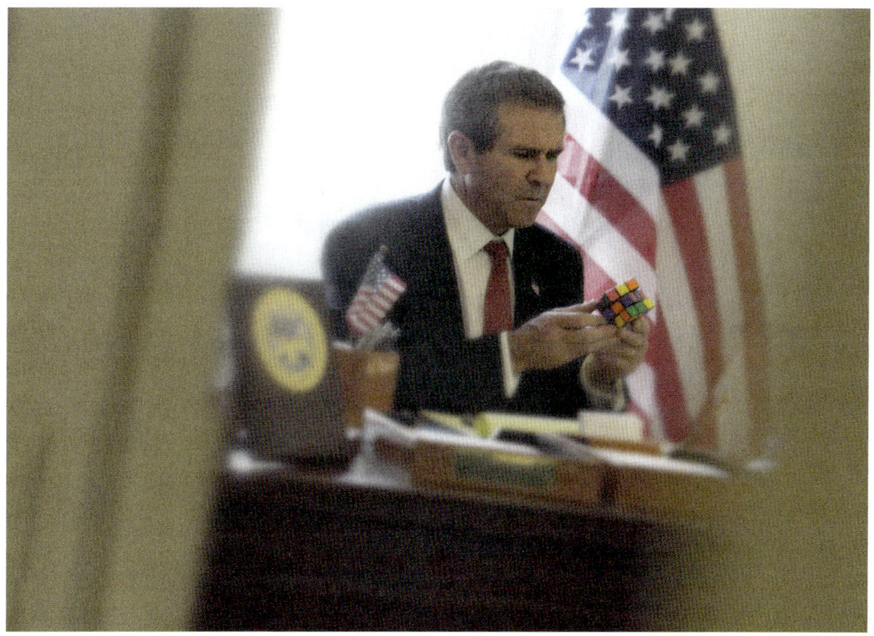

ALISON JACKSON
Bush with Rubik's Cube
2008

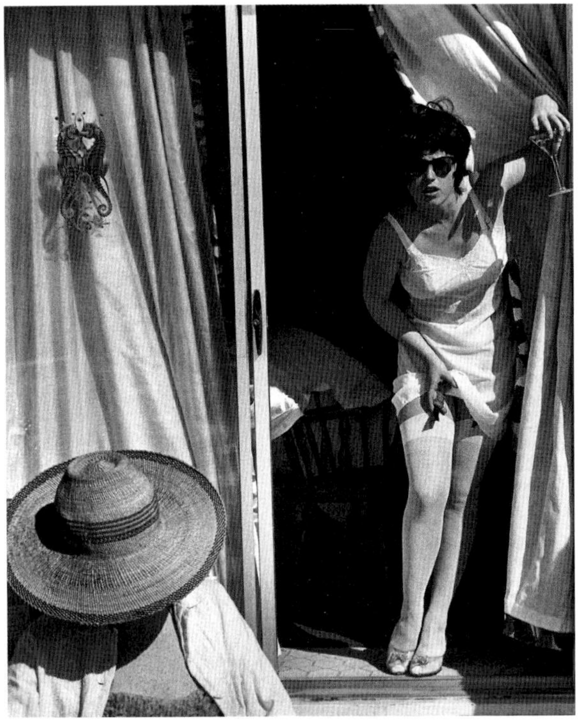

CINDY SHERMAN
Untitled Film Still #7
1978

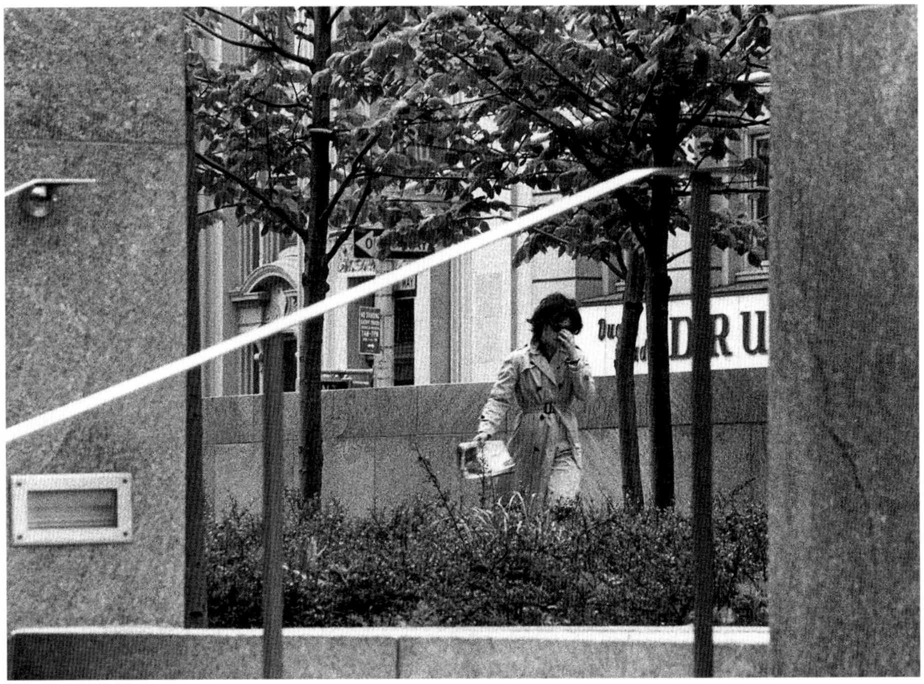

CINDY SHERMAN
Untitled Film Still #83
1980

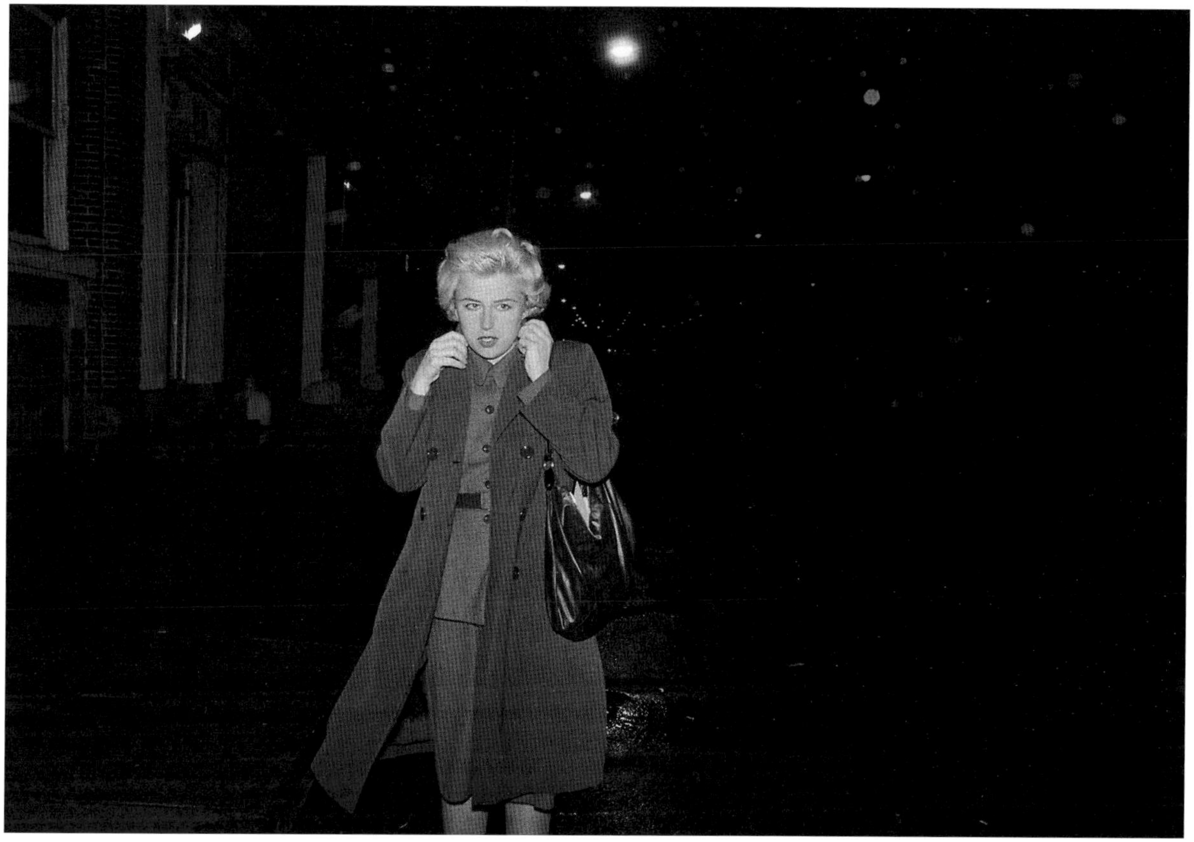

CINDY SHERMAN
Untitled Film Still #54
1980

CINDY SHERMAN executed *Untitled Film Stills* between 1977 and 1980. This was a series of sixty-nine black-and-white photographs featuring the artist in different situations. The images were inspired by various feminine stereotypes conveyed by popular culture through television, film, and the illustrated press. She played with scenes that are embedded in our collective memory. Although it may not be possible to precisely identify the source images, Cindy Sherman's work unmistakably evokes a sense of déjà vu among those who study it. Some of the source photos, publicized to the point of tedium by the media, are pictures of stars being hounded, struggling to conceal themselves and to escape the predatory gaze of the watching paparazzi. Appropriating the visual codes of media overexposure and restaging them for her own purposes, Cindy Sherman ingeniously deconstructs them in a genuinely postmodern spirit.

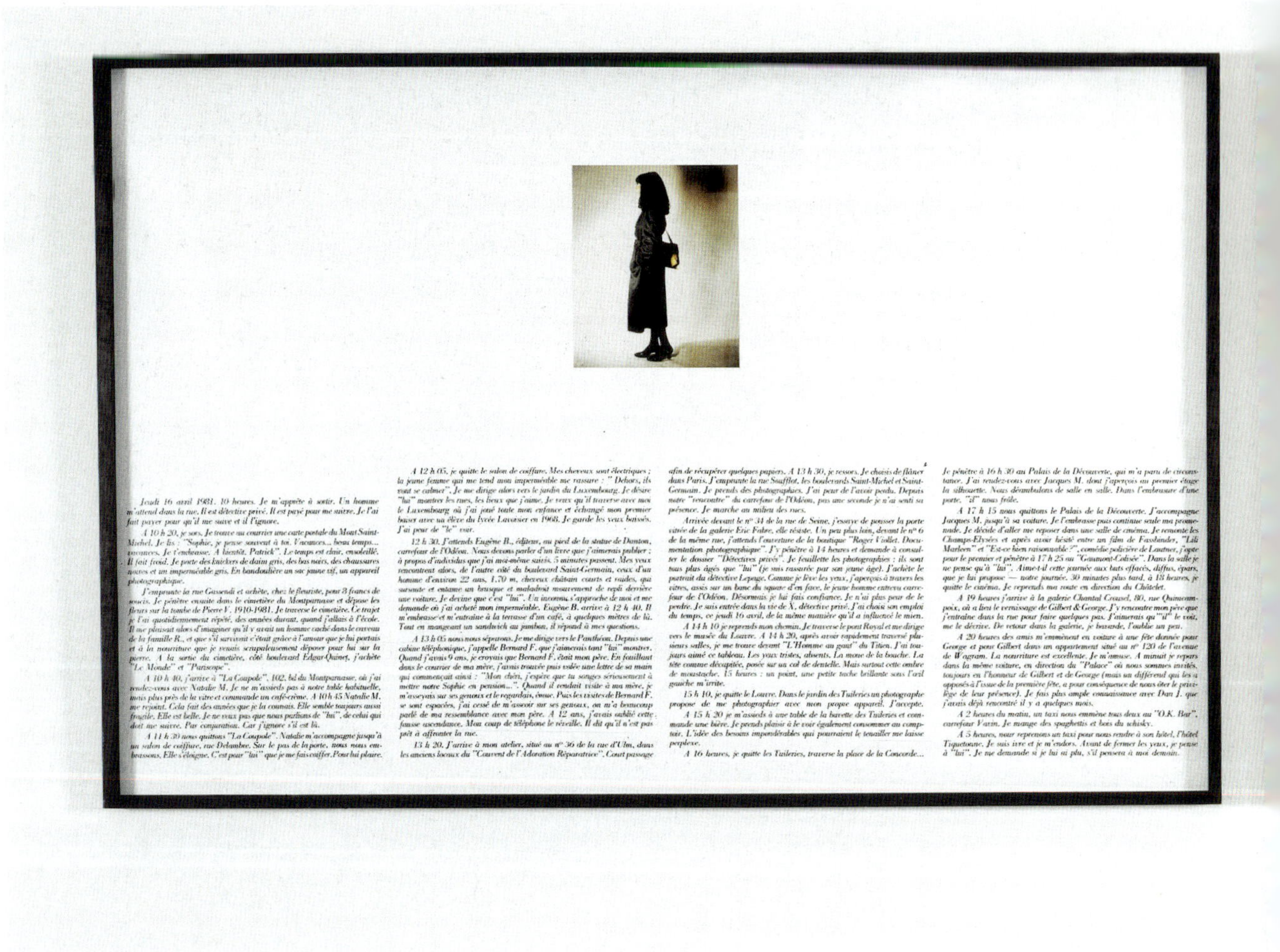

SOPHIE CALLE. In April 1981, Sophie Calle asked her mother to go to the private detective agency Duluc and instruct them to track her daughter like a suspect. During the course of a day, an investigator shadowed the artist, photographing her constantly and systematically recording her activities, movements, and encounters. This was the basis for the installation entitled *La Filature* (*The Shadow*). These written and photographic pieces of "evidence" instituted a dialectic between the visible and the tellable. The banality of the daily routine they depicted was the antithesis of sensationalism. Instead they spoke eloquently of the triviality that the paparazzi aesthetic often represents. Appropriating images and forms associated with the world of private investigators, surveillance, and espionage, Sophie Calle created a work in which she distanced herself, blurring the lines between the worlds of the artist and the paparazzi.

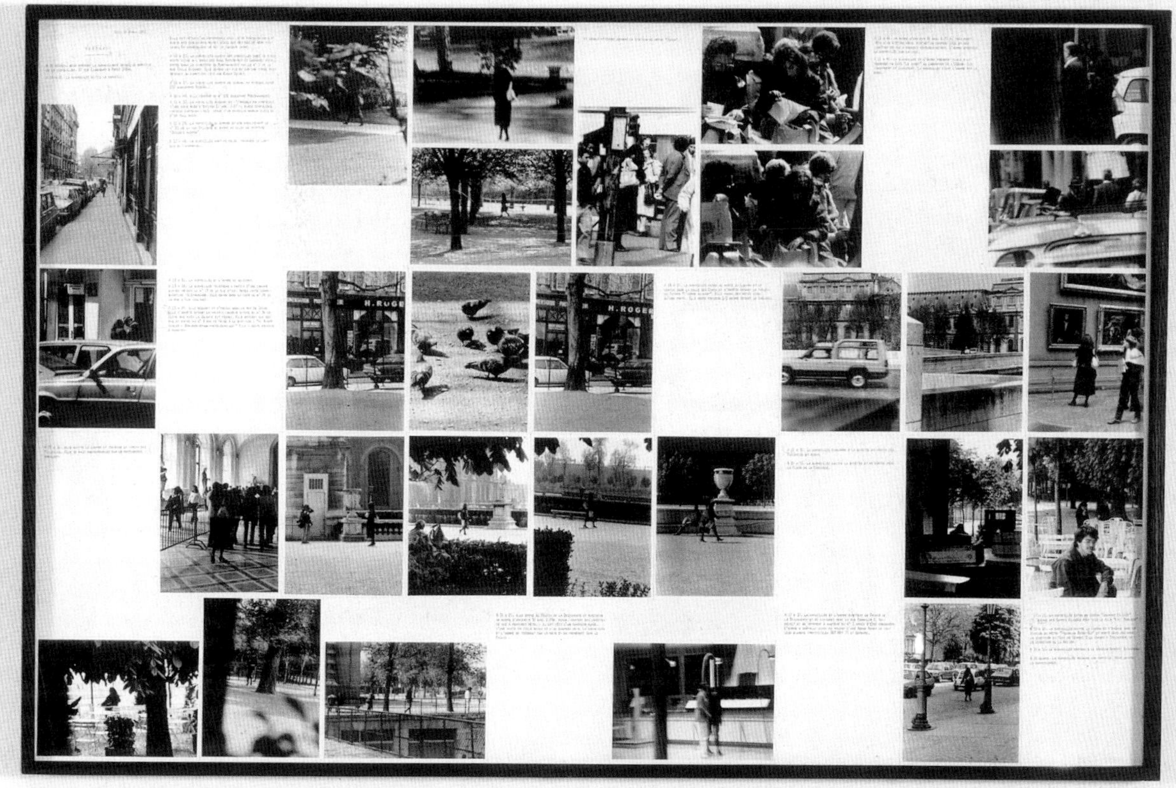

SOPHIE CALLE
La Filature (*The Shadow*)
1981

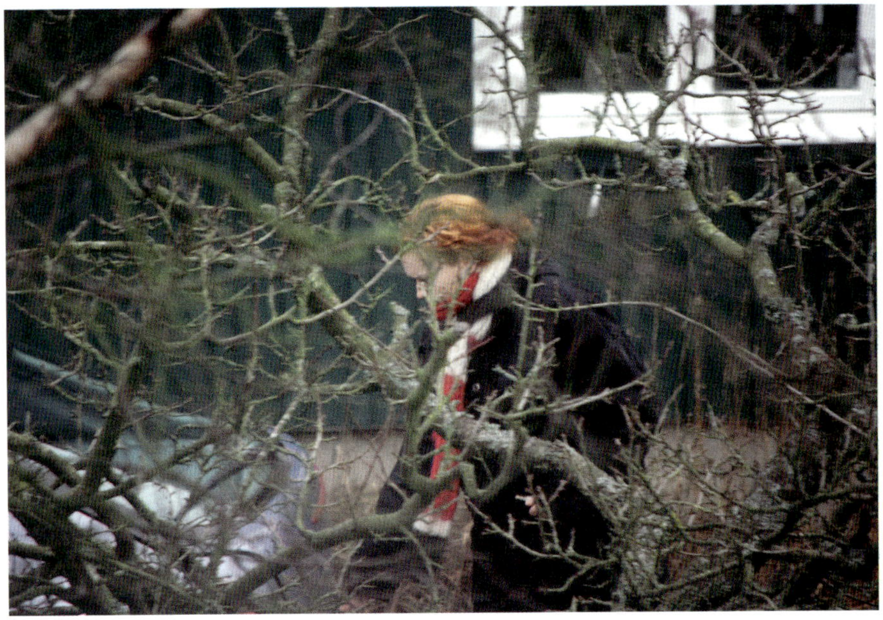

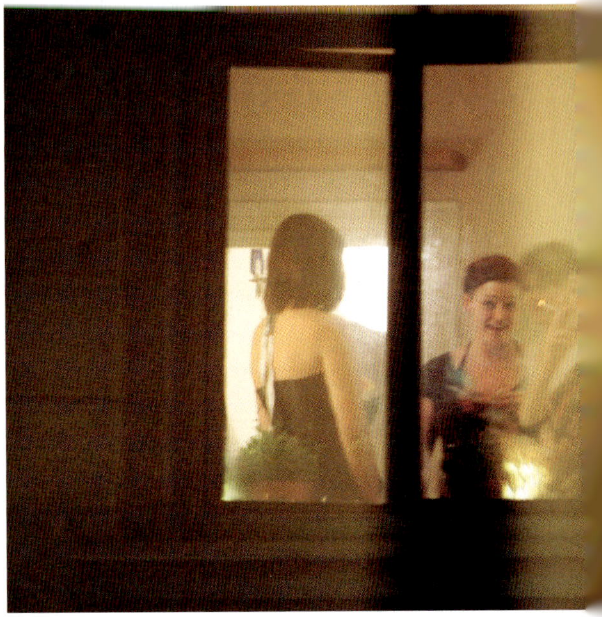

MALIN ARNESSON. A Swedish artist born in 1976, Malin Arnesson is a graduate of the Umeå Academy of Fine Arts. She worked for the Swedish paper *Aftonbladet* photographing public figures, usually without their knowledge. In reaction to this activity, she initiated an artistic project in 2004 that involved asking several paparazzi to follow and photograph her for almost a year and a half. The resulting images show the artist at various moments in her private life, on the sidewalk, at her home, among her friends. The series recognizes the phenomenon of stalking and surveillance that victimizes celebrities, and her work is titled *The Penance*. For the artist, it is both a work of introspection and a plea for redemption. She raises the issue of culpability and invites us to debate the existence of a paparazzi code of ethics.

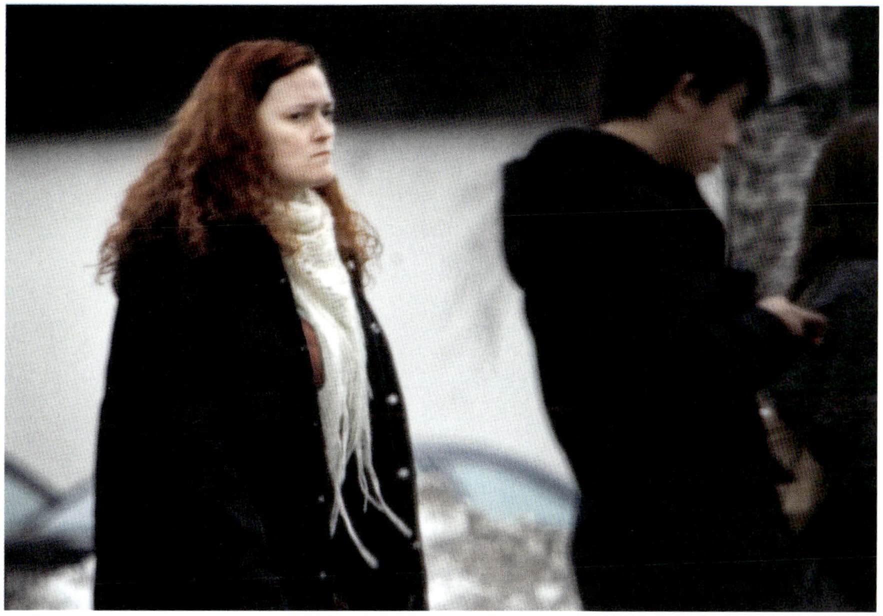

MALIN ARNESSON
Botgöringen/The Penance,
2008
(Photographs:
Pelle Wikström,
Gustav Mårtensson,
Anders Carlsson)

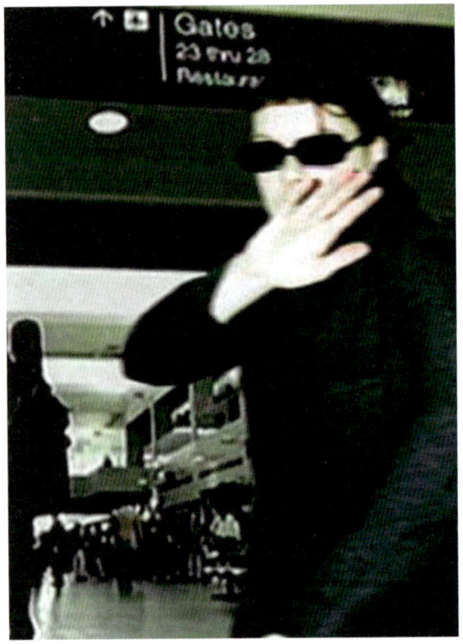

KATHRIN GÜNTER
Airport, from the series *Star Shots*
2007

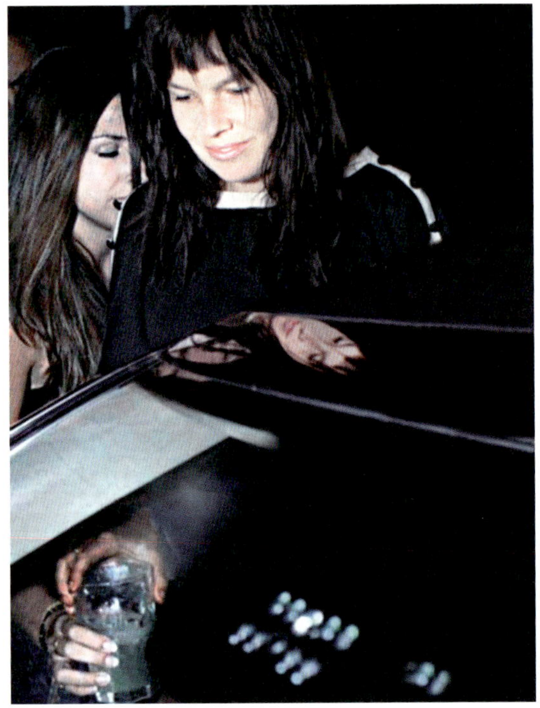

KATHRIN GÜNTER
Another One for the Road, from the series *Star Shots*
2007

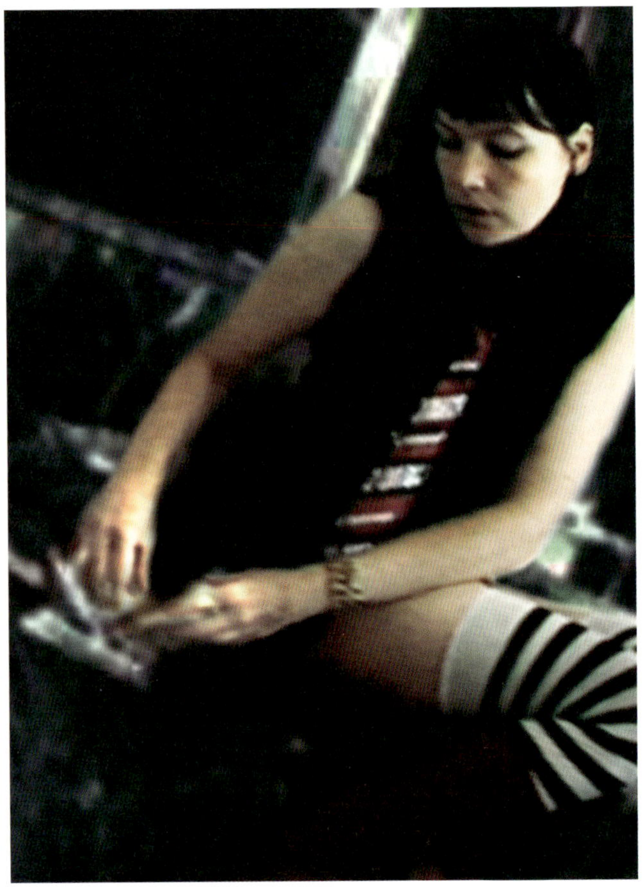

KATHRIN GÜNTER
Co-Kate, from the series *Star Shots*
2007

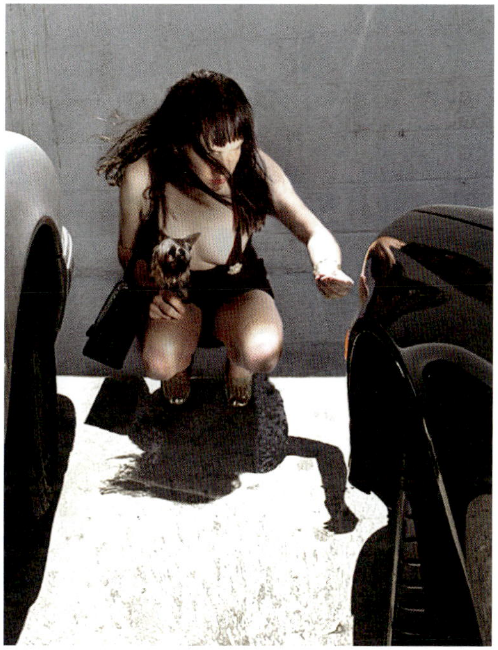

KATHRIN GÜNTER
Fender Bender, from the series *Star Shots*
2007

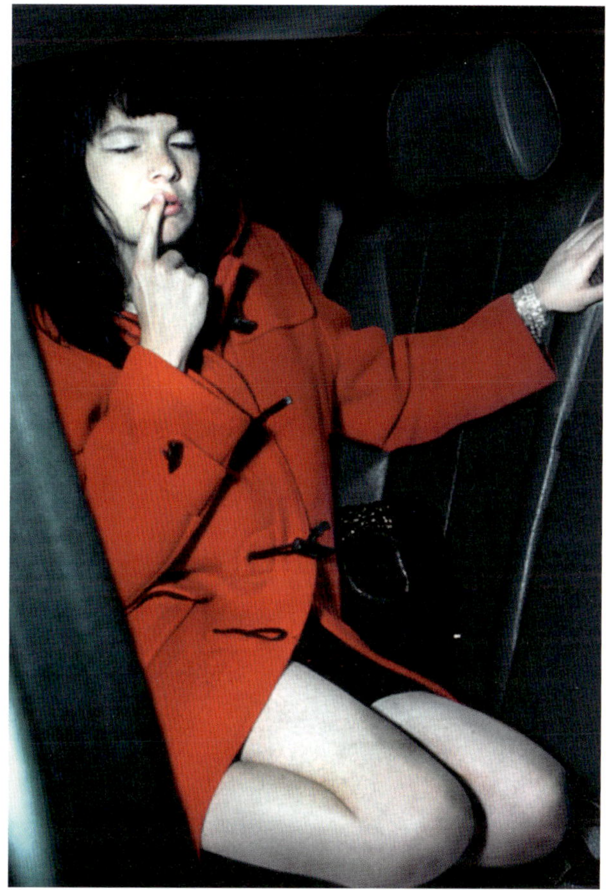

KATHRIN GÜNTER
Worse for Wear, from the series *Star Shots*
2007

KATHRIN GÜNTER is a German artist who lives and works in Berlin. She practices an intensive form of self-portraiture, challenging her own identity fantasies as well as the visual codes of celebrity. Her images are carefully composed and staged to mimic paparazzi shots in every detail. With a certain sense of mockery, she echoes typical celebrity poses, media-staged situations, and stereotypes of the celebrity press. She also calls into question the process by which an artist becomes a star, due to the growing media coverage since art has become an investment product, or even a form of financial speculation. Her work culminates in the creation of magazines in which she is the sole person to be photographed and interviewed. Pushed to its limit, her approach borders on the absurd. Star and artist merge in the viewer's perception in an infinite game of mirrors.

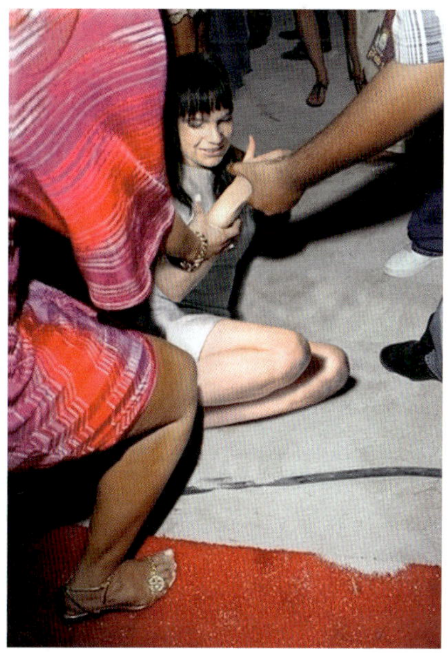

KATHRIN GÜNTER
Toe-Up, from the series *Star Shots*
2007

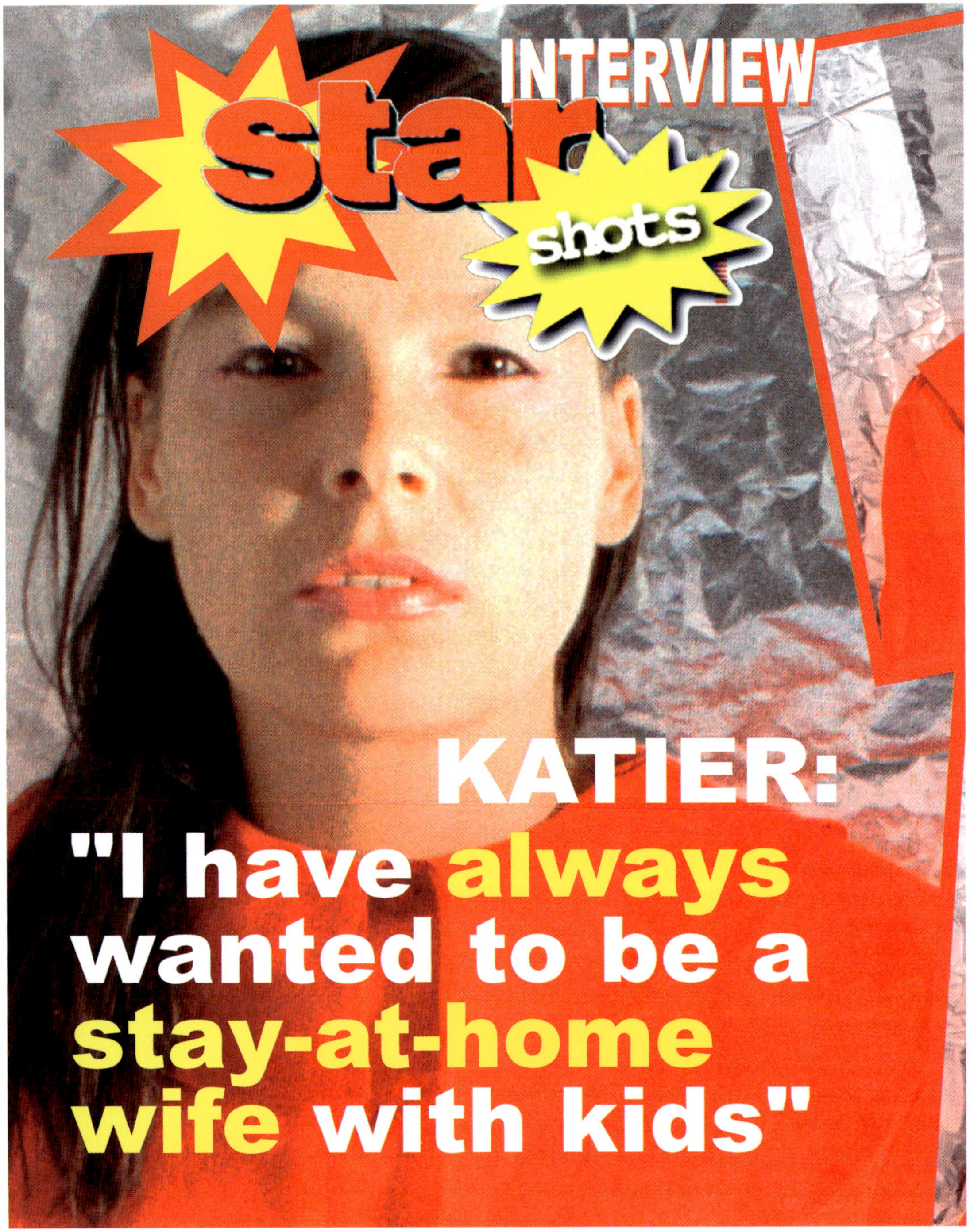

Star Shots Magazine
December 2007, p. 10
(Photograph:
Kathrin Günter)

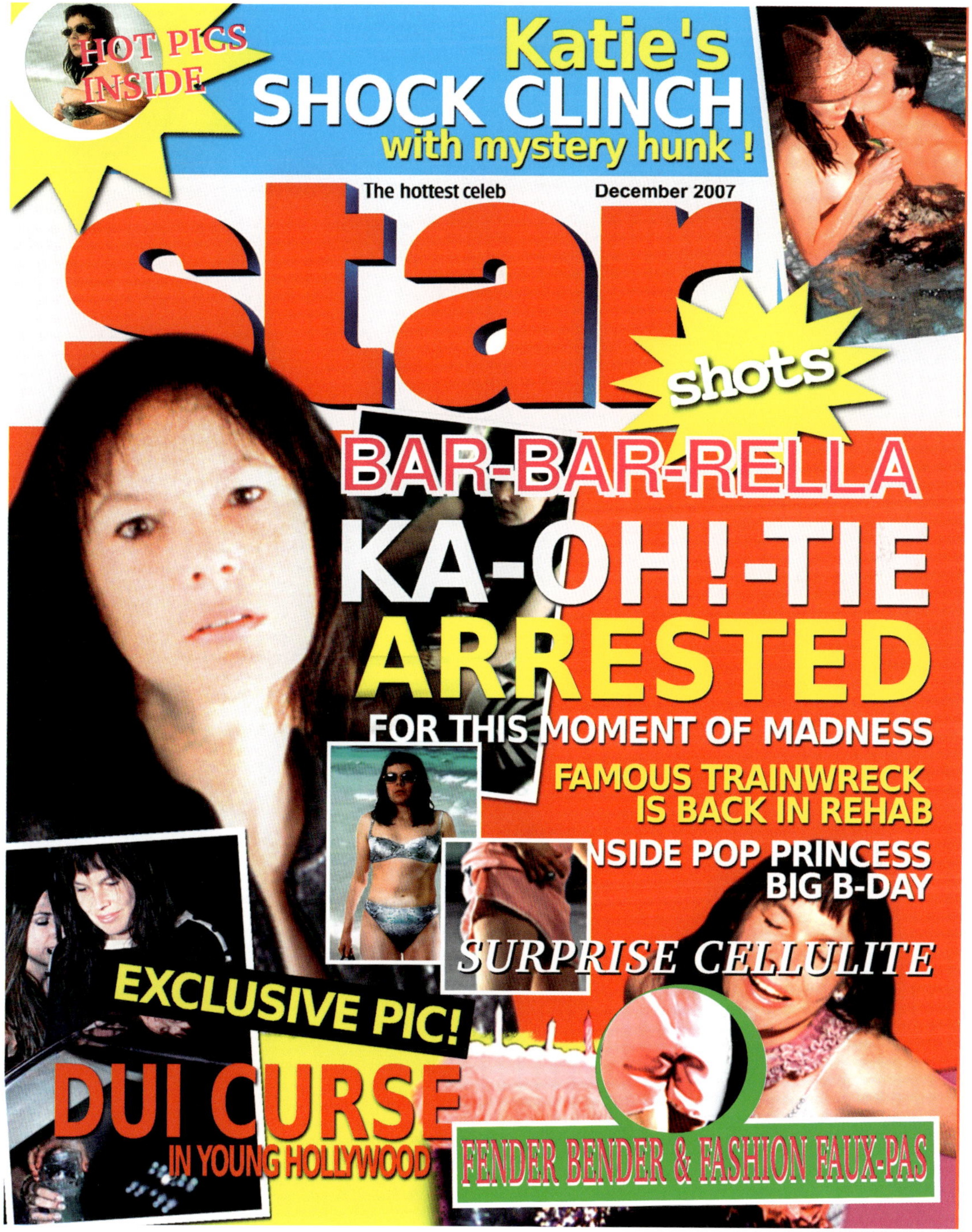

Star Shots Magazine
December 2007, front cover
(Photographs:
Kathrin Günter)

GAVIN TURK was born in 1967 and studied at the Royal College of Art in London. He is a member of the generation of Young British Artists supported by Prince Charles, and has rapidly assumed a prominent place in the international art market. Turk's work, which consists primarily of sculptures and installations, questions the myth of the artist in an overtly postmodern fashion. What is the artist's place in society, and what are the processes that lead to recognition? Consider his 1994 work *Identity Crisis*, in which he reflects on the impact of a child's birth on the life of an artist. In an ironic imitation of the media hype surrounding the artists of his generation, he poses with a woman and child—we have no idea whether they are actually his own—on the cover of an entirely fabricated celebrity magazine. The work raises several fundamental questions on the authenticity of art, its vulgarization, and its relationship with celebrity.

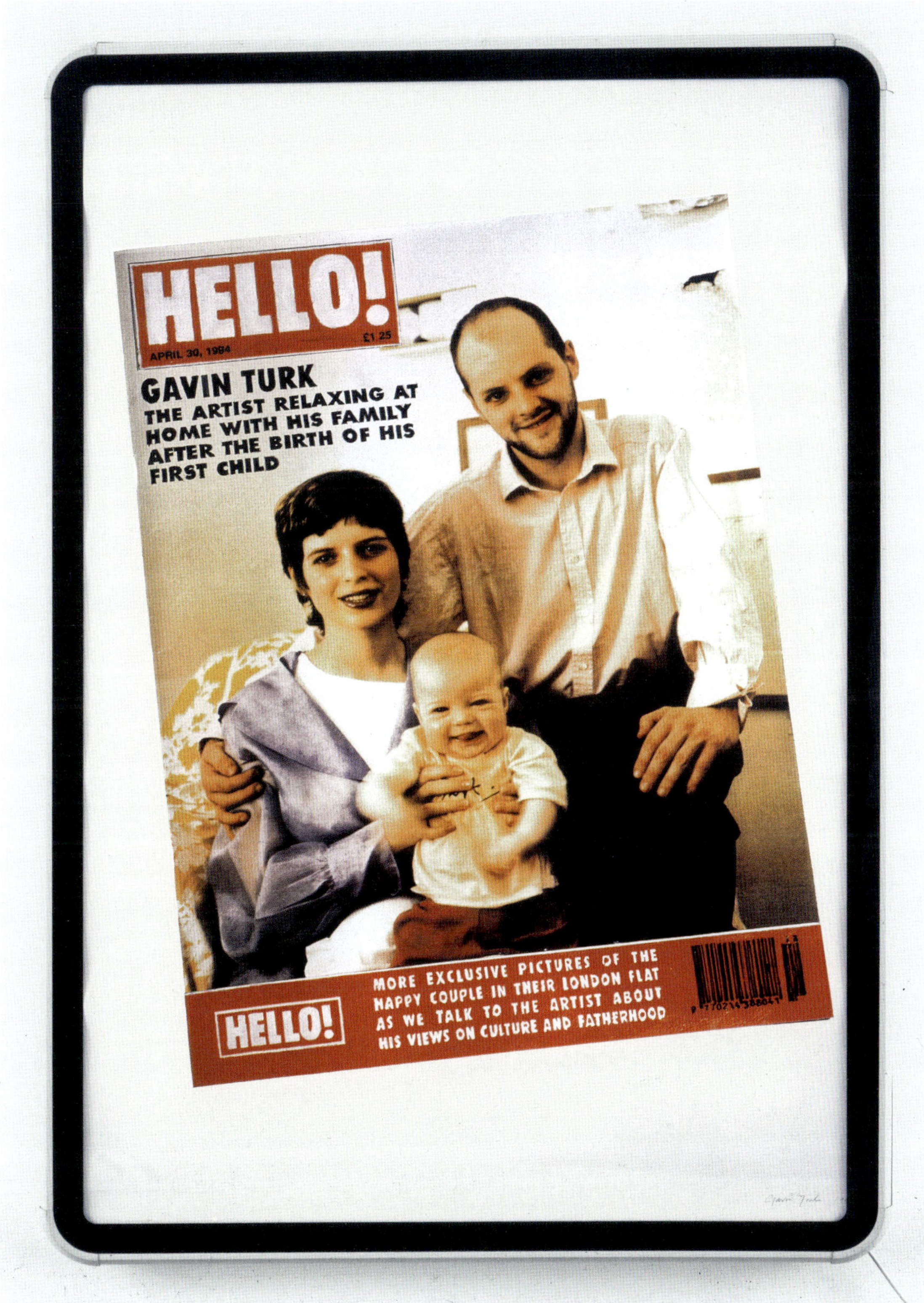

GAVIN TURK
Identity Crisis
1994

Paparazzi are financed by an industry that operates according to its own customs, rules, and codes: the celebrity press. It is a sector that has undergone substantial change since it originated almost a century ago. Now, in the age of the Internet, it is one of the last remaining bastions of profitability for the surviving publishers of printed material. These papers and magazines, unabashedly devoted to sensationalism and scandal, are easily recognizable by a number of distinctive visual signs: garish colors, crude graphics, flashy page layouts, vulgar content, and, of course, blatant photographic indiscretions. Reviewing the art of Andy Warhol, Paul McCarthy, Barbara Kruger, Armin Linke, and Jonathan Horowitz, this chapter concludes with the issues raised by the practices and customs of publications that print paparazzi photographs.

ON THE NEWSSTANDS

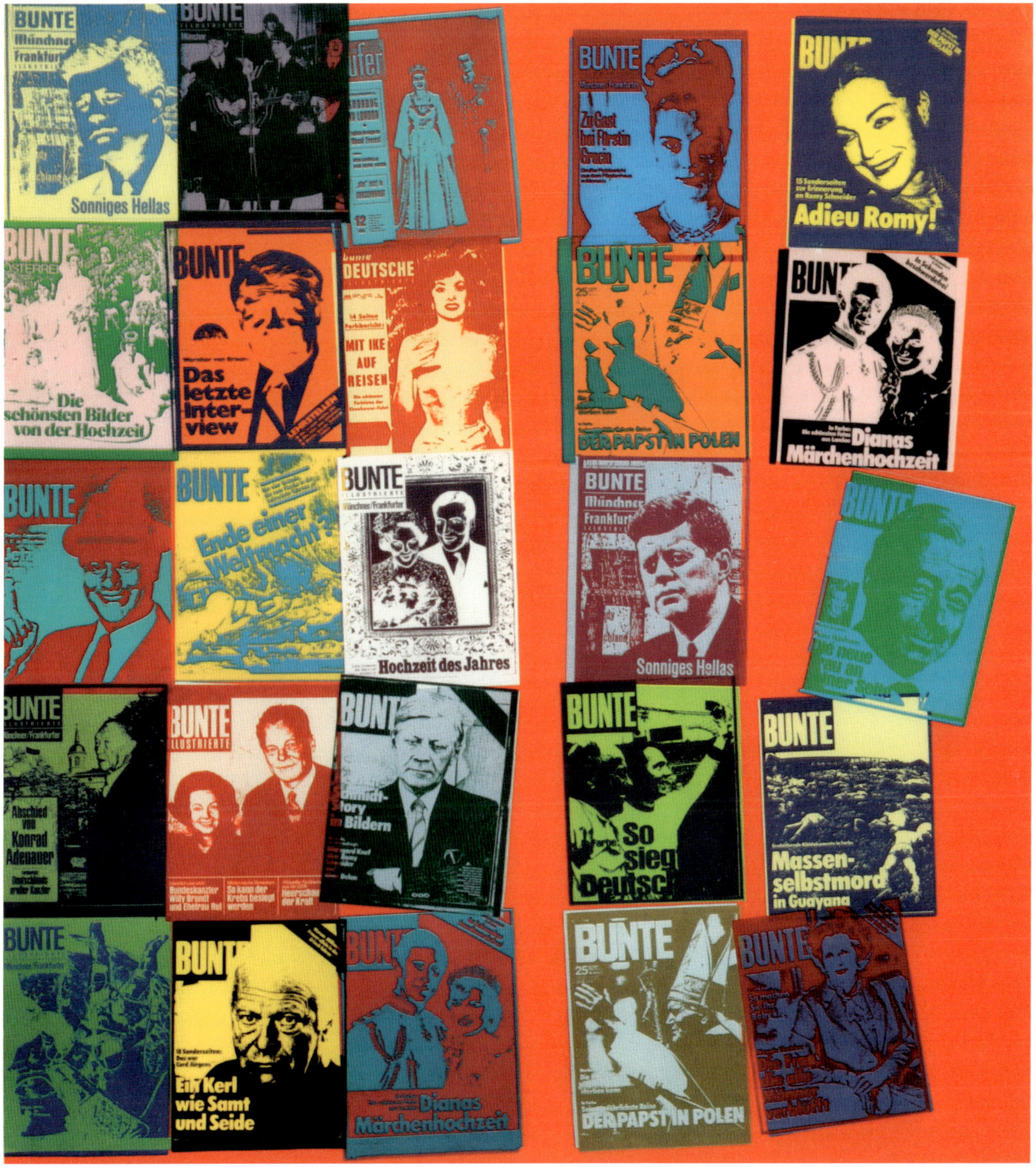

ANDY WARHOL
Magazine and History
(0290)
1983

PAGE 283

ANDY WARHOL. In 1983, Andy Warhol created *Magazine and History*, a montage based on twenty-five covers from *Bunte*, the era's most popular German illustrated magazine. It routinely published paparazzi photographs. Intended as a corporate gift, this work was commissioned by Hubert Burda, one of the sons of the German press magnate Franz Burda. It used the silk-screen technique to enlarge the cover pages of the weekly publication. In its style and brightly colored palette, *Magazine and History* is characteristic of pop art. It draws our attention to the links between art and the press and focuses on the fascination exerted by the world of stardom. Oriented toward the sensationalism of the tabloid press, it calls into question the nature of celebrity. Both successful businessmen in the worlds of art and publishing respectively, Andy Warhol and Hubert Burda represent a generation of prominent individuals who were highly influential in the creation and dissemination of images.

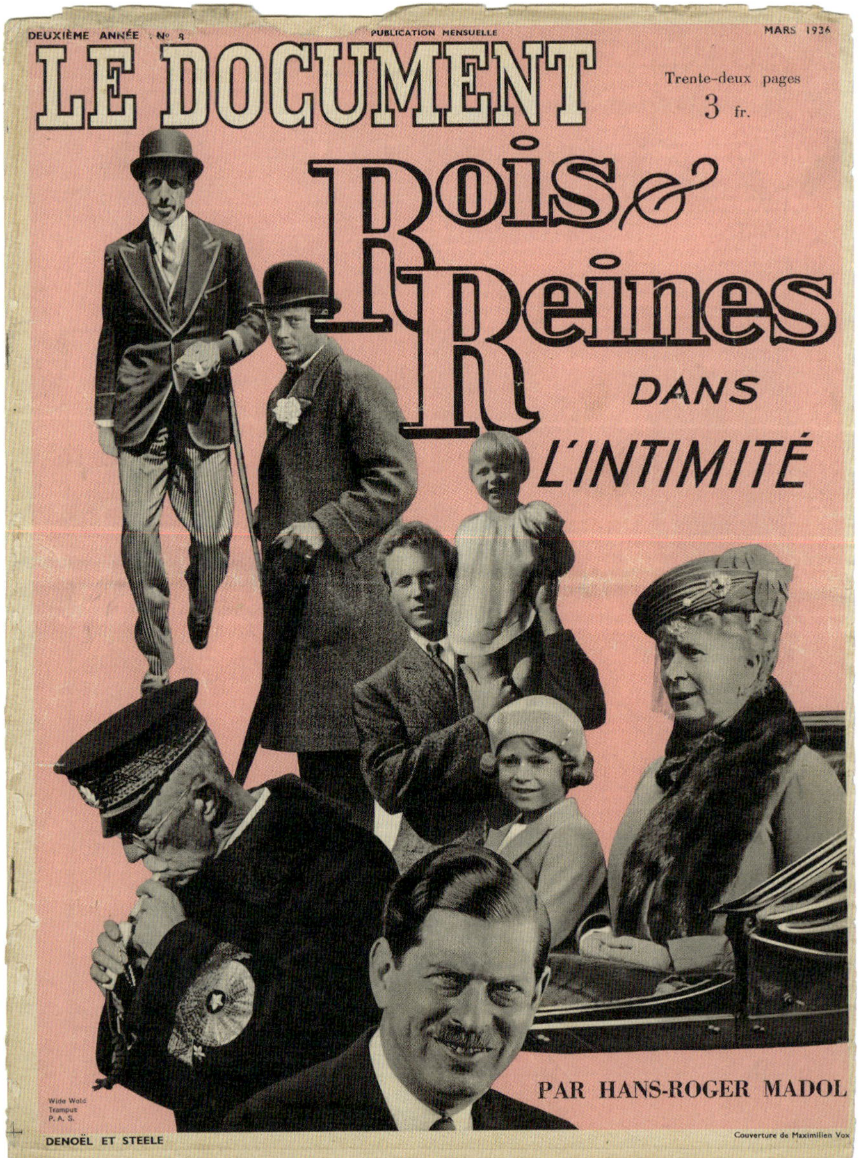

"Rois et reines dans l'intimité" (The Private Lives of Kings and Queens), *Le Document*, vol. 2, no. 8, March 1936, front cover (Photomontage: Maximilien Vox)

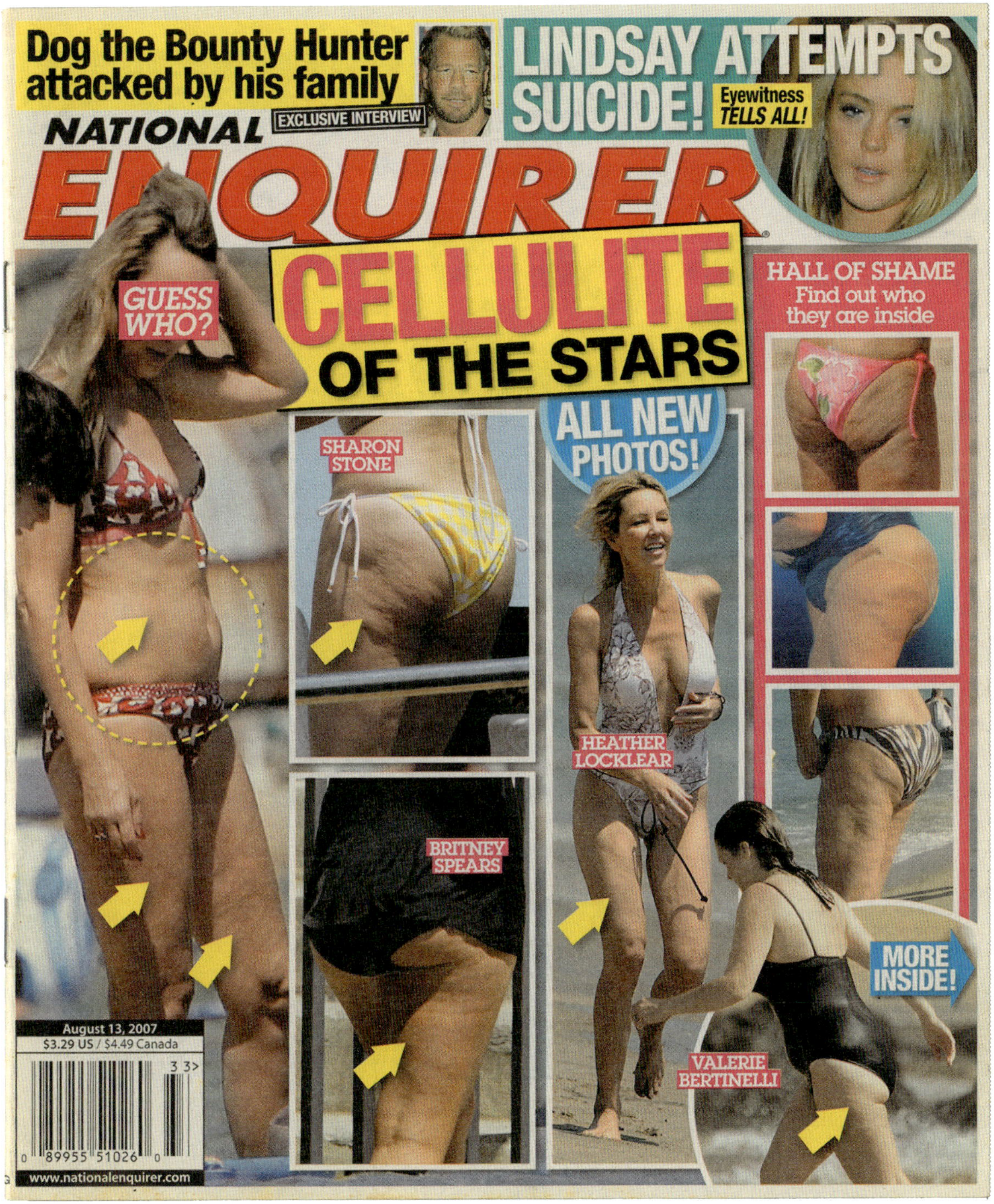

"Cellulite of the Stars," *National Enquirer*, vol. 82, no. 33, August 13, 2007, front cover (Photographs: anonymous)

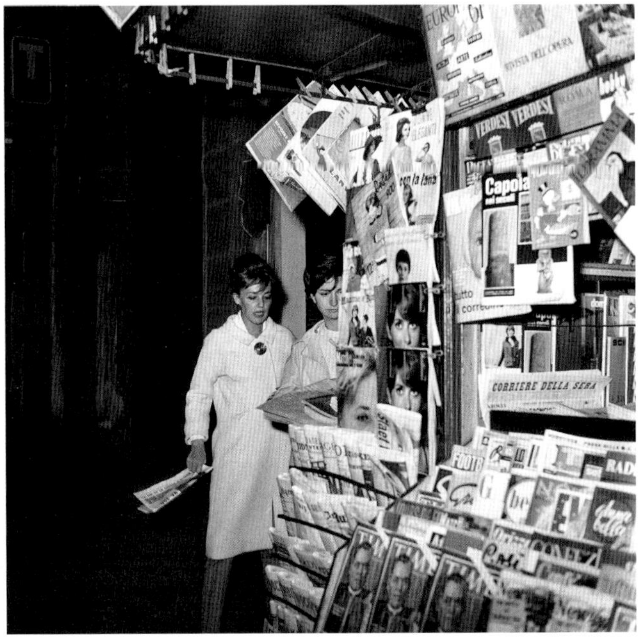

MARCELLO GEPPETTI
Jeanne Moreau at a Kiosk,
Via Veneto, Rome
February 1962

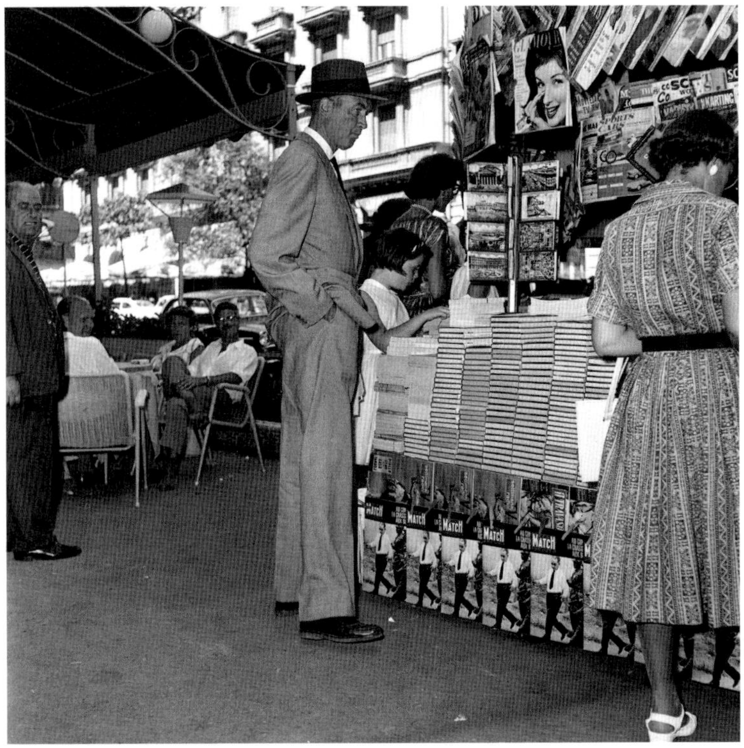

MARCELLO GEPPETTI
James Stewart at a Kiosk,
Via Veneto, Rome
1960

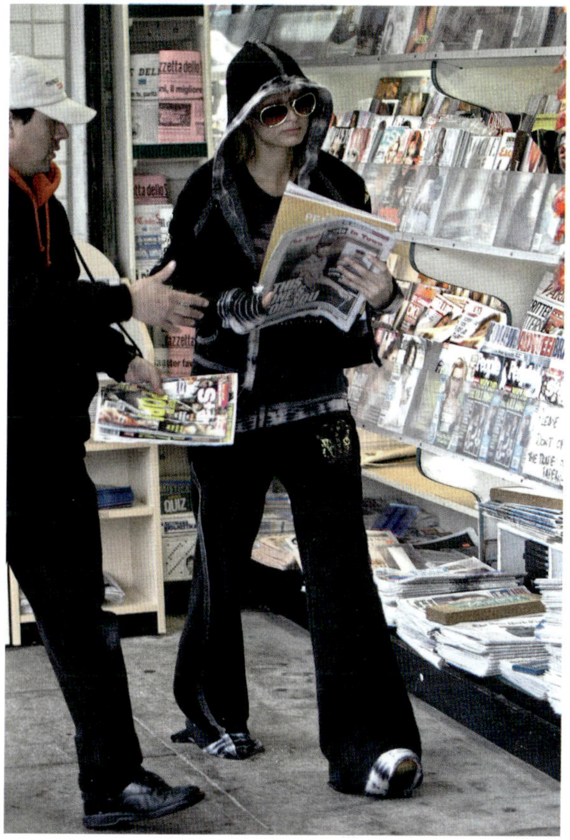

SÉBASTIEN VALIELA AND VINCENT LEPRESLE
Paris Hilton at a Newspaper Kiosk
April 5, 2006

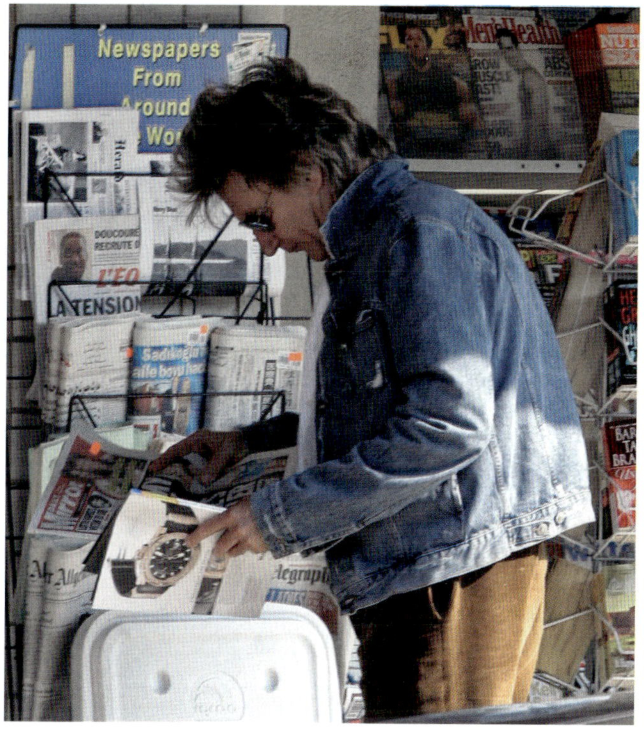

SÉBASTIEN VALIELA AND VINCENT LEPRESLE
Rod Stewart Buying Celebrity Magazines
October 8, 2005

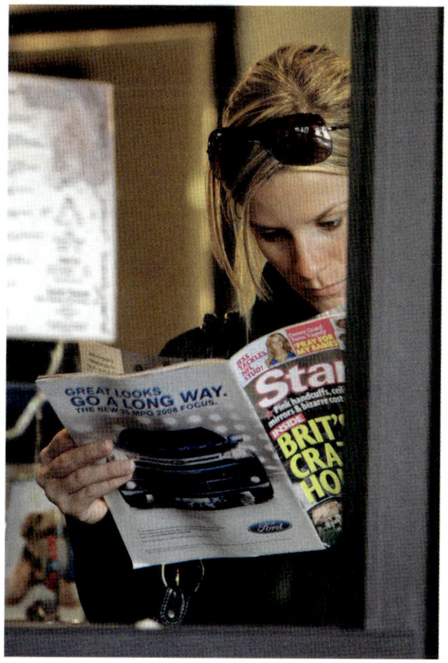

SÉBASTIEN VALIELA
Monika Casey, George Eads' Girlfriend, during One of Their First Public Outings, Los Angeles
December 1, 2007

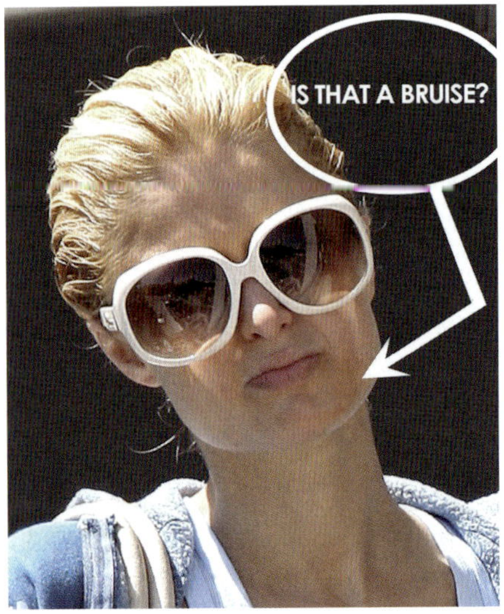

SÉBASTIEN VALIELA AND VINCENT LEPRESLE
Paris Hilton
March 29, 2006

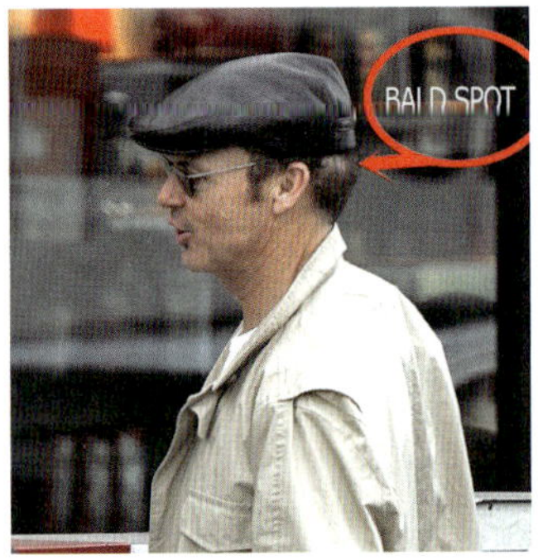

SÉBASTIEN VALIELA
Michael Keaton
February 9, 2006

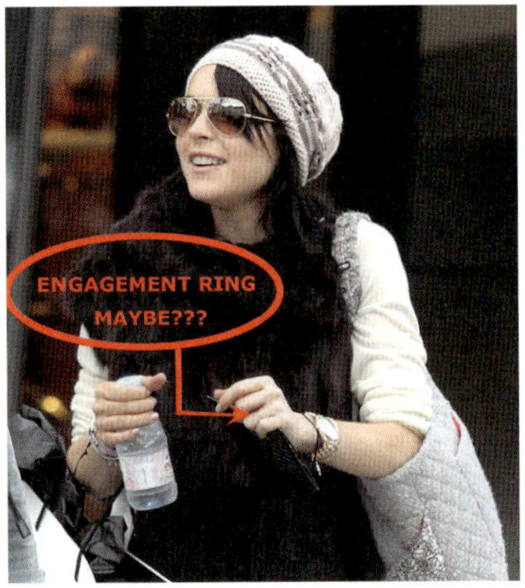

SÉBASTIEN VALIELA
Lindsay Lohan
December 27, 2005

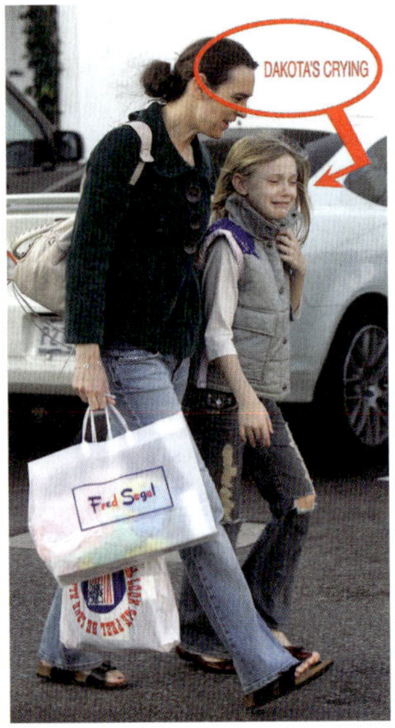

SÉBASTIEN VALIELA
Dakota Fanning
November 3, 2005

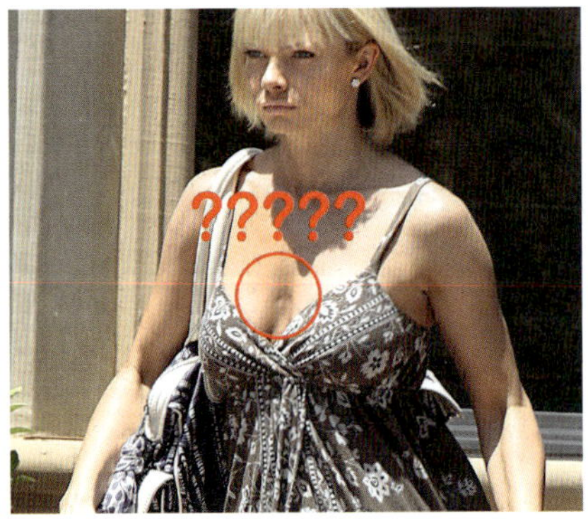

SÉBASTIEN VALIELA
Jaime Pressly
May 4, 2008

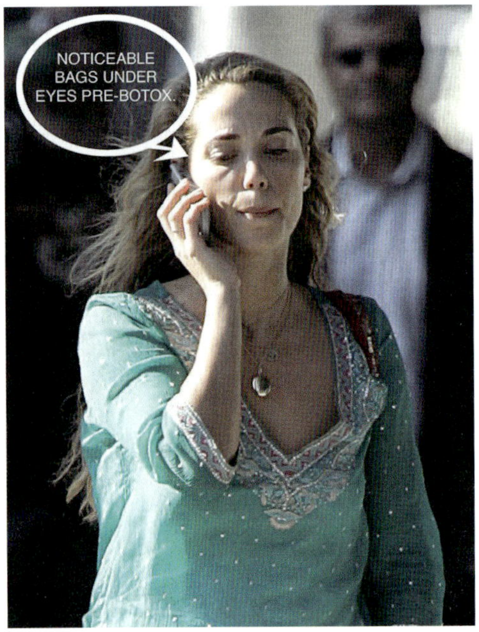

SÉBASTIEN VALIELA
Elizabeth Berkley
September 26, 2005

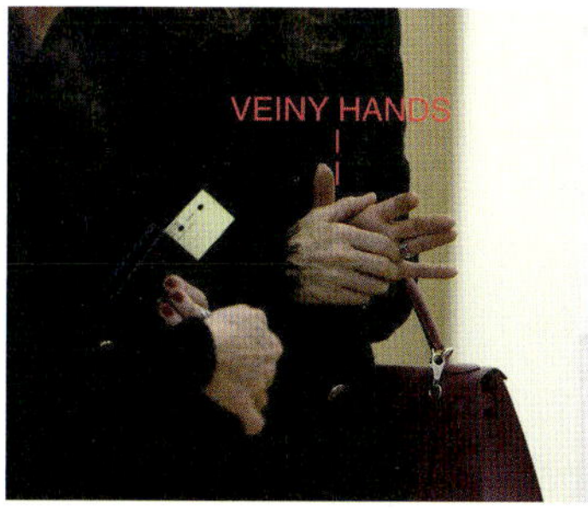

SÉBASTIEN VALIELA
Jaclyn Smith
December 15, 2006

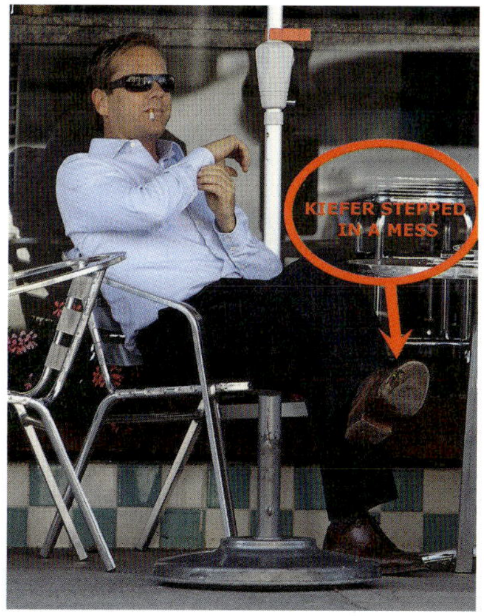

SÉBASTIEN VALIELA
Kiefer Sutherland Has Stepped in Something
September 25, 2005

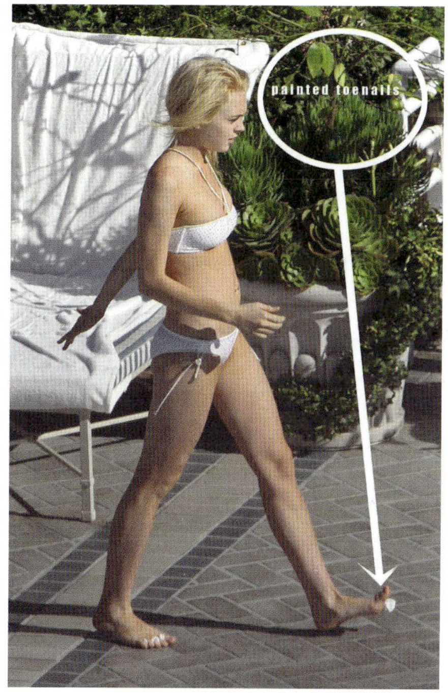

SÉBASTIEN VALIELA
Lindsay Lohan
June 18, 2005

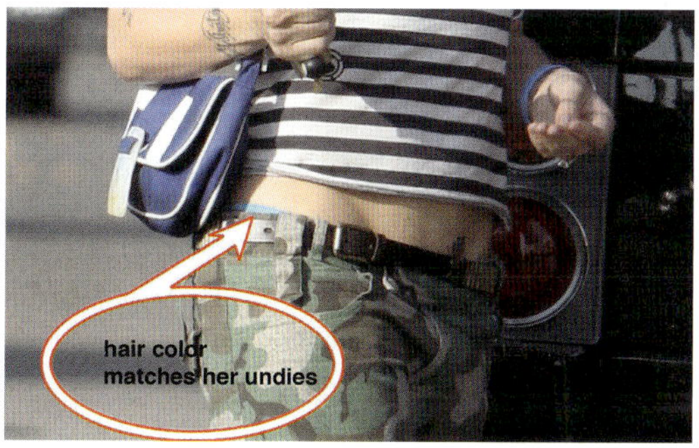

SÉBASTIEN VALIELA
Pink's Style in Beverly Hills
November 4, 2005

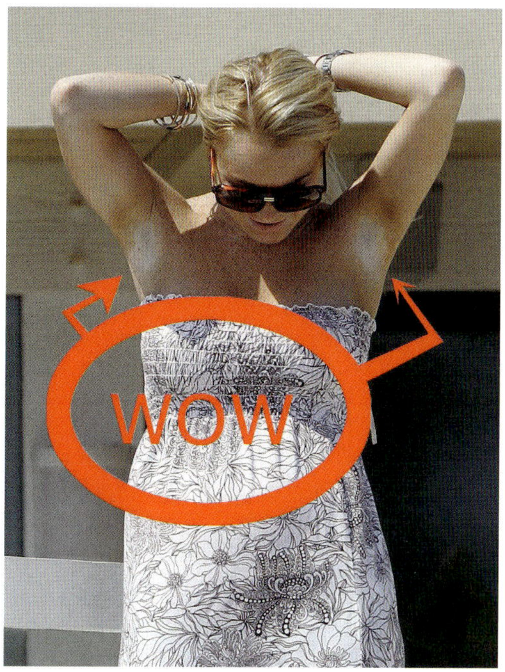

SÉBASTIEN VALIELA
Lindsay Lohan
July 22, 2007

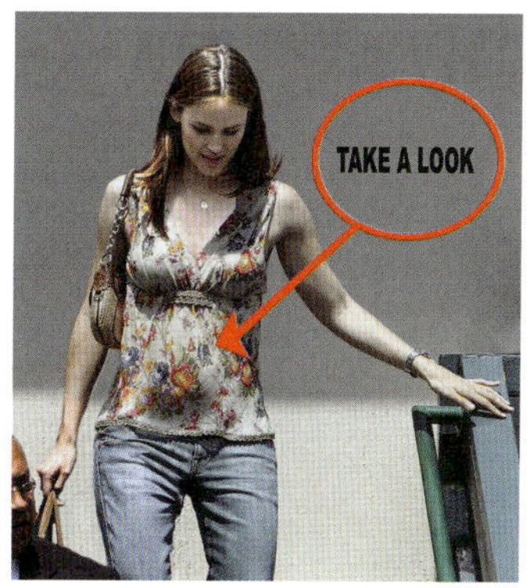

SÉBASTIEN VALIELA
Jennifer Garner
May 1, 2005

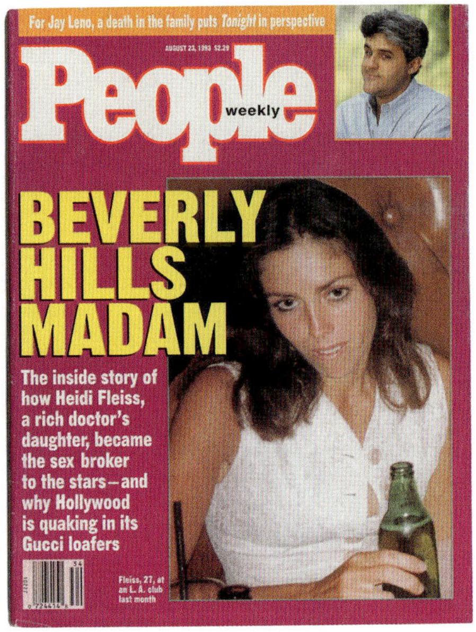

"Beverly Hills Madam,"
People Weekly, vol. 40, no 8,
August 23, 1993, front cover
(Photograph: E.L. Woody/
Ramey Photo Agency)

PAUL MCCARTHY. Born in 1945, Paul McCarthy is an American artist known for his radical, irreverent, and extreme criticism of Western values. In 2000, the Californian artist executed *People*, a work devoted to the scandal surrounding Heidi Fleiss, who had just been arrested for operating a Beverly Hills brothel frequented by stars. Based on the cover of the aptly named *People*, the most popular American celebrity magazine, and playing with collages and cut paper in a spirit that recalled Dadaist photomontages, McCarthy deconstructed Heidi Fleiss's face. In one of the series' images, he masks everything but the young woman's first name, reminding us of the beloved Swiss children's book *Heidi*. The innocence of the young girl in the story and the presumed culpability of the actual young woman in question are telescoped in a convergence of meaning that is disturbing to say the least.

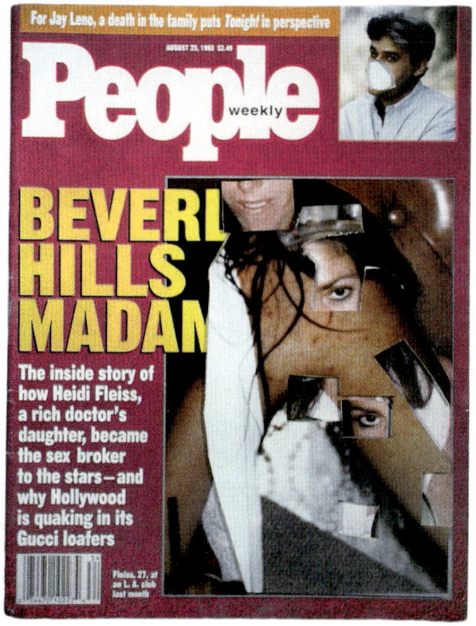

PAUL MCCARTHY
People 1
2000

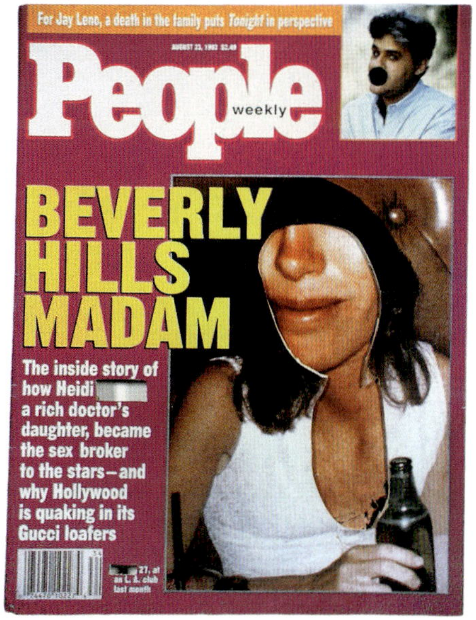

PAUL MCCARTHY
People 2
2000

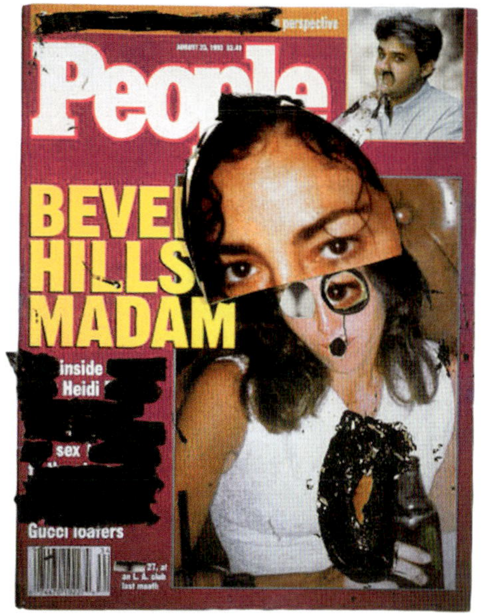

PAUL MCCARTHY
People 3
2000

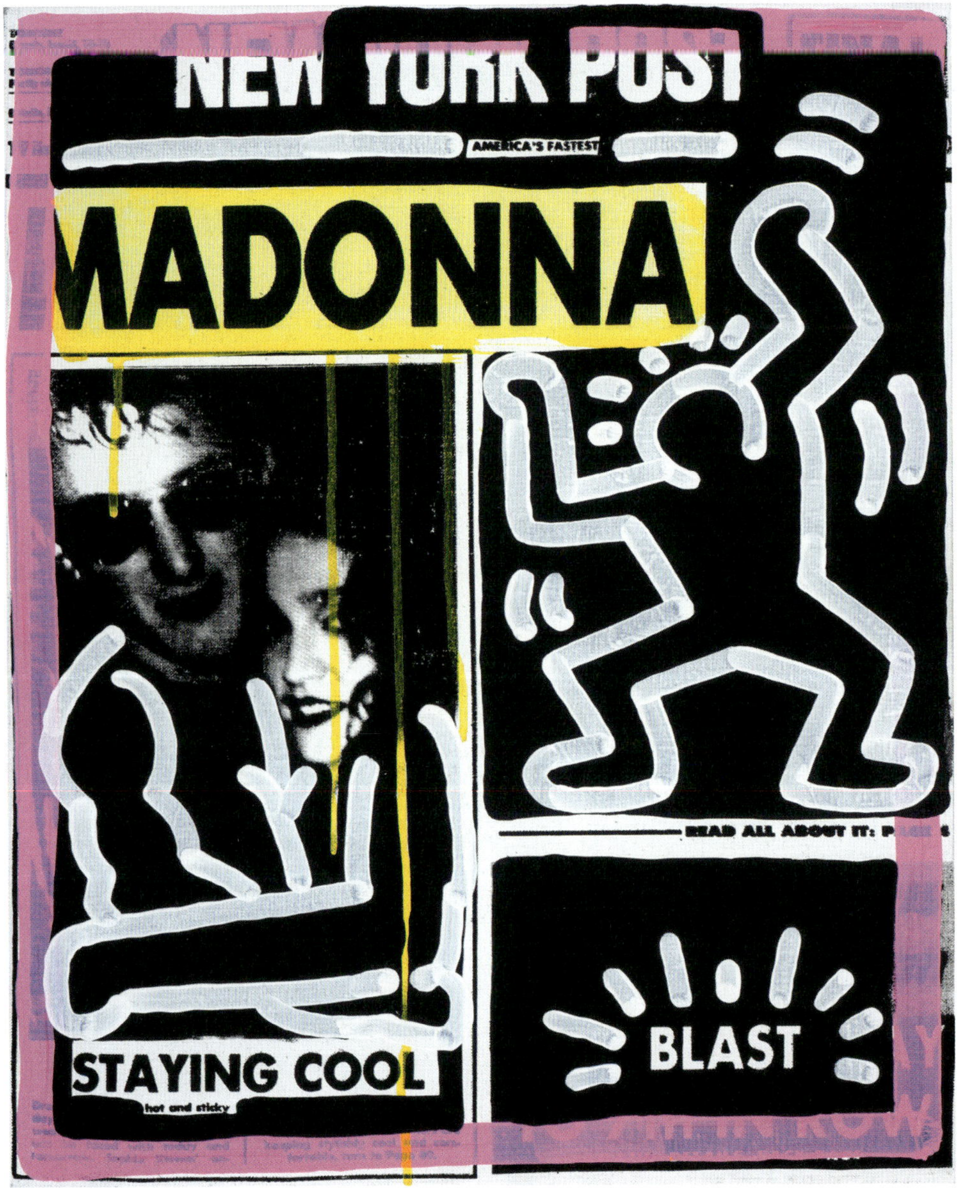

ANDY WARHOL AND KEITH HARING
Untitled (New York Post *Front Page—Madonna)*
1984–85

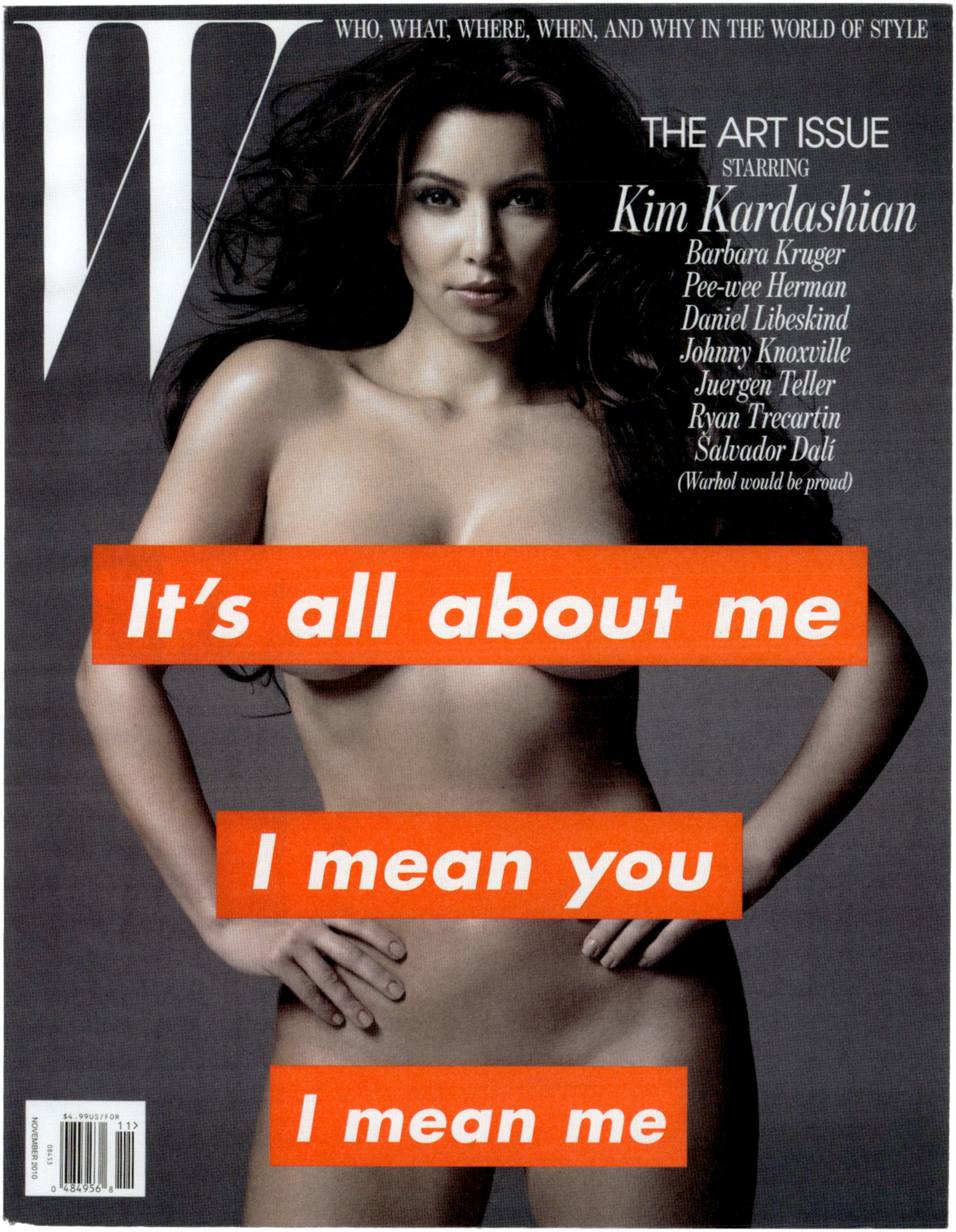

BARBARA KRUGER
"It's All About Me," front cover of *W* magazine, featuring Kim Kardashian
November 2010
(Photograph: Mark Seliger)

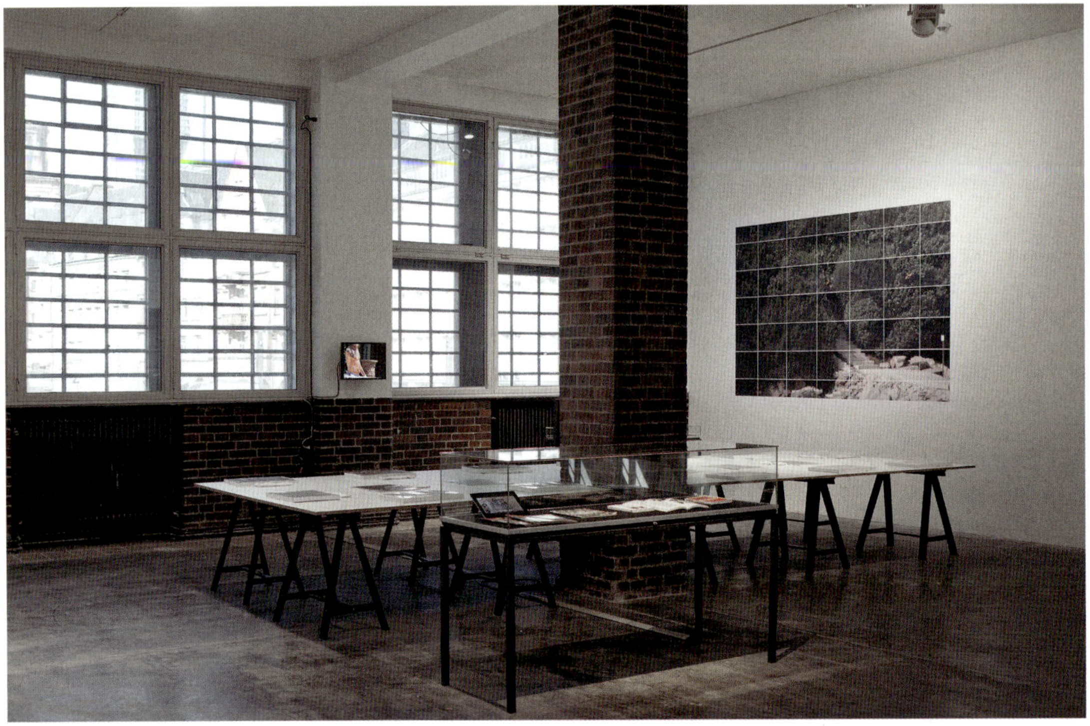

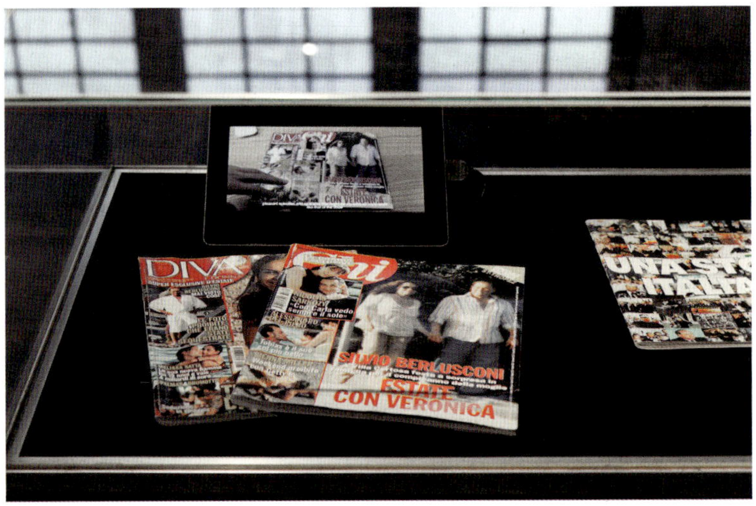

ARMIN LINKE
Paparazzi—What Is Revealed Is the Obviousness of the Visibility to the Others,
installation views
2012

ARMIN LINKE. Born in 1966, Armin Linke divides his time between Berlin and Milan. His installation entitled *Paparazzi*, composed of photographs, videos, and documents, challenges the relationship between media and politics. Analyzing Silvio Berlusconi's orchestration of the Italian media, he targets the complicity that exists between politicians and paparazzi. Armin Linke unveils the political and economic backdrop of a market system that is based on the power of images. He also studies the forms of these photographs. A new language is emerging from this surge of media propaganda, a vocabulary not so different from that of film or dance. The repetitive nature of these sequences gives us food for thought on the medium of photography itself. They are all elements that can be used to assess the relevance and challenges of the paparazzi aesthetic.

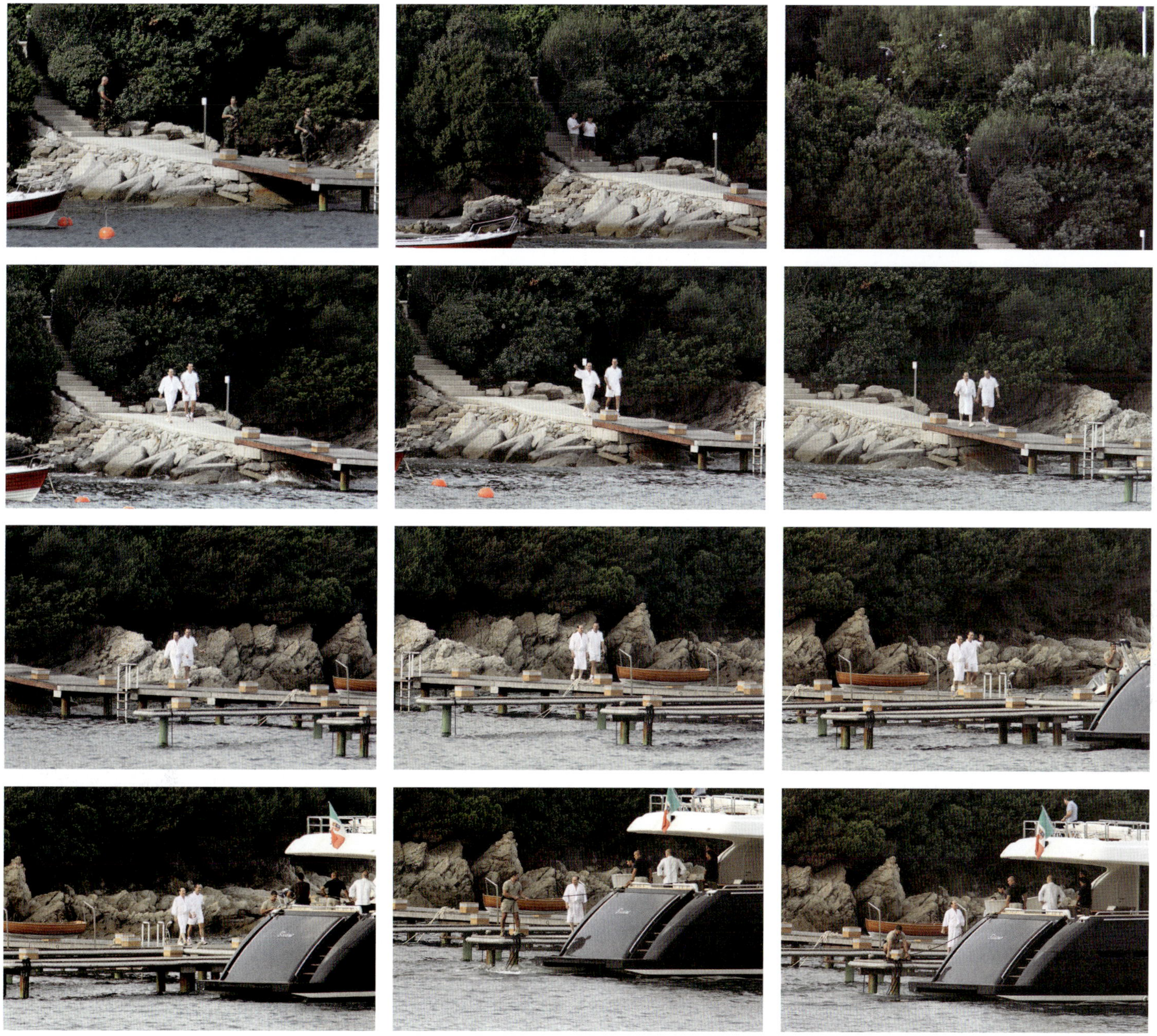

CORRADO CALVO
Silvio Berlusconi,
Villa Certosa
2009

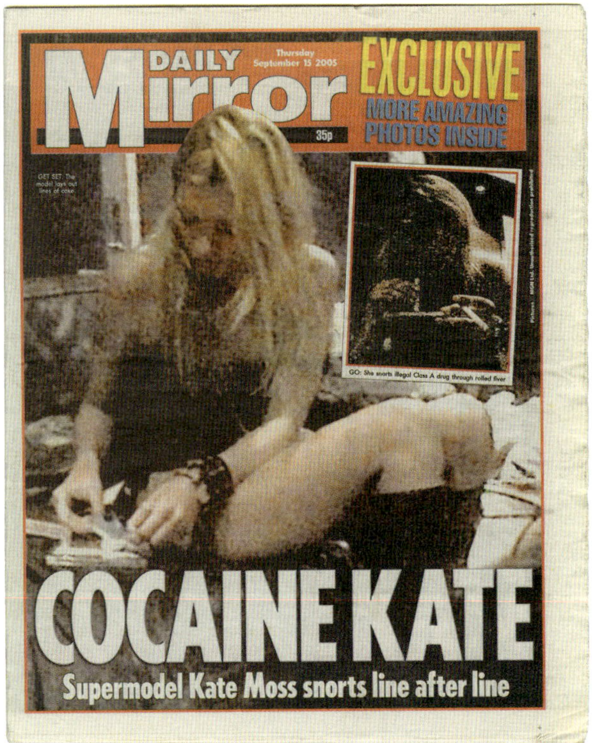

"Cocaine Kate," *Daily Mirror*, September 15, 2005, front page (Photograph: anonymous)

JONATHAN HOROWITZ. An American artist born in 1966, Jonathan Horowitz lives and works in New York. Active in the realms of sculpture, video, installation, and photography, he casts a critical eye over a hyperconsumerist society and its modes of communication. In his 2006 work entitled *Daily Mirror*, he hijacked the cover of the eponymous newspaper dated September 15, 2005, which had printed a photo of the model Kate Moss caught snorting cocaine at a private party. He had the graphics and headline typeface of the newspaper silk-screened onto a mirror. The viewer standing in front of the work becomes the subject featured on the front page—in other words, a star. Through this aptly named "daily mirror," the artist invites us into a speculative game where multiple levels of meaning intersect in the space between the public and private spheres.

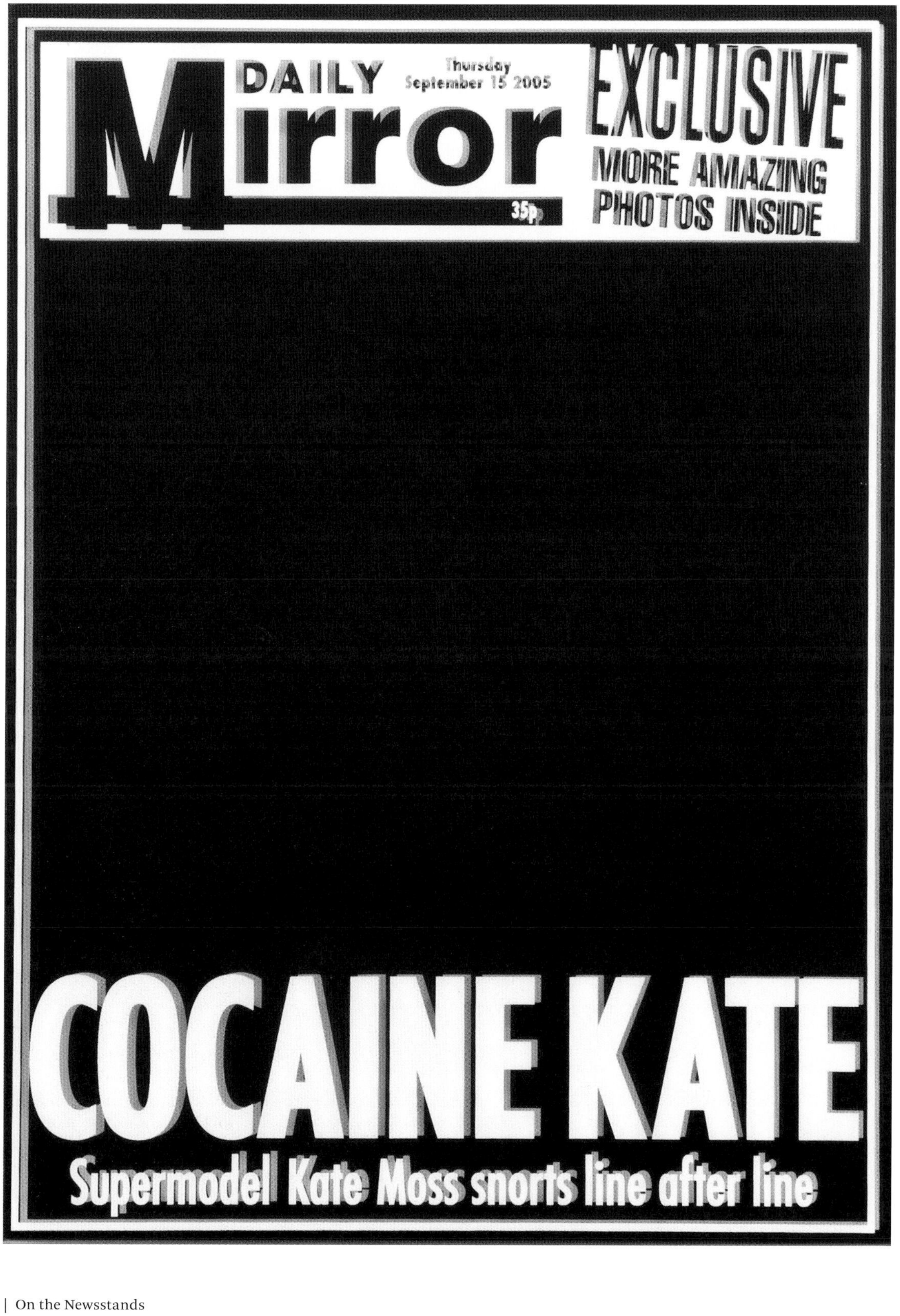

JONATHAN HOROWITZ
Daily Mirror
2006

APPENDI

XES

Bibliography

PERSONAL ACCOUNTS

ABENHAIM, William
Profession paparazzo
Paris: Nouveau Monde éditions, 2009

ANGELI, Daniel
Objectif Une: souvenirs d'un photographe de stars
Foreword by Raymond Depardon
Neuilly-sur-Seine: Michel Lafon, 2010

BARTOLONI, Adriano
Le Pape: dans l'intimité d'un homme
Paris: Robert Laffont, 2001

BUREAU, Henri
"Paparazzi," Bouclages: une vie de reporter
Paris: Florent Massot, 2010

CHICH, Jean-Paul
Paparazzo 1er
Lyon: Jacques André éditeur, 2009

COLIN, Jacques
Voilà! 1663 jours dans les coulisses de Voici
Paris: Ramsay, 2002

ELTERMAN, Brad
Shoot the Stars: How to Become a Celebrity Photographer
Beverly Hills: California Features, 1985

FOX, Joshua
Confessions of a Paparazzo: Some Call It Stalking, I Call It Love
Kindle e-book, 2012

HENROTTE, Hubert
(in collaboration with Jean-Louis Gazignaire)
Le Monde dans les yeux: Gamma-Sygma, l'âge d'or du photojournalisme
Paris: Hachette Littératures, 2005

LHOTE, Gilles
Voleurs d'images: les dessous des scoops
Paris: Michel Lafon, 1995

LYONS, Darryn
Mr Paparazzi: My Life As the World's Most Outrageous Celebrity Photographer
London: John Blake, 2008

MOURON, Bruno
ROSTAIN, Pascal
(in collaboration with Hervé Prudon)
Paparazzi: chasseurs de stars
Paris: Michel Lafon, 1988

MOURON, Bruno
ROSTAIN, Pascal
(in collaboration with Guy Benhamou)
Scoop: révélations sur les secrets d'actualité
Paris: Flammarion, 2007

POIVRE D'ARVOR, Patrick
Lettre ouverte aux violeurs de vie privée
Paris: Albin Michel, 1996

SALOMON, Erich
"Une documentation unique à conserver. Les plus extraordinaires photographies du docteur Salomon, le 'roi des indiscrets'"
In BAQUÉ, Dominique, Les Documents de la modernité: anthologie de textes sur la photographie de 1919 à 1939
Nîmes: Jacqueline Chambon, 1993

SOPOGLIAN, Fabrice
Confessions d'un paparazzi: d'après une histoire vraie
Nice: France Europe éditions, 2007

YOUNG, Richard
(with Sally Moulsdale)
Paparazzo! The Photographs of Richard Young
London: Virgin, 1989

STUDIES

1. Works on paparazzi

BONITO OLIVA, Achille
FACCIOLI, Davide
A Flash of Art: Action Photography in Rome, 1953–1973
Milan: Photology, 2004

BURGESS, Anthony
(Introduction)
ANGELI, Daniel
DOUSSET, Jean-Paul
(Photographs)
Private Pictures
New York: Viking Press, 1980

COSTANTINI, Paolo (ed.)
Paparazzi, Fotografie 1953–1964, exh. cat.
Florence: Alinari, 1988

DALTON, D. M.
"Historical Look at the Paparazzi Phenomenon of the Twentieth Century"
Master's thesis in performance arts, submitted in 2000 to San Jose State University, under the supervision of Kimb Massey

GREBE, Stefanie
SCHNEIDER, Sigrid
(eds.)
Wirklich Wahr! Realitatsversprechen von Fotografien, exh. cat.
Essen: Ruhrlandmuseum / Ostfildern-Ruit: Hatje Cantz, 2004

HOWE, Peter
Paparazzi: And Our Obsession with Celebrity
New York: Artisan, 2005

MATUSEK, Piros
Paparazzo or Journalist? The Role of Corpus Linguistics in the 21st Century
Sarrebruck: VDM Verlag, 2009

PINKUS, Karen
The Montesi Scandal: The Death of Wilma Montesi and the Birth of Paparazzi in Fellini's Rome
Chicago: University of Chicago Press, 2003

TARONI, Francesca
Paparazzi
Translated by Gilles Schaufelberger
Paris: Assouline, 1998

2. Articles on paparazzi

ANCERY, Pierre
GUILLET, Clément
"Le monde selon Oops!: nos conseils pour réussir un bon journal people"
Slate, August 21, 2012
http://www.slate.fr/story/59323/recettes-presse-people

BALAKRISHNAN, Angela
"The Press Pack That Chased Diana"
The Guardian, April 7, 2008

BOGGIO, Philippe
"Enquête au pays des scoops"
Le Monde, November 18, 1988

CARR, David
"Hot Photos, High Prices for Paparazzi"
The New York Times Arts & Styles / Le Monde, November 10 and 11, 2002

COCHRANE, Kira
"Creepshots and Revenge Porn: How Paparazzi Culture Affects Women"
The Guardian, September 22, 2012

DIFORTI, Massimo
"Flash Warning: The Paparazzi Are Coming"
Aperture, no. 132 (1993): 20–25

FOSSARD, Aurore
"La blonde plantureuse sous l'objectif du paparazzi: évolution d'un sujet cinématographique"
Culturevisuelle, July 3, 2012
http://culturevisuelle.org/paparazzi/archives/32

FOSSARD, Aurore
"Britney contre l'homme-machine"
Culturevisuelle, February 17, 2012
http://culturevisuelle.org/paparazzi/archives/21

FOSSARD, Aurore
"Du photoreporter au paparazzi: genèse d'une "personnagification"
Culturevisuelle, February 10, 2012
http://culturevisuelle.org/paparazzi/archives/9

GIRARD, Laurence
"Dans les pas des paparazzi"
Le Monde, June 3, 2008

GUERRIN, Michel
"Chasse à l'homme privé"
Le Monde, September 24, 1996

GUERRIN, Michel
"Felice Quinto"
Le Monde, February 14 and 15, 2010

GUERRIN, Michel
"Paparazzi"
In GUERRIN, Michel, *Profession photoreporter. Vingt ans d'images d'actualité*
Paris: Centre Pompidou / Gallimard, 1988, 212–27

GUERRIN, Michel
"La presse à scandales a relancé le phénomène des paparazzi"
Le Monde, September 2, 1997

GUILLOT, Claire
"Un paparazzi au musée"
Le Monde, July 10 and 11, 2011

JOUBERT, Flora
"L'insaisissable: archéologie de la photographie de paparazzi dans le magazine *Cinémonde* (1928–1940)"
Histoire de l'art, no. 70 (May 2012): 93–102

KOESTENBAUM, Wayne
"Shooting Stars"
Artforum International, no. 36 (November 1997): 9–10

NAUDET, Jean-Jacques
"Paparazzi!"
Photo, no. 122 (September 1977)

PHILLIPS, Sandra S.
"Celebrity and the Public Gaze"
In PHILLIPS, Sandra S., (ed.), *Exposed: Voyeurism, Surveillance, and the Camera Since 1870*, exh. cat.
London: Tate Publishing, 2010, 89–92

POIRIER, Agnès-Catherine
"L'âge d'or des paparazzi"
Libération, August 21, 2004

PRAT, Louis
"De l'actualité des célébrités aux photographies volées"
Le Monde, November 4, 2003

REVEL, Renaud
"Paparazzi, un métier en voie de disparition?"
L'Express, May 19, 2011

ROLLAT, Alain
"Les Pitbulls"
Le Monde, September 2, 1997

SANDBYE, Mette
"Paparazzien er kommet for at blive"
In GREVE, Irene, Vidnerne historien: dansk pressefotografi i 100 år
Copenhagen: Pressefotografforbundet, 2012

SATTA, Gloria
"The Buzz About Paparazzi: Marcello Mastroianni Remembers Working With Federico Fellini and Tazio Secchiaroli, the First Paparazzo"
Aperture, no. 150 (1998)

SCHWARTZ, Vanessa R.
"Grand angle sur la plage"
Études photographiques, no. 26 (November 2010)

SEKULA, Allan
"Paparazzo Notes,"
In SEKULA, Allan, (ed.), *Photography Against the Grain: Essays and Photo Works 1973–1983*
Halifax: The Press of the Nova Scotia College of Art and Design, 1984, 23–31

SPINDLER, Amy M.
"Fashion's Affair with the Paparazzi"
The New York Times, September 9, 1997

SQUIERS, Carol
"Class Struggle: The Invention of Paparazzi Photography and the Death of Diana, Princess of Wales"
In SQUIERS, Carol, (ed.), *Over Exposed: Essays on Contemporary Photography*
New York: The New Press, 1999, 269–303

SQUIERS, Carol
"Original Sin: The Birth of the Paparazzo"
In PHILLIPS Sandra S., (ed.), *Exposed: Voyeurism, Surveillance, and the Camera Since 1870*, exh. cat.
London: Tate Publishing, 2010, 220–27

TASSEL, Fabrice
"La presse *people* punie en une"
Libération, October 28, 1997

TOURANCHEAU, Patricia
"Chasseurs de scoops, pas tueurs de stars"
Libération, September 4 and 5, 1999

ZANNIER, Italo
"Un fotografo chiamato paparazzo"
Fotologia, no. 7 (1987): 39–90

3. Works and articles on the star system and celebrities

BARDELOT, Estelle
"Lire la 'presse people'"
Dissertation for a postgraduate degree in information and communications science, submitted in September 1999 at the Université Lyon II , under the supervision of Jean-François Tétu

BECKMANN, Anne-Marie (ed.)
Making History, exh. cat.
Frankfurt: Frankfurter Kunstverein / Ostfildern-Ruit, Hatje Cantz, 2012

BOORSTIN, Daniel J.
The Image: A Guide to Pseudo-Events in America
New York: Atheneum, 1987. First published 1962

GENESTAR, Alain
Artistes et stars par les photographes de Paris Match, exh. cat.
Levallois-Perret: Filipacchi / Paris: Culturespaces, 2006

HADEN-GUEST, Anthony
KUMMER, Niels
QUINTO, Felice
Studio 54: The Legend
Kempen: teNeues, 1997

HEIFERMAN, Marvin
KISMARIC, Carole
Fame After Photography, exh. cat.
New York: The Museum of Modern Art, 1999

HEINICH, Nathalie
De la visibilité. Excellence et singularité en régime médiatique
Paris: Gallimard, 2012

HENDERSON, Amy
"Media and the Rise of Celebrity Culture"
Organization of American Historians Magazine of History 6, no. 4 (Spring 1992): 49–54

HINERMAN, Stephen
LULL, James
Media Scandals: Morality and Desire in the Popular Culture Marketplace
New York: Columbia University Press, 1997

LUTAUD, Léna
DROMARD, Thiébault
Les Dessous de la presse people
Paris: Éditions de La Martinière, 2006

MACMILLAN, Katie
EDWARDS, Derek
Who Killed the Princess? Description and Blame in the British Press
Loughborough: Loughborough University, 1998

MARION, Philippe
"Petite phénoménologie de la photo people"
Communication 27, no. 1 (2009)

MENDELSON, Andrew L.
"On the Function of the United States Paparazzi: Mosquito Swarm or Watchdogs of Celebrity Image Control and Power"
Visual Studies 22, no. 2 (September 2007): 169–83

RUGOFF, Ralph
The Painting of Modern Life: 1960s to Now, exh. cat.
London: Hayward Gallery Publishing, 2007

THOMPSON, Douglas
"The Liberation of Jackie O"
The Times, November 7, 2009

WALKER, John A.
Art and Celebrity
London: Pluto Press, 2002

WALLS, Jeanette
Dish: How Gossip Became the News and the News Became Just Another Show
New York: Perennial, 2000

4. Documentaries on paparazzi

GAST, Leon
Smash His Camera
New York: Magnolia Pictures, Home Box Office, 2010, 87 min.

GRENIER, Adrian
Teenage Paparazzo
New York: Reckless Productions, 2010, 91 min.

DEPARDON, Raymond
Reporters
Clamart: Palmeraie et désert / Paris: BPI Centre Pompidou, 1981, 90 min.

WORKS on the photographers and artists presented in this exhibition

Valerio ADAMI

ALBORCH, Bataller Carmen et al.
Adami, exh. cat.
Valencia: IVAM, Generalitat Valenciana, 1991

GLUSBERG, Jorge
Valerio Adami en el Museo Nacional de Bellas Artes de Buenos Aires, exh. cat.
Milan: Skira, 1998

PACQUEMENT, Alfred et al.
Adami, exh. cat.
Paris: Centre Pompidou, 1985

PADOVANO-FRIEDMAN, Alisa
Valerio Adami, exh. cat.
Tel Aviv: Tel Aviv Museum of Art, 1997

Daniel ANGELI

ANGELI, Daniel
Plus près des étoiles
Preface by Raymond Depardon
Neuilly-sur-Seine: Michel Lafon, 2010

HEBEL, François
DEPARDON, Raymond et al.
Rencontres d'Arles 2006: 37th edition, exh. cat.
Arles: Actes Sud, 2006

PHILIPPE, Bénédicte
"Le premier paparazzi"
Télérama, June 6, 2012

POLI, Elisa
"Storia di un paparazzo"
La Reppublica, June 8, 2012

POLI, Elisa
"Daniel Angeli: les icones du maître du genre"
Le Journal de la photographie, June 6, 2012, accessed March 18, 2013
http://lejournaldelaphotographie.com/archives/by_date/2012-06-06/6997/daniel-angeli-les-icones-du-maitre-du-genre (site discontinued)

Malin ARNESSON

BERG, Erik
AILLY, Stella d'
Masters of Fine Art Graduate Show 2008, exh. cat.
Umeå: Academy of Fine Arts, 2008, 10–17

Richard AVEDON

STEVENS, Norma (ed.)
Avedon Fashion, exh. cat.
New York: International Center of Photography / Paris: Éditions de La Martinière, 2009

François-Marie BANIER

BANIER, François-Marie (ed.)
Francois-Marie Banier, exh. cat.
Paris: Maison européenne de la photographie / Gallimard, 2003

BANIER, François-Marie
Samuel Beckett
Göttingen: Steidl, 2009

MOBILIO, Albert
"Beckett: Photographs by François-Marie Banier"
Bookforum, April–May 2010

NAKAZAWA, Shinichi
ORGEVAL, Martin d'
François-Marie Banier, exh. cat.
Tokyo: Tokyo Metropolitan Museum of Photography / Asahi Shimbun, 2000

ORGEVAL, Martin d' (ed.)
Banier: perdre la tête, exh. cat.
Rome: Villa Médicis / Paris: Gallimard, 2005

PALAZZOLI, Daniela
STELLA, Dominique
François-Marie Banier, exh. cat.
Milan: Fondazione Mudima, 2000

Julián BARÓN

BARÓN, Julián
CENSURA
Mexico: Editorial RM, 2011

Christophe BEAUREGARD

THÉL, Nicolas
"Photographe des passions ordinaires"
on the artist's personal website, accessed May 15, 2013
http://www.christophe-beauregard.com/publications.php?id_page=6

Viktoria BINSCHTOK

BINSCHTOK, Viktoria
World of Details
Berlin: Distanz Verlag / Gestalten, 2013

BINSCHTOK, Viktoria (photographs)
HARDER, Matthias
BENN MICHAELS, Walter (text)
Viktoria Binschtok: Suspicious Minds, exh. cat.
Berlin: Klemm's, 2009

Gary Lee BOAS

BOAS, Gary Lee
Celebrity
Amsterdam: Reflex, 2008

BOAS, Gary Lee
New York Sex, 1979–1985
Paris: Kamel Mennour, 2003

BOAS, Gary Lee (photographs)
MCCORMICK, Carlo (text)
Starstruck: Photographs from a Fan
Los Angeles: Dilettante Press, 1999

HAINLEY, Bruce
"Gary Lee Boas: Karyn Lovegrove Gallery"
Artforum International 44, no. 2 (October 1, 2005)

JOHNSON, Ken
"Art in Review; Gary Lee Boas 'Starstruck'"
The New York Times, February 18, 2000

RUGOFF, Ralph
"Gary Lee Boas' Starstruck: Photographs from a Fan"
Frieze, no. 52 (May 2000)

Sophie CALLE

CALLE, Sophie
Doubles-jeux (livre IV): A suivre...: Préambule, Suite vénitienne, La Filature
Arles: Actes Sud, 1998

CALLE, Sophie
BESSON, Christian (afterword)
Sophie Calle, book by the artist designed for the exhibition
Nevers: Association pour l'art contemporain, 1985

CLOT, Manel
GUIBERT, Hervé
Sophie Calle: Relatos, exh. cat.
Barcelona: Fundación La Caixa, 1996

MACEL, Christine (ed.)
Sophie Calle. M'as-tu vue?, exh. cat.
Paris: Centre Pompidou / Xavier Barral, 2003

Raymond DEPARDON

LARDEAU, Yann
"Dramaturgie de la photo"
Cahiers du cinéma, no. 326 (July–August 1981): 58–59

LE PERON, Serge
"L'oeil du reporter"
Cahiers du cinéma, no. 306 (December 1979): 20–22

TOUBIANA, Serge
"Reporters. Le photographe sur le qui-vive"
Cahiers du cinéma, no. 326 (July–August 1981): iii, iv, vi

Georges DUDOGNON

DUDOGNON, Georges (photographs)
GÉLIN, Daniel (text)
Comme on s'aimait à Saint-Germain-des-Près
Paris: Bordas, 1993

Brad ELTERMAN

ELTERMAN, Brad
Like It Was Yesterday
Los Angeles: Seventy Seven Press, 2010

Malachi FARRELL

Culture Meets Culture, Korea Busan Biennale, exh. cat.
Busan: Busan Biennale, 2002

DINKLA, Söke
MAGNAGUAGNO, Guido
PAKESCH, Peter
et al.
Bewegliche Teile: Formen des Kinetischen / Moving Parts: Forms of the Kinetic, exh. cat.
Cologne: Walther König, 2004

FRANCBLIN, Catherine
MACEL, Christine
Malachi Farrell, l'art à état vif. Entretien avec Malachi Farrell
December 13, 2007, accessed May 15, 2013
http://fondationentreprise-ricard.com/conferences/entretiens/art/malachi_farrell/

GRIM, Ruth
Shortcuts between Reality and Fiction: Video, Installations and Painting from Le Fonds national d'art contemporain
Miami Beach: Bass Museum of Art, 2005

SCHAFHAUSEN, Nicolaus (ed.)
Neue Welt, exh. cat.
Frankfurt: Frankfurter Kunstverein / Berlin, Lukas & Sternberg Inc., 2001

Federico FELLINI

STOURDZÉ, Sam (ed.)
Federico Fellini. La Dolce Vita, l'album
Paris: Fondation Jérôme Seydoux-Pathé / Xavier Barral, 2009

STOURDZÉ, Sam
Fellini. La Grande Parade, exh. cat.
Paris: Jeu de Paume / Anabet, 2009

Henry FLORES

FLORES, Henry
A Day in the Life of the Paparazzi
Manchester: Out Of Sight Media, LLC (printed on demand), 2011

FLORES, Henry
Alluring Desire
Manchester: Out Of Sight Media, LLC (printed on demand)

FLORES, Henry
My Plastic Camera
Manchester: Out Of Sight Media, LLC (printed on demand)

Ron GALELLA

BLUTTAL, Steven (ed.)
The Photographs of Ron Galella
New York: Greybull Press, 2002

GALELLA, Ron
Jackie: My Obsession
New York: Ron Galella Ltd., 2012

GALELLA, Ron
No Pictures
New York: Powerhouse Books, 2008

GALELLA, Ron
Off-Guard: A Paparazzo Look at the Beautiful People
New York: McGraw-Hill, 1976

HOFFMAN, Felix (ed.)
Ron Galella: paparazzo extraordinaire!, exh. cat.
Ostfildern-Ruit: Hatje Cantz, 2011

Settimio GARRITANO

GARRITANO, Settimio (photographs)
SCARAFFIA, Giuseppe (text)
Un Mito nel mito. Jacqueline a Capri
Capri: La Conchiglia, 2011

Marcello GEPPETTI

BARABERA, Alberto
CASELLI, Stefano (introduction)
KEZICH, Tullio
MOLITERNI, Rocco (text)
Glianni della dolce vita: fotografie di Marcello Geppetti e Arturo Zavattini, exh. cat.
Turin: Museo nazionale del Cinema / Fondazione Solares, 2010

GEPPETTI, Marcello (photographs)
MALIPIERO, Ana Maria (text)
Paparazzo senza tregua
Paris: Librairie Serge Plantureux, 2007

Michel GINIÈS

GINIÈS, Michel
Promenades
Paris: Dreamland, 2002

GINIÈS, Michel (preface)
SOLAL, Isabelle (ed.)
Icônes: 1960–1990
Paris: Hugo & Cie, 2006

G.R.A.M.

G.R.A.M. (photographs)
BRAUN, Reinhard
FRANCK, Georg
SBELIG, Thomas (text)
Paparazzi, exh. cat.
Salzburg: Fotohof, 2009

MATRAY, Maxime
G.R.A.M., Côte noire, exh. cat.
Nice: Villa Arson / Centre national des arts plastiques, 1998

PIJARSKI, Krzysztof
"G.R.A.M.: Gestures of Ironic Profanation / Gesten ironischer Profanierung"
Camera Austria International, no. 119 (2012): 27–38

STADLER, Eva Maria
TRUMME, R. Thomas (eds.)
G.R.A.M.
Vienna: Osterreichische Galerie Belvedere / Graz: Grazer Kunstverein, 1997

ULRICH, Wolfgang
G.R.A.M., Reenactements 1998–2011
Barcelona: Poligrafa, 2011

Kathrin GÜNTER

GREBE, Stefanie
SCHNEIDER, Sigrid (eds.)
Wirklich Wahr! Realitatsversprechen von Fotografien, exh. cat.
Essen: Ruhrlandmuseum / Ostfildern-Ruit: Hatje Cantz, 2004

GÜNTER, Kathrin
Star Shots
Newmilns: Aglu, 2012

SCHUBART, Rikke
Hollywood Revisited: Aarhus Kunstmuseum, exh. cat.
Aarhus: ARoS Aarhus Kunstmuseum, 2002

WIEHAGER, Renate (ed.)
Moving Pictures: Photography and Film in Contemporary Art
Ostfildern-Ruit: Hatje Cantz, 2001

Richard HAMILTON

WILSON, Andrew
Richard Hamilton Swingeing London 67 (f)
London: Afterall Books, 2011

Jonathan HOROWITZ

BIESENBACH, Klaus (ed.)
Jonathan Horowitz: And/Or, exh. cat.
New York: PS1 Contemporary Art Center / Zurich: JRP|Ringier, 2009

CRAM, Gabrielle
ZYMAN, Daniela
Other Than Yourself: An Investigation Between Inner and Outer Space, exh. cat.
Vienna: Thyssen-Bornemisza Art Contemporary / Cologne: Walther König, 2008

Alison JACKSON

JACKSON, Alison
Kate and Wills Up the Aisle: A Right Royal Fairy Tale
London: Quadrille Publishing Ltd, 2011

JACKSON, Alison
Private
London: Penguin Books, 2003

JACKSON, Alison (photographs)
SELF, Will (text)
Confidential
Cologne: Taschen, 2007

Johannes KAHRS

BEAUMELLE, Agnès de la
Collection art graphique. La collection du Centre Pompidou, Musée national d'art moderne
Paris: Centre Pompidou, 2008, 517

BLANCKAERT, Amélie
"L'essentiel en jeu. 1903–2003: le centenaire de la Société des amis du Musée national d'art moderne"
Les Cahiers du Musee national d'art moderne, no. 86 (Winter 2003–2004): 110

DUPLAIX, Sophie (ed.)
Collection art contemporain. La collection du Centre Pompidou, Musée national d'art moderne
Paris: Centre Pompidou, 2007, 240

RUGOFF, Ralph
Johannes Kahrs
Ostfildern-Ruit: Hatje Cantz, 2009

William KLEIN

KLEIN, William (photographs)
Mode In & Out
Paris: Seuil, 1994

SAYAG, Alain
BAJAC, Quentin (eds.)
William Klein, exh. cat.
Paris: Centre Pompidou / Marval, 2005

Barbara KRUGER

ALBERRO, Alexander
et al.
Barbara Kruger
New York: Rizzoli, 2010

Alexi LUBOMIRSKI

LUBOMIRSKI, Alexi
Alexi Lubomirski – Decade
Bologna: Damiani Editore, forthcoming March 2014

Ulf LUNDIN

BRIND, Susan
MCKENZIE, Ray
SUTTON, Damian
The State of the Real: Aesthetics in the Digital Age
London: IB Tauris, 2007, 32

KARALLUS, Christine
"Ulf Lundin: Pictures of a Family"
In FROHNE Ursula, LEVIN Thomas Y., WEIBEL Peter (eds.)
CTRL [SPACE]: Rhetorics of Surveillance from Bentham to Big Brother, exh. cat.
Karlsruhe: Zentrum fur Kunst und Medientechnologie / Cambridge (Mass.): MIT Press, 2002, 310–11

LUNDIN, Ulf
BLANK, Gil
"Pictures of a Family: Gil Blank and Ulf Lundin in Conversation"
Influence, no. 1 (2003): 92–111

TOZER, John
"Annelies Strba/Ulf Lundin"
Art Monthly, no. 223 (February 1999): 26–28

Paul MCCARTHY

PHILLIPS, Lisa (introduction)
CAMERON, Dan
JONES, Amelia
VIDLER, Anthony (text)
Paul McCarthy, exh. cat.
Ostfildern-Ruit: Hatje Cantz, 2000

RITTER, Peter
"Let's Entertain: Sex, Celebrity, and Television"
Flash Art, no. 214 (October 2000): 98–99

ROSENBERG, Jeremy
"Los Angeles: Paul McCarthy"
Art and Auction, November 1, 2000

RUGOFF, Ralph
STILES, Kristine
DI PIETRANTONIO, Giacinto
Paul McCarthy
London: Phaidon, 1996

Olivier MIRGUET

GARANDEAU, Coralie
"Les cachots secrets d'Hassan II"
Libération, June 9, 2005

GUERRIN, Michel
"Olivier Mirguet dans la Maison ronde"
Le Monde, April 30, 2005

Bruno MOURON and Pascal ROSTAIN

DEMOULE, Jean-Paul (text)
MOURON, Bruno
ROSTAIN, Pascal (photographs)
Autopsie
Paris: Editions de La Martinière, 2013

GUERRIN, Michel
"Bruno Mouron et Pascal Rostain: paparazzis de haut vol"
Le Monde, March 14, 2007

LIZE, Hubert
"Exposition: les 400 coups des paparazzis"
Le Parisien, September 14, 2012

MOURON, Bruno
REGNAULT, Christophe
ROSTAIN, Pascal
Chasseurs de scoops. L'histoire vraie des photos qui ont secoué la République
Issy-les-Moulineaux: Glenat, 2012

MOURON, Bruno
ROSTAIN, Pascal (photographs)
GARNER, Philippe (preface)
Famous
Paris: Robert Laffont, 2012

MOURON, Bruno
ROSTAIN, Pascal (photographs)
MALLE, Loïc (text)
Trash, exh. cat.
Paris: Maison européenne de la photographie / Editions du Regard, 2007

REVEL, Renaud
"Des poubelles et des hommes"
L'Express, March 13, 2007

Jeremiah PALECEK

"Painter Spreads Internet Memes in Oil"
NPR News, March 12, 2008
http://www.npr.org/templates/story/story.php?storyId=88131536

JEPPESEN, Travis
"Jeremiah Palecek @ STYX Project Space"
White Hot Magazine, September 2008
http://www.whitehotmagazine.com/index.php?action=articles&wh_article_id=1546

Jean PIGOZZI

HARDER, Matthias (text)
Pigozzi and the Paparazzi, exh. cat.
Berlin: Helmut Newton Foundation, 2008

PIGOZZI, Jean (photographs)
Catalogue déraisonné
Göttingen: Steidl, 2010

PIGOZZI, Jean (photographs)
SOTTSASS, Ettore (introduction)
A Short Visit to Planet Earth
New York: Aperture, 1991

PIGOZZI, Jean (photographs)
WENNER, Jann (introduction)
Pigozzi's Journal of the Seventies
New York: Doubleday, 1979

Barbara PROBST

IRVINE, Karen (introduction)
BATE, Davis (text)
MEINHARDT, Johannes (interview)
Barbara Probst: Exposures
Göttingen: Steidl, 2007

Terry RICHARDSON

HALLSTRÖM, Bornold Salka et al.
Fashination, exh. cat.
Stockholm: Moderna Museet, 2004

HANSON, Dian
Terryworld
Cologne: Taschen, 2004

RICHARDSON, Terry
Son of Bob
Tokyo: Little More, 1999

RICHARDSON, Terry (photographs)
MILLER, Harland (text)
Feared by Men, Desired by Women
Chicago: Guiding Light, 2000

Gerhard RICHTER

BLOCK, René
VOGEL, Carl (text)
Grafik des Kapitalistischen Realismus
Berlin: René Block, 1971, 144

GODFREY, Mark
SEROTA, Nicholas (eds.)
Gerhard Richter, Panorama, exh. cat.
Paris: Centre Pompidou, 2012

MOORHOUSE, Paul
Gerhard Richter Portraits. Painting Appearances, exh. cat.
London: National Portrait Gallery, 2009

PAOLETTI, John T.
"Gerhard Richter: Ambiguity as an Agent of Awareness"
Print Collectors' Newsletter 19, no. 1 (March–April 1988): 1–6

STORR, Robert
Gerhard Richter: Forty Years of Painting, exh. cat.
New York: The Museum of Modern Art, 2002

Tate Gallery: Illustrated Catalogue of Acquisitions 1986–88
London: Tate Publishing, 1996

Alicia ROSS

MASSIER, John
Alicia Ross: Samplers, exh. cat.
Buffalo: Hallwalls Contemporary Art Center, 2007

ROSS, Alicia
Alicia Ross, 2002–2010
Blurb (printed on demand), 2010.

"Samples of Tension"
The Buffalo News, June 15, 2007

Jacques ROZIER

BURDEAU, Emmanuel
"Courts métrages"
Les Cahiers du cinéma, no. 508 (December 1996)

BURDEAU, Emmanuel (ed.)
Jacques Rozier, le funambule
Paris: Les Cahiers du cinéma / Centre Pompidou, 2001

ROZIER, Jacques
"Paparazzi, réalisation, scénario et montage de Jacques Rozier"
L'Avant-scène, double issue on Contempt, no. 412–413 (May–June 1992)

Erich SALOMON

HUNTER, Peter
Erich Salomon
New York: Aperture, 1979

MORAND, Sylvain (ed.)
Erich Salomon, 1886–1944, exh. cat.
Strasbourg: Musée d'art moderne et contemporain / Musées de Strasbourg, 2004

Jaclyn SANTOS

"Two Alumni Compete on New Bravo Series"
Maryland Institute Collage of Art (MICA), April 22, 2010, accessed May 15, 2013
http://www.mica.edu/news/two_alumni_compete_on_new_bravo_series.html

Tazio SECCHIAROLI

BENZIO, Fabio
MORMORIO, Diego
Tazio Secchiaroli, Dagli Anni della Dolce Vita Al Miti del Set, Fotografie 1958–1979
Milan: Frederico Motta Editore, 1998

BERTELLI, Giovanna
Tazio Secchiaroli. Il cinema negli occhi. Fotografie 1953–1983, exh. cat.
Reggio Calabria: Villa Genoese Zerbi, 2005

GHEZZI, Enrico
LOREN, Sophia
Tazio Secchiaroli: The Original Paparazzo, exh. cat.
Milan: Galleria Photology, 1996

MORMORIO, Diego
Tazio Secchiaroli: Greatest of the Paparazzi
New York: Harry N. Abrams Inc., 1999

MORMORIO, Diego
Tazio Secchiaroli: le photographe de la dolce vita
Arles: Actes Sud, 1998

PLANTUREUX, Serge
Tazio Secchiaroli. Cinquante épreuves originales
Paris: Serge Plantureux / Patrimoine photographique, 2000

Cindy SHERMAN

SHERMAN, Cindy
The Complete Untitled Film Stills
New York: The Museum of Modern Art, 2003

SHERMAN, Cindy
DANTO, Arthur C.
Cindy Sherman: Untitled Film Stills
Paris / Munich: Schirmer-Mosel, 1990

SHERMAN, Cindy
ROSENZWEIG, Phyllis
Cindy Sherman: Film Stills, exh. cat.
Washington, DC: Hirshhorn Museum and Sculpture Garden, 1995

Liam TICKNER

TICKNER, Liam
London 2008
Amsterdam: Gerrit Rietveld Academie, 2008

Gavin TURK

BARRETT, David
Gavin Turk
London: Royal Jelly Factory, 2004

FARQUHASON, Alex
COMPSTON, Joshua
Gavin Turk: Collected Works 1994–98, exh. cat.
London: South London Gallery / Jay Jopling / White Cube, 1998

"My Week: Gavin Turk"
The Guardian, October 11, 2009

TURK, Gavin (ed.)
COLLINS, Judith
SINCLAIR, Iain (text)
Gavin Turk
Munich / London: Prestel, 2013

WITHERS, Rachel
"Gavin Turk"
Frieze, no. 43 (November–December 1998)

Nick UT

HUTCHINSON, Bill
"From 'Napalm Girl' to a Crying Paris Hilton: Nick Ut Captures Iconic Photos"
New York Daily News, June 8, 2012
http://www.nydailynews.com/news/world/napalm-girl-cryingparis-hilton-nick-ut-captures-iconicphotos-article-1.1091579

LE SOMMIER, Régis
"Nick Ut, deux filles et notre époque dans l'objectif"
Paris Match, June 20, 2012

LUYKEN, Reiner
"Vom Kriegsreporter zum Paparazzo"
Zeitmagazin Leben, June 5, 2008

Andy WARHOL

CUEFF, Alain (ed.)
Warhol: le grand monde d'Andy Warhol, exh. cat.
Paris: RMN, 2009

DONOVAN, Molly (ed.)
Warhol Headlines, exh. cat.
Washington: National Gallery of Art / New York: Prestel, 2011

FELDMAN, Frayda
DEFENDI, Claudia
Andy Warhol Prints: A Catalogue Raisonné 1962–1987
4th ed. New York: Ronald Feldman Fine Arts / Andy Warhol Foundation for the Visual Arts / Munich: Schellman, 2003

WEEGEE

LEE, Anthony W.
MEYER, Richard
Weegee and Naked City
Berkeley: University of California Press, 2008

WEEGEE
Naked City
New York: Da Capo Press, 1975 [1945]

List of Exhibited Works and Publications

PAUL ABASCAL
Paparazzi
2007
Cinematographic film, 35 mm, color, sound (extracts)
TF1 VIDEO
Repr. p. 93

VALERIO ADAMI
Il Vecchio Timido e l'Adulterio in Piscina
1966
Acrylic on canvas, 3 ft. 3 in. × 4 ft. 2 in. (99.5 × 127 cm)
PRIVATE COLLECTION
Repr. p. 220

ALPA (camera)
KILFITT (telephoto lens)
Reflex Camera, Alpa 10D, and Kilfitt Telephoto Lens, Zoomar Sport-Fern-Kilar
c. 1968
Lens: 30 ¼ in. (770 mm), dia. 5 ½ in. (140 mm), case: 5 ¾ × 3 ¾ × 4 ½ in. (148 × 95 × 112 mm)
MUSÉE SUISSE DE L'APPAREIL PHOTOGRAPHIQUE, VEVEY, ALPA-BOURGEOIS-COLUMBERG COLLECTION
Repr. p. 41

DANIEL ANGELI
Claude François in a Car
Undated
Gelatin silver print
7 ¾ × 11 ¾ in. (20 × 30 cm)
CÉCILE ANGELI COLLECTION

Brigitte Bardot and Gunter Sachs
c. 1967
Gelatin silver print
7 ¾ × 11 ¾ in. (20 × 30 cm)
PHILIPPE GARNER COLLECTION
Repr. p. 202

Mick's Opinion: Mick Jagger at the Byblos Hotel after His Wedding with Bianca Moreno in Saint-Tropez
May 12, 1971
Gelatin silver print
11 ¾ × 7 ¾ in. (30 × 20 cm)
CÉCILE ANGELI COLLECTION
Repr. p. 172

Johnny Hallyday, Leaving a Concert
1972
Gelatin silver print
7 ¾ × 11 ¾ in. (20 × 30 cm)
CÉCILE ANGELI COLLECTION
Repr. p. 201

Caroline of Monaco
c. 1974
Gelatin silver print
3 ¾ × 5 ¾ in. (10 × 15 cm)
BIBLIOTHÈQUE NATIONALE DE FRANCE

Jacqueline Onassis in Paris
1974
Gelatin silver print
11 ¾ × 15 ¾ in. (30 × 40 cm)
CÉCILE ANGELI COLLECTION

Marlene Dietrich Attacks a Photographer [Francis Apesteguy] at Orly Airport
1975
Gelatin silver print
11 ¾ × 7 ¾ in. (30 × 20 cm)
CÉCILE ANGELI COLLECTION
Repr. p. 189

Jack Nicholson Showing His Buttocks, Saint-Tropez
July 1976
2 gelatin silver prints
7 ¾ × 11 ¾ in. (20 × 30 cm)
CÉCILE ANGELI COLLECTION

Giovanni Agnelli Diving Naked from His Boat off the Shore of Saint-Tropez
1977
Gelatin silver print
7 ¾ × 11 ¾ in. (20 × 30 cm)
CÉCILE ANGELI COLLECTION

Brigitte Bardot at La Madrague, Saint-Tropez
1979
Gelatin silver print
7 ¾ × 11 ¾ in. (20 × 30 cm)
CÉCILE ANGELI COLLECTION

Elizabeth Taylor in Gstaad
December 24, 1979
Chromogenic print
7 ¾ × 11 ¾ in. (20 × 30 cm)
CÉCILE ANGELI COLLECTION
Repr. p. 108

Brigitte Bardot at La Madrague, Saint-Tropez
July 6, 1981
Gelatin silver print
7 ¾ × 11 ¾ in. (20 × 30 cm)
CÉCILE ANGELI COLLECTION
Repr. p. 113

ANONYMOUS
(Underwood & Underwood)
The German Delegates Mueller and Bell, Leaving Versailles after Having Signed the Peace Treaty
1919
Gelatin silver print
4 ¾ × 7 ¼ in. (12.1 × 18.2 cm)
THE MUSEUM OF MODERN ART, NEW YORK
THE NEW YORK TIMES COLLECTION
Repr. p. 201

ANONYMOUS
(Fox Photos)
Reporter Hanging off Scaffolding, London
c. 1930
Gelatin silver print
9 ½ × 7 in. (24 × 18 cm)
THIERRY VALLETOUX COLLECTION
Repr. p. 31

ANONYMOUS
Photograph Taken on the Film Set of Le Gamin de Paris *by Gaston Roudès*
1932
Gelatin silver print
6 ¾ × 9 in. (17 × 23 cm)
COURTESY GALERIE LUMIÈRE DES ROSES
Repr. p. 43

ANONYMOUS
(Service des agences françaises d'actualité et de reportage associées—Service of French Associated News and Reporting Agencies)
Photographer Hiding in a Sentry Box
c. 1938
Gelatin silver print
3 ¾ × 5 ¾ in. (10 × 15 cm)
BIBLIOTHÈQUE NATIONALE DE FRANCE
Repr. p. 43

ANONYMOUS
(Keystone)
It's Not a Bazooka!
c. 1952
Gelatin silver print
3 ¾ × 5 ¾ in. (10 × 15 cm)
BIBLIOTHÈQUE NATIONALE DE FRANCE

ANONYMOUS
Michèle Morgan and Gérard Philipe
1953
Gelatin silver print
5 × 7 in. (13 × 18 cm)
ZK IMAGES GALLERY COLLECTION

ANONYMOUS
(Reporters Associati)
Group of Photographers Playing a Game While Waiting for a Star to Leave the Theater, Rome
1954
Gelatin silver print
7 ¾ × 7 ¾ in. (20 × 20 cm)
REPORTERS ASSOCIATI
Repr. p. 44

ANONYMOUS
(Reporters Associati)
Marlon Brando in Rome (Crowd of Photographers at Fiametta)
1956
Gelatin silver print
11 ¾ × 11 ¾ in. (30 × 30 cm)
REPORTERS ASSOCIATI

ANONYMOUS
(Reporters Associati)
Anita Ekberg and Anthony Steel Surprised by Photographers: Anthony Steel Fights with Two Photographers, Tazio Secchiaroli and Paolo Pavia, Via Veneto, Rome
1958
4 gelatin silver prints
7 ¾ × 7 ¾ in. (20 × 20 cm)
REPORTERS ASSOCIATI

ANONYMOUS
(Reporters Associati)
Photographers Attempting to Enter Lea Padovani's Villa during a Cocktail Party
1958
Gelatin silver print
11 ¾ × 11 ¾ in. (30 × 30 cm)
REPORTERS ASSOCIATI
Repr. p. 46

ANONYMOUS
(Reporters Associati)
Soraya Esfandiary-Bakhtiari Meets Raimondo Orsini
1958
Gelatin silver print
7 ¾ × 7 ¾ in. (20 × 20 cm)
REPORTERS ASSOCIATI

ANONYMOUS
(Pierluigi Agency)
Anita Ekberg Getting Off an Airplane
1959
Gelatin silver print
7 ¼ × 9 ½ in. (18.3 × 24 cm)
MICHEL GINIÈS COLLECTION
Repr. p. 27

ANONYMOUS
Don Gussoni and Marcello Geppetti
1959
Gelatin silver print
8 × 10 in. (20.5 × 26.2 cm)
MICHEL GINIÈS COLLECTION
Repr. p. 189

ANONYMOUS
(Reporters Associati)
Ingrid Bergman at Santa Marinella near Rome
1959
Gelatin silver print
7 ¾ × 7 ¾ in. (20 × 20 cm)
REPORTERS ASSOCIATI

ANONYMOUS
(Pierluigi Agency)
Photographers Waiting for Anita Ekberg at an Airplane Boarding Ramp
1959
Gelatin silver print
9 ¼ × 11 ¾ in. (23.7 × 30 cm)
MICHEL GINIÈS COLLECTION
Repr. p. 26

ANONYMOUS
(Reporters Associati)
Photographers Waiting for the Arrival of Soraya Esfandiary-Bakhtiari at Ciampino Airport
1959
Gelatin silver print
7 ¾ × 11 ¾ in. (20 × 30 cm)
REPORTERS ASSOCIATI
Repr. p. 42

ANONYMOUS
Reportage on the Paparazzi in Rome during the Shooting of La Dolce Vita
September 24, 1959
4 gelatin silver prints
10 ¼ × 8 in. (26.2 × 20.8 cm);
8 × 10 in. (20.8 × 25.6 cm);
10 ¼ × 8 in. (26.3 × 20.4 cm);
10 ¼ × 8 in. (26.4 × 20.8 cm)
MICHEL GINIÈS COLLECTION
Repr. p. 45

ANONYMOUS
Federico Fellini Looking at a Magazine
c. 1960
Gelatin silver print
CINETECA DEL COMUNE DI BOLOGNA, BOLOGNA
Repr. p. 73

ANONYMOUS
(United Press International)
Eddie Fisher Holding Back Elizabeth Taylor as a Car Comes Past While She Is Walking along the Via Condotti, Rome
November 10, 1960
Gelatin silver print
3 ¼ × 5 ¾ in. (10 × 15 cm)
BIBLIOTHÈQUE NATIONALE DE FRANCE

ANONYMOUS
Elizabeth Taylor and Richard Burton
March 16, 1961
Gelatin silver print
7 ¾ × 11 ¾ in. (20 × 30 cm)
COURTESY SPHINX AGENCY

ANONYMOUS
Brigitte Bardot's Apartment and Terrace
April 1961
Gelatin silver print
3 ¾ × 5 ¾ in. (15 × 10 cm)
BIBLIOTHÈQUE NATIONALE DE FRANCE

ANONYMOUS
(Report-Attualità-Fotografica)
Elizabeth Taylor, Eddie Fisher, and Richard Burton
July 16, 1962
Gelatin silver print
2 ½ × 3 ¼ in. (6.5 × 8.5 cm)
JAMES HYMAN GALLERY COLLECTION

ANONYMOUS
(Reporters Associati)
Photographers Waiting for Brigitte Bardot, Rome
1963
Gelatin silver print
7 ¾ × 7 ¾ in. (20 × 20 cm)
REPORTERS ASSOCIATI

ANONYMOUS
(Keystone)
Brigitte Bardot during the Shooting of Le Mépris (Contempt)*, Rome*
April 18, 1963
Gelatin silver print
9 ½ × 7 ¼ in. (24 × 18 cm)
PHILIPPE GARNER COLLECTION
Repr. p. 115

ANONYMOUS
Alfred Hitchcock and Tippi Hedren, Palais des Festivals, Cannes
May 11, 1963
Gelatin silver print
7 × 5 in. (18 × 12.7 cm)
ZK IMAGES GALLERY COLLECTION

ANONYMOUS
(Keystone)
Christine Keeler, Witness in the Stephen Ward Affair, Arrives at Court with Her Lawyer in a Police Car
July 24, 1963
Gelatin silver print
8 × 6 in. (20.5 × 15.2 cm)
PHILIPPE GARNER COLLECTION

ANONYMOUS
Jacqueline Kennedy
November 22, 1963
Gelatin silver print
3 ¾ × 5 ¾ in. (10 × 15 cm)
BIBLIOTHÈQUE NATIONALE DE FRANCE

ANONYMOUS
(Roma Press Photo)
Brigitte Bardot
April 14, 1964
Gelatin silver print
11 × 8 in. (27.5 × 20.8 cm)
PHILIPPE GARNER COLLECTION

ANONYMOUS
Elizabeth Taylor and Richard Burton
c. 1965
Gelatin silver print
5 ¾ × 7 ¾ in. (15 × 20 cm)
BIBLIOTHÈQUE NATIONALE DE FRANCE

ANONYMOUS
(Reporters Associés)
Brigitte Bardot
c. 1965
Gelatin silver print
6 × 9 in. (15.2 × 22.9 cm)
COURTESY JAMES HYMAN GALLERY

ANONYMOUS
Jackie Onassis
February 17, 1965
3 gelatin silver prints
7 ¾ × 11 ¾ in. and 11 ¾ × 7 ¾ in. (20 × 30 cm and 30 × 20 cm)
COURTESY SPHINX AGENCY

ANONYMOUS
(United Press International Photo)
Brigitte Bardot Resting at Her Hotel after Having Been Slightly Wounded in the Eye by the Explosion of a Photographer's Flash, New York
December 20, 1965
Gelatin silver print
3 ¾ × 5 ¾ in. (10 × 15 cm)
BIBLIOTHÈQUE NATIONALE DE FRANCE
Repr. p. 192

ANONYMOUS
Brigitte Bardot on the Set of the Film À Coeur Joie (Two Weeks in September)*, London*
September 17, 1966
Gelatin silver print
10 × 7 ½ in. (25.5 × 19 cm)
PHILIPPE GARNER COLLECTION

ANONYMOUS
Brigitte Bardot with Gunter Sachs at La Madrague, Saint-Tropez
1967
Gelatin silver print
7 ¾ × 11 ¾ in. (20 × 30 cm)
PHILIPPE GARNER COLLECTION
Repr. p. 111

ANONYMOUS
(Associated Press)
Jacqueline Onassis and Her Son John
c. 1968
Gelatin silver print
3 ¾ × 5 ¾ in. (10 × 15 cm)
BIBLIOTHÈQUE NATIONALE DE FRANCE

ANONYMOUS
(Reporters Associati)
Photographers Chased from the Restaurant Taverna Flavia, Rome
1968
Gelatin silver print
11 ¾ × 7 ¾ in. (30 × 20 cm)
REPORTERS ASSOCIATI

ANONYMOUS
(Reporters Associati)
Paparazzi Hiding in front of Gina Lollobrigida's House
1972
Gelatin silver print
7 ¾ × 11 ¾ in. (20 × 30 cm)
REPORTERS ASSOCIATI
Repr. p. 43

ANONYMOUS
(United Press International)
A Crowd Gathers in Rome around the Latest Issue of the Magazine Playmen *to Look at the Photographs of Jacqueline Onassis Naked on the Island of Skorpios*
November 1972
Gelatin silver print
3 ¾ × 5 ¾ in. (10 × 15 cm)
BIBLIOTHÈQUE NATIONALE DE FRANCE

ANONYMOUS
(Associated Press)
At a Newsagent's in Rome, a Man Looks at an Italian Magazine in which Photos of Jacqueline Onassis Naked on the Island of Skorpios Were Published
November 27, 1972
Gelatin silver print
3 ¾ × 5 ¾ in. (10 × 15 cm)
BIBLIOTHÈQUE NATIONALE DE FRANCE

ANONYMOUS
(Reporters Associati)
Photographers Fighting at Night in Rome
1973
Gelatin silver print
7 ¾ × 11 ¾ in. (20 × 30 cm)
REPORTERS ASSOCIATI

ANONYMOUS
(Bettmann Collection)
Lady Diana Spencer Walking in Kensington, London
November 22, 1980
Gelatin silver print
11 ¾ × 7 ¾ in. (30 × 20 cm)
BETTMANN/CORBIS/ASSOCIATED PRESS
Repr. p. 136

ANONYMOUS
Nicolas Cage and His Second Wife, Lisa Marie Presley
2002
Chromogenic print
11 ¾ × 7 ¾ in. (30 × 20 cm)
KCS PRESSE

ANONYMOUS
(Rex Features)
Paris Hilton Going to the Party Organized at Rogue for the Kerrang! Awards, London
August 21, 2003
Chromogenic print
8 × 6 in. (20.2 × 15.5 cm)
PHILIPPE GARNER COLLECTION

ANONYMOUS
Paris Hilton in a Bikini, Malibu
July 16, 2007
Chromogenic print
7 ¼ × 9 ½ in. (18.5 × 24 cm)
PHILIPPE GARNER COLLECTION
Repr. p. 140

ANONYMOUS
Britney Spears with No Panties
2008
Chromogenic print
7 ¾ × 11 ¾ in. (20 × 30 cm)
PRIVATE COLLECTION
Repr. p. 148

ANONYMOUS
Britney Spears with Her Boyfriend, the Paparazzo Adnan Ghalib, Studio City, California
January 14, 2008
Chromogenic print
15 ¾ × 11 ¾ in. (40 × 30 cm)
PREMIÈRE PHOTO/CAMERA PRESS/GAMMA

ANONYMOUS
Britney Spears with No Panties
February 19, 2008
Chromogenic print
11 ¾ × 7 ¾ in. (30 × 20 cm)
FAMEFLYNET/BESTIMAGE
Repr. p. 145

ANONYMOUS
Kendra Wilkinson Crying While Carrying Her Baby Out of the Super Bowl, after the Defeat of the Colts, the Team for which Her Husband, Hank Baskett, Plays
February 8, 2010
Chromogenic print
11 ¾ × 7 ¾ in. (30 × 20 cm)
MAVRIX PHOTO

FRANCIS APESTEGUY
Caroline of Monaco Taking Her Baccalauréat Exam in a High School in the West Suburbs of Paris
June 10, 1975
Gelatin silver print
7 ¾ × 11 ¾ in. (20 × 30 cm)
FRANCIS APESTEGUY COLLECTION
Repr. p. 130

Romy Schneider, Surprised while Walking Her Dog, Hides from the Camera
October 29, 1975
Gelatin silver print
15 ¾ × 11 ¾ in. (40 × 30 cm)
FRANCIS APESTEGUY COLLECTION

Brigitte Bardot on the Pontoon at La Madrague, Saint-Tropez
June 14, 1976
Gelatin silver print
7 ¾ × 11 ¾ in. (20 × 30 cm)
FRANCIS APESTEGUY COLLECTION
Repr. p. 113

Robert Redford Escaping from Photographers in Paris
September 21, 1976
Gelatin silver print
11 ¾ × 15 ¾ in. (30 × 40 cm)
FRANCIS APESTEGUY COLLECTION

Sophia Loren Sunbathing on the Terrace of Her Chalet in Megève
February 24, 1977
Gelatin silver print
7 ¾ × 11 ¾ in. (20 × 30 cm)
FRANCIS APESTEGUY COLLECTION

Reza Pahlavi, the Exiled Iranian Shah, Bathing in the Sea among Tourists at Nassau, in the Bahamas
May 20, 1979
Gelatin silver print
11 ¾ × 15 ¾ in. (30 × 40 cm)
FRANCIS APESTEGUY COLLECTION
Repr. p. 163

Madonna in the Streets of Paris, Protected By Her Bodyguards
October 10, 1992
Chromogenic print
7 ¾ × 11 ¾ in. (20 × 30 cm)
FRANCIS APESTEGUY COLLECTION

FRANCIS APESTEGUY AND PATRICK SICCOLI
(Gamma Agency)
Richard Gere
1980
7 gelatin silver prints
7 ¾ × 11 ¾ in. (20 × 30 cm) each
© POOL APESTEGUY-SICCOLI/ GAMMA RAPHO
Repr. p. 60

DARIO ARGENTO
Il Gatto a nove code (*The Cat With Nine Tails*)
1971
Cinematographic film, 35 mm, color, sound, 114 min. (extract)
WILD SIDE FILMS
Repr. p. 93

MALIN ARNESSON
Bötgoringen/The Penance
2008
(Photographs: Pelle Wikström, Gustav Mårtensson, Anders Carlsson)
3 inkjet prints
27 ½ × 39 ¼ in. (70 × 100 cm) each
MALIN ARNESSON COLLECTION
Repr. pp. 274–75

MASSIMO ASCANI
Gina Lollobrigida at the Maschere d'Argento (Silver Ribbon) Ceremony, Rome
March 29, 1962
Gelatin silver print
6 ¾ × 9 ¼ in. (17.2 × 23.8 cm)
PHILIPPE GARNER COLLECTION
Repr. p. 27

Elizabeth Taylor and Richard Burton after the Announcement of Liz's Divorce
April 3, 1962
Gelatin silver print
3 ¾ × 5 ¾ in. (10 × 15 cm)
BIBLIOTHÈQUE NATIONALE DE FRANCE

RICHARD AVEDON
Dovima, Hat by Balenciaga, Maxim's, Paris
August 1955
Gelatin silver print
18 × 14 in. (45.7 × 35.6 cm)
THE RICHARD AVEDON FOUNDATION

Mike Nichols and Suzy Parker, Suit by Dior, Paris
July 20, 1962
Gelatin silver print
11 ¾ × 15 ¾ in. (30 × 40 cm)
THE RICHARD AVEDON FOUNDATION

Suzy Parker and Mike Nichols, Dress by Lanvin-Castillo, Maxim's, Paris
July 28, 1962
Gelatin silver print
36 × 36 in. (91.4 × 91.4 cm)
THE RICHARD AVEDON FOUNDATION
Repr. p. 250

Mike Nichols and Suzy Parker, Hat by Dior, Chez Anna, Paris
July 29, 1962
Gelatin silver print
16 × 20 in. (40.6 × 50.8 cm)
THE RICHARD AVEDON FOUNDATION
Repr. p. 249

Suzy Parker and Mike Nichols, Ladies' Suit by Simonetta-Fabiani, Rue François-Ier, Paris
July 30, 1962
Gelatin silver print
14 × 18 in. (35.6 × 45.7 cm)
THE RICHARD AVEDON FOUNDATION
Repr. p. 248

Mike Nichols and Suzy Parker Rock Europe, Paris
July 31, 1962
Gelatin silver print (contact sheet)
6 ¼ × 6 ¼ in. (16 × 16 cm)
THE RICHARD AVEDON FOUNDATION
Repr. p. 250

Mike Nichols and Suzy Parker, Coat by Laroche, Bois de Boulogne, Paris
July 31, 1962
Gelatin silver print
20 × 16 in. (50.8 × 40.6 cm)
THE RICHARD AVEDON FOUNDATION

Suzy Parker and Mike Nichols, Coat by Yves Saint Laurent, American Hospital of Paris, Neuilly-sur-Seine
July 31, 1962
Gelatin silver print
20 × 19 in. (50.8 × 48.3 cm)
THE RICHARD AVEDON FOUNDATION
Repr. p. 248

FRANÇOIS-MARIE BANIER
Samuel Beckett, Paris
September 1989
9 gelatin silver prints
15 ¾ × 11 ¾ in. (40 × 30 cm) each
PRIVATE COLLECTION
Repr. pp. 228–29

JULIÁN BARÓN
C.E.N.S.U.R.A., Spain
November 2011
7 carbon prints
19 ½ × 13 ¾ in. (50 × 35 cm) each
JULIÁN BARÓN COLLECTION
Repr. pp. 236–37

CHRISTOPHE BEAUREGARD
Bois de Boulogne, from the series *Hush . . . Hush*
2013
Chromogenic print
14 × 9 ¼ in. (35.7 × 23.75 cm)
CHRISTOPHE BEAUREGARD COLLECTION
Repr. p. 69

Hôpital Européen Georges-Pompidou, Paris, from the series *Hush . . . Hush*
2013
Chromogenic print
14 × 9 ¼ in. (35.7 × 23.75 cm)
CHRISTOPHE BEAUREGARD COLLECTION
Repr. p. 68

Hôtel Lutetia, Paris, from the series *Hush . . . Hush*
2013
Chromogenic print
14 × 9 ¼ in. (35.7 × 23.75 cm)
CHRISTOPHE BEAUREGARD COLLECTION
Repr. p. 68

Town Hall, 7th Arrondissement, Paris, from the series *Hush . . . Hush*
2013
Chromogenic print
14 × 9 ¼ in. (35.7 × 23.75 cm)
CHRISTOPHE BEAUREGARD COLLECTION
Repr. p. 68

Town Hall, 7th Arrondissement, Paris, from the series *Hush . . . Hush*
2013
Chromogenic print
14 × 9 ¼ in. (35.7 × 23.75 cm)
CHRISTOPHE BEAUREGARD COLLECTION

VIKTORIA BINSCHTOK
Flash #1
2008
Lightjet print
21 ½ × 28 ¼ in. (55 × 72 cm)
COURTESY VIKTORIA BINSCHTOK AND KLEMM'S, BERLIN

Flash #2
2008
Lightjet print
3 ft. 8 in. × 5 ft. 5 in. (1.13 × 1.66 m)
COURTESY VIKTORIA BINSCHTOK AND KLEMM'S, BERLIN

Flash #3
2008
Lightjet print
3 ft. 5 in. × 4 ft. 11 in. (1.04 × 1.49 m)
COURTESY VIKTORIA BINSCHTOK AND KLEMM'S, BERLIN

Flash #4
2008
Lightjet print
2 ft. 5 in. × 3 ft. 5 in. (73 × 104 cm)
FRIEDHELM HEITLAND COLLECTION

Flash #5
2008
Lightjet print
4 ft. 2 in. × 5 ft. 11 in. (1.26 × 1.81 m)
COURTESY VIKTORIA BINSCHTOK AND KLEMM'S, BERLIN

Flash #6
2008
Lightjet print
3 ft. 1 in. × 4 ft. 5 in. (94 × 134 cm)
COURTESY VIKTORIA BINSCHTOK AND KLEMM'S, BERLIN
Repr. p. 235

Flash #7
2008
Lightjet print
2 ft. 9 in. × 3 ft. 11 in. (83 × 119 cm)
COURTESY VIKTORIA BINSCHTOK AND KLEMM'S, BERLIN

Flash #8
2008
Lightjet print
18 ½ × 26 ¼ in. (47 × 67 cm)
COURTESY VIKTORIA BINSCHTOK AND KLEMM'S, BERLIN

PHILIPPE BLET
Brangelina (Brad Pitt and Angelina Jolie) in Paris
2010
Inkjet print
15 ¾ × 19 ½ in. (40 × 50 cm)
COURTESY PHILIPPE BLET
Repr. p. 151

GARY LEE BOAS
Katharine Hepburn, Mark Hellinger Theater, Broadway
January 31, 1970
Chromogenic print
3 × 3 in. (7.5 × 7.5 cm)
KAMEL MENNOUR COLLECTION
Repr. p. 182

Elizabeth Taylor at the Lombardy Hotel, New York
February 24, 1976
Chromogenic print
3 × 3 in. (7.5 × 7.5 cm)
KAMEL MENNOUR COLLECTION
Repr. p. 109

Barry Manilow at the St. Regis Hotel, New York
July 26, 1978
Chromogenic print
3 × 3 in. (7.5 × 7.5 cm)
KAMEL MENNOUR COLLECTION
Repr. p. 203

A Moment Caught
1966–79
Installation: chromogenic prints
Variable number
3 × 3 in. (7.5 × 7.5 cm) each
COURTESY GARY LEE BOAS AND KAMEL MENNOUR, PARIS
Repr. pp. 262–63

MAURICE-LOUIS BRANGER
King George V in Paris
1914
Gelatin silver print
7 × 5 in. (18 × 13 cm)
COURTESY GALERIE LUMIÈRE DES ROSES
Repr. p. 42

JACK BURLOT
Elizabeth Taylor and Richard Burton, Le Bourget Airport
January 22, 1968
Inkjet print
11 ¾ × 17 ¾ in. (30 × 45 cm)
JACK BURLOT COLLECTION
Repr. p. 106

SOPHIE CALLE
La Filature (The Shadow)
1981
Diptych, texts, color and black-and-white photographs
3 ft. 7 in. × 5 ft. 4 in. (1.10 × 1.62 m) each
COURTESY GALERIE PERROTIN
Repr. pp. 272–73

DANIEL CANDE
Brigitte Bardot Leaving Court during the Trial opposing the Nouvelle Vague and Roger Vadim, Paris
1961
Gelatin silver print
9 × 11 ¾ in. (23 × 30 cm)
DANIEL CANDE COLLECTION
Repr. p. 97

JEAN-JACQUES CECCARINI
Brigitte Bardot during a Demonstration against the Massacre of Baby Seals in front of the Norwegian Embassy, Paris
April 1976
Gelatin silver print
3 ¾ × 5 ¾ in. (10 × 15 cm)
BIBLIOTHÈQUE NATIONALE DE FRANCE
Repr. p. 27

CHAPMAN
(Rex Features)
Paris Hilton during the Launch Party for Her Perfume "Paris Hilton," Il Bottaccio, Grosvenor Place, London
May 16, 2005
Chromogenic print
8 × 5 ¼ in. (20.2 × 13.5 cm)
PHILIPPE GARNER COLLECTION

UMBERTO CICCONI
Liz Taylor in Her Car, Leaving the Frank Sinatra Concert at Teatro Eliseo, Rome
May 24, 1962
Gelatin silver print
7 ¾ × 7 ¾ in. (20 × 20 cm)
ARCHIVIO FOTOGRAFICO STORICO ITALIANO UMBERTO CICCONI, ROME

Paparazzi Photographing Sophia Loren at the Premiere of the Film Marriage Italian Style *by Vittorio De Sica at the Teatro dell'Opera, Rome*
December 18, 1964
Gelatin silver print
11 ¾ × 11 ¾ in. (30 × 30 cm)
ARCHIVIO FOTOGRAFICO STORICO ITALIANO UMBERTO CICCONI, ROME
Repr. p. 24

PASCAL DANZ
1972 (Paparazzi)
2007
Oil on canvas
27 ½ × 31 ½ in. (70 × 80 cm)
FRAC ALSACE COLLECTION
Repr. p. 25

THOMAS DEMAND
Junior Suite
2012
Inkjet print
4 ft. 7 in. × 3 ft. 9 in. (1.40 × 1.15 m)
SPRUTH MAGERS COLLECTION
Repr. p. 227

BRIAN DE PALMA
Femme Fatale
2001
Cinematographic film, 35 mm, color, sound, 115 min. (extracts)
QUINTA COMMUNICATIONS
Repr. p. 92

RAYMOND DEPARDON
Roger Vadim Did Not Leave Her Side during the Whole Stay
c. 1955
Gelatin silver print
7 ¾ × 7 ¾ in. (20 × 20 cm)
MAGNUM PHOTOS

The Ballets Roses Affair
1959
Gelatin silver print
7 ¾ × 7 ¾ in. (20 × 20 cm)
MAGNUM PHOTOS

Brigitte Bardot Visits Jacques Charier at the Meudon Clinic
1960
Gelatin silver print
11 ¾ × 7 ¾ in. (30 × 20 cm)
MAGNUM PHOTOS

Reporters
1981
Cinematographic film, color, sound, 90 min. (extract)
PALMERAIE ET DÉSERT
Repr. p. 61

DUSKO DESPOTOVIC
Princess Diana in Malaga
May 2, 1994
2 chromogenic prints
7 ¾ × 11 ¾ in. (20 × 30 cm) each
© DUSKO DESPOTOVIC/SYGMA/CORBIS
Repr. p. 137

CHARLES DESSOUDEIX
Tie camera
1890
Metal, fabric, glass
11 × 4 ¾ × 2 in. (28 × 12 × 5 cm)
MUSÉE FRANÇAIS DE LA PHOTOGRAPHIE—CONSEIL GÉNÉRAL DE L'ESSONNE

JESSICA DIMMOCK
Jessica Alba, from the series *Paparazzi!*
2009
Inkjet print
16 × 24 in. (40.6 × 61 cm)
JESSICA DIMMOCK/VII PHOTO
Repr. pp. 64–65

Jessica Simpson, from the series *Paparazzi!*
2009
Inkjet print
16 × 24 in. (40.6 × 61 cm)
JESSICA DIMMOCK/VII PHOTO

Lauren Bosworth, from the series *Paparazzi!*
2009
Inkjet print
16 × 24 in. (40.6 × 61 cm)
JESSICA DIMMOCK/VII PHOTO

Leonardo DiCaprio, from the series *Paparazzi!*
2009
Inkjet print
16 × 24 in. (40.6 × 61 cm)
JESSICA DIMMOCK/VII PHOTO

Madonna, from the series *Paparazzi!*
2009
2 inkjet prints
16 × 24 in. (40.6 × 61 cm) each
JESSICA DIMMOCK/VII PHOTO
Repr. pp. 66–67

Tom Cruise, from the series *Paparazzi!*
2009
Inkjet print
16 × 24 in. (40.6 × 60.96 cm)
JESSICA DIMMOCK/ VII PHOTO
Repr. p. 66

GEORGES DUDOGNON
Greta Garbo at the Club Saint-Germain, Paris
c. 1952
Gelatin silver print
7 × 7 in. (18.1 × 17.9 cm)
GEORGES DUDOGNON FAMILY COLLECTION
Repr. p. 181

ROMAIN DUSSAULX AND BENJAMIN LALANDE
L.A. 2006
2013
PAL video, color, sound, 3 min. 30 sec.
ROMAIN DUSSAULX AND BENJAMIN LALANDE COLLECTION
Repr. pp. 70–71

BRAD ELTERMAN
The Tape Measure (Jacqueline Onassis and Ron Galella)
1976
Gelatin silver print
7 ¾ × 11 ¾ in. (20 × 30 cm)
BRAD ELTERMAN COLLECTION
Repr. p. 120

Iggy "No Photos" Pop
1978
Gelatin silver print
16 × 11 ¾ in. (40 × 30 cm)
BRAD ELTERMAN COLLECTION
Repr. p. 171

PHILIPPE D'EXEA
Paparazzi on Strike in front of Brigitte Bardot's Apartment, Avenue Paul-Doumer, Paris
1965
Gelatin silver print
7 ¾ × 11 ¾ in. (20 × 30 cm)
COURTESY SPHINX AGENCY
Repr. pp. 48–49

Brigitte Bardot and Gunter Sachs at La Madrague, Saint-Tropez
1966
Gelatin silver print
11 ¾ × 7 ¾ in. (30 × 20 cm)
COURTESY SPHINX AGENCY

Brigitte Bardot and Gunter Sachs at La Madrague, Saint-Tropez
1966
Gelatin silver print
16 × 11 ¾ in. (40 × 30 cm)
COURTESY SPHINX AGENCY
Repr. p. 112

MALACHI FARRELL
Interview (Paparazzi)
2000
Mixed installation
Variable dimensions
CENTRE NATIONAL DES ARTS PLASTIQUES—MINISTÈRE DE LA CULTURE ET DE LA COMMUNICATION, PARIS
INV: FNAC 01-037
Repr. p. 21

FEDERICO FELLINI
La Dolce Vita
1960
Cinematographic film, 35 mm, black and white, sound, 172 min. (extracts)
FONDATION JÉRÔME SEYDOUX-PATHÉ, PARIS
Repr. pp. 82–85

Photographic Albums of *La Dolce Vita*
c. 1960
3 photographic albums
14 × 10 ¾ and 12 ½ × 10 ½ in. (35.5 × 27.5 and 32 × 27 cm)
FONDATION JÉRÔME SEYDOUX-PATHÉ, PARIS

Walter Santesso, Paparazzo, the Photographer of La Dolce Vita
c. 1960
Ink on paper (facsimile)
SAM STOURDZÉ COLLECTION
Repr. p. 73

HENRY FLORES
Avril Lavigne and a Friend
2011
Chromogenic print
7 ¾ × 11 ¾ in. (20 × 30 cm)
HENRY FLORES COLLECTION
Repr. p. 173

RON GALELLA
Jackie Onassis Goes Back to Her Apartment after a Walk in Central Park, New York
January 3, 1971
Gelatin silver print
10 × 8 in. (25.4 × 20.3 cm)
COURTESY RON GALELLA/A. GALERIE

Jackie Onassis Glimpsed in Central Park, New York
October 4, 1971
Gelatin silver print
16 × 20 in. (40.6 × 50.8 cm)
COURTESY RON GALELLA/A. GALERIE
Repr. p. 121

"Windblown Jackie": Jackie Onassis, on the Corner of 91st Street and Madison Avenue, New York
October 4, 1971
Gelatin silver print
13 ½ × 8 in. (34.3 × 20.3 cm)
COURTESY RON GALELLA/A. GALERIE
Repr. p. 119

Jackie Onassis and Ron Galella on Madison Avenue, New York
October 7, 1971
Gelatin silver print
8 × 10 in. (20.3 × 25.4 cm)
COURTESY RON GALELLA/A. GALERIE
Repr. p. 120

Al Pacino at a Party Given by Elia Kazan at the Lyceum for the Publication of The Understudy, *New York*
December 9, 1974
GELATIN SILVER PRINT
14 × 11 in. (35.6 × 27.9 cm)
Courtesy Ron Galella/A. Galerie

Warren Beatty at the 31st Writers Guild of America Awards at the Beverly Hilton Hotel, Beverly Hills
April 5, 1979
14 × 11 in. (35.6 × 27.9 cm)
COURTESY RON GALELLA/A. GALERIE
Repr. p. 171

Woody Allen and Mia Farrow at the Box Tree Restaurant, New York
September 18, 1980
Gelatin silver print
10 × 8 in. (25.4 × 20.3 cm)
COURTESY RON GALELLA/A. GALERIE

Mick Jagger Returns to His Home after a Rolling Stones Concert at Madison Square Gardens, New York
November 12, 1981
Gelatin silver print
10 × 8 in. (25.4 × 20.3 cm)
COURTESY RON GALELLA/A. GALERIE

Mick Jagger and Jerry Hall Leaving the Mizuno Gallery, Beverly Hills
January 16, 1983
Gelatin silver print
11 × 14 in. (27.9 × 35.6 cm)
COURTESY RON GALELLA/A. GALERIE
Repr. p. 172

Sean Penn and Madonna on a Break during Rehearsals for Goose and TomTom *at the Mitzi Newhouse Theater, New York*
August 13, 1986
Gelatin silver print
10 × 8 in. (25.4 × 20.3 cm)
COURTESY RON GALELLA/A. GALERIE

After a Showing of Goose and TomTom *at the Mitzi Newhouse Theater, Sean Penn Punches and Throws the Photographer Anthony Savignano out of His Home on 64th West Street, New York*
August 29, 1986
Gelatin silver print
10 × 8 in. (25.4 × 20.3 cm)
COURTESY RON GALELLA/A. GALERIE
Repr. p. 189

Bruce Springsteen Makes an Entrance at the Party Held after a Sting Concert at the Canal Bar, New York
August 24, 1988
Gelatin silver print
14 × 11 in. (35.5 × 27.9 cm)
COURTESY RON GALELLA/A. GALERIE
Repr. p. 203

PHILIPPE GARNER
Richard Avedon and Princess Diana at a Private Opening at the National Portrait Gallery, London
March 21, 1995
Gelatin silver print
20 × 24 in. (50.8 × 61 cm)
PHILIPPE GARNER COLLECTION
Repr. p. 135

SETTIMIO GARRITANO
Jacqueline Onassis Naked, Skorpios
1972
Slide
KATIA BEDE GARRITANO COLLECTION
Repr. p. 122

Jacqueline Onassis Naked, Skorpios
1972
Gelatin silver print
15 ¾ × 20 in. (40 × 50 cm)
KATIA BEDE GARRITANO COLLECTION
Repr. p. 123

MARCELLO GEPPETTI
Anna and Lucia Placido, and Sandra Tesi Fight with a Photographer, Rome
1960
Gelatin silver print
11 ¾ × 11 ¾ in. (30 × 30 cm)
MARCELLO GEPPETTI MEDIA COMPANY

James Stewart at a Kiosk, Via Veneto, Rome
1960
Gelatin silver print
7 ¾ × 7 ¾ in. (20 × 20 cm)
MARCELLO GEPPETTI MEDIA COMPANY
Repr. p. 286

Tullio Piacentini Chased by Paparazzo James Alexis, Rome
1960
Gelatin silver print
7 ¾ × 7 ¾ in. (20 × 20 cm)
MARCELLO GEPPETTI MEDIA COMPANY

Anita Ekberg with Bow and Arrows
October 20, 1960
4 gelatin silver prints
11 ¾ × 11 ¾ in. (30 × 30 cm) each
MARCELLO GEPPETTI MEDIA COMPANY
Repr. p. 186

Anita Ekberg Threatens Photographers with Her Bow and Arrow
October 20, 1960
Gelatin silver print
9 ½ × 7 in. (24.1 × 17.8 cm)
PIERRE APRAXINE COLLECTION
Repr. p. 187

Jacqueline Kennedy at Princess Irene Galitzine's Boutique, Rome
1961
Gelatin silver print
11 ¾ × 19 ¾ in. (30 × 50 cm)
MARCELLO GEPPETTI MEDIA COMPANY

Jacqueline Kennedy on the Stairs, Surrounded by Paparazzi
1961
Gelatin silver print
7 ¾ in. × 7 ¾ in. (20 × 20 cm)
MARCELLO GEPPETTI MEDIA COMPANY

Elizabeth Taylor Tries on Her Cleopatra Costume in the Cinecittà Studios
September 1961
Gelatin silver print
11 ¾ × 7 ¾ in. (30 × 20 cm)
MARCELLO GEPPETTI MEDIA COMPANY
Repr. p. 105

Hanna Rasmussen after the Call-Girls Scandal
January 1962
5 gelatin silver prints
7 ¾ × 7 ¾ in. (20 × 20 cm) each
MARCELLO GEPPETTI MEDIA COMPANY
Repr. pp. 178–79

Jeanne Moreau at a Kiosk, Via Veneto, Rome
February 1962
Gelatin silver print
7 ¾ × 7 ¾ in. (20 × 20 cm)
MARCELLO GEPPETTI MEDIA COMPANY
Repr. p. 286

Elizabeth Taylor and Richard Burton Kissing on the Island of Ischia
June 18, 1962
Gelatin silver print
7 ¾ × 11 ¾ in. (20 × 30 cm)
MARCELLO GEPPETTI MEDIA COMPANY
Repr. p. 107

Brigitte Bardot Leaving the Set of the Film Le Mépris (Contempt), *Rome*
1963
Gelatin silver print
7 × 9 ½ in. (18 × 24 cm)
JAMES HYMAN GALLERY COLLECTION
Repr. p. 114

Franco Nero Attacks Rino Barillari in front of the Trevi Fountain, Rome
1965
Gelatin silver print
11 ¾ × 7 ¾ in. (30 × 20 cm)
MARCELLO GEPPETTI MEDIA COMPANY

Elizabeth Taylor and Richard Burton Going to the Teatro Quirino, Rome
1966
Gelatin silver print
11 ¾ × 7 ¾ in. (30 × 20 cm)
MARCELLO GEPPETTI MEDIA COMPANY
Repr. p. 106

Brigitte Bardot and Gunter Sachs Naked in the Pool at their Villa, Via Appia
June 2, 1967
Gelatin silver print
7 ¾ × 11 ¾ in. (20 × 30 cm)
MARCELLO GEPPETTI MEDIA COMPANY

Rita Pavone, Via Condotti, Rome
1972
Gelatin silver print
15 ¾ × 11 ¾ in. (40 × 30 cm)
MARCELLO GEPPETTI MEDIA COMPANY
Repr. p. 181

MICHEL GINFRAY
(Gamma)
Caroline of Monaco, in an Austin Driven by the Famous DJ Hubert, Arrives at L'Aventure Nightclub
March 20, 1975
Gelatin silver print
3 ¾ × 5 ¾ in. (10 × 15 cm)
BIBLIOTHÈQUE NATIONALE DE FRANCE

MICHEL GINIÈS
Birth of Chiara Mastroianni, Paris
May 1972
Gelatin silver print
8 × 11 ¾ in. (20.2 × 30 cm)
MICHEL GINIÈS COLLECTION
Repr. p. 202

Stéphanie of Monaco Refusing to Pose for the Photographer, Followed by Her Bodyguard
1974
Gelatin silver print
7 ¾ × 11 ¾ in. (20 × 30 cm)
MICHEL GINIÈS COLLECTION
Repr. p. 131

Brigitte Bardot Rushing in Anger at the Photographer
June 4, 1975
Gelatin silver print
12 × 7 ¾ in. (30.2 × 20 cm)
MICHEL GINIÈS COLLECTION
Repr. p. 117

Brigitte Bardot Walking Her Dogs in the Bois de Boulogne
June 4, 1975
3 gelatin silver prints
7 ¾ × 11 ¾ in. (20 × 30 cm) each
MICHEL GINIÈS COLLECTION
Repr. p. 116

Actor Robert Redford, in the Company of Costa-Gavras, Leaving the Lapérouse Restaurant, Paris
September 1976
Gelatin silver print
9 ½ × 12 in. (24 × 30.5 cm)
MICHEL GINIÈS COLLECTION
Repr. p. 200

John Travolta Going to the Premiere of Grease
1978
Gelatin silver print
12 × 7 ¾ in. (30.5 × 20 cm)
COLLECTION MICHEL GINIÈS
Repr. p. 203

G.R.A.M.
(Günther Holler-Schuster, Ronald Walter, Armin Ranner, Martin Behr)
Café Paparazzi
2009/2014
Mixed installation
Variable dimensions
COMMISSIONED BY CENTRE POMPIDOU-METZ
COURTESY CHRISTINE KÖNIG GALERIE, VIENNA
Repr. pp. 241, 264–65

FRATELLI GRAPPASONNI (GRAPPASONNI BROTHERS)
Elizabeth Taylor and Richard Burton Leaving a Restaurant in Spoleto, Italy
July 12, 1962
Gelatin silver print
7 × 9 ½ in. (18 × 24 cm)
PHILIPPE GARNER COLLECTION

KATHRIN GÜNTER
Star Shots Magazine
(cover and page 10, photographs Kathrin Günter)
December 2007
Offset prints
17 × 11 in. (43.2 × 27.9 cm)
COLLECTION KATHRIN GÜNTER
Repr. pp. 278–79

Star Shots 2007: Airport, Another One For The Road, Blue Royal, (Back)side on the Scene, Co-Kate, Fender Bender, Home, Hotel, Pull Over, Toe-Up, Worse for Wear, and Yacht
2007
12 inkjet prints
11 ¾ × 7 ¾ in. and 16 × 11 ¾ in. (30 × 20 cm and 40 × 30 cm)
KATHRIN GÜNTER COLLECTION
Repr. pp. 276–77

Star Shots 2012, The Go-Between: Double "Victoria Beckham" 05
2012
Inkjet print
23 ½ × 15 ¾ in. (60 × 40 cm)
KATHRIN GÜNTER COLLECTION
Repr. p. 209

Star Shots 2012, The Go-Between: Double "Victoria Beckham" 07
2012
Inkjet print
23 ½ × 15 ¾ in. (60 × 40 cm)
KATHRIN GÜNTER COLLECTION
Repr. p. 208

Star Shots 2012, The Go-Between: Double "Victoria Beckham" 09
2012
Inkjet print
23 ½ × 15 ¾ in. (60 × 40 cm)
KATHRIN GÜNTER COLLECTION
Repr. p. 208

RICHARD HAMILTON
Release
1972
Silk-screen print, stencil, and collage
27 ½ × 37 ¼ in. (69.9 × 94.5 cm)
THE ALAN CRISTEA GALLERY, LONDON
Repr. p. 222

HARUKAWA TRADING CO.
Septon Pen Camera
c. 1953
1 ¼ × 5 × 1 ¼ in. (3.5 × 13 × 3.5 cm)
FRÉDÉRIC HOCH COLLECTION
Repr. p. 40

GLENN HARVEY
Princess Diana and Prince Charles Kissing at the Guards Polo Club, Windsor
July 1986
Gelatin silver print
7 ¾ × 11 ¾ in. (20 × 30 cm)
© GLENN HARVEY/CAMERA PRESS/GAMMA

SHAHROKH HATAMI
Brigitte Bardot
c. 1965
Gelatin silver print
9 ½ × 11 ¾ in. (24 × 30 cm)
PHILIPPE GARNER COLLECTION

JONATHAN HERNÁNDEZ
Vulnerabilia (Covers Under Arrest)
2011–13
Collage on paper
33 ¼ × 37 × 1 ¾ in. (84.5 × 94 × 4.5 cm)
JONATHAN HERNÁNDEZ COLLECTION
Repr. p. 224

JONATHAN HOROWITZ

Daily Mirror
2006
Silk-screen print on a mirror
14 ¾ × 11 ½ × ¼ in.
(37.5 × 29.3 × 0.6 cm)
COURTESY JONATHAN HOROWITZ AND GAVIN BROWN'S ENTERPRISE, NEW YORK
Repr. p. 207

CBS Evening News/www. britneycrotch.org
2008
Inkjet prints
4 ft. 9 in. × 3 ft. 2 in. (1.44 × 0.97 m)
COURTESY JONATHAN HOROWITZ AND GAVIN BROWN'S ENTERPRISE, NEW YORK
Repr. p. 149

ALISON JACKSON

Charles, Camilla, and Diana (1, 2, and 3/3)
1999
3 inkjet prints
11 ¾ × 16 ½ in. (30 × 42 cm) each
ALISON JACKSON COLLECTION

Diana Finger-Up
2000
Inkjet print
7 × 8 ½ in. (18 × 22 cm)
ALISON JACKSON COLLECTION
Repr. p. 267

Diana and Marilyn Shopping
2000
Inkjet print
30 ¾ × 21 ¼ in. (78 × 54 cm)
ALISON JACKSON COLLECTION
Repr. p. 266

Marilyn Wank Window Bars
2002
Inkjet print
11 ¾ × 16 ½ in. (30 × 42 cm)
ALISON JACKSON COLLECTION
Repr. p. 267

Queen on the Loo
2003
Inkjet print
8 ½ × 7 in. (22 × 18 cm)
ALISON JACKSON COLLECTION
Repr. p. 267

Bush with Rubik's Cube
2005
Inkjet print
11 ¾ × 16 ½ in. (30 × 42 cm)
ALISON JACKSON COLLECTION
Repr. p. 269

Bush Target Practice
2007
Inkjet print
21 ¼ × 30 ¾ in. (54 × 78 cm)
ALISON JACKSON COLLECTION
Repr. p. 269

Bush with Rubik's Cube
2008
Silicone sculpture
PRIVATE COLLECTION

Nicholson Rage
2007
5 inkjet prints
7 × 8 ½ in. (18 × 22 cm) each
ALISON JACKSON COLLECTION
Repr. p. 268

JOHANNES KAHRS

I Finally Accept Fate
2002
Charcoal and pastel on paper
2 joined pages
5 ft. 11 in. × 9 ft. 6 in. (1.80 × 2.90 m)
CENTRE POMPIDOU, MUSÉE NATIONAL D'ART MODERNE, PARIS
Repr. p. 223

JEAN KER

Elizabeth Taylor
October 22, 1962
Gelatin silver print
17 ¾ × 17 ¾ in. (45 × 45 cm)
BIBLIOTHÈQUE NATIONALE DE FRANCE

KIEV

Vega Spy Camera used by the KGB
1962
3 ¼ × 1 ½ × ¾ in. (8.5 × 4.2 × 2.2 cm)
KAMERAMUSEUM WESTLICHT, VIENNA

John Player Special Spy Camera
1970
4 × 2 × 1 in. (10 × 5.5 × 2.5 cm)
KAMERAMUSEUM WESTLICHT, VIENNA
Repr. p. 40

WILLIAM KLEIN

Anne Sainte Marie + Cruiser, fashion photograph for *Vogue, New York*
1962
Chromogenic print
19 ½ × 15 ¾ in. (50 × 40 cm)
WILLIAM KLEIN COLLECTION
Repr. p. 252

Antonia + Yellow Taxi, fashion photograph for *Vogue,* New York
1962
Chromogenic print
19 ½ × 15 ¾ in. (50 × 40 cm)
WILLIAM KLEIN COLLECTION
Repr. p. 252

Kadidjah, "Exile" fashion series for *Vanity Fair,* Paris
1988
Chromogenic print
15 ¾ × 19 ½ in. (40 × 50 cm)
WILLIAM KLEIN COLLECTION
Repr. p. 253

BARBARA KRUGER

"It's All About Me," front cover of *W* magazine with Kim Kardashian (photograph: Mark Seliger)
November 2010
13 × 10 in. (33 × 25.4 cm)
PRIVATE COLLECTION
Repr. p. 293

BRANIMIR KVARTUC

Beyoncé and Jay-Z, on Vacation in Dubrovnik, Leaving a Restaurant Protected by Their Bodyguards
August 18, 2009
Chromogenic print
11 ¾ × 11 ¾ in. (30 × 30 cm)
© KVARTUC/CROPIX/SIPA
Repr. p. 183

JACQUES LANGEVIN

Last Photograph of Princess Diana
August 31, 1997
Chromogenic print
11 ¾ × 15 ¾ in. (30 × 40 cm)
COURTESY MUSÉE DE L'ELYSÉE, LAUSANNE
Repr. p. 133

LEICA (CAMERA) ASTRO (LENS)

Telephoto rifle
1940
31 ½ × 6 × 11 in. (80 × 15 × 28 cm)
KAMERAMUSEUM WESTLICHT, VIENNA
Repr. p. 41

CHRISTIAN LESEMANN

Famous When Dead
2001
Inkjet print
15 ¾ × 11 ¾ in. (40 × 30 cm)
CHRISTIAN LESEMANN COLLECTION
Repr. p. 254

Giorgio Armani
2001
Inkjet print
11 ¾ × 15 ¾ in. (30 × 40 cm)
CHRISTIAN LESEMANN COLLECTION
Repr. p. 255

Intersection #0
2001
Artist's book
13 ¾ × 9 × ¾ in. (35 × 23 × 2 cm)
CHRISTIAN LESEMANN COLLECTION

Monaco Grand Prix
2001
Inkjet print
11 ¾ × 15 ¾ in. (30 × 40 cm)
CHRISTIAN LESEMANN COLLECTION
Repr. p. 255

LIMITED COMPANY

Ticka Watch: camera in the form of a pocket watch, "Focal Plane" model
c. 1910
1 × 3 in. (3 × 8 cm)
FRÉDÉRIC HOCH COLLECTION

ARMIN LINKE

In collaboration with Corrado Calvo. Texts and contributions by Estelle Blaschke, Marco Belpoliti, Franco Bonera, Giulia Bruno, Giovanna Calvenzi
Paparazzi—What Is Revealed Is the Obviousness of the Visibility to the Others
2009–2013
Mixed Installation
Variable dimensions
COMMISSIONED BY CENTRE POMPIDOU-METZ
Repr. p. 294

ALEXI LUBOMIRSKI

Downtown LA
2007
3 inkjet prints
7 ¾ × 11 ¾ in. (20 × 30 cm) each
ALEXANDRE LAMARE COLLECTION
Repr. pp. 256–57

ULF LUNDIN

Pictures of a Family
1996
9 chromogenic prints
28 ¼ × 39 ¼ in. (72 × 100 cm) each
COURTESY ULF LUNDIN AND GALLERI MAGNUS KARLSSON
Repr. pp. 230–31

XAVIER MARTIN

Jackie Onassis, Avenue Montaigne, Paris
1975
Gelatin silver print
11 ¾ × 7 ¾ in. (30 × 20 cm)
XAVIER MARTIN COLLECTION

Jackie Onassis, Avenue Montaigne, Paris
1975
Gelatin silver print
11 ¾ × 7 ¾ in. (30 × 20 cm)
XAVIER MARTIN COLLECTION

Jean-Paul Belmondo and Laura Antonelli, The Kiss, Paris
1976
3 gelatin silver prints
7 ¾ × 11 ¾ in. (20 × 30 cm) each
XAVIER MARTIN COLLECTION
Repr. pp. 164–65

Jack Nicholson Showing His Buttocks, Saint-Tropez
July 1976
2 gelatin silver prints
7 ¾ × 11 ¾ in. (20 × 30 cm) each
XAVIER MARTIN COLLECTION
Repr. p. 175

Caroline of Monaco and Philippe Junot, Tahiti
July 1978
3 gelatin silver prints
8 × 12 in. (20.5 × 30.5 cm) each
XAVIER MARTIN COLLECTION

PAUL MCCARTHY

Girls 2
2000
Cibachrome print
4 ft. × 5 ft. 10 in. (1.22 × 1.78 m)
DEICHTORHALLEN, HAMBURG
FALCKENBERG COLLECTION
COURTESY PATRICK PAINTER, INC.
Repr. p. 225

People 1
2000
Cibachrome print
5 ft. 10 in. × 4 ft. × 1 in.
(177.8 × 121.9 × 3.5 cm)
PRIVATE COLLECTION
COURTESY PATRICK PAINTER, INC.
Repr. p. 291

People 2
2000
Cibachrome print
5 ft. 10 in. × 4 ft. × 1 in.
(177.8 × 121.9 × 3.5 cm)
PRIVATE COLLECTION
COURTESY PATRICK PAINTER, INC.
Repr. p. 291

JONAS MEKAS

Shaving Her Head, from the series *365 Day Project*
February 21, 2007
Video, color, sound, 5 min. 45 sec.
COURTESY JONAS MEKAS
Repr. p. 147

OLIVIER MIRGUET

Paparazzi #4 – Los Angeles
2009
Inkjet prints
7 ¾ × 11 ¾ in. (20 × 30 cm)
© OLIVIER MIRGUET/VU
Repr. p. 63

Paparazzi #14 – Los Angeles
2009
Inkjet prints
7 ¾ × 11 ¾ in. (20 × 30 cm)
© OLIVIER MIRGUET/VU
Repr. p. 62

Paparazzi #21 – Los Angeles
2009
Inkjet prints
7 ¾ × 11 ¾ in. (20 × 30 cm)
© OLIVIER MIRGUET/VU
Repr. p. 62

Trash #0049
2009
Inkjet print
15 ¾ × 15 ¾ in. (40 × 40 cm)
© OLIVIER MIRGUET/VU
Repr. p. 226

Trash #0067
2009
Inkjet print
15 ¾ × 15 ¾ in. (40 × 40 cm)
© OLIVIER MIRGUET/VU
Repr. p. 226

Trash #6024
2009
Inkjet print
15 ¾ × 15 ¾ in. (40 × 40 cm)
© OLIVIER MIRGUET/VU
Repr. p. 226

Trash # Affleck 3
2009
Inkjet print
15 ¾ × 15 ¾ in. (40 × 40 cm)
© OLIVIER MIRGUET/VU

Trash # ROK8739
2009
Inkjet print
15 ¾ × 15 ¾ in. (40 × 40 cm)
© OLIVIER MIRGUET/VU

PATRICK MORIN

Brigitte Bardot during the Shooting of Le Mépris (Contempt), *Rome*
1963
Gelatin silver print
8 × 9 ¾ in. (20.8 × 24.8 cm)
MICHEL GINIÈS COLLECTION
Repr. p. 115

BRUNO MOURON

Catherine Deneuve and Her Daughter Chiara Mastroianni, Going Back to School, Paris
September 16, 1980
Gelatin silver print
7 ¾ × 11 ¾ in. (20 × 30 cm)
COURTESY BRUNO MOURON/SPHINX AGENCY
Repr. p. 162

Stéphanie of Monaco at the Beach with a Friend
June 10, 1981
Gelatin silver print
9 ½ × 11 ¾ in. (24 × 30 cm)
COURTESY BRUNO MOURON/SPHINX AGENCY
Repr. p. 128

Princess Diana, Prince Charles, and William, Leaving St. Mary's Hospital, London
June 27, 1982
Gelatin silver print
7 ¾ × 11 ¾ in. (20 × 30 cm)
COURTESY BRUNO MOURON/SPHINX AGENCY
Repr. p. 134

Kate Moss during Fashion Week, Paris
1992
Gelatin silver print
15 ¾ × 11 ¾ in. (40 × 30 cm)
COURTESY BRUNO MOURON/SPHINX AGENCY
Repr. p. 174

JEREMIAH PALECEK

Britney Spears Upskirt
2008
Oil on Masonite
11 ¾ × 15 ¾ in. (30 × 40 cm)
JEREMIAH PALECEK COLLECTION
Repr. p. 148

ERIC C. PENDZICH

(Rex Features)
Paris Hilton Arrives at the Studios of The Late Show, *New York*
May 8, 2008
Gelatin silver print
8 × 5 ¼ in. (20.2 × 13.5 cm)
PHILIPPE GARNER COLLECTION

FRANK PERRIN

The Big Shot #01, #03, #04 (Postcapitalism section 14)
2013
3 chromogenic prints
4 ft. 11 in. × 4 ft. 11 in.
(1.50 × 1.50 m) each
FRANK PERRIN COLLECTION
Repr. pp. 22–23

JEAN PIGOZZI

Mick Jagger and Arnold Schwarzenegger, Hôtel du Cap, Antibes
1990
Gelatin silver print
11 × 14 in. (27.9 × 35.6 cm)
CENTRE POMPIDOU, MUSÉE NATIONAL D'ART MODERNE, PARIS
Repr. p. 181

MAX CHRISTIAN PRIESTER AND WILLY WILCKE
Otto von Bismarck on His Deathbed
July 31, 1898
Gelatin silver print
(Facsimile)
DENKMALSCHUTZAMT HAMBURG—BILDARCHIV, HAMBURG
Repr. p. 204

BARBARA PROBST
Exposure #9: N.Y.C., Grand Central Station, 12.18.01, 1:21 p.m.
2001
6 inkjet prints
2 ft. 10 in. × 4 ft. 3 in. (0.86 × 1.30 m)
CENTRE POMPIDOU, MUSÉE NATIONAL D'ART MODERNE, PARIS
Repr. pp. 238–39

PHIL RAMEY
Madonna and Sean Penn's Wedding
1985
Chromogenic print
11 ¾ × 7 ¾ in. (30 × 20 cm)
PHIL RAMEY COLLECTION

Michael Jackson Accompanying Liz Taylor
1991
Chromogenic print
11 ¾ × 7 ¾ in. (30 × 20 cm)
PHIL RAMEY COLLECTION

PHIL RAMEY AND SÉBASTIEN VALIELA
Paparazzo Phil Ramey's Sock, Driven Over by Britney Spears, for Sale on eBay
October 19, 2007
2 inkjet prints
7 ¾ × 11 ¾ and 11 ¾ × 7 ¾ in.
(20 × 30 cm and 30 × 20 cm)
EYEWITNESS COLLECTION
Repr. p. 147

PAUL J. RICHARDS
Princess Diana Swimming
January 4, 1993
Chromogenic print
7 ¾ × 11 ¾ in. (20 × 30 cm)
AGENCE FRANCE-PRESSE
Repr. p. 136

GERHARD RICHTER
Herr Heyde
1965
Oil on canvas
21 ½ × 25 ½ in. (55 × 65 cm)
PRIVATE COLLECTION
Repr. p. 221

Elizabeth II
1966
Photolithograph
27 ½ × 23 ¼ in. (70 × 59.4 cm)
THE MUSEUM OF MODERN ART, NEW YORK GIFT OF THE COSMOPOLITAN ARTS FOUNDATION
INV.: 445.1978
Repr. p. 213

ALICIA ROSS
The Origin of the World (Britney)
2010
Inkjet print on canvas
Gold frame
31 × 35 ¼ in. (78.7 × 89.9 cm)
ALICIA ROSS COLLECTION
Repr. p. 149

PASCAL ROSTAIN
Mick Jagger and Jerry Hall at the Pré Catelan, Paris
June 19, 1980
Gelatin silver print
7 ¾ × 11 ¾ in. (20 × 30 cm)
COURTESY PASCAL ROSTAIN/SPHINX AGENCY
Repr. p. 188

Alexandre Solzhenitsyn Playing Tennis at His Vermont Property in the United States
August 1981
Gelatin silver print
11 ¾ × 15 ¾ in. (30 × 40 cm)
COURTESY PASCAL ROSTAIN/SPHINX AGENCY
Repr. p. 163

Caroline and Guillermo Vilas on the Island of Maui in Hawaii
June 1982
Chromogenic print
9 ½ × 11 ¾ in. (24 × 30 cm)
COURTESY PASCAL ROSTAIN/SPHINX AGENCY
Repr. p. 129

PASCAL ROSTAIN AND BRUNO MOURON
Marlene Dietrich
Undated
Gelatin silver print
7 ¾ × 7 ¾ in. (20 × 20 cm)
COURTESY PASCAL ROSTAIN AND BRUNO MOURON/SPHINX AGENCY

Michael Jackson
Undated
Gelatin silver print
7 ¾ × 11 ¾ in. (20 × 30 cm)
COURTESY PASCAL ROSTAIN AND BRUNO MOURON/ SPHINX AGENCY

Stéphanie of Monaco, First Cigarette after School, Paris
February 9, 1981
Gelatin silver print
7 ¾ × 11 ¾ in. (20 × 30 cm)
COURTESY PASCAL ROSTAIN AND BRUNO MOURON/SPHINX AGENCY
Repr. p. 130

Madonna 2
March 1990
Inkjet print
3 ft. 11 in. × 5 ft. 11 in. (1.20 × 1.80 m)
COURTESY PASCAL ROSTAIN AND BRUNO MOURON/SPHINX AGENCY
Repr. p. 258

Woody Allen and Soon-Yi at the Tuileries Gardens, Paris
October 1994
Gelatin silver print
7 ¾ × 11 ¾ in. (20 × 30 cm)
COURTESY PASCAL ROSTAIN AND BRUNO MOURON/SPHINX AGENCY
Repr. p. 162

George Clooney Playing Softball in Santa Monica, California
1996
Gelatin silver print
7 ¾ × 11 ¾ in. (20 × 30 cm)
COURTESY PASCAL ROSTAIN AND BRUNO MOURON/SPHINX AGENCY
Repr. p. 188

Pierre Soulages
June 2008
Inkjet print
3 ft. 11 in. × 5 ft. 11 in. (1.20 × 1.80 m)
COURTESY PASCAL ROSTAIN AND BRUNO MOURON/SPHINX AGENCY
Repr. pp. 260–61

Jeff Koons
July 15, 2008
3 inkjet prints
8 ft. 2 in. × 5 ft. 11 in.
(2.50 × 1.80 m) each
COURTESY PASCAL ROSTAIN AND BRUNO MOURON/SPHINX AGENCY
Repr. p. 259

Paris Hilton 6
c. 2010
Chromogenic print
7 ¾ × 11 ¾ in. (20 × 30 cm)
COURTESY PASCAL ROSTAIN AND BRUNO MOURON/SPHINX AGENCY

Mel Gibson
2010
Gelatin silver print
3 ft. 11 in. × 5 ft. 11 in. (1.20 × 1.80 m)
COURTESY PASCAL ROSTAIN AND BRUNO MOURON/SPHINX AGENCY

JACQUES ROZIER
Paparazzi
1963
Documentary film, 35 mm, black-and-white, sound, 18 min.
LES FILMS DU COLISÉE

ERICH SALOMON
Aristide Briand Just Before He Points at Erich Salomon, Quai d'Orsay, Paris
August 1931
Gelatin silver print
7 ½ × 8 in. (18.9 × 20.4 cm)
BERLINISCHE GALERIE, LANDESMUSEUM FÜR MODERNE KUNST, FOTOGRAFIE UND ARCHITEKTUR, BERLIN

Aristide Briand Pointing At Erich Salomon and Shouting, "Ah! There he is! The King of Indiscretion!", Quai d'Orsay, Paris
August 1931
Gelatin silver print
6 × 8 in. (15.3 × 20.4 cm)
BERLINISCHE GALERIE, LANDESMUSEUM FÜR MODERNE KUNST, FOTOGRAFIE UND ARCHITEKTUR, BERLIN
Repr. p. 170

JACLYN SANTOS
Super Star
2009
Oil on canvas
4 ft. 11 in. × 3 ft. 4 in. (1.51 × 1.02 m)
JACLYN SANTOS COLLECTION
Repr. p. 149

PAUL SCHMULBACH
Marlon Brando and Ron Galella at the Charity Ball for the American Indians Development Association at the Waldorf Astoria Hotel, New York
November 26, 1974
Gelatin silver print
8 × 10 in. (20.3 × 25.4 cm)
COURTESY RON GALELLA/A. GALERIE
Repr. pp. 190–91

TAZIO SECCHIAROLI
The Paparazzi
c. 1950
2 gelatin silver prints
DAVID SECCHIAROLI COLLECTION

Ava Gardner Chased by Paparazzi, Rome
1958
Gelatin silver print
19 ½ × 19 ½ in. (50 × 50 cm)
DAVID SECCHIAROLI COLLECTION
Repr. p. 47

Behind Bars: Brigitte Bardot on the Set of Le Mépris (Contempt)
1963
Gelatin silver print
9 ½ × 11 ¾ in. (24 × 30 cm)
COURTESY JAMES HYMAN GALLERY
Repr. p. 115

Brigitte Bardot on the Set of Le Mépris (Contempt)
1963
Gelatin silver print
9 ½ × 11 ¾ in. (24 × 30 cm)
COURTESY JAMES HYMAN GALLERY

Sophia Loren with Her Son Carlo Jr. in a Pram, in the Gardens of Her Villa in Marino, near Rome
1968
4 gelatin silver prints
7 ¾ × 11 ¾ in. (19.7 × 29.8 cm);
7 ¾ × 12 in. (20 × 30.5 cm);
7 ¾ × 12 in. (20 × 30.2 cm);
8 × 12 in. (20.3 × 30.2 cm)
DAVID SECCHIAROLI COLLECTION
Repr. p. 168

CINDY SHERMAN
Untitled Film Still #7
1978
Gelatin silver print
10 × 8 in. (25.4 × 20.3 cm)
COURTESY CINDY SHERMAN AND METRO PICTURES, NEW YORK
Repr. p. 270

Untitled Film Still #54
1980
Gelatin silver print
8 × 10 in. (20.3 × 25.4 cm)
COURTESY CINDY SHERMAN AND METRO PICTURES, NEW YORK
Repr. p. 271

Untitled Film Still #83
1980
Gelatin silver print
8 × 10 in. (20.3 × 25.4 cm)
COURTESY CINDY SHERMAN AND METRO PICTURES, NEW YORK
Repr. p. 270

PATRICK SICCOLI
Grace, Albert, and Caroline of Monaco in a Car
1976
Gelatin silver print
7 ¾ × 11 ¾ in. (20 × 30 cm)
PATRICK SICCOLI COLLECTION
Repr. p. 127

Isabelle Adjani Pointing Her Finger
1976
Gelatin silver print
15 ¾ × 11 ¾ in. (40 × 30 cm)
PATRICK SICCOLI COLLECTION
Repr. p. 171

Stéphanie of Monaco as a Child
1976
Gelatin silver print
15 ¾ × 11 ¾ in. (40 × 30 cm)
PATRICK SICCOLI COLLECTION

Jerry Hall with Mick Jagger at the Wheel, Giving the Finger
1982
Gelatin silver print
7 ¾ × 11 ¾ in. (20 × 30 cm)
PATRICK SICCOLI COLLECTION
Repr. p. 172

Mick Jagger at the Wheel, Sticking Out His Tongue
1982
Gelatin silver print
7 ¾ × 11 ¾ in. (20 × 30 cm)
PATRICK SICCOLI COLLECTION

Serge Gainsbourg and Catherine Deneuve
1982
Gelatin silver print
11 ¾ × 15 ¾ in. (30 × 40 cm)
PATRICK SICCOLI COLLECTION
Repr. p. 202

Brigitte Bardot on the Beach
1983
Gelatin silver print
7 ¾ × 11 ¾ in. (20 × 30 cm)
PATRICK SICCOLI COLLECTION

Stéphanie of Monaco Jumping into a Pool
c. 1984
Chromogenic print
11 ¾ × 15 ¾ in. (30 × 40 cm)
PATRICK SICCOLI COLLECTION
Repr. p. 129

JIM SMEAL
(BEImages)
Paris Hilton at the Gay Pride Parade, West Hollywood, Los Angeles
June 12, 2005
Chromogenic print
8 × 5 ¼ in. (20.3 × 13.5 cm)
PHILIPPE GARNER COLLECTION
Repr. p. 139

ELIO SORCI
Walter Chiari and Tazio Secchiaroli, Rome
1958
Gelatin silver print
7 × 9 ¼ in. (17.71 × 23.57 cm)
DAVID SECCHIAROLI COLLECTION
Repr. p. 189

STEINECK CAMERA
Steineck ABC Camera in the form of a strap watch
c. 1948
2 × 6 × 2 in. (5 × 15 × 5 cm)
FRÉDÉRIC HOCH COLLECTION

SUZUKI OPTICAL CO.
Cigarette Lighter Camera Echo-8
c. 1955
2 ¼ × 1 ½ × ½ in. (5.5 × 4.0 × 1.5 cm)
KAMERAMUSEUM WESTLICHT, VIENNA
Repr. p. 40

JUERGEN TELLER
OJ Simpson, Miami
2000
Chromogenic print
11 ¾ × 15 ¾ in. (30 × 40 cm)
JÜRGEN TELLER COLLECTION
Repr. pp. 184–85

LIAM TICKNER
London
2008
Artist's book
LIAM TICKNER COLLECTION
Repr. pp. 232–33

GAVIN TURK
Identity Crisis
1994
Silk-screen print on paper
Light box
5 ft. 8 in. × 3 ft. 8 in. (1.72 × 1.12 m)
MURDERME COLLECTION
Repr. p. 281

NICK UT
Paris Hilton Seen through a Police Car Window before Appearing in Court
2007
Inkjet print
7 × 5 ¼ in. (18 × 13 cm)
© NICK UT/THE ASSOCIATED PRESS/SIPA
Repr. p. 192

SÉBASTIEN VALIELA
Bill Clinton
March 11, 2004
Inkjet print
7 ¾ × 11 ¾ in. (20 × 30 cm)
EYEWITNESS COLLECTION
Repr. p. 201

Stars' Houses
2005–8
Slides
EYEWITNESS COLLECTION
Repr. pp. 160–61

Britney Spears's Belly Pokes Out
April 2, 2005
Inkjet print
7 × 5 ¼ in. (18 × 13 cm)
EYEWITNESS COLLECTION

Jennifer Garner
May 1, 2005
Inkjet print
7 × 5 ¼ in. (18 × 13 cm)
EYEWITNESS COLLECTION
Repr. p. 289

Renée Zellweger Wearing Her New Wedding Ring
May 19, 2005
Inkjet print
5 ¼ × 7 in. (13 × 18 cm)
EYEWITNESS COLLECTION

Brad Pitt
June 5, 2005
Inkjet print
5 ¼ × 7 in. (13 × 18 cm)
EYEWITNESS COLLECTION

Heather Locklear
June 7, 2005
Inkjet print
7 × 5 ¼ in. (18 × 13 cm)
EYEWITNESS COLLECTION

Lindsay Lohan
June 18, 2005
Inkjet print
7 × 5 ¼ in. (18 × 13 cm)
EYEWITNESS COLLECTION
Repr. p. 289

Jennifer Garner's Belly
June 25, 2005
Inkjet print
7 × 5 ¼ in. (18 × 13 cm)
EYEWITNESS COLLECTION

Kate Hudson
August 14, 2005
Inkjet print
7 × 5 ¼ in. (18 × 13 cm)
EYEWITNESS COLLECTION

Toni Braxton
August 15, 2005
Inkjet print
7 × 5 ¼ in. (18 × 13 cm)
EYEWITNESS COLLECTION

Pierce Brosnan
August 31, 2005
Inkjet print
7 × 5 ¼ in. (18 × 13 cm)
EYEWITNESS COLLECTION

Nicky Hilton
September 7, 2005
Inkjet print
7 × 5 ¼ in. (18 × 13 cm)
EYEWITNESS COLLECTION

Justin Timberlake
September 8, 2005
Inkjet print
7 × 5 ¼ in. (18 × 13 cm)
EYEWITNESS COLLECTION

Kevin Federline
September 9, 2005
Inkjet print
7 × 5 ¼ in. (18 × 13 cm)
EYEWITNESS COLLECTION

Alyssa Milano
September 20, 2005
Inkjet print
7 × 5 ¼ in. (18 × 13 cm)
EYEWITNESS COLLECTION

Paris Hilton in Rainbows and Diamonds
September 23, 2005
Inkjet print
7 × 5 ¼ in. (18 × 13 cm)
EYEWITNESS COLLECTION

Ben Affleck Smoking
September 25, 2005
Inkjet print
7 × 5 ¼ in. (18 × 13 cm)
EYEWITNESS COLLECTION

Kiefer Sutherland Has Stepped in Something
September 25, 2005
Inkjet print
7 × 5 ¼ in. (18 × 13 cm)
EYEWITNESS COLLECTION
Repr. p. 289

Elizabeth Berkley
September 26, 2005
Inkjet print
7 × 5 ¼ in. (18 × 13 cm)
EYEWITNESS COLLECTION
Repr. p. 288

Dakota Fanning
November 3, 2005
Inkjet print
7 × 5 ¼ in. (18 × 13 cm)
EYEWITNESS COLLECTION
Repr. p. 288

Pink's Style in Beverly Hills
November 4, 2005
Inkjet print
5 ¼ × 7 in. (13 × 18 cm)
EYEWITNESS COLLECTION
Repr. p. 289

Jake Gyllenhaal
November 17, 2005
Inkjet print
5 ¼ × 7 in. (13 × 18 cm)
EYEWITNESS COLLECTION

Lindsay Lohan
December 27, 2005
Inkjet print
7 × 5 ¼ in. (18 × 13 cm)
EYEWITNESS COLLECTION
Repr. p. 288

Keanu Reeves
January 27, 2006
Inkjet print
5 ¼ × 7 in. (13 × 18 cm)
EYEWITNESS COLLECTION

Michael Keaton
February 9, 2006
Inkjet print
5 ¼ × 7 in. (13 × 18 cm)
EYEWITNESS COLLECTION
Repr. p. 288

Nicole Richie and Paris Hilton (in the background) during the Shooting of the Fourth Season of the TV Show The Simple Life
February 27, 2006
Inkjet print
7 × 5 ¼ in. (18 × 13 cm)
EYEWITNESS COLLECTION

Paris Hilton during the Shooting of the Fourth Season of the TV Show The Simple Life
February 27, 2006
Inkjet print
11 ¾ × 7 ¾ in. (30 × 20 cm)
EYEWITNESS COLLECTION
Repr. p. 142

Actor Ryan Reynolds Driving the Same Motorbike as Brad Pitt
March 12, 2006
Inkjet print
5 ¼ × 7 in. (13 × 18 cm)
EYEWITNESS COLLECTION

Paris Hilton Has a New Toy: A $500,000 Mercedes
March 21, 2006
Inkjet print
11 ¾ × 7 ¾ in. (30 × 20 cm)
EYEWITNESS COLLECTION

Paris Hilton on a Lawn Mower
March 21, 2006
Inkjet print
7 ¾ × 11 ¾ in. (20 × 30 cm)
EYEWITNESS COLLECTION
Repr. p. 143

Mischa Barton
April 22, 2006
Inkjet print
7 × 5 ¼ in. (18 × 13 cm)
EYEWITNESS COLLECTION

Jude Law
May 5, 2006
Inkjet print
5 ¼ × 7 in. (13 × 18 cm)
EYEWITNESS COLLECTION

Jennifer Aniston's Bodyguard
May 22, 2006
Inkjet print
7 × 5 ¼ in. (18 × 13 cm)
EYEWITNESS COLLECTION

Shera Danese and Peter Falk
October 27, 2006
Inkjet print
7 ¾ × 11 ¾ in. (20 × 30 cm)
EYEWITNESS COLLECTION

Actor Dominic Monaghan, from the Series Lost, *Shopping in Hawaii*
November 3, 2006
Inkjet print
11 ¾ × 7 ¾ in. (30 × 20 cm)
EYEWITNESS COLLECTION

Paris Hilton and Britney Spears Shopping
November 26, 2006
Inkjet print
7 ¾ × 11 ¾ in. (20 × 30 cm)
EYEWITNESS COLLECTION
Repr. p. 140

Paris Hilton Out of Order
November 27, 2006
Inkjet print
11 ¾ × 7 ¾ in. (30 × 20 cm)
EYEWITNESS COLLECTION
Repr. p. 141

Jaclyn Smith
December 15, 2006
Inkjet print
5 ¼ × 7 in. (13 × 18 cm)
EYEWITNESS COLLECTION
Repr. p. 289

Paris Hilton
January 31, 2007
Inkjet print
5 ¼ × 7 in. (13 × 18 cm)
EYEWITNESS COLLECTION

Paris Hilton Surrounded by the Media
June 7, 2007
Inkjet print
7 ¾ × 11 ¾ in. (20 × 30 cm)
EYEWITNESS COLLECTION

Lindsay Lohan
July 22, 2007
Inkjet print
7 × 5 ¼ in. (18 × 13 cm)
EYEWITNESS COLLECTION
Repr. p. 289

Actress Elisha Cuthbert, from the Series 24, Taking a Photo of Paris Hilton
August 11, 2007
Inkjet print
11 ¾ × 7 ¾ in. (30 × 20 cm)
EYEWITNESS COLLECTION

Britney Spears Decides to Go Shopping
October 10, 2007
Inkjet print
7 ¾ × 11 ¾ in. (20 × 30 cm)
EYEWITNESS COLLECTION
Repr. p. 146

Britney Spears Pulls a Face while We Take Photographs
October 12, 2007
Inkjet print
7 ¾ × 11 ¾ in. (20 × 30 cm)
EYEWITNESS COLLECTION
Repr. p. 146

Monika Casey, George Eads' Girlfriend, during One of Their First Public Outings, Los Angeles
December 1, 2007
Inkjet print
11 ¾ × 7 ¾ in. (30 × 20 cm)
EYEWITNESS COLLECTION
Repr. p. 287

Fergie and Josh Duhamel
December 22, 2007
Inkjet print
5 ¼ × 7 in. (13 × 18 cm)
EYEWITNESS COLLECTION

Kathy Griffin in a Car with Adnan Ghalib
April 10, 2008
Inkjet print
7 × 5 ¼ in. (18 × 13 cm)
EYEWITNESS COLLECTION

Jaime Pressly
May 4, 2008
Inkjet print
5 ¼ × 7 in. (13 × 18 cm)
EYEWITNESS COLLECTION
Repr. p. 288

Paris Hilton at the Zoo
June 28, 2008
Inkjet print
7 ¾ × 11 ¾ in. (20 × 30 cm)
EYEWITNESS COLLECTION

Jack Nicholson's House
June 30, 2008
Inkjet print
5 ¼ × 7 in. (13 × 18 cm)
EYEWITNESS COLLECTION

Liliane Bettencourt in Her House in Mallorca
August 15, 2010
3 inkjet prints
7 ¾ × 11 ¾ in. (20 × 30 cm) each
EYEWITNESS COLLECTION

Loana Working Out
February 25, 2011
Inkjet print
7 ¾ × 11 ¾ in. (20 × 30 cm)
EYEWITNESS COLLECTION
Repr. p. 169

Loana on Exceptional Leave from Sainte-Anne's Clinic for Two Hours
January 13, 2012
Inkjet print
7 ¾ × 11 ¾ in. (20 × 30 cm)
EYEWITNESS COLLECTION

Loana on a Relaxing Weekend at La Baule
April 1, 2012
Inkjet print
7 × 5 ¼ in. (18 × 13 cm)
EYEWITNESS COLLECTION

SÉBASTIEN VALIELA AND JULIEN DOORNAERT

Paris Hilton Arrested for Speeding
September 20, 2005
Inkjet print
7 ¾ × 11 ¾ in. (20 × 30 cm)
EYEWITNESS COLLECTION
Repr. p. 142

Pamela Anderson Partying
September 2, 2006
Inkjet print
7 × 5 ¼ in. (18 × 13 cm)
EYEWITNESS COLLECTION

Paris Hilton, Britney Spears, and Her Son, Sean Preston, Shopping
November 26, 2006
Inkjet print
11 ¾ × 7 ¾ in. (30 × 20 cm)
EYEWITNESS COLLECTION

SÉBASTIEN VALIELA AND VINCENT LEPRESLE

The Twins Ashley and Mary-Kate Olsen
August 15, 2005
Inkjet print
7 × 5 ¼ in. (18 × 13 cm)
EYEWITNESS COLLECTION

Britney at Breaking Point
August 25, 2005
Inkjet print
11 ¾ × 7 ¾ in. (30 × 20 cm)
EYEWITNESS COLLECTION

Rod Stewart Buying Celebrity Magazines
October 8, 2005
Inkjet print
11 ¾ × 7 ¾ in. (30 × 20 cm)
EYEWITNESS COLLECTION
Repr. p. 287

Rod Stewart
October 8, 2005
Inkjet print
7 × 5 ¼ in. (18 × 13 cm)
EYEWITNESS COLLECTION

George Clooney and Krista Allen, Holding Hands in front of a Sushi Restaurant, Beverly Hills
March 4, 2006
Inkjet print
7 ¾ × 11 ¾ in. (20 × 30 cm)
EYEWITNESS COLLECTION
Repr. p. 163

Paris Hilton
March 29, 2006
Inkjet print
7 × 5 ¼ in. (18 × 13 cm)
EYEWITNESS COLLECTION
Repr. p. 288

Paris Hilton at a Newspaper Kiosk
April 5, 2006
Inkjet print
11 ¾ × 7 ¾ in. (30 × 20 cm)
EYEWITNESS COLLECTION
Repr. p. 287

Paris Hilton Running in the Rain
April 5, 2006
Inkjet print
11 ¾ × 7 ¾ in. (30 × 20 cm)
EYEWITNESS COLLECTION
Repr. p. 142

Brad Pitt
June 15, 2006
Inkjet print
7 × 5 ¼ in. (18 × 13 cm)
EYEWITNESS COLLECTION

Britney Spears, Single Woman
November 9, 2006
Inkjet print
11 ¾ × 7 ¾ in. (30 × 20 cm)
EYEWITNESS COLLECTION

Drew Barrymore
May 18, 2007
2 inkjet prints
11 ¾ × 7 ¾ in. (30 × 20 cm)
EYEWITNESS COLLECTION

Fergie and Josh Duhamel Visiting the Ranch Where Their Wedding Will Be Held
December 22, 2007
Inkjet print
7 ¾ × 11 ¾ in. (20 × 30 cm)
EYEWITNESS COLLECTION

SÉBASTIEN VALIELA AND PIERRE SUU
Mazarine Pingeot and Her Father, François Mitterrand, in front of Le Divellec Restaurant, Paris
September 21, 1994
Inkjet print
7 ¾ × 11 ¾ in. (20 × 30 cm)
EYEWITNESS COLLECTION
Repr. p. 162

ANDY WARHOL
Magazine and History (0290)
1983
Acrylic and silk-screen print on canvas
13 ft. 9 in. × 12 ft. 2 in. (4.18 × 3.70 m)
HUBERT BURDA MEDIA SAMMLUNG
Repr. p. 283

Paparazzi
1986
Gelatin silver print
8 × 10 in. (20.3 × 25.4 cm)
PRIVATE COLLECTION
Repr. p. 26

WEEGEE
Hairdresser Salvatore Ossido, Charged with the Murder of Einer Sporrer, Is Taken to a Police Station, New York
March 21, 1937
Gelatin silver print
8 × 10 in. (20.6 × 25.4 cm)
INTERNATIONAL CENTER OF PHOTOGRAPHY, NEW YORK

Maxine Tursen
c. 1938
Gelatin silver print
6 ¼ × 8 ¼ in. (16.2 × 20.8 cm)
INTERNATIONAL CENTER OF PHOTOGRAPHY, NEW YORK
Repr. p. 176

A Customer Leaving a Casino, Wrapped in Her Ermine Fur Coat, New York
December 22, 1940
Gelatin silver print
8 × 10 in. (20.6 × 25.4 cm)
INTERNATIONAL CENTER OF PHOTOGRAPHY, NEW YORK

Young Women Arrested at Anna Swift's after a Vice Squad Raid
1941
Gelatin silver print
10 × 8 in. (25.4 × 20.6 cm)
INTERNATIONAL CENTER OF PHOTOGRAPHY, NEW YORK
Repr. p. 176

Waxy Gordon
c. 1942
Gelatin silver print
6 ½ × 8 ¼ in. (16.5 × 21 cm)
INTERNATIONAL CENTER OF PHOTOGRAPHY, NEW YORK

Charles Sodokoff and Arthur Webber Using Their Hats to Hide Their Faces, New York
January 27, 1942
Facsimile
11 × 14 in. (27.9 × 35.6 cm)
INTERNATIONAL CENTER OF PHOTOGRAPHY, NEW YORK
Repr. p. 176

Robert Redwing Is Taken for Questioning by the New York Police as Part of the Inquiry into the Murder of Albert Langford
June 1945
Gelatin silver print
8 × 6 ¼ in. (20.3 × 15.6 cm)
INTERNATIONAL CENTER OF PHOTOGRAPHY, NEW YORK
Repr. p. 176

Henry Rosen and Harvey Stemmer Are Arrested for Having Bribed Brooklyn University Basketball Players, New York
July 25, 1945
Gelatin silver print
8 × 10 in. (20.3 × 25.4 cm)
INTERNATIONAL CENTER OF PHOTOGRAPHY, NEW YORK
Repr. p. 177

WILLIAM WYLER
Roman Holiday
1953
Cinematographic film, 35 mm, black and white, sound, 119 min. (extracts)
PARAMOUNT PICTURES
Repr. p. 92

RICHARD YOUNG
(Rex Features)
Paris Hilton Celebrates Her 21st Birthday at the Stork Rooms, a London Nightclub
May 2, 2002
CHROMOGENIC PRINT
8 × 5 ¼ in. (20.2 × 13.2 cm)
Philippe Garner Collection

ANDRZEJ ZULAWSKI
The Most Important Thing: Love
1975
Cinematographic film, 35 mm, color, sound, 112 min. (extract)
STUDIO CANAL
Repr. p. 92

PUBLICATIONS
(listed by section)

PHOTOGRAPHERS

Mythologies

Epoca, November 16, 1958, pp. 38–39
13 ¼ × 20 ½ in. (33.5 × 52 cm)
PRIVATE COLLECTION

La Domenica del Corriere, May 15, 1955
15 ¼ × 11 ½ in. (39 × 29 cm)
PRIVATE COLLECTION

La Domenica del Corriere, July 8, 1956, back cover
15 ¼ × 11 ½ in. (39 × 29 cm)
PRIVATE COLLECTION

Le Ore, September 6, 1958, pp. 52–53
PRIVATE COLLECTION

L'Espresso, July 29, 1956, front cover
21 ½ × 16 ¼ in. (55.1 × 41 cm)
PRIVATE COLLECTION

L'Espresso, August 26, 1956
21 ½ × 16 ¼ in. (55.1 × 41 cm)
PRIVATE COLLECTION

L'Espresso, February 17, 1957, back cover
21 ½ × 16 ¼ in. (55.1 × 41 cm)
PRIVATE COLLECTION

L'Espresso, February 24, 1957, back cover
21 ½ × 16 ¼ in. (55.1 × 41 cm)
PRIVATE COLLECTION

L'Espresso, November 16, 1958, front cover (facsimile)
11 × 15 ¾ in. (28.1 × 40.1 cm)
PRIVATE COLLECTION

L'Europeo, September 17, 1958, pp. 58–59
14 ¾ × 21 ¼ in. (37.4 × 54.4 cm)
PRIVATE COLLECTION

L'Europeo, September 28, 1958, cover and pp. 54–55 (facsimile)
14 ¾ × 21 ¼ in. (37.5 × 54.4 cm)
PRIVATE COLLECTION

L'Europeo, November 1958, inside pages
15 ¼ × 22 in. (38.7 × 55.7 cm)
PRIVATE COLLECTION

Lo Specchio, November 16, 1958 (facsimile)
12 × 9 in. (30.4 × 22.8 cm)
PRIVATE COLLECTION

Paris Match, no. 570, March 12, 1960
13 ¾ × 10 ¼ in. (35 × 26.3 cm)
PRIVATE COLLECTION

STARS

In the Spotlight: Jackie

Documenti di Attualità, "Jacqueline tutta nuda!", May 1972, front cover and pp. 39 and 41 (anonymous photomontage)
10 ¾ × 7 ½ in. (27 × 19 cm)
Michel Giniès Collection
Repr. p. 125

Life, vol. 72, no. 12, March 31, 1972, front cover (photograph: Art Zelin), pp. 64–65 (photographs: Joy Smith and Ron Galella), pp. 68–69 (photographs: Ron Galella)
13 × 20 ¾ in. (33.2 × 53 cm) (open)
PRIVATE COLLECTION
Repr. p. 120

Playmen, vol. 6, no. 12, December 1972, cover and double spread (photograph: Settimio Garritano)
11 ¼ × 16 ½ in. (28.5 × 42 cm) (open)
PRIVATE COLLECTION
Repr. p. 124

In the Spotlight: Caroline and Stéphanie

Oggi, January 2, 1975, pp. 16–17 (photographs: Michel Giniès)
13 ¾ × 20 in. (35 × 51 cm) (open)
Michel Giniès Collection
Repr. p. 131

Voici, no. 868, June 28, 2004, front cover
11 ½ × 9 in. (29 × 23 cm)
PRIVATE COLLECTION
Repr. p. 131

Behind the Scenes: It's Perfectly Innocent

Paris Match, no. 1727, July 2, 1982, front cover (anonymous photograph)

Paris Match, no. 1769, April 22, 1983, front cover (anonymous photograph)

Paris Match, no. 1775, June 3, 1983, front cover (anonymous photograph)

Paris Match, no. 1964, January 16, 1987, front cover (anonymous photograph)

Paris Match, no. 2389, March 9, 1995, front cover (anonymous photograph)

Paris Match, no. 2517, August 21, 1997, front cover (anonymous photograph)

Paris Match, no. 2700, February 22, 2001, front cover (anonymous photograph)

Paris Match, no. 2936, August 25, 2005, front cover (anonymous photograph)

Paris Match, no. 3325, February 7, 2013, front cover (anonymous photograph)
11 ¾ × 9 ¼ in. (30.1 × 23.6 cm) each (closed)
PRIVATE COLLECTION
Repr. pp. 166–67

Behind the Scenes: No Photos!

Détective, no. 773, April 21, 1961, front cover (anonymous photograph)

Détective, no. 805, December 1, 1961, front cover (anonymous photograph)

Détective, no. 812, January 19, 1962, front cover (anonymous photograph)

Détective, no. 814, February 2, 1962, front cover (anonymous photograph)

Détective, no. 824, April 13, 1962, front cover (anonymous photograph)

Détective, no. 827, May 4, 1962, front cover (anonymous photograph)

Détective, no. 841, August 10, 1962, front cover (anonymous photograph)

Détective, no. 847, September 21, 1962, front cover (anonymous photograph)

Détective, no. 1244, June 11, 1970, front cover (anonymous photograph)
16 ¼ × 11 ½ in. (41 × 29.3 cm) each
PRIVATE COLLECTION
Repr. p. 180

Behind the Scenes: The Other Side of the Coin

Globe, vol. 39, no. 20, May 19, 1992, front cover (anonymous photograph)
11 ¾ × 10 ¼ in. (29.8 × 25.7 cm)
PRIVATE COLLECTION
Repr. p. 193

Globe, vol. 39, no. 37, September 15, 1992, front cover (anonymous photograph)
11 ¾ × 10 ¼ in. (29.8 × 25.7 cm)
PRIVATE COLLECTION
Repr. p. 193

¡ Hola !, no. 2498, June 25, 1992, front cover (anonymous photograph)
13 × 9 ½ in. (33 × 24 cm)
PRIVATE COLLECTION
Repr. p. 193

Behind the Scenes: The Last Portrait

Ici Paris, no. 3069, May 27, 2004, pp. 4–5
11 × 18 ¾ in. (28 × 48 cm) (open)
PRIVATE COLLECTION
Repr. p. 207

Illustrirte Zeitung, no. 2876, August 11, 1898, front cover (facsimile)
20 ½ × 13 ¾ in. (52 × 35 cm)
Stiftung Deutsches Historisches Museum, Berlin
Repr. p. 205

National Enquirer, vol. 52, no. 4, September 6, 1977, front page (anonymous photograph)
13 ¾ × 10 ¾ in. (35 × 27.5 cm)
PRIVATE COLLECTION
Repr. p. 206

National Enquirer, vol. 55, no. 21, December 30, 1980, front cover (anonymous photograph)
12 ½ × 9 ¾ in. (32 × 25 cm)
PRIVATE COLLECTION

National Enquirer, vol. 87, no. 10, March 5, 2012, front cover and pp. 30–31 (anonymous photograph)
10 ½ × 18 ½ in. (27 × 47 cm) (open)
PRIVATE COLLECTION
Repr. p. 206

OK !, vol. 5, no. 28, July 13, 2009, front cover (anonymous photograph)
10 ½ × 7 ¾ in. (26.5 × 19.8 cm)
PRIVATE COLLECTION
Repr. p. 206

Paris Match, no. 1442, January 14, 1977, pp. 38–39 (anonymous photograph)
12 ¼ × 18 ½ in. (30.8 × 47.4 cm) (open)
PRIVATE COLLECTION

Paris Match, no. 2435, January 25, 1996, pp. 36–37 (anonymous photograph)
11 ¾ × 18 ½ in. (30.1 × 47.26 cm) (open)
PRIVATE COLLECTION
Repr. p. 207

ARTISTS

In the Skin of a Paparazzo

"Mike Nichols and Suzy Parker Rock Europe," layout for *Harper's Bazaar*, September 1962 (photographs: Richard Avedon)
THE RICHARD AVEDON FOUNDATION
Repr. p. 251

H&M Magazine Germany, fall 2010, pp. 60–61 (photographs: Alexi Lubomirski)
11 ½ × 17 ¾ in. (29 × 45 cm) (open)
PRIVATE COLLECTION
Repr. p. 256

On the Newsstands

Daily Mirror, September 15, 2005, front page (anonymous photograph)
14 ½ × 11 ½ in. (37 × 29.5 cm)
PRIVATE COLLECTION
Repr. p. 296

Le Document, vol. 2, no 8, March 1936, front cover (photomontage: Maximilien Vox)
15 ½ × 11 ½ in. (39.5 × 29 cm)
PRIVATE COLLECTION
Repr. p. 284

National Enquirer, vol. 82, no. 33, August 13, 2007, front cover (anonymous photographs)
11 ¼ × 9 ¼ in. (28.5 × 23.5 cm)
PRIVATE COLLECTION
Repr. p. 285

People Weekly, vol. 40, no 8, August 23, 1993, front cover (photograph: E.L. Woody/ Ramey Photo Agency)
10 ¾ × 8 in. (27.3 × 20.3 cm)
PRIVATE COLLECTION
Repr. p. 290

Museum Credits

PAPARAZZI! PHOTOGRAPHERS, STARS, ARTISTS

February 26–June 9, 2014
Centre Pompidou-Metz
Galerie 3

June 27–October 12, 2014
Schirn Kunsthalle Frankfurt

November 2014–February 2015
Heydar Aliyev Center, Baku

EXHIBITION

The exhibition *Paparazzi! Photographers, Stars, Artists* was designed and organized by the Centre Pompidou-Metz.

CURATOR
Clément Chéroux, *Curator at the Centre Pompidou, Musée national d'art moderne, Chief Curator of the Photography Department*

ASSOCIATE CURATORS
Quentin Bajac, *Chief Curator of the Photography Department, The Museum of Modern Art, New York*
Sam Stourdzé, *Director of Les Rencontres d'Arles*

PROJECT MANAGER
Irene Pomar

RESEARCH AND EXHIBITIONS OFFICER
Camille Lenglois

RESEARCH OFFICER
Lucie Le Corre

EXHIBITION DESIGN
Agence NC: Nathalie Crinière, Mathilde Le Coutour

GRAPHIC DESIGN
P&J: Laurent Pinon and Aurore Jannin with the collaboration of Sofia Chaoui

EDITOR
Claire Bonnevie

ARTWORKS REGISTRAR
Charline Becker
Julie Schweitzer

GALLERIES REGISTRAR
Alexandre Chevalier

EXHIBITION DESIGN COORDINATION
Christian Bertaux
Stéphane Leroy

LIGHTING
Julia Kravtsova
Vyara Stefanova

AUDIOVISUAL CONCEPTION AND COORDINATION
Christian Heschung
Jean-Pierre Del Vecchio
Christine Hall

INSTALLATION OF AUDIOVISUAL AND LIGHTING EQUIPMENT
JCD Communication: Jean-Christophe Accorsi, Frédéric Pernot, and their team
Cottel: David Cottel and his team
MPM Éclairage: Laurent Capron and his team
Sébastien Bertaux
Vivien Cassar
Jean-Philippe Currivant
Pierre Hequet

GALLERIES LAYOUT CONSTRUCTION
Volume International: Christophe des Dorides, Marc Froissard, and their team

PAINTING
Debra Frères: Jacques Debra and his team
Jean-David Puttini

ELECTRICAL INSTALLATION
Cofely Ineo GDF Suez: Christophe Lere and his team

PHOTOGRAPHIC PRINTS
Rainbow Color: Catherine Brunet-Rossini, Cédric Viviani, and their team

FRAMING AND MOUNTING FOR THE PRESENTATION OF ARTWORKS
Aïnu: Stéphane Pennec, Alix Camus, Ana Pennec, Simona Calza, and their team

ARTWORK PACKAGING AND TRANSPORTATION
LP Art: Gwenaël Rimaud, Nicolas Rimaud, David Pierucci, Laurine Derval, and their team

ARTWORK HANGING
Axal-Artrans: Wahiba Khenifi, Sébastien Schaeffer, and their team

ARTWORK INSURANCE
Blackwall Green: Robert Graham and his team

BUILDING CONTROL OFFICER
Socotec: François Jimenez

SAFETY AND SECURITY
André Martinez
SGP Lorraine

FIRE CONTROL
Service Départemental d'Incendie et de Secours de la Moselle

EDUCATIONAL ACTIVITIES OFFICER
Phone Régie

EDUCATIONAL DOCUMENTS
Anaïs Feyeux
Anne Horvath
Camille Lenglois
Dominique Oukkal

INTERNS
Max Bonhomme
Amélie de Dianous
Gabrielle De la Selle
Camille Grateau
Flora Joubert
Judith Langendorff
Céline Laurent
Véra Léon
Mathilde Petit
Jeanne Rethacker
Julia Rey

CENTRE POMPIDOU-METZ

The Centre Pompidou-Metz is a public establishment for cultural cooperation whose founding members are the French State, the Centre Pompidou, the Lorraine Region, the Communauté d'Agglomération de Metz Métropole, and the City of Metz.

BOARD OF DIRECTORS
Alain Seban, *President*
Jean-Marie Rausch, *Honorary President*
Jean-Luc Bohl, *Vice President*

REPRESENTATIVES OF METZ MÉTROPOLE
Jean-Luc Bohl, *President*
Arlette Mathias, *Vice President*
Margaud Antoine-Fabry, *Community Counselor*
Patrick Grivel, *Delegated Community Counselor*
Hacène Lekadir, *Community Counselor*
Pierre Muel, *Delegated Community Counselor*
Patrick Thil, *Community Counselor*

REPRESENTATIVES OF THE CENTRE POMPIDOU
Alain Seban, *President*
Denis Berthomier, *Chief Executive Officer*
Jean-Marc Auvray, *Legal and Financial Director*
Bernard Blistène, *Director of the Musée national d'art moderne*
Brigitte Leal, *Assistant Director of the Musée national d'art moderne*

REPRESENTATIVES OF THE LORRAINE REGIONAL COUNCIL
Nathalie Colin-Oesterlé, *Regional Counselor*
Josiane Madelaine, *Vice President*
Jean-Pierre Moinaux, *Vice President*
Rachel Thomas, *Vice President*
Roger Tirlicien, *Regional Counselor*

FRENCH STATE REPRESENTATIVE
Nacer Meddah, *Prefect for the Lorraine Region, Prefect for the Eastern Zone of Defense and Safety, Prefect for Moselle*

REPRESENTATIVES OF THE CITY OF METZ
Dominique Gros, *Mayor of Metz, home to the gallery*
William Schuman, *Delegated Counselor*

QUALIFIED INDIVIDUALS
Frédéric Lemoine, *President of the Wendel Group Board of Directors*
Patrick Weiten, *President of the Moselle General Council*

REPRESENTATIVES OF THE CENTRE POMPIDOU-METZ STAFF
Djamila Clary, *Visitor Relations and Sales Officer*
Élodie Stroecken, *Programming Coordinator*

MANAGEMENT
Laurent Le Bon, *Director*
Claire Garnier, *Personal Assistant and Project Coordinator*

GENERAL SECRETARIAT
Pascal Keller, *Acting Secretary General*
Hélène De Bisschop, *Legal Advisor*
Cécilia Zunt-Radot, *Administrative Coordinator*
Émilie Engler, *Secretarial Assistant*
Anne Horvath, *Secretarial Assistant*

DEPARTMENT OF ADMINISTRATION AND FINANCE
Rodolphe Di Sabatino, *Head of Department*
Jérémy Fleur, *Chief Accountant*
Mathieu Grenouillet, *Accounts Assistant*
Audrey Jeanront, *Human Resources Management Assistant*
Alexandra Morizet, *Public Contracts Advisor*
Véronique Muller, *Accounts Assistant*

DEPARTMENT OF BUILDING MAINTENANCE AND OPERATION
Philippe Hubert, *Technical Director*
Mouhamadi Ascani-Bacar, *Information Systems Assistant*
Christian Bertaux, *Head of Building Maintenance*
Sébastien Bertaux, *Chief Electrician*
Vivien Cassar, *Technical Coordinator*
Jean-Philippe Currivant, *Technical Registrar*
Christian Heschung, *Head of Information Systems*
Stéphane Leroy, *Operation Manager*
André Martinez, *Head of Security*
Jean-David Puttini, *Technician Painter*

DEPARTMENT OF COMMUNICATIONS AND DEVELOPMENT
Annabelle Türkis, *Head of Department*
Charline Burger, *Communications and Events Officer*
Noémie Gotti, *Communication and Press Relations Officer*
Marie-Christine Haas, *Multimedia Communications Officer*
Anne-Laure Miller, *Communications Officer*
Amélie Watiez, *Communications and Events Officer*

DEPARTMENT OF PRODUCTION
Olivia Davidson, *Head of Department*
Charline Becker, *Project Manager*
Alexandre Chevalier, *Galleries Registrar*
Jean-Pierre Del Vecchio, *Systems and Networks Administrator*
Jennifer Gies, *Project Manager*
Christine Hall, *Audiovisual Technician*
Thibault Leblanc, *Performing Arts Registrar*
Éléonore Mialonier, *Project Manager*
Fanny Moinel, *Project Manager*
Marie Pessiot, *Performing Arts Production Officer*
Irene Pomar, *Project Manager*
Marianne Pouille, *Production Assistant*
Julie Schweitzer, *Project Manager*
Jeanne Simoni, *Project Manager*
Amandine Such, *Production Assistant*

DEPARTMENT OF PROGRAMMING
Hélène Guenin, *Head of Department*
Claire Bonnevie, *Editor*
Géraldine Celli, *Wendel Auditorium and Studio Programming Officer*
Héléne Meisel, *Research and Exhibitions Officer*
Alexandra Müller, *Research and Exhibitions Officer*
Dominique Oukkal, *Manufacturing Coordinator*
Élodie Stroecken, *Programming Coordinator*

DEPARTMENT OF VISITOR RELATIONS
Aurélie Dablanc, *Head of Department*
Fedoua Bayoudh, *Visitor Relations and Tourism Officer*
Djamila Clary, *Visitor Relations and Sales Officer*
Jules Coly, *Visitor Relations, Information and Accessibility Officer*
Anne-Marine Guiberteau, *Youth Programming and Educational Activities Officer*
Benjamin Milazzo, *Visitor Relations and Membership Officer*
Anne Oster, *Schools Relations Officer*

ACCOUNTING OFFICER
Jean-Eudes Bour

FRIENDS OF CENTRE POMPIDOU-METZ

Friends of Centre Pompidou-Metz is a non-profit organization whose purpose is to accompany the Centre in its cultural projects and to enlist the support of the business world and private individuals who wish to make their contribution.

Jean-Jacques Aillagon, *Former Minister of Culture, President*
Ernest-Antoine Seillière, *Vice President*
Philippe Bard, *President of Demathieu & Bard, Treasurer*
Lotus Mahé, *Secretary General*
Lisa Cartus, *Assistant to the Secretary General*

ACKNOWLEDGMENTS

We would like to give our sincere thanks to all those listed in the credits together with those who helped to make this event possible, in particular the Centre Pompidou, Metz Métropole, the City of Metz, the Lorraine Regional Council, the Moselle General Council, the Lorraine and Moselle Regional Prefecture, their respective departments and the following:

PARTNERS

Schirn Kunsthalle Frankfurt
Max Hollein, *Director*
Katharina Kanold, *Directorial Assistant*
Inka Drögemüller, *International Relations Officer*
Esther Schlicht, *Exhibitions Officer*
Katharina Dohm, *Curator*
Karin Grüning, *Chief Registrar*
Jessica Keilholz, *Assistant Registrar*
Axel Braun, *Press Relations Officer*
Simone Krämer, *Press Relations Officer*
Katharina Siegmann, *Editor*
Daniela Schmidt, *Assistant*

Heydar Aliyev Center, Baku
Thanks to the team of the Heydar Aliyev Center, Baku

ARTISTS AND PHOTOGRAPHERS

Paul Abascal
Valerio Adami
Daniel Angeli
Francis Apesteguy
Dario Argento
Malin Arnesson
Massimo Ascani
François-Marie Banier
Julián Barón
Christophe Beauregard
Martin Behr
Viktoria Binschtok
Philippe Blet
Gary Lee Boas
Jack Burlot
Sophie Calle
Corrado Calvo
Daniel Cande
Jean-Jacques Ceccarini
Pascal Danz
Thomas Demand
Brian De Palma
Raymond Depardon
Dusko Despotovic
Jessica Dimmock
Julien Doornaert
Romain Dussaulx
Brad Elterman
Philippe d'Exea
Malachi Farrell
Henry Flores
Ron Galella
Philippe Garner
Michel Ginfray
Michel Giniès
Kathrin Günter
Richard Hamilton
Glenn Harvey
Shahrokh Hatami
Jonathan Hernández
Günther Holler-Schüster
Jonathan Horowitz
Alison Jackson
Johannes Kahrs
Jean Ker
William Klein
Barbara Kruger
Branimir Kvartuc
Benjamin Lalande
Jacques Langevin
Vincent Lepresle
Christian Lesemann
Armin Linke
Alexi Lubomirski
Ulf Lundin
Xavier Martin
Paul McCarthy
Jonas Mekas
Olivier Mirguet
Bruno Mouron
Jeremiah Palecek
Eric C. Pendzich
Frank Perrin
Jean Pigozzi
Barbara Probst
Phil Ramey
Armin Ranner
Paul J. Richards
Gerhard Richter
Alicia Ross
Pascal Rostain
Jacques Rozier
Jaclyn Santos
Paul Schmulbach
Cindy Sherman
Patrick Siccoli
Jim Smeal
Pierre Suu
Jürgen Teller
Liam Tickner
Gavin Turk
Nick Ut
Sébastien Valiela
Ronald Walter
Richard Young
Andrzej Zulawski

LENDERS

AUSTRIA
VIENNA

WestLicht
Peter Coeln, *Director*
Rebekka Reuter, *Chief Curator*
Lisa Riebenbauer, *Project Assistant*

FRANCE
AIX-EN-PROVENCE

Hôtel de Gallifet
Nicolas Mazet, *Director*

BIÈVRES

Musée français de la photographie
Julie Corteville, *Chief Curator*
Rémi Calzada, *Deputy Director*
Nathalie Barriat, *Collections Registrar*

BOULOGNE-BILLANCOURT

Canal Plus
Delphine Beillard, *Production Management*
Muriel Sadoun, *Production Management*

TF1 Vidéo
Margaux Tournemire

CLAMART

Palmeraie et désert
Raymond Depardon
Claudine Nougaret
Sarah Froux

ISSY-LES-MOULINEAUX

Studio Canal
Dominique Hascoet-Brunet, *Sales Officer—Clips and Festivals*

LEVALLOIS-PERRET

Bestimage
Céline Bonnarde

MONTREUIL

Galerie Lumière des Roses
Marion and Philippe Jacquier

NEUILLY-SUR-SEINE

Collection Cécile Angeli
Cécile Angeli
Jean-Jacques Naudet, *Chief Editor of the Journal de la photographie*

OFFWILLER

Frédéric Hoch

PARIS

A. Galerie
Arnaud Adida
Corinne Franza

Agence France-Presse
Anne Lorré, *Manager of Corporate Editions for Photographs*
Philippe Collette, *Sales Officer for Photographs France*

Sphinx Agency
Bruno Mouron
Pascal Rostain
Liliane Leclerc

Bibliothèque nationale de France
Bruno Racine, *Director*
Jacqueline Sanson, *Managing Director*
Sylvie Aubenas, *Director of the Prints and Photographs Department*
Dominique Versavel, *Curator of Modern Photography, Department of Prints and Photographs*
Brigitte Robin-Loiseau, *Exhibitions Department—Office of External Exhibitions*
Julien Spinner, *Assistant of the Office of External Exhibitions*
Frank Bougamont, *Reproductions Department*

Centre Pompidou, Musée national d'art moderne
Alain Seban, *President*
Agnès Saal, *Managing Director*
Bernard Blistène, *Director*

Georges Dudognon Family Collection
Thierry de Beaumont

Collection Michel Giniès

Collection T. Valletoux

Corbis France
Célia Challal

Eyewitness
Sébastien Valiela

Fondation Jérôme Seydoux-Pathé
Stéphanie Salmon

Fonds national d'art contemporain
Richard Lagrange, *Director of the Centre national des arts plastiques*
Aude Bodet, *Head of the Conservation and Distribution Department*
Pascal Beausse, *Head of the Photography Collection*
Pascale Cassagnau, *Head of the Audiovisual and New Media Collection*
Sébastien Faucon, *Head of the Visual Arts Collection*
Laetitia Dalet, *Loans Officer*
Amélie de Dianous, *Restorer*

Galerie Perrotin
Emmanuel Perrotin, *Director*
Lara Blanchy, *Arts Officer*

Gamma-Rapho
Isabelle Sadys, *Publications and Exhibitions Officer*

Getty Images
Martine Guillemain

Institut national de l'audiovisuel
Mathieu Gallet, *President-Managing Director*
Dominique Thiercelin, *Cultural and Educational Activities Department*

Kamel Mennour
Kamel Mennour, *Director*
Marie-Sophie Eiché, *Director*
Meriadek Caraes, *Loans Officer*
Emma-Charlotte Gobry-Laurencin, *Communications*

KCS Presse
Christian Blachier

Magnum Photos
Nikandre Koukoulioti, *Sales Director, Archives*
Eva Bodinet, *Head of Editions and the Cultural Sector*

Management + Artists
Alexandre Lamare

Pathé
Pascale Paulet

Quinta Communications
Sophie Verlière, *Distribution and Post-Production Coordinator*

Sipa Press
Philippe Meyssat
Cristelle Doveri
Macha Gorina Bellanger

Wild Side Films
Malvina Marque, *TV, Projections, and Festivals Sales*

ZK Images Gallery
Serge and Florence Zreik, *Directors*

SÉLESTAT

Frac Alsace
Olivier Grasser, *Director*
Pascal Bion, *Collections Officer*
Katia Gagnard, *Exhibitions Manager*

GERMANY
BERLIN

Berlinische Galerie – Landesmuseum für Moderne Kunst, Fotografie und Architektur
Dr. Thomas Köhler, *Director*
Ulrich Domröse, *Scientific Manager of the Photography Collection*
Tanja Keppler, *Photography Collection Officer*

Klemm's
Sebastien Klemm
Silvia Bonsiepe
Arielle Bier

Sprüth Magers Berlin London
Philomene Magers
Monika Sprüth
Franziska von Hasselbach
Esther Dörring

Stiftung Deutsches Historisches Museum
Prof. Dr. Alexander Koch, *President*
Anne Dorte Krause, *Iconographical Archives*

HAMBURG

Deichtorhallen Internationale Kunst und Fotografie Hamburg
Dirk Luckow, *Artistic Director*
Bert Antonious Kaufmann, *Sales Director*
Uwe Lewitzky, *Loans Manager*

Kulturbehörde Denkmalschutzamt Bildarchiv
Milena Del Duca
Evelyn Möcking

MUNICH

Hubert Burda Media Sammlung
Dr. Hubert Burda
Fiona Seidler

Zwingenberg
Friedhelm Heitland

ITALY
BOLOGNA

Cineteca del Comune di Bologna
Carlo Mazzacurati, *President*
Gian Luca Farinelli, *Director*
Anna Fiaccarini, *Head of Library and Archives except Film*

ROME

David Secchiaroli Collection
David Secchiaroli
Giovanna Bertelli

Fondazione Allori – Archivio Fotografico Storico Italiano Umberto Cicconi
Luca Di Garbo
Edoardo Dionea Cicconi
Marcello Geppetti Foundation, srl
Andrea Dezzi, *Director*
Camilla Macro, *Director*
Marco Geppetti
Monica Geppetti

Katia Bede Garritano Collection
Katia Bede Garritano
Eva Lengyel
Massimo Vicinanza

Reporters Associati
Emanuela Acito
Alessandro Canestrelli

MEXICO
MEXICO CITY

Kurimanzutto
Mónica Manzutto, *Director*
José Kuri, *Director*
Martha Reta, *Registrar*
Fatima Gonzalez Martinez Parente, *Assistant*
Amelia Hinojosa, *Head of Communications*

SWITZERLAND
LAUSANNE

Sam Stourdzé Collection

Musée de l'Élysée
Sam Stourdzé, *Director*
Daniel Girardin, *Curator*

VEVEY

Musée suisse de l'appareil photographique
Pascale and Jean-Marc Bonnard Yersin, *Directors*

UNITED KINGDOM
LONDON

Collection Philippe Garner

James Hyman Gallery
James Hyman, *Director*
Mary Pelletier, *Head of the Gallery*
Valerie C. Whitacre, *Sales Officer*

Murderme Collection
Kate Davies

The Alan Cristea Gallery
Alan Cristea, *Director*
Hanna Sorrell, *Head of Exhibitions*

UNITED STATES
CLOSTER (NJ)

Rainer Ganahl and Lilly Hull

LOS ANGELES

Mavrix Photo

Paramount Pictures
Larry McCallister, *Clip & Still Department*

NEW YORK

Gavin Brown's Enterprise
Gavin Brown, *Director*
Jamie Kenyon

International Center of Photography
Mark Lubell, *Director*
Barbara Woytowic, *Registrar*
Erin Barnett, *Assistant Curator of Collections*
Claartje van Dijk, *Assistant Curator of Collections*
Pauline Vermare, *Assistant Curator of the Robert Capa Archives*

Metro Pictures
Janelle Reiring
Helene Winer
Tom Heman
Karine Haimo

Museum of Modern Art
Glenn D. Lowry, *Director*
Ramona Bronkar Bannayan, *Director, Collection Management and Exhibition Registration*
Quentin Bajac, *Chief Curator of the Photography Department*
Hope Cullinam, *Coordination Officer for Collection Management and Exhibition Registration*
Lucy Gallun, *Assistant Curator of the Photography Department*
Christophe Cherix, *The Abby Aldrich Rockefeller, Chief Curator of Prints and Illustrated Books*
Katherine Alcauskas

Pierre Apraxine Collection
Pierre Apraxine
Denis Canguilhem

RBS Collection
Nicole Grammatico

Richard Avedon Foundation
Michelle Franco, *Program Director*
James Martin, *Executive Director*
Eugenia Bell, *Permissions and Publications Officer*
Katrina Dumas, *Registrar*
Christopher Nesbit, *Editor*

As well as the lenders who preferred to remain anonymous.

We would also like to thank:
Philippa Adams
Camille Aguignier
Grégoire Alexandre
Sarah Allen
Meri Atkin
Alexandre Barthet
Tony Basset
Chantal Berck
Sylvain Besson
Achille Bonito Oliva
Cyril Brody
Kate Callahan
François Cheval
Marine Colliard
Nicholas Cullinan
Pascal Dalbon
Kate Davies
Chris Deacon
Pierre-Louis Denis
Daniel Entwistle
David Facioli
Filip Firlej
Giovanna Fornarelli
Aurore Fossard-De Almeida
Thierry Gervais
Mark Godfrey
Didier Grandsart
Anna Gray
Michel Guerrin
Joe Hage
Julie Heath
Lauren Hechel
Nathalie Heinich
Eva Hofler
Danny Howell
Tim Jefferies
Peter Jukadofsky
Sonja Junkers
Maimouna Kaba
Ahmad Khan
Christine König Galerie

Carina Krause
Marie-Louise Laband
Luce Lebart
Pierre Leguillon
Luc Lessertisseur
Karin Lindmark
Loïc Malle
Paola Massardi
Nicolas Maubert
Frédéric Monneyron
Michel Moortgat
Camille Morineau
Patricia Morvan
Benjamin Musset
Virginie Otth
Alfred Pacquement
David Peckman
Andrea Pereira
Serge Plantureux
Sarah Poppel
Annelise Ream
Kelly Reynolds
Alexandra Ribeiro de Azevedo
Terry Richardson
Paul Roth
André Rouillé
Georg Rulffes
Mira Schröder
Sonia Schuller
Nina Schwenke
Karin Seinsoth
Giuliano Sergio
Gregory Spencer
Valentine Suc
Alexandra Theiler
Valérie Théveniaud-Violette
Patricia Topolsky Lambert
Leslie Van Damme
Marion Varinot
Agnès Vergez
Dragana Vujanovic
Roxie Warder
Elisabeth Whitelaw
Hannah Winchester

Centre Pompidou-Metz would like to thank all of its service providers and their teams:
Cofely Services GDF Suez
Librairie Flammarion
Lustral Clean Alliance
Phone Régie
Restaurant La Voile Blanche
SGP Lorraine

SPONSORS AND PARTNERS

Wendel, Founder Sponsor
Frédéric Lemoine, *President of the Board of Directors*

Groupe Galeries Lafayette
Philippe Houzé, *President of the Board of Directors*
Guillaume Houzé, *Director of Sponsorship and Image*
Florence Brachet Champsaur, *Head of Sponsorship – Heritage Director*
François Quintin, *Executive Manager of the Fondation d'entreprise Galeries Lafayette*

Rivedroit Avocats (Lawyers)
Maître Nicolas Maubert

Friends of Centre Pompidou-Metz
Jean-Jacques Aillagon, *President*
Ernest-Antoine Seillière, *Vice President*
Lotus Mahé, *General Secretary*

CENTRE POMPIDOU

The Centre Pompidou-Metz has the status of an Établissement public de coopération culturelle (EPCC: Public Establishment for Cultural Co-operation) associated with the Centre national d'art et de culture Georges Pompidou, National Public Establishment of a Cultural Nature under the administrative supervision of the French Ministry of Culture and Communication (law no. 75-1 January 3, 1975).

Alain Seban, *President*
Denis Berthomier, *Managing Director*
Jack Lang, *President of the Association for the Development of the Centre Pompidou*
Jacques Boissonnas, *President of the Musée national d'art moderne's Friends Society*

MUSÉE NATIONAL D'ART MODERNE / CENTRE DE CRÉATION INDUSTRIELLE (NATIONAL MUSEUM OF MODERN ART, CENTER FOR INDUSTRIAL CREATION)
Bernard Blistène, *Director*
Brigitte Leal, *Deputy Director, Collections Manager*
Catherine David, *Deputy Director, Research and Globalization Manager*
Frédéric Migayrou, *Industrial Creation Manager*
Didier Ottinger, *Cultural Programming Manager*
Catherine Grenier, *Research and Globalization Manager*
Catherine Perdrial, *Adminstrator*
Olga Makhroff, *Loans and Deposits Officer*

CONSERVATION OF ART COLLECTIONS

Modern Art Department
Jean-Michel Bouhours, *Head of Department, by interim*

Contemporary Art Department
Sophie Duplaix, *Head of Department*

Contemporary and Prospective Creation Department
Christine Macel, *Head of Department*
Emma Lavigne, *Curator*

Drawings and Graphic Art Department
Jonas Storsve, *Head of Department*
Macha Daniel, *Assistant Curator*

Photography Department
Clément Chéroux, *Head of Department*
Emmanuelle Etchecopar-Etchart, *Assistant Curator*
Carole Hubert, *Assistant Curator*
Julie Jones, *Assistant Curator*
Camille Lenglois, *Assistant Curator*
Véronique Landy, *Restorer*
Jean-Gabriel Massardier, *Operations Coordinator*

Experimental Cinema Department
Philippe-Alain Michaud, *Head of Department*

New Media Department
Sylvie Douala-Bell, *Assistant Curator*
Florence Parot, *Assistant Curator*

Restoration Department
Véronique Sorano-Stedman, *Head of Department, Restorer*

Collections Department
Ariane Coulondre, *Head of Department*

INDUSTRIAL CREATION

Architecture Department
Olivier Cinqualbre, *Head of Department*

KANDINSKY LIBRARY

Didier Schulmann, *Head of the Kandinsky Library*

PRODUCTIONS DEPARTMENT
Stéphane Guerreiro, *Director*
Anne Poperen, *Deputy Director, Head of Administration and Finance*

Architectural and Museum Production Department
Katia Lafitte, *Head of Department*

Artworks Management Department
Hélène Vassal, *Head of Department*
Émilie Choffel, *Collections Registrar*

Audiovisual Department
Laurie Szulc, *Head of Department*

Studios and Technical Resources
Gilles Carle, *Head of Studios and Technical Resources*

Events Department
Yvon Figueras, *Head of Department*

Gallery Management Department
Hugues Fournier-Montgieux, *Head of Department*

CULTURAL DEVELOPMENT DEPARTMENT
Roger Rotmann, *Deputy Director*
Bakta Thirode, *Administrator*

The Spoken Word Department
Jean-Pierre Criqui, *Head of Programs, Head of Department*

Performing Arts Department
Serge Laurent, *Head of Programs, Head of Department*

Cinema Department
Sylvie Pras, *Head of Department*

COMMUNICATIONS AND PARTNERSHIP DEPARTMENT
Benoît Parayre, *Director*
Marc-Antoine Chaumien, *Deputy Director*
Stéphanie Hussonnois-Bouhayati, *Deputy Director*
Alexandre Colliex, *International Relations Officer*

PUBLICATIONS DEPARTMENT
Nicolas Roche, *Director*
Jean-Christophe Claude, *Deputy Director*

VISITOR AND EDUCATIONAL DEPARTMENT
Patrice Chazotte, *Deputy Director*
Cléa Richon, *Deputy Director*

Photographic Credits

FRONT COVER
© Jean Pigozzi/Centre Pompidou, Mnam-Cci, Dist. RMN-Grand Palais/image Courtesy of CAAC – The Pigozzi Collection

p. 9: © Shigeru Ban Architects Europe and Jean de Gastines Architectes with Philip Gumuchdjian for the design of the winning competition project/Metz Métropole/Centre Pompidou-Metz
From top left: photos 1, 4, 8, 13, 15, 16, 20, 25, 27, 28 by Philippe Gisselbrecht; photo 31 by Arge Lola, Kai Loges, and Andreas Langen for Regiofactum; All Rights Reserved for all other images

p. 10: © Centre Pompidou-Metz/Photos by Beatrice Hatala
p. 12: All Rights Reserved
p. 14: © Mazel & Cauvin
p. 15: © Mamarazzi Photography
p. 16: © Publicis Graffiti/All Rights Reserved
p. 17: All Rights Reserved
p. 18: © Archivo/Revista Noticias

Red Carpet
p. 21: © Adagp, Paris 2014/Photo by Malachi Farrell
pp. 22–23: © Frank Perrin
p. 24: © Archivio Fotografico Storico Italiano Umberto Cicconi, 2014 – All Rights Reserved – www.archiviocicconi.com
p. 25: © Adagp, Paris 2014/Collection Frac Alsace
p. 26 top, p. 27 top: © Reporters Associati/Courtesy of Michel Giniès
p. 26 bottom: © The Andy Warhol Foundation for the Visual Arts, Inc. /Adagp, Paris 2014/Courtesy of Hauser & Wirth
p. 27 bottom left: © UPI Photo/Massimo Ascani/Courtesy of Michel Giniès
p. 27 bottom right: © Jean-Jacques Ceccarini/Figarophoto/Bibliothèque nationale de France, Paris

PHOTOGRAPHERS

A Profession
p. 31: © Cyclope & Compagnie/Collection T. Valletoux
p. 40 top: © Kameramuseum Westlicht
p. 40 center: © Frédéric Hoch
p. 40 bottom: © Kameramuseum Westlicht
p. 41 top: © Kameramuseum Westlicht
p. 41 bottom: © Collection Alpa-Bourgeois-Columberg – Musée suisse de l'appareil photographique, Vevey
p. 42 top: Courtesy of Galerie Lumière des Roses
p. 42 bottom: © Reporters Associati
p. 43 top: Courtesy of Galerie Lumière des Roses
p. 43 center: © Reporters Associati
p. 43 bottom: © Bibliothèque nationale de France, Paris
p. 44: © Reporters Associati
p. 45: Courtesy of Michel Giniès/All Rights Reserved
p. 46: © Reporters Associati
p. 47: © Tazio Secchiaroli/David Secchiaroli
pp. 48–49: © Philippe d'Exea/Agence Sphinx
p. 60: © Pool Apesteguy-Siccoli/Gamma Rapho
p. 61: © Raymond Depardon/Magnum Photos
pp. 62–63: © Olivier Mirguet/VU
pp. 64–67: © Jessica Dimmock/VII/Corbis
pp. 68–69: © Christophe Beauregard
pp. 70–71: © Romain Dussaulx and Benjamin Lalande

Mythologies
p. 73 left: © Cinetica del Comune di Bologna/All Rights Reserved
p. 73 left: All Rights Reserved
p. 80–81: © 1959 – La Dolce Vita – Pathé Production – Riama Film/Collection Fondation Jérôme Seydoux-Pathé/All Rights Reserved
p. 82 left: All Rights Reserved
p. 82 right, top and bottom: © Reporters Associati
p. 83 top: © Tazio Secchiaroli/David Secchiaroli/All Rights Reserved
p. 83 bottom: © Reporters Associati
p. 84 top left: All Rights Reserved
p. 84 top right: © Reporters Associati
p. 84 bottom, left and right: © Tazio Secchiaroli/David Secchiaroli/All Rights Reserved
p. 85, top and bottom: © Reporters Associati
p. 92 top: © Quinta Communications/All Rights Reserved
p. 92 center: © Studio Canal/Rizzoli Film/All Rights Reserved
p. 92 bottom: © Paramount Pictures Ltd/All Rights Reserved
p. 93 top: © Icon/20th Century Fox/The Kobal Collection/Myles Aronowitz
p. 93 bottom: © Mondial Te-Fi/Seda Spettacoli/Terra Filmkunst/Labrador Film/All Rights Reserved

STARS

In the Spotlight
p. 97: © Daniel Cande
p. 105: © Marcello Geppetti Media Company
p. 106 top: © Marcello Geppetti Media Company
p. 106 center: © Pascal Rostain and Bruno Mouron/Agence Sphinx
p. 106 bottom: © Jack Burlot/Corbis
p. 107: © Marcello Geppetti Media Company
p. 108: © Daniel Angeli
p. 109: © Gary Lee Boas/Courtesy of the artist and Kamel Mennour, Paris
p. 111: Courtesy of Phillipe Garner/All Rights Reserved
p. 112: © Philippe d'Exea/Agence Sphinx
p. 113 top: © Daniel Angeli
p. 113 bottom: © Francis Apesteguy
p. 114: © Marcello Geppetti Media Company
p. 115 top: © Tazio Secchiaroli/David Secchiaroli/Courtesy of James Hyman Gallery
p. 115 center: © Patrick Morin/Rue des Archives/Courtesy of Michel Giniès
p. 115 bottom: Courtesy of Michel Giniès/All Rights Reserved
pp. 116–17: © Michel Giniès
p. 119: © Ron Galella/Courtesy of A. Galerie
p. 120 top: © Ron Galella, Ltd/Courtesy of A. Galerie
p. 120 center: © Brad Elterman
p. 120 bottom: © Art Zelin
p. 121: © Ron Galella/Courtesy of A. Galerie
pp. 122–24: © Settimio Garritano/Katia Bede Garritano
p. 125: Courtesy of Michel Giniès/All Rights Reserved
p. 127: © Patrick Siccoli
p. 128: © Bruno Mouron/Agence Sphinx
p. 129 top: © Pascal Rostain/Agence Sphinx
p. 129 bottom: © Patrick Siccoli
p. 130 top: © Francis Apesteguy
p. 130 bottom: © Pascal Rostain and Bruno Mouron/Agence Sphinx
p. 131 top: © Michel Giniès
p. 131 center: © Michel Giniès/All Rights Reserved
p. 131 bottom: © Prisma Presse
p. 133: © Jacques Langevin/Courtesy of Musée de l'Élysée, Lausanne
p. 134: © Bruno Mouron/Agence Sphinx
p. 135: © Philippe Garner
p. 136 top: © Paul J. Richards/AFP
p. 136 bottom: © Bettmann/Corbis/Associated Press
p. 137: © Dusko Despotovic/Sygma/Corbis
p. 139: © Jim Smeal/BEImages/MAXPPP
p. 140 top: © Sébastien Valiela/Eyewitness
p. 140 bottom: All Rights Reserved
p. 141: © Sébastien Valiela/Eyewitness
p. 142 top: © Sébastien Valiela and Vincent Lepresle/Eyewitness
p. 142 center: © Sébastien Valiela/Eyewitness
p. 142 bottom: © Sébastien Valiela and Vincent Lepresle/Eyewitness
p. 143: © Sébastien Valiela/Eyewitness
p. 145: © FameFlynet/Bestimage
p. 146: © Sébastien Valiela/Eyewitness
p. 147 top: © Jonas Mekas
p. 147 bottom: © Phil Ramey/Sébastien Valiela/Eyewitness
p. 148 top: All Rights Reserved
p. 148 bottom: © Jeremiah Palacek
p. 149 top: © Jonathan Horowitz/Courtesy of Gavin Brown's Enterprise
p. 149 center: © Alicia Ross
p. 149 bottom: © Jaclyn Santos

Behind the Scenes
p. 151: © Philippe Blet
pp. 160–61: © Sébastien Valiela/Eyewitness
p. 162 top: © Sébastien Valiela and Pierre Suu/Eyewitness
p. 162 center: © Bruno Mouron/Agence Sphinx
p. 162 bottom: © Pascal Rostain and Bruno Mouron/Agence Sphinx
p. 163 top: © Francis Apesteguy
p. 163 bottom left: © Sébastien Valiela and Vincent Lepresle/Eyewitness
p. 163 bottom right: © Pascal Rostain/Agence Sphinx
pp. 164–65: © Xavier Martin
pp. 166–67: © Paris Match, All Rights Reserved
p. 168: © Tazio Secchiaroli/David Secchiaroli
p. 169: © Sébastien Valiela/Eyewitness
p. 170: © BPK, Berlin, Dist. RMN-Grand Palais/Erich Salomon
p. 171 top: © Brad Elterman
p. 171 center: © Ron Galella/Courtesy of A. Galerie
p. 171 bottom: © Patrick Siccoli
p. 172 top: © Ron Galella/Courtesy of A. Galerie
p. 172 center: © Patrick Siccoli
p. 172 bottom: © Daniel Angeli
p. 173: © Henry Flores, http://www.henryflores.com
p. 174: © Bruno Mouron/Agence Sphinx
p. 175: © Xavier Martin
pp. 176–77: © Weegee (Arthur Fellig)/International Center of Photography/Getty Images
pp. 178–79: © Marcello Geppetti Media Company
p. 180: © Éditions Nuit et Jour/All Rights Reserved
p. 181 top: © Marcello Geppetti Media Company
p. 181 center: © Jean Pigozzi/Centre Pompidou, Mnam-Cci, Dist. RMN-Grand Palais/image courtesy of CAA – The Pigozzi Collection
p. 181 bottom: © Georges Dudognon
p. 182: © Gary Lee Boas/Courtesy of the artist and Kamel Mennour, Paris
p. 183: © Kvartuc/Cropix/Sipa
pp. 184–85: © Juergen Teller
pp. 186–87: © Marcello Geppetti Media Company
p. 188 top: © Pascal Rostain/Agence Sphinx
p. 188 bottom: © Pascal Rostain and Bruno Mouron/Agence Sphinx
p. 189 top left: © David Secchiaroli
p. 189 top right: Courtesy of Michel Giniès/All Rights Reserved
p. 189 bottom left: © Daniel Angeli
p. 189 center right: © Ron Galella/Courtesy of A. Galerie
pp. 190–91: © Ron Galella, Ltd/Courtesy of A. Galerie

p. 192 top: © UPI Photo/Bibliothèque nationale de France, Paris
p. 192 bottom: © Nick Ut/AP/Sipa
p. 193 left: © Globe/American Media, Inc./All Rights Reserved
p. 193 center: Hola S.L. /All Rights Reserved
p. 193 right: © Globe/American Media, Inc./All Rights Reserved
p. 200: © Michel Giniès
p. 201 top: © 2013. Digital image, The Museum of Modern Art, New York/Scala, Florence/Agence Réa
p. 201 center: © Sébastien Valiela/Eyewitness
p. 201 bottom: © Daniel Angeli
p. 202 top: © Daniel Angeli
p. 202 center: © Michel Giniès
p. 202 bottom: © Patrick Siccoli
p. 203 top left: © Ron Galella/Courtesy of A. Galerie
p. 203 top right: © Michel Giniès
p. 203 bottom: © Gary Lee Boas/Courtesy of the artist and Kamel Mennour, Paris
p. 204: © Denkmalschutzamt Hamburg – Bildarchiv/Photographers: Priestler and Wilke/Photo: 00031350
p. 205: © Stiftung Deutsches Historisches Museum, Berlin
p. 206 top: © National Enquirer/American Media, Inc./All Rights Reserved
p. 206 center: © Ok! /American Media, Inc./All Rights Reserved
p. 206 bottom: © National Enquirer/American Media, Inc./All Rights Reserved
p. 207 top: © Paris Match/All Rights Reserved
p. 207 bottom: © Ici Paris/Hachette Filipacchi/All Rights Reserved
pp. 208–9: © Kathrin Günter

ARTISTS

Forms of Appropriation

p. 213: © Gerhard Richter, 2014/© 2014. Digital image, The Museum of Modern Art, New York/Scala, Florence
p. 220 top: © Adagp, Paris 2014/Photos by Nathalie de Bournet-Becdelièvre
p. 220 bottom: © Time Inc./All Rights Reserved
p. 221 top: © Gerhard Richter, 2014
p. 221 bottom: © Spiegel/All Rights Reserved
p. 222 top: © R. Hamilton. All Rights Reserved, Adagp, Paris 2014/Courtesy of The Alan Cristea Gallery
p. 222 bottom: © Daily Sketch/Associated Newspapers Ltd/Bibliothèque nationale de France, Paris
p. 223 top: © Adagp, Paris 2014/Centre Pompidou, Mnam-Cci, Dist. RMN-Grand Palais/ image Centre Pompidou, Mnam-Cci
p. 223 bottom: © Spiegel/Reuters
p. 224: © Jonathan Hernandez
p. 225: Courtesy of the artist and Hauser & Wirth, in collaboration with Patrick Painter Inc.
p. 226: © Olivier Mirguet/VU
p. 227: © Thomas Demand/Adagp, Paris 2014/Courtesy of Sprüth Magers Berlin London
pp. 228–29: © Adagp, Paris 2014
pp. 230–31: © Adagp, Paris 2014/Courtesy of Ulf Lundin and Galleri Magnus Karlsson
pp. 232–33: © Liam Tickner
pp. 234–35: © Viktoria Binschtok and Klemm's, Berlin
pp. 236–37: © Julián Baron
pp. 238–39: © Adagp, Paris 2014/Centre Pompidou, Mnam-Cci, Dist. RMN-Grand Palais/Philippe Migeat

In the Skin of a Paparazzo

p. 241: © G.R.A.M. /Courtesy of Christine König Galerie, Vienna
pp. 248–51: © The Richard Avedon Foundation
pp. 252–53: © William Klein
pp. 254–55: © Christian Lesemann
pp. 256–57: © Alexi Lubomirski
pp. 258–61: © Pascal Rostain and Bruno Mouron/Agence Sphinx
pp. 262–63: © Gary Lee Boas/Courtesy of the artist and Kamel Mennour, Paris
pp. 264–65: © G.R.A.M. /Courtesy of Christine König Galerie, Vienna
pp. 266–69: © Alison Jackson
pp. 270–71: © Cindy Sherman/Courtesy of the artist and Metro Pictures, New York
pp. 272–73: © Adagp, Paris 2014/Courtesy of Galerie Perrotin, Paris
pp. 274–75: © Adagp, Paris 2014
pp. 276–79: © Kathrin Günter
p. 281: © Live Stock Market/Gavin Turk

On the Newsstands

p. 283: © The Andy Warhol Foundation for the Visual Arts, Inc./Adagp, Paris 2014/Courtesy of Hubert Burda Media Sammlung
p. 284: All Rights Reserved
p. 285: © National Enquirer/American Media, Inc./All Rights Reserved
p. 286: © Marcello Geppetti Media Company
p. 287 center and right: © Sébastien Valiela and Vincent Lepresle/Eyewitness
p. 287 bottom: © Sébastien Valiela/Eyewitness
p. 288 top left: © Sébastien Valiela and Vincent Lepresle/Eyewitness
pp. 288–89: © Sébastien Valiela/Eyewitness
p. 290: People/Time Inc./E.L. Woody/Ramey Photo Agency
p. 291: Courtesy of the artist and Hauser & Wirth, in collaboration with Patrick Painter Inc.
p. 292: © The Andy Warhol Foundation for the Visual Arts, Inc./Adagp, Paris 2014 © Keith Haring Foundation Photo Collection of The Andy Warhol Museum,Pittsburgh
p. 293: © Condé Nast/Barbara Kruger/Mark Seliger
p. 294: © Armin Linke/Photos by Corrado Calvo
p. 295: © Corrado Calvo, 2009
p. 296: © Daily Mirror/Mirrorpix
p. 297: © Jonathan Horowitz/Courtesy of Gavin Brown's Enterprise

GENERAL EDITOR
Clément Chéroux,
with the assistance of Camille Lenglois

CENTRE POMPIDOU-METZ
Editor: Claire Bonnevie,
with the assistance of Camille Aguignier

DESIGN
P&J: Laurent Pinon and Aurore Jannin,
with the assistance of Sofia Chaoui

Translated from the French by
Anna Hiddleston-Galloni (essays and chapter openers pp. 7–91,
list of works and publications, and credits and acknowledgments)
and
Elizabeth Heard (essays and chapter openers pp. 96–282,
texts accompanying the images, and bibliography)
Copyediting: Helen Adedotun and Marc Feustel
Typesetting: Thierry Renard
Proofreading: Penelope Isaac
Color Separation: Les Artisans du Regard, Paris

Printed in Slovenia by Gorenjski Tisk Storitve

Originally published in French as *Paparazzi! Photographes, stars et artistes*

English-language edition

ISBN: 978-2-08-020193-5

ISBN: 978-2-35-983033-0

87, quai Panhard et Levassor
75647 Paris Cedex 13

editions.flammarion.com

14 15 16 3 2 1

Dépôt légal: 07/2014